THE
AGRARIAN FOES
OF
BOLSHEVISM

STUDIES OF THE RUSSIAN INSTITUTE

COLUMBIA UNIVERSITY

The
Agrarian Foes
of
Bolshevism

PROMISE AND DEFAULT

OF THE

RUSSIAN SOCIALIST REVOLUTIONARIES

FEBRUARY TO OCTOBER

1917

By Oliver H. Radkey

COLUMBIA UNIVERSITY PRESS

NEW YORK   1958

THE system of transliteration from the Russian employed in this book is based on that of the Library of Congress with certain modifications. Familiar names of German or Jewish origin are given in the German form (Rosenblum, Richter), whereas less familiar ones or names the original form of which is doubtful, are transliterated from the Russian (Gendelman, Shreider); in a few instances names are simply given in the form most familiar to the author. The soft and medial hard signs and the two dots over stressed *e*, pronounced *yo* in Russian, have been confined to Russian text or titles and do not appear in the case of proper names in the English text or in the citation of authors, the only exceptions being names of some significance that are frequently mispronounced (Slëtov, Pugachëv).

Dates are given in the Old Style.

THE RUSSIAN INSTITUTE
OF COLUMBIA UNIVERSITY

———

THE Russian Institute was established by Columbia University in 1946 to serve two major objectives: the training of a limited number of well-qualified Americans for scholarly and professional careers in the field of Russian studies, and the development of research in the social sciences and the humanities as they relate to Russia and the Soviet Union. The research program of the Russian Institute is conducted through the efforts of its faculty members, of scholars invited to participate as Senior Fellows in its program, and of candidates for the Certificate of the Institute and for the degree of Doctor of Philosophy. Some of the results of the research program are presented in the Studies of the Russian Institute of Columbia University. The faculty of the Institute, without necessarily agreeing with the conclusions reached in the Studies, believe that their publication advances the difficult task of promoting systematic research on Russia and the Soviet Union and public understanding of the problems involved.

The faculty of the Russian Institute are grateful to the Rockefeller Foundation for the financial assistance which it has given to the program of research and publication.

STUDIES OF THE RUSSIAN INSTITUTE

COLUMBIA UNIVERSITY

SOVIET NATIONAL INCOME
AND PRODUCT IN 1937 *Abram Bergson*

THROUGH THE GLASS OF SOVIET LITERATURE:
VIEWS OF RUSSIAN SOCIETY *edited by Ernest J. Simmons*

THE PROLETARIAN EPISODE
IN RUSSIAN LITERATURE, 1928-1932 *Edward J. Brown*

MANAGEMENT OF THE INDUSTRIAL FIRM IN THE USSR:
A STUDY IN SOVIET ECONOMIC PLANNING *David Granick*

SOVIET POLICIES IN CHINA, 1917-1924 *Allen S. Whiting*

UKRAINIAN NATIONALISM, 1939-1945 *John A. Armstrong*

POLISH POSTWAR ECONOMY *Thad Paul Alton*

LITERARY POLITICS
IN THE SOVIET UKRAINE, 1917-1934 *George S. N. Luckyj*

THE EMERGENCE OF RUSSIAN
PANSLAVISM, 1856-1870 *Michael Boro Petrovich*

BOLSHEVISM IN TURKESTAN, 1917-1927 *Alexander G. Park*

THE LAST YEARS OF THE GEORGIAN
MONARCHY, 1658-1832 *David Marshall Lang*

LENIN ON TRADE UNIONS
AND REVOLUTION, 1893-1917 *Thomas Taylor Hammond*

THE JAPANESE THRUST INTO SIBERIA, 1918 *James William Morley*

SOVIET MARXISM: A CRITICAL ANALYSIS *Herbert Marcuse*

THE AGRARIAN FOES OF BOLSHEVISM: PROMISE
AND DEFAULT OF THE RUSSIAN SOCIALIST
REVOLUTIONARIES, MARCH TO OCTOBER, 1917 *Oliver H. Radkey, Jr.*

TO THE MEMORY OF

MY MOTHER AND FATHER

Sarah Hewlett and

Oliver H. Radkey

FOREWORD

FROM undergraduate days the author has been interested in the fate of the large but little-known movement which spoke for the peasantry in the Revolution of 1917. There was a certain mystification about the subject: Why this collapse of a movement which defended the peasant interest in one of the great peasant lands of the world? Why this beheading of a class so imposing in numbers and why its enforced servitude to a cause not its own? There was no answer to the problem, only the raw material for an answer, and this scattered in distant places and unavailable in Western tongues. All this simply added to the interest. It was apparent, even to the immature mind, that Western writers had nothing to offer, and Russian writers seemed hopelessly prejudiced, when they dealt with the subject at all.

The paradox of peasant loss in a peasant land, then so baffling, is now quite easy to understand, but first the blank in the record had to be filled and the myth of mass rule exploded in the mind of the author. For it must be said that the triumph of a minority in Russia in 1917 was not in defiance of the nature of human society, but in accordance with it. No lesson of history is more illuminating, or appalling, than the ability of a small group hungry for power to subjugate and victimize the mass of their fellow beings—the rural mass more easily than the urban. Always the peasantry has borne the brunt of fiscal extortion and military sacrifice, from the crushing incidence of church and state in ancient Egypt to the dictum of a Prussian king that the rural toiler is the "beast of burden of human society." The story of the feeble enterprise of the peasants' partisans in Russia and of their failure is the subject of this book.

These partisans were called Populists. With the older Populism of

the nineteenth century this study is not concerned; others have dealt
with it at greater length than it deserves. It seems incredible that a
tiny band of adult children should have claimed so much attention
while the broad movement of neo-Populism in our own century has
been neglected. The only explanation is that under the influence of
the German school of *Kulturgeschichte*, slavishly followed elsewhere
by intellectuals who damn everything that is German, attention has
been riveted upon the high-flown abstractions of a few individuals,
and particularly upon the vastly overpublicized antithesis between
East and West, instead of upon the conflict of social groups, national
or class, Eastern or Western, out of which this vapor arises. Enough
has been said in this book about the ideology of neo-Populism (we
shall see how lightly it rested upon the Socialist Revolutionaries in
1917), but no time has been wasted on tracing its philosophical
origins. In the last analysis, it sprang from the emotions of those who
embraced it and from the mind of V. M. Chernov, who took from
the older Populism and from Marxian socialism, from Western revisionism and Russian reality, from Comte, Avenarius, Mach, and
others, whatever he found suitable for his purpose, throwing the rest
away and adding much of his own, in a ceaseless endeavor to construct an ideology that would be pleasing to people who practiced
terrorism and loved the peasantry, yet wished to preserve it from the
inequalities of a regime of private property such as had grown out
of the French Revolution and might conceivably grow out of the
revolution which they were fomenting in Russia.

In accordance with the author's view that too much attention has
been paid to the ideology of movements and too little to their practice, his treatment has centered on the events of 1917 and on an
analysis of why these events were so little in harmony with the stated
purposes of the neo-Populist movement. The emphasis throughout
has been on men and their actions, their foibles and failures, rather
than on the theories they threw up to justify their feelings or conceal
their actions. In short, the author has set himself the task of writing
a history of Social Revolutionism in 1917, sometimes in more detail
than the reader will relish, for the purpose of presenting a full record
of the movement whose failure forms the complement of Bolshevik

success in an agrarian society, a success that has since been repeated elsewhere, above all in China, with the knowledge and techniques first amassed or worked out in Russia. Merely because the agrarian opposition to Bolshevism failed and has shared the oblivion of lost causes does not deprive it of significance for Russian or even for world history.

The earlier history of Social Revolutionism, from the turn of the century to 1917, has been treated in cursory fashion, more to provide background for 1917 than for its own sake; the war years, however, have for that very reason received more attention. The Socialist Revolutionary party (PSR) did not exist as a mass organization before 1917, and as it was more than half dead after 1917, its corporate existence in the true sense of the word was compressed within the limits of a single year. It is upon that year that our account is centered.

The author has had the pleasure (in some cases, drudgery) of examining virtually every important source for that year, some of them of great rarity, so rare, in fact, that at times he has dispensed with the conventional "see so and so" in the footnotes because of the manifest absurdity of such recommendation. The minutes of the party congresses and the party press, right, left, and center, provide the framework of this study; the illumination has come from memoirs and private papers, from bits of information pieced together, from a book that was torn from the press, and from oral testimony. Primary sources have been used almost exclusively. The author desired to approach the material directly and reach his own conclusions even in those rare instances when some aspect of the subject was touched upon in a secondary source not disfigured by prejudice or ignorance. Only certain fringes of the field had been plowed; the subject itself was virgin soil, and for the most part the question of secondary sources did not arise.

In addition to the printed sources, scattered in libraries from Moscow to California, the author has had the privilege of meeting party leaders, of discussing with them points of mutual interest, and of being permitted to inspect certain manuscripts in their possession. His good fortune in this respect began in 1934 when V. M. Chernov generously placed at his disposal materials that disclosed the inner recesses of party life. Interviews with A. A. Argunov and S. P. Postnikov followed, and later with V. M. Zenzinov and V. V. Rudnev, in Paris, each adding something to an understanding of the subject or presenting a different point of view. Mark V. Vishniak from the right sector of party opinion and I. Z. Steinberg from the left have helped orally as well as through their writings, while Zenzinov continued from time to time to discuss even the most intimate questions until his death in 1953. As Chernov had died in the previous year, two major sources of enlightenment henceforth were denied the author, but enough had been given already to add to the worth of this study. To his friend-enemy Vishniak, still flourishing and still ready to spring to the defense of policies that are so little defensible, the author wishes to express his thanks for the assistance rendered despite the clash of opinions.

In recent years the author has had the pleasure of coming to know A. F. Kerenski and of benefiting from the observations and judgments of this elder statesman who has done so much to broaden and deepen the author's understanding, not only of events in 1917, but of other aspects of Russian society. While adhering to his own point of view in respect to the course of the Provisional Government, the author has often speculated on how different things might have been had Kerenski's opportunity come later in life and had he acted more in accord with his own genius and less under the whip of external compulsions, chief among them the rule or ruin policy of his country's allies.

It has not been easy to criticize, at times severely, the actions of men who have given so generously of their time and knowledge to an unknown student, just as it has been grievous to see them go to the grave with their hopes unrealized and their story untold. Nothing that is said in this book should be taken as indicating any lack of esteem for them personally or as questioning their devotion to the people's cause. If one might wish that they had had more of the realism of Western political leaders, one might also wish that Western political leaders had their honesty.

Two men from the Menshevik camp have graciously extended

assistance: Boris I. Nikolaevski, from his fund of knowledge concerning the bibliography and personalities of the revolution, and Irakli Tsereteli, with significant disclosures about the actions of Chernov and his position in the government in the summer of 1917. Tsereteli's brief characterization of the SR movement in that year was a masterpiece in itself.

The author owes an especial debt of gratitude to the supervisor of his doctoral dissertation and his friend of later years, Professor Michael Karpovich of Harvard, who spent a great deal of time in counseling and guidance, more than university systems afford their professors, and who displayed a tolerance of other points of view as broad as his knowledge of the field. Professor G. T. Robinson of Columbia University has inspected the manuscript of the present work and given the benefit of his criticism, both generally and in respect to agrarian conditions. No one has done more to bring this project to fruition than Professor Philip E. Mosely of Columbia. And Professor Anatole G. Mazour of Stanford University has aided with suggestions and friendly advice, but especially with steady encouragement over a period of years.

To his friends in the Hoover Library, where most of this work was done, the author is indebted for innumerable favors and kindnesses: to Philip T. McLean, Ruth Perry, Arline Paul, and Helena Sworakowski, for the location of improbable sources; to Xenia J. Eudin and Olga Hess Gankin, for a willingness at any time to discuss difficult problems, aid with the Russian language, and suggest helpful sources; to Harold H. Fisher, Inez Richardson, Easton Rothwell, Witold Sworakowski, and Winifred Teague, for working conditions the least distracting from duty and the most pleasant in the country. To all these and others go heartfelt thanks. It has been an unforgettable experience in this clearinghouse of knowledge to step down the hall and settle in a few moments' time some obscure and vexing question that otherwise would have required an inordinate amount of time and effort or more probably would have remained unanswered.

Finance is always of crucial importance in projects of this kind, and however unsatisfactory the remuneration of his profession in general, the author cannot complain of ungenerous treatment in this instance. The European side of the research was financed by a grant from Harvard University. The first chapters of this work were written on the proceeds of a fellowship in Slavic Studies awarded by the Hoover Institute and Library under the direction of Professor Harold H. Fisher. The chapters on 1917, comprising the heart of the work, were written with the financial assistance of the Russian Institute of Columbia University, which has also assumed the cost of publication. In the case of so large a sum, this generous decision on the part of the Institute alone has made possible the appearance of this book, and to it the author will always be grateful.

The Deans of the College, H. T. Parlin and H. H. Ransom, and the Department of History at the University of Texas have helped with a liberal policy on leaves, and the Graduate School, with authorization of a research grant.

Columbia University Press has performed its work with a maximum of thoroughness and a minimum of interference, and Miss Barbara Melissa Voorhis has proved to be not only a competent but also a liberal editor with whom it has been a pleasure to work.

Last but not least, the author wishes to see in print a word of appreciation to his wife, upon whom much of the drudgery has devolved, and who has borne it without a murmur of protest or dismay. In many ways she has helped to ease the burden of what was foreordained to be a long and difficult task.

The Hoover Institution on War,
Revolution, and Peace
Stanford, California
July 23, 1957

OLIVER H. RADKEY

CONTENTS

I THE ESSENCE OF RUSSIAN POPULISM 3

II THE PROGRAM OF SOCIAL REVOLUTIONISM 24

III THE ORIGIN AND DEVELOPMENT OF THE SR PARTY, 1900-1914 47

IV THE IMPACT OF THE WAR: FISSURES AND FEUDS IN THE PARTY 88

V THE FEBRUARY REVOLUTION AND THE GENESIS OF COALITION 127

VI THE THIRD PARTY CONGRESS 185

VII THE FIRST COALITION 240

VIII THE JULY CRISIS AND THE BIRTH OF THE SECOND COALITION 279

IX THE STERILE RECORD OF THE SECOND COALITION 322

X THE SR DESCENT TO DISASTER 362

XI THE RISING TIDE OF EXTREMISM 429

XII MISTAKES AND WEAKNESSES IN 1917 455

LIST OF SOURCES 486

INDEX 501

THE
AGRARIAN FOES
OF
BOLSHEVISM

I

THE ESSENCE OF
RUSSIAN POPULISM

IN Russia before the revolution there were two kinds of socialism and four socialist parties as a result of the conflict between moderates and extremists, or evolutionists and activists, within each of the warring camps. Two Social Democratic (SD) factions, which later became parties, the Mensheviks and Bolsheviks, bore the banner of Marxian socialism, while the Socialist Revolutionaries (SR) and Popular Socialists (Narodnye Sotsialisty) embraced an older belief known as Populism. Both wings of the Social Democracy agreed on one thing, if on little else: that the Populists (Narodniki) were really not socialists at all but representatives of a class of small producers which as yet had not fully crystallized, either socially or ideologically, amid the backward conditions of the Russian Empire. The Marxists derided the opposing philosophy as "utopian," "nebulous," "eclectic," "disjointed," "petty bourgeois," when they did not use even harsher terms, and it must be admitted that the Populists never succeeded in working out a doctrine as precise or watertight as that of their rivals. But Populism was less an ideology than a state of mind which brought men together in the absence of concrete formulas and held them together despite divergences over program and tactics. The state of mind was induced by a desire to make a revolution quickly in an agrarian country where the regime of private property did not rest upon a broad foundation, and where the existence of precapitalist forms afforded hope that the individualist order of the West could be circumvented in favor of an early approach to the collectivist society of the future.

In the course of its evolution Populism passed through three stages. It was in its childhood in the 1870s when the failure of the people to respond to youthful evangelists of the *v narod* ("into the people") movement diverted some of these into the path of terrorism, and when belief in the socialist emanations of the village commune (*obshchina*) and faith in the ability to guide the "dark people" in the desired direction, once the emperor had been assassinated, featured an ideology best described as children's socialism. In the 1890s Populism had to contend with the newer or Marxian brand of socialism, and thought to do so by denying the evidence of the senses in respect to the growth of capitalism in Russia under Witte's industrialization program. This stage exhibited all the obstinacy, all the gawkiness and blundering self-assertiveness, of adolescence. So completely was it worsted and so patently had the bankruptcy of the Chernyshevski-Lavrov-Mikhailovski-ostrich school of socialism been demonstrated that Populism would have died in adolescence had it not been for the genius of V. M. Chernov and the requirements of revolution-making in a peasant land.

When Chernov began to rear the edifice of neo-Populism or Social Revolutionism in the early years of the twentieth century, he inherited from the older Populism little more than a razed site and certain ideals, foremost among them a sense of dedication to the rural masses. Many of the bricks he used came from Western socialism, not so much from Marx himself as from the revisionism that had developed as a consequence of the persistence of the small producer, particularly in agriculture, and a broader distribution of the benefits of capitalism. The mortar Chernov supplied himself, and also the cornerstone, in the form of an agrarian program which neither Herzen nor Chernyshevski nor Lavrov nor Mikhailovski had known how to devise. By some curious distortion of history these men have figured as the founders of Populism whereas in reality they contributed nothing more than inspiration and a utopian ideology which by 1900 had either decently to be embalmed or thrown on the refuse heap. The serious and viable Populism of the twentieth century was the creation of the man who died in New York in 1952, in the bitterness and obscurity of a second exile. So little resemblance did Chernov's handiwork bear to what went before, in fact, that one keen observer would deny it the name of Populism, contending that it was an entirely new enterprise operating under an established trade name.[1] We are not prepared to go so far, since emotionally there was still a tie to the past; but intellectually Populism not only matured under Chernov but in part originated with him. If in harmonizing it with Western thought and fitting it into the ranks of world socialism he drew heavily upon Marxism and its revisionist offshoot, the reverse is also true, and Russian Marxism after 1900 betrays increasing evidence of the influence of the rival ideology. This influence was negligible in the case of Menshevism, which adhered closely to the original Marxist pattern, but weighty in the case of Bolshevism, the wing of Marxism that sought to adapt to Russian conditions and so could not neglect the peasantry. Though Lenin denounced Populism as "stinking carrion" and must be reckoned as its mortal foe, there was a certain affinity between his willingness to anticipate historical development in order to speed the revolution and a movement which thought to use for the purposes of revolution not only the class contradictions of the capitalist order but also the mass of toilers who had as yet been preserved from its polarizing influence. Both had in mind the restive, land-hungry mass of peasantry, so different in situation and outlook from its counterpart in Western Europe. Wherever the Populists had marked out a short cut to revolution, Lenin was sure to follow, tearing down their property signs and putting up his own. Far from acknowledging the debt, he silently appropriated what was useful while plotting the death of the owner.

But the readiness with which evidence of the interaction between Populism and Marxism may be established does not mean that either altered its essence or went over to the enemy in all except name. There were certain basic positions or predilections which were never surrendered, no matter how eclectic Chernov proved to be in constructing his neo-Populism or how flexible Lenin's tactics may have become while maintaining his rigid adherence to the dogma that only the proletariat could be entrusted with the task of social reconstruction. The points of distinction will now be singled out for brief discussion, but the reader should bear in mind that sometimes they

[1] Sukhanov, *Marksizm i Narodnichestvo*.

became rather blurred as a result of the readiness of the Bolsheviks to appropriate for their own purposes ideas belonging to the Socialist Revolutionaries. Each time the latter fired on the Marxist fortress, they hit the Mensheviks but not necessarily the Bolsheviks, who might be either inside the fortress or outside in the field, maneuvering with great skill and even occupying some of the same positions as the Populists. Similarly, the Marxists often trained their guns on the wrecked castle of nineteenth-century Populism, though Chernov's neo-Populists were not always inside the ruins. Each tended to reduce the enemy to a stereotype and preferred a fixed position on which to fire to a moving target in the field.

In general it may be observed that, in contrast to Marxism, which came from the industrial West and regarded the urban proletariat as the chosen class or hegemon of the revolution, Populism was native in inspiration and agrarian in emphasis. Four specific features of Populism set it off sharply from classical Marxism and two of these from Bolshevism as well.

First, the Narodnik interpretation of history varied widely from the Marxian. Since it is not proposed to venture into the philosophical background of Populism here, suffice it to say that the Populists viewed historical causation in terms of the interaction of two factors: one objective, comprising the natural environment; the other subjective, comprising man and his thoughts and actions, not, indeed, as a divine creation but as a complex force of nature in his own right. Man is influenced by his environment and in turn reacts upon it to produce the phenomena of history. Economic, political, and intellectual systems are all three derivative from this fundamental process and hence cannot be ranked as to primacy, but must be viewed as coordinate with each other. A given society is in part the product of nature and in part the product of social habit; the first component is fixed but the second is subject to change, and the change occurs as a result of the implementation of ideas conceived by critically thinking individuals. The individual, then, becomes an object of priceless worth in the Narodnik ideology, and to accord him maximum latitude for developing his capabilities, not less than to harmonize his relations with other individuals, is the ultimate purpose of socialism. The Populists admitted that elemental or impersonal forces in large part govern the course of history, but they contended, first, that these forces could not be reduced to the economic category, as the Marxists would have it, and second, that the course of history is also influenced by the conscious and purposeful intervention of the individuals who make up society.

The content of history, therefore, is not exhausted by the class struggle; there are other social units besides classes, equally valid in point of historical effect and equally productive of antagonism (for example, the demon of class hatred must share the stage with the demon of national hatred) and this conflict of social forces, economic and noneconomic, is complemented by a conflict of ideas and ideals. These are not conceived in a vacuum; rather, they reflect their social origin, but can transcend that origin and so assume an independent value: thus the very idea of socialism was formulated in large part by men of the middle class. The class struggle itself takes on ideological form; it seeks justification in ideals and becomes more acute as a result of the inspiration it derives from them. If ideas did not influence the course of history, then there would be no purpose in schemes of social betterment. A movement addressed to that end can not abdicate in favor of the elemental forces of nature, for the outcome of the cosmic process—the extinction of life on the planet—can never serve as a goal of human endeavor. A socialist philosophy must synthesize a realism of perception of the phenomena of life with an idealism of their evaluation and active transformation. Thus did the neo-Populists oppose their "realistic" interpretation of history to Marx's "materialistic" interpretation, by broadening the concept of materialist causation while refusing to ascribe to it exclusive significance because of their belief in the ability of man to influence his destiny.[2]

[2] "K voprosu o teoreticheskom obosnovanii sotsializma," *Revoliutsionnaia Rossiia*, No. 36 (November 15, 1903), pp. 1-5 (this article, though unsigned, was undoubtedly written by V. M. Chernov); Polianski, *Narodnicheskii sotsializm*, pp. 22-47; Masaryk, *Spirit of Russia*, II, 372-77.

A second fundamental distinction between the two types of socialism, and the most significant of all, lay in the fact that each was interested primarily in a different segment of the population. Many of the Populists had as strong a predilection for the peasantry and the intelligentsia as the Marxists for the proletariat, though they might be less open in avowing it. The Narodnik concept of "toil" permitted its adherents to advocate a union of the working class with the "toiling" peasantry and the "toiling" intellectuals as the three component elements of contemporary society which suffered from exploitation at the hands of "nontoilers" (i.e., those who did not work themselves but lived from the labor of others). The Marxists contended that their rivals were trying to yoke together elements which lacked a community of economic interests, in as much as they were overlooking the distinction between ownership and nonownership of the means of production, between the sale of the products of labor and the sale of labor itself. But the Populists maintained that such distinctions were subordinate to the common bond of toil and the common grievance of exploitation. Thus the Narodnik conception of the class struggle was much broader than the Marxist, but also more diffuse.

Essentially, however, it was the peasantry that engaged the attention of the Populists. They were lovers of the people, and most of the Russian people were peasants. Furthermore, they wanted to make a revolution, and without peasant support no revolution could possibly succeed. Fortunately for the makers of revolution, Russia was not a land of peasant proprietors but one in which the mass of the rural population had been preserved from the development of property instincts by the communal system of landholding prevalent in Great Russia. At the same time the deep-seated antagonism between the village population and the gentry opened the widest perspectives before a band of determined revolutionists. The situation in Russia was as unlike that in the West as it was possible to imagine: the Russian peasantry constituted an asset to the revolution, not only in the negative sense that it was not committed to the defense of a regime of private property, but also in the positive sense that it could be transformed into an active force for the overthrow of the existing order. To effect that transformation was the primary task of the Populists.

It was in this connection that the role of the intelligentsia assumed paramount significance. Narodnik ideology in general assigned an important position to the group in society whose critical thinking was the leaven of social progress; as Lavrov expressed it, "Progress is the process of developing in mankind the consciousness and realization of truth and justice by means of the working of the critical thought of individuals upon contemporary culture."[3] But it was the attempt to revolutionize the peasantry which placed a special premium on the services of the intelligentsia. The peasantry was not only "dark," it was inert and amorphous; even after it had been aroused, it was all too prone, as the record of the past had shown, to dissipate its strength in wild thrashings and undisciplined violence. What the Populists wanted was not a Pugachëv rebellion but a modern agrarian revolution. Only the intelligentsia, with its self-sacrificing zeal, could enlighten the peasantry and stir it to action; only the intelligentsia could provide it with purposeful direction and save it from bloody defeat. Thus the inclusion of the peasantry in the ranks of the revolution strengthened the need for the inclusion of the intelligentsia, or rather that portion of it which had the vision and idealism to break with its class origin and assume the leadership of the live forces of the future, in preference to remaining with a decadent social order and fighting a rear-guard action in the name of economic selfishness and political reaction. This sloughing-off process, whereby the most idealistic elements of a dominant social group abandon it in order to help the oppressed, was viewed as a supreme manifestation of the subjective factor in history. So it was that Populism, for all its association of the proletariat with the other two components of the army of toil, never made itself the champion of the workers as did Marxism; fundamental to its ideology was the stake it placed on the revolutionary

[3] Quoted in Polianski, *Narodnicheskii sotsializm*, p. 37.

spirit of the rural masses and the exalted conception it had of the role of the intelligentsia.[4]

A third major distinction between Populism and Marxism concerned the road to socialism: the two movements proposed to arrive at a common goal by different routes. While the early Marxists and the later Mensheviks believed that the historical development of Russia would be, in essence, a recapitulation of what had taken place in more advanced countries, the Populists held that the way of the West was not to be the way of Russia. We have seen that they viewed the historical process in terms of the interaction of subjective and objective factors, of the growth of man's dominion over the forces of nature. The process was complex and in it there were many variables. Natural conditions varied, and individuals varied, and groups of individuals living under certain conditions did not evolve in the same way as other groups dwelling in different environments. Nations, in other words, have their individuality and cannot all be expected to follow the same path of historical development. In the case of Russia there were two peculiar circumstances which made it quite certain that her society would not experience the same evolution as that of Western Europe. One of these was the agrarian system; the other, the political regime.

The Great Russian peasant shared ownership of the land with his fellow villagers but tilled it on an individual basis. This combination of collective ownership and individual cultivation suggested to the Populists a stage intermediate to (a) the individual ownership and individual cultivation of a regime of private property, and (b) the collective ownership and collective cultivation of the socialist era. Here in Russia, in the form of the *obshchina* or village commune, was an institution with features suitable to a period of transition, a kind of natural bridge over which Russian society could move from

---

[4] *Protokoly pervago s"ezda P.S.-R.*, pp. 133, 357; P. Novobrantsev (probably a pseudonym), "Osnovnye voprosy russkoi revoliutsionnoi programmy" (Basic Problems of the Russian Revolutionary Program), *Revoliutsionnaia Rossiia*, No. 33 (October 1, 1903), p. 8; "Sotsialdemokraty i sotsialisty-revoliutsionery" (Social Democrats and Socialist Revolutionaries), *ibid.*, No. 16 (January 15, 1903), pp. 1-2.

the grievous order then existing to the socialist millennium of the future without falling into the quicksands of capitalism below. Why throw away this inestimable advantage and expose the Russian countryside to the destructive influence of capitalism; why break down the commune and permit the rise of mutually antagonistic classes—the peasant proprietor on the one hand, and the agricultural laborer or village pauper on the other? That was the desire of the Marxists, of those who denied that Russia could evolve in her own way and who insisted that everything, the village as well as the town, must come under the laws of capitalist development, particularly the laws of the increasing concentration of wealth and the intensification of the class struggle, which alone could prepare the ground for the advent of socialism. Not so, replied the Populists—and on this question they generated plenty of heat: to bring capitalism into the Russian village was wholly unnecessary and, more than that, it would be positively ruinous to the cause of socialism.

It was unnecessary because the Russian peasantry, thanks to the existence of communal tenure, had evolved a concept of landholding radically different from that of its Western counterpart. The mind of the Russian people, it was claimed, had been deeply furrowed by a consciousness of the right of toil (*trudovoe pravosoznanie*), according to which land was viewed as a free commodity not subject to private appropriation, as no one's (*nich'ia*) or as God's (*bozh'ia*). The right of use of the land inhered only in those who worked it with their own hands and only so long as they worked it in that way. The Russian peasant, then, knew the individual use of the land, but possession was conveyed not by title but by toil. Of individual ownership in the Western legal sense there was virtually no conception. And the Populists meant to keep it that way. In the writings and speeches of V. M. Chernov, founder and leader of the Socialist Revolutionary party, we encounter frequent expressions of gratitude that the Roman law, with its principle of absolute ownership of property, had only superficially penetrated the Russian Empire, together with expressions of determination never to permit it to poison the toilers' mind, unspoiled as it yet was by notions of private appropriation.[5] While it might be questioned whether the village commune inculcated a kind of latent socialism in the minds of its members—the Socialist Revolutionaries were less sanguine on this point than the earlier Populists—it at least had kept the road clear for socialism, preserving the rural population, and so the vast majority of the people, from that passionate attachment to a plot of ground, that *Eigentumsfanatismus* as Marx called it, which had proved so grave a stumbling block to the progress of socialism in the West. Once the autocracy had been disposed of, the Populists never doubted but that the whole complex of practices and habits of mind centering around the village commune, of which the consciousness of the right of toil was by all odds the most important, could serve as the basis for a new social order which would gradually mature into the collectivist society of the future without having to pass through an intervening stage of capitalism. The raw material for socialism did not have to be created through the capitalist process; it was already there, in the form of a village population revolutionary in tradition and outlook and devoid of a property consciousness.[6]

It was foolish to overlook these peculiar conditions and insist on bringing capitalism and the class war to the village. The effect would only be to destroy the solidarity of the peasants and set them at each other's throat. Moreover, such a course would be ruinous to the cause of socialism. The Populists never accepted, at least with reference to agriculture, the Marxian thesis that the end of capitalist development would find a few immensely wealthy individuals con-

---

[5] See especially *Protokoly pervago s"ezda P.S.-R.*, p. 211; *Zemlia i pravo*, pp. 130-31, 133-34, 167.

[6] "Russkaia krest'ianskaia obshchina i blizhaishiia zadachi revoliutsii" (The Russian Peasant Commune and the Immediate Tasks of the Revolution), *Revoliutsionnaia Rossiia*, No. 53 (September 30, 1904), pp. 3-6; "Agrarnaia programma russkoi sotsial-demokratii" (The Agrarian Program of Russian Social Democracy), *ibid.*, No. 40 (January 15, 1904), p. 9; "Sotsialdemokraty i sotsialisty-revoliutsionery," *ibid.*, No. 16 (January 15, 1903), pp. 3-4; *Protokoly pervago s"ezda P.S.-R.*, pp. 206-7, 220-22; Polianski, *Narodnicheskii sotsializm*, p. 49; Chernov, *P.S.-R. v epokhu Gershuni*, p. 1. These are the more pertinent sources upon which the brief summary above is based. For Marxist rebuttal see N. Egorov, "Marksistskaia kritika narodnicheskikh vzgliadov na russkuiu obshchinu," *Istoricheskii Zhurnal*, XII (1938), 35-47.

fronting a horde of dispossessed. On the contrary, they contended, the small landed proprietor or farmer seemed to be holding his own with remarkable tenacity: where he did not have enough land, he hired himself out part of the time, selling his surplus labor but keeping his plot intact; where he had a sufficient amount to absorb his labor, the productiveness of that labor did not suffer when compared with the results on large estates, because the tendency of the small owner was to carry on a more intensive cultivation than frequently was the case where men worked, not for themselves, but for someone else. Hence the small owner held his own in competition with large-scale agricultural economy or even extended his acreage at the expense of the type upon which Marx had wagered in predicting that capitalism would run its course and encompass its own destruction.[7]

The result of the introduction of capitalism into the Russian village, therefore, would be the elimination of communal tenure, together with the distinctive psychology which it had bred, and the creation of a class of peasant proprietors whose numbers would not diminish with the passage of time but, on the contrary, would remain constant or grow even larger. The individual cultivator would cease to regard the land as a natural good at the disposal of those who worked it, and would come to regard it as an object of private appropriation, as something to be accumulated in as large a quantity as possible for the exclusive benefit of the titleholder, whether he worked it himself or employed others for that purpose. Thus the strong peasants would exploit the weaker ones, and the class war would come to the village, even as Marx had foretold; but the strong peasants would not eat each other, since the inherent advantages of personal toil impose a limitation upon the capitalist process. As for

[7] L. Shishko, "K voprosu ob agrarnoi programme v sviazi s teoriei nauchnago sotsializma" (The Question of the Agrarian Program in Connection with the Theory of Scientific Socialism), *Vestnik Russkoi Revoliutsii*, No. 4 (March, 1905), pp. 324-44; Polianski, *Narodnicheskii sotsializm*, p. 52, citing the study of V. A. Kosinski. Professor Kosinski's conclusion was that the old-type, extensively cultivated estate everywhere was giving way to the small farm and could be saved only by conversion to the intensively cultivated, scientifically managed estate; this superior type of large-scale economy could arrest the progress of the small cultivator, but not even it could reclaim or take from him the land already in his possession. See his *Osnovnyia tendentsii v mobilizatsii zemel'noi sobstvennosti*, pp. 301-7.

the weak peasants, the agricultural laborers or hired hands, they would not be concentrated like factory workers in the towns but would be widely dispersed, and this lack of cohesion, together with their degraded status, might cause them to hearken as readily to the voice of reaction as to the call of revolution.[8] The net effect would be an immense strengthening of the institution of private property without any compensatory advantage in the field of labor organization. The consciousness of the right of toil would be replaced by a consciousness of private possession; the thousands of squires would be joined by millions of petty landowners. A natural foundation for socialism would be destroyed, and the strongest possible barrier to its progress would be erected. If the Russian revolution were to succeed, capitalism must be kept out of the village or, failing that, its development must be arrested at the earliest possible moment.[9]

The Narodnik attitude toward capitalism and the class struggle was neatly formulated by a member of the Socialist Revolutionary party (PSR) when he wrote that "in the refounding of society on socialist principles, the party makes use not only of the class contradictions of the capitalist order, but also of the whole reserve of spiritual forces which have been preserved in the toiling people of Russia from the polarizing influence of industrial capital."[10] By that he meant the toiling peasantry and its distinctive psychology under

---

[8] "Programmnye voprosy: Proletarii-batraki v russkoi derevne" (Programmatic Questions: Proletarian Hired Labor in the Russian Village), *Revoliutsionnaia Rossiia*, No. 12 (October, 1902), pp. 5-7.

[9] Expressions of Populist opinion as to the destructive role of capitalism in the village may be found in "Programmnye voprosy: Sotsializatsiia zemli i kooperatsiia v sel'skom khoziaistve" (Programmatic Questions: Socialization of the Land and Cooperation in Agriculture), *ibid.*, No. 15 (January, 1903), pp. 6-7; "Klassovaia bor'ba v derevne" (The Class Struggle in the Village), *ibid.*, No. 11 (September, 1902), pp. 7-9; "Sotsialdemokraty i sotsialisty-revoliutsionery," *ibid.*, No. 16 (January 15, 1903), p. 4; "Agrarnaia programma russkoi sotsial-demokratii," *ibid.*, No. 40 (January 15, 1904), p. 9. The Stolypin land legislation forced a revision of viewpoint upon the Socialist Revolutionaries, causing them to shift the emphasis from the primitive collectivism of the commune to its equalizing tendencies as a basis for their agrarian program. The other Populists were either too ridden by dogma or too little viable to make any readjustment.

[10] A. Gukovski, "Pis'ma sotsialist-revoliutsionera: Partiinye voprosy" (Letters of a Socialist Revolutionary: Party Questions), *Delo Naroda*, No. 113 (July 29, 1917).

communal tenure, which made it possible to claim the great mass of
the Russian people not only for the revolution but also for socialism.
This brings us to the heart of the controversy between the two
schools of Russian socialism.

The Marxists conceded that the peasantry was a revolutionary
force because of the survival of precapitalist or feudal forms of
exploitation, but they regarded that class as bourgeois in essence,
and believed that its true colors would show as soon as the old order
had passed from the scene. They compared the Populists in Russia
with the revisionists of the West and found that both addressed their
appeal to petty bourgeois elements, though in a different manner,
the revisionists by emasculating the class position of Marxism, and
the Populists by ascribing socialist proclivities to those whom they
would enlist in the revolutionary cause. The one course was oppor-
tunistic; the other, utopian. Only in Russia, where the class contradictions of the capitalist order were as yet imperfectly understood,
could such illusions be cherished and a movement arise which, in
seeking to synthesize interests that inherently were incompatible,
would think to make an original contribution to the cause of socialism. The desire of the Populists to see their principle of class synthesis accepted by the world movement might be viewed as an
interesting recrudescence, in revolutionary trappings, of the old
Slavophile messianism.[11]

In addition to the agrarian system and its far-reaching effects upon
Russian society, there was a second peculiar feature of that society
which the Populists considered imparted a special content to Russian
history and caused the paths of Russian and Western socialism to
diverge. This was the political regime. The Marxian concept of the
political order as derivative from the economic broke down completely in Russia, where the autocracy had called capitalism into
being and sustained it with subsidies, monopolistic privileges, and
tariff protection. This hothouse capitalism could not compete in
the world markets with the robust capitalism of the West, the
product of natural forces, nor could it thrive at home because of

[11] P. P. Maslov, "Narodnicheskiia partii" (Narodnik Parties), in *Obshchestvennoe dvizhenie v Rossii*, III, 89-95.

the weakness of the internal market, a consequence of the chronically depressed condition of agriculture. It could not stand on its own feet but must continue to rely on official favor, so that nothing in the way of independent political action could be expected of it: for it to strike at the autocracy would be to strike at the source of its own prosperity. This alliance between capitalism and absolutism in Russia, so at variance with their traditional antagonism in Western Europe, was reinforced by the pressure of the working class upon the entrepreneurs. Russian capitalism, parasitical in being and reactionary in spirit, confronted a proletarian movement that was all the more aggressive because of the harsh exploitation to which it was subjected. Denied a legal status for its combinations and smarting under miserable living conditions, the Russian proletariat, in truth, had nothing to lose but its chains; unrestrained by considerations which imposed caution on working-class movements elsewhere, it had developed a fighting spirit and a recklessness unique in Europe, which drove the servile bourgeoisie into still greater dependence on the autocracy. The rise of a proletariat in Russia under the scepter of absolutism, in the absence of political liberalism but in the presence of a maximalist-minded intelligentsia rich in the experience of other lands, was a development "fraught with the gravest historical consequences."[12] The SR leader (V. M. Chernov) who uttered these words in 1906 could scarcely have realized their full import.[13]

The nature of the political regime in Russia not only decreed that the revolutionary movement must follow an independent road to socialism but also governed the choice of methods to be used in clearing that road of obstructions. Though seemingly of less fundamental significance than the points of difference already discussed, the divergence between Populism and Marxism on tactical matters became so sharply defined as to provide the general public with a graphic symbol of their differences. Hence it may be ranked as a major distinction, the fourth in the present outline. The Populists, or rather the activists among them, embraced a cult of ultrarevolu-

[12] *Protokoly pervago s"ezda P.S.-R.*, p. 146.
[13] *Ibid.*, pp. 142-46, 247-48, 344, 359-60.

tionism.[14] They magnified the weak and ineffectual autocracy into a monster of evil, and felt that the singular oppressiveness of its rule justified a resort on their part to the most extreme measures. According the freest play to individual initiative in keeping with their ideology, they recognized acts of political assassination as valid in the revolutionary struggle, and acclaimed them as throwing confusion into the ranks of the bureaucracy while at the same time inspiring the people to resistance and bringing nearer the day of mass insurrection. Terrorism, then, was a prominent feature of Narodnik tactics, and the bomb-throwers of the Russian Revolution were either Populists or anarchists. Marxian socialists eschewed such methods as barren of permanent effect and as detrimental to the constructive aspects of revolutionary activity; with them, only the mass movement counted, or, as some would say, only mass terrorism. It should be pointed out that the Populist camp itself was sharply divided on the question of tactics and that a minority, organized after 1906 into the Popular Socialist party, not only rejected terrorism but in general displayed a Fabian spirit so unlike the ultra-radicalism of the Socialist Revolutionaries as to make it difficult to believe that both were rooted in the same tradition.

In the foregoing pages an attempt has been made to summarize under four headings the broad and basic differences which account for the existence in Russia of two distinct types of socialism, in contrast to the situation in a country like Germany, where the contest lay between two factions of the same socialist movement, in as much as both revisionism and orthodoxy were rooted in a common Marxian doctrine. Nothing more has been attempted than to present the main features of Populism, without delving overmuch into its theory. In the last analysis, the Populists were people who wanted to make a revolution in a land where society was overwhelmingly agrarian in character, where the state had always overshadowed the individual,

[14] See brief discussion of this point in Polianski, *Narodnicheskii sotsializm*, pp. 53-54.

and where the concept of property was still in a primitive stage. Hence it is not necessary to explore the misty recesses of their philosophy in order to understand why they emerged with a program of agrarian collectivism. They came out with what they desired from the beginning; it is not the philosophical background, but the socio-political setting of this movement that is fundamental to its under-standing. The Narodnik system of thought may, in fact, be viewed simply as a philosophical defense against which it was hoped that opposing knights of theory, whether liberal or Marxist, would splinter their lances in vain.[15]

In a pamphlet intended for popular consumption, and hence couched in simple and elemental terms, the Socialist Revolutionaries explained to their followers the reasons for the cleavage in the Russian socialist movement. Let us see what these reasons were and in what order they were given. The SR's could not go with the SD's, the pamphlet declared, because the Marxists (1) regarded the peasantry as an enemy of socialism, (2) did not acknowledge terror-ism, and (3) in general disparaged the role of the individual in his-tory, resting their hopes on the elemental course of economic development.[16] One notes what comes first in this exposition and what last. Whether knowingly or unknowingly, the SR's herein reveal what was uppermost in their minds. We have followed another order in our outline and have introduced a fourth distinction, the controversy over the peculiarity of Russian historical development and the road to socialism, which may, of course, be viewed as derivative from Points (1) and (3) above.

When all is said and done, Populism was, in essence, a movement composed of intellectuals who championed the cause of the peas-antry, and Marxism, a movement composed of intellectuals who

[15] As Chernov himself once said, " 'It is not the word, but the deed that counts.' How people explain, formulate, motivate their conduct is always less important than how they actually conduct themselves." "Otkrytyi vopros" (An Open Question), in *Internatsional i voina*, p. 73.

[16] "Iz partiinoi deiatel'nosti: Programma dlia kruzhkov pervago tipa (ele-mentarnykh)" (From the Work of the Party: A Program for Circles of the First Type [Elementary]), *Revoliutsionnaia Rossiia*, No. 53 (September 30, 1904), Appendix, p. 12. Program drawn up by group of propagandists of Kiev Committee of the PSR.

championed the cause of the proletariat. The Populists liked to contrast their broad and catholic "people's socialism" with the narrow "industrial socialism" of their rivals. But the impartial observer knows that the intelligentsia thoroughly dominated both socialist movements, and that neither the peasants nor the workers were masters in what was supposed to be their own house. The Narodnik thesis as to the significance of the intelligentsia is thus confirmed, but not in a manner from which its adherents would have derived much satisfaction. In the case of the workers this circumstance may not have been of great importance, since they had a highly effective champion in the person of Lenin (an intellectual who was not overly fond of intellectuals), but in the case of the peasants the domination of the intelligentsia eventuated in disaster, as an examination of the events of 1917 will demonstrate.

We may pause, after this inspection of the Populist background of Social Revolutionism, to note certain corollaries or by-products of the guiding principles discussed above. These corollaries manifested themselves in the life of the party and, while they do not appear on the surface and may, in fact, be denied official recognition, they nevertheless are of great historical moment—sometimes more so, one is tempted to say, than the principles from which they derive.

First, the emphasis on the individual in Narodnik ideology was no lightly held article of faith but the result of deep-seated conviction. In the field of tactics, as we have seen, it found expression in the approval of terrorism, that most characteristic of weapons in the SR arsenal. In the field of party organization it accounts for the almost incredible freedom of opinion and even of action which prevailed under the SR label, converting the party into a babel of discordant voices and reducing its discipline to the vanishing point. The Socialist Revolutionaries retained in fullest measure their freedom of dissent in 1917, but only at the cost of infirmity of decision and paralysis of execution. The outcome of a contest for power between such a party and the smaller but well-knit and superbly disciplined organization headed by Lenin could never be in doubt. Likewise in the field of political theory the SR's favored the most scrupulous observance of personal rights, and went in for all such features of the ultraliberal state as decentralization, national self-determination, bills of rights, and so on, which would afford maximum security to the untrammeled development of individuality in all of its manifold aspects.[17] So much concern was lavished on political liberties, in fact, that in 1917 they came to overshadow the demands of the social revolution in the minds of many of the intellectuals at the party helm.

Amid so much emphasis on individualism, however, there was one inconsistency: the individual was not to be free to unfold his talents in economic enterprise except within the narrow limits of his own labor, for any activity resulting in the employment of one man by another was regarded as exploitation and severely condemned. On this point the SR's were quite fanatical and wholly unwilling to make any concession to economic reality.[18] Again the reader is reminded: This was only nominally a peasants' party; in essence it was a party of doctrinaire intellectuals, as purblind in its devotion to shibboleths as any such movement always will be.

In the second place, there is a highly significant corollary of the Populist belief in the distinctiveness of Russian historical development and the peculiar fitness of the Russian people for socialism. It followed that the homeland must be suffered to go its own way, without interference from external forces seeking to impair its integrity or foist upon it a course alien to its genius; it followed, also, that a people who marched, or at least could easily be drawn, in the direction of socialism stood morally on an elevated plane and was to be cherished highly. All of this is but one step removed from nationalism. In 1917 many SR's took this step, some knowingly and others probably without realizing it, so natural was the change-over from aversion to the Russian state as they had known it to acclaim of the fatherland after the overthrow of tsarism and the dawn of an era of political freedom. The shift from internationalism to patriotism by so many members, particularly those in high position,

---

[17] A good illustration of this point may be found in the speech of Mark V. Vishniak, in *Protokoly pervago s"ezda P.S.-R.*, pp. 172-73.

[18] It is true that the First Congress refused to impose a specific ban on hired labor in agriculture. It was expected, however, that this type of labor would soon disappear under the program of land socialization (*Protokoly pervago s"ezda P.S.-R.*, pp. 211-12, 237-39, 252).

created acute tension within the party, impeded collaboration with the Ukrainian SR's, and made it impossible for the membership to present a united front on any number of issues, from matters of domestic economy to questions of war and peace. A situation where one section of an organization undergoes a change of character and another hews to the original line can have but one result—schism— and the wonder is that it was so long delayed.

In the third place, the Marxists and the Populists could not contend with one another without each being influenced by the opposing point of view. Neither liked to acknowledge anything valid in the other, but Marxism was in accord with the facts of economic development while Populism fitted the needs of revolution-making in a peasant land. Only the Mensheviks and the antediluvian Populists resisted the tendency to effect a synthesis. Populism as tempered in the heat of conflict with Marxism is neo-Populism or Social Revolutionism. Without going over to the materialist interpretation of history, the neo-Populists under Chernov moved away from idealism onto the middle ground of "realism"; they became reconciled to the advent of capitalism and accepted the class struggle, while redrawing its lines to suit their own convenience; they turned away from the artel to the factory, from the artisan to the proletarian, according the latter an honored place in the army of toil and a firm position on the scale of their solicitude. On the other hand the Marxists, who had always maintained, with considerable justification, that their rivals mistook for peculiarities of Russian historical development what actually were evidences of its backwardness, came to see that such conditions might be made to serve the purposes of a revolution which would duplicate neither the process nor the outcome of social upheavals in the West. Lenin's alliance system bears the imprint of Populism in its play for the peasantry and its depreciation of the Russian bourgeoisie, just as his activism, his willingness to anticipate the laws of historical development, bears traces of the Populist doctrine of the purposeful intervention of individuals as a factor in social progress, though in this case he may have been influenced more by the emotional tie with the older Populism, in whose service his brother died, than by intellectual controversy with its SR heirs. The executive committee of the Narodnaia Volia (the People's Will Group)[19] may have been the prototype of the organization sought by Lenin through application of the rules of democratic centralism and merited authority. Whether in evolving his theory of the rapid deepening of the political into a social revolution Lenin owed anything to Chernov's teaching that the coming revolution would overstep the bounds of a bourgeois order, and be limited only by the powers of achievement of the Russian people, is an open question.

In any event the interaction of Marxism and Populism did not change the essence of either. While using the peasantry as a steppingstone to power, Bolshevism retained in full measure that aversion for the independent tiller of the soil which is so characteristic of Marxian socialism, and never surrendered its purpose of reducing him to the level of a worker in the field, which, since its rise to power, it has pursued with tireless fanaticism. On the other hand, all the concessions made by the neo-Populists to capitalist development did not lessen their determination to exclude it from the village, not because of solicitude for the village commune, as so many intellectuals like to think, but in order to preserve the class unity of the peasantry in the face of the dangers that beset it, even more from the left than from the right, once the revolution had materialized. It was not the practice of terrorism, the nature of the revolution, the role of the individual versus the impersonal forces of history, and least of all the vastly overpublicized controversy about the divergence of the Russian and Western paths of historical development, which formed the watershed between Populism and Marxism; it was their attitude toward the peasantry. In 1917 the spiritual heirs of those who had made the most noise about preserving the folk virtues of Russia from Western corruption showed least resistance to the Western influences that were shoving their country into an abyss, and the more steeped they were in Slavophile tradition, the more frantically they clung to the Western powers and the more avidly they sought the alliance of Russian capitalism. When they descended from the clouds onto earth, their vaunted ideology dis-

---

[19] The terrorist wing of early Populism; see pp. 48-49.

solved like a wisp of smoke, leaving only a residue of nationalism. All the intellectual foam was gone—except from the minds of intellectuals who write history and love to dabble in purely intellectual constructions. But neo-Populism is not to be confused with the Slavophile froth of a minority of individuals who had never freed themselves from the aberrations of the past, and the prominence of these individuals must not blind us to the valid core of neo-Populism as the political expression of the peasant movement. As such the latter's fate was as tragic as that of the Slavophile vestige was ludicrous.

II

THE PROGRAM OF
SOCIAL REVOLUTIONISM

THE Socialist Revolutionary program was adopted at the First Party
Congress, held in the town of Imatra in Finland early in 1906, and
remained virtually unchanged through the ensuing years. Not even
the Revolution of 1917 produced anything to take its place, so
that it was still the official program at the time of the party's death.
Acclaimed as the product of a collective conscience, it was actually
the handiwork of a single man, and the congress gratefully acknowledged the labors of V. M. Chernov by according an ovation to "the
young giant who has borne on his shoulders for five years the whole
burden of the theoretical elaboration of our program."[1] The practiced eye easily detects the imprint of the author's personality at
every turn; unfortunately for his party, the deficiencies of Chernov
are also only too faithfully reflected in the program which he
formulated.

The division of the program into maximum and minimum sections
reflected the consensus as to the nature of the new order to be
erected on the ruins of tsarism. The SR's envisaged neither a triumph of socialism nor the establishment of a purely capitalist regime
such as the original Marxists and, later, the Russian Mensheviks had
in mind. The SR's believed that historical forces would deposit the
revolution somewhere between classic liberalism and the collectivist
society of the future, which could not be created by fiat but must
grow organically from the increasing consciousness, organization,
and economic achievement of the toilers themselves. To clear the
way for this organic development and to hasten its progress was

---

[1] *Protokoly pervago s"ezda P.S.-R.*, p. 294.

the purpose of the minimum program. Instituted for the duration of the in-between stage, it had been framed without regard for the interests of capitalism, in contrast to the solicitude of the Marxists for the maximum extension of the capitalist system. In fact, the SR's considered it possible to assume an attitude of hostility toward capitalism from the outset, restricting it to the narrowest possible limits and denying it access to fields where any alternative form of economic organization seemed feasible. In the sphere of industry they felt that capitalism must be tolerated for some time to come until conditions had ripened for its overthrow, but in the sphere of agriculture they believed that its exclusion was both feasible and necessary.[2]

The fruit of this belief was the famous proposal for socialization of the land, the heart of the SR program and the subject of many a bitter controversy with Marxists and liberals alike. Its purpose was, first, to preserve the Russian peasantry from class divisions and the contagion of property instincts which would have accompanied the triumph of capitalism in the village—one notes here the unwilling confession of weakness in the resolve to prevent the peasant even from tasting the fruits of private property lest he be seduced by their sweetness—and, second, to open an irreparable breach in the dike of bourgeois society through which the waters of socialism would flow until eventually everything had been inundated.

It is not easy to explain the meaning of this term, "socialization of the land," if for no other reason than that it was never fully clarified in the minds of the SR's themselves. Land was no longer to be bought or sold, nor was it to remain an object of private ownership, either by individuals or by groups; instead, it was to become a "belonging of all the people" (*obshchenarodnoe dostoianie*). This was the kind of phrase the SR's delighted in—high-flown, ponderous,

[2] *Ibid.*, pp. 141, 156-57, 254-69, 360-61; "Programmnye voprosy: Programma-maksimum i programma-minimum" (Programmatic Questions: A Maximum Program and a Minimum Program), *Revoliutsionnaia Rossiia*, No. 41 (February 15, 1904), pp. 5-8; A. Egorov, "Zarozhdenie politicheskikh partii i ikh deiatel'nost'" (The Origin of Political Parties and Their Activity), in *Obshchestvennoe dvizhenie v Rossii*, I, 419; A. Potresov, "Evoliutsiia obshchest-venno-politicheskoi mysli v predrevoliutsionnuiu epokhu" (The Evolution of Social and Political Thought in the Prerevolutionary Period), *ibid.*, pp. 631, 633-34.

and vague—and it was the kind of phrase that Chernov knew so well how to devise, for if he could not settle an issue he could always mask it with words. Attempts to render the formula more conventional, as by substituting the word "property" (*sobstvennost'*) for "belonging" (*dostoianie*), encountered steady resistance from its author, on the ground that the concepts of the Roman law had not as yet penetrated the consciousness of the Russian people and that it was the duty of the party to do everything in its power "to cause that legal system to wither away on our soil without ever having come to bloom."[3] Socialism must make its own law and not try to fit its reforms into the framework of Roman law, impregnated as this was with the individualist spirit.[4] The land would be the property neither of individuals nor of societies, neither of the state nor of the locality; "we shall make it no one's," explained Chernov, "and precisely as no one's does it become the belonging of all."[5] Basically, the SR objective seems to have been to make land as nearly like air as possible. Once the Roman legal terminology had been discarded and the very concept of property excluded from Russian minds, the local organs of self-government entrusted with the administration of the land fund would appear, not as sovereign proprietors of the land, but as regulators of the relations between individuals or associations with equal rights to the use of the land.[6] The term

[3] *Protokoly pervago s"ezda P.S.-R.*, p. 221.

[4] In this task the socialists could build upon folk concepts of justice surviving from earlier times in which the community interest was uppermost. "The socialist law of the future may boldly extend its hand to the toilers' sense of right, now in revolt against bourgeois private law, in order to pervade it with the light of scientific knowledge and overcome by common efforts the common foe" (Chernov, *Zemlia i pravo*, p. 167; see also p. 142). Both capitalism and the Roman law were to be vanquished with the aid of primitive forces which had survived in Russia after being extinguished in the West; primitive collectivism and ultramodern collectivism were to unite against the individualist present, reducing the era of private rights to an interlude in the history of man.

[5] *Protokoly pervago s"ezda P.S.-R.*, p. 220.

[6] Chernov argued that up to the present the individual had had both private rights and private obligations, but only public obligations without public rights (save in the political sphere, and there only quite recently). Socialism proposed to extend his public rights to the economic sphere (in the case of the SR's, to the use of the land, thereby compensating him, so far as was compatible with the interests of his fellow men, for the surrender of private rights to the land) (*Zemlia i pravo*, pp. 161-62).

"socialization" was preferred to "nationalization" in order to lend emphasis to the party stand in favor of decentralized control of the land fund, and in order to avoid confusion with the Henry George school of "bourgeois nationalizers," whose program contravened some of the fundamentals of SR ideology.[7]

Who was to have the right to use the land, how was it to be distributed among the users, and upon what agency would administration of the land fund devolve? The question can be answered only in the most general terms, for the SR land program was never more than a declaration of principles into which the necessary details were never sketched. Not even the events of 1917 induced the SR's to take this step.

Use of the land was to be granted on equal terms to those who worked it with their own hands (*uravnitel'no-trudovoe pol'zovanie*), whether they did so on an individual basis or collectively, as members of an agrarian commune. The SR's insisted that by socialization of the land they did not mean collectivization of production, for no basic overturn in that sphere was involved; the cultivation of the land would continue on a predominantly individual or household basis for some time to come, perhaps for a number of decades, until such time as the inherent advantages of cooperative effort had been demonstrated before the eyes of the peasants and they had joined in collective enterprises of their own free will. Here it is interesting to note that the SR's had vaguely sensed, a quarter of a century beforehand, the possibility of a program of enforced collectivization such as was instituted in the Soviet Union under the Five-Year Plans, and had taken a stand against it. They were uncompromising democrats, and remained so to the end; the people were not to be

---

[7] *Ibid.*, pp. 131-37; *Protokoly pervago s"ezda P.S.-R.*, pp. 219-28; "Programmnye voprosy: Sotsializatsiia zemli i kooperatsiia v sel'skom khoziaistve" (Programmatic Questions: Socialization of the Land and Cooperation in Agriculture), *Revoliutsionnaia Rossiia*, No. 15 (January, 1903), pp. 5-8; "K sporam o sotsializatsii zemli" (On the Controversies over Socialization of the Land), *ibid.*, No. 75 (September 15, 1905), pp. 5-7.

driven into the collectivist fold, but were to enter voluntarily, convinced of the superiority of that form of economic organization. The SR's harbored no distrust of the small individual cultivator:

We consider it as both inevitable and fully compatible with socialist principles to extend the holdings (on a basis of use, not of ownership) of those peasants who cannot be engaged in large-scale, socially organized farming, for want of the material prerequisites for such enterprise, and who will prefer a small-scale, individualistic economy. It will be our task gradually to draw them into socialism through the intrinsic attractiveness of a collectivist society.[8]

Inevitable it certainly was; but whether such a course was fully, or even partially, compatible with socialist principles is quite another matter. The SR spokesman on the floor of the Second Duma even went so far as to state that the party did not desire "at this time" to do away with individually owned plots (*podvornoe vladenie*), proposing merely to extend to these, also, the principle of equality in the use of the land.[9]

Socialization apparently would have erased the distinction between communal ownership (*obshchinnoe vladenie*), the prevalent form of peasant tenure in Great Russia, and ownership by households (*podvornoe vladenie*), the prevalent form in Little Russia, in as much as cultivation in both cases had always been on a household basis and now, under the reform, neither the commune nor the household would hold title to the land. Further, the function of equalization, hitherto performed at intervals through repartition by some of the communes, would devolve upon the local and higher organs of self-government as a constant duty. It would seem, therefore, that after socialization had taken place there would be a great mass of petty individual cultivators and a few communes of the new or higher type, the members of which would practice collective farming—would form a kolkhoz, in Soviet terminology. Some

[8] "Sotsialdemokraty i sotsialisty-revoliutsionery" (Social Democrats and Socialist Revolutionaries), *ibid.*, No. 16 (January 15, 1903), p. 4.

[9] P. P. Maslov, "Narodnicheskiia partii (Narodnik Parties), in *Obshchestvennoe dvizhenie v Rossii*, III, 124; *Gosudarstvennaia Duma, Vtoroi sozyv, Stenograficheskie otchëty, 1907 god: Sessiia vtoraia*, I (State Duma, Second Convocation, Stenographic Reports, 1907: Second Session, I) (St. Petersburg, 1907), 1330.

members of the party seemed to hope that the old-type commune could be transformed into the new without disrupting its corporate existence,[10] but in view of the fact that coercion was ruled out, it is difficult to find any grounds for their optimism. In the face of such a situation it required faith, indeed, in the "toiling conscience" to believe that the Russian peasants would retain the old, at best nebulous, notions regarding the soil and would not strive to become a class of peasant proprietors owning in full right the land that they used.

Yet whatever the future might have held in store, the situation itself could have been created—all that was necessary was for the revolution to triumph, the landowners to be expropriated, and the state properties to be turned over to the peasants. So far all, or nearly all, of the toilers would have made common cause. But then the second aspect of socialization—equalization of use—would have come to the fore, dividing the toilers and arraying them against one another. The SR's never made any progress toward settling this thorniest of problems, certain to arise because of the dearth of land in relation to population in some parts of Russia and its relative abundance in other parts. They were warned of the danger at the First Congress,[11] for many communes already regarded the land in their possession as their own property because of the redemption payments they had made, and would undoubtedly strive to add to it at the time of the revolution by seizing as much of the squire's property as they could, later refusing to yield any excess to the common land fund of "all the people"; thus the party might have to take property from its own supporters. In Siberia some Socialist Revolutionaries, in the name of regional autonomy, were already demanding that exclusive control of land resources be reserved to the regional authority, thinking in this way to fence off unappro-

---

[10] *Protokoly pervago s"ezda P.S.-R.*, pp. 119-20.

[11] In two ringing speeches by the agronomist Shvetsov, delegate from Tomsk (the "Pashin" of the congress) (see *Protokoly pervago s"ezda P.S.-R.*, pp. 184-86, 205-12). As the party was on a conspiratorial footing, only pseudonyms are given in the minutes. Many years later, at the request of this author, several participants undertook to list the real names from memory, but only V. M. Chernov had any success, and he had forgotten most of them.

priated tracts as the preserve of those who were already there, and in effect closing the door to the land-hungry population in the black-earth zone of European Russia. Elsewhere, also, autonomist pretensions might serve as a cloak for economic selfishness, and the whole program of land reform might bog down in anarchy and in bloody strife among the toilers themselves. Obviously, a clear head and a firm hand were indispensable to the success of the party's agrarian program. But clearness of vision was not an SR asset, and the party membership contented itself with the idea that the amount of land allotted the toiler should neither fall below the subsistence level nor exceed the level beyond which hired labor would have to be engaged.[12] How this was to be achieved and how the use of the land was to be equalized over all of Russia, it never said.[13]

Nor was a firm hand to be available—for the SR's refused to concede to the central organs of government the full measure of authority that would have been necessary to ensure an equitable and uniform implementation of their reform. Instead, authority was to be divided between the central and local organs without the competence of either being clearly defined. Outright proponents of national control and supporters of a solution along anarcho-syndicalist lines were both voted down, the majority point of view being expressed by Chernov when he said that "superstitious fear of the state is foreign to us, but for all that we are great friends of decentralization."[14] One reason for this was that the SR's expected to have control of some of the local organs long before they secured a majority in the central institutions of government, where bour-

[12] *Ibid.*, p. 363 and *passim*. It is true that a concise formula to this effect was rejected, for technical reasons, at the congress (p. 252); nevertheless, this was in essence what the SR's believed.

[13] That is, not officially. One of the party specialists in agrarian matters, however, worked out a scheme which would probably have been followed but for the October Revolution, and which was published in pamphlet form (Vikhliaev, *Kak uravniat' pol'zovanie zemlëi*). The pressure of events in 1917 prevented it from receiving the party's formal endorsement. A brief analysis of the Vikhliaev plan will be found in my study, "Chernov and Agrarian Socialism," in *Continuity and Change in Russian and Soviet Thought*, pp. 72-73, 77-79; on socialization in general, see pp. 69 ff.

[14] *Protokoly pervago s"ezda P.S.-R.*, p. 235.

geois influence would be predominant for some time to come.[15] Another reason was that they favored decentralization in principle. But they were constrained to admit that supervision from above could not be ruled out entirely; the higher organs must equalize the use of the land "in one way or another" (no way was ever specified, aside from a vague reference to differential taxation); these organs must also administer the land reserve and look after the problem of resettlement. But how were conflicts to be resolved when the local organs of self-government, administering the land already in use, contravened the principles of the reform? These local organs were defined in the party program as democratically organized, self-governing communes free of class distinctions (*bessoslovnye*)[16]—in other words, reformed *obshchinas*.[17] In numberless instances during the revolution these communes would have seized in anarchic fashion more land than was their due. How were the higher organs entrusted with supervisory authority to reclaim this land on behalf of the less fortunate—or less predatory—elements of the Russian people, in keeping with the program of socialization? By moral suasion? The question was posed at the First Congress in 1906 and was still unanswered in 1917, when such seizures were taking place all over the country.[18]

One of the few clear-cut features of the SR land program was

---

[15] See, for example, Chernov's opinion in *ibid.*, p. 234; note contradiction below, pp. 35-37.

[16] That is, not purely peasant, but inclusive of all social elements in the village.

[17] On this point see also Chernov, *Zemlia i pravo*, pp. 197, 209, 230.

[18] "K sporam o sotsializatsii zemli," *Revoliutsionnaia Rossiia*, No. 75 (September 15, 1905), p. 4; "Programmnye voprosy: Sotsializatsiia zemli i kooperatsiia v sel'skom khoziaistve," *ibid.*, No. 15 (January, 1903), pp. 7-8, where uncertainty as to the nature of the regime that would replace tsarism is cited in explanation of the failure to draw up a more detailed program. There was more to it than that, however; month after month went by in 1917 without any attempt being made to reduce the program of socialization to concrete terms (see later chapters). The SR's were simply not practical-minded people (once more the reader is reminded that theirs was, in essence, a party not of peasants but of intellectuals). On the subject of land administration, see also *Protokoly pervago s"ezda P.S.-R.*, pp. 91-92, 181-84, 198-201, 210, 231-36, 363-64. Subsoil resources were reserved to the state; presumably the central authority would have enjoyed in this sphere the authority which it lacked in respect to the administration of the land.

the provision for expropriation without compensation. Private owners of land were to lose their property and were to receive nothing in return except the right to be supported at public expense until such time as they could readjust their lives to changed conditions. The element within the party which later seceded to form the Popular Socialist party opposed the ban on compensation, desiring to leave the question open for the future to decide; but sentiment ran strongly the other way, partly because of revolutionary fanaticism and partly because the peasantry was believed to be dead-set against any form of payment—as very likely it was. Even so slight a mitigation of the lot of the landowner as that implied by temporary maintenance grants drew fire from some of the members. "A philanthropic matter cannot be the concern of our party," exclaimed O. S. Minor. "Even if all the squires should perish, what of it? A philanthropist's point of view is not pertinent to the social struggle, which is merciless."[19] Ordinarily, the SR's were not cruel folk, they were even imbued with a kind of sentimental softheartedness, but this gave way to callousness such as only moral indignation can produce whenever they had to deal with two elements of the opposition: with tsarist bureaucrats and noble landowners. The harshness of their stand on expropriation was, of course, directed at the gentry; with reference to peasants who had bought land or inherited it in full right, they meant to deal gently, as we have seen.[20]

A seeming contradiction in the SR program, and a fruitful source of dissension within the party, was the refusal to advocate the socialization of industry along with socialization of the land. Whereas the one was placed in the minimum program—in fact, constituted the heart of it—the other was deferred to the maximum program—that is, to the more or less remote future. The SR's promised the working class immediate improvement of its status

[19] *Protokoly pervago s"ezda P.S.-R.,* p. 205.
[20] See above, p. 28. For debate on compensation, see *Protokoly pervago s"ezda P.S.-R.,* pp. 90, 192, 201-2, 205, 209, 214, 249-52, 364.

through benefits and privileges, such as a comprehensive system of insurance at no cost to the workers, shorter hours, freedom of combination, a voice in factory operation, and so on; they plumed themselves on being able to champion the principle of the minimum wage and a further reduction of the workday below the eight-hour standard, since they did not share the Marxist concern for unimpeded capitalist development; but they were not willing to advocate the taking-over of industry at the outbreak of revolution. Extremists within the party protested the inconsistency of a program revolutionary in relation to agriculture but reformist in relation to industry, and demanded the socialization of both sectors of the national economy at the same time. When they did not get their way, they split off and formed the Union of Maximalists, a small, ultrarevolutionary group on the fringe between Social Revolutionism and anarchism.[21]

The majority opinion held that the two measures were not complementary. Socialization of the land was still a far cry from socialism in agriculture, for it related only to possession of the land and not to the production or exchange of agricultural commodities, which must continue to be in private hands for a long while to come. While the framework of bourgeois economy would be shaken and gradually undermined, since land, the most basic means of production, would no longer be subject to private appropriation, it would not be destroyed. On the other hand, socialization of industry affected not only property relationships but entailed collectivization of production and distribution; it was a far more intricate matter, and could not be thought of until industrial society had advanced beyond the present stage. In the words of V. M. Chernov, "the socialization of plants and factories is the sum of measures which logically lie within the scope of the maximum program and historically follow upon the definitive triumph of the working class, organized in the socialist party."[22] Thus did the SR's restrict social-

---

[21] For a concise discussion of Maximalism see Maslov, "Narodnicheskiia partii," in *Obshchestvennoe dvizhenie v Rossii*, III, 133-35; V. I. Gorev, "Apoliticheskiia i antiparlamentskiia gruppy" (Nonpolitical and Antiparliamentary Groups), in *ibid.*, pp. 511-23.

[22] *Protokoly pervago s"ezda P.S.-R.*, p. 158.

ization under their minimum program to the agrarian sphere, contending that the measure analogous to it in the towns was not the socialization of industry but simply municipal ownership of the land upon which factories and other buildings stood. The economic reasoning behind the position of the majority was no doubt sound, but more would appear to be involved here than economic reasoning: though the members never acknowledged preferential treatment for the rural toilers, it was only natural that the SR party should have been more concerned with agrarian reform than with urban questions, only natural that it should have had more to offer the peasants than the workers. And, finally, it was only natural that in 1917, after a hard and prolonged struggle (for the SR's were strong in the cities as well as in the country), the Russian proletariat should have prevailingly cast its lot with the Bolshevik wing of Social Democracy, turning away from a party which could not match Lenin in bidding for its support.[23]

The SR minimum program embodied the *political* principles common to most Continental socialist parties: the rights of man; universal, direct, equal, and secret suffrage; free public instruction; direct taxation; a fiscal policy calculated to encourage all forms of cooperation; free trade; and the replacement of the standing army by a people's militia. The SR's were anticlerical: they desired an educational system free from clerical influence, and they stood for the complete separation of church and state. They favored proportional representation and all the devices of direct democracy (initia-

[23] For discussion of the socialization of industry see *Protokoly pervago s"ezda P.S.-R.*, pp. 106-7, 111-12, 115, 121, 148-58, 268-69, 281, 284, 362-63. Two prominent SR leaders, Altovski and N. I. Rakitnikov, went part of the way with the Maximalists, favoring socialization of the more concentrated branches of industry at the time of the revolution. On the same general subject, see also "Programmnye voprosy: Sotsializatsiia zemli i programma-minimum" (Programmatic Questions: Socialization of the Land and the Minimum Program), *Revoliutsionnaia Rossiia*, No. 42 (March 1, 1904), pp. 3-7; L. Shishko, "Neskol'ko myslei po povodu proekta partiinoi programmy" (Some Thoughts on the Draft of the Party Program), *ibid.*, No. 53 (September 30, 1904), Appendix, pp. 9-11.

tive, referendum, and recall), believing that there was no reason to fear the rural vote, in view of the special character of the Russian peasantry, which would rule out manipulation by reactionary interests.[24]

In certain respects, however, the Socialist Revolutionaries went further in their political demands than other socialist parties. That they should have done so was in keeping with the maximalism commonly displayed by political movements in Russia, which caused them to be pitched further to the left—or right—than comparable movements elsewhere. Unlike those socialists who professed indifference to the form of the state so long as constitutional rights were secured (thus tacitly accepting the principle of limited monarchy), the SR's were ardent republicans who rejected the whole concept of dynasticism, and not simply its absolutist form.[25] Here was another point of divergence from the moderate Populists, who seceded in 1906 to form their own party. At the First Congress of the Socialist Revolutionary party their representative, Miakotin, opposed raising the issue of monarchy, lest propaganda among the peasants be impeded. As he saw it, the throne still had a strong hold on the loyalties of that class and any attempt to mix in republican ideas with the propagation of economic views could have only disastrous results. His protest fell on deaf ears. The political section of the program, calling in unambiguous terms for the establishment of a democratic republic, was passed without a dissenting vote.[26]

In opposition to the centralizing tendencies of many socialist parties, the SR's favored maximum decentralization. This feature has already been noted in connection with the administration of the land fund. During the period of the minimum program the SR's were prepared to accept an abnormal degree of decentralization—

---

[24] "Novyia sobytiia i starye voprosy" (New Events and Old Problems), *ibid.*, No. 74 (September 1, 1905), p. 6; *Protokoly pervago s"ezda P.S.-R.*, pp. 361-62.

[25] "Sotsialisty-revoliutsionery i nesotsialisticheskaia demokratiia" (Socialist Revolutionaries and the Nonsocialist Democracy), *Revoliutsionnaia Rossiia*, No. 56 (December 5, 1904), p. 7.

[26] *Protokoly pervago s"ezda P.S.-R.*, pp. 93, 292. Miakotin and his associates, Annenski and A. V. Peshekhonov, the founders of the Popular Socialist party, had the right to speak but not to vote at this congress.

even by their own standards—which they would be the first to rescind with the advent of a fully developed socialism. Not the anarchist's "superstitious" fear of the state,[27] but the calculation that for a long while after the overthrow of autocracy, control of the central government would rest in the hands of the "bourgeois minority" dictated this attitude of "exceptional caution" toward the central organs of state. As to the local organs, the party might expect to win a majority in some of them well before it could hope to duplicate that feat in the country at large. Apparently the dominance of the bourgeois minority on the upper levels of society might express itself either directly, through actual political control, or indirectly, through the influence of its ideology and economic power.[28]

It is not easy to reconcile this forecast of the future with the party's stand in favor of direct democracy and its optimism in respect to the views of the peasantry. There was to be universal suffrage, and the peasantry was imbued with the "toilers' sense of right"; yet the bourgeois minority would be in control of the central government. Obviously, it was not expected that the rural vote would place the SR party in power. Probably the SR's had in mind the situation that prevailed during the first revolution, at the time of the elections to the First and Second Dumas, when the peasant suffrage went for the most part to the Group of Toil, a parliamentary club rather than a party, consisting of deputies, mainly peasants, who embraced a watered-down version of the Narodnik land program but who were essentially reformers rather than revolutionaries, and democrats rather than socialists. Part of the time the members of this group, lacking clear-cut views and firm convictions of their own, had been taken in tow by the Kadets and

---

[27] The Socialist Revolutionary party was never free of a tinge of anarchism. One of the delegates at the First Congress declared that "we fear the state as the devil fears holy water." Chernov denied this in the name of the majority (*ibid.*, pp. 233-34; *Zemlia i pravo*, pp. 137 ff.). The official position was that the party rejected both the dogmatic antiparliamentarianism of the anarchists and the fetish of bourgeois legality developed by the German socialists ("Novyia sobytiia i starye voprosy," *Revoliutsionnaia Rossiia*, No. 74 [September 1, 1905], p. 6).

[28] *Protokoly pervago s"ezda P.S.-R.*, pp. 233-36, 264-66.

thus had succumbed to bourgeois influence. The SR's may have been right in thinking that in the face of such a situation something like socialization of the land could nevertheless be carried through— the program was predicated upon the assumption that it could be fitted into the framework of capitalism—but they seem never to have considered seriously the danger of perversion at the hands of a regime controlled by the bourgeoisie or subject to its influence, which could only have been exerted in the direction of making peasant proprietors out of the myriads of smallholders and thus of giving a turn to the land reform which the party desired above all else to avoid. If the SR's were relying upon the peasants' "consciousness of the right of toil" and upon communal practices restrictive of individual enterprise to resist such a temptation as this, they were standing on shaky ground. Nor do they seem to have envisaged circumstances like those of 1917, when, under the spur of war conditions and the collapse of the monarchy, the bourgeoisie lost command of the situation, the Group of Toil faded away, and the peasant suffrage was given directly to their own party.

Besides republicanism and decentralization, which they emphasized, there was another political matter, and one of great moment in Russia, in relation to which the SR's were prepared to go beyond European socialism as a whole. Their program extolled the principle of federalism in dealing with the nationalities problem and promised its widest possible application within the Russian Empire; it went on to declare that the party recognized for the peoples of that empire the "unconditional right" of national self-determination.[29] The SR's hoped that all nationalities would accommodate themselves within the framework of a federal state; but if any were determined to go their own way it was the intent of the First Congress to give them this right rather than to mar the principle of federalism by a resort to coercion. Their stand on this issue brought the SR's into sharp conflict with the Social Democratic

[29] *Ibid.*, p. 361.

point of view prevalent at the turn of the century, which favored
the preservation of existing states on the very understandable
grounds that the world unity of the proletariat could be more
easily achieved from the vantage-ground provided by a few large
empires than if these were knocked apart into a jumble of small
and feuding nation-states. *Iskra*, the Social Democratic organ, an-
grily accused the SR's of working great mischief to the cause of
international socialism by stressing a divisive principle instead of a
unifying one.

The SR's answered that, in view of the artificial and morally
indefensible ways in which multinational states had been put together, the existing boundaries could have little claim on the socialist
conscience; furthermore, restrictions on the right of self-determination would serve rather to awaken antagonism than to strengthen
the bonds among nations. They differentiated between two types
of nationalism: the one aggressive and prone to deny to others the
rights it claimed for itself; the other pacific and intent only on
national regeneration, which could proceed according to forms that
were historical and distinctive, and yet retain a spirit that was
socialist and universal. The second type they viewed as wholly
legitimate, and concluded that the demand of a people for independence was not at all incompatible with the cause of socialism.[30]

This acceptance of the right of national self-determination in the
broadest sense did not pass unchallenged at the first or founding
congress. What would the party do, asked A. I. Gukovski and
others, if a people exercising this right after being released from
the bonds of the Russian Empire should fall under the sway of a
native oligarchy? Would it not be better to devise some system of
minimum guarantees, binding on all the component nationalities of
the present empire, whereby the Russian democracy would be em-
powered to intervene in the affairs, say, of Poland in case that
country came to have a regime that flouted the principle of uni-

---

[30] "Natsional'nyi vopros i revoliutsiia" (The National Question and Revolution), *Revoliutsionnaia Rossiia*, No. 35 (November 1, 1903), pp. 1-3; comment
of the editorial board on manifesto of Armenian Dashnaktsutiun, "K revo-
liutsionnym partiiam Rossii (To the Revolutionary Parties of Russia), *ibid.*,
No. 71 (July 15, 1905), pp. 12-13.

versal suffrage? One way of securing such guarantees would be to insist that every nationality should take part in the All-Russian Constituent Assembly before convening one of its own; several members of the congress defended this procedure, and a decade later, in 1917, it became a burning question, both within and without the party. The most extreme position of all was taken by V. V. Rudnev, future mayor of Moscow and in 1917 a prominent right-wing leader, when he refused to concede the unconditional right of self-determination even to such cultured peoples as the Finns and the Poles, and then went on to declaim:

More than that. The Great Russian Revolution has a great world task to perform, a transcending mission for all of humanity, in the name of which it has the right of revolutionary dictatorship—the right to violate the guarantees of peoples—and not only of those peoples associated by fate with Russia, but also of those elsewhere throughout the world.[31]

Here was Russian messianism with a vengeance. No better example could be found of how reformers with a world mission to perform open wide the gates to imperialism, militarism, and a host of other evils which in theory they denounce, but in practice accept —like a man who sees a false label on a bottle of poison and swallows the contents without blinking.

Another set of objections to the absolute freedom of nationalities did not concern the injury which a liberated people might do itself so much as the economic disadvantages that would arise from the disruption of a great political entity like the Russian Empire. New tariff barriers would be erected in a world already cursed with a superabundance of them. And at least one delegate bethought himself of the loss of the rich petroleum fields of Transcaucasia and of what that would mean to the interests of the state. Here a note of nationalism, if not of imperialism, is clearly sounded.[32]

In reply to these arguments, the proponents of national-minority emancipation without reservations warned that the party must not enter upon the slippery path of coercion in dealing with national

[31] *Protokoly pervago s"ezda P.S.-R.*, p. 172.
[32] *Ibid.*, p. 173. The discussion here is based on the debate at the congress (*ibid.*, pp. 163 ff.).

minorities. Chernov distinguished between the right of self-determination and the use to which it might be put: the party might
strive to correct abuses by all means in its power, short of coercion,
except in cases where a people had succumbed to autocratic rule;
if that happened, then the revolutionary intervention of the Russian
people would not in reality constitute a violation of the principle
in question. Chernov summoned the party to remain faithful to the
tradition first established by Alexander Herzen when he promised
Poland in the name of the Russian Revolution that it was to have the
privilege, not merely of autonomy, but even of separation. In the
end, a motion to delete the word "unconditional" from the clause in
the party program bearing on self-determination received only three
votes in its favor.[33]

This was a deceptive vote. The issue in question had called forth
an extended and heated debate at the congress, and the fact that the
opposition folded up when the showdown came is no accurate indication of its weight in the party councils. In 1906 the SR's were a
party without responsibility; in 1917 they had achieved responsibility; and, as they surveyed the nationalities problem from the
vantage-ground of offices of state, they came to conceive of it in a
less generous spirit than during the years preceding the triumph of
the revolution. As the party in 1917 never presented a united front
on any issue, it is difficult to describe its position; and though the
SR's rather frequently shifted ground from an old position, they
never liked to admit it. All factions retained their belief in federalism,
but by 1917 the right SR's were openly hostile to anything smacking
of separatism, the center tacitly so (except in the case of Finland and
Poland), while only the left wing was able to contemplate a seces-
sionist movement with any degree of equanimity. Self-determination
for the peoples comprising the old empire was a question of
capital significance in 1917, and one that occasioned no end of grief
for the party.

[33] *Dobavlenie k protokolam pervago s"ezda P.S.-R.*, pp. 8 ff. The statement in
Bernard Pares, *Russia and Reform* (New York, 1907), p. 340, to the effect that
the SR's opposed the division of Russia into racial areas, and would accept
autonomy even for Poland with reluctance, is wholly erroneous.

With this, the discussion of the main features of the minimum program adopted in 1906 by the First or Imatra Congress of the party comes to a close. The SR's proposed not only to defend this program in the constituent assembly toward which they were working, but also to attempt to implement it through direct action during the period of revolution.[34]

The maximum program requires little comment. It would be put into effect when the toiling masses were sufficiently conscious, sufficiently well-organized and sufficiently matured in the economic sense to desire the extension of the collectivist principle to all phases of the national economy, and when they had lodged the power of state firmly in the hands of their social revolutionary party. The socialization of land having already been realized under the minimum program, the party would proceed to the collectivization of agriculture, to the socialization of industry, and to the elimination of all aspects of private economy. In case of need, the program expressly sanctioned the resort to a "temporary revolutionary dictatorship." Some members of the party, not liking the connotations of the word "dictatorship" under any circumstances, argued that this implied the manifest absurdity of the people's establishing a dictatorship over itself; but Chernov, citing the example of the French Revolution and Thiers's regime in 1871, maintained that recourse to dictatorial methods on the part of a majority was by no means unknown to history, and that it was necessary to have a reliable weapon in the arsenal of socialism for use against the plottings and intrigue of the dispossessed minority. After considerable bickering, the point was retained in the program by a vote of 44 against 10 with 2 abstentions.[35]

Thus in the Socialist Revolutionary program, as in the Social Democratic, there was a provision for dictatorship under certain

---

[34] *Protokoly pervago s"ezda P.S.-R.*, p. 365.

[35] *Ibid.*, pp. 87, 158-60, 248, 360. The program speaks of a dictatorship of the "working class," but here the term does not have its customary connotations, for in the Chernovian phraseology it is synonymous with "people" (see statement on p. 87).

conditions. But the SR concept differed widely from the revision which the Marxian formula underwent at the hands of Lenin. The SR program envisaged no departure from democracy until the hour of the definitive triumph of socialism, when dictatorship would serve merely as a temporary expedient of the majority, to be laid aside as soon as the immediate purpose had been achieved. Lenin, on the other hand, advanced the hour to a point shortly past the outbreak of the revolution against tsarism, to a time when society would still be unripe for socialism and when the dictatorship must inevitably rest upon a restricted popular basis. In the first case, dictatorial methods could be discarded, safely and with despatch (in theory, at any rate), whereas in the second case they would have to be prolonged, creating a vested interest and feeding upon themselves, in as much as any relaxation would invite an uprising of the most formidable proportions. In the light of these profound differences, the assertion of a Menshevik writer[36] that the Bolshevik theory of dictatorship actually originated with the SR's must be rejected; the seed of the idea was there in the original Marxist theory, and its cultivation was chiefly the work of Lenin, who on this occasion would seem to have owed little or nothing to the SR's.[37]

When the SR program is critically analyzed, it is obvious that if the large admixture of optimism regarding the peasantry were taken away, the whole structure would crash to the ground. Basic to everything else was the assumption that this class, besides being revolutionary in spirit, was already semicollectivist in outlook and could be made wholly so with the passage of time. In keeping with this outlook, and in order to preserve the peasant mentality against the temptations of a capitalist economy which otherwise would remain intact, the program of land socialization had been conceived. It was in the harmony of the village outlook with the heart

[36] A. Egorov, "Zarozhdenie politicheskikh partii," in *Obshchestvennoe dvizhenie v Rossii, I*, 419-20.

[37] This is not to deny that he may have been influenced by the example of the Narodnaia Volia, the terrorist movement which flourished in the late 1870s and early 1880s as the lineal predecessor of Social Revolutionism. Despairing of the peasantry, the Narodnaia Volia had pinned its hopes on a strong-armed, conspiratorial group for action as the only means of breaking up the old order in Russia. Believing in the peasantry, the SR's could renounce the counsels of despair in favor of a democratic solution.

of the SR program that the party beheld the secret of "its strength, its invincibility, and its fascination for the minds of the people."[38] That the program had very great appeal for the Russian people, there can be no doubt. In the only authentic election in Russian history, they gave this party, even under the adverse conditions of late 1917, an absolute majority in the Russian core of the empire, and very nearly gave it a majority in the empire as a whole.[39]

But the utopian character of the program appears in the belief that such primitive, half-baked notions regarding the possession of land would have continued to thrive in the postrevolutionary era, despite the contagion of a private-enterprise economy, breached in this one respect, but in no other. The SR's acknowledged that in the field of industry the role of capitalism was still far from being exhausted—hence their refusal to contemplate the early socialization of industry—and they acknowledged that bourgeois influence would long be powerful in the councils of state—hence their insistence on decentralization, though they also favored it on principle. Are we to suppose, then, that the representatives of the bourgeoisie would have sat with folded hands and permitted the socialization of the land gradually to undermine their order of society, as the SR's claimed it would? Or would not these representatives, forced to acquiesce in the measure at the time of the revolution, have done everything in their power to subvert it later, dangling before the eyes of the peasants, now in possession of the landowners' estates, the sweet fruits of ownership in fee simple? According to the Mensheviks, this is precisely what would have happened, whether or not land socialization had initially been decreed; once the peasants had acquired a taste for property, the Narodnik ideology would be blown sky-high, and the lengthy process of capitalist development, ending in the polarization of rural society, would set in. The Bolsheviks were unwilling to wait so long; seeking a short-cut, they eventually hit upon the device of instituting a minority dictatorship

[38] *Protokoly pervago s"ezda P.S.-R.*, p. 207.

[39] See the author's study, *Election to the Russian Constituent Assembly*, pp. 20-22. If the seats won by the national SR groups (principally Ukrainian) be added to those of the main party, including the left wing, a clear majority of the whole assembly is obtained for the agrarian program, the only point on which all SR's still agreed.

with the aid of the peasants during the first flush of revolution, and then of turning this power against them in order to drive great numbers of them into collectivism against their will.

The SR's could agree with neither wing of the Social Democracy. They did not hold with the Mensheviks that the small peasant owner would disappear under capitalism, but believed that he would remain as a bulwark of private property. And they would have regarded anything resembling the agrarian program of Bolshevism under the Five-Year Plans with deepest repugnance; after all, they meant to serve the people, not to beat and starve them. They could only cling to their faith in the "toilers' sense of right" as being stronger than any property consciousness that might arise to challenge it after the peasantry had taken over the estates of the nobility. It would seem that this was a vain hope; it must be admitted, however, that it would have been sustained by one powerful factor— the egalitarian sentiment of the average communal peasant, who would have seen in a program for equalized use of the land without property title a means of holding his more capable or less indolent fellow on the same level with himself.[40] Whether this would have sufficed to arrest the development of a concept of land possession analogous to that of the Western farmer is doubtful.

Would the SR party, therefore, under its own program have eventually lost its peasant following to the liberals or the conservatives? That is a matter of speculation. The estimate of this investigator, based upon a close study of the party's character, is that it would have retained its following but shed its socialism, becoming the political expression of a class of small democratic owners and cultivators like the Radical Socialist party of France in the departments south of the Loire. As we have seen, the SR's drew much satisfaction from the stability of small holdings in the West, feeling that here was a phenomenon which controverted the Marxian thesis

---

[40] It was precisely this factor which Chernov seized upon as the main support for the agrarian program after the Stolypin reform had threatened the commune with extinction (see p. 84). Naturally, the SR's derived egalitarianism from noble impulse rather than from jealousy of success.

of proletarianization as applied to the village. In their view, the small cultivator in Russia, working without hired labor on land that belonged to "all the people," could be similarly successful. They expected him not to ask for title. But if he did, and if they were ever faced with the alternative of seeing him drift away to the right or of resorting to some compulsory and artificial program of collectivization, quite possibly they would have granted title. Regard for the free cultivator was perhaps stronger with them than aversion to private ownership.

Of all these implications in their program, and of the multitude of difficulties that would beset the scheme of land socialization, even more after its realization than before,[41] the SR's at their First Congress seemed blissfully unaware. They were devoted to their ideology, and pleased with the formulation which Chernov had given it. It is true that some voices were raised in criticism of the program as being unduly influenced by Marxism, the "fateful stove around which Chernov and many others had chosen to dance."[42] There is little substance to such criticism. Chernov always professed to be a sincere admirer, but never a blind worshipper, of the founder of scientific socialism; as he said at the congress, "Marx is our great common teacher in the realm of economics, but we do not feel constrained to make of him an idol."[43] The SR's accepted the idea of the class struggle, but so diminished its significance and so diluted its content as to change it beyond recognition. They believed to a certain extent in the theory of the increasing concentration of wealth[44] but not in its application to small-scale enterprise in agriculture. About the only Marxian doctrine they accepted whole-

---

[41] For a concise, nonsocialist appraisal of the land program and its effects, see article by L. Litoshenko in *Russkiia Vedomosti*, No. 9 (January 17, 1918).

[42] *Protokoly pervago s"ezda P.S.-R.*, p. 87. The words are Miakotin's.

[43] *Ibid.*, p. 136; Chernov, *Zapiski*, I, 105; Masaryk, *Spirit of Russia*, II, 372-73.

[44] Iu. Gardenin (pseud. of V. M. Chernov), "Nekotoryia osobennosti nashei programmy: Programma P.S.-R. i teoriia obnishchaniia" (Some Features of Our Program: The SR Party Program and the Theory of Impoverishment), *Revoliutsionnaia Rossiia*, No. 53 (September 30, 1904), Appendix, pp. 6-9; *Protokoly pervago s"ezda P.S.-R.*, pp. 103, 137.

heartedly was the labor source of value.[45] Only extreme Narodnik doctrinaires like the founders of Popular Socialism could discover an excessive amount of Marxism in the SR program.[46]

There can be no doubt that the SR program faithfully reflected the will of the overwhelming majority of party members. It was their misfortune, and the misfortune of their popular following, that it was more a declaration of general principles than a carefully thought-out plan of action, more a statement of objectives than an indication of how they were to be attained; and this weakness neither the Second Congress, which met in 1907 and dealt with tactical matters, nor the Third and Fourth Congresses, which convened in the storm and stress of 1917, succeeded in overcoming.

[45] See, for example, the model program prepared by a Kievan committee, in "Iz partiinoi deiatel'nosti: Programma dlia kruzhkov pervago tipa (elementarnykh) (From the Work of the Party: A Program for Circles of the First Type [Elementary]), *Revoliutsionnaia Rossiia*, No. 53 (September 30, 1904), Appendix, pp. 11-12.

[46] A. Komov (pseud.?), "Nashi zadachi i ikh formulirovka" (Our Tasks and Their Formulation), *ibid.*, pp. 1-3; Gardenin (pseud. of Chernov), "Nekotoryia osobennosti nashei programmy: Chto takoe partiinaia programma" (Some Features of Our Program: What a Party Program Means), *ibid.*, pp. 3-6; *Protokoly pervago s"ezda P.S.-R., passim.*

III

THE ORIGIN AND DEVELOPMENT
OF THE SR PARTY, 1900–1914

THE program of Social Revolutionism discussed in the preceding chapter was not adopted until after the party had been in existence for more than four years. Indeed, at the time of the party's birth the views of its members were very far from being crystallized, and even on so cardinal a question as what to do about the peasantry there was no unanimity of opinion. The party came first, and then the program, the theoretical elaboration of which was the work of a single man. It is true that Chernov drew inspiration and ideas from such men as Chernyshevski, Mikhailovski, and Lavrov, and also from Marx, but the fact remains that the celebrated Narodnik philosophy could not provide a platform upon which a political party could stand, or even a plank for the agrarian section of its platform. What is important as the source of the party is not the theories spun by a few individuals but the state of mind which brought men together in the first place and made it possible for them to agree on a program as a kind of afterthought.

The state of mind first became evident in the 1870s, and in essence it remained the same thenceforward. Something new was united with something very old, and the connecting link between the two was the village commune. The something new was the socialism of the intelligentsia, which began then to bestir itself, at a time when the ideals of the French Revolution were growing cold and in a country where they somehow did not seem to fit, the middle class being undeveloped, and the condition of the peasantry being such as to place the emphasis upon social rather than political reform. Maximalist-minded from the outset, the Russian intelligentsia was prepared to accept the boldest conclusions of contemporary thought, and that could mean only socialism. But there was already a revolutionary tradition in Russia, one that had demonstrated its power in furious though spasmodic uprisings in the past: the peasants' movement, compounded of greed for the land and social hatred such as only serfdom in the East European form could breed. How was this elemental force to be reconciled with a socialist goal? Here is where the *obshchina* or village commune enters the picture. The existence of this institution afforded hope to the intelligentsia that they might harness the age-old agrarian movement to the needs of an ultramodern revolution without compromising the society of the future through the creation of a vast number of small landowners. In other words, they hoped to avoid the solution of the French Revolution in favor of one where the peasant would work the land without owning it. All that was necessary was to incite the peasants to action, but that was no easy task; it would require the services of "critically thinking" individuals from the ranks of the intelligentsia to spark the agrarian movement. Hence the worth of the individual and the role of the intelligentsia in the oncoming revolution. Here are the basic ingredients of Populism; one need go no further to grasp its essence.

Populism began in the 1870s with the *v narod* or "into the people" movement. The naive propagandists of this movement had soon discovered that the government was not minded to stand aside and let them encompass its ruin; they also discovered with even greater pain that the peasantry was not ready for their message. Stung to desperation by official repression and disillusioned in the peasantry, a part of them turned to political action, believing that not until they had seized control of the state could they overcome the inertia of the people. Such was the genesis of the Narodnaia Volia. Its numbers were small but its will was strong. The terrorism to which it resorted accorded with both the weakness of the movement and the temperament of its members. Spectacular as was the success of the campaign, it accomplished nothing of permanent value, its essential futility becoming apparent in the replacement of the Tsar Liberator by Alexander III; but the Narodnaia Volia left to posterity a tradition of vain though heroic struggle which never ceased to fascinate the minds of youthful revolutionaries.

The center was soon knocked to pieces, the fire extinguished, but here and there embers smoldered until a generation later, when they burst anew into the flame of Social Revolutionism. Meanwhile, the rival movement of Marxian socialism sprang up and competed for the allegiance of the intelligentsia. So strong was the infatuation for this new doctrine, supported as it was by the visible progress of the industrial revolution and the rise of a new social class, that it seemed for a time as though Populism might be reduced to ashes. Losses were sustained, but the older movement managed to keep glowing, and in the later nineties there is evidence that Narodnik circles of a more or less active tendency existed in the black-earth zone at Saratov, Voronezh, Tambov, and Kursk; in Little Russia at Kiev, Chernigov, Poltava, Kharkov, Ekaterinoslav, and Odessa; in St. Petersburg and Moscow; in Perm province; and at Viatka, Vladimir, and Nizhni Novgorod.[1] It was a case of each circle for itself, however, for even more serious than the lack of organizational unity was the absence of ideological agreement.

In view of the dispersion and dissension that prevailed, how was it that the revolutionary wing of Populism withstood the Marxist onslaught and succeeded in preserving its identity? The answer is that these Populists, wherever they were and whatever they believed, regarded themselves as the heirs of the Narodnaia Volia; as such, they acknowledged terrorism as a legitimate form of struggle and believed that political liberation must be kept in the foreground of revolutionary demands. Furthermore, despite the disillusionment over work in the village which had come down from the Narodnaia Volia, they were unwilling to write off the peasantry as a loss to socialism; in fact, one of their main reasons for seeking the speedy overthrow of the autocracy was to open the way to the village. Thus the Populists were congenitally unable to accept the class theory of Marxism, nor could they accept its eco-

---

[1] Slětov, *K istorii vozniknoveniia P.S.-R.*, p. 50. The primary source. Slětov was one of the founders of the PSR. So also was his sister, Anastasia Nikolaevna Slětova, who became the first wife of V. M. Chernov.

nomic materialism, so that it might be said of them that, while they had not agreed on their own articles of faith, they were at one in rejecting those of their rivals. All of these factors helped to bind the Populists together in a rough sort of unity, at the same time serving to set them off from the Marxists.[2] But more was involved than disagreement over tactics and program. Populism was rooted in one tradition and Marxism in another. Having different backgrounds, the adherents of each tended to stand apart, jealously guarding their identity and seeking recruits for their cause, as much out of pride as out of conviction. Presently they were hotly competing with each other, and the animosity bred by this competition, in the opinion of one observer,[3] had more to do with estranging the two movements than their theoretical differences, which at that time were not nearly so acute or so clearly defined as they later became.

Even under the spur of Marxist rivalry, however, it was no easy task to bring the Populists together. They did not share even a common name. In some localities they continued to refer to themselves as "Narodovoltsy,"[4] while in others they were content to carry on their activities without any specific designation. In still others, however, the term employed was "socialist revolutionary," which also had a tradition behind it, since it was the generic term used in the 1870s to describe the whole movement from which specific organizations like the Zemlia i Volia (Land and Liberty) or the Narodnaia Volia were formed.[5] This term also had the advantage of avoiding the connotations of centralism and excessive concentration on terrorism which went with the name "Narodnaia Volia," while at the same time it stressed the greater activism of the radical

[2] *Ibid.*, pp. 38-39; Slëtov, *Sto let bor'by za narodnoe delo*, pp. 35-37; A. Egorov, "Zarozhdenie politicheskikh partii i ikh deiatel'nost' " (The Origin of Political Parties and Their Activity), in *Obshchestvennoe dvizhenie v Rossii*, I, 415. The last authority, a Menshevik, states that belief in political terrorism was the chief common bond of the various groups which merged to form the PSR.

[3] Argunov, "Iz proshlago P.S.-R." (From the SR Past), *Byloe*, No. 10/22 (October, 1907), p. 108.

[4] Meaning "those of the Narodnaia Volia."

[5] Thus the first terrorist acts of the Narodnaia Volia were committed in the name of the "Executive Committee of the Russian Social Revolutionary Party."

Populists as compared with the Social Democrats, who were thought to be bogged down in a slough of "evolutionism" or "economism." It was natural, therefore, that this name gained increasing currency in Populist circles and eventually came to be applied to the nascent party.[6]

In the late nineties two organizations of more than local significance adopted this nomenclature. One of them, centering first at Saratov on the Volga and then at Moscow, came to be known as the Union of Socialist Revolutionaries, or "northern union," to distinguish it from the other, which bore the pretentious title of Party of the Socialist Revolutionaries but which would more aptly have been termed the "southern union," as it was confined almost wholly to Little Russia. Although neither was more than a very small society, the formation of these unions represents a distinct step forward, since it came at a time when conditions were more favorable to revolutionary action than in the early nineties, a period during which every scheme for organization on a more than local scale either had not gotten beyond the paper stage or else had come to prompt and inevitable ruin. The conjunction of a weak reign with growing industrialization, the revival of unrest in the towns, and the return from exile of old-line rebels created an atmosphere of impending change.

It was obvious that if the two unions could be brought together, there would be an all-Russian Narodnik party. By the end of 1901 the fusion had been consummated: the conclusion of an agreement in Berlin between Evno Azef, representing the "northern union," and Gregory Gershuni, acting in the name of the Saratov organization and the southern "party," marked the birth of the PSR. Strongly supported by M. R. Gotz and V. M. Chernov, they succeeded in drawing in the rather temperamental elements of the Narodnik emigration abroad and in working out an arrangement whereby the organ of the "northern union," the *Revoliutsionnaia Rossiia*, would be transferred abroad and placed under the editorial direction of Chernov and Gotz. The new party also acquired its fighting

[6] Slëtov, *K istorii vozniknoveniia P.S.-R.*, pp. 41-42.

slogan at this time: "V bor'be obretësh ty pravo svoë!" (In Struggle
Thou Shalt Win Thy Rights!)[7]

All of this, however, was merely the formal aspect of unification;
the real spadework had been done at home. The truth of the matter
is that the northern "union" and the southern "party" had both
fallen to pieces before the birth of the PSR, and the center of
gravity had shifted to the flourishing local at Saratov, which performed the actual work of unification. There was an unusually
large number of intellectuals of Narodnik bent in the "Athens of
the Volga," from the ranks of whom the nascent party drew a disproportionate share of its leadership. Men and women such as N. I.
Rakitnikov, his wife (born Altovskaia), L. P. Bulakov, Sebastian
V. Arefev, and others helped lay the cornerstone of the PSR and
always occupied posts of eminence in its councils. From Saratov
province, though not from the city, came the single most outstanding member of the party, V. M. Chernov.[8] The array of local
talent was powerfully reinforced by veteran revolutionists like
E. K. Breshko-Breshkovskaia and younger leaders such as Gregory
Gershuni, M. M. Melnikov, and P. P. Kraft, who were drawn
thither from other parts of the country. Operating out of Saratov
in the course of 1901, Breshkovskaia, who was already something
of a venerated relic, made the rounds from one end of the country
to the other, from Vologda and Viatka through the Urals and the
valley of the Volga to the south of Russia, everywhere calling the
elder generation of revolutionaries back into service and inspiring
the younger with a zeal for the underground. Following in the
footsteps of this "holy ghost of the revolution" came Gershuni
to give organizational form to the enthusiasm evoked by her presence. That is how the PSR was put together, and the negotiations
abroad were more the effect than the cause of unification. By the

---

[7] *Ibid.,* pp. 107-8; *Zakliuchenie sudebno-sledstvennoi komissii,* pp. 18-19; A.A.
Argunov, "Azef v partii S.-R." (Azef in the SR Party), *Na Chuzhoi Storone*
(In a Foreign Land), VI (1924), 170, 174; Chernov, P.S.-R. v epokhu Gershuni,
pp. 8-9; Nikolaevski, *Istoriia odnogo predatelia,* pp. 48-50; Spiridovich, *Histoire
du terrorisme russe,* pp. 102-5.

[8] His home was at Kamyshin, a river town below Saratov. Part of his
education was received in that city. At this time (1901) Chernov was living
abroad in the emigration.

end of 1901 all the tiny rivulets of Populism were flowing into a single stream, as yet of no great breadth or depth, but already running swiftly and beginning to undercut the foundations of the traditional social order.[9]

There are several features of this process of unification which deserve to be underscored. The formation of the PSR came at a time when both subjective and objective factors favored such a development, when it was no longer necessary either to corral kindred spirits or go counter to the trend of the times. There was no attempt to impose a ready-made scheme of union from above or to force the pace of events. The organic growth of the new party secured it against the fate of those phantom organizations which had cluttered the preceding decade with the wreckage of their plans. There was nothing ephemeral or artificial about this union; it had come to stay.

Of equal, if not greater, significance was the geographical aspect of the new party. Unlike its rivals, the Social Democratic and Constitutional Democratic parties, which were always centered in the metropolitan areas, the PSR arose in the provinces and remained primarily a phenomenon of the black-earth and Volga regions. Even though it extended its conquests into other parts of the country, it never rested on such solid foundations there as where it had been born and where its core of leadership had been assembled. Not Petersburg or Moscow, but Saratov on the Volga was its capital or nerve-center. Until such time as an all-party congress could be convened, the functions of a central committee devolved upon the Saratov organization.[10] Narodnik groups in Moscow had exhibited

[9] Slëtov, *K istorii vozniknoveniia P.S.-R.*, pp. 42-44, 103-6; Breshkovskaia, *Hidden Springs of the Russian Revolution*, pp. 278-80; Chernov, *P.S.-R. v epokhu Gershuni*, pp. 7-8; Nikolaevski, *Istoriia odnogo predatelia*, pp. 50-51; Argunov, "Iz proshlago P.S.-R.," *Byloe*, No. 10/22 (October, 1907), pp. 111-12; Argunov, "Azef v partii S.-R.," *Na Chuzhoi Storone*, VI (1924), 168-74; Spiridovich, *Histoire du terrorisme russe*, pp. 101-2.

[10] Nikolaevski, *Istoriia odnogo predatelia*, p. 50; Chernov, *P.S.-R. v epokhu Gershuni*, p. 8; Slëtov, *K istorii vozniknoveniia P.S.-R.*, p. 104.

neither strength nor stability, and in St. Petersburg an organization was not even effected until 1902, after the party's formation.[11] Similarly in 1917, when nothing impeded partisan activity and a conclusive test was possible, the SR organizations in the capitals never rested on a secure basis and were exploded with comparative ease. It was only natural that Social Revolutionism should have thrived in those sections of the country where the intelligentsia could not have escaped the agrarian problem even had it been minded to do so, and should have lagged behind, or failed to attain stability, in places where other class interests occupied the foreground. In Saratov province, though the household allotments were of average size, the yield per unit of land was unusually low for the black-earth zone, so that the degree of peasant impoverishment must have been greater than elsewhere.[12] This may perhaps explain why Saratov was just about the most turbulent province in all of Russia and why even before 1902 people had come to speak of the state of disaffection of the Saratov countryside as chronic.[13] Viewed in a broader sense, the strength of Social Revolutionism along the Volga was a natural consequence of conditions which had caused successive outbursts of elemental wrath on the part of the peasantry to center in this region. The roots of Social Revolutionism as a truly popular phenomenon go deep into history, and in this sense the SR's may be viewed as the heirs of Stenka Razin and Emilian Pugachëv.

The geographical aspect of Social Revolutionism suggests a parallel with the history of the Republican party in the United States. That party arose in the heart of the farming country as an expres-

---

[11] A. Egorov, "Zarozhdenie politicheskikh partii," in *Obshchestvennoe dvizhenie v Rossii*, I, 415. As the Marxist historian observes, it should have been easy to make headway there, in view of the current obsession of Marxist circles with "economism," which led them to combat the natural pull of workers and intellectuals toward political action.

[12] See statistics in *Sel'skoe khoziaistvo Rossii v XX veke*, pp. 69, 134-40, 156. The contrast between Voronezh and Saratov is especially striking. The yield was also relatively low in Samara province and the Don region, but there the allotments were larger.

[13] V. Gorn, "Krest'ianskoe dvizhenie do 1905 g." (The Peasant Movement Up to 1905), in *Obshchestvennoe dvizhenie v Rossii*, I, 236, n. 3; 249-50. Saratov was also more exposed to drought and famine than a central black-earth province like Kursk or Voronezh. In general, it was more of a marginal farming area and the population lived more on the edge of the knife.

sion of the determination of the Northwestern democracy to keep the western domain free, and only thereafter was it transplanted to the Northeast on the wings of abolitionist sentiment. The original dualism in its nature has never been overcome, and the party has generally remained in a sounder condition in that part of the country where it first struck root, its acquisition of—or more aptly, its appropriation by—the Eastern plutocracy having been a gain of very dubious value.

A third feature of the process of unification was that the members of the new party were drawn together by common sentiment rather than by adherence to a rigid program, which would have served only as a stumbling-block to unification. A tacit understanding prevailed with regard to the burning issues of the day, while other matters of a more detailed or theoretical nature were simply ignored for the time being. The members accepted political liberation as the immediate goal of their endeavor and were willing to enter into a temporary alliance with liberalism[14] in order to achieve it. They acknowledged terrorism in principle and proposed to engage in it wherever practicable, but only as a means of inciting the toilers to active resistance, not as an all-absorbing and self-sufficient enterprise as in the days of the Narodnaia Volia. So far there is no contradiction between the initial attitude of the party members and their later convictions. It is in relation to the peasantry that we find an astonishing discrepancy between the opinion of the party at the outset of its career and the official position which it later assumed. As they set forth to war upon autocratic Russia, the SR's determined to concentrate their efforts on those elements of the population which promised to respond most quickly to the call of revolution, leaving for some future occasion the task of inciting to action the more inert elements. "The party devotes its attention primarily to work among two layers of the population: the industrial workers in large centers

---

[14] In view of the abuse to which this term is subjected in contemporary American usage, it seems advisable to caution the reader that here and throughout this study the term "liberalism" is used in the classic sense of the nineteenth century to denote a movement which combined a belief in constitutional government with defense of the institution of private property.

and the intelligentsia. Within the intelligentsia the party concentrates . . . on the student youth." The peasantry was not entirely to be ignored—wide-awake individuals and groups were to be enlisted wherever possible in the cause—but the party members admittedly had no hope of stirring up the mass of the peasantry and were disposed to wait until political liberation had been won with the aid of other forces and the way to the village cleared before turning their main attention to the peasantry.[15]

This dominant note of disillusionment in the peasantry, which stemmed from the reaction of the Narodnaia Volia against the naive faith of the *v narod* movement, had never been suffered to pass unchallenged by certain individuals who persevered in their efforts to arouse the countryside despite the lessons of past experience. The newly formed party acclaimed their initiative while failing to share their optimism.[16] Breshkovskaia was one of those who had not despaired of the peasantry, reaffirming her faith in it upon her return from exile in 1896.[17] Of actual work in the village, even during the period when this negative attitude was strongest, there are a number of examples.

The best-known is the Tambov group of the middle nineties, consisting of V. M. Chernov, his wife, A. N. Slëtova, her brother, S. N. Slëtov, P. A. Dobronravov, and the brothers Volski—all figures of prominence in SR history. They initiated the first revolutionary peasants' organization in Russia during the years 1896-97 in the village of Pavlodar, Borisoglebsk *uezd* (district), whence the movement gradually spread to surrounding districts of Tambov province until the multiplication of "brotherhoods," as these revolutionary units were called, culminated in the large-scale insurrection of 1905. Here was a kind of training ground for men and women who would later make the PSR the mouthpiece of peasant aspirations. Here

---

[15] See especially "Neotlozhnaia zadacha" (An Urgent Task), *Revoliutsionnaia Rossiia*, No. 3 (January, 1902), pp. 8-9; "Nasha programma" (Our Program), *Vestnik Russkoi Revoliutsii*, No. 1(1902), pp. 8-9. These were the two official organs of the new party; hence their statements may be accepted as authoritative.

[16] *Ibid.*

[17] Slëtov, *K istorii vozniknoveniia P.S.-R.*, pp. 52-53.

they laid the foundations for that virtual monopoly of political
influence which the PSR was destined to enjoy in the central black-
earth region. Here they learned that rationalistic religious sects could
sometimes be made the vehicle of revolutionary propaganda, and
even that lay defenders of Orthodoxy would hearken to schemes of
social betterment, but that nothing could be done with the Stundists
or Baptists, who were slaves to their mania for literal interpretation
of the Bible. Most valuable, perhaps, of all the lessons they learned
was that the old bugaboo of the revolutionists, the peasants' loyalty
to the throne, could be overcome by skillful propaganda which
taught the peasants to look upon the tsar, not as a compassionate
father deceived by wicked squires, but as himself the first of the
squires and the greatest landowner in all Russia. That was the entering wedge devised by Chernov to split the people from the throne,
and it must be admitted that it was an efficacious one. The only
trouble was that Chernov did not harvest the fruits of his labor; they
were gathered in by the Bolshevik foe.[18]

Other examples of early work among the peasants may be cited.
In Saratov province the groundwork for the powerful agrarian
movement of the future appears to have been laid by Sebastian V.
Arefev and his sons, whose unflagging zeal neither official repression
nor peasant lethargy could thwart. Little is known of their work,[19]
but it must have accomplished a great deal, judging from the results.
From other provinces came reports of similar, if less sustained, activity. In Poltava province, however, the widespread disorders of 1902
were preceded by a dozen years or so of molelike work in the villages, on a small scale and uncoordinated, it is true, but attuned to
the needs of the peasantry through the use of the native idiom, and
featuring an admixture of republican and Ukrainophile sentiments
with the message of social reform.[20]

It was these disorders in Poltava province in the spring of 1902

[18] The story of the Tambov enterprise is told by Chernov in *Zapiski*, I,
249-335.

[19] See Slëtov, *K istorii vozniknoveniia P.S.-R.*, pp. 55-56; also obituary of
V. S. Arefev in *Vestnik Russkoi Revoliutsii*, No. 2, Sec. III, pp. 114-16.

[20] Slëtov, *K istorii vozniknoveniia P.S.-R.*, pp. 56-57.

which changed the whole course of party history.[21] The spirit of
revolt spread to Kharkov province, while in the Saratov district a
simultaneous though independent outbreak assumed even more formidable proportions in the sense that the movement was more complex, less naive, and wholly free of illusions as to sympathy on the
part of the tsar.[22] This double-barreled blast at either end of the
black-earth zone convinced the SR's overnight, as it were, that they
had been on the wrong track in nursing small groups of workers in
railroad shops and elsewhere,[23] and that those individuals were right
who had maintained all along that the most fertile field for the application of the party's energies lay in the rural communities. So the
SR's turned around and joyfully faced the village. That is what they
had really wanted to do all along, for they had never written the
peasantry off as a total loss, intending to turn to it as soon as political
conditions were favorable; and now they were promised a reward
for their efforts which would dwarf anything to be obtained from
the towns. Within a few years the fertile brain of Chernov had
evolved the program of land socialization, and the party had the
theoretical justification for dedicating itself to the village[24]—a course
of action which the individual members had always desired, however
they might differ as to its feasibility, and which the party, as a corporate enterprise, had already embarked upon before the program

[21] The whole eighth number (June 25, 1902) of *Revoliutsionnaia Rossiia* is
given over to the peasant movement. See especially "Krest'ianskoe dvizhenie,"
pp. 1-5, and the report from Poltava province, pp. 17-19. See also "Programmnye voprosy: Kharakter sovremennago krest'ianskago dvizheniia" (Programmatic Questions: The Nature of the Contemporary Peasant Movement),
ibid., No. 13 (November, 1902), pp. 4-6; A. Egorov, "Zarozhdenie politicheskikh
partii," in *Obshchestvennoe dvizhenie v Rossii*, I, 418; Gorn, "Krest'ianskoe
dvizhenie," in *ibid.*, pp. 245-49.

[22] *Ibid.*, p. 250.

[23] In Saratov the local Populists had been assiduously cultivating the employees of a few small factories and shops, to the neglect of the peasants, who
even in this hotbed of disaffection had been left to the individual ministrations
of a few perennial workers like the Arefevs. The gradual process whereby the
rural population was being revolutionized went unnoticed by these intellectuals.
See Argunov, "Iz proshlago partii," *Byloe*, No. 10/22 (October, 1907), pp.
103-4.

[24] On this point see especially Chernov's comment in *Zemlia i pravo*, p. 236.

was formulated.[25] That all of this amounted to a reversal of the initial attitude offered no difficulty; the PSR was an organization of intellectuals, and intellectuals often reverse themselves.

Of the disillusionment bequeathed by the Narodnaia Volia, nothing whatever remained. And this was entirely in accord with the changed aspect of the Russian village. Where once the revolutionists had encountered a blank wall of inertia and suspicion in the village, they now struck something that was soft and yielding. The village was no longer what it had been; the Alexandrinian reforms, especially the institution of the zemstvos, had set in motion a process whereby an intelligentsia of service had been introduced into the village at the same time that the villagers themselves were becoming increasingly literate as a result of the establishment of schools. The gulf between agitators and peasants had been too great in the 1870s, but when the revolutionists came back to the village, in driblets before 1902 and in droves thereafter, they found a literate stratum to which it was easy to talk and through which it was possible to reach all the rest of the peasantry. In fact, the intellectuals in public service and the educated peasants did not wait to be subverted but themselves often took the initiative, so that in the end the SR's became par excellence a party of the rural intelligentsia.

In every instance of early activity referred to above,[26] and in others not mentioned, the center of agitation was invariably some intellectual sojourning in the village, either a teacher, a physician, a medical assistant, the son of a church official, a seminary student, or some other member of the educated class, whose ranks had been swelled so greatly by the reform legislation of Alexander II.[27]

To this subjective factor of change was joined a powerful objective factor: the growing impoverishment of the peasantry as a result of the pressure of population upon the available land fund, the stag-

[25] The reader will observe the sequence of developments: first came the party, then the agrarian movement, and only subsequently the theory. In respect to the cardinal tenet of Social Revolutionism, theory occupies a secondary and derivative position.

[26] See pp. 56-57.

[27] See especially Slëtov, *K istorii vozniknoveniia P.S.-R.*, pp. 56-59.

nation induced by the commune, and the one-sided fiscal policy of S. I. Witte, beneficial to industry and detrimental to agriculture. Under the double impact of cultural progress and economic misery the old order began to give way, the throne and the altar no longer cast a spell over the minds of the people,[28] and the SR's, discarding the pessimism of the Narodnaia Volia and reverting to the original dream of the Zemlia i Volia, found that they could go to the people and that the people would respond. The agrarian revolution henceforth engrossed their attention, and if they did not entirely abandon the towns to the Social Democrats, they at any rate regarded them as a secondary theater of operations.[29]

With the about face on the peasant problem, the party had found itself, so to speak, and henceforth it grew rapidly, passing from a stage of "domestic economy" into one of large-scale enterprise. Both ancillary societies and the party organization per se expanded from year to year as the ferment of public opinion brought the country nearer the crisis of 1905. The chief ancillary society was the Peasants' Union of the PSR,[30] founded in 1902 at Saratov by Breshkovskaia, Gershuni, and Rakitnikov, and later introduced into other parts of the country, where it proved hardly less of a success than along the Volga.[31] Linking economic reform with political liberation, the union called the peasants "through land to freedom and through freedom to land." Proposing to attract as wide a following as possible—depth was admittedly a minor consideration—the union was not fastidious in the choice of methods and its appeal to the peasants' land hunger

[28] Interesting observations on this subject in S. Nechëtnyi (pseud. of S. N. Slëtov), "U zemli (zametki i vospominaniia)" (Close to the Soil [Notes and Recollections]), *Vestnik Russkoi Revoliutsii*, No. 2, Sec. II, pp. 58-65.

[29] So swift and complete was the change-over that of 57 titles published by the PSR in 1902, only one dealt with the problems of the working class. See P. P. Maslov, "Narodnicheskiia partii" (Narodnik Parties), in *Obshchestvennoe dvizhenie v Rossii*, III, 98-99.

[30] Not to be confused with the nonpartisan Peasants' Union, formed in 1905 and revived in 1917.

[31] Bykhovski, *Vserossiiskii Sovet Krest'ianskikh Deputatov*, p. 63n.

was couched in primitive and demagogic terms.[32] Another ancillary organization worthy of note was the Union of Public Schoolteachers, which merged in 1905 with the national Teachers' Union. Nonpartisan in form, the enlarged Teachers' Union actually was dominated by the SR's.[33] The party laid great store by the village schoolteachers, seeing in them excellent conveyers of its message to the people,[34] and no group gave more unified or more steadfast support. The student youth likewise furnished many recruits to the SR cause, though here the party faced sterner competition from rival political movements which also had their branches in the main educational centers.[35] As for the workers, the weakness of the party effort is seen more in the failure to create stable ancillary organizations than in any lack of popularity, for the SR's enjoyed what for the SD's must have been an embarrassing vogue in proletarian circles, due to the appeal of their terrorist tactics and the agrarian background of the working class.[36]

The growth of the party organization itself kept pace with the extension of its influence over the population. During the first year of its existence the PSR comprised nine full-fledged committees and

[32] "Ot Krest'ianskago Soiuza P.S.-R. ko vsem rabotnikam revoliutsionnago sotsializma v Rossii" (From the Peasants' Union of the PSR to All Workers for Revolutionary Socialism in Russia), *Revoliutsionnaia Rossiia*, No. 8 (July 25, 1902), pp. 5-14. Much of the illegal literature distributed came from the Agrarian Socialist League abroad. See letter of Saratov Committee to the League's Second Congress, *ibid.*, No. 31 (September 1, 1903), pp. 22-23.

[33] "Otchët komiteta soiuza narodnykh uchitelei P.S.-R." (Report of the Committee of the Union of Public Schoolteachers of the PSR), *ibid.*, No. 40 (January 15, 1904), p. 22.

[34] See, for example, the pamphlet of the Voronezh Committee, *K narodnym uchiteliam i uchitel'nitsam* (To the Nation's Male and Female Teachers) (Voronezh, 1904).

[35] Nikolaevski, *Azew*, pp. 63-64; Chernov, P.S.-R. v epokhu Gershuni, p. 27; A. Egorov, "Zarozhdenie politicheskikh partii," in *Obshchestvennoe dvizhenie v Rossii*, I, 419-20. Nikolaevski points out that the officers' corps of practically all revolutionary parties was made up to a large extent of participants in student disorders at the turn of the century who had been called to the colors as punishment for their actions.

[36] Chernov, P.S.-R. v epokhu Gershuni, pp. 30-31; Maslov, "Narodnicheskiia partii," in *Obshchestvennoe dvizhenie v Rossii*, III, 100-101. The Marxian historian attempts to depict the popularity of the PSR in working-class circles as an infatuation soon outlived. This is simply not true. The popularity was as great in 1917 as in 1905, perhaps more so.

ten lesser organizations or "groups"; by 1906 it embraced no less than seventy-five organizations, and many more were formed in that year, though a goodly number of these, no doubt, betrayed the softness of their mushroom growth. The increasing effectiveness of the party's work can be seen in the fact that illegal literature was distributed to the peasants of six provinces in 1902, and to those of forty-two provinces in 1903.[37] The money needed for expansion came not from the dues of party members, as in the case of Western socialist groups, but from the donations of wealthy sympathizers in intellectual or business circles who were hostile to the regime.[38] One of the surest storm signals of approaching revolution is the readiness on the part of some elements of a class whose property is to be expropriated to help along the cause of expropriation. These "fat boys"—or girls—who work for the destruction of their class, oftentimes without realizing what they are doing, are an inevitable, if not too familiar, concomitant of social unrest, whether in prerevolutionary Russia or in present-day America. From one point of view these financial angels of subversion are high-minded people who desert the camp of the exploiters to help those who are oppressed, but from another point of view they are so many symbols of decadence of a class that is marked for extinction. However that may be, we find Gershuni speaking of persons who gave tens of thousands of rubles to the party and performed inestimable services on its behalf, yet never once thought of becoming members.[39] The party also drew considerable support from the United States,[40] where in centers like New York, Chicago, and Boston there were large colonies of Russian Jews bitterly hostile to tsarism. And at least one contribution was received from a lodge of the Grand Orient of France.[41]

Though statistics on membership are neither accurate nor com-

[37] Statistics on growth from Chernov, P.S.-R. v epokhu Gershuni, pp. 9-11; see also Protokoly pervago s"ezda P.S.-R., p. 340.

[38] Protokoly vtorogo . . . s"ezda, pp. 135-36; Maslov, "Narodnicheskiia partii," in Obshchestvennoe dvizhenie v Rossii, III, 108.

[39] Protokoly vtorogo . . . s"ezda, p. 119.

[40] See especially "Russkoe dvizhenie v Amerike" (The Russian Movement in America), Revoliutsionnaia Rossiia, No. 60 (March 1, 1905), pp. 21-22, and No. 62 (March 25, 1905), pp. 15-16. A tour by Breshkovskaia in 1905 netted 40,000 francs.

[41] See financial statement of the SR Committee Abroad, ibid., No. 60 (March 1, 1905), p. 24.

plete, it appears that the PSR at the height of its development during the first revolution (i.e., toward the fall of 1906) comprised a core of 50,000 actual members and a camp following of some 300,000 persons who were continuously within the orbit of party influence and accepted its program, yet were not formally affiliated with any of its local branches.[42] This may be compared with the 150,000 members in full standing of the Russian Social Democratic party at the time of its Fifth Congress (May, 1907).[43] Deeply fissured though it was by the cleavage between Mensheviks and Bolsheviks, the Marxian party was much stronger than its Narodnik rival, even in point of numbers, not to speak of discipline or solidity of organization.

We know from admissions of the SR's themselves how little confidence was inspired by the large "periphery" or camp following and how little satisfaction was felt over the state of the party organization. A delegate at the Second Congress declared that his hair stood on end at the thought of things that were being done and said in the name of the party, for Duma electors whose standing in ancillary peasant "brotherhoods" and even in the party membership itself had passed unchallenged were carrying on in the vein of the Black Hundreds[44]—presumably an allusion to outbursts of anti-Semitism. A general demand arose for some method of demarcation between conscious elements and the raw intake from the outside, but the definition of membership contained in the provisional code[45] remained more often than not a dead letter, with everything depending on local practice, as some branches counted as members only those who were steadily in service while others accorded that status to the whole loose category of sympathizers.[46] The backbone of the organizational structure was the Central Committee at the top and the local committees in each provincial capital at the bottom, but the gap beween these levels was too great, and the attempt to put something in between had resulted in failure.[47] Chaos might be termed the nor-

---

[42] *Protokoly vtorogo . . . s"ezda*, p. 120.

[43] N. Popov, *Outline History of the Communist Party of the Soviet Union* (New York, 1934), I, 208, 213.

[44] *Protokoly vtorogo . . . s"ezda*, p. 116.

[45] Text of code in *Protokoly pervago s"ezda P.S.-R.*, pp. 366-68; *Protokoly vtorogo . . . s"ezda*, pp. 130-32.

[46] *Protokoly vtorogo . . . s"ezda*, p. 110.

[47] *Ibid.*, p. 158.

mal state of affairs within the SR organization, and the severest criticism that can be made of the party was its inability to remedy a situation deplored on every hand.[48] In fact, it never overcame its organizational weakness, the final catastrophe of 1917-18 being in part due to the superiority of the Bolsheviks in this respect.[49]

The Marxist historian Maslov is unquestionably correct in depicting the rapid growth of the PSR up to 1907 and its precipitous decline thereafter as simply a reflection of the rise and fall of the general revolutionary spirit of the times, as more an elemental tide than a conscious process of adherence and withdrawal on the part of articulate individuals.[50] But the contribution of the PSR to the revolution is not to be measured by the number of its members or by the strength or weakness of its organization; its service primarily was to inflame the spirit of revolt in the rural masses, and it had accomplished a great deal along this line before the first wave of revolution broke against the military bastions of autocracy and the genius of Witte, Durnovo, and Stolypin. In some parts of the country, notably in the black-earth region, the PSR had taken deep root, and in its Saratov stronghold there was not a single village in nine out of ten *uezds* without its contingent of SR's.[51] Under the blows of reaction the movement soon fell apart, but the groundwork had been laid for an overwhelming comeback in 1917.

Experiencing a vigorous growth in the first years of its existence, the party had not escaped the schismatic tendencies common to most revolutionary movements. The year 1906 witnessed a twofold seces-

[48] See especially *ibid.*, pp. 109-34, 170.

[49] On organizational matters see also *Protokoly pervago s"ezda P.S.-R.*, pp. 302-7; "Organizatsionnyi vopros" (The Organizational Question), *Revoliutsionnaia Rossiia*, No. 68 (June 1, 1905), pp. 6-9; "Iz partiinoi deiatel'nosti: Programma dlia kruzhkov pervago tipa (elementarnykh)" (From the Work of the Party: A Program for Circles of the First Type [Elementary]), *ibid.*, No. 73 (August 15, 1905), p. 27; Maslov, "Narodnicheskiia partii," in *Obshchestvennoe dvizhenie v Rossii*, III, 111-12.

[50] "Narodnicheskiia partii," in *Obshchestvennoe dvizhenie v Rossii*, III, 125, 128.

[51] *Bericht der Russischen S.-R. Partei*, p. 59.

sion from the PSR, the Popular Socialists splitting off on the extreme
right and the Maximalists on the extreme left. The Popular Socialists[52] desired to emasculate the SR movement by playing down or
eliminating such features as terrorism, republicanism, and expropriation without compensation in order to attain legal status and thus
be free to convert what was essentially a conspirative society into a
mass party. They also wanted to throw overboard the internationalist
tenets of socialism in favor of an exclusively Russian brand of collectivism, thus carrying to a logical extreme one of the basic proclivities of Populism. Moderation and nationalism were the keynotes
of their program. More doctrinaire in theory than the SR's, the
Popular Socialists were far more willing to compromise in practice,
and the tsar could have granted them the coveted legality with very
little danger to his throne. The old regime did not make compro-
mises, however, and the movement that aspired to the fruits of revolution while rejecting its methods was destined to remain a head
without a body, existing only as an ideological current until 1917,
when it became a distinct and stable, though numerically insignifi-
cant, party. The secession of the Popular Socialists took very little
strength from the PSR, as their debacle at the First Congress clearly
shows, the loss being felt principally on the intellectual plane, for
the oratorical and literary skill of these people was out of all proportion to their numbers.[53]

As for the Maximalists, their point of departure was the demand
for simultaneous socialization of both land and industry; in the field
of tactics they stood for the broadest application of terrorism, going
in for the "agrarian" as well as the political brand through their
advocacy of pillage and incendiarism in respect to the estates of the
nobility. They proposed to finance their movement by indiscrimi-
nate seizure of public or private property, especially bank funds;
this practice was spoken of as "expropriation," though prejudiced
observers preferred to call it "robbery." With the Maximalists

---

[52] Narodnye Sotsialisty, whence abbreviation NS.
[53] V. V. Rudnev, "Pochemu oni ushli?" (Why Did They Leave?), *Narodovlastie*, No. 3 (1918), pp. 34-47; *Protokoly pervago s"ezda P.S.-R.*, pp. 46 ff. and
passim; Chernov, *P.S.-R. v epokhu Gershuni*, pp. 26-27; Maslov, "Narodnicheskiia partii," in *Obshchestvennoe dvizhenie v Rossii*, III, 151-58.

action was everything and theory, a kind of afterthought, but they fashioned for themselves—or borrowed from Western anarcho-syndicalism—an ideology that was antiparliamentarian and decentralist in emphasis, with full powers of economic administration as well as political autonomy vested in the rural or urban communes. The Maximalists wobbled about the nature of the peasantry more than the SR's, feeling that perhaps the individualistic strain might get the better of the collectivist; in view of that possibility, their contention that the workers ought to take the factories while the peasants were taking the land was not devoid of a certain logic. Nor was their conception of the revolution, which postulated a clear-cut victory of the toilers: bourgeois influence on the state would be eliminated with the overthrow of bourgeois economy in both the industrial and agricultural sectors, and there would be no need of a second revolution, for society could attain by peaceful evolution the stage where socialism would be the conscious desire of everyone. Thus the inconsistency in the SR program between continued bourgeois control of the state and the abolition of private property in land did not exist for the Maximalists. Even the Marxists could not deny the originality and logical consistency of their theory, but the fact remained that the Maximalists were pretty wild people: they had to struggle at all times—and without conspicuous success—to keep a line between themselves and the anarchists, and oftentimes it was hard to distinguish them from ordinary bandits. By 1908 the movement had collapsed with only a year's lurid history behind it, and in 1917 it failed to stage a comeback, if for no other reason than that there was not sufficient ground to stand on between the powerful left wing of the PSR and the black-bannered anarchists.[54]

The SR's went through the first revolution (1905-7) with far

[54] V. I. Gorev, "Apoliticheskiia i antiparlamentskiia gruppy" (Nonpolitical and Antiparliamentary Groups), in *Obshchestvennoe dvizhenie v Rossii*, III, 511-23; Antonov, "Po povodu 'Vol'nago Diskussionnago Listka'" (Apropos "The Free Discussion Pamphlet"), *Revoliutsionnaia Rossiia*, No. 76 (October 15, 1905), pp. 12-14; Chernov, *P.S.-R. v epokhu Gershuni*, pp. 25-26; *Protokoly pervago s"ezda P.S.-R.*, pp. 147, 271-77, 310-12; Maslov, "Narodnicheskiia partii," in *Obshchestvennoe dvizhenie v Rossii*, III, 133-35.

greater cohesion in their ranks than later, during the Revolution of 1917, since the withdrawal of the Maximalists and the Popular Socialists cannot be compared, either in scope or in effect, with the bolt of the Left SR's. In part the cohesion was due to the limited numbers of the earlier period and the absence of the strains that come with power, but primarily it was due to the failure of the war in the Far East to stir the passions of the later European conflict which was to awaken all the latent nationalism in the Populist movement and set the "defencists" and the "internationalists" at each other's throat. The Manchurian war occasioned no such dissension, owing to the unanimous decision of party members to regard it as an odious venture in imperialism which ought to be frustrated by every means in their power. The party unblushingly encouraged subversive activity among the troops, declaring that "it is better to be shot for insurrection against violence and lies than to die for the glory of the 'sacred monarch'!"[55] But when Germany became the enemy, and war struck closer home, it was a different matter. The party split wide open, and the cleavage could never subsequently be overcome.

Throughout the period of its early growth and the years of the first revolution, the fortunes of the PSR are inseparably linked with terrorism. No other form of activity shed more luster on its name, and no other failure produced more devastating results. The bomb-throwers of the Russian Revolution were Socialist Revolutionaries, in so far as they were not anarchists. The Social Democrats eschewed terrorist tactics, and no sharper line between the two parties was ever drawn than on this issue.[56] The SR's inherited the tradition from the Narodnaia Volia but always maintained that in their hands the dread

[55] "Otechestvo v opasnosti!" (The Fatherland in Danger!), *Revoliutsionnaia Rossiia*, No. 41 (February 15, 1904), pp. 1-2; Chernov, P.S.-R. v epokhu Gershuni, pp. 34-35.

[56] A convenient summary of Lenin's views on terrorism—and very pronounced views they were—can be found in Pavlovich, "Lenin i es-ery," *Pod Znamenem Marksizma*, X (October, 1923), 155-62.

weapon was wielded solely to further the cause of a mass insurrection, never to take its place.[57]

In how far was this claim justified? Resounding feats like the assassinations of Minister of the Interior Pleve (July, 1904) and the Grand Duke Sergius (February, 1905) undoubtedly quickened the spirit of revolt and increased the momentum of the oncoming tide of revolution. On the other hand, terrorism as practiced by the SR's detracted from the prosaic but primary tasks of propagandizing the masses and building up the party organization; moreover, it was not coordinated with other forms of activity but flourished in isolation from the rest of the party. It was the boast of the leaders that the terror was never stinted in funds. In the words of the treasurer:

> We observed in general this rule, that the Fighting Organization was never to be denied anything. Whether money were on hand or not, it was necessary to supply it; we had to arrange matters so that this enterprise would never suffer for want of funds. We economized on literature and on other things, but never curtailed expenses as far as terrorism was concerned.[58]

Whatever the party publications might be saying about keeping the interests of the mass movement in the foreground, the fact remains that the party leaders regarded terrorism as the big thing.[59] So enthralled were they with the feats of the Fighting Organization that they accorded it full autonomy, not even presuming to dictate the choice of victims, to say nothing of regulating its internal affairs or selecting its personnel.[60] It was not until 1907 that the Central Committee assumed jurisdiction over projects of national significance.[61] We can only conclude that if the PSR did not degenerate into a conspirative society, isolated from the people and similar in all respects to the Narodnaia Volia, it was due solely to the temper of the times and not to any merit on the part of the leadership. Viewed in its broadest aspect, however, the terrorist campaign neither helped to bring on the revolution nor detracted from the

[57] See especially "Terror i massovoe dvizhenie" (Terror and the Mass Movement), *Revoliutsionnaia Rossiia*, No. 24 (May 15, 1903), pp. 1-3.
[58] *Zakliuchenie sudebno-sledstvennoi komissii*, p. 12.
[59] *Ibid.*, p. 13. Official admission.
[60] Savinkov, *Memoirs*, pp. 74-75; Nikolaevski, *Azew*, pp. 52-53, 85, 90.
[61] *Protokoly vtorogo s"ezda*, pp. 14-15, 23, 29 ff., 93-95, 162.

mobilization of public forces, for it pulsated in perfect harmony with the heartbeat of the people, waxing with the rising tide of disaffection and waning with its fall.[62]

The statistics of terrorism are revealing. They attest the deadliness of the chosen form of combat of this "party of assassins." An analysis[63] of over 200 outrages, of which but 13 were accounted for by the "central terror," the celebrated Fighting Organization, the rest being perpetrated either by regional Mobile Detachments of Combat or by local brigades, reveals that only 16 of the human targets escaped unharmed, as against 85 who were wounded and 139 who were killed. The list of victims is long, and sparkles with illustrious names: Minister of the Interior Sipiagin, Minister of the Interior Pleve, Grand Duke Sergius Alexandrovich, uncle of the emperor and "vice tsar" of Russia, together with numerous governors and other high-ranking members of the bureaucracy, generals and admirals, police and prison officials, and the smaller fry of the administration. The weakness of that administration is shown by the fact that the majority of perpetrators made good their escape. Deadliness, however, is not necessarily synonymous with effectiveness. One misses the names of men like Witte, Durnovo, and Stolypin,[64] who were primarily responsible for turning back the tide of revolution. Witte was never slated for assassination, as he was known to be an opponent of absolutism (it would be more accurate to say that he was an opponent of incompetent absolutism); Stolypin escaped partly because he was tackled later than others; as for Durnovo, the terrorists were after him for a long time, but the "old fox" always eluded them.

What kind of people went in for terrorism? Contrary to expectations, we find that less than 30 percent belonged to the intelligentsia as against the more than 70 percent who were workers, peasants,

---

[62] *Boevyia predpriiatiia sotsialistov-revoliutsionerov v osveshchenii okhranki*, pp. 96-97, reprinting a study of terrorism first published in the *Pamiatnaia Knizhka Sotsialista-Revoliutsionera* (Notebook of a Socialist Revolutionary), (Paris, 1914). Only 6 acts were perpetrated in 1902-04, while 51 are recorded for 1905, 78 for 1906, 62 for 1907, and 3 for 1908.

[63] Chernov, P.S.-R. v epokhu Gershuni, pp. 32-33. The analysis is evidently based upon the study referred to in the footnote above.

[64] The assassination of Stolypin some years later, in 1911, was not the work of the PSR. In fact, however, it is not easy to say whose work it was.

soldiers, and sailors—further evidence that the phenomenon of terrorism cannot be divorced from the popular movement. A goodly number of the participants were women (Russian, and Jewish, women have never been particularly retiring). Both normal and abnormal individuals took part. Whereas some of the terrorists had a sensible approach to their work, viewing it as a tactical device to be suspended immediately upon the attainment of constitutional liberty, others tended to make a cult of the practice, occupying, as it were, a twilight zone between idealism and criminality; and still others were plainly unbalanced.[65] The cultists among them had little use for parliamentary action, disdained the mass movement, and looked upon the main body of their party comrades, including the Central Committee, with ill-concealed contempt. They were pursuing a course which could easily lead to anarchism—or to something that eventually would be known as Fascism. Yet oftentimes the spirit of destruction was combined with moral sensibilities of a very high order; some of the terrorists did not seek to live beyond the accomplishment of their mission, believing that, while assassination was justified from the social standpoint by the service it rendered the revolution, from the personal standpoint it was still a grievous thing, which must be atoned for through the sacrifice of one's own life.[66] Of the bravery and persistence of these men and women who relentlessly tracked their foe by day and returned to their quarters at night with overwrought nerves to work with the volatile and inferior chemicals at their disposal, it is idle to speak. We read that on the thirteenth of October, 1906, in the dynamite laboratory of the PSR at Kazan, an explosion occurred which claimed the lives of four

[65] See especially Savinkov, *Memoirs*, pp. 39, 76-78, 277; Nikolaevski, *Azew*, p. 98; *Protokoly vtorogo . . . s"ezda*, pp. 94-95. Sazonov, the assassin of Pleve, seems to have been emotionally unstable; Dulebov died in a hospital for the insane at the age of twenty-five; Boris Vnorovski had suffered a nervous breakdown as a student.

[66] Savinkov, *Memoirs*, pp. 254, 279. Some had a passion for self-effacement: Chernov was once requested, as editor of the central organ, not to print obituaries for those who fell in the line of duty, since it was their wish "to go to our death as nameless soldiers of the party" (Nikolaevski, *Azew*, p. 205).

members of the Volga *druzhina* (armed band), a terrorist group responsible for the murders of the governors of Simbirsk, Penza, and Samara; the bride of one of the participants had been killed in a previous explosion, but that had not deterred him from carrying on his work.[67] In terrorism both the lighter and the darker aspects of human nature came to the fore.

The darker aspect is exemplified in the career of Evno Fishelevich Azef, who has no equal in the annals of espionage. The shock was great when, at the close of 1908, the party learned that for years it had nourished at its bosom a traitor who at one and the same time had been a member of the Central Committee, the connecting link between that body and the Fighting Organization, and the head of the Fighting Organization itself. Even today, as the investigator treads through the maze of evidence, he is assailed by doubts at certain points, and is inclined to view with indulgence the legends that have clustered about the name of this man. Apparently Azef played a double game, now betraying the terrorists to the police and now withholding information so as to permit them to score a success, as a consequence of which he made himself indispensable to both sides and milked both of funds. Yet a key figure in the espionage system, A. V. Gerasimov, maintains that Azef collaborated loyally with the police, certainly after 1905 if not before, and that he was no provocator but only an informer, whose duty it was to furnish leads to the authorities, leaving it to their ingenuity to unearth the details of an impending action.[68] In the specific instance of the Pleve affair, Gerasimov claims that Azef gave enough of a lead to have enabled a more competent force to forestall the assassination;[69] Nikolaevski, however, asserts that Azef desired the death of Pleve, both for personal advantage and because he held the minister responsible for anti-Semitic excesses (Azef was a Jew);[70] while a prominent member of the party, V. M. Zenzinov, told this writer that he per-

[67] *Delo Naroda*, No. 179 (October 13, 1917).
[68] *Erinnerungen*, pp. 200-203.
[69] *Ibid.*, pp. 199-200.
[70] *Azew*, pp. 62 ff.

sonally had knowledge of how Azef refused to divulge the where-
abouts of Sazonov on the eve of the fatal assault.[71]

Nor is there agreement concerning the motives of this fat and
cunning man. Nikolaevski argues that Azef was interested only in
feathering his nest at the expense of both sides, and estimates the
total profits accruing to him at from 200,000 to 250,000 marks,[72]
but Zenzinov, who had some experience with terrorism, contends
that cupidity alone is not a sufficient explanation, and that the ego-
tistical satisfaction that came from being a key figure in two opposed
camps and from holding so many threads in his hands must have been
of equal importance[73]—all of which, of course, is simply another
passage at arms between Marxist materialism and Narodnik subjec-
tivism. Azef's greed for money was no doubt great—one look at his
swinish countenance would probably convince anyone of that—but
Azef was not a brave man, and the impartial observer can only
wonder whether avarice alone would have overridden the fears engendered by so hazardous a profession.[74]

But if there is still some uncertainty regarding the motives and
conduct of Azef, the historically more important question of how he

[71] Interview in Paris (September, 1935). Such action, of course, does not
necessarily constitute a betrayal of the police. If Azef had told the tsarist police
everything he knew, his services would soon have been over, and very likely
his days on earth as well. The espionage system was full of leaks, and it was
only an elementary precaution, as Gerasimov freely admits, to have withheld
all but the most basic information. The question of whether Azef was guilty
of simple or double betrayal is one of extraordinary complexity; the consensus
is that he was false to both sides, but the testimony of Gerasimov lies in the
way of a definitive conclusion. Another police official, L. A. Rataev, considered
Azef guilty of treachery, but Rataev's account in reality supports the thesis of
Gerasimov. See his memorandum in *Provokator: Vospominaniia i dokumenty o
razoblachenii Azefa* (Agent Provocateur: Memoirs and Documents on the
Unmasking of Azef), ed. P. E. Shchëgolev (n.p., 1929), especially pp. 161-63,
170-71. Azef's earnestness in the affair of the cruiser *Riurik* (an attempt at
tsaricide) does not necessarily reflect on his previous activity, as it came after
retirement and represented a last desperate attempt to rehabilitate himself and
so avert death at the hands of the party.

[72] *Istoriia odnogo predatelia*, p. 357.

[73] See Zenzinov's criticism of Nikolaevski's account in *Sovremennyia Zapiski*,
L, 480-84.

[74] For Gerasimov, also, the motives of Azef remained a riddle (*Erinnerungen*,
pp. 208-9). The sketch that he draws of Azef (pp. 197-209) is rather favorable.
Nikolaevski's is wholly negative.

was able to play this game for so many years can be answered with assurance. An Azef could have flourished only in the PSR. The amazing credulity of the party leaders shielded him as with impenetrable armor against the shafts of his detractors. He gained the "boundless confidence" of Gershuni and Michael Gotz[75]—the most authoritative personage in the party—and after they had passed from the scene, Chernov, Natanson, and Argunov were always ready to spring to his defense against comrades like Slëtov, who sensed that something was wrong.[76] The Central Committee turned back one accusation after another with the stock rejoinder that it was all a police intrigue to compromise Azef and destroy the moral prestige of the terror, in blind disregard of the fact that the police had had no end of opportunities to establish the identity of Azef and decree his arrest.[77] The professional pride of the terrorists was another factor sustaining Azef, and one is led to suspect that the members of the Central Committee stood somewhat in awe of the monster they had created. The traitor had accumulated so much capital by permitting the plots against Pleve and the grand duke to succeed—or at any rate by failing to frustrate them—that his game might have gone on indefinitely had it not been terminated by disclosures from the ranks of the bureaucracy itself, in the form of testimony proffered by A. A. Lopukhin.[78] It took the intervention of a tsarist functionary to rescue the party from the fatuousness of its own leaders. The mere presence of a person like Azef in a position of responsibility would have occasioned a scandal in any well-regulated party. By conviction he was a moderate liberal and never bothered to conceal his views from other members, brazenly inquiring of Peshekhonov on one occasion whether he really believed in socialism.[79] He was not even a strong proponent of terrorism, at times opposing its continuance in the

---

[75] *Zakliuchenie sudebno-sledstvennoi komissii*, p. 91.

[76] Slëtov tried to develop the "agrarian current" as an offset to the hypnotic hold of terrorism upon the party mind. He was rewarded for his common sense by being shouldered out of the Central Committee (Nikolaevski, *Azew*, pp. 68-69, 77).

[77] *Zakliuchenie sudebno-sledstvennoi komissii*, pp. 66, 92.

[78] Stolypin railroaded Lopukhin through to Siberia in punishment for his disclosures.

[79] Nikolaevski, *Azew*, pp. 86-87, 159; Gerasimov, *Erinnerungen*, p. 208.

Central Committee, though he naturally accepted the commission to head the campaign when it was thrust upon him by that fantastic body.[80] As to the police, one has only to bear in mind the administrative confusion and moral rottenness of that branch of the government in order to understand how Azef kept the upper hand, if we are to assume with Nikolaevski and others that he actually betrayed his employers. Gerasimov claims that things improved a great deal after he took office, as apparently they did, but Gerasimov believed in protecting his secret agents and never expected Azef to communicate minute details such as could easily have led to his unmasking.

The bottomless swamp of the Azef affair is an awful example of what can happen when revolutionists undertake to combat by terroristic means a regime that has lost its moral authority and is forced to rely upon police measures as its primary line of defense. The unmasking of Azef gave the *coup de grâce* to the terrorist campaign. It was so hopelessly discredited that the SR's could not even carry out the sentence of death which the Central Committee pronounced against Azef, much less renew the campaign on its former scale, or, indeed, on any scale at all. An attempt by Slëtov and Savinkov to restore the luster of this sadly tarnished weapon, which the SR's had always regarded as something peculiarly their own, ended in complete failure.[81] Treachery is probably inseparable from terrorist conspiracy, certainly so when supervision of the enterprise devolves upon men like the leaders of the PSR, who were gullible to an extent that can scarcely be believed. Constituted as they were, they ought to have stayed as far away as possible from so deep and desperate a game, instead of which they were attracted to it like moths to a candle. The wounds inflicted on the monarchy, severe though they had been, cannot be compared to the blow sustained by the party when the news of Azef's treachery became known. The conclusion is inescapable that the practice of terrorism had not paid off in the long run, all the more so since its primary purpose, at least in theory, had been to provoke a popular uprising which would sweep the old regime into the dustbin of history.

[80] Gerasimov, *Erinnerungen*, p. 202.
[81] Chernov, P.S.-R. v epokhu Gershuni, p. 41; Spiridovich, *Histoire du terrorisme russe*, pp. 589, 624-25.

Such an uprising never occurred, though on several occasions it seemed to be in the offing. The SR's lived in sanguine expectation of an elemental outbreak from below in relation to which their role would be one of coordination and leadership in conjunction with other revolutionary parties. For this purpose they sought a permanent understanding with national socialist groups like the Polish Socialist party (PPS) and the Armenian Dashnaktsutiun, while being prepared to concede only a temporary alliance to the rival Social Democrats, who found in this preferential treatment for movements tinged with chauvinism[82] further support for their claim that the SR brand of socialism was at best a dubious thing.[83] For this purpose, also, the SR's sought to collect arms by every available means, by stealing weapons from state foresters in order to arm their peasant following in Saratov province,[84] and by engaging in gunrunning across the Finnish border on the proceeds of contributions sent to Russian extremist groups through that country, supposedly by "American millionaires" but actually by agencies of the Imperial Japanese government.[85] The party members did what they could to subvert the armed forces, meeting with rather more success in the navy than in the army; although nearly all of the military units stationed in the capital contained individual sympathizers, the factor of dispersion reduced their significance to the vanishing point, since soldiers either move all together or else not at all.[86] Throughout these feverish preparations the attitude of the party was more anticipatory than initiatory; first would come the popular rising and then the party with its allies would move in and provide arms and guidance. In the last analysis, the initiative devolved upon the people itself. Thus the First Congress, after prolonged and heated discus-

---

[82] The PPS was the party of Pilsudski.

[83] *Protokoly pervago s"ezda P.S.-R.*, pp. 338-42.

[84] S. Mazurenko, "Eshchë po povodu s"ezda Saratovskikh krest'ian 18-go dekabria 1905 g." (More about the Conference of Saratov peasants of December 18, 1905), *Byloe*, No. 8 (1908), p. 149.

[85] Nikolaevski, *Azew*, p. 102; Savinkov, *Memoirs*, pp. 126-27.

[86] L. Deich, "Voennye vo vremia pervoi nashei revoliutsii" (Military Personnel during Our First Revolution), *Byloe*, No. 12 (June, 1918), pp. 215-21; Akhun and Petrov, *Bol'sheviki i armiia*, pp. 72-73, 130-31; Savinkov, *Memoirs*, pp. 185-86.

sion, resolved not to force the pace of developments but to await the expected agrarian insurrection in the spring of 1906.[87] The SR's cannot be blamed for such a decision, for neither their organizational strength nor the technical resources at their command justified independent action ahead of a spontaneous upsurge from below.

This inability to dictate the course of events meant, however, that the party was at the mercy of elemental forces, and when the first Russian Revolution culminated in the Moscow uprising of December, 1905, neither the PSR nor the Social Democrats were able to crystallize their strength and bring the rest of the country to the aid of the workers against the smoothly functioning machinery of repression in the hands of Witte and Durnovo.[88] The SR's could only wring their hands in despair at the tragic isolation of the Moscow proletariat,[89] which had chosen to rise at a time when the party was least prepared to lend assistance, since it had gone on the defensive after the October Manifesto and was regrouping its forces in anticipation of the agrarian revolt in the spring. But later on, when the party assumed the initiative and tried actively to foment an uprising in conjunction with the dissolution of the First Duma, the results were equally disappointing.[90] Even less could be done in answer to

[87] *Protokoly pervago s"ezda P.S.-R.*, pp. 308-32; *Dobavlenie k protokolam pervago s"ezda P.S.-R.*, pp. 16-40.

[88] Zenzinov, *Iz zhizni revoliutsionera*, pp. 20-23; Savinkov, *Memoirs*, pp. 186-87; *Protokoly vtorogo . . . s"ezda P.S.-R.*, pp. 139-40; Spiridovich, *Histoire du terrorisme russe*, pp. 281 ff.

[89] *Protokoly pervago s"ezda P.S.-R.*, pp. 340-41. General Min, the pacificator of Moscow, was killed in the following year by the SR village schoolmistress, Zinaida Konopliannikova. The party members most prominently identified with the fighting in Moscow were Maximalists, though stalwarts like Zenzinov, Rudnev, and Bunakov-Fondaminski also took part. On the role of the SR's see Spiridovich, *Histoire du terrorisme russe*, pp. 271 ff.

[90] Spiridovich, *Histoire du terrorisme russe*, pp. 317 ff. The SR's had boycotted the election to the First Duma, partly out of fear that it would dampen the spirit of the people, mainly out of fear that it would expose their own weakness. The boycott was a failure, and the party, reversing its stand, campaigned as best it could for the Second Duma, securing a total of 35 seats as against nearly thrice that number for the moderate Trudoviks. In view of the electoral restrictions, however, especially in the case of a terrorist party, this cannot be accepted as a definitive test of strength. The boycottist tactics were resumed in connection with the Third and Fourth Dumas. On the relations between the party and the Duma see *Bericht der Russischen S.-R. Partei*, pp. 66-70; *Protokoly pervago s"ezda P.S.-R.*, pp. 9-23; *Protokoly vtorogo . . . s"ezda*, pp. 14-96, 160-63; Maslov, "Narodnicheskiia partii," in *Obshchestvennoe dvizhenie v Rossii*, III, 116-25.

Stolypin's provocative assault upon the Fundamental Laws in connection with the dissolution of the Second Duma.[91] It would seem that the SR's were confronted by a task beyond their strength in striving to bring down a regime which still maintained its grip on the instruments of coercion and had not been too severely shaken by a distant colonial war. Fundamentally, their strategy had been sound: the party had never lost sight of the necessity for concerted action which would prevent the town from getting too far ahead of the village and which would rally elements of the army and navy to the assistance of both; the trouble was that the agrarian revolution never materialized on the hoped-for scale.

Nevertheless, the PSR must shoulder a part of the blame for the debacle that overtook the revolution. All along, as Gershuni admitted, the party had overestimated the strength of the popular movement, largely because it confused the spirit of some thousands of propagandized peasants with the mood of the millions as yet untouched.[92] Hence decisions had been taken in the face of a fundamental miscalculation. The central authority had never been properly linked with the cells in the provinces, so that when the call came to take up arms after the dismissal of the First Duma, the local committees, according to the testimony of Breshkovskaia, had been caught unawares.[93] Most grievous of all were the faults of leadership. Prospects for an armed uprising had been so encouraging in 1905 that the party had engaged in rather extensive preparations, despite the objections of Savinkov, Azef, Gotz, and other proponents of terrorism, for whom an experiment in mass action could only come as an unwelcome diversion. More than professional jealousy was involved, for neither by temperament nor by political conviction were these men disposed to stake their cause on a popular movement. But the Central Committee for once overruled them, and then, with a fatuousness not often exhibited even in SR circles, turned around and entrusted the supervision of the whole enterprise to Azef and Savinkov, the one a traitor, the other a cynical and shifty individualist, and both opponents of the project committed to their care.

[91] Spiridovich, *Histoire du terrorisme russe*, pp. 437-41.
[92] *Protokoly vtorogo . . . s"ezda*, pp. 81-82.
[93] *Ibid.*, pp. 1, 139.

Azef lost no time in communicating the details of the undertaking to the police; he seems to have withheld nothing on this occasion (after all, he would have been in a bad way if the revolution had triumphed). A series of disasters shook the party: its two dynamite laboratories were seized in the capital, and a number of key figures were caught in the dragnet: Vedeniapin, whom the party had chosen to lead the peasants' rebellion in Saratov province; Troitski, slated for a similar role among the troops in Samara; and others of lesser consequence.[94]

Thus the isolation of the Moscow proletariat at the time of its rising is not to be ascribed solely to the lack of strategic planning; the PSR would have been in a position to render substantial (though doubtlessly still ineffectual) assistance had it not been for the incredible folly of its leaders. To entrust the execution of a mission to those who had opposed it from the outset is an inexplicable sort of wrongheadedness which seems to have flourished in SR circles.[95] The impression one gets of the party leadership in relation to the task before it is one of complete ineptitude; not only could it not cope with problems of personnel but at no time does it seem to have had a clear conception of what to expect in the way of an armed uprising or of how to go about ensuring its success. "We are revolutionists of the idea, revolutionists of the word, and the technique of insurrection quite escapes us"; such was the verdict of one of the party workers who had passed through the searing experience of 1905.[96] Throughout the period of its existence, in 1917 as in 1905, the party struggled under the handicap of incompetent leadership and organizational disunity, and although there were other reasons for the disaster that came upon it with the October Revolution, scarcely any can be said to have outweighed these two perennial weaknesses.

[94] Nikolaevski, *Azew*, pp. 102-5, 122-24; Savinkov, *Memoirs*, pp. 125 ff., 183-89; Chernov, P.S.-R. v epokhu Gershuni, pp. 36-37; P. P. Maslov, "Krest'ianskoe dvizhenie," in *Obshchestvennoe dvizhenie v Rossii*, II, Part II, 234-35; Maslov, "Narodnicheskiia partii," in *ibid.*, III, 107.

[95] See pp. 408-10.

[96] Victor Voennyi (pseud.), "K voprosu o prichinakh neudach voennykh vozstanii," *Sotsialist-Revoliutsioner*, No. 2 (1910), p. 224.

Under the double impact of the defeat of the revolution and the disclosure of Azef's treachery, the PSR staggered from one internal crisis to another in the years between 1907 and the outbreak of the war. The spirit of the party was wounded more grievously than its body. With devastating effect its enemies circulated rumors that the members of the Central Committee had known all along of Azef's duplicity but had tolerated it in order to insure their own safety; another calumny was that the favored instrument of terrorism, far from serving the cause of the revolution, had skillfully been manipulated by one faction at the Russian court in order to decimate the ranks of another.[97] The poison engendered by this affair spread through the ranks, inducing panic and disorder and causing the party members to lose confidence in one another. Though faith in terrorism was officially reaffirmed,[98] this method of combat had been discredited beyond redemption. Nor was it possible to set in motion any other form of activity. The Fifth Council of the party, convened in May, 1909, strove desperately to repair the mischief that had been done by accepting the collective resignation of the Central Committee[99] and electing to it an entirely new membership[100] with the proviso that it must function henceforth on Russian soil; but before anything could be accomplished, the committeemen were swept up and sent to Siberia. By the end of the year the attempted revival had failed, and the party lapsed into a state of demoralization and physical enervation.

Chernov has made the claim that the losses sustained by the PSR, principally because of the drain of its terrorist campaign but also because of its generally militant policy, exceeded those of all other parties combined.[101] Certainly the core of veteran workers had been sadly decimated, but the phenomenal shrinkage in party membership

---

[97] Chernov, P.S.-R. v epokhu Gershuni, p. 41.
[98] *Izveshchenie o V-m s"ezde soveta P.S.-R.*, pp. 3-4, 21.
[99] Composed at that time of Argunov, Avksentiev, Chernov, Natanson, and Rakitnikov.
[100] The only outstanding figure was V. M. Zenzinov.
[101] P.S.-R. v epokhu Gershuni, p. 40.

is to be attributed mainly to the loss of all the excess fat accumulated during the years of mushroom growth; for the ebbing tide of revolution had carried away most of the strength which the incoming tide had brought, and the Azef affair went far toward alienating the sympathies of the more stable element. It would not be too wide of the mark to compare the party to a corpse from which all the flesh had been stripped and of which not even the skeleton was intact. Zenzinov has recorded his impressions of a tour through Russia in 1909: everywhere the organization had fallen apart, though here and there something remained; more disheartening than the wreckage surveyed, however, were the conversations he had with former comrades and sympathizers, in whom a reluctance to return to service was all too obviously underlain by a spiritual estrangement from party affairs, the most disastrous of all the consequences of the ill-fated terrorist enterprise. Doors that once had opened readily to the knock of a party functionary were now closed in his face, and where personal contacts could be established, all sorts of excuses were offered to justify the retirement from partisan activity.[102]

Within Russia the organization had been shattered beyond repair. Yet not everything had been lost. During the years of frenzied agitation, many peasants had been taught to connect their economic grievances with political conditions, and this lesson was not forgotten. Particularly in the black-earth provinces, where the numerous "brotherhoods" bore witness to the success of SR work in the villages, the undermining of loyalty to old institutions outlived the "brotherhoods" themselves and created an atmosphere of smoldering disaffection in which the party might readily revive, once the repressive power of the regime began to abate.[103] Former party workers immured themselves in zemstvo and cooperative institutions as the only available means of serving the people's cause until such time as membership in a revolutionary organization might again become feasible—and safe. In the cities there was little or no activity, except in St. Petersburg, where in the years immediately preceding

[102] "Iz nedalëkago proshlago" (Out of the Recent Past), *Delo Naroda*, No. 126 (August 13, 1917).

[103] See especially N. Egorov, "Krest'ianskoe dvizhenie v Tsentral'noi Chernozëmnoi oblasti v 1907-1914 godakh," *Voprosy Istorii*, V (May, 1948), 10-12; Spiridovich, *Histoire du terrorisme russe*, pp. 515-17.

the war of 1914 newspapers of a left Narodnik tendency made their appearance, addressed to the interests of the working class and distributed in sufficient quantity, despite recurrent confiscations, to lift the enterprise out of the category of an isolated affair of the intelligentsia onto the level of a popular undertaking.[104]

Outside of Russia the leadership in exile divided into three groups, of which one approached the Maximalist position, another leaned toward Popular Socialism, and a third stood in between. The intermediate group under Chernov hewed to the orthodox SR line in spite of hell and high water. The tiny group on the left, at first known as the "minority of initiative" and then as the SR Union of the Left, concerned itself principally with tactical matters, one of its favorite projects being the obliteration of the Romanov dynasty, but since it never accomplished anything and is not the progenitor of the powerful Left SR movement of 1917, it has no real significance in party history.

The same cannot be said of the so-called "liquidators" or "Pochinists" on the right, for this group was directly connected, both in personnel and in ideology, with the influential right wing of the party as constituted in 1917. In fact, the right wing of the PSR may be said to have originated with the "liquidationist" current in the prewar emigration, to have been strengthened by the controversy over the war itself, and to have reached its full flower with the defense of Kerenski's position in 1917. On the surface, the "liquidators" seemed to be divided from the rest of the party more by tactical disputes than by fundamental issues. In their organ, the *Pochin*, they defended the thesis that the revolution had sustained a crushing defeat and that for the foreseeable future nothing remained for the party to do except to exploit the possibilities of legal action by contesting elections for the Duma and by causing its followers to infiltrate the cooperatives, the zemstvos, and various professional societies so as to seed the ground with SR doctrines, albeit in denatured form. But actually an undercurrent of disillusionment runs through their writings; these men were tired of making revolu-

---

[104] N. Kopytovski, "Eshchë o nashikh gazetakh" (More about Our Newspapers), *Delo Naroda*, No. 13 (March 30, 1917); Spiridovich, *Histoire du terrorisme russe*, pp. 633-34.

tion, and their preference for legal action was not simply a tactical matter, dictated by the exigencies of the moment, but tended more and more to ascend to the level of a principle that was to be adhered to even in case a resumption of revolutionary activity became feasible. Thus did men like Avksentiev and Bunakov-Fondaminski prepare themselves for the transition from old-line Social Revolutionism to something akin to liberalism—a development fraught with the gravest consequences for the future of their party.[105]

There remains to be noted one other development of the prewar years which not only swelled the tide of disillusionment but threatened for a time to give the party its *coup de grâce*. Under the leadership of Prime Minister Stolypin the Imperial government embarked upon a program of land reform which struck at the very foundations of Populism by promoting the breakup of the commune and the reconstruction of Russian agriculture on a thoroughgoing individualist basis. Under this program, the collectivist viewpoint of the communal peasantry would give way to the instinct of private property; the solidarity of the village would give way to class war, and no matter whether Stolypin's stake on the peasant proprietor or Lenin's wager on the landless farmworker prevailed in the end, the Populist ideal would be hopelessly shattered. The alarm in party ranks was very great. Here, truly, was a mortal threat. Some members were ready to bury the SR agrarian plan along with the commune; others believed it would have to be relegated to the maximum program, thereby erasing the chief difference between themselves and the Marxists, a prospect which only added to their discomfort. It was in the midst of a visibly shaken party that V. M. Chernov set his hand to the task of restoring faith in the SR program.

[105] It should be pointed out that notwithstanding its affinity with Popular Socialism, the *Pochin* group was made up of party stalwarts devotedly attached to the SR label and devoid of any intention of bolting the organization. On the subject of factionalism, see especially Chernov, P.S.-R. v epokhu Gershuni, pp. 41-42; Maslov, "Narodnicheskiia partii," in *Obshchestvennoe dvizhenie v Rossii*, III, 135-37; Spiridovich, *Histoire du terrorisme russe*, pp. 531-33, 594-95, 605-6.

His own grave concern is manifest in his writings, yet he managed to steer the party away from the reefs of disaster. Chernov did not attempt to play down the connection between the commune and SR doctrine, nor did he seek comfort in the notion, then so popular, that habits of thought bred by the commune would survive the institution itself. Delving into party history to show that such a turn of events had not been unexpected, he could point to the obvious argument that agitation in the village would always pay dividends so long as the Imperial regime did not contradict its own nature by bringing the estates of the nobility within the scope of the land reform. From this point onward, however, the SR leader had to break new ground.

Though he does not admit it, Chernov saw that it was necessary to refound the agrarian program. The first thing to do was to draw a line, more sharply and clearly than ever before, between Social Revolutionism and old-line Populism, the connection with which was acknowledged, but only in the sense of organic development from a lower to a higher form of life. The outworn propositions of nineteenth-century Populism could no more be permitted to dominate party thinking in the twentieth century than its surviving adherents could be permitted to dictate the policies of an organization in which their proper position was that of honored guests rather than executive directors.[106]

Having thus decently interred the remains of Populism, Chernov was free to reappraise the *obshchina* and shift the emphasis from one set of values, now of dubious validity, to another of unquestioned vitality. It was not true, he argued, that the SR land program rested upon the existing communal system. "In the communal traditions of the village we see a complex conglomerate of both positive and negative features."[107] There was something of value which could be turned to account, but there was also much that was wholly incompatible with the socialist conscience, for the *obshchina* had served the autocracy as an instrument of fiscal oppression and had pre-

[106] Here Chernov was striking at the influence of men like N. K. Chaikovski, which he rightly held to be incompatible with making a revolution amid new conditions.

[107] *Zemlia i pravo*, p. 210.

served patriarchal forms of life which submerged individuality, youth, and womanhood alike. Even the positive aspect of the commune was regarded in the light of a "wild plant which could bear fruit only after skillful grafting by socialist hands."[108] It was far from the SR intent to blow up the cultural and economic backwardness of the country into a great historical advantage. "Those honeysweet lovers of the people who are carried away with the charms of the existing *obshchina* are only ridiculous in our eyes."[109]

What was of value in the commune was not its primitive collectivism but its equalizing tendency, as a result of which the peasant was imbued with the feeling that the individual toiler must have access to the land on equal terms with his fellows. If freed of the incrustations of backward forms and extended in scope beyond the narrow confines of the commune, this egalitarianism could become the basis of agrarian socialism, for then the collectivist principle would appear, not as a hang-over from an institution doomed to extinction, but as the only feasible means of keeping the use of the land equalized after redistribution. Thus Chernov abandoned the former stress on the services of the *obshchina* in conditioning the peasantry against private property and sought support for the agrarian program in its egalitarian features; the collectivist principle he reintroduced as a kind of handmaiden to equalization instead of deriving that principle from the communal tradition. With this shift in emphasis the party had taken a long step away from the utopian socialism of early Populist days and in the direction of that society of small independent cultivators enjoying the useful, if not the ultimate, ownership of the land toward which it had been steadily though unconsciously gravitating.

Finally, Chernov was able to demonstrate that the SR land program was not dependent upon the commune at all. For this purpose he advanced what might be called the Ukrainian argument. Socialization was applicable equally to regions with communal tenure (*obshchinnoe vladenie*) and to those with household tenure

[108] *Ibid.*, p. 208.
[109] *Ibid.*, p. 230.

(*podvornoe vladenie*),[110] even though the latter type might interpose somewhat greater obstacles, and the propagation of the party's program had met with as great success in the land of Little Russian individualism[111] as in the Great Russian domain of communal tenure. The scheme of socialization had been taken over by kindred parties of other nationalities which had no institution resembling the commune. If the central theme of the party had so much appeal where the *obshchina* did not exist, why should its fortunes in Great Russia be inseparably linked to the fate of that institution?

One must concede that Chernov had escaped from a bad, even a desperate, situation. He had extricated his party from a quagmire where it soon must have perished and brought it out onto solid ground. The only thing was that in throwing overboard the excess baggage of Populism and refounding the land program on the vital forces of contemporary society, he would seem to have moved his party still further away from its announced goal of socialism and still closer to a small farmers' paradise, in which the individual[112] holders might or might not have been content to use the land without aspiring to ultimate ownership.[113]

It should be noted that Lenin, writing in the heyday of the Stolypin reform and with as little liking for SR doctrines as ever, nevertheless realized the potentialities of the land program which so many regarded as bankrupt, and acclaimed the great historic mission

[110] The SR leader chided his comrades for despairing of the party's position because of the government's campaign to transform communal into household tenure. As a matter of fact, the Stolypin reform aimed at something higher than household tenure—it envisaged a type of holding on the order of the American farmstead, which almost certainly would have stimulated a desire for private property.

[111] Party workers claimed to have heard expressions of sentiment on the part of Ukrainian peasants to the effect that landholding should be communal as among the Great Russians ("obcheska, iak u katsapov"). It must be remembered that the peasants were being worked on by the intellectuals and were willing to fall in with any scheme that promised them the landowners' estates.

[112] Chernov is at pains to leave no doubt that his party guaranteed individual rights to the land; in fact, he even underscores the word "individual." See *Zemlia i pravo*, p. 235.

[113] The foregoing exposition is based on the article, "Sotsializatsiia zemli, kak takticheskaia problema" (Socialization of the Land as a Tactical Problem), *Zemlia i pravo*, pp. 198-240. This is a long and substantial essay, and one in which the author's polemical skill appears to best advantage.

it was destined to perform, not, indeed, in any constructive sense but as a powerful destructive force in breaking up the old form of land tenure in Russia and clearing the ground for the swift evolution of the capitalist process. In its constructive aspect the program of the left Narodniks (i.e., the Socialist Revolutionaries) was the height of absurdity, according to Lenin, for if all the land were distributed equally among all the toilers it would not be a year before it would begin to pass, by means of rental contracts or otherwise, into the hands of those who possessed capital and could best accommodate themselves to market requirements. Yet in the negative sense the Narodnik program offered a most efficacious means of leveling obstructions to this process of land mobilization under capitalism. The land would be swept free of feudal encumbrances and made ready for redistribution, wrote Lenin, but the redistribution would be, not "by souls," as the SR's imagined, but by capital, as the market decreed. Thus already in 1912 Lenin had begun to warm up to the program which, five years later, he would lift bodily from its context and make one of the first decrees of his new Soviet government, without, of course, in any way prejudicing his future policy toward the peasantry.[114]

Leaving aside the question of the ultimate tendencies locked within the socialization program, it can be said that Chernov had preserved the faith of the revolutionary wing of his party. His art and logic were equally lost on those confirmed pessimists, the "liquidators," who saw in the Stolypin measures only further justification for the course they had taken—namely, away from revolution. These men had neither the flexibility of mind nor the will to revolution which would have enabled them to follow Chernov in his readjustment of the party program. They were still emotionally wedded to the Populist shibboleths of yore, yet no longer believed in their feasibility, either in respect to the agrarian question or in respect to terrorism. They could not keep pace with the revolutionary wing, yet they were unwilling to divest themselves of their SR raiments

---

[114] "Sravnenie stolypinskoi i narodnicheskoi agrarnoi programmy" (Comparison of the Agrarian Programs of Stolypin and the Narodniks), in *Sochineniia*, XVI, 10-14, and "Poslednii klapan" (The Last Valve), in *ibid.*, pp. 87-91.

and go over boldly to the liberal side. In 1905 many of them had been ultrarevolutionists of the "now-or-never" school, which held that the overturn must occur before bourgeois influences seeped into the peasantry, a confession of weakness, as Chernov observed;[115] with the failure of the revolution they lost heart, and the Azef affair and the Stolypin offensive were but added stones on the grave of their faith. Thus there was never any question of restoring the faith of the whole party, but only of its revolutionary wing.

[115] *Zemlia i pravo*, pp. 202 ff.

IV

THE IMPACT OF THE WAR: FISSURES
AND FEUDS IN THE PARTY

IF anything were wanting to complete the picture of disunity and decrepitude presented by the party at this stage of its history, it was furnished by the outbreak of war. The principle of working-class solidarity, shared by the PSR with other socialist parties, now came into violent conflict with the element of nationalism latent in Populism. Where formerly there had been only a fissure, there now developed a gulf, and it should not have required the experience of 1917 to demonstrate that this gulf was unbridgeable, save by flimsy and temporary structures created in the name of a unity which had vanished forever in 1914. The First Congress had pledged the party to oppose by the "most decisive means" in its power the entrance of Russia into war,[1] but the strength of prowar sentiment within the membership, now composed almost wholly of intellectuals since the people had fallen away, made it idle to think of implementing this resolution, with the result that the fate of the party conformed to that of other groups affiliated with the Second International. Argunov has compared the Paris center after the outbreak of war to a demolished ant heap, except that these ants, instead of rebuilding, ran off in all directions, biting each other on the way.[2]

We shall now proceed to analyze the line-up with respect to the war, noting the various stands of the contending factions, together with the considerations which impelled them to take those stands. It must always be borne in mind that the Socialist Revolutionary Party, as it existed during the interrevolutionary period

[1] *Protokoly pervago s"ezda P.S.-R.*, pp. 290-91.
[2] Pravoe i levoe, p. 8.

(1907-17), was a head without a body. The factionalism about to be described is, therefore, an affair of the intellectuals at the top and not of the ordinary people, who do not enter the picture until the February Revolution has created the conditions essential to the formation of a mass organization, this time on a far more ambitious scale than in 1905.

It is impossible to gain a clear impression of what was going on within Russia. Apparently the intellectuals for the most part accepted the war as a national enterprise from which they could not stand apart, while the SR's of working-class origin (relatively few of whom could have been actual members of the party) gravitated more and more toward an antiwar position. With regard to the peasant following, the record is a complete blank. The cleavage between the intellectuals and the workers was especially well-defined in Petrograd, where the great majority of intellectuals who had been or still were members of the party championed the cause of national defense, in contrast to the growing internationalism, not untinged with defeatism, which the SR workingmen shared with their Bolshevik comrades.[3] S. P. Postnikov told this writer that at a meeting of some twoscore party members and sympathizers in a private apartment in Petrograd soon after the outbreak of war, only he and R. V. Ivanov-Razumnik breasted the overwhelming tide of patriotism.[4] At Saratov a similar sentiment prevailed, most of the SR's being described as definitely "defensist" in outlook.[5] Yet the attitude of the intelligentsia does not appear to have exerted a decisive influence upon whatever was left of the party organization, and Chernov was able to claim, in support of his internationalist position, that no local group in Russia had sided with the opposing or prowar faction, although the evidence he adduced of a positive stand in favor of halting the war through a restored International was vague and inconclusive.[6] Chernov's assertion that the remnants of the Petrograd

[3] Sviatitski, "Voina i predfevral'e," *Katorga i Ssylka*, LXXV (II, 1931), 9-10, 13.

[4] Interview in Prague (August, 1935).

[5] Antonov-Saratovski, *Pod stiagom proletarskoi bor'by*, I, 7-8, 11.

[6] See his article "Novyi politicheskii blok" (A New Political Bloc), in *Chuzhimi putiami*, pp. 58-59.

organization adopted an internationalist point of view is confirmed by other sources, which state that a conference of party members in the capital accepted a resolution couched in Zimmerwaldist terms on the motion of A. F. Kerenski.[7] In the last analysis, however, the status of the party was such that its collective opinion could not be ascertained, and it was largely to overcome this state of affairs, and to secure an authoritative pronouncement on the war, that an attempt was made shortly before the February Revolution to revive the corporate existence of the PSR. This attempt, like all others, ended in failure.[8]

Of that part of the SR leadership which passed the war years on home soil we know relatively little. We know that Abram R. Gotz in his Siberian exile entertained views that might be described as right Zimmerwaldian—in other words, similar to those of V. M. Chernov—and that his close associate in 1917, V. M. Zenzinov, was definitely on the other side; we know that prominent SR's in the capital like N. V. Sviatitski and N. S. Rusanov shared Gotz's internationalism, and that the nucleus of leadership in Moscow, including M. V. Vishniak and M. Ia. Gendelman, was already committed to the "defensist" ideology of Zenzinov, who was the most influential member of the party in that city. Already the lines were being traced for the cleavage in 1917, when the two metropolitan organizations would be on opposite sides of the controversy dividing the party. It may be inferred that N. I. Rakitnikov, chief of the Saratov SR's, had assumed before 1917 the position of moderate internationalism to which he consistently adhered during the revolution. For those whose knowledge is confined to the events of 1917 it will come as a surprise to learn that A. F. Kerenski had stood quite close to the Zimmerwaldist line as long as the conduct of the war lay in the hands of the Imperial regime. On the far left mention should be made of S. Mstislavski in Petrograd and I. Z. Steinberg in Moscow, men of the younger generation whose extremism would ultimately find an

---

[7] *Aleksandr Fëdorovich Kerenskii: Po materialam Departamenta Politsii* (Kerenski: On the Basis of Police Department Records) (Petrograd, 1917), pp. 35-36; Spiridovich, *Histoire du terrorisme russe*, pp. 650-51; Sviatitski, "Voina i predfevral'e," *Katorga i Ssylka*, LXXV, 24.

[8] Sviatitski, "Voina i predfevral'e," *Katorga i Ssylka*, LXXV, 39 ff.

outlet in the party of the Left Socialist Revolutionaries. The main nest of leftists, however, was in the Kharkov-Voronezh region, where the South Russian committee, consisting of Kogan-Bernstein, Kachinski, Chaikin, and others, was already laying the foundations of the movement which would later, in 1917, convert Kharkov province into a citadel of left-wing Social Revolutionism.[9]

Many of the SR leaders had made their way abroad after the failure of the Revolution of 1905 and it was there, in the free climate of Western Europe, that the opposing viewpoints of internationalism and "defensism" received their definitive formulation. The majority of party workers in exile were prowar in sentiment. Among the more prominent "defensists," as they came to be known, were founders of the party, such as S. N. Slëtov and A. A. Argunov, tribunes, such as N. D. Avksentiev and Ilia I. Bunakov-Fondaminski, V. V. Rudnev, the future mayor of Moscow, B. V. Savinkov, Azef's understudy in the terrorist organization, and I. A. Rubanovich, representative of the party in the International Socialist Bureau. Against these party luminaries the internationalist camp could oppose the well-known name of Mark Natanson, a link with the early days of Populism, and lesser lights such as B. D. Kamkov (whose real name was Katz), Dalin (whose real name was Levenson), and Peter Alexandróvich; towering above all other internationalists, however, was the figure of V. M. Chernov, whose polemical skill and erudition went far to offset the numerical preponderance on the other side.

At first the contending factions were not so far apart as they later became under the spur of controversy. Their representatives could still talk to each other, and three weeks after the outbreak of war, on the twenty-second of August, 1914, a conference of the leading personalities on both sides was held in the Swiss village of Beaugy-sur-Clarens for the purpose of threshing out the issues and exploring the possibilities of united action. The identity of all of the participants cannot be established owing to the use of pseudonyms,[10] but Avksentiev, Bunakov, Argunov, and Rudnev represented the "defen-

---

[9] *Ibid., passim.*

[10] Rudnev, "Iz istorii partii," *Svoboda*, No. 4 (December, 1935), pp. 13-14. This practice appears to have been carried further than was necessary and to have become somewhat childlike in its application.

sist" point of view, and Chernov and Natanson, the internationalist. The conference was a fiasco. Chernov, as usual, took the initiative and proposed two lines of action: one inside Russia, directed toward crystallizing public opinion around an SR mission to be sent from abroad; the other European in scope, and addressed to restoring the International, as a first step toward which he proposed to convene, on the initiative of Russian socialists, a conference of the socialists of neutral countries which would draw in the levelheaded elements of belligerent powers and at least prick the conscience of the backsliding elements. The leaders assembled at Beaugy approved, with a noticeable lack of enthusiasm, the first proposal by a vote of six to three, after Avksentiev had criticized Chernov for his failure to indicate clearly the course which the mission would follow upon its arrival in Russia. The obvious rejoinder would have been that any clear-cut formula would split the conference wide open. Against such a background it is small wonder that nothing ever came of the scheme. As for the second proposal, it was killed outright (two favored it, with six opposed).[11]

The conference at Beaugy-sur-Clarens thus had no practical effect whatever, yet it is of significance as marking the emergence of the various factions into which the emigration and eventually the whole party were to be divided. At this early date there was still an area of agreement: all conceded that the war was an immeasurable evil, all felt that an Allied triumph would be the lesser evil, and all opposed a vengeful peace directed against the German people. But beyond this point there was already a sharp division of opinion which could only be accentuated with the progress of the war. For some the interests of national defense overruled all other considerations; for others, the orthodox precepts of socialism retained their full validity. Whereas some would suspend the revolutionary struggle in order to further the prosecution of the war, others would step up the revolutionary struggle while throttling the war by the combined pressure of toilers everywhere. The line was being drawn between

[11] Protokol'naia zapis'. Nearly all of the material in this typewritten manuscript has been published by Rudnev in the journal *Svoboda*, No. 4 (December, 1935), pp. 14-17, and No. 5 (July, 1936), pp. 6-10, under the title "Iz istorii partii."

"defensism" and internationalism, but at the same time another line was being drawn within each major faction between moderates and extremists. Thus Bunakov, Rudnev, and Argunov would have renounced all revolutionary activity during the war, but Avksentiev was unwilling to go so far: he would keep a free hand and be prepared to take advantage of any break, while in general subordinating the making of revolution to the claims of national defense. Though this particular issue was later effaced when all "defensists" became reconciled to the thought of revolution in wartime, we have here a clear indication of the difference in outlook which would divide them into a right and a right center.[12]

Likewise on the other side: with Chernov insisting that active opposition to the war in Russia must be conditioned upon similar activity in Germany,[13] Natanson took the stand that considerations of reciprocity must be put aside[14] in favor of encompassing the overthrow of tsarism by any means that were feasible, regardless of the effect upon the war.[15] Military defeat he quite openly regarded as a prelude to revolution.[16] In this divergence of viewpoint between Chernov and Natanson, the moderate antiwar or internationalist position of the one being opposed to the extreme antiwar or defeatist position of the other, we observe the beginning of the cleavage between the left center and the left which eventually wrecked the SR party at the very moment when the Bolsheviks were coming into power.

Thus the debate at Beaugy-sur-Clarens discloses the existence, not simply of two, but actually of four currents within the *émigré* leadership in respect to the war. Up to the time of the revolution the subfactions held together, arrested in their development by the

[12] Protokol'naia zapis', *passim.*
[13] *Ibid.,* pp. 14, 20.
[14] *Ibid.,* p. 18.
[15] This is the inference to be drawn from his remarks at the conference (pp. 10 ff.). It is true that he wobbled somewhat, at one point conditioning a political overturn upon the maintenance of the country's defenses (p. 26). Whether he was being hypocritical or illogical on this occasion is not known, but certainly it was a case of one or the other, for this statement cannot be reconciled with the general tenor of his remarks.
[16] *Ibid.,* p. 11.

fact that the whole controversy was restricted to a theoretical plane; but once the party took on the flesh of a mass organization and assumed power, they moved rapidly into the foreground and produced a double schism. The conference at Beaugy is also the point of departure for the development of both the main lines of thought, as both underwent a process of clarification and elaboration which produced significant changes with the passage of time.

Let us consider first the evolution of "defensism." It was a belief compounded of several elements, of concern for the fatherland, of sympathy for the Western Allies, and of antipathy for Germany. Narodnik ideology had always been pregnant with nationalism because it depended for its validity upon the distinctive character of Russian society, and hence indirectly upon the preservation of its national base. Avksentiev saw the country's very existence at stake in a war with the powerful and immediate neighbor, Germany, as had not been the case in the earlier conflict with Japan.[17] Some of the SR "defensists," loath to renounce the old internationalism despite the upsurge of patriotism, worked out a concept of the fatherland as a necessary stage in the evolution of a world order,[18] but this attempt to reconcile two opposing principles cannot be termed a success, for the "defensist" wing of the party had in effect shifted its stand onto national grounds, even though many of its adherents might not wish to admit it. At the Beaugy conference Rudnev had offered a defense of the shattered International which Chernov termed worse than any burial;[19] twenty years later Rudnev was to admit that, gravely concerned as he was for the future of his country, he had been to a high degree indifferent to the fate of the International.[20]

[17] *Ibid.*, pp. 9-10. The contrast between the party's attitude in 1904 and ten years later is brought out in Chernov's articles, "Prezhde i teper'" (Before and Now) and "Istoriko-literaturnaia spravka" (Historical and Literary Information), reprinted in the pamphlet, *Istinnye i mnimye porazhentsy*, pp. 5-8, 14-16.
[18] Argunov, *Pravoe i levoe*, pp. 13-14.
[19] *Protokol'naia zapis'*, pp. 35-37.
[20] "Dvadtsat' let tomu nazad," *Sovremennyia Zapiski*, LXI, 378.

But it was not only Russia whose security the SR "defensists" viewed with trepidation. The affection they cherished for liberal England and especially for republican France cannot be explained wholly on the basis of the democratic institutions which these countries possessed, but must also be attributed in part to the fact that these exiles had come to identify themselves, at least to some extent, with the lands in which they lived. Thus we find Avksentiev arguing the inadmissibility of a German victory because of the effect it would have on the internal situation in France, where the republicans already had to contend with a reactionary movement the seriousness of which he could vouch for, owing to his position in the ranks of freemasonry.[21] To such an extent had a Russian revolutionist become involved in the affairs of the Grand Orient of France. Another SR presented a revealing formula for determining his attitude to the war: he was for the victory of the side on which France fought and did not fear the victory of the side on which Russia was engaged.[22] Was this Russian nationalism or was it Francophilism, carried to a point where it became spiritual allegiance to the Republic? The "defensists" conceded the possibility that the Allied governments might seek to inflict a bad peace upon the defeated enemy, but such was their faith in the Western democracies that they believed the public conscience would force the governments to return to a reasonable basis for the conclusion of peace. If that belief were not justified, an Allied victory would still be preferable to a triumph of German arms.[23]

Toward Germany the "defensist" attitude was one of hostility, tempered only by their socialist distaste for chauvinism. This territorially restricted but strongly knit state in the heart of Europe was disliked as the hearth of militarism and the land of efficient autocracy. Russian socialists had very little to say about Austria, so it must have been that the propinquity and power of Germany inspired in them a kind of subconscious dread which was reflected in their judgments concerning the war. Those judgments were also

[21] Protokol'naia zapis', p. 10.
[22] Ibid., p. 12.
[23] Bunakov (pseud. of I. I. Fondaminski), "Chto nas razdeliaet?" (What Divides Us?), Prizyv, No. 12 (December 18, 1915).

influenced, though to a lesser degree, by moral considerations which received much greater publicity: Germany bore the guilt for having started the war as well as the opprobrium for ravaging other countries, upon whose soil, for the most part, the war was being waged. As time went on, emotionalism began to color the "defensist" viewpoint, and it became increasingly difficult to maintain the distinction between the German ruling classes and the German people, one right-winger (V. Lebedev) going so far as to view with indulgence the French use of the term "boche."[24] Thus the rising tide of Germanophobia brought some elements of the party within measurable distance of that chauvinism of which their enemies accused them, but in as much as there is no record of their championing anything other than a fair peace, the SR "defensists" in general may be acquitted of this charge.

In the light of their attitude toward the homeland, the Allies, and Germany, it is easy to understand the "defensist" formula with respect to the war. International socialism had not proved equal to the task of averting the war. All sections were to blame for the debacle, but none so much as the German, which had consistently blocked all efforts to concert a program of effective resistance and had rallied with alacrity to the support of its own aggressive government. Once started, the war must conform to the iron logic of history *(sic)* and continue until one side or the other had achieved a victory. Efforts to halt it by the intervention of a "third force" consisting of the antiimperialist, toiling elements of European society were doomed to futility: the time was too short, the socialists too weak, their forces too dispersed, and the German socialists too uncooperative. Though they could not hope to stop the war, the socialists might incline the scales in favor of the coalition whose hegemony would be more compatible with culture and progress, and that meant the Triple Entente. The defeat of the Central Powers would free Europe from the incubus of militarism by eliminating the chief military establishment and thus depriving all the others of their *raison d'être;* it would create a more favorable climate for

[24] Chernov, "Na odnom primere" (As One Example), in *Chuzhimi putiami,* pp. 25-26.

the solution of the nationalities problem; and it would destroy the one truly formidable absolutism in Europe, leaving the Russian autocracy with nothing to fall back upon, an isolated anachronism upon which all the forces of the new order would beat with unimpeded vigor. Hence it was the duty of socialists everywhere to work for an Allied victory, and since that could not be achieved without the assistance of Russia, the socialists of that country must support its war effort, quieting their conscience with the thought that victory, far from redounding to the credit of the hated autocracy, would actually hasten its end.[25]

There was one other consideration dictating acceptance of the war—namely, its popular character. To have listened to the SR "defensists," one would have thought that the Russian people were red-hot for war. Men such as Rudnev, Argunov, and Fondaminski never tired of reiterating from the beginning of the war to the end that the people were wholly absorbed in the struggle and had no thought of socialism or indeed of anything but national defense. "There can be no doubt," said Rudnev, "that the entire Russian people, like other peoples, is drawn to the war and lives by it."[26] For the party to stand aside, refusing to participate in the war effort, would mean to cut itself off from the people, and for it actively to oppose the war, opposing its fractious will to the majestic course of the Russian nation, would not only be presumptuous but might be suicidal. So this group of SR's urged very strongly that the party members "go along" with the people, submerging their specific objectives in the common task of preserving the integrity and independence of the country.[27]

All this, of course, was based on a fundamental miscalculation. The war was anything but a popular cause, as the sequel would show. The leaders in exile were in no position to judge the temper of the Russian people, least of all the peasantry, whose psychology

<hr>

[25] Bunakov, "Chto nas razdeliaet?", *Prizyv*, No. 12 (December 18, 1915) and No. 13 (December 25, 1915); Jan Slavík, "Ruské strany politické za světové války," *Slovanský Přehled*, XVII, 477; Argunov, Pravoe i levoe, pp. 10-12.

[26] Protokol'naia zapis', p. 26.

[27] "Defensist" literature is replete with this line of argument. It is strongly presented in *ibid.*, pp. 19, 23, 25-28.

has never been easy to fathom. Admitting the delusion, Argunov writes that from afar the nation seemed to be solid in support of the war, especially since all the noise was being made by the pro-war element, with no avenue open for the expression of dissent.[28] But the observer can only wonder whether the SR "defensists" were deluded by circumstances or by the fervor of their own convictions. What they did not see, or did not want to see, was plainly visible to a conservative like Bishop Nikon when he noted with dismay how little the war had captured the soul of the Russian peasant.[29] In simplest terms, the SR "defensists" had imputed to the Russian people their own cherished convictions, either never realizing what they were doing or else in time falling victim to their own propaganda. The delusion is of the utmost importance, for as we shall see in a moment, it governed their whole approach to the question of revolution in time of war.

There was one other faulty link in the chain of reasoning whereby the "defensists" arrived at their stand in support of the war. As pointed out above, they denied the possibility of stopping the war by any concerted action on the part of the toilers of all countries, one reason being that they had no faith in the antiwar sentiment or revolutionary enterprise of the German working class. Yet it must be said that SR "defensists" were unwilling to take any step calculated to evoke a fraternal response from the other side of the trenches. With them, it was not a question of reciprocity but one of one-sided action by the German socialists to atone for their sins, after which the Allied socialists would reconsider their stand in favor of prosecution of the war. This attitude, it goes without saying, was not calculated to assist the German proletariat in shaking off the hypnosis of the front. The truth is that the emotionalism which crept into judgments concerning the enemy destroyed any possibility that a bridge might be thrown over to the other side. A classic example of an emotional approach to the problem of dealing with German socialism is presented by Fondaminski, an authoritative

[28] Pravoe i levoe, pp. 16-17.
[29] Chernov, "Voina i revoliutsiia" (War and Revolution), in *Chuzhimi putiami*, p. 67.

spokesman for SR "defensism," when he frankly states that "it would be hard for me, both morally and psychologically, to come to an international socialist conference and shake the hand that is stained with my people's blood."[30] And Rudnev was completely uninhibited in condemning Karl Liebknecht for pitting his individual conscience against the collective conscience of the German people in seeking a revolutionary way out of the bloodbath.[31] A more complete abdication of the traditional socialist position, or a greater willingness to submit to mob psychology, could scarcely be imagined.[32] Small wonder that the SR "defensists" professed to see no hope for a sensible solution of the crisis, but only for a lessening of its evil through an Allied victory:[33] they not only had no formula for ending the war, they did not find it congenial even to search for such a formula.

In this connection, it should be pointed out that the SR "defensists" abroad were more extreme than those at home. Superficially, their position seemed to be the same, for the émigrés approved Kerenski's speech in the Duma in which he summoned the people to protect the national soil, yet refused to vote in favor of the war credits requested by the tsar's ministers.[34] Actually, however, there was a difference in emphasis: while the "defensists" at home, including even the moderate Trudoviks and Popular Socialists, stressed the united front of toilers everywhere as the goal to be achieved, pending which the Russian people must look to its own defense, the exiles abroad stressed only defense. Contact with Russian reality and the absence of sentimental ties to foreign lands, such as arise from prolonged residence abroad, held the party members at home closer to the original spirit of Social Revolutionism than was the case with their colleagues in exile.[35]

---

[30] "Chto nas razdeliaet?" *Prizyv*, No. 13 (December 25, 1915).

[31] "Iz istorii partii," *Svoboda*, No. 5 (July, 1936), p. 7; Protokol'naia zapis', p. 27.

[32] At the same time, one must note the absence of hypocrisy in Rudnev's stand: he concedes to German socialists the same right which he claims for himself.

[33] Protokol'naia zapis', p. 36.

[34] Argunov, Pravoe i levoe, pp. 11-12.

[35] See Chernov, "O narodnicheskoi konferentsii" (About the Narodnik Conference), in *Chuzhimi putiami*, pp. 79-80.

After following this analysis of "defensist" opinion with respect to the war, we have next to consider the "defensist" position with respect to the revolution which many foresaw as the inevitable result of the war. In general it can be said that the relation of the "defensists" to the revolution was governed by their relation to the war. Underlying the whole "defensist" ideology and imparting unity to its following, despite some disagreement over secondary issues, was the conviction, stated in so many words by Rudnev at the Beaugy conference,[36] that the interests of revolution must be subordinated to the successful conduct of the war. In the early months of the conflict the "defensists" were divided, some urging a complete suspension of revolutionary activity, others favoring its continuation, but in a modified form so as not to impede the military effort. This is the first indication of a divergence in viewpoint which would eventuate in a right and a right center. Among those on the right were the exterrorist Savinkov, who equated any active opposition to the tsar and capitalism with aid to the enemy,[37] and Fondaminski, who argued that there could be no partisan objectives in time of war and beseeched the party to cast off the old habits of thought which caused it to regard the Russian government as the first enemy of the Russian people.[38] More moderate was the position of men like Avksentiev and Rubanovich, who could not bring themselves to execute a somersault with relation to the autocracy.[39]

But by the end of 1915 a significant change had taken place. The crushing defeats sustained by Russian arms in the course of that year had convinced the extreme "defensists" that they had been on the wrong track in advocating victory before revolution and that, in fact, it might be necessary for revolution to precede victory because of the hopeless incompetence of the existing regime and its inability to organize a successful defense. They admitted they

[36] Protokol'naia zapis', p. 22.
[37] See his letter published in the *Mysl'* as quoted in Chernov, "Dve pozitsii" (Two Positions), in *Chuzhimi putiami*, p. 11.
[38] Protokol'naia zapis', pp. 2-3, 14, 19-20.
[39] *Ibid.*, p. 22; Argunov, Pravoe i levoe, p. 15; Slavík, "Ruské strany politické za světové války," *Slovanský Přehled*, XVII, 478.

had overdrawn the perils of revolutionary action in time of war.[40] But having come to accept the idea of revolution, they proceeded to fashion it in their own image. "A revolution is brewing in Russia," wrote Fondaminski, "which will be national rather than international, democratic rather than social, and prowar rather than pacifist."[41] History does not record a more erroneous prediction. The revolution now in the offing was going to be everything that Fondaminski said it would not be. Yet these words deserve to be engraved on the reader's memory, for they are the key to much that happened in 1917.

How did the SR "defensists" intend to put over the revolution? And what kind of a revolution would it be? The guiding consideration was to avoid any dislocation of the military effort, and the primary purpose of the revolution would be to insure a more efficient conduct of the war. Hence it could not be a social revolution but must be confined to the political sphere so that the indispensable class truce would not be disturbed. Popular participation in the work of defense must be carried to the highest possible degree so that the government would fairly be enveloped by popular forces prepared to assume authority as it slipped from the hands of a discredited regime. Once the requisite degree of infiltration and envelopment had been attained, and once the regime was no longer capable of withstanding public pressure, the way would be open to a painless transfer of power at the higher level without any need for an upheaval from below, which could only cause a disastrous reaction on the front. Something on the order of events that transpired in France in 1870, when the regime of Napoleon III gave way to a new government dedicated to national defense, was what these SR's had in mind, only there was to be nothing resembling the Paris Commune. The fruits of such a revolution would be military triumph and political freedom; property relationships would remain as before. Obviously, then, these Socialist Revolutionaries had renounced social revolution in favor of something which might

[40] Chernov, "Nerevoliutsionnaia revoliutsiia" (A Nonrevolutionary Revolution), in *Chuzhimi putiami*, p. 61.
[41] "Chto nas razdeliaet?", *Prizyv*, No. 13 (December 25, 1917).

be termed a "revolution for victory" or, as V. M. Chernov, the leader of the opposing faction, chose to express it, a "castrated" revolution.[42]

Where had the evolution of their views on war and revolution deposited the SR "defensists"? The answer is, in the back yard of Menshevism, for their formula of revolution for victory was, in essence, nothing more nor less than the old Menshevik concept of a purely bourgeois revolution. This basic affinity in point of view, though arrived at over a different road, is the foundation of the alliance between Social Revolutionism and Menshevism which would be consummated in 1917 and which was destined to have such profound—and disastrous—consequences for the PSR. Collaboration on this basis began during the war, both in Russia and abroad. In Russia the SR "defensists" joined hands with the Mensheviks in urging workers' participation in the war industrial committees, despite the boycottist tactics of the Bolsheviks, supported by the SR internationalists. Abroad, the right-wing fringe of Menshevism and the SR prowar elements founded as a joint enterprise the newspaper *Prizyv*, even though they did not always see eye to eye on specific issues, as, for example, the voting of war credits by the Duma, which Plekhanov approved but Avksentiev opposed.[43] Thus the collaboration between the "defensist" wings of both parties had already commenced and was functioning in a dual aspect by the time of the revolution. It was sustained by another potent factor besides the common purpose with respect to the war: the prowar faction of the PSR was also the right wing of the party, having as its nucleus the "liquidationist" or *Pochin* group of tired revolutionists, whose moderation in social and economic matters disposed

---

[42] See his articles "Nerevoliutsionnaia revoliutsiia," "Voina i revoliutsiia," and "Ot sotsial-patriotizma k neo-kadetstvu" (From "Socialist" Patriotism to Neo-Constitutional-Democratism), in *Chuzhimi putiami*, pp. 60-78; "Gde zhe nastoiashchie porazhentsy?" (But Where Are the Real Defeatists?), in *Istinnye i mnimye porazhentsy*, pp. 28-29, 30-32.

[43] "Sotsialisty i golosovanie voennykh kreditov" (Socialists and the Voting of War Credits), *Prizyv*, No. 17 (January 22, 1916), and reply of Plekhanov in same issue; Argunov, *Pravoe i levoe*, pp. 10, 15. Avksentiev favored a motivated abstention, not as a matter of principle, but in the name of national defense, as a protest against the ineptitude of the administration.

them to accept, in fact if not in theory, the Menshevik position on such issues. It was withal a stable alliance. The Menshevik influence within this bloc, largely because of superior leadership, was disproportionate to its numerical weight, just as the influence of the SR "defensists" within their party exceeded the strength of their popular following. Herein lies the explanation of the success of the Provisional Government in steering a relatively conservative course without forfeiting the support of the majority socialists in control of the soviets.

Having noted the main features of SR "defensism," we now turn to an examination of the ideology and evolution of the internationalist faction of the party, also known as the "defeatist" faction, despite the inaccuracy of this term with reference to the left center. If the "defensist" ideolgy was compounded of incipient nationalism, of adulation of the Allies and aversion for Germany, the sources of the opposing belief are to be found in hatred of tsarism, devotion to the principle of working-class solidarity, repugnance to imperialism in any form, and a clear understanding of the senselessness of war. We may say that the SR internationalists cherished a deeper antipathy for Russian autocracy than for the more distant semi-absolutism of Germany, that they denounced impartially both the Allied and the German brands of imperialism, and that they had rather more regard for the toilers of Germany and Austria than for the democratic but nonsocialist features of Western political life. As in the case of the "defensists," their views on war and revolution shifted somewhat with the passage of time.

Their conception of the character of the war determined their relationship to it. For the SR internationalists the war was an incalculable evil, menacing the very fabric of civilization and opening before the eyes of toilers everywhere broad vistas of slaughter in pursuance of objectives which were incompatible with their class interests and disruptive of their class organizations. It was as though the workers' movement should be drowned in the blood of its sundered national sections. Moral aversion to bloodshed was strongly emphasized by this group: "For us human blood is equally precious, no matter from whose veins and arteries it flows, whether from German or Russian, from Bulgarian or Serbian."[44] The initial preference for a victory of the Western powers was founded upon the belief that, in the absence of a single will backed by overwhelming military force, the Allied hegemony could not be as solid or as enduring as the German, and would result in an unstable equilibrium conducive to social progress.[45] But owing to the presence of tsarist Russia in the Allied ranks, the SR internationalists could muster no enthusiasm for victory, even in the early days of the war; they always maintained that Russian militarism was no less nefarious than German.[46] As time went on and predatory instincts gained the ascendancy everywhere, the mild preference for an Allied victory yielded to the conviction that the war had lost any aspect of a defensive struggle and had become a contest in which all the participants were equally guilty of harboring aggressive designs.[47]

The imperialism implicit in Russian policy had been denounced from the very beginning. On this subject Chernov had expended much of his polemical art. In the twenty years or so of his political activity there are some equivocations and many deviations, but in one particular he never wavered: he was invincibly determined that Russia should not have the Straits. Not even the land question could strike such fire from the SR leader. In part he was motivated by moral indignation at the thought of the people's blood being expended in pursuit of a venture about which they cared nothing,

[44] Chernov, "K obosnovaniiu nashego lozunga" (On Providing a Basis for Our Slogan), in *Voina i "tret'ia sila,"* p. 50.

[45] Analysis of Chernov, Protokol'naia zapis', pp. 4-5; concurrence of Natanson, *ibid.*, p. 10.

[46] See declaration of Chernov and Natanson on the London Conference of 1915 in Chernov, *Internatsional i voina*, p. 53; Chernov, "Dve pozitsii," in *Chuzhimi putiami*, p. 12; Chernov, "Prezhde i teper'," in *Istinnye i mnimye porazhentsy*, pp. 8-9.

[47] Chernov, "Logika odnogo grekhopadeniia" (The Logic of a Certain Transgression), in *ibid.*, p. 42; Chernov, "Imperativy morali i imperativy zhizni" (The Imperatives of Morality and the Imperatives of Life), in *Voina i "tret'ia sila,"* p. 59.

in part by the realization that Russia's acquisition of the Straits would bring on endless complications with Great Britain and open up new prospects of slaughter for the Russian people. Chernov and his associates likewise directed their fire at Russian policy in Galicia, condemning especially the persecution of Ukrainian culture and the excesses against the Jews.[48]

British and French imperialism received more attention as the controversy with the "defensists" developed and the internationalists sought to counter the argument that the Allied coalition merited socialist support because the virtues of Western liberalism outweighed the sins of Russian absolutism. They took up the cudgels on behalf of oppressed colonial peoples; they talked of Morocco and Egypt, of Persia and India, and they did not overlook symptoms of imperialism in Europe itself. They spoke of the hypocrisy involved in claims that a "war of liberation" was being conducted by such powers, and of the futility of thinking that these powers could exert, or would care to exert, a liberalizing influence upon their tsarist partner. Soon voices were raised protesting against even an academic preference for one side or the other as foreign to SR ideology,[49] and by the middle of 1917 the initial mild sympathy for the Western Allies had given way to sentiments ranging from irritation to open hostility. The internationalists addressed themselves to the task of overthrowing the "legend of liberation" which served the "defensists" as a basis for their "idealization" of the war. The Triple Entente, uniting such seemingly incompatible elements as autocratic Russia, liberal England, and democratic France, was in reality no fluke of circumstance, according to V. M. Chernov; in essence it represented a combination of the dynastic imperialism of Russia with the capitalistic imperialism of Great Britain and the finance imperialism of France to withstand the thrust of a mighty rival.[50]

[48] "Maska sbroshena" (The Mask Is Dropped), *Na Chuzhbine*, No. 13, pp. 23-25; Protokol'naia zapis', pp. 6, 13; "Nashi deklaratsii" (Our Declarations), *Internatsional i voina*, p. 52.

[49] So Dalin (Levenson) in *Zhizn'*, No. 29, as referred to in Argunov, Pravoe i levoe, p. 20.

[50] "Nebyvalyi prizyv" (An Unprecedented Appeal), in *Chuzhimi putiami*, pp. 9-10.

Wars were not waged in bourgeois society except with predatory designs.[51]

Such being the character of the present war, what stand should socialists take in respect to it? According to the SR internationalists, they should hold fast to the orthodox tenets of socialism, refusing to identify themselves with a cause not their own. They should accept the war as a grievous necessity, complying with its dictates to the extent of securing their country's defenses but otherwise refusing to be swayed by it, until such time as popular disillusionment and the resurrection of the socialist movement would make it possible to cry halt to the carnage. Defense was sanctioned, but not victory. The socialist must stand guard, warding off the thrusts of the enemy but not seeking to strike him down. The pursuit of victory would inevitably becloud the socialist conscience, for it would require callousness to further bloodshed, compromise with the class enemy in the name of national unity, encouragement to neutrals to enter the fray, thus widening the circle of horror, and, worst of all, the cultivation of ill-feeling for the enemy population, which could lead only to an intensification of national hatreds and the setting back of the cause of socialism, international in essence, for generations to come. Furthermore, none of the existing governments, Allied or enemy, could be trusted to refrain from abuse of a decisive victory; the temptation that would arise would be altogether too great for their weak moral sense to withstand. If it was madness to seek the defeat of one's own country, as the "defensists" urged, it was also madness to seek the ruin of another country; not only Russia, but also the Central Powers, should be spared the ravages of a conqueror's peace, with all the hell that would flow therefrom. The internationalists denounced Germanophobia as being no less grievous a fault than anti-Semitism; they wanted neutrals to remain on the side lines, reserving for Rumania's entrance into the

---

[51] "Lozungi momenta: I, Patsifizm i sotsializm" (Slogans of the Moment: I, Pacifism and Socialism), in *Voina i "tret'ia sila,"* p. 34. See also "Maska sbroshena," *Na Chuzhbine*, No. 13, p. 22; Chernov, "Nashi deklaratsii," in *Internatsional i voina*, pp. 48-49; Chernov, "Velikii raskol" (The Great Schism), in *Voina i "tret'ia sila,"* pp. 8-9; Protokol'naia zapis', pp. 12-13, 17-17a.

war a venomous polemic such as only a jackal state would invite;[52] and in general, they felt that the interests of humanity would best be served by a peace without victors or vanquished.[53]

The next thing to consider is how they would promote such an outcome. The answer lies in Chernov's doctrine of the "third force," enunciated by him as early as the Beaugy conference in August, 1914. Chernov compared the contending coalitions to two giant trusts in whose death grapple a third force, born of the sufferings of humanity, must intervene in order to force a settlement that would be fair and equitable, and hence beyond the capacity of either imperialist trust to achieve. The basis of the settlement would be the renunciation of annexations and indemnities, of vengeance and humiliation, with the right of national self-determination secured to every people. The third force would comprise the toiling masses of all countries, roused to action by the whip of privation and the instinct of self-preservation, and given conscious direction by a revived socialist international, now resolved to exemplify in deeds the hitherto empty phrases of its grandiloquent manifestoes.[54]

But the third force would not embrace all antiwar elements, for it did not aim at a restoration of the *status quo ante bellum* but at the creation of something new, and it was directed not simply against the war itself but at the whole order of society which had produced the war. Hence no collaboration with bourgeois forces opposed to the war was contemplated. Chernov drew a sharp distinction, in both spirit and purpose, between revolutionary socialism with its militancy and concern for justice, and bourgeois pacifism, with its softness and comfort-seeking, its one-sided emphasis and its

[52] "Novaia 'zashchitnitsa svobody'" (A New "Defender of Freedom"), *Na Chuzhbine,* No. 10, pp. 9-11.

[53] See especially Chernov, "Dva techeniia" (Two Trends), in *Voina i "tret'ia sila,"* pp. 13-15; Chernov, "Voina i revoliutsiia," in *Chuzhimi putiami,* pp. 71-72; Chernov, "Dopol'nitelnyia zatraty" (Additional Expenditures), in *ibid.,* pp. 44-49; Chernov, "Na odnom primere," in *ibid.,* p. 25; Argunov, Pravoe i levoe, p. 19.

[54] See especially Chernov, "Tret'ia sila" (The Third Force), in *Voina i "tret'ia sila,"* pp. 23-26; Chernov, "Dva techeniia," in *ibid.,* p. 13; Chernov, "Nashi deklaratsii," in *Internatsional i voina,* pp. 49-51; Protokol'naia zapis', p. 17.

willingness to sacrifice other considerations to the attainment of peace. Not a temporary stay of the manifestations of militarism but an eradication of the evil itself was posed as the task of the third force. And while peace must be considered a boon of inestimable value, it ought not be procured by surrendering other objectives of the working-class movement, as, for example, the right of national self-determination. Socialism did not abjure all forms of war but only those that were historically sterile.[55] Thus the socialists, like reformers of all ages, closed one door upon an evil and opened wide another. The same maximalist spirit which ruled out any collaboration with bourgeois pacifism also precluded an alliance with those rather influential elements in capitalist society which, without being pacifist in ideology, nevertheless desired to halt the war because of a higher moral sense or because they realized in full measure its undermining effects upon the order they represented.[56] The third force could not work with bourgeois statesmen of the type of Witte or Caillaux, Lansdowne or La Follette, since they were only against war and not against private property. In their efforts to preserve the revolutionary purity of the third force, its advocates undeniably weakened that force as a factor for peace by rejecting out of hand any thought of collaboration with influences working in the same direction on the other side of the class barrier.

The third force, thus restricted to revolutionary socialist elements, would first manifest itself in simultaneous or at any rate parallel action in each country against the class truce, the disruption of which would leave the toilers free to assemble under their own banner. When the gathering of forces had been completed and ties established with the same movement in other countries, the third force would then proceed to storm the battlements of the order sustaining the war. Apparently in the first or defensive stage only pressure tactics were to be used in working for peace; whereas

[55] "Lozungi momenta: I. Patsifizm i sotsializm," in *Voina i "tret'ia sila,"* pp. 33-35; "K obosnovaniiu nashego lozunga," in *ibid.,* pp. 44-49.

[56] The SR internationalists ignored, or were blind to, the existence of such elements. According to Chernov, nothing whatever was to be expected of the ruling classes by way of ending the war ("K obosnovaniiu nashego lozunga," in *ibid.,* p. 46).

in the second or offensive stage, open revolution was contemplated.[57] The most difficult aspect of the task of swinging the third force into action, of course, was the coordination of the movement in the various countries. The SR internationalists wrestled with this problem and at length came forth with a definite formula.

According to them, the German toilers might be expected to make the first move in view of the initial fault of their country, their own failure to act decisively in restraint of imperialism, and the superior military position of Germany, whose armies were more the hammer than the anvil. But there were considerations militating against the assumption of the initiative by the German working class: its lack of revolutionary traditions, its habits of moderation and orderliness, the enervating influence of the party bureaucracy, transmitted through the powerful trade-union organization, and the presence of an aristocracy of skilled labor, enmeshed in the toils of capitalism. Moral incumbency of action did not create the objective possibility of action. The Independent Socialists in Germany had already stirred from the patriotic trance and were heading down the road toward illegal action, disrupting the *Burgfrieden* and everywhere contesting the position of the Majority Socialists. More could not be expected for the moment, and revolutionary initiative devolved upon a country where fewer obstacles would be encountered than in Germany, which had never been to the fore in this respect and had ever stood in need of an external stimulus. It could not be England, for there the hardships of war had been felt less acutely than elsewhere and class friction was at a minimum, nor could it be France, a power long sunk in decadence and no longer capable of standing in the vanguard of European developments.[58]

Who, then, was to take the lead? The SR internationalists believed that the honor of beginning the world revolution as well as the risk of making the first move would fall to Russia. The crisis brewing there went deeper and would break sooner than elsewhere, and for socialists to refuse to take advantage of it merely because

[57] See *ibid.*, pp. 47-48; "Nashi deklaratsii," in *Internatsional i voina*, pp. 49-50.
[58] Chernov, "Imperativy morali i imperativy zhizni," in *Voina i "tret'ia sila,"* pp. 59-63; Chernov, "Komu nachat'?" (Who Shall Begin?), in *ibid.*, pp. 56-57.

the country was at war would be to have fish's blood in their veins. It was the war that gave them their opportunity. The accumulated pressure of an abortive revolution and reforms long delayed, the administrative ineptitude and moral corrosion of the regime, and the whole vast strain of the war upon an anachronistic state combined to produce a situation which could not fail to eventuate in revolution, whether it were consciously planned or not. Socialists must be prepared to exploit the crisis in the firm conviction that an upheaval in a great country like Russia would not remain without effect in other lands, especially in enemy countries, where the ending of the "Cossack danger" would strengthen the hand of those independent groups which already were displaying commendable energy in the task of weaning the masses away from the government socialists. In a word, the strategy must be the transformation of the war crisis into a revolutionary crisis, not only in Russia but everywhere else, so that the Russian revolution would not remain in dangerous isolation but would be complemented by revolutions in Germany and Austria, states whose political affinity to Russia rendered them vulnerable to infection from that quarter.[59]

It has been claimed that the SR internationalists were powerfully influenced in the construction of their ideology by Lenin—in fact, that he was the fountainhead of their inspiration. Their original stand in favor of resurrecting the International and bringing pressure to bear upon existing regimes in the interests of peace is said to have deepened into a demand for the violent overthrow of those regimes under the influence of the Bolshevik example. The turning point in this evolution of the concept of the third force was allegedly the Zimmerwald Conference, following which it is said to have assumed more concrete form and advanced to a bolder position. The acceptance of the vanguard role of Russia in the European revolution is cited as conclusive evidence of Chernov's indebtedness to Lenin.[60]

---

[59] Chernov, "Komu nachat'?", in *ibid.*, pp. 53-58; Chernov, "Imperativy morali i imperativy zhizni," in *Voina i "tret'ia sila,"* pp. 63-67; Chernov, "Voina i revoliutsiia," in *Chuzhimi putiami,* pp. 68-69.

[60] Slavík, "Ruské strany politické za světové války," *Slovanský Přehled,* XVII, 480-82; Argunov, Pravoe i levoe, pp. 19, 22-23.

Yet it would be foolhardy to deny originality to Chernov in the realm of theory, however completely he may have been overshadowed by his Bolshevik rival in the realm of action. It is quite probable that he arrived at similar conclusions through independent analysis. Chernov's estimate of imperialism and of the situation created by the war does bear a marked resemblance to Lenin's,[61] as does also his prescription of tactics for the new International,[62] but one does not have to assume that he simply borrowed his ideas from Lenin. At the very beginning of the war Chernov realized that the socialists confronted a situation of extreme fluidity in which it was possible to play for the highest stakes; he foresaw that the war would have "stupendous consequences," and even while he spoke in modest terms of "international pressure" by socialists to halt the struggle, he was fully conscious of the possibility of "elemental developments" before the end of the war which would overturn the governments responsible for it and cast down the thrones of Eastern Europe.[63] Thus long before the Zimmerwald Conference (September, 1915), the fertile brain of Chernov contained all the ideas necessary to the construction of his theory of the third force in its ultimate form. While it is quite likely that the example of Lenin's "hatchet Bolshevism" emboldened the SR internationalists to proceed more rapidly along the road to revolution, the clarification and deepening of their program may likewise be attributed to the progress of the war itself, with its exposure of tsarism as a worm-eaten system of government, now ready to pass from the scene.

In order to exculpate Chernov entirely from the charge of theoretical subservience to Lenin, it is necessary only to remember that affinity does not constitute identity. There was one profound difference between the two men in relation to the war: Chernov was not a defeatist. Desertion, sabotage, and refusal to serve in the army did not meet with the sanction of the SR leader, who felt that

[61] "Lozungi momenta: II, Nash takticheskii lozung" (Slogans of the Moment: II, Our Tactical Slogan), in *Voina i "tret'ia sila,"* pp. 38-40; "Komu nachat'?" in *ibid.,* pp. 53-56.

[62] "Otkrytyi vopros" (An Open Question), in *Internatsional i voina,* pp. 71-75.

[63] Protokol'naia zapis', pp. 13, 16-17.

such actions fell within the scope of the old adage, "travailler pour le roi de Prusse."[64] The Leninist slogan calling for the defeat of one's own government in the imperialist war was expressly rejected as favoring the victory of another government, equally hostile to the toiling democracy of Russia, for it was not always true that "the enemy of our enemy is our friend"; he could be "our enemy also, with whom no conciliation, even tacit, is possible."[65] Since the weakening of one regime through defeat entailed the strengthening of another through victory, Chernov argued that the "pan-defeatism" of Lenin and Zinoviev was self-contradictory, and went on to characterize it as a "primitive and stereotyped" theory, founded upon "hatchet logic." The true socialist, he submitted, could not wish for the defeat of any one power in particular simply because he could not wish for the victory of any other power.[66] War must be accepted as a necessary evil until such time as enough strength had been assembled to counteract it with help from the opposite side. Basic to Chernov's plan of action was the principle of reciprocity:

If on one side of the boundary the proletariat rises as one man against the war and deranges the whole machinery of mobilization, but on the other side the proletariat as one man shoulders its rifles and marches docilely into action, then it turns out that the revolutionarily inclined proletariat has done something that is not at all revolutionary but has simply played into the hands of an alien ravisher.[67]

As we have seen, Chernov was willing for Russia to take the first plunge into the revolutionary sea, but he expected the toilers of Germany and Austria to follow suit, and until they did, the war would go on, for revolutionary Russia could not come to terms with imperial Germany. The revolutionary provisional government would not meet a conqueror's army with bread and salt. But the war it would conduct would be a different kind of war, in which the new Russia, having renounced all international commitments

---

[64] Chernov, "Dva techeniia," in *Voina i "tret'ia sila,"* p. 11.

[65] Chernov, "K obosnovaniiu nashego lozunga," in *ibid.*, pp. 49-50.

[66] "Pan-porazhenchestvo" (All-around Defeatism), in *Istinnye i mnimye porazhentsy*, pp. 22-26.

[67] "Komu nachat'?" in *Voina i "tret'ia sila,"* p. 52.

springing from the predatory designs of tsarist Russia *or from the hidden imperialist aims of its allies*,[68] could appeal to the German people to overthrow the Hohenzollerns without fear of ensuing disaster at the hands of a foreign invader.[69] In this manner revolutionary Russia would maintain its guard against imperial Germany at the same time that it would place a premium upon revolutionary action within that country by offering the German people a way out of the slaughter. The Bolsheviks failed in the first respect, and the SR "defensists" in the second. Chernov's ground was well chosen.

Certain misconceptions regarding this position, which, as nearly as we can tell, was that of the majority of the party in 1917, may now be pointed out. The demand for reciprocal action on the other side of the trenches knocks out the charge of defeatism which has so often and so ignorantly been preferred against Chernov and his following within the party. The SR leader was fully cognizant of the difficulties attendant upon a stand for reciprocity but he firmly rejected the short cut of defeatism because of three substantial considerations. First, socialists had no right to speculate upon a catastrophe which would engulf not only the government of their country but the entire population as well. Second, the defeat of imperial Russia at the hands of imperial Germany would mean that the crash of the one would be purchased at the price of strengthening the other, a price which socialists could not pay, in as much as the cultural superiority of the Hohenzollern regime could not compensate for the more formidable character of its warmaking apparatus. Third, a revolution growing out of the demoralization induced by military disaster would never enjoy stability. Only gains which had been fought for and won could be lasting, and, in the final analysis, the liberation of the people must be the work of the people itself. The defeatist stand of the Bolsheviks, far from being a manifestation of revolutionary boldness, was actually a con-

[68] Italics added. This phrase has far-reaching implications, both for the party and the Provisional Government, in 1917.

[69] Chernov, "O narodnicheskoi konferentsii," in *Chuzhimi putiami*, pp. 81-82; Chernov, "Logika odnogo grekhopadeniia," in *ibid.*, pp. 41-42; Chernov, "Imperativy morali i imperativy zhizni," in *Voina i "tret'ia sila*," pp. 67-68.

fession of weakness. For socialists to depend upon an alien imperialism to accomplish their task was neither honorable nor necessary, nor could it in the long run be efficacious. Alien hands would inevitably serve alien interests.[70]

Closely allied with the charge of defeatism is that of pro-Germanism. It had duly cropped up with reference to Chernov in the war years, well in advance of the Revolution of 1917, at which time the chauvinists would seize upon it to raise a terrific din in the organs of public opinion for the purpose of driving the SR leader from the Provisional Government. The accusation was wholly unfounded. Chernov never betrayed any softness toward imperial Germany, which he consistently placed on the same level with tsarist Russia. In rejecting the pacifist stand, he proclaimed the necessity of using the sword which history had placed in the hands of socialism to cut the two Gordian knots holding up a rational solution of the European crisis: one of these was in St. Petersburg, the other in Berlin.[71] Even with reference to the social democracy of enemy countries, he was sharply critical,[72] but he never forgot that if the German and Austrian socialists, like Eve, had tasted the war-apple first, the Allied socialists, like Adam, had been quick to follow suit; both had partaken of the forbidden fruit.[73] Chernov never imputed a monopoly of oppression to the Central Powers and was wholly free of that chauvinism, hidden or avowed, which has disgraced the intellectual class on both sides of the hoary controversy between Teuton and Slav. He insisted on the inalienable rights of the German people, wished to spare them a conqueror's peace, and fought with all his strength against the monstrous doctrine of collective guilt.[74]

[70] "Na kogo i na chto nam nadeiat'sia" (On Whom and on What Shall We Base Our Hopes), in *Istinnye i mnimye porazhentsy*, pp. 10-13; "Istoriko-literaturnaia spravka," in *ibid.*, pp. 14-16; "Pan-porazhenchestvo," in *ibid.*, pp. 25-26; Protokol'naia zapis', p. 6.

[71] "Lozungi momenta: I, Patsifizm i sotsializm," in *Voina i "tret'ia sila*," p. 36.

[72] See especially his open letter to Victor Adler in *Internatsional i voina*, pp. 27-32; "Tri konferentsii" (Three Conferences), in *ibid.*, pp. 44-45.

[73] "Logika odnogo grekhopadeniia," in *Chuzhimi putiami*, pp. 36, 40-41.

[74] *Ibid.*, pp. 42-43; "Voina i revoliutsiia," in *ibid.*, p. 71; "Dva techeniia," in *Voina i "tret'ia sila*," p. 13.

Finally, a widespread misconception as to his position in general should here be laid at rest. Chernov's detractors—and they are legion—have urged that cowardice and hypocrisy underlay his approach to the war question, that under a fog of casuistry and verbosity he preached a message the essence of which he had taken— or stolen—from Lenin. Those who are more charitably inclined ascribe his position to fuzzy thinking rather than to crafty design.[75] On the other hand the Bolsheviks derided the internationalism of the Chernovian SR's, and Lenin characterized their position as wholly lacking in stability.[76] The truth of the matter is that Chernov preached an antiwar doctrine which was logical and legitimate, and which was refused recognition by the Bolsheviks only because for them nothing was antiwar which was not also defeatist.[77] Between the rival camps of unconditional acceptance of war and uncompromising rejection of national defense there was ample ground on which an independent doctrine could arise, dedicated to combating the imperialism of both warring trusts without falling into the clutches of either. Admittedly, it was not so simple a doctrine as that preached on either extreme, but Chernov contended with much validity that "defensism" and defeatism were crassly simplified formulas which did not accord with the complexities of the situation.[78] The trouble with his doctrine was that it would be subject to the stress and strain of its intermediate position, to the process of polarization, and to misrepresentation by fanatics on either extreme. In propagating the SR brand of internationalism, in striving to end the war by encouraging the peace movement in Germany while teaching his own people the difficult discipline of defense without victory, Chernov was attempting something which the common man would probably never understand and certainly would never accept as a guide to his own actions. But that is no excuse for the minority

[75] For typical judgments see Slavík, "Ruské strany politické za světové války," *Slovanský Přehled*, XVII, 481; Argunov, Pravoe i levoe, pp. 19-23.
[76] *Sochineniia*, XVIII, 128; translation in Olga H. Gankin and H. H. Fisher, *The Bolsheviks and the World War*, p. 186; see also p. 200.
[77] See his polemical exchange with Zinoviev, "Plennoe narodnichestvo" (Captive Populism), in *Chuzhimi putiami*, p. 93.
[78] "Prezhde i teper'," in *Istinnye i mnimye porazhentsy*, pp. 9-10.

of intellect and character to' have distorted the purpose or denied the virtue of his endeavor. If SR internationalism became in time a feeder for Bolshevism, that was not the intent of Chernov but rather was due to the deterioration which any belief undergoes when it is communicated to ordinary individuals.[79]

Already in the bosom of the internationalist wing of the party there was forming a group of extremists which would constitute the core of the future schismatic party of the Left Socialist Revolutionaries (Internationalists). The venerable Mark Natanson was their leader, assisted by Boris D. Kamkov (real name Katz) and G. Dalin (real name M. Levenson). These men were not troubled by Chernov's scruples against defeatism; they were Jews, and their hatred of imperial Russia knew no bounds.[80] Natanson had never shared Chernov's belief in reciprocity.[81] A German victory in the East would not have evil consequences, he believed, because it would be followed by a German defeat in the West.[82] Natanson thus shares with Durnovo the distinction of having foreseen the outcome of the war at its beginning, though in Natanson's case perspicacity and prejudice coincided. Here undoubtedly was a flash of genius, but otherwise the left SR's were singularly undistinguished, either in intellect or literary skill, and ideologically followed in the wake of Chernov, regarding him with something akin to reverence even after they no longer accepted his teachings in their hearts. But the retention of their ideological independence did not prevent these SR's from drawing nearer to Bolshevism in their practical conduct, so that by the time of the revolution they actually stood closer to Lenin than to Chernov, albeit such was the obfuscation in this party that even such a prominent Left SR as Alexandróvich seemed

[79] In a series of articles, Chernov marked off his position from the Bolsheviks in "Pan-porazhenchestvo," in *ibid.*, pp. 22-26; from the SR defeatists in "Na kogo i na chto nam nadeiat'sia," in *ibid.*, pp. 10-13; from Alexinski, Plekhanov, and the "defensists" in "Spetsialist razoblachitel'nago tsekha" (A Specialist in the Unmasking Guild), in *ibid.*, pp. 16-21, and "Gde zhe nastoiashchie porazhentsy?", in *ibid.*, pp. 26-32.

[80] Right in the beginning of the war Natanson had termed a Russian victory the worst of all possible outcomes (Protokol'naia zapis', p. 10).

[81] *Ibid.*, p. 18.

[82] *Ibid.*, p. 11.

not to be aware of it.[83] In effect, SR internationalism had lost its unity before the revolution began, one group under Natanson gravitating steadily toward Bolshevism while the other continued to follow Chernov. It required the revolution to reveal how deep the cleavage had become. In terms of party factionalism, the Natanson group became the left and Chernov's group, the left center; in the parlance of international socialism, the Natanson group formed a part of the Zimmerwaldian left while Chernov's group adhered to the Zimmerwaldian right. In the case of the left alone is it possible to speak of a tinge of defeatism, yet it should be borne in mind that once the bitter fruits of that policy had been tasted, the recovery of the left SR's was rapid indeed, as is seen in their violent reaction to the Treaty of Brest-Litovsk.

One of the first indications of a rift in the ranks of Socialist Revolutionaries opposed to the war came in connection with the celebrated Zimmerwald Conference. Of the two SR representatives, Natanson ("Bobrov") signed the manifesto without reservation but Chernov withheld his signature, not because he disagreed with the main content of the document or disregarded the advantages of a united front but because it did not meet with his views on two side issues to which he assigned much importance. As the custodian of agrarian socialism, Chernov could not approve an appeal which summoned the proletariat to rise against war but ignored the peasant masses of Eastern Europe as an equally potent factor of peace. Quite rightly he pointed to the unpopularity of the war in the villages of Russia and Bulgaria, even of France, and concluded that no movement against the war would get very far in such countries unless it knew how to capitalize upon this sentiment. In the second place, the SR leader desired that the war guilt of the three imperial dynasties be singled out for especial condemnation instead of being obscured in a generalized attribution of guilt to the capitalist order of society. He wanted more material for republican propaganda than the Zimmerwald manifesto gave, partly no doubt to needle the Western socialists in a weak point, but mainly to demonstrate to the

[83] Sviatitski, "Voina i predfevral'e," *Katorga i Ssylka* (II, 1931), LXXV, 41.

people the connection between their sufferings and monarchical institutions, with the overthrow of which the social revolution must begin. In short, Chernov felt that the manifesto suffered from the Marxian myopia of its framers, as very likely it did. He and Natanson submitted amendments in the SR spirit, not because of partisan truculence but in order to make it more effective as an instrument against war, and both also supported the Radek-Lenin resolution on tactics, but in the final act their paths diverged, for Natanson and his group were already moving into the orbit of Bolshevism.[84]

With this the discussion of SR internationalism, its ideology and inner state, has been concluded. If its cohesiveness was less than that of social patriotism, its tenets were as passionately embraced. Something must now be said of the relations between the internationalist and "defensist" camps during the prerevolutionary period.

The lines of division traced by the war hardened into rigid barriers as personal animosity was joined to ideological controversy. If at first amenities were still observed and the leaders of both the international and the "defensist" factions could assemble at Beaugy-sur-Clarens, it was not long before matters reached the stage of open breach; already at the time of the London Conference of Allied socialists (February, 1915) the representatives of the two currents no longer were exchanging greetings.[85] Efforts to convene an all-party conference to work out some formula of unity came to naught,[86] and henceforth the paths of the warring factions diverged, the cleavage within the party over the war proving stronger than the cleavage between Populism and Marxism, as is seen in the fact that the "defensists" teamed up with like-minded Menshevik elements while the internationalists participated in the

---

[84] See Chernov's account, "Moi otchët" (My Account), in *Internatsional i voina*, pp. 59-70.

[85] Argunov, *Pravoe i levoe*, p. 18. Argunov and Rubanovich attended for the "defensists," Chernov and Natanson for the internationalists.

[86] Slavík, "Ruské strany politické za světové války," *Slovanský Přehled*, XVII, 479.

Zimmerwald and Kienthal conferences together with the antiwar Marxists. Polemical exchanges between the two SR factions waxed hotter and hotter, and the air was filled with harsh epithets: the social patriots hurled charges of defeatism and pro-Germanism, and the antiwar group countered with terms such as "Pharisees," "Kadets," "barbarians," and "counterrevolutionaries." At no time did the command of invective and the formidable polemical skill of V. M. Chernov show to better advantage than in his flagellation of the "defensists" in general and of I. I. Bunakov-Fondaminski in particular. He spoke of his opponents as political bushmen who could never understand the distinction between the desire to spare the enemy a conqueror's peace and the desire for an enemy victory; using the national drinks as symbols of chauvinism, he berated equally the "kvass socialists" of Russia and the "beer socialists" of Germany, showing how each played into the other's hands. By 1916 Chernov could attest the spiritual alienation of the two factions and the fact that the moral judgments of the one had become virtually incomprehensible to the other.[87]

Besides the verbal controversy there were several developments during the war which served to embitter relations. One of these was volunteerism. About 600 Russian political émigrés, among them a number of Socialist Revolutionaries, volunteered for service in the republican army of France.[88] Some of them were killed and others wounded. The most prominent member of the party to lose his life was Stephen Slëtov.[89] The internationalist wing of the party greeted the wave of volunteerism with studied hostility as a manifestation

[87] "Voina i revoliutsiia," in *Chuzhimi putiami*, pp. 71-72; "Nerevoliutsionnaia revoliutsiia," in *ibid.*, pp. 60-66; "Novyi politicheskii blok," in *ibid.*, p. 60; "Logika odnogo grekhopadeniia," in *ibid.*, pp. 40-41, 43; "Ot sotsial-patriotizma k neo-kadetstvu," in *ibid.*, pp. 74-75.

[88] A group of 68 volunteers was selected for analysis. In respect to political affiliation, 35 were SD's, 17 were SR's, 9 were anarchists, and 7 were something else. The disproportion of Jews is startling: 33 volunteers were of that community as against only 29 Russians and 6 of other communities (Argunov, *Pravoe i levoe*, p. 32).

[89] At Vauquois, June 6, 1915 (N.S.). Slëtov was one of those intellectuals who never master the soldier's art. His sergeant said of him, "O, c'est un bon type, mais peu intelligent." See *ibid.*, pp. 32-34; L. Rossel', "Pamiati S. N. Slëtova" (In Memory of S. N. Slëtov), *Volia Rossii*, No. 6 (1925), pp. 84-96; *Pamiati Stepana Nikolaevicha Slëtova, passim.*

of the mass psychosis which had overborne the socialist conscience. In connection with the death of Slëtov, Chernov expressed regret that his brother-in-law and cofounder of the party had not fallen under the red flag of international socialism.[90] The cold detachment with which their opponents sat in their editorial offices and passed strictures upon men in imminent danger of their lives naturally aroused the indignation of the social patriots.

Another development leading to an exacerbation of feelings was the institution of the war industrial committees in Russia as a means of strengthening the productive effort. As workingmen were granted representation along with the employers, the question of class collaboration arose in acute form. The SR internationalists, who appear to have enjoyed real influence in Petrograd, put forth every effort, in conjunction with the Bolsheviks, to induce the workers to boycott the election of representatives to these committees. Whether the Bolsheviks or the SR's were more responsible it is impossible to say, but at any rate the opponents of participation won a victory in the first elections, later reversed when the government invalidated the results and ordered a new vote. The "defensists," of course, had favored participation, and in attempting to get their views before the workers in Russia, they had permitted a manifesto of the *Prizyv* group to be printed in newspapers of various tendencies, including a section of the capitalist press. This circumstance drew down upon their heads a hail of abuse from the internationalists.[91]

A third development, and the one provocative of the most embittered controversy of all, concerned the publication by the internationalist SR group at Geneva of a series of brochures bearing the title, *Na Chuzhbine* (In a Foreign Land). The purpose of this modest publication was to win converts to the stand of its authors from among the Russian prisoners of war in German and Austrian camps. Some time previously a "society for intellectual assistance to Russian prisoners of war" had been formed to minister to the

[90] "Stepan Nikolaevich Slëtov," *Zhizn'*, No. 1 (Geneva series; No. 63 from the start in Paris), June 20, 1915; Argunov, Pravoe i levoe, p. 34.
[91] Argunov, Pravoe i levoe, pp. 16-18; *Bulletin of the International Socialist Committee in Berne*, No. 5 (July 10, 1916), pp. 11-12; Slavík, "Ruské strany politické za světové války," *Slovanský Přehled*, XVII, 482-83.

cultural needs of these hitherto neglected compatriots in such a manner as to awaken their political conscience and recruit them as warriors for the future liberation of the homeland. *Na Chuzhbine* was the fruition of this enterprise. It preached a thoroughly subversive message, directed against the government, the order of society, and especially against the war effort. According to the "defensists," it was "a hash of crude demagogy with defeatist injunctions in the Zimmerwald spirit," calculated to give its readers a false impression of conditions at home and filled with coarse attacks upon the officers' corps. The indignation provoked in patriotic circles by the appearance of *Na Chuzhbine* can be compared only with the reverberations of the sealed-car episode in Bolshevik history. The opposition alleged that, besides being packed with lies about Russia, the brochures contained nothing about German imperialism and so served the enemy as a means of decomposing the war spirit of Russian soldiers. In as much as they could not be distributed without the permission of the enemy authorities and as they bore on the outer cover the device, "distributed gratis in camps," there followed the inevitable charge about German gold. When proof was demanded, then and later, the "defensists" were constrained to admit they could not substantiate the charge, but they continued to regard the publication of *Na Chuzhbine* as morally and politically a criminal act. Stalinski wrote in *Prizyv* that the deeds of the Russian internationalists helped only the Prussian king, the worst enemy of the revolution, and cited these brochures in support of his argument.[92]

An inspection of representative issues of *Na Chuzhbine* fails to disclose any softness toward German imperialism. All governments are condemned for their part in the war and its ill-effects are brought out with reference to Germany and Austria as well as other powers.[93] But the editors admittedly concentrated their fire on the home front, leaving the evils of Germany to the socialists thereof: "Is it for us to concern ourselves with the enlightenment

---

[92] Argunov, Pravoe i levoe, pp. 23-24.
[93] See, for example, "Novaia 'zashchitnitsa svobody,'" No. 10, pp. 9, 11; A. Gorski, "Po puti k miru" (On the Road to Peace), No. 1, pp. 14-15.

of our neighbors, when in our own land the murk is impenetrable and slavery unshaken? We feel that it is the duty of the socialists of each country to contend with the internal enemy, to struggle against existing conditions."[94] Despite the emphasis on Russian affairs, enough was said about Germany to cause certain numbers to be confiscated, and soldiers, in writing of the pleasure with which they read the booklets, expressly requested that all mention of Germany be omitted so that there would be no interference with their distribution. Owing to the fact that some enterprising individuals had cornered copies and charged for letting them be read, it had been decided to indicate on the cover that they were free. As to the charge of enemy subventions, the Geneva SR's published the balance sheet for *Na Chuzhbine*, showing that most of the modest funds involved had been raised by entertainment or lottery.[95] Finally, in defense of the revolutionary honor of this enterprise, it was pointed out that the Austrian authorities, as a rule and not as an exception, forbade the distribution of *Na Chuzhbine.* among their prisoners of war.[96]

As a result of these various developments and of the incessant press warfare, the relations between the "defensist" and internationalist wings of the Socialist Revolutionary party on the eve of the February Revolution could not conceivably have been worse. If, in their more charitable moments, the "defensists" conceded that the opposition had the same goal of a just peace without forcible seizures of territory, and differed only as to the path to be chosen,[97] they never really divested themselves of the view that the intermediacy of the internationalists' position was more apparent than real, and that, in essence, the policy of Chernov was the policy of Lenin, only more hazy in concept and more devious in execution. Furthermore, it might be said that in one sense they considered Chernov even worse than Lenin, for in their eyes the insidious, doubt-stirring phrases of their erstwhile comrade gained a hearing

---

[94] "K nashim chitateliam" (To Our Readers), No. 13, p. 5.
[95] See No. 14, p. 32.
[96] Letter of M. Levenson (G. Dalin) in *Delo Naroda*, No. 118 (August 4, 1917); see also letters of B. Kamkov in *ibid.*, No. 112 (July 28, 1917) and No. 117 (August 3, 1917).
[97] Bunakov, "Chto nas razdeliaet?" *Prizyv*, No. 12 (December 18, 1915).

in quarters which would have turned a deaf ear to the harsh and bludgeon-like words of Lenin.[98] Chernov went ahead, breaking the ground, and Lenin followed after, sowing the dragon's teeth of a crop that only he could harvest. V. V. Rudnev, one of the most uncompromising of "defensists," told this writer, with great sincerity and great bitterness, that what Chernov had done to extinguish national sentiment in the breasts of the armed defenders of a youthful and immature people was the one thing that could never be forgiven him.[99]

On the other hand, the internationalists could not divest themselves of the view that their party opponents were renegades from the cause of socialism and backsliders from the principle of the brotherhood of all peoples. The cardinal sin of the "defensists" was not their stand for defense, the necessity of which was acknowledged, but their moral acceptance of the war and of everything to which it led. They brought to the war a much greater tribute than was exacted by mere defense. Not only had they accepted the defensive implications of war but they had gone far afield to embrace many of its aggressive features as well, including the enticement of neutrals into the fray, the cultivation of bad feeling toward the enemy populations, and the whitewashing of Allied imperialism. Rejecting an alliance with the German working class unless positive and unilateral guarantees of revolutionary action were forthcoming, they had given their support to notoriously imperialist regimes without asking any guarantees whatever.[100]

Equally as bad as the moral acceptance of war, and closely associated with it, was the determined effort to set victory above revolution. According to Chernov, the "defensists" would have renounced the very idea of revolution if only the tsarist generals had been more successful; once convinced of its inevitability, they sought to denature it of its social content so as to leave undisturbed the class collaboration essential to victory. This attempt to prostitute

---

[98] Interview with Argunov in Prague (June, 1935).
[99] Interview in Paris (September, 1935).
[100] Chernov, "Logika odnogo grekhopadeniia," in *Chuzhimi putiami*, pp. 36-41; Chernov, "Dopolnitel'nyia zatraty," in *ibid.*, pp. 44-49.

the sacred cause of revolution to an alien purpose, this specter of a "castrated" revolution, enraged the internationalists. With them, revolution definitely came before victory, for an upheaval of the type they had in mind would either make victory unnecessary or else would change the character of the war so as to legitimatize it for the socialist conscience.[101]

Finally, in their indictment of social patriotism, the internationalists charged a gross breach of party discipline. No authoritative party organ, or even any organ at all, had sanctioned such wide departures from the hallowed traditions of Social Revolutionism, nor had the "defensists" any right to enter into such intimate relations with like-minded Social Democratic elements, swallowing as they did so a sizable potion of Marxist doctrine.[102]

If the two wings of the party had been less intent on belaboring each other and less blinded by socialist dogma, they might have perceived that both were caught in a current the depth of which they could not fathom. Socialism simply did not have the strength needed to cope with the war in the manner prescribed by its principles. The "defensists" had no formula for ending the bloody business except to hack their way through to victory. The full bankruptcy of their position, however, appears only in their fond belief that the pressure of public opinion in the Western democracies would prevent abuse of the victory. It was precisely this new force of public opinion, inflamed and intolerant, ignorant and incapable of restrained judgments, even more than the chancelleries of the old order, which endangered the future peace and rendered a just and even-handed settlement out of the question.

On the other hand, the internationalists, in proposing to halt the struggle before it had run its course, were forced to bank upon the revolutionary will to action of the German as well as the Russian people, and their optimism in this respect was greater than circumstances justified. Chernov spoke in glowing terms of the Independent

---

[101] "Voina i revoliutsiia," in *ibid.*, pp. 67-71; "Nerevoliutsionnaia revoliutsiia," in *ibid.*, pp. 60-66; "Imperativy morali i imperativy zhizni," in *Voina i "tret'ia sila,"* pp. 67-68.

[102] Chernov, "Novyi politicheskii blok," in *Chuzhimi putiami*, pp. 49-60.

Socialist movement in Germany, of how it had become a serious force and everywhere was disputing the positions of the Majority,[103] yet even after the revolution, in the elections to the National Assembly in 1919, the Independents secured only 22 seats against 163 for the Majority Socialists and 236 for the parties of private property.[104] Only in a few districts—in Berlin, Leipzig, the middle German industrial region, and along the lower Rhine—did they display real strength; elsewhere their organization was still too weak for serious inroads to be made upon the position of the Majority.[105] And in the flood tide of radicalism in 1920 the Independents and Communists together polled barely 20 percent of the total vote.[106] Manifestly, therefore, the main ally of the internationalists in Germany was not the organized force of the Independents but the elemental force of war weariness, which was indeed a powerful factor, but one that required a lengthy period and magnified suffering to work itself out in the face of deeply ingrained habits of obedience.

Thus both wings of the Socialist Revolutionary party were caught beyond their depth. The one could no more insure a fair peace than the other could stop the war. Each could see the flaws in the other's armor but not those in its own. A common feeling of futility, or at least a greater sense of humility, might have assuaged the bitterness of their controversy, but the self-righteousness so characteristic of SR's was now turned against their own breed. Soon there was an end of mutual understanding or sympathy, for neither side was capable of perceiving in full measure the tragedy in which both were involved.

It is remarkable, therefore, that the fiction of unity should have survived. Lenin accused the SR internationalists of bad faith in not making a clean break with the "defensist" element in their party; in his customarily brutal language, he denounced their "rotten diplomacy" in signing the Zimmerwald Manifesto while keeping up the

[103] "Imperativy morali i imperativy zhizni," in *Voina i "tret'ia sila,"* pp. 62-63.
[104] *Statistisches Jahrbuch für das Deutsche Reich 1921/22* (Berlin, 1922), p. 355.
[105] E. Prager, *Geschichte der U.S.P.D.*, p. 188.
[106] *Statistisches Jahrbuch für das Deutsche Reich 1921/22*, p. 357.

connection with "social-chauvinism."[107] Levenson ("Dalin") voiced
the same protest from within the party.[108] But neither the left center
nor the social patriots were ready for a final break. In spite of everything, a common tradition, common attachment to a label, and
common cloudiness of ideology prevented them from laying the
ghost of unity after the substance had withered and died. Apparently the internationalists toyed with the idea of excluding their
opponents from the party, but nothing ever came of it, if for no
other reason than that there was no agency of excommunication.
The Central Committee had ceased to exist, no congress or conference could be convened, and the Delegation Abroad of the
Central Committee, which had come to have an antiwar majority,[109]
lacked the requisite authority for such drastic action, besides which
it broke down in the course of the struggle and renounced all political functions.[110] Thus the Revolution of 1917 found the party in a
state of chaos, with unity in name but not in fact. It would have
been better had the battling factions dissolved partnership and gone
their respective ways. But both clung to the family house and attempted cohabitation during the honeymoon stage of the revolution.
The result was mutual paralysis. As one member of the party has
observed, "the experience of 1917 proved that there was very little
sense in striving to bring about a mechanical union of people who
had been spiritually estranged by the war."[111]

[107] Gankin and Fisher, *The Bolsheviks and the World War*, p. 356, n. 63;
Sochineniia, XVIII, 89.
[108] Argunov, Pravoe i levoe, p. 20.
[109] In 1914 the Delegation consisted of eight members, evenly divided over
the war issue. By 1916 the balance had altered in favor of the internationalists,
owing to the voluntary withdrawal of two of the four "defensists" (*Interna-
tionale sozialistische Kommission zu Bern: Bulletin* No. 4 [April 22, 1916], p. 15,
note).
[110] See statement issued by the Delegation in *ibid.*, pp. 14-15; see also
A. Kubov (A. A. Argunov?) "O simvole edinstva partii" (On the Symbol of
Party Unity), *Prizyv*, No. 37 (1916); Argunov, Pravoe i levoe, p. 18; Chernov,
"Plennoe narodnichestvo," in *Chuzhimi putiami*, pp. 93-94; Slavík, "Ruské
strany politické za světové války," *Slovanský Přehled*, XVII, 483; Sviatitski,
"Voina i predfevral'e," *Katorga i Ssylka*, LXXV (II, 1931), 23.
[111] Sviatitski, "Voina i predfevral'e," *Katorga i Ssylka*, LXXV (II, 1931), 46.

V

THE FEBRUARY REVOLUTION AND
THE GENESIS OF COALITION

THE February Revolution was in the fullest sense a popular phenomenon. It proceeded from the people itself, in a purely spontaneous and wholly unorganized fashion. In fact, it was not so much a
revolution in the accepted sense of the term as simply the toppling
over, under slight external pressure, of a structure which had rotted
away. The restricted nature of the popular movement in its early
stages, however, was no gauge of its potentiality, for if it is true
that a relatively small number of people in one corner of the Empire
produced the revolution, it is also true that an even smaller number
resisted the change. Herein lay the deception of those moderate
socialists who all through 1917 lived in mortal fear of a counterrevolution, never realizing that the circumstances of the February
overturn signified not so much the vulnerability of their own cause
as the baselessness of the old regime.

As little as their rivals could the Socialist Revolutionaries claim
to have initiated the events which culminated in the overthrow of
tsarism. The party leaders freely acknowledged the unattended birth
of the revolution. In his opening address before the Third Congress,
Rakitnikov declared that the revolutionists had little reason to plume
themselves over the ease with which the momentous change had been
brought about, for the peasant soldiers and the workers themselves
had assumed the initiative and achieved the victory.[1] He would have
been doing his party a service had he gone on and added that since
the intellectuals had not made the revolution, they could scarcely
hope to impose their concept of its nature and results upon the

[1] *Tretii s"ezd P.S.-R.*, pp. 3-4.

people. "The revolution caught us, the party men of that time, like the foolish virgins of the Scriptures—fast asleep," wrote an officer of the General Staff, S. Mstislavski, who added that later it seemed unbelievable that they should have failed to sense the approaching storm.[2] At a conference of radical leaders late in December, 1916, no one realized what was in the offing and even the most extreme among the participants counseled against an attempt to organize a demonstration on the anniversary of Bloody Sunday;[3] as late as the middle of February the professional revolutionaries still were not keyed up, seeing in the incipient strike movement nothing more than an ordinary manifestation of discontent. In the words of Zenzinov, the revolution came like lightning from the sky. "Let us be frank: it was a great and joyful event, unexpected even by those of us who had been working toward it for many years and waiting for it always."[4]

From what has previously been said, it is obvious that the PSR was in no condition to lead a revolution even had it known one was coming. Like other radical organizations in Russia, it had never been a political party in the real sense but rather a secret society, locked within itself, one of those "socialist sects, overflowing with fanatical idealism, which usually crystallized about a single outstanding thinker."[5] Its membership had consisted of a small but fervent group of active warriors, recruited mainly from the ranks of the intelligentsia. Since the first revolution this organization had been steadily deteriorating, passing through one major crisis after another, until on the eve of the February Revolution, as Zenzinov admits, not only the foes of the party but some of its friends had been ready to bury it.[6] By then it had been reduced to a skeleton of a few illegal groups with no generally recognized center, with an inert constituency, and with the bulk of its best workers forcibly immobilized as exiles, pris-

---

[2] *Piat' dnei*, p. 12.
[3] Sviatitski, "Voina i predfevral'e," *Katorga i Ssylka*, LXXV (II, 1931), 44-46.
[4] "Smysl sobytii" (The Meaning of Events), *Delo Naroda*, No. 1 (March 15, 1917). See also Zenzinov, *Iz zhizni revoliutsionera*, p. 81.
[5] Chernov, manuscript commentary on the minutes of the Central Committee, p. 27.
[6] "Posle partiinago s"ezda" (After the Party Congress), *Delo Naroda*, No. 70 (June 9, 1917); see also "Iz nedavniago proshlago" (From the Recent Past), *ibid.*, No. 126 (August 13, 1917).

oners, or suspects.[7] According to confidential police reports which are partially confirmed in SR sources, the system of espionage had attained such proficiency that the work of underground revolutionary circles was paralyzed, and all attempts to build up an effective SR organization had been nipped in the bud.[8]

Outside the capital an observer who had become convinced of the party's extinction would have found in the months preceding the revolution very little to disturb his view. A Bolshevik source states that the SR's had no organization worthy of the name in any of the large industrial centers; they had never put the transport of literature from abroad on a satisfactory basis and had centered their attention primarily upon students and other intellectuals.[9] In Moscow prominent party members like V. M. Zenzinov, M. Ia. Gendelman, D. S. Rosenblum, and M. V. Vishniak were living on a legal basis and looking forward to nothing more exciting than participation in the elections to the Fifth Duma, now that the party ban, imposed since the dissolution of the Second Duma, was to be removed.[10] There is some evidence of activity in Baku, where a number of arrests had been made,[11] in Nizhni Novgorod, where an extremist group had issued a call for an armed uprising (December, 1916),[12] and in Kharkov, the scene of a newspaper enterprise,[13] but nothing of real importance either here or elsewhere can be recorded. No

[7] Chernov, manuscript commentary on the minutes of the Central Committee, p. 3.

[8] "V ianvare i fevrale 1917 g. (Iz donesenii sekretnykh agentov A. D. Protopopova)" (In January and February, 1917 [from the Reports of the Secret Agents of A. D. Protopopov]), Byloe, No. 13 (No. 7, 1918), p. 95; "Politicheskoe polozhenie Rossii nakanune fevral'skoi revoliutsii v zhandarmskom osveshchenii" (The Political Situation of Russia on the Eve of the February Revolution according to Police Records), Krasnyi Arkhiv, XVII (IV, 1926), 35.

[9] Shliapnikov, Kanun semnadtsatogo goda, Part II, p. 106.

[10] Sviatitski, "Voina i predfevral'e," Katorga i Ssylka, LXXV, 31 ff.

[11] "V ianvare i fevrale 1917 g.," Byloe, No. 13 (No. 7, 1918), pp. 95-96; Rathauser, Revoliutsiia i grazhdanskaia voina v Baku, Part I, p. 44.

[12] Shliapnikov, Kanun semnadtsatogo goda, Part I, pp. 270-71.

[13] N. Kopytovski, "Eshchë o nashikh gazetakh" (More about Our Newspapers), Delo Naroda, No. 13 (March 30, 1917). At the close of 1915, according to a Bolshevik source, the party was not functioning in Kharkov and sympathizers were working strictly as individuals. See A. Baltin (T. Blum), "Khar'kovskaia organizatsiia R.S.-D.R.P. (b-kov) vo vremia voiny" (The Kharkov Organization of the R.S.-D.R.P. [b-kov] during the War), Letopis' Revoliutsii (Chronicle of the Revolution) (Kharkov), No. 5 (1923), p. 16.

testimony is more revealing than Sviatitski's account of a tour which he made of the Ural and Volga regions in the spring of 1916, in the course of which he could find no trace of the underground organization that once had flourished in this birthplace of Social Revolutionism, nor detect any inclination on the part of the Narodnik intellectuals with whom he conversed to undertake its reconstruction.[14] Many of these men had entered the public service and had no intention of jeopardizing their legal status by taking up the old game; as he admits, they constituted an element which was "burnt out in the revolutionary sense," the domestic counterpart and natural ally of the tired revolutionaries of the *Pochin* or "liquidationist" group abroad, with whom they would soon be merged in an effective combination directed against the revolutionary initiative of the party in the months that lay ahead.

In the capital party life had never entirely ceased but it had remained at a rudimentary level, efforts to constitute an all-city committee—the most recent one at the end of 1916—having come to naught. Activity in the capital was greatly impeded not only by the police infiltration which continued to be the bane of the party's existence but also by the sharp division over the war,[15] which aligned the working-class SR's against the intellectuals and foreshadowed the eventual conflict between the Petrograd organization and the Central Committee. This cleavage along class lines as well as on ideological grounds had been deepened by the arrival from abroad of Peter Alexandróvich (Pëtr Aleksándrovich Dmitrievskii),[16] who came as the emissary of the Geneva group of internationalists to rally antiwar sentiment and build up an underground organization. Very little had been accomplished, however, before the outbreak of the February Revolution.[17]

More than thirty years later it is still not possible to speak with any assurance regarding political conditions in the Petrograd garrison, to determine the degree of conscious revolutionary feeling that

---

[14] "Voina i predfevral'e," *Katorga i Ssylka*, LXXV (II, 1931), 32-33.

[15] See pp. 89, 120.

[16] Date of birth not known; died in the Left SR rising in Moscow, July, 1918. Alexandróvich was one of the founders of the Left SR party.

[17] Sviatitski, "Voina i predfevral'e," *Katorga i Ssylka*, LXXV (II, 1931), 39-46.

may have existed, or to evaluate the respective efforts of Social
Democrats and Socialist Revolutionaries. The "defensist" element,
of course, had nothing in particular to say to the garrison; as for the
left SR's, we know from police reports[18] that they were claiming
marked success for their propaganda in the army, especially among
mobilized workers and presumably for the most part within the
garrison, yet Shliapnikov asserts that he had heard nothing about
SR activity in the barracks nor had any overtures been addressed to
the Bolsheviks for coordination of efforts (his testimony is the more
plausible in that he admits that the Bolsheviks themselves were
entrenched only in the navy).[19]

In general it may be said that neither in the capital nor elsewhere,
even as late as the second month of 1917, were the Socialist Revolutionaries encouraging popular demonstrations, since they regarded
these as futile in time of war; they had not advanced beyond the stage
of propagandist activity to the stage of concrete plans for insurrection when the workers and the soldiers took matters into their
own hands and set in motion the process which ended in the overthrow of the monarchy. In the words of Chernov, "neither the
Bolsheviks nor the Mensheviks nor the 'workers' group' nor the
Socialist Revolutionaries, whether severally or all together, drew
the Petrograd workingmen into the streets, but Someone more
mighty than they: Tsar Hunger."[20]

While the distinction of having initiated the February Revolution
will remain forever beyond the reach of partisan claims, it is otherwise with regard to the indirect responsibility for this fateful development, which made it certain that, for better or for worse, a new
Europe would emerge from the war. The SR spokesman can urge
with a show of justice that the revolution was the legitimate fruit of
that long campaign in which his party played so prominent and
so indispensable a role.[21] The speed with which hunger riots turned

---

[18] "Politicheskoe polozhenie Rossii nakanune fevral'skoi revoliutsii," *Krasnyi
Arkhiv*, XVII (IV, 1926), 7-8; Chernov, *Rozhdenie revoliutsionnoi Rossii*, pp.
213-15.
[19] *Semnadtsatyi god*, I, 131-32; *Kanun semnadtsatogo goda*, Part II, p. 106.
[20] Chernov, *Rozhdenie revoliutsionnoi Rossii*, pp. 213, 215.
[21] Zenzinov, "Smysl sobytii," *Delo Naroda*, No. 1 (March 15, 1917).

into demonstrations against the political order bespeaks the presence of elements in both the civilian and military population which had at some time in the past acquired a political consciousness, although in the majority of cases one not acute enough to admit of a choice between parties. As a concrete example, the young soldier who burst into the soviet to announce the adherence of the Semenovski Regiment to the revolution had obviously passed through some school of subversion.[22] It is not necessary to agree with Trotski that such types for the most part bore the stamp of Bolshevism.[23] The PSR would soon demonstrate that the popularity it had once enjoyed in working-class circles had by no means been dissipated, and as for the garrison, composed so largely of rebellious peasants, there is no doubt that the bulk of conscious revolutionaries leaned in the direction of "agrarian socialism."

It was to the SR's, moreover, and specifically to the remnants of their military organization that the soviet turned for assistance in the task of restoring order among the troops in the city so that the revolution would be in a position to counter a thrust from the old regime. Both the commissioned officers who presided over the hastily constituted military staff of the soviet—the librarian of the General Staff Academy, S. D. Mstislavski (S. D. Maslovski), and the naval lieutenant, V. N. Filippovski—had been members of the defunct SR officers' organization of 1905. Under their direction some obvious precautions were taken, some strategic posts occupied, but the result of much hard labor[24] was merely to reduce chaos to confusion (a feeling of helplessness is apparent in Mstislavski's account of how those who received orders did not obey them and those who acted did so without orders). When, as a result of Rodzianko's intervention, the functions of this staff were transferred to the military commission of the Duma's Provisional Committee, and nominal control of the garrison passed from the soviet to the Duma, these radical officers together with their noncommissioned colleagues simply re-

---

[22] Sukhanov, *Zapiski o revoliutsii*, I, 133-34; see also p. 83.

[23] *The History of the Russian Revolution* (New York, 1932), I, 152. For discussion of this question see pp. 142 ff.

[24] Filippovski is said to have remained uninterruptedly at his post for 72 hours (Stankevich, *Vospominaniia*, p. 85).

tired into the military section of the soviet, whence they continued to work for the consolidation of that body's authority over the armed forces, realizing with sure instinct that herein lay the gage of security in case of a conflict between the Provisional Government and the revolution.[25]

As for the main body of the soviet, the contribution of the SR's in the early days is less marked. All parties played a minor role at the outset. The early period of the Petrograd Soviet was the heyday of independent radicalism, when such men as Steklov and Sukhanov secured election to the Executive Committee by thirty-seven or more votes against a mere twenty or so for partisan candidates like Shliapnikov and Alexandróvich.[26] If partisanship had as yet made little headway among the workers, it had scarcely touched the peasants in uniform, whose representatives were now admitted on very generous terms into the soviet, transforming it into a joint organ of the workers and soldiers, to the very great advantage of its prestige and physical power but to the detriment of its political consciousness. The modest numbers of the original SR delegation did not protect it against disunion, for the cleavage over the war previously noted was duly reflected in the Petrograd Soviet by the presence of two distinct groups, a nucleus of intellectuals led by Zenzinov and a small band of SR workingmen under Alexandróvich. It is significant that while Zenzinov entered the Executive Committee as the representative of the party organization,[27] Alexandróvich secured election from the floor as the choice of the workers themselves.[28] Here already is

[25] Mstislavski, *Piat' dnei*, pp. 17-48, 73-75; Sukhanov, *Zapiski*, I, 88, 102-4, 143-44, 151-53, 191, 251; II, 34; Akhun and Petrov, *Bol'sheviki i armiia*, pp. 28, 196; "Fevral'skaia revoliutsiia v Petrograde" (The February Revolution in Petrograd), *Krasnyi Arkhiv*, XLI-XLII (IV-V, 1930), 62-63. Reports to the staff and its orders are printed here, pp. 63 ff.

[26] Sukhanov, *Zapiski*, I, 134, 148-49, 176-83; Shliapnikov, *Semnadtsatyi god*, I, 146-49, 190-91. The two accounts differ in certain respects. See also *Ocherki po istorii Oktiabr'skoi revoliutsii*, II, 87-88.

[27] N. S. Rusanov was named along with Zenzinov. Later others were accredited as party representatives (N. D. Avksentiev and A. R. Gotz). See list of members in *Petrogradskii Sovet*, pp. 361-62. Kerenski automatically became a member of the Executive Committee through his election as a presiding officer of the soviet at the time of its formation.

[28] Sukhanov, *Zapiski*, I, 124-25; II, 204.

an indication of the maximalism of the Petersburg proletariat which eventually would throw the city organization into the hands of the left-wing extremists.

By the end of March the era of partisanship had begun and the SR delegation swelled in numbers. At the same time its complexion changed. The small and intensely radical workers' group about Alexandróvich was forced into the background as members drawn from the liberal professions gathered about the official party nucleus under Zenzinov and Gotz, and as the soldier mass, succumbing to the lure of the SR agrarian program, moved away from its originally non-partisan position in the same direction. It was to this soldier constituency that the SR's owed their preponderance in the Petrograd Soviet. Shliapnikov tells us that at first the SR's and Mensheviks opposed the admission of soldiers on the ground that the armed forces should not be exposed to the disrupting influence of politics, but adds that they speedily abandoned this position in favor of cultivating the soldiers when they saw the danger of resisting their wishes.[29] Apparently the desire to keep the soldiers in their own soviet where they would not be contaminated by the Social Democratic influence prevalent in working-class circles did not figure in the calculations of the Petrograd SR's, as it did in the case of certain other party organizations. So successful were the SR's in controlling the soldiers' section that they had no interest in rectifying the system which grossly overweighted representation in favor of the military,[30] especially not when it was realized, by the early part of May, that fully a third of the Petersburg proletariat already followed the banner of Bolshevism and that this strength would be augmented rather than diminished in the future as a result of the by-elections even then running in favor of Lenin's party. The soldier element,

[29] *Semnadtsatyi god*, I, 192-94; II, 90.
[30] The basis of representation was one delegate for each thousand workers and one for each company of soldiers. Originally the companies in question had been those of the swollen reserve regiments, as each counted a thousand or more soldiers, but soon every company, regardless of size, was sending one deputy to the soviet. As a result 150,000 troops in the garrison had double the representation of 450,000 workers in the city. See *Ocherki po istorii Oktiabr'-skoi revoliutsii*, II, 116; Shliapnikov, *Semnadtsatyi god*, I, 193-94; Sukhanov, *Zapiski*, II, 226.

radical in matters pertaining to military discipline but otherwise less extremist and seemingly more docile than its proletarian counterpart, appeared to provide the SR leaders with a stable basis for the conduct of soviet policy. How firm this support proved to be in the face of the party's record on crucial issues—principally those of land and peace—we shall presently see.[31]

The SR delegation in the Petrograd Soviet, numerically the most powerful and hence chiefly responsible for the decisions taken in the name of this key institution, consisted of more than 400 members in full standing (i.e., registrants who accepted the party whip), and could count on sympathizers from among those who were not inscribed on the rolls of any party to bring its voting strength on important issues to well over a thousand. This appears to have been enough to override the whole Social Democratic vote on the rare occasions when the dominant SR–Menshevik bloc went to pieces (as it did on the agrarian question and the reelection of the Executive Committee), and the old alignment of Marxist versus Populist reappeared for the moment in place of the more recent and meaningful alignment of moderate versus extremist. There was no division of strength in the Populist camp, for the small Trudovik–Popular-Socialist delegation soon melted away as the PSR came to monopolize the allegiance of those who were attracted to the Narodnik ideology. The touchstone of success was, of course, the agrarian program, equally appealing to the peasants in uniform as to those in the villages. It was claimed on behalf of the SR delegation that it had much to do with bringing order out of the initial chaos which prevailed in the soviet: it was the first to adopt the practice of thrashing out matters in caucus and of making the decisions there arrived at binding upon the membership so that dissent could not be voiced in the plenum. When other delegations followed the SR example, the stimulus for endless speechmaking on the floor of the plenum was removed and the transaction of business greatly facilitated. As to its political line, the SR delegation adhered consistently to a middle-of-the-road position, avoiding the pitfalls of extremism and, through friendly tolerance of dissenting opinion, managing to

[31] Sukhanov, *Zapiski*, I, 182; II, 227, 260-61, 289, 377; III, 362-63.

preserve its unity even after other party agencies had been rent by schism.[32]

The SR delegation owed its prominence in the soviet solely to numbers, for its leadership can at best be described as mediocre. In a party which could never boast of adequate talent, all but one of the eminent figures subordinated work in the soviet to other activities. Kerenski found the atmosphere of the cabinet more to the taste of a radical lawyer than the orthodox socialist deliberations of the soviet, where men such as Steklov—whom he heartily detested—held forth. Yet even after control passed into more friendly hands, he continued to hold aloof, whether because of the pressure of ministerial duties or because of inward repulsion, it is not possible to say.[33] Chernov arrived late on the scene but could have played an important role in the soviet, following his elevation to the Executive Committee, had he not preferred to turn to literary activity before being swallowed up in the Ministry of Agriculture. Avksentiev likewise became a member of the Executive Committee, but his attention was soon diverted to the affairs of the All-Russian Peasants' Soviet. Of the two original leaders, Zenzinov became engrossed in party organizational matters and in the management of the *Delo Naroda*, and Alexandróvich shared the momentary eclipse of the left wing, his determination to have nothing to do with the "defensists" causing him to bolt the SR caucus and sit as a guest with the Bolsheviks.[34]

The field was left to A. R. Gotz and his two lieutenants, Boldyrev and Livshits, who were hopelessly outclassed in point of intellect, personality, forensic ability, and scent for maneuver by that galaxy of Menshevik leaders in which Tsereteli, Dan, and Chkheidze were the brightest luminaries. These men were the real dictators of soviet policy, first in the Petrograd and later in the All-Russian Soviet of Workers' and Soldiers' Deputies. The "group of the presidium," as

---

[32] N. Livshits, "Fraktsiia S.-Rov petrogradskago Soveta Rabochikh i Sold. Deputatov" (The SR Delegation in the Petrograd Soviet of Workers' and Soldiers' Deputies), *Partiinyia Izvestiia*, No. 5 (January 20, 1918), pp. 27-31.

[33] Sukhanov, *Zapiski*, II, 285-87; Stankevich, *Vospominaniia*, pp. 95-96; V. D. Nabokov, "Vremennoe Pravitel'stvo," in *Arkhiv Russkoi Revoliutsii*, I, 35, 66.

[34] Sukhanov, *Zapiski*, II, 270; III, 407-8.

they were modestly called, having no wide popular following immediately behind them and forced to grapple with the lively internationalist wing of their own party under Martov,[35] found a convenient pedestal for their policies in the form of the large, amorphous mass of SR deputies, whose own leaders seemed content to leave the direction of affairs to others and themselves to stand aside as though sizing up the situation.[36] Sukhanov contends that the weakness in leadership of the PSR compelled it, if not to invite, then at least to acquiesce in the rule of the Varangians who came to it in the guise of Menshevism, and adds that history long ago showed the result of such an experiment.[37]

The mainsprings of the SR–Menshevik coalition in 1917 will presently be examined in some detail; at this point it need only be said that too much should not be made of the ostensible power of the Menshevik leaders to impose their will upon the SR's, for the plain facts of the matter are, first, that many of the differences between the two parties had disappeared by this time or at least had been relegated to the background; and, second, that figures like Tsereteli, having more forceful personalities and disposing of greater oratorical talent, naturally came to voice opinions on the issues of the day which were held in common by the leadership of both parties. Yet it cannot be denied that the Socialist Revolutionaries never wielded in soviet councils the influence which their numerical strength would have warranted, and this was as true of the All-Russian Soviet organization, after its formation, as of the most important local soviet in the country. Only in the peasants' soviets were the SR's masters of the situation.

From an examination of the relationship of the party to the soviet we now turn to the party organization itself and to the issues which confronted it in the early months of the revolution.

[35] See *ibid.*, III, 359-61.
[36] Stankevich, *Vospominaniia*, p. 84.
[37] *Zapiski*, III, 240.

The men and women who would occupy positions of influence and responsibility were widely dispersed at the outbreak of the revolution. Some enjoyed legal status in various urban centers of European Russia: thus M. Ia. Gendelman, D. S. Rosenblum, and M. V. Vishniak were living in Moscow, and N. I. Rakitnikov, in Saratov. Some were in Siberian exile: Abram Gotz, Maria Spiridonova, M. A. Vedeniapin, and the "grandmother of the revolution," E. Breshko-Breshkovskaia. The main contingent, as we have seen, was abroad, in Switzerland or in France, Geneva being the headquarters of the antiwar faction and Paris, of the "defensists."

Russian socialists who favored the war had no trouble in returning home[38] but in the case of the internationalists the way back was strewn with obstacles, for the conventions between the Allied and tsarist police, under which the whole of the Geneva group had been set down as suspect of working in the enemy cause, remained in effect, and the English authorities seemed determined to use their control of communications to shut out elements unsympathetic to the prosecution of the war. On the proscribed list were Boris D. Kamkov (Katz), M. A. Natanson, and Chernov himself. In the name of the party Zenzinov called the attention of the foreign minister to the unsatisfactory state of affairs and demanded the immediate admission of all émigrés who were being detained.[39] After being turned back in England on his first attempt, Chernov managed to attach himself to a party including such well-known "defensists" as A. A. Argunov, N. D. Avksentiev, I. I. Bunakov (Fondaminski), and B. V. Savinkov, and so concealed behind a "thick front of chauvinism," to reach Petrograd on April 8. Kamkov was held up by the English authorities despite the amnesty proclaimed by the Provisional Government.[40]

When the exiles remaining in Switzerland learned of the difficulties that would be encountered, they arranged an interparty conference at which Natanson spoke for the SR's and Martov for the SD's. The

[38] See Argunov's manuscript, Pravoe i levoe, pp. 36 ff.
[39] "Chto eto znachit?" (What Does This Mean?), Delo Naroda, No. 15 (April 1, 1917).
[40] See his letter in Delo Naroda, No. 15 (April 1, 1917); Argunov, Pravoe i levoe, pp. 39-40; Sukhanov, Zapiski, III, 145-48.

idea of returning through Germany in exchange for an equal number of German nationals interned in Russia was broached by Martov, and after a fortnight of waiting to see what Petrograd would do, part of the group availed themselves of the graciousness of the German authorities, while the remainder chose to wait a while longer.[41] Eventually all found their way back to Russia. Natanson's journey across Germany in the "sealed train" caused him to share the odium which descended upon Lenin and so embittered relations with the right wing of his party that its unity ceased to be a matter of concern for him, and in the end he turned against even the most sacred of SR symbols, the Constituent Assembly. The internationalists arrived on the scene exasperated at the humiliating experience they had undergone and more than ever convinced that neither side in the bloody conflict had any claim on the socialist conscience.

While the émigrés were making their way home as best they could, the first steps toward party organization had been taken and the first internal crisis surmounted—for the time being. As we have seen, the revolution found the SR's of the capital already divided into two factions. The question whether the extremists or moderates would control the city organization came to a head on March 1, when a manifesto appeared over the signature of the "Petersburg Committee of Socialist Revolutionaries," calling on the soldiers to take matters into their own hands and force an immediate showdown with the Duma over the questions of land and peace. Still more alarming was the attack upon military discipline, the soldiers being warned, with respect to officers who professed loyalty to the revolution only in order to reimpose their authority, that "the fox's tail is more fearful than the wolf's fang."[42] The manifesto threatened to unhinge the new order at its weakest point by rendering futile all efforts to bridle the garrison and establish an equilibrium between the rival centers of authority, the soviet and the Duma committee. The Provisional Government then being formed could not exist in the face of such tactics. No wonder that Kerenski was beside himself at the news and that moderate SR's in general were taken aback

---

[41] Shliapnikov, *Semnadtsatyi god*, III, 376.
[42] Text in *ibid.*, I, Appendix 24, 261-62.

at what had been done in the party name, for the manifesto was the handiwork of Alexandróvich, acting in conjunction with like-minded Bolshevik elements.[43]

Had this violent revolutionary spoken for the party or had he usurped its authority? That was the question which faced the first Petrograd city conference as it convened on March 2. The decision went against Alexandróvich: the conference "strongly condemned the proclamation as most unfortunate in content, as being calculated to inspire mistrust and discord among the popular masses, and as having been issued without the knowledge of duly constituted party authorities."[44] At the same time Alexandróvich received a stern reprimand, though this was not made public.[45] In general it can be said that for the time being the all-city conference wanted the revolution stopped where it was, and this disposition was confirmed two days later when the first Petrograd regional conference adopted resolutions of a similar nature. Both these party assemblies voiced support of the Provisional Government in the conviction that it would carry out its program of consolidating the political conquests of the revolution, and more was not asked for at the moment. Even in the political field, the party claimed for itself merely the right to agitate in favor of a republican form of government preparatory to the Constituent Assembly, making no attempt to foreclose the question of monarchy or to bind the Provisional Government with respect to the economic and diplomatic issues growing out of the revolution.[46]

It is unfortunate that the records do not admit of a reconstruction of these early conferences which overruled the nascent left wing of the party and made so few demands upon the Provisional Government. Very often the circumstances under which party resolutions were formulated are more revealing than the resolutions themselves. Apparently the conferences were convened on the spur of the

[43] *Ibid.*, pp. 153, 190-91, 199-200; Sukhanov, *Zapiski*, I, 292-95; *Ocherki po istorii Oktiabr'skoi revoliutsii*, II, 107-8. The soviet hastened to suppress the manifesto, confiscating the remaining supply in the possession of Molotov.

[44] See report of conference in *Delo Naroda*, No. 1 (March 15, 1917).

[45] Interview with Zenzinov in Paris (September, 1935).

[46] Texts of resolutions in *Delo Naroda*, No. 1 (March 15, 1917). Sukhanov, *Zapiski*, II, 97-98; Miliukov, *Istoriia vtoroi russkoi revoliutsii*, I, Part I, 53, 78.

moment, in *ad hoc* fashion, without observing any fixed rules of representation, for one of the first tasks of the new city committee was "to convoke an all-city conference on a truly representative basis."[47] This strengthens the assumption that the intellectual forces then streaming into the party dominated the proceedings to the exclusion of the cruder proletarian elements, handicapped as these were in respect to mobility and self-expression.[48] The only spokesman for the left whose name has been preserved was Alexandróvich, and he was notably deficient in the qualities of a tribune.[49] It must be remembered that this was the honeymoon stage of the revolution, that men of some prestige in party circles, particularly Zenzinov, lent the weight of their influence to the moderate side, and that the example of Kerenski, who had entered the ministry, worked in the same direction. So it is not surprising that the moderates should have won the first passage at arms and that in the newly chosen city committee such men as Kerenski, Zenzinov, Sviatitski and B. O. Flekkel should have occupied the seats of authority.[50] They would never do so well again. The subsequent enrollment of large numbers of workers and enlisted men, counterbalancing the earlier influx of intellectuals, together with the advent of articulate leadership in the person of Alexandróvich's superior, Boris D. Kamkov, converted the metropolitan and Northern Regional organizations into strongholds of extremism, whence the opponents of compromise conducted their vendetta against the official party line until, in conjunction with

[47] See under heading, "Iz zhizni partii s.-r." (From the Life of the SR Party), *Delo Naroda*, No. 1 (March 15, 1917).

[48] Alexandróvich spoke in this vein to Sukhanov (*Zapiski*, II, 96-97). From his remarks it is to be inferred that the radicals were well represented at the city conference, yet the official report in *Delo Naroda* states that unanimous support of the Provisional Government was voiced. Perhaps the radicals were mute. Sukhanov says that in the soviet they not only could not defend their viewpoint but could not even express it (I, 292).

[49] Although a man of very limited ability, Alexandróvich is a significant figure. He was of the hard-shelled, inflexible type which knows neither hesitation nor mercy, the type which does not play at revolution, but actually makes it, heedless of anything save its own fanaticism—a finished product of the Russian underground. For characterization see Sviatitski, "Voina i predfevral'e," *Katorga i Ssylka*, LXXV (II, 1931), 40-42; Sukhanov, *Zapiski*, I, 124 and *passim*.

[50] Sviatitski, "Voina i predfevral'e," *Katorga i Ssylka*, LXXV (II, 1931), 43. The sole reference to the committee's personnel. The central organ is silent on this point; nothing is added in *Rech'*, No. 56 (March 7, 1917), p. 6, or in *Revoliutsiia 1917 goda (Khronika sobytii)*, I, 55-56, 64.

like-minded provincial organizations, of which note will be taken later, they had amassed enough strength to produce the October schism.

The question of power had been the first to confront the party as it emerged from underground into the light of legal activity. The decision to support the Provisional Government had occasioned little difficulty, for the left wing existed as yet only in embryonic form, and all the rest of the party was a unit in desiring to avoid the burdens of authority. Why this flight from responsibility? Whence this self-effacement?

One reason for refusing to make a bid for power was the shadowy existence the party had been leading since 1907, suggesting to all who had its interests at heart that instead of disputing the position of bourgeois parties with the advantage of twelve years of legal status behind them, the SR's should first concentrate on achieving a comparable state of organization so that the party would be able to mobilize its following and assimilate the flood of new members in accordance with its principles and traditions. Another reason was the fear of counterrevolution, then very lively and, indeed, never absent from the minds of party members, even after the definitive triumph of the February Revolution. Socialist Revolutionaries simply could not understand how an order which had withstood so many assaults in the past could have crumbled so completely, and went on peering into the shadows for the lurking monster of counterrevolution, never realizing the change wrought in the folk psychology as a result of the war or the ease with which elements mobilized under the banner of reaction in 1905 and directed against Jews and revolutionists could be brought over to the red flag in 1917 and directed against squires and army officers. The best means of averting the danger seemed to lie in permitting the liberals to take over the government lest the specter of socialism drive them into a common front with the reactionaries for the preservation of property rights; this policy of forbearance was all the more natural in that the liberals were then regarded as comrades in arms, for it was not realized, in the first flush of victory over tsarism, how little stomach the members of the Progressive Bloc had had for any but a palace revolution. Finally, it should be pointed out that many SR's were determined to do nothing that would rock the boat in time of war, and for that reason above all others, were disposed to follow a course which promised a minimum of friction in the political life of the country.[51]

These considerations found expression in resolutions adopted at SR meetings in various parts of the country, in the great cities, in Kiev, Minsk, Nizhni Novgorod, Kazan, Tomsk, and elsewhere.[52] There was no visible dissent from the proposition that the Provisional Government should continue in office until the Constituent Assembly, subject to the fulfillment of a program of political reform which would leave the revolutionary parties absolute freedom in respect to organization and propaganda. The qualifications and reservations which accompanied the pledge of support indicated, however, that the party meant to keep the government on short leash and that relations between the two would never be free of friction. The resolutions bristle with phrases like "constant control over," "organized pressure upon," "in so far as," "as long as," and so on. Socialist Revolutionaries might deny the existence of a "dual power" (dvoevlastie),[53] but no amount of quibbling could conceal the fact that, whatever the formal aspect of the situation might be, the SR conception of a government functioning under the constant supervision and prodding of another agency, and subject to overthrow whenever the revolutionary democracy might feel it was defaulting on its obligations, certainly entailed a dispersion of authority and stressed a divided loyalty. In committing the party to simultaneous support of both the soviet and the ministry, the leading editorial in the first issue of the central organ had termed the Provisional Government the product of a contract or understanding between the Executive Committee of the Duma and the Petrograd Soviet, imply-

[51] General analyses in Chernov, *Rozhdenie revoliutsionnoi Rossii*, pp. 242-49; *Ocherki po istorii Oktiabr'skoi revoliutsii*, II, 99-110.
[52] *Delo Naroda*, Nos. 1, 3-6 (March 15, 17-19, 21, 1917).
[53] "Vremennoe Pravitel'stvo i Sovet Rabochikh i Soldatskikh Deputatov" (The Provisional Government and the Soviet of Workers' and Soldiers' Deputies), *ibid.*, No. 14 (March 31, 1917); see also speech of N. P. Pumpianski, in *Vserossiiskoe Soveshchanie Sovetov*, p. 153.

ing that if the experiment did not succeed, the power must be handed back to its dual source.[54] Before long Chernov would say this in so many words.[55]

As though to demonstrate that acceptance of a nonsocialist interim regime did not involve an abandonment of revolutionary principle, the Socialist Revolutionaries at first rejected the idea of a coalitional ministry. While the opposite point of view found some expression,[56] reflecting an early trend toward coalition in right-wing circles, majority opinion seemed determined to avoid a course which in the West had been synonymous with emasculation of the socialist position. In the words of a party spokesman (Pumpianski of Chita):

To accept a coalitional ministry at this time means to lower the crest of the revolutionary wave on which you are borne aloft; it means that the Constituent Assembly will not be convened in a revolutionary atmosphere such as now exists and such as is extremely important for the democracy to have. A coalitional ministry involves the pacification, the softening and lowering of the revolutionary spirit, and that is something that we must guard against.[57]

Another spokesman (Gendelman of Moscow) warned the revolutionary democracy against being maneuvered into a position where it would be lending the weight of its authority to measures of a bourgeois character.[58] Yet within a month and a half that is exactly what had happened, and this same Gendelman had become a steadfast defender of the principle of collaboration with the Russian liberals. But that is running ahead of the story; for about two months after the February Revolution, majority sentiment in the PSR definitely opposed the idea of participation in the Provisional Government.[59]

[54] "Velikii perevorot i partiia" (The Great Overturn and the Party), *Delo Naroda*, No. 1 (March 15, 1917).
[55] See below, p. 161.
[56] See especially speeches of D. M. Titov and P. P. Usov on April 1 in *Vserossiiskoe Soveshchanie Sovetov*, pp. 164-65, 168-69.
[57] *Ibid.*, pp. 152-53; Shliapnikov, *Semnadtsatyi god*, III, 240-41.
[58] *Vserossiiskoe Soveshchanie Sovetov*, p. 158.
[59] See also speech of N. S. Rusanov at the Second Petrograd City Conference (April 4) in *Delo Naroda*, No. 17 (April 6, 1917); speech of Zenzinov at the Fourth Party Congress (December, 1917) in *Kratkii otchët o rabotakh chetvërtago s"ezda P.S.-R.*, p. 68.

How, then, to explain the presence of A. F. Kerenski in the first cabinet as minister of justice? The answer is that Kerenski had entered the government without the formal consent of either the party or the soviet, and that this precipitous action on the part of one of their nominal leaders did not sit well with large numbers of Socialist Revolutionaries who were going to have reason enough to be displeased with Kerenski in any event. It is true that the first Petrograd city and regional conferences of March 2 and 4 gave Kerenski a mandate in everything except name when they issued a blanket indorsement of his course of action during the February Days and specifically approved his entrance into the ministry as champion of the people's rights and as the medium through which popular control over the administration could be realized,[60] but this action taken by assemblies uniquely conservative in their make-up was later contravened by the Second Petrograd City Conference (April 3-5),[61] which held it to be inadmissible for party representatives to sit in a bourgeois ministry. This decision, embodied in a formal resolution,[62] underscored the rather pointed statement of Rusanov that Kerenski had discharged his duties in commendable fashion without being an "official representative of the PSR."[63] Rakitnikov's assertion at the Third Congress that Kerenski had joined the ministry "on his own initiative"[64] is borne out by Kerenski's own account of how he had suffered no partisan scruples to influence

---

[60] *Delo Naroda*, No. 1 (March 15, 1917).

[61] As a regularly constituted convention with 152 voting delegates in attendance, this conference was undoubtedly more authoritative than the hastily assembled ones of the preceding month. Scheme of representation in *ibid.*, No. 13 (March 30, 1917).

[62] Printed in *ibid.*, No. 18 (April 7, 1917).

[63] See his report on the Provisional Government in *ibid.*, No. 17 (April 6, 1917). As though to take the edge off its action, the conference sent Kerenski a telegram acclaiming him as a comrade and praising his services to the revolution. See *Revoliutsiia 1917 goda (Khronika sobytii)*, I (2d ed.), 171. SR's often did things like this. When the Menshevik organ, *Den'*, noted the discrepancy between resolution and telegram, the *Delo Naroda* explained that the resolution had merely pronounced against having an official representative in the cabinet, and that it was entirely permissible for a party member to join the cabinet as an individual. See under column "Pechat' i zhizn'" (The Press and Life), No. 20 (April 9, 1917).

[64] *Tretii s"ezd P.S.-R.*, p. 4.

his decisions: "I could plainly see," he writes, "the absurdity of the attitude of the revolutionary democracy. . . . During those critical days in the destiny of Russia, considerations of dogma or of party simply did not exist for me. It seemed to me that in any case no party program was any longer applicable."[65]

Kerenski, moreover, had taken out a very effective form of insurance against the possibility of a conflict with the party on whose rolls his name was now formally inscribed. After indicating to the Duma committee his willingness to assume the portfolio of justice but before announcing his decision in public, he had taken Zenzinov into his confidence and had received the blessing of this influential SR leader, who throughout 1917 would be the mediator between the party and the minister, reconciling their differences and holding them together in much the same way that A. R. Gotz would serve as the buffer between the minister and the soviet.[66] To the steadfast support and patient intervention of these two men, intellectually less gifted but organizationally more influential than Chernov, Kerenski owed his good fortune in averting a breakdown in relations with the party until after the Kornilov rebellion.

Even so, the tension arising from Kerenski's action and the party's aversion to coalition was not finally allayed until the last days of the first Provisional Government, when Kerenski published a letter which Chernov had written for him, stating that his acceptance of a cabinet post on his own initiative as well as the exclusion of the revolutionary democracy from a share in forming the government had been due to its then-existing state of disorganization; now that the socialist parties had reversed their stand on coalition and contemplated sending their representatives into the ministry on a basis of accountability for the work there performed, he promised for the future to accept only such a commission.[67] This satisfied the SR

---

[65] *Crucifixion of Liberty*, p. 291.
[66] Interview with Zenzinov in Paris (September, 1935). Sukhanov notes that already by March 2 Zenzinov had become Kerenski's faithful arms-bearer and his active helpmate behind the scenes (*Zapiski*, I, 307). It is because of such information that Sukhanov's memoirs are indispensable to a study of the revolution.
[67] Chernov, *Rozhdenie revoliutsionnoi Rossii*, p. 372; Chernov, manuscript of chapter, Partiia S.-R.; Sukhanov, *Zapiski*, II, 98.

leaders and tided the situation over until the Third Congress could vote Kerenski a mandate in the name of the whole party.

It was not only the forwardness of Kerenski in the matter of collaboration with the nonsocialist camp but some of his official actions as well which occasioned a measure of dissatisfaction in party circles. Many SR's looked upon Kerenski as a lever with which to pry concessions from the Provisional Government, not realizing at first that the process could be reversed and that, through Kerenski, his ministerial colleagues might press upon the democracy to moderate or even forego its demands.[68] Indeed, this was the more probable outcome because of Kerenski's belief in the superiority of a minister's prerogatives over the dictates of the soviet, and because of his strained relations with that organ. Although a vice chairman of the Petrograd Soviet, Kerenski had left its leaders in the dark concerning the negotiations over the fate of the monarchy, saying nothing about the dispatch of the Guchkov-Shulgin mission to arrange for a regency.[69] His subsequent solicitude for the monarch and his family aroused some adverse comment in extremist quarters.[70] Yet Kerenski had been largely responsible for the decision which made inevitable the triumph of the republican cause, in this respect going beyond the stand of his own party, which had not sought to determine the nature of the interim regime leading up to the Constituent Assembly.[71] Seconded by Rodzianko and aided behind the scenes by Nekrasov, Kerenski had overcome Miliukov's bid for the preservation of the "traditional symbol of power" as a kind of sheet anchor for the new regime by dissuading the Grand

[68] See, for example, Sukhanov, *Zapiski*, III, 225-26.

[69] *Ibid.*, I, 336-37; II, 35, 46-47.

[70] Before the revolution Kerenski had once expressed to V. P. Antonov, a fellow attorney in Saratov and a Bolshevik, his admiration for Mirabeau, whom he considered nobler and wiser than Danton or Robespierre. "If Louis had not been such a fool, if he had listened to Mirabeau, the revolution would have taken an entirely different course." Antonov says he remembered this conversation when Kerenski became so attentive to Nicholas (*Pod stiagom proletarskoi bor'by*, I, 38-39). The statement in question, while thoroughly characteristic of Kerenski, has reference more to his distaste for extremism and bloodshed than to any regard for monarchy. Kerenski was certainly a republican in 1917, and may have been one all along.

[71] See above, p. 140.

Duke Michael Alexandrovich from ascending the throne prior to the manifestation of the will of the Russian people in the Constituent Assembly.[72]

In the light of this yeoman service to the revolution and of the pledge given the soldiers' section of the soviet that he would not quit his post before the democratic republic was assured,[73] Kerenski's concern as minister of justice for the safety of the Imperial family, particularly his sponsorship of the plan to send its members abroad to England,[74] appears to be the outgrowth of a compassionate nature or the treatment of a fallen foe according to the laws of chivalry, certainly not an indication of furtive sympathy for the cause of monarchy. Yet this was an attitude which found no support, either in the soviet or in Kerenski's own party, and after the Executive Committee had quietly despatched the left SR officer, Mstislavski, to Tsarskoe Selo to make sure the august prisoners were safely caged,[75] the government recognized the futility of the project and shelved it. A serious crisis had been averted, and the precarious balance of power realized in the first Provisional Government continued for a while longer before being shattered on the shoals of the war issue.

The war issue was the second great problem which confronted the Socialist Revolutionaries at the outset of their venture in statecraft. It was not their fault that this issue which divided them most

[72] V. V. Shul'gin, *Dni*, pp. 299-300, 303; Miliukov, *Istoriia vtoroi russkoi revoliutsii*, I, Part I, 53-55.

[73] Sukhanov, *Zapiski*, II, 358.

[74] The story is told in Kerenski's *Road to Tragedy*, pp. 109-18.

[75] Mstislavski, *Piat' dnei*, pp. 73-106; Sukhanov, *Zapiski*, II, pp. 131 ff.; *Petrogradskii Sovet*, pp. 29-30, 32-33; B. N. (B. Nikolaevski), "Novoe o proshlom v zarubezhnoi pechati: K istorii 1917 goda: martovskie dni" (New Information about the Past in the Foreign Press: For the History of the Year 1917: The March Days), *Katorga i Ssylka*, XXX (I, 1927), 228. Kerenski's version of the affair (Road to Tragedy, p. 110) is inaccurate. It goes without saying that the soviet leaders did not inform Kerenski; he learned of the action later, and most likely in a distorted form. The Executive Committee and the "hostage of democracy" in the cabinet were playing fast and loose with one another, each in turn withholding vital information from the other.

profoundly should have been the one least capable of solution. The prerevolutionary background of the fateful cleavage between "defensism" and internationalism has been given in the preceding chapter; henceforth only the immediate aspects of the controversy will engage our attention. The bitter dissension in the ranks of the emigration was now transferred in magnified form onto Russian soil and soon the whole party was riven from head to foot. For a brief moment, it is true, a certain tolerance prevailed, a feeling that, after all, the "defensists" and the internationalists were comrades who ought to do all in their power to find a formula which would hold the party together, for whatever illusions the SR's might cherish on other matters, they understood only too well the depth and the danger of the division over the war. Nor were elements of concordance entirely lacking: if, on the one hand, most of the internationalists had no desire for the defeat of Russia,[76] most of the "defensists," on the other hand, accepted the fundamental theses of Zimmerwaldism,[77] if not the tactical deductions therefrom, and both groups denounced as repugnant to the socialist conscience any thought of annexation and indemnities.[78]

If the one side had been less sanguine regarding the prospects of a social upheaval which would divide the Continent along class instead of national lines, and the other had been less convinced of the virtue of Western democracy, something might have come of the effort to find a common language. As it was, these points of divergence could not be overcome. Far from removing them, or even lessening their acuteness, the February Revolution merely projected them onto a larger scale. The upheaval which to the one side prom-

---

[76] See reference in *Delo Naroda*, No. 17 (April 6, 1917) to speech of Bolshakov at the Second Petrograd Conference, in which he asserted that not one of the internationalists wanted Russia beaten. Yet as we have seen, the Natanson group at Geneva skirted the edge of defeatism, to say the least. Apparently the Bolshakov referred to was the left SR workingman who in 1914 was chairman of the St. Petersburg tanners' union. He himself is described as a defeatist; see Sviatitski, "Voina i predfevral'e," *Katorga i Ssylka*, LXXV (II, 1931), 11-12.

[77] Steinberg, *Ot fevralia po oktiabr'*, pp. 13-14. The author was one of the leaders of the left wing.

[78] This point, already developed in chap. IV, is stressed in the editorial, "Vopros o mire i soiuznaia burzhuaziia" (The Problem of Peace and the Allied Bourgeoisie), *Delo Naroda*, No. 36 (April 29, 1917).

ised the solution of all difficulties besetting the new Russia was to the other side a chimera distracting attention from the menace of German imperialism, against which the maintenance of the Russian front and continued association with the Western powers were the only sure means of protection. One observer remarked that the whole controversy centered around the imminence of world revolution.[79] But the differing evaluations of Russia's allies were perhaps of equal importance: while at one end of the SR spectrum the aging Breshkovskaia declared at Samara that it was an honor to be associated with the "upright and enlightened peoples of France and England" in pursuing the war to a victorious conclusion,[80] the extremists at the other end blasted away at the predatory designs of the Allied governments, and even the more moderate Chernov could find only harsh words to characterize the readiness of the Allied democrats to welcome anything at all on the eastern front—even an army of gorillas—provided it promised to abet their selfish purposes.[81]

The revolution had injected some new elements into the controversy, though fewer than might have been expected. Both sides clung to their respective positions, reshaping their arguments or inventing new ones to accord with the altered circumstances. The prowar faction could now urge that in defending the country the revolutionists were defending their own cause as well; it consistently sought to link the fortunes of the Russian Revolution with the outcome of the war, and its theme song became the danger of a Romanov restoration on the points of Hohenzollern bayonets.[82] Just why the two imperial dynasties, partners in the service of world reaction, should have warred upon each other for two and a half years, the "defensists" did not explain. Another argument consistently put forward was that if Russia backed out of the war, defaulting on her international obligations, she would not only be plunged into dangerous

---

[79] A. Gizetti at the Second Petrograd Conference; see report in *ibid.*, No. 17 (April 6, 1917).

[80] See under dispatches in *ibid.*, No. 6 (March 21, 1917).

[81] "Do polnoi pobedy!" (To a Complete Victory!), *ibid.*, No. 27 (April 18, 1917).

[82] See, for example, A. Gukovski's article, "Sotsializm, voina i otechestvo" (Socialism, War, and the Fatherland), *ibid.*, No. 1 (March 15, 1917).

isolation but would be exposed to attack by her former allies, or at least to a general pacification effected at her expense.[83] Just how this could be squared with the virtues of the Western powers or with their zeal for the destruction of Prussian militarism is not immediately apparent. The antiwar faction maintained that the character of the struggle had not been altered by the Russian Revolution; that for Russia to continue the war in association with powers which had not followed her example in renouncing imperialist ambitions meant to force her sons to shed their blood in the interest of foreign squires and capitalists.[84]

The prevailing opinion in party circles may best be described as a cross between moderate "defensism" and moderate internationalism, resting upon three basic ideas: restoration of the International; adherence to the soviet peace formula of no annexations and indemnities with the right of national self-determination assured to all peoples; and, in the meantime, continued defense of the homeland. Resolutions in this vein were passed by local organizations all over the country, in Petrograd, Moscow, Minsk, Tiflis, Baku, and elsewhere,[85] but it is not difficult to detect a change in emphasis on turning from the internationalist-minded capital to the Transcaucasus, where the shadow of the Moslem menace induced a strongly "defensist" mood.[86] In other cases, also, the language used is stronger than in the typical centrist resolution: the Odessa SR conference (March 30) called for a "tenacious struggle against German militarism until it shall have been completely destroyed by the free armies of the Allied democracies";[87] the Tver conference (March 30) branded desertion as a crime;[88] and even in the capital, a district meeting (March 6) advocated "active defense" and denounced as

[83] See, for example, speeches of Lebedev and Sorokin at the Second Petrograd Conference, *ibid.*, No. 17 (April 6, 1917).
[84] See Kamkov's speech in *Vserossiiskoe Soveshchanie Sovetov*, pp. 103-4; Shliapnikov, *Semnadtsatyi god*, III, 227-29.
[85] *Delo Naroda*, Nos. 1, 4, 8, 9, 11, 12, 14 (March 15, 18, 23, 25, 28, 29, 31, 1917).
[86] See especially report from Tiflis in column on party affairs, *ibid.*, No. 15 (April 1, 1917).
[87] *Ibid.*, No. 20 (April 9, 1917).
[88] *Ibid.*, No. 19 (April 8, 1917).

"empty and devoid of content" the slogan, "Down with the War!"[89] Less articulate at first than the "defensists," the extreme internationalists found their tongue when B. D. Kamkov arrived from Geneva and took over the leadership from Alexandróvich; by the time of the All-Russian Soviet Conference (March 29-April 3) they were strong enough to split the SR delegation, forming a minority which made common cause with the Bolsheviks against the dominant SR–Menshevik bloc. The radicals withdrew their resolution directed against the Provisional Government but on the war question they fought to the end, the declaration of the Executive Committee being adopted by a vote of 325 against 57 with 20 abstentions.[90] Here was the first clear indication of a growing community of interest between the left-wing SR's and the Bolsheviks in answer to the tendency of the moderate SR's to bloc with the Mensheviks on all important issues: it was as though the Social Democracy, having lost all semblance of unity itself, was determined that its Narodnik rival should not escape a similar fate.

By April the pot was boiling furiously in the party organization at Petrograd, the largest in the country. At the second city conference (April 3-5)[91] a full-dress debate on the war question was held with all shades of opinion participating. The battle lay between the left and the center, for the out-and-out champions of war, though vocal at the conference, did not possess enough voting strength to make them a serious factor. The moderate position was presented by A. R. Gotz,[92] who urged the party members to follow the path already marked out by the soviet and to embrace the cause of national defense while continuing their efforts to end the war by means of a general settlement based on the renunciation of annexations and indemnities and the recognition of the right of national self-determination. The new position in which the Russian democracy found itself as a result of the revolution had led it to change its

[89] *Ibid.*, No. 1 (March 15, 1917).
[90] *Vserossiiskoe Soveshchanie Sovetov*, pp. 103-4, 106; *Delo Naroda*, No. 14 (March 31, 1917); Steinberg, *Ot fevralia po oktiabr'*, p. 16. It is not possible to divide the negative vote into its component elements.
[91] See above, p. 145, n. 61.
[92] Text of his speech in *Delo Naroda*, No. 16 (April 5, 1917).

tactics in relation to the war but not its conviction that the war was an imperialist struggle in which both coalitions were tarred with the same brush. By placing the real, if not the formal, power in the hands of the socialists, the revolution imposed upon them the double task of acting as the vanguard of international socialism in the quest for peace and as the shield of the revolutionary fatherland against German imperialism; much had already been done in the first direction by advancing the soviet peace formula and by forcing the Provisional Government to break with tsarist foreign policy, and now it behooved the socialists to take a firm stand in favor of national defense by acknowledging that a breakdown at the front would be equivalent to a breakdown of the revolution. Moderate opinion quite obviously meant to hold fast to the Allied connection and expected the German people to make some move toward meeting the Russian democracy halfway.

In a lengthy rebuttal, B. D. Kamkov developed the left-wing thesis that Russia was conducting an imperialist rather than a defensive war as long as she adhered to a coalition the other members of which had not renounced expansionist aims exceeding in scope those of the Central Powers (the first instance of a differentiation in favor of one of the coalitions). The shedding of Russian blood in the interest of French and English capital was intolerable, and the Russian democracy, which so far had fulfilled only a minimum of its international obligations, must press for a world socialist congress, the publication of secret treaties, and a peace conference to which the Provisional Government would summon its allies after having framed a peace program of its own. The task confronting the party was not the elaboration of "defensist" formulas but the kindling of a "world conflagration" in which contemporary bourgeois society would be consumed and the collectivist society of the future would be forged. Boldest and most farsighted of all the internationalists was V. E. Trutovski, who enunciated a kind of Russian isolationism based upon the rejection of Western tutelage, the contraction of ties with the backward countries of the East, and the conclusion of a separate peace with Germany if that power were willing to renounce annexations and indemnities.

From the controversy it is possible to elucidate a few cardinal differences which either were not clearly formulated or else were purposely muffled at the conference. With regard to the front, the left wing favored a standstill that would keep the army in being but would exclude offensive action; the SR's of the center did not believe that the morale of the troops could be sustained under such an arrangement, and favored an "active defense" admitting of occasional thrusts at the enemy on the order of the June offensive, which aroused a storm of indignation on the left and greatly widened the breach between it and the center. With regard to the diplomacy of peace, the left SR's obviously meant to dictate their will to Russia's allies or else go ahead without them, convening first a socialist congress and then abruptly summoning the Western powers to a peace conference on a take-it-or-leave-it basis; whereas the center proposed first an Allied conference to work out a peace program in accordance with the soviet formula, and then a socialist congress to popularize this program in all countries, with the peace conference itself relegated to the more distant future. But what if the Allies would not accept the soviet formula? What if they persevered in their plans for a peace of vengeance, thus rendering futile the whole campaign to convince the German people that only the imperialist pretensions of its own government stood in the way of a just and reasonable settlement? Silence on this aspect of the problem gravely weakened the whole centrist position, as one spokesman for the left duly pointed out; and months later, after the Bolsheviks had overwhelmed the moderates and the party structure lay in ruins, the center still had not broken out of the "magic circle" created by the obduracy of its allies.

The spirited debate at the Second Petrograd Conference, charged with emotion and carrying with it undertones of a schism, first revealed how strongly the tide of extremism was running in the party's largest and most influential organization. The right wing recoiled in shock and dismay before the specter of a separate peace, and the center, fighting to maintain its grip upon party affairs in the capital, had to strain every nerve to avert a disastrous defeat. Notwithstanding Kerenski's intervention on behalf of the Gotz resolution, it was forced into a conciliation commission from which it emerged with a concession to the left in the form of a demand for the publication of secret treaties, and with agreement secured on all other provisions save only the last, which emphasized the duty of conducting a defensive war. On this there could be no agreement, and on the crucial test of strength at the conference the amended resolution prevailed by the narrow margin of 68 votes against 56 with 13 abstentions.[93] The center had gained a Pyrrhic victory, and when Mstislavski announced that the left was not minded to provoke a schism over its discomfiture, he only revealed how narrowly the party had averted in April the fate that came to it in October.[94]

While the party was struggling to discover its physiognomy with respect to the war, its leaders decided that the time had come to force the Provisional Government to accept the antiimperialist program of the revolutionary democracy and so to conduct its diplomacy as to bring the question of peace into the foreground of the world's attention. It was an eventful decision, for it precipitated the downfall of the first Provisional Government and led to the experiment in coalition with all of its manifold consequences, for both the party and the nation. This first grave crisis in the history of the revolution cannot, of course, be attributed solely to the Socialist Revolutionaries—both wings of the Social Democracy worked in the same direction; yet despite the vigorous and fruitful agitation of Lenin's Bolsheviks, to whom Soviet literature assigns virtually all of the credit, and the emergence of the Georgian Menshevik, Irakli Tsereteli, as the most influential socialist leader in government circles, the man who led the concerted assault upon Miliukov's foreign

[93] Votes in which the number of abstentions exceeds the margin of decision are not a rarity in SR annals. This was a party of individualists, and very conscientious individualists, it must be said. On this occasion the abstentions represented either waverers between the left and the center or right-wingers dissatisfied with the centrist resolution, or both.

[94] Proceedings and debates of the conference in *Delo Naroda*, Nos. 16-19, 23-24 (April 5-8, 13-14, 1917). Only the last issue cited contains nothing on the war question.

policy and who more than any other was responsible for the minister's resignation was the SR generalissimo, V. M. Chernov. Newly arrived on the scene, full of elation over the February victory, with his spirit as yet undampened by the factional strife in his party, Chernov then stood at the zenith of his influence and prestige. He resolved to strike while the iron was hot in the interest of his Zimmerwaldian program, hoping to convert the new Russia into a base for the mobilization of that "third force" whose intervention in the death grapple of the rival imperialist "trusts" would result in a peace without victors or vanquished.

The campaign for a more promising foreign policy than Miliukov's prescription of peace through total victory had not awaited Chernov's arrival from abroad. The minister's statement on Russian war aims in his interview with the press on March 23, his stubborn insistence upon the dismemberment of Austria-Hungary and the annexation of the Straits and Galicia, had called forth a stiff rejoinder from V. M. Zenzinov on the front page of the SR organ: although an adherent of the right center and strongly prowar in his sentiments, this authoritative spokesman was a real "defensist," not a chauvinist masquerading as one. He now summoned the Provisional Government to make up its mind whether it was waging a war of revolutionary defense or a war of imperialist aggression, for if the latter were the case, the country must know it and must prepare for civil war.[95] The editors of the *Delo Naroda* had welcomed the ministerial declaration of March 28 as a renunciation of predatory designs, but had based their approval upon the assumption that the pledge to observe Russia's obligations to her allies excluded the observance of annexationist treaties, and that the rejection of a separate peace implied a willingness to enter upon peace negotiations once both sides had given up plans for conquest.[96] For this strained interpretation of clauses that ought to have been taken at face value they had no justification whatever except their eagerness to avoid a rupture with the Provisional Government. The coauthors of the

[95] "Vremennoe Pravitel'stvo i tseli voiny" (The Provisional Government and War Aims), *Delo Naroda*, No. 9 (March 25, 1917).
[96] No. 11 (March 28, 1917).

declaration have both admitted in their memoirs that it was framed for the express purpose of deluding soviet opinion into believing that its wishes were being observed while in reality leaving the government free to engage in conventional European diplomacy.[97] With this display, first of grim vigilance, then of naive optimism, on the part of the SR's, matters had rested until the return of Chernov.

With his arrival the campaign against Miliukov began in earnest.[98] Months later, after the abortive coup of General Kornilov had blown the lid off the cauldron of factionalism, SR's of the extreme right would formally accuse their party comrade of having caused the downfall of the first Provisional Government by his "loud and blatant" campaign against its foreign policy.[99] Chernov used as sounding boards both the Petrograd Soviet and the party press. Entering into the most intimate relationship, after his election to the Executive Committee, with the "group of the presidium" led by Tsereteli, Chernov began to press upon it with all the means at his disposal. Besides his zeal and eloquence he had one other weapon in his armory—the votes of the SR soldiers in the committee. Almost unwillingly Tsereteli and his associates were pushed into action. Chernov first went before the Executive Committee with a report on how the Foreign Ministry was managing to convey one impression as to its aims and methods in Russia and quite another impression abroad, how every effort had been made to convince the foreign public that the revolution had involved no change in external policy or in the prosecution of the war, and how nothing was known abroad concerning the declaration of March 28, so obviously intended for home consumption and for nothing more. He then crossed swords with Miliukov at a joint session of the cabinet and the Soviet contact commission, demonstrating that he could meet the minister on his own ground.[100]

[97] V. D. Nabokov, "Vremennoe Pravitel'stvo," in *Arkhiv Russkoi Revoliutsii,* I, 59-60; Miliukov, *Istoriia vtoroi russkoi revoliutsii,* I, Part I, 86.
[98] V. D. Nabokov, "Vremennoe Pravitel'stvo," in *Arkhiv Russkoi Revoliutsii,* I, 62.
[99] "Nedostoinaia igra" (An Unworthy Game), *Volia Naroda,* No. 110 (September 5, 1917).
[100] Sukhanov, *Zapiski,* III, 201-5; Chernov, *Rozhdenie revoliutsionnoi Rossii,* pp. 360-61.

At the same time a press campaign was launched, no doubt at Chernov's instigation.[101] On April 11 (Chernov returned on the eighth) the Moscow *Zemlia i Volia* called on the Allies to define their war aims, and the *Delo Naroda* summoned the government to communicate to these powers the contents of its recent pronouncement on the war.[102] On April 15 the central organ repeated its demand with the pointed observation that it was the personal policy of Miliukov which stood in the way of compliance, an attempt being made in this fashion to drive a wedge between the Provisional Government and its foreign minister—"that reincarnation of Guizot who will persevere in his doctrinaire stand until history shows him the door."[103] Chernov did not hide behind the anonymity of the editorial board but lashed out at Miliukov in a series of signed articles, drawing upon his formidable polemical skill to send shaft after shaft into the body of the obdurate professor. Quoting from Miliukov's own writings and utterances to show how he was committed body and soul to imperialism, Chernov argued that the foreign minister, whom he sardonically called "Miliukov-Dardanelski," would yield only to force, and asked whether the Russian people had freed itself from the willful impulses of dictators of the Stolypin brand only to fall under the sway of dogmatists in error like Miliukov.[104] The Russian revolutionists also sought the defeat of the Hohenzollerns and the Habsburgs, he declared, not, however, by wading through a sea of blood but by building up against these dynasties an internal front through so clear and unmistakable a renunciation of predatory designs on the part both of Russia and her allies that the veil would be torn from before the eyes of the Teutonic peoples and they would come to see in their own governments the real obstructions to peace.[105]

Besides the person of the foreign minister, another object of attack

[101] He refers to it in his memoirs: *Zapiski*, I, 16.

[102] See under column, "Pechat' i zhizn'," No. 21.

[103] "Kogo zhe, nakonets, podderzhivat'?" (Who, Then, Is to Be Supported?), No. 25.

[104] "Miliukov Zavoevatel'" (Miliukov the Conqueror), *Delo Naroda*, No. 25 (April 15, 1917).

[105] "Do polnoi pobedy!" (On to Total Victory!), *ibid.*, No. 27 (April 18, 1917).

in this offensive against imperialism was the continuity of personnel in the diplomatic service, which had experienced no purge despite the change in regime. In urging that the time had come to clean out the "Augean stables" of Russian diplomacy, an anonymous author wrote that it would be easier to lead a camel through the eye of a needle than to conduct an external policy worthy of the new Russia with tsarist functionaries like Izvolski, Sazonov, Neratov, and Poklevski-Kozel still filling positions of authority.[106] Chernov re-echoed this demand a few days later when he challenged the ministry to make the conduct of foreign affairs a matter of collective concern, replacing the representatives of the former regime by commissars of the Provisional Government.[107]

While this hammer and tongs offensive was being mounted from without, Miliukov was being subjected to pressure from within the cabinet. For the first and about the only time during the revolution, the public was treated to the spectacle of the two most prominent figures of the PSR, Kerenski and Chernov, working together in pursuit of a common objective. Already on April 6 Kerenski had taken sharp issue with Miliukov's stand in an address to the Allied socialist delegation which smacked of Zimmerwaldist ideology.[108] He next tried to force the minister's hand by informing the press that the note bringing to the attention of foreign powers the declaration on war aims of March 28 was then in the stage of preparation, when actually this was not the case.[109] The matter began to take on the aspect of a personal duel between the two ministers, a duel, however, in which Kerenski had as his seconds certain very influential colleagues who could carry with them the majority of this "bourgeois"

[106] "Avgievy koniushni" (The Augean Stables), *ibid.*, No. 25 (April 15, 1917). The article is signed "Svobodny."

[107] See postscript to his article, "Na dve stezi" (On Two Roads), *ibid.*, No. 30 (April 22, 1917).

[108] The present ecstatic mood of the Russian democracy, he assured his listeners, did not arise from any conception of the fatherland in the conventional sense but from a vision of the impending triumph of the brotherhood of nations. See Chernov, *Rozhdenie revoliutsionnoi Rossii*, p. 362; Miliukov, *Istoriia vtoroi russkoi revoliutsii*, I, Part I, 91-92.

[109] Miliukov, *Istoriia vtoroi russkoi revoliutsii*, I, Part I, 92; V. D. Nabokov, "Vremennoe Pravitel'stvo," in *Arkhiv Russkoi Revoliutsii*, I, 63.

cabinet in support of the "lone hostage of [socialistic] democracy." For Kerenski was by no means so isolated in the cabinet as one might conclude from an examination of its political complexion, his socialistic internationalism being powerfully reinforced by the Slavophile idealism of Prince Lvov and the Masonic internationalism of Nekrasov and Tereshchenko.[110] Nekrasov in particular played a major role in the formulation of official policy, the obscurity which has surrounded his name by no means reflecting the weight of his influence in councils of state; and Nekrasov and Kerenski were very close to each other.

Miliukov found the pressure too great and had to give in, but in sending the text of the declaration of March 28 to the Allied capitals on April 18, he added a note couched in language which could not fail to strike fire from the soviet democracy. War to "decisive victory" in "full agreement" with the Western Allies was the theme of this note, and the only reference to peace was the indorsement of "sanctions and guarantees" to be imposed by the victorious democracies in preventing future wars. In the framing of the note all ministers had taken part, and all accepted the final draft, not excluding Kerenski, whose objections had been withdrawn after certain changes had been made and Nekrasov had signified his approval.[111]

The belligerent Petersburg proletariat and the war-hating soldiers of the garrison instinctively realized that Miliukov had no thought of peace short of total victory, that by "sanctions and guarantees" he meant one-sided measures against the Teutonic powers to prevent their resurgence, and that he intended to support the imperialist pretensions of France and Great Britain while holding fast to his own despite the ostensible renunciation of such aims in the text of the declaration. Their reaction was prompt and impressive. The April Days began. The persuasive powers of the SR and Menshevik leaders were strained to the utmost to prevent grave excesses from

[110] Chernov, *Rozhdenie revoliutsionnoi Rossii*, p. 363; Miliukov, *Istoriia vtoroi russkoi revoliutsii*, I, Part I, 85, 92.

[111] Miliukov, *Istoriia vtoroi russkoi revoliutsii*, I, Part I, 92; V. D. Nabokov, "Vremennoe Pravitel'stvo," in *Arkhiv Russkoi Revoliutsii*, I, 63; Sukhanov, *Zapiski*, III, 307-8. An example of Nekrasov's influence. For Kerenski's version see below, p. 163.

arising out of the demonstrations of workers and soldiers and the counterdemonstrations of propertied and white-collar elements in support of the minister. The soviet spokesmen were caught between two fires, for whereas they were less desirous than ever of supplanting the government in the performance of its thankless task,[112] they felt compelled to put up a strong outward front in order to force at once some concession to antiwar sentiment lest their following get out of hand. Pleading for the calmness that comes from a knowledge of strength, Chernov assured the soviet that if the Provisional Government persisted in disregarding the will of the democracy, the authority derived from the soviet and the Duma must be handed back to its source.[113]

On the evening of April 20, when the Provisional Government and the Soviet Executive Committee met together to settle the crisis, the main burden of formulating the soviet demands devolved upon the SR leader. Chernov declared it to be the democracy's conviction that Russia must cease to speak the language of a "poor relation" when dealing with other European powers, that once having disclaimed any intent of territorial seizures, she must bring this to the world's attention in terms of unmistakable clarity. Finally, it must be made evident that Miliukov spoke only for himself, that his views did not reflect the collective will of the cabinet. Tactfully and cautiously, with much outward deference and softness of expression, Chernov developed his idea of transferring Professor Miliukov to some other post, such as the Ministry of Education, where his genius would find unrestricted scope and his opinions would no longer constitute a chronic weakness for the Provisional Government and a constant irritant to the revolutionary conscience.[114]

This devious attack played its part in further weakening Miliukov's position, but the only immediate result of the conference was the

---

[112] Chernov, *Rozhdenie revoliutsionnoi Rossii,* p. 365; Shliapnikov, *Semnadtsatyi god,* III, 108.

[113] Sukhanov, *Zapiski,* III, 274-75. See above, pp. 143-44.

[114] *Rozhdenie revoliutsionnoi Rossii,* pp. 365-66; *Delo Naroda,* No. 30 (April 22, 1917); Miliukov, *Istoriia vtoroi russkoi revoliutsii,* I, Part I, 103; V. D. Nabokov, "Vremennoe Pravitel'stvo," in *Arkhiv Russkoi Revoliutsii,* I, 62-63; Shliapnikov, *Semnadtsatyi god,* III, 106; Sukhanov, *Zapiski,* III, 286.

issuance by the cabinet of a statement interpreting in an innocuous manner the more controversial passages of the note of April 18: thus "sanctions and guarantees" were defined as limitation of armaments, international tribunals, and so forth. This concession pacified the soviet majority. Chernov had already published a denunciation of the note as blocking the road to peace, as dodging the issue of notifying other signatories of the partial revision of rapacious treaties through annulment of the sections involving Russia, and, above all, as misrepresenting the will of the Russian people; he now greeted the ministry's "explanation" but warned that the toiling democracy would watch vigilantly over the translation of words into deeds, for "each partial success it achieves does not entail a lapse into passivity but rather serves as a point of departure for a fresh application of its pulsating energy."[115]

These words, more ominous, perhaps, than their author realized, were indicative of how rapidly the crisis over the war question was passing into the succeeding stage of a crisis over power. The collision between General Kornilov and the soviet over control of the garrison, the ludicrous situation arising from the government's exercise of authority without power and the soviet's exercise of power without authority, could no longer be tolerated.[116] The quaking of the ground beneath the existing ministry grew stronger and stronger as the revolutionary press chanted in unison, "Miliukov must go!"[117] and as the butt of the offensive shifted from the minister himself to the party he represented.[118]

But Miliukov was not the only minister in difficulty. Kerenski's acquiescence in the note of April 18 placed him in an embarrassing position and threatened to cost him some of his popularity. A Bolshevik trade-union leader charges that Kerenski lay low while the

[115] "Na dve stezi," *Delo Naroda*, No. 30 (April 22, 1917), and postscript to same.
[116] Chernov, *Rozhdenie revoliutsionnoi Rossii*, pp. 368-69.
[117] See Mstislavski's article, "A vsë zhe . . ." (Nevertheless . . .), *Delo Naroda*, No. 30 (April 22, 1917), and editorial, "Argumentum ad hominem," *ibid.*, No. 31 (April 23, 1917).
[118] For attacks upon the Constitutional Democratic party, see Chernov, "Istoriia, Isteriia i Misteriia" (History, Hysteria, and Mystery), *ibid.*, No. 32 (April 25, 1917), and editorials in same number and in No. 30 (April 22, 1917).

storm raged, avoiding the state conference on the twentieth, while his party spread the rumor that he had taken no part in preparing the note or even that he had opposed it.[119] According to Miliukov, Kerenski himself tried to deny responsibility, but all attempts to escape an awkward situation were spiked when it was announced that the final draft had been approved unanimously. This enforced solidarity with Miliukov irked Kerenski still more and sharpened his antagonism for the Kadet statesman. He now demanded that the conduct of foreign policy be withdrawn from the exclusive competence of Miliukov and placed in commission, thus giving tangible form to one of the proposals advanced by Chernov. There is no certainty as to what transpired behind the scenes in connection with the note of April 18,[120] for the accounts of Miliukov[121] and Nabokov[122] vary widely in certain respects from the report[123] which Kerenski presented to the Bureau of the Executive Committee on April 24. On the basis of this report, Kerenski offered much sterner resistance to the original draft than Miliukov and Nabokov are willing to concede; in fact, by threatening to resign, he had vetoed this draft with its assertion that only through victory could peace be approached, and his assent to the final draft had been procured by concessions in substance which outweighed certain remaining defects in wording. Though not entirely satisfied with the note as issued, Kerenski had deemed it compatible with the declaration of March 28 and confessed that the reaction of the soviet had come as a complete surprise. On this occasion, of course, Kerenski felt obliged to square himself with the soviet, and it may be that Miliukov and Nabokov have left a more accurate account of the cabinet proceedings.

In his speech before the soviet organ, Kerenski openly championed the principle of a coalitional government, with representatives of the revolutionary democracy assuming formal responsibility for the conduct of official policy. Two days later, on April 26,

[119] Shliapnikov, *Semnadtsatyi god*, III, 105.
[120] See also above, p. 160.
[121] *Istoriia vtoroi russkoi revoliutsii*, I, Part I, 92, 95-96.
[122] "Vremennoe Pravitel'stvo," in *Arkhiv Russkoi Revoliutsii*, I, 63-64.
[123] *Petrogradskii Sovet: Protokoly zasedanii*, pp. 216-18.

he sent to party headquarters, to the soviet, and to other agencies the open letter previously alluded to,[124] in which he conditioned his further participation in the government upon receipt of a definite mandate from party and soviet.[125] This step brought to a head the question of reorganizing the Provisional Government on a broader basis. The radical liberal clique[126] in the cabinet, consisting of Premier Lvov and Ministers Nekrasov and Tereshchenko, which for some time had been working hand in glove with Kerenski, had already determined upon a coalition with the soviet parties as the best way out of the impasse.[127] It remained to be seen whether the original aversion to coalition on the part of the Socialist Revolutionary as well as the Menshevik party could be overcome.

Actually, the April crisis had caused a shift in SR sentiment away from the traditional principle of no collaboration with the class enemy in the direction of a venture in statecraft in association with the Constitutional Democrats. The situation will be clearer if it is borne in mind that the left wing of the PSR always opposed coalition with bourgeois elements while the right wing always favored such coalition. The center, therefore, decided the issue, at first in the negative and then, after the April Days, in the affirmative. The crisis convinced the middle-of-the-road SR's that the attempt to graft a socialist program onto a nonsocialist ministry had failed, and that if they expected to realize their cherished ambitions, they must assume a part of the burden of governing. With the authority of the Provisional Government hopelessly undermined, and with

[124] See above, pp. 146-47; see also next chapter, p. 230.

[125] *Catastrophe*, p. 138 (for background, see pp. 133 ff.); Miliukov, *Istoriia vtoroi russkoi revoliutsii*, I, Part I, 105-7; *Revoliutsiia 1917 goda (Khronika sobytii)*, II, 75.

[126] It could usually count on a majority with the support of Konovalov, Godnev, and V. N. Lvov—men supposedly standing to the right of the Kadets. It was these who formed the solid core of opposition. See, for example, Kerenski, *Catastrophe*, p. 134, note; Miliukov, *Istoriia vtoroi russkoi revoliutsii*, I, Part I, 102-3.

[127] Miliukov, *Istoriia vtoroi russkoi revoliutsii*, I, Part I, 102 ff.; V. D. Nabokov, "Vremennoe Pravitel'stvo," in *Arkhiv Russkoi Revoliutsii*, I, 64n.

class antagonisms dangerously accentuated, both considerations of national defense and fears of counterrevolution induced a willingness to combine with the liberal bourgeoisie in order to isolate the elements of reaction and force them to bow to the popular will without the necessity of fighting a civil war that would wreck the national cause.[128]

Something deeper and more fundamental than the circumstances of the hour, however, impelled the Socialist Revolutionary party to move toward acceptance of coalition. For important segments of party opinion entrance into a coalitional ministry was not a means but an end, not a steppingstone toward the attainment of social revolutionary objectives but a realization of the "union of all vital forces" to bolster the war effort and consolidate the political revolution which already had taken place. Though the Third Party Congress would shortly reaffirm the traditional SR view[129] on the revolution as ushering in a regime of toil based on socialization of the land, and hence as distinct from both the Menshevik and the Bolshevik concepts, the truth was that the influential right wing no longer believed in social revolution and so could accept collaboration with the bourgeoisie as a long-term commitment rather than as a short-term expedient.

Evidence of this attitude can be adduced, though it was more a frame of mind than a clearly formulated theory. Early in the revolution, at an SR conference in Moscow attended by Breshkovskaia— the nature of the conference is not revealed but it must have been strictly a right-wing affair—the participants agreed that the purpose of the revolution was not to produce an overturn in economic relations for the benefit of the proletariat or even the toiling peasantry (!) but merely to establish a democratic republic which would then become the arena for the developing social struggle.[130] The implication is that socialization of the land would be indefinitely postponed, which was rank heresy from the traditional point

---

[128] Such was the defense of their course offered years later by a number of SR leaders, including A. R. Gotz, who were on trial for their lives before a Soviet tribunal. See *Dvenadtsat' smertnikov*, pp. 108-9.

[129] See p. 210.

[130] See report in *Delo Naroda*, No. 7 (March 22, 1917).

of view. With respect to individual opinions we have seen how Bunakov-Fondaminski already in 1915 had defined the character of the coming revolution in terms of his own prejudices,[131] and when it came, he refused to revise his interpretation even though it stood at an astronomical distance from reality. Avksentiev, likewise, persisted in construing the February overturn in a narrow sense, ascribing to it a purely patriotic and political motivation. In Kerenski's opinion, it was "precisely the wish to prevent defeat that gave birth to the revolution"—[132] a point of view representing no sober analysis of reality, but rather the substance of what an unenthusiastic Duma hoped to snatch from a movement which had not been of its making and which it regarded with grave misgivings. The baldest statement of all reflecting the altered conception was made at the Third Congress by Kovarski, who flatly declared the revolution to be bourgeois in character.[133]

The right wing of the party, recruited from the "liquidationist" or *Pochin* group abroad and from officials of the cooperatives and other public-service institutions at home, had in effect embraced the Menshevik theory of revolution, finding in the "defensist" credo with its emphasis on class collaboration the surrogate for their burnt-out faith in social revolution. Close association with the Marxist "defensists" abroad and in the war industrial committees at home had no doubt helped the spread of Menshevik influence, against which SR ideology had always offered a weaker defense than the SR spirit. With the decay of that spirit increasing numbers of Socialist Revolutionaries began to succumb to the intellectual brilliance and aggressive leadership which distinguished the Menshevik party.

It was the misfortune of Social Revolutionism that this alien influence, so enervating in its effect upon revolutionary enterprise, could not be restricted to the right wing of the party but pervaded the core as well. The SR's of the center differed from their rightist brethren in that they still believed in a social revolution, and if they,

[131] See p. 101.
[132] *Crucifixion of Liberty*, pp. 265-66.
[133] *Tretii s"ezd P.S.-R.*, pp. 81-82.

too, agreed to a coalition with the archbourgeois Constitutional Democratic party, it was not because they accepted the Menshevik theory of bourgeois hegemony in the revolution but because they saw no other means of coping with the adverse circumstances of the moment. Yet they also deferred to the Mensheviks, especially in tactical matters, and here the factor of personal association would seem to have played a decisive role.

The flood of literature on the Russian Revolution has shed almost no light on the subject of "Siberian Zimmerwaldism," yet in it, apparently, are to be found the roots of that intimate relationship between the centrist leadership and the Menshevik high command which had such profound and disastrous consequences for the Socialist Revolutionary party. A colony of numerous exiles had been living before the revolution in distant Eniseisk province, in and about the town of Irkutsk. Some were SR's and some SD's, but cutting squarely across party lines was another division in relation to the war. The majority continued to embrace the moderate internationalism characteristic of the Second International before its disruption.[134] Men of this persuasion embarked upon journalistic enterprises in order to get their views before the public. On the pages of the Irkutsk *Sibir'*, a considerable newspaper of regional significance which had come under his control,[135] Abram R. Gotz opened up a campaign against chauvinism and preached the waste and senselessness of war. His collaborators, including E. M. Timofeev and (A. A.?) Krakovetski, were for the most part SR's, and there is no indication that leading Social Democrats took a hand in the enterprise.[136] It is not unlikely that their role was restricted to their own short-lived ventures with the *Sibirski Zhurnal* and the *Sibirskoe*

---

[134] Answers to a questionnaire in 1916 disclosed that of the 30 SR's who replied, 25 harbored internationalist convictions, 2 were nationalists, and 3 were noncommittal. In all, 141 of the 350 exiles sent in replies. See Il. Vardin (Mgeladze), "Politicheskaia ssylka nakanune revoliutsii" (Political Exile on the Eve of the Revolution), *Proletarskaia Revoliutsiia*, V (1922), 93-94, 119-20.

[135] As has been pointed out, the Gotz family was very wealthy.

[136] Voitinski, *Gody pobed i porazhenii*, II, 404; see also article of A. Turunov on prerevolutionary newspapers in *Sibirskaia Sovetskaia Entsiklopediia* (Siberian Soviet Encyclopedia), I, 599.

Obozrenie, to which Irakli Tsereteli and F. I. Dan were the chief contributors.[137]

However that may be, the proximity of the two groups with similar views on the war encouraged personal contacts, and it was here, apparently, that Gotz and his colleagues first came under the spell of Tsereteli's magnetic personality and accepted his clear-cut distinction between "internationalism" and "defeatism," along with his conviction that the prohibitive cost to Russia of a separate peace precluded any attempt on the part of the Russian democracy to liquidate the conflict independently of the working-class movement in other countries.[138] When the revolution released them from exile, Gotz and Tsereteli traveled together to St. Petersburg and there plunged into the thick of political life, maintaining intimate contact with each other through the medium of the "star chamber" *(zvëzdnaia palata),*[139] a small circle of influential socialist leaders which in conjunction with the other, advanced liberal clique around Nekrasov and Kerenski, really dictated the course of the revolution until both were thrust aside by Lenin's seizure of power.[140]

Such was the origin and such were the mainstays of the alliance in 1917 between the Socialist Revolutionaries, a vast army with inadequate leadership, and the Mensheviks, a galaxy of strong-willed and self-assured leaders with but a slender following. The Mensheviks needed a base to stand on and the SR's, a leadership to follow. Each had what the other lacked; it was a natural, and hence a stable, alliance. But the SR's bought this alliance at a very high

[137] S. M. Levin, "Sotsialisticheskaia pechat' vo vremia imperialisticheskoi voiny" (The Socialist Press during the Imperialist War), *Krasnyi Arkhiv,* II (1922), 211-12; Voitinski, *Gody pobed i porazhenii,* II, 390 ff.

[138] For Tsereteli's formulation of these views see Voitinski, *Gody pobed i porazhenii,* II, 392, 395. Sukhanov claims that on his arrival in St. Petersburg Gotz already stood at an "astronomical distance" from Zimmerwaldism (*Zapiski,* II, 290).

[139] Dan and Chkheidze were other members. Gotz seems to have been the only SR in this predominantly Menshevik group. Zenzinov and Chernov did not belong to it. Although Gotz and Zenzinov were the dominant figures of the right center and usually in agreement on the issues of the day, they were not of the same feather.

[140] Interview with Nikolaevski in Prague (May, 1935); Sukhanov, *Zapiski,* II, 288, 291.

price, for it was the larger but weaker party representing the peasantry which became the beast of burden, and it was the party of the trade-union aristocracy and of the Jewish and Georgian intellectuals which very definitely became the rider in the saddle. The right wing of the PSR, with more influence than either its numbers or its political acumen justified, had tacitly capitulated to the basic Menshevik doctrine of the hegemony of the middle class, and the center, while retaining its belief in a social revolution in the agrarian sphere, deferred everything to the Constituent Assembly, thereby removing any ideological barrier in the interval to the extension of Tsereteli's influence, already great because of his ability to captivate and lead by the nose not only A. R. Gotz of the right center but also V. M. Chernov of the left center.

The consummation of this durable but ill-fated alliance is said to have occurred at the All-Russian Soviet Conference (March-April) in the form of a soviet bloc destined soon to become the foundation for the coalitional structure of the Provisional Government.[141] It is interesting to note that at the beginning of the revolution, before leaving Irkutsk, Arkhangelski for the SR's and Dan for the Mensheviks had joined in a plea for the fusion of the two parties.[142] Though the organizations were never merged, relations continued through the year to be so harmonious that in some towns joint papers were issued,[143] and in virtually all parts of the country an absence of recriminations between the SR and Menshevik press could be noted.[144]

Nothing like this cordiality existed to smooth the way for collaboration with the Constitutional Democrats, the third main component of a ministry of national union, and yet elements of an understanding were not wanting even here. Aside from a brief flirtation with the liberals in 1904, when it seemed possible to mount a common offensive against the government,[145] the Socialist

---

[141] Sukhanov, *Zapiski*, II, 398; III, 300, 359, 378.
[142] *Delo Naroda*, No. 4 (March 18, 1917).
[143] The *Bor'ba* (Struggle) of Smolensk is an example.
[144] See P. Fabrichny's article on the press in *God russkoi revoliutsii*, pp. 151-52.
[145] See *Revoliutsionnaia Rossiia* (1904-5), *passim*, and Steklov, *P.S.-R.*, p. 4.

Revolutionaries had abstained from contact with the bourgeois opposition until the rise of the liquidationist current with its taste for legal methods had narrowed the distance between the two camps. The war brought them still closer together in that the right-wing SR's embraced the cause of national defense with all the fervor which they no longer could muster for revolution, and the Kadets moved leftward in their opposition to official conduct of the war. Prominent SR "defensists" like Avksentiev and A. A. Argunov virtually identified themselves with the Kadet tactics of blanketing the regime with public-spirited forces so as to prepare its conversion to a limited monarchy; this phenomenon, known to SR's of the center as "neo-Kadetism," has already been touched upon in connection with the war.[146] The triumph of the revolution brought still another development which strengthened the ties between Constitutional Democracy and one section of the PSR: the large number of professional people, white-collar workers, and petty burghers who were streaming into the PSR because the Kadet party was too high-toned or too conservative or simply not fashionable enough for their taste, nevertheless were much more disposed, by their social origin and framework of loyalties, to seek an understanding with that party than with Bolshevism or even with the left wing of their own party. These "March Socialist Revolutionaries," together with the veteran corps of "defensists," imparted considerable stability to a working agreement with the Kadets.

Thus a basis for coalition existed even while majority opinion in the PSR still opposed entrance into a government over whose decisions the socialists could exert but a partial influence. From what has been said it might be concluded that the Mensheviks would lead the procession toward a coalitional form of government with the SR's tagging along in the rear. Yet the reverse was the case. To assist the bourgeoisie in fulfilling—and exhausting—its historical mission would have seemed to be the natural course for Menshevism

[146] See p. 101.

to follow, but this wing of the Russian Social Democracy could never move without an eye to the actions of its terrible twin, nor could it harbor any illusions as to Bolshevik policy in the face of a discredited coalition. The left wing of the Socialist Revolutionary party, on the other hand, did not yet stand forth in sharp enough relief to impose similar caution upon the rest of that organization. There were two elements pushing for coalition: the right wing, now feeling its oats with the return of the leaders in exile, many of them with the prestige of distinguished service in the past, and the soldiers, who saw in the assumption of office the guarantee of progress toward the goal of peace. It will at once be observed that coalition did not mean the same thing to the two elements most forward in its support; in fact, the benefits they thought to derive from it were mutually exclusive, for while the right wing valued a ministry of national union as the most efficacious means of strengthening the war effort, the soldiers looked upon socialist participation in the government as the best means of bringing the war to an end. Thus the experiment in coalition would surely disappoint one or the other of these elements, and so vastly increase the strain under which the party was laboring. What happened was that the soldiers were disillusioned and went over en masse to the left wing, if, indeed, they did not switch directly to Bolshevism.

Shortsightedness cursed SR policy throughout 1917, however, and thus we find party opinion generally running ahead of the Mensheviks in acceptance of the principle of coalition. For example, the Committee of Soldiers' Soviets of the Western Front on April 28 favored the admission of socialists into the cabinet by the strictly partisan vote of 26 SR's against 25 SD's.[147] On the same day the Moscow regional congress of the PSR resolved not "to exclude the possibility" of entering the ministry "in case of extreme necessity," provided that other socialist parties did likewise and the soviet formula for peace was accepted.[148] In the Petrograd Soviet, where crucial decisions were taken in 1917, the party membership late in April swung over to the stand of the Trudoviks and Popular

---

[147] *Revoliutsiia 1917 goda (Khronika sobytii)*, II, 84.
[148] *Ibid.*

Socialists, who from the outset had favored coalition. But the Mensheviks still hung back, and the Executive Committee on April 28 witnessed the temporary disruption of the soviet bloc when the Mensheviks parted company with the SR's to join with the extremists in rejecting coalition by a one-vote margin.[149]

Matters could not rest here, however. With the resignation of Guchkov the crisis became more acute instead of abating. As the necessity for reorganizing the government became increasingly evident, a tendency on the part of middle-of-the-road SR's to rationalize the discrepancy between their initial attitude and present inclination could be noted. The organization of the revolutionary democracy, which at first had been so unsatisfactory that the plenitude of power had to be conceded to the bourgeoisie, was now represented as having advanced to the level where the assumption of part of the burden of governing was a natural and desirable development.[150] Some of the leaders displayed considerable agility in making the change-over. Thus on April 21 Chernov advised the soviet that only when he should have confidence in the organized democratic forces at their backs would he be prepared to welcome a coalitional ministry,[151] yet on May 5 he merely cautioned the same body that it was still too weak in an organizational sense to take all of the power.[152] Apparently a fortnight had been enough for him to acquire this confidence. With many SR's a consideration that weighed heavily was the obligation not to leave Kerenski out on the end of the limb where the publication of his letter of April 26 had placed him by making his continuance in office dependent upon a mandate from both the party and the soviet. These SR's exerted pressure upon their Menshevik allies to revise the negative stand from which they were receding in any event under the same compelling circumstances which had induced the SR center to re-

[149] *Ibid.*, p. 82; *Ocherki po istorii Oktiabr'skoi revoliutsii*, II, 199; Sukhanov, *Zapiski*, III, 385, 398-99.

[150] See Chernov's speech before the First All-Russian Peasants' Congress in *Revoliutsiia 1917 goda (Khronika sobytii)*, II, 112-13; see also his speech before the Fourth Party Congress in *Kratkii otchët o rabotakh chetvërtago s"ezda P.S.-R.*, p. 15.

[151] *Delo Naroda*, No. 30 (April 22, 1917).

[152] *Revoliutsiia 1917 goda (Khronika sobytii)*, II, 112.

verse its position. The soviet bloc was restored in a very short space
of time and on May 1 the Executive Committee rescinded by a
vote of 44 to 19 the decision of April 28 opposing coalition. Neither
party presented a united front on this occasion, the extremist
minority being composed of four left SR's and three Menshevik
internationalists in addition to the Bolshevik delegation. But majority
opinion in both was now committed to coalition in principle; conditions were formulated in the name of the soviet, and a commission
chosen to negotiate with the ministry, Gotz, Avksentiev, and Filippovski serving as the SR representatives.[153]

In the ensuing negotiations the voice of the PSR was heard not
only through the commission from the Petrograd Workers' and
Soldiers' Soviet but also through the representatives of the All-
Russian Congress of Peasants' Soviets, a body entirely under the
domination of the SR party and more particularly of its right wing.
All of the members of the congress who took part in the negotiations
seem to have been of that persuasion, yet they exhibited more
radicalism in their demands than their confreres from the Petrograd
Soviet, insisting upon socialist tenure of no less than seven portfolios, among them the key post in the centralized and excessively
governed countries of Europe—that of the Ministry of the Interior.
Although lacking the wholehearted support of the other soviet delegation, the representatives of the peasants' congress stood their
ground with some tenacity in the face of pleas by Kerenski and
others not to upset the delicate equilibrium, only in the end to agree
that it would be unseemly to contest the interior post with the
incumbent, Prince Lvov, who at the same time was head of state
and a staunch advocate of socialist participation in the government.
It was further decided not to press for more than six posts.[154]

At this juncture a competition of singular character arose between
the SR and Menshevik parties, each seeking to induce the other to
accept a maximum number of portfolios. The explanation of this

---

[153] Ibid., pp. 95-96; Petrogradskii Sovet, pp. 130-31; Sukhanov, Zapiski, III,
404-9.
[154] Gurevich, "Vserossiiskii Krest'ianskii S"ezd," in Letopis' Revoliutsii, I,
180-83; Bykhovski, Vserossiiskii Sovet Krest'ianskikh Deputatov, pp. 60-62;
Chernov, Rozhdenie revoliutsionnoi Rossii, p. 373.

forbearance and touching solicitude for one's partner lay in the fear of the Menshevik leaders that Bolshevism would succeed in turning the workers against them if they became too prominently identified with a ministry dedicated to the maintenance of a class truce, as well as in the fact that they were by no means averse to giving the SR's enough rope to hang themselves. The Mensheviks especially desired to inveigle Chernov into the cabinet. The crafty SR leader, however, was not deceived by this maneuver; he decided that his party, also, should exercise forbearance, in no case accepting more than three posts, and he insisted that Tsereteli enter the ministry with him.[155]

Once these preliminary decisions had been taken, the juggling of portfolios and personalities began. To reconcile the ambitions and animosities now rising to the surface was comparable to squaring the circle. Much of the controversy centered about the person of Chernov. The left wing of his party, hostile in general to the idea of coalition, would have been gratified to see him assume the direction of foreign affairs, now that Miliukov was vacating that post; but majority opinion held him better befitted for the Ministry of Agriculture because of his authorship of the program for socialization of the land and because his presence there would insure a land reform in accord with the party's views. Since there were weighty considerations—mainly the pressure of Russia's allies—in favor of a nonsocialist occupancy of the Ministry of Foreign Affairs, and since Kerenski endorsed the government's choice, the French-speaking connoisseur of ballets, M. I. Tereshchenko, as an exponent of democratic methods in diplomacy, the soviet delegations permitted this key position to go by default. Having thus been quietly shunted aside from consideration as foreign minister, Chernov nevertheless faced stern opposition as his party's choice for the post of Minister of Agriculture, not only from the Constitutional Democrats, who could never forgive him his part in the Zimmerwald Conference or his present campaign against Miliukov, but also from the Popular

---

[155] Chernov, *Rozhdenie revoliutsionnoi Rossii*, p. 373; Gurevich, "Vserossiiskii Krest'ianskii S"ezd," in *Letopis' Revoliutsii*, I, 182; Bykhovski, *Vserossiiskii Sovet Krest'ianskikh Deputatov*, p. 57.

Socialists, who had their own candidate, A. V. Peshekhonov, but who were willing to take virtually anyone but Chernov. This was a matter, however, on which the Socialist Revolutionaries could not compromise,[156] and the assembling delegates of the All-Russian Peasants' Congress were dead set against having an advocate of landowners' compensation in so strategic a position. As a last resort, the enemies of Chernov thought to defeat his candidacy by advancing the name of his right-wing party colleague, N. D. Avksentiev. But the "star chamber," unknown to Chernov himself, had earmarked the post for him;[157] the Menshevik leaders supported his candidacy, and Gotz, in the name of the PSR, gave it the force of an ultimatum.[158]

There were other difficulties. Kerenski's shift to the crucial Ministries of War and Marine encountered only the doctrinaire opposition which the Kadets would offer to the appointment of any socialist as head of the armed forces, since the rest of the government saw clearly enough that if the jaded troops were to be whipped into action, as was so ardently desired, the services of a revolutionary hero with great moral authority must be employed. The difficulty in this connection came in filling the post of Minister of Justice which Kerenski was relinquishing. The mathematics of coalition called for an SR, but no candidate could be found among the leaders and in the end, thanks largely to Kerenski's influence, the appointment went to the Petrograd attorney, P. N. Pereverzev, whose customary designation as an SR[159] has no substance in fact. Pereverzev was one of those radical lawyers who hovered in the twilight zone

[156] Sukhanov, ever a caustic critic of the "very biggest party," says that the SR leaders saw as the ideal solution having a prominent party name grace the ministry with Peshekhonov as his assistant to do the actual work (Zapiski, III, 425).

[157] Interview with Nikolaevski in Prague (May, 1935).

[158] Stankevich, Vospominaniia, pp. 128-32; Gurevich, "Vserossiiskii Krest'-ianskii S"ezd," in Letopis' Revoliutsii, I, 182-83; Bykhovski, Vserossiiskii Sovet Krest'ianskikh Deputatov, pp. 60-61; Sukhanov, Zapiski, III, 408, 415; Chernov, Rozhdenie revoliutsionnoi Rossii, p. 373. The statement in Revoliutsiia 1917 goda (Khronika sobytii), II, 103-4, as to the ease with which Chernov's nomination was agreed upon in open conference is misleading unless one knows what went on behind the scenes preceding the conference.

[159] See, for example, Revoliutsiia 1917 goda (Khronika sobytii), II, 106.

between liberalism and Populism,[160] and the failure to assume responsibility for the new Minister of Justice or even to mention his
name on the occasion when the Third Party Congress voted mandates to Kerenski and Chernov is conclusive evidence that he was
not regarded as a member of the party.[161] The desire of A. I.
Shingarev (Constitutional Democrat) to retain the Food Ministry
and gather the fruits of his labor in that field occasioned a deadlock
which was resolved in favor of A. V. Peshekhonov (Popular
Socialist), largely as a result of Chernov's firm stand for socialist
tenure of an office with jurisdiction overlapping that of his own.[162]
When all the pieces of the puzzle had been fitted together,[163] it
was found that on a basis of nominal party allegiance six socialists
faced nine nonsocialists in this first coalitional ministry. Thus, even
had the socialist ministers formed a cohesive group—which was very
far from being the case—they still would have been overbalanced in
cabinet deliberations by their bourgeois colleagues. The Executive
Committee of the Petrograd Soviet had voted down Sukhanov's
motion favoring a socialist majority, and his caustic observation that
the soviet leaders were desperately determined to remain in the
minority has more than a grain of truth in it.[164]

On the surface, however, the socialist democracy and particularly
the SR party would appear to have scored a major triumph. Miliukov
was no longer in the cabinet, having in effect been forced into
retirement by the desire of his colleagues to relegate him to the
Ministry of Education and by his own disinclination to work with
socialists in the government.[165] In the provinces the news of his

[160] Sviatitski, "Voina i predfevral'e," *Katorga i Ssylka*, LXXV, 14. See also
Demianov, "Moia sluzhba pri Vremennom Pravitel'stve," in *Arkhiv Russkoi
Revoliutsii*, IV, 82; Sukhanov, *Zapiski*, III, 425-26, 430; Bykhovski, *Vserossiiskii
Sovet Krest'ianskikh Deputatov*, p. 62; Gurevich, "Vserossiiskii Krest'ianskii
S"ezd," in *Letopis' Revoliutsii*, I, 184.

[161] See *Tretii s"ezd P.S.-R.*, pp. 374-76, and below, p. 212.

[162] See his article, "Istorik ili isterik?", *Volia Rossii*, III (1925), 94-95; Chernov,
Rozhdenie revoliutsionnoi Rossii, p. 373; Sukhanov, *Zapiski*, III, 427 ff.,
especially pp. 438-39; Gurevich, "Vserossiiskii Krest'ianskii S"ezd," in *Letopis'
Revoliutsii*, I, 183-84; Stankevich, *Vospominaniia*, p. 130.

[163] Around 2 A.M. on May 5.

[164] *Zapiski*, III, 410, 416.

[165] V. D. Nabokov, "Vremennoe Pravitel'stvo," in *Arkhiv Russkoi Revoliutsii*,
I, 64.

fall had been received with elation or dejection, depending on the views of the persons concerned, but all regarded it as a development of fateful significance, redounding to the prestige of the Socialist Revolutionaries, who in the public eye had quite outstripped the other parties in weight of influence as in the vigor of their attack.[166] The new foreign minister as well as the cabinet as a whole appeared to be committed to an antiimperialist course, judging from the declaration issued in the name of the reconstituted Provisional Government.[167] The PSR had also scored heavily on two other fronts, taking over control of the armed forces in the person of its then most popular figure, A. F. Kerenski, and placing its titular leader, V. M. Chernov, in the Ministry of Agriculture, where he could proceed to give satisfaction to the mass of his party's supporters by implementing the land program which many years before his fertile brain had conceived. Such was the attractive picture that presented itself to the average member of the party on the morrow of Miliukov's resignation and the formation of the first coalition.

Never were appearances more deceiving. The power of the Socialist Revolutionary party was indeed great as long as the two basic elements personified by Kerenski and Chernov pulled in the same direction. But the sober truth was that the party had emerged from the underground and had magnified its organization without in any way removing the fateful wedge which the war had driven into that organization. The "defensists" still proposed to continue the war at any cost, preserving the class truce at home and the ties with the Allies abroad, while the "internationalists" were looking for a way out of the war with Germany so as to engage in social revolution at home. Neither element was imperialist and both could oppose the policy of Miliukov in so far as it was addressed to territorial acquisitions. But in that policy the attainment of specific advantages for Russia was linked with sustaining the war effort of the Western Allies; the "defensists" were willing to subscribe to a self-denying ordinance for Russia but they held invincibly to the alliance with France and Great Britain, and if supporting the war

[166] Pasmanik, *Revoliutsionnye gody v Krimu*, p. 46.
[167] Text of declaration in *Revoliutsiia 1917 goda (Khronika sobytii)*, II, 271-73, and in the contemporary press.

effort of the "valiant allies" meant supporting their war aims as well, then it must be said that the SR "defensists," and "defensists" in general, despite all their turnings and twistings, were prepared to condone in France and Great Britain the tendencies which they condemned in Germany and even in Russia herself.

And this, of course, was precisely what His Majesty's Government desired. For the truth of the matter is that Great Britain had not been sorry to see Miliukov lose his duel with Kerenski and retire from the cabinet. That far-seeing and coldly calculating power realized that by his open and honest diplomacy, by his bull-headed insistence upon expanding the borders of Russia, Miliukov was building up a resentment in the army and elsewhere which might explode with terrific force, relieving Germany of her fateful problem of the double front and endangering the Allied victory which the entrance of the United States into the war had disclosed as a still rather distant but definite probability. Furthermore, by pursuing the glittering prize of Constantinople and the Straits in spite of hell and high water, but in conformity with treaties to which British signatures were affixed, Miliukov would place his country in a position where it must inevitably collide with British interests in the Mediterranean and the Near East. The London cabinet could survey distant as well as immediate perspectives, even if the professor of Russian history could not. If a man could be found who would persevere in the concentric pressure upon Germany, restore the Russian army as an effective fighting force through the exercise of his revolutionary authority, and yet forego these disquieting aspects of Russian imperialism, then he would enjoy the support of His Majesty's Government and of the financial power which it wielded in preference to a minister who, though a loyal friend, had outlived his usefulness. Kerenski was that man. Already on April 10, Sir George Buchanan had taken soundings to ascertain the views and convictions of Kerenski and Tereshchenko and had found them eminently satisfactory. The French government, with its customary narrowness of vision and its disinterest in the Straits, was more favorable to Miliukov, but Albert Thomas, the government socialist who had been sent to Russia to dispel the antiwar prejudices of the working class, helped to grease the skids for the Kadet leader.[168]

Thus in throwing their weight onto the scales against Miliukov, the SR "defensists" were by no means running counter to their allies' wishes. With the replacement of Miliukov by Tereshchenko and with Kerenski's transfer to the defense ministries, the features of Russian foreign policy obnoxious to Great Britain were eliminated but the features essential to British diplomacy remained. In fact, they were strengthened, for one of the main objectives of Prince Lvov and his associates in drawing socialists into the government had been to produce a change in army morale preparatory to launching an offensive, and the prime minister had been careful to denature the effect of accepting the soviet peace formula by tying the peace diplomacy of the cabinet firmly to the war chariot of the Western Allies.[169] Miliukov himself on a previous occasion had toyed with the idea of retiring in favor of Tereshchenko ("he is not entirely ignorant in these matters and will at least be able to converse with the ambassadors");[170] the two men differed in method rather than in motivation, except perhaps for the Straits. Tereshchenko set himself the task of continuing his predecessor's policy but in such a way as to pull the wool over the eyes of the soviet. He was committed body and soul to the war, and his complacency in regard to national interests as well as his good manners and "complete dilettantism in matters of foreign policy" endeared him to Russia's allies.[171]

No fundamental change had occurred as a result of the Socialist Revolutionary victory over Miliukov, at least so far as ending the war was concerned. If Russia had now been brought to renounce

[168] Ocherki po istorii Oktiabr'skoi revoliutsii, II, 377-84; V. D. Nabokov, "Vremennoe Pravitel'stvo," in Arkhiv Russkoi Revoliutsii, I, 62, 64. Nabokov, who was very close to Miliukov, comments on his devotion to England (p. 55).

[169] Ocherki po istorii Oktiabr'skoi revoliutsii, II, 202; Sukhanov, Zapiski, III, 412; Stankevich, Vospominaniia, pp. 199 ff., 132; see also text of official declaration, May 6, in Revoliutsiia 1917 goda (Khronika sobytii), II, 271-72.

[170] V. D. Nabokov, "Vremennoe Pravitel'stvo," in Arkhiv Russkoi Revoliutsii, I, 62.

[171] Ibid., pp. 45-47. These strictures, it will be remembered, are not voiced by some biased socialist but by a member of the Central Committee of the Constitutional Democratic party.

all imperialist pretensions, the shift in foreign ministers would prove to be a positive disadvantage in another sense, for Miliukov had been a firm and tangible obstacle into which the partisans of peace could sink their teeth, whereas Tereshchenko, with his outward deference and clandestine obstruction of their efforts, threw them off guard and created in their minds the illusion of progress toward the goal of peace. Had the fall of Miliukov entailed a full revision of foreign policy, then it would not have come about, for in that case the prowar faction in the party would not have made common cause with the antiwar faction and the semblance of unity would have been exploded in April instead of after the Kornilov putsch in September. As it was, the right center could continue the dance with the left center for four months longer until the intransigence of the wings had been communicated to the core. Only if the left Socialist Revolutionaries had been able to realize their desire to have Chernov succeed Miliukov would the inauguration of a real peace policy have been feasible, and it may well have been that the zeal displayed by A. R. Gotz and the right center in pushing Chernov's candidacy for another post even to the point of an ulti- matum had concealed their alarm over an agitation which, unless headed off, would assuredly have produced not only a new de- parture in external relations but also a first-class crisis in both country and party.

The hollowness of the SR victory extended beyond the field of diplomacy into the whole realm of social revolution. The socialist minority in the cabinet had no cohesion whatever. Kerenski had always identified himself with the interests of state rather than of party, and with the overthrow of Miliukov he sought to arrest the leftward course of revolution; Pereverzev was a nonentity; Tsereteli and Skobelev were right-wing Mensheviks, for whom the interests of socialism would long be inseparable from those of a liberal bour- geois regime; and Peshekhonov belonged to the Popular Socialist party—of all nominally socialist groups, the one standing farthest to the right. Chernov was left alone to carry the banner of social revolution, and he was too soft and pliant by nature, too mindful of party harmony, and too much under the influence of men like

Tsereteli to buck the liberal majority of the cabinet without support from his socialist colleagues. Already the doom of an energetic agrarian policy directed toward satisfying the ambitions—or greed— of the peasantry had been foreshadowed in the text of the government's declaration, where the solution of the land question was left to the Constituent Assembly and the new ministry was pledged to secure the "maximum production of grain" and to regulate the use of the land in the "interest of the public economy and of the toiling population."[172] When invited by Sukhanov to press for alterations in the text to render it more in accord with the SR land program, Gotz readily agreed that the main thing was not the "production of grain" or regulation in some vague general interest, but he either could not or did not know how to secure the desired amendment.[173]

Far from being the spearhead of an agrarian offensive, Chernov was more a captive in a body where not one colleague agreed with his deep-seated convictions as to what to do about the war and the land. An unwilling convert to coalition—he had said that if the situation were not so bad, the revolutionists even now would refuse to serve[174]—he minimized the dangers on the ground that control of the instruments of coercion had slipped from the hands of the bourgeoisie,[175] and he plainly intimated before the peasants' congress that when the revolutionary forces had gained in organization and experience they would take more power. A party comrade suspects that Chernov did not have his heart in defending coalition on this occasion, but states that his attitude of taking what could be gotten now and trying for more later reflected exactly the mood of the peasant delegates.[176] The SR representation in the Petrograd Soviet, a tractable and moderate group on the whole, comforted itself with the same thought.[177] This point of view, undoubtedly reflecting majority opinion within the party, could not be recon-

[172] The last phrase is unjustly omitted in Sukhanov's account.
[173] *Zapiski*, III, 413.
[174] Bykhovskii, *Vserossiiskii Sovet Krest'ianskikh Deputatov*, p. 67.
[175] *Revoliutsiia 1917 goda (Khronika sobytii)*, II, 112.
[176] Gurevich, "Vserossiiskii Krest'ianskii S"ezd," in *Letopis' Revoliutsii*, I, 190.
[177] *Delo Naroda*, No. 50 (May 16, 1917).

ciled with that of the liberals or the other socialist ministers or of right-wing socialists in general, for whom the formation of a coalitional ministry represented the final step in the evolution of government toward a class truce in which the interests of the contracting parties would be subordinated to the cause of national defense.[178] Once more it must be pointed out that within the Socialist Revolutionary party itself coalition meant one thing to the right wing and quite another thing to the rest of the party. The structure of coalition was raised on a foundation of sand.

More than anything else it was Chernov's acceptance of the portfolio of agriculture which rendered the experiment in coalition palatable to the majority of Socialist Revolutionaries and caused them to reverse their earlier stand in the hope that the man who had conceived the program of land socialization and acquired repute as a champion of peace could both realize the age-old aspirations of the peasantry and satisfy its new-found longing for an end to war. Many expected that the influence of A. F. Kerenski would be exerted in the same direction. The divergence between the points of view of the two men had not yet registered upon the consciousness of the party, at least not upon that of the rank and file: had they not just made common cause against the leading exponent of Russian imperialism, with the result that he had been driven from power? Small wonder, then, that the left wing of the party made no headway in its arguments against coalition, not even in Petrograd, where its influence was strongest and where, only a month before, it had all but unhorsed the center on the question of war and peace. On May 3 a joint conference of SR organizations in the capital sanctioned party representation in the government by a vote of 172 to 37 with 5 abstentions, this top-heavy margin standing in marked contrast to the close division at the Second Petrograd Conference. The two gatherings are not commensurate, however, for this time it was simply the city and regional committees meeting with the delegational leaders in the soviet instead of a regular conference composed of representatives elected by the rank and file in local assemblies.

---

[178] See especially Steinberg, *Ot fevralia po oktiabr'*, pp. 21-22; clear formulation of the right SR point of view in editorial in the *Volia Naroda*, No. 6 (May 5, 1917).

Since only the leadership and not the membership of the Petrograd organization was consulted, the voice of the center and the right was correspondingly magnified, for party offices were as yet largely filled by men with distinguished service records, who tended to be moderate in their point of view. Chernov helped the cause along, though with a noticeable lack of enthusiasm, by addressing the conference and telling it there was nothing to do but enter the government.[179]

At the All-Russian Peasants' Congress, his presence in the Ministry of Agriculture, symbolizing the ascendancy of the party concept of land reform, gave the right SR's in control of the congress all the ammunition they needed to refute the arguments of Kamkov, Natanson, and Steinberg (the leaders of the left wing) that only a government composed entirely of socialists could secure the toilers' interests. Though by no means satisfied with what had been obtained, the mass of delegates believed that a fair start had been made and, having as yet no sympathy for the slogan of "All power to the soviets!" and no objection in principle to coalition, they ratified the new ministry by a tremendous majority.[180] There is no reason to doubt that the delegates were animated by the same spirit as their constituents. Telegrams of congratulation pouring in from peasant and party groups in widely separated localities attested the popularity of Chernov at the outset of his ministerial career and bore witness to the lift of spirit which the news of his appointment had given to the Russian people.[181] Agreement with the course of the party leadership in the capital was expressed, now in blanket form, now with substantial reservations, by regional and local assemblies throughout the country.[182]

[179] Report of conference in *Delo Naroda*, No. 40 (May 4, 1917), and in *Volia Naroda*, No. 5 (May 4, 1917); speech of Chernov in *Delo Naroda*, No. 42 (May 6, 1917).

[180] Bykhovski, *Vserossiiskii Sovet Krest'ianskikh Deputatov*, p. 71; Gurevich, "Vserossiiskii Krest'ianskii S"ezd," in *Letopis' Revoliutsii*, I, 190. The only region to dissent was White Russia, consistently a stronghold of extremism in 1917.

[181] See *Delo Naroda*, No. 58 (May 26, 1917), for a whole sheaf of these telegrams.

[182] *Ibid.*, No. 54 (May 20, 1917), and No. 58 (May 26, 1917); *Volia Naroda*, Nos. 12, 14, 16, 18, 23, 25 (May 12, 14, 17, 19, 26, 28, 1917).

In all these resolutions, however, it was more a question of elation over partisan gains than appreciation for the advantages and duties of coalition. Genuine enthusiasm over the prospects of collaboration with other public forces, whether socialist or nonsocialist, was confined to right-wing circles, which argued that the interim nature of the Provisional Government justified the suspension of partisan controversy and beseeched party members to cease giving only half-hearted support to the regime, now that it had been made over into a worthy repository of the people's confidence.[183] Some SR organizations betrayed their fear that association with the class enemy would weaken socialist convictions by insisting upon strict subordination of representatives in the cabinet to party instructions. To allay such fears Chernov announced before the peasants' congress that the PSR would assume formal responsibility for those of its members who entered the cabinet.[184] All of these pronouncements and assertions of opinion, however, were not in themselves conclusive. Definitive confirmation of the party's venture in coalition as well as the formulation of its position on other pressing questions of the hour awaited the convocation of the Third Party Congress at the end of May in Moscow. This highest instance of party authority would survey the field after three months of revolution and chart the course through the shoals and reefs that lay ahead.

[183] See the editorial in *Volia Naroda*, No. 6 (May 5, 1917).
[184] Bykhovski, *Vserossiiskii Sovet Krest'ianskikh Deputatov*, p. 68.

VI

THE THIRD PARTY CONGRESS

WE have seen that the "party of assassins" had been forced to hold its first two congresses in Finland, since even in the midst of revolution the tsarist bureaucracy had not been reduced to the point where it would tolerate such gatherings on Russian soil. In closing the Second Congress, Gershuni had promised his comrades that next time they would meet on the banks of the Neva and, while they actually assembled in Moscow, he was correct in thinking that the country would be in the throes of a successful revolution and his party in a position of power. What he had not foreseen was that ten years would elapse before that time. It was to this long interruption in the corporate existence of the party that Chernov attributed the absence at Moscow of the comradely feeling which had pervaded the Imatra and Tammerfors meetings;[1] yet actually two other factors were of at least equal moment: the influx of new elements in the wake of the February Revolution, and the estrangement within the old core of leadership produced by the war.

Since the beginning of the revolution the party spokesmen had awaited with trepidation the forthcoming congress. They feared the ideological content of the movement might be altered beyond recognition as a result of the inability of the veteran cadres—"ridiculously" small in numbers because of the attrition of terrorism[2]—to absorb the flood of recruits which free conditions and the popularity of its slogans were bringing the party. Old-line partisans from exile or from prison, reinforced by those who had fallen away in time of adversity, saw their grip on the machinery endangered not only by newcomers unschooled in the traditions of the move-

[1] *Tretii s"ezd P.S.-R.*, pp. 426-27.
[2] Chernov, manuscript of chapter entitled Partiia S.-R.

ment but also by elements whose social background aroused suspicion and promised to act as a barrier against assimilation. It is not necessary to draw upon hostile sources, which tell us that the fad of membership spread rapidly in higher army circles and among landowners,[3] or within the humbler stratum of shopkeepers and mistresses of girls' gymnasia;[4] the SR's themselves admit that the horde of adventurers, careerists, and "unsettled minds" streaming into the organization had introduced a strain of opportunism into its decisions.[5]

But they could not agree as to the political tendency of this undesirable element or as to the factional advantage conferred by its presence. Throughout 1917 the phrase "March Socialist Revolutionary" was bandied about as a term of opprobrium, serving either extreme against the other, the left charging that chauvinism and a covert opposition to changing the economic order had crept into the party as a result of this type of membership, and the right denouncing it as the natural support of every kind of demagoguery. To the accusation that it was attempting to pervert the ideology of Social Revolutionism by packing meetings with spurious converts,[6] the right replied that its opponents welcomed new members as long as these were drawn from the less conscious strata of society, becoming concerned about ideological purity only when it was a question of admitting intellectuals.[7] The organizational chaos[8] in the PSR was such that no one could be sure what was happening, but the sequel would disclose that, in so far as they did not become dead wood on the party tree, the new members tended to divide according to their outlook and interests, adhering as they became orientated in party affairs to one or another of the groups already existing. There was, in other words, no cohesion among the "March SR's," and in time the vastly extended organization was fractured along

[3] Sukhanov, *Zapiski*, I, 108-9, 125; and IV, 14.
[4] *Oktiabr' na Odeshchine*, pp. 160-61.
[5] Chernov, manuscript of chapter Partiia S.-R.
[6] M. L. Kogan-Bernstein, "Organizatsionnye voprosy" (Organizational Problems), *Delo Naroda*, No. 46 (May 11, 1917).
[7] M. M. Engelhardt, "Na rasput'i" (At the Crossroads), *Volia Naroda*, No. 21 (May 24, 1917).
[8] See below, pp. 233 ff.

the same lines as the small prerevolutionary core. Chernov was no doubt correct when he asserted that the March tide had washed into the party a goodly number of Philistines on the right and ochlocrats on the left.[9]

Amid much jockeying for position and a welter of organizational problems the Sixth National Conference met on April 30 to prepare for the congress. It soon became apparent that local organizations did not all compute membership in the same manner and that there was no yardstick for determining their relative strength. Originally the plan had been to apportion representation according to membership, but when it was discovered that certain vital provincial organizations with rigid standards of admission reckoned their members by hundreds, while lesser groups (*uezd* or local) which had been only sporadically active claimed a strength running into the thousands or even tens of thousands, the conference abandoned its plan in favor of a more or less arbitrary allotment of delegates based on a scrutiny of the nature and scope of activities.[10] In an effort to make the congress spring from the rank-and-file membership instead of from the party officialdom, it was provided that delegates should be chosen by the convention method[11] rather than by committee appointment, but the maze of dubious mandates through which the credentials committee had to wade[12] suggests that this injunction was not always obeyed.

Factionalism was stimulated by the approaching congress, which would determine control of the party through the election of a central committee and formulate policy on the issues of the day, first and foremost the question of war and peace. Such was the general uncertainty that each faction could hope to make its point of view official and relegate that of its opponents to the rank of a heresy,

[9] "Ochishchenie partii" (Purging the Party), *Delo Naroda*, No. 218 (November 24, 1917).

[10] *Volia Naroda*, No. 5 (May 4, 1917). The list of organizations with their representation is given here.

[11] As an example, the Petersburg city convention (or conference) may be cited. Mass meetings of the membership were held in each ward; these elected representatives to the all-city conference, which in turn chose the delegates to the Third Congress. See *Delo Naroda*, No. 54 (May 20, 1917).

[12] See the report in *Tretii s"ezd P.S.-R.*, pp. 135-39.

tolerated, perhaps, but subject to crippling restrictions. That the congress would witness a struggle between left and right was a foregone conclusion; the question was whether the center could bind the extremes to the party and itself avoid being polarized.

The right had already hardened into a faction before the congress. In fact, it had come measurably close to forming a separate party. Rooted in the émigré "defensism" of the war period, this current of opinion had won support after the revolution among intellectuals who had worked with the party in the past or were employed in institutions serving the peasantry, like the cooperatives. Especially did it command a following among the elder generation of Populists, many of whom like E. E. Lazarev had seen their fondest dreams come true with the overthrow of the autocracy and the attainment of political freedom; such men had little stomach for a social upheaval in the midst of a war that enlisted their undivided support.[13] But it was not to be expected that their views would carry much weight in the capital, where the intellectuals were under heavy pressure from the radical masses, and where the right wing had been virtually ostracized in the local organization. After its helplessness had been exposed at the Second City Conference,[14] it asserted its freedom of action and withdrew its representatives, A. I. Gukovski and P. A. Sorokin, from the Delo Naroda, announcing in a letter signed by thirty-six party members that the conference had been out of step with party opinion as a whole.[15] The statement was accompanied by a declaration of principles suggesting that the signatories had embraced a brand of national socialism and attached no conditions whatever to their support of the Provisional Government.[16]

The next step in combatting what the right termed anarchistic demagogy under the guise of socialism was to set up its own organ of propaganda; and on the last day of April the first number of the

[13] Interview with Argunov in Prague (June, 1935).
[14] See preceding chapter, p. 152.
[15] No. 30 (April 22, 1917); Tretii s"ezd P.S.-R., pp. 358, 360; Kratkii otchët o rabotakh chetvërtago s"ezda P.S.-R., p. 70.
[16] See editorial comment in Delo Naroda, No. 30 (April 22, 1917).

Volia Naroda appeared. A. A. Argunov served as editor and E. K. Breshko-Breshkovskaia supplied the funds for this venture. Like many another veteran of the movement, the "grandmother of the revolution" had made the transition from Populism to nationalism, becoming an ardent champion of the war and even, in the heat of the conflict with the Teutonic powers, something of a Pan-Slavist.[17] Any effort to keep Russia in the war at the side of the Western Allies was sure to command her support, and from the considerable funds placed at her disposal by American friends she advanced 600,000 rubles to Argunov to defray the expenses of publication and insure the distribution without cost of his newspaper.[18] Argunov's collaborators, among whom were Boris V. Savinkov, Sergei S. Maslov, V. I. Lebedev, P. A. Sorokin, A. I. Gukovski, E. A. Stalinski, L. P. Bulanov, I. I. Mainov, V. S. Pankratov, the brothers Sigov (A. S. and I. S.), L. Ia. Sternberg, N. S. Tiutchev, and Vladimir M. Chernov (the elder brother of Victor), were all hard-bitten "defensists"; their journal contained none of the verbiage of compro-

[17] See the excerpt from her appeal for Russo-Czech collaboration in 1918 printed in Makarov, *Oktiabr' i grazhdanskaia voina v Udmurtii*, p. 52.

[18] Interview with Argunov in Prague (June, 1935). Breshkovskaia was the good fairy godmother of "defensist" undertakings in 1917. Among the recipients of her largess, in addition to Argunov, were the Popular Socialists (50,000 rubles) and S. L. Maslov, editor of the right-wing *Zemlia i Volia* of Moscow (20,000 rubles). After the October Revolution her private secretary, V. Bakrylov, deserted to the Left SR's and published in their organ, the Petersburg *Znamia Truda*, an account of the considerable funds which in the course of the year had passed through her hands. According to him, Breshkovskaia had received 100,000 rubles from certain persons (apparently compatriots) on the understanding that opinion-molding organs under her control would advocate postponement of basic reforms until the Constituent Assembly, and American sources had contributed 2,100,000 rubles. It was stressed that this money had been given *before* an appeal was addressed to the American public at large. The Bolsheviks seized upon these disclosures as a means of turning back upon the SR "defensists" the charge that had been leveled against themselves—subservience to a foreign power. See Meshcheriakov's résumé and comment on Bakrylov's article in *Izvestiia moskovskago soveta rabochikh i soldatskikh deputatov*, No. 221 (December 3, 1917). Subsequent to the arrival in July of the American Red Cross mission to Russia, large sums were advanced to the Committee on Civic Education in Free Russia, of which Breshkovskaia was chairman, by the American capitalist, William B. Thompson. See the testimony of Raymond Robins in *Bolshevik Propaganda: Hearings*, pp. 774-77.

mise that filled the columns of other SR papers. A hostile source observes that the SR staff of the Parisian "defensist" organ, the *Prizyv*, had moved over bodily to the *Volia Naroda*.[19]

It was not to be expected that so determined a band of men would stop at propaganda. When the editors of the *Volia Naroda*, still paying lip service to the shibboleth of unity, declared that "the appearance of our paper should in no wise be interpreted as a symptom of centrifugal forces within the party,"[20] they grossly misrepresented the situation, for they were making an open break with the Petersburg organization and surreptitiously initiating separatist action on a national scale. Factionalism reached a new high in the capital with the effort of the Petersburg Committee to strike the party slogan from the masthead of the *Volia Naroda* on the ground that, since none of the district organizations had any hand in its founding, it was the organ of a private group without official standing;[21] the Northern Regional Conference, reflecting the anti-war sentiment of a military constituency, went still further and refused its representatives even the right to be heard.[22] Not at all intimidated by this evidence of majority disfavor, the *Volia Naroda* continued its denunciations of "party Bolsheviks" whose tactics, it declared, would lead to "slavery without and anarchy within";[23] and more and more it served as the point of crystallization for that element within the party for whom prosecution of the war meant more than preservation of unity. A few days before the opening of the Third Congress, the *Volia Naroda* issued a call to sympathizers to attend a special meeting, ostensibly for the purpose of discussing for the first time in SR history the setting up of a factional organization.[24]

Far from restricting themselves to this purpose, however, the forty-odd partisans who answered the call took the bull by the

[19] B. D. Kamkov, "Bor'ba 'tsennosti'" (A Conflict of Value), *Nash Put'*, No. 2 (1917), p. 9.
[20] "Vo imia edinstva" (In the Name of Unity), No. 11 (May 11, 1917).
[21] No. 14 (May 14, 1917); *Tretii s"ezd P.S.-R.*, pp. 360-61.
[22] *Delo Naroda*, No. 55 (May 21, 1917); *Volia Naroda*, No. 21 (May 24, 1917).
[23] No. 14 (May 14, 1917).
[24] Chernov, manuscript of chapter Partiia S.-R.; *Kratkii otchët o rabotakh chetvërtago s"ezda P.S.-R.*, p. 70.

horns and boldly debated the advisability of withdrawing from the
PSR and forming a separate party. The aged L. P. Bulanov favored
this course as did also Tiutchev, Mainov, Pankratov, and the
brothers Sigov, but others felt the time had not yet come for so
drastic an action, and Argunov, seconded by Lebedev and Stalinski,
threw the weight of his influence against the proposal. The hot-
heads were restrained and outwardly, at any rate, the old song and
dance went on about the totem pole of unity. Yet eighteen years
after the event in question Argunov told this author that it was
not any lingering hope of preserving the fellowship of the past
but strictly practical considerations, such as the desire to maintain
contacts with the "friendly enemies" of the right center and the
fear of "flooding the market" with a new political party of untested
strength, which on this occasion had stayed the hands of his group.
According to him, the spiritual unity of the party had already been
so undermined by the war that the ties of sentiment stressed by other
SR's as the chief restraining influence no longer had any effect. It
is interesting to note that in retrospect Argunov had come to feel
that his opposition to forming a new party in the spring of 1917
had been a mistake."[25]

The fact that only forty-odd partisans had responded to the call
of the *Volia Naroda*, and that most of these did not have voting
privileges, is evidence that the numerical strength of the right did
not match the level of its consciousness. Even so, what had been
done formed an inauspicious prelude to the congress. For now that
the other side had made a move, the left, not wishing to be taken
at a disadvantage, began to mobilize its strength. And it had strength,
even in the honeymoon stage of the revolution. Originally an intellectual movement with one center abroad in the editorial offices of the
Na Chuzhbine and another at home in the Petersburg literary circle
around R. V. Ivanov-Razumnik, left-wing Social Revolutionism soon
became a mass movement as a result of the extremist but non-
Marxist sentiment among Petersburg workers which had sent P.
Alexandróvich to the local soviet, and as a result of the bitter feeling

[25] Interview in Prague (June, 1935). The debate on secession must have been
held in complete secrecy, for there is no mention of it in the printed sources.

against the war in the barracks and naval centers of the Northern Region. Nor was its strength confined to that region and to the capital. By autumn the tide of peasant discontent, the green wave that washed out the foundations of the traditional order of Russian society, would have floated the Left SR's onto the level of a major party; but already in the period before the Third Congress they had acquired dominion over the peasant movement in certain provinces of Great and Little Russia, in Kazan and Ufa, in Kharkov and Kherson, and here and there were other islands of strength. Not until near the end of the year did the left overcome the spotty character of its support, though by the time of the May congress it was already a factor to be reckoned with.

At the head of the movement stood a band of youthful extremists, some of them from the emigration, some from prison or places of exile, and some from the depths of the people. Boris Kamkov represented the antiwar section of the Populist emigration, and Maria Spiridonova, the Siberian prison contingent; P. P. Proshian and A. N. Ustinov attained prominence as agitators in the military camps of the north, and L. A. Kalegaev and Ilia Maiorov, as organizers of the Kazan peasant movement; while the radical intelligentsia of Kharkov province found a leader in V. A. Karelin. Kamkov had about him the transplanted editorial staff of *Na Chuzhbine*, and Spiridonova was the central figure in the so-called Maltsevo circle of extremists who had been sentenced to long terms of imprisonment for terrorist activity,[26] and who were now returning to European Russia to settle accounts with whatever was left of the old regime, their zeal unabated by the snows of Siberia. Spiridonova had celebrated her liberation by causing the prisons of Chita to be blown into the air, and the frame of mind revealed by this incident was hardly less characteristic of her boon companions, Anastasia Bitsenko, Alexandra Izmailovich, and Irina Kakhovskaia. Other nuclei of leadership were to be found in the provincial centers of Kazan, Kharkov, and Ufa.

Somewhat in the background but holding the threads in his hand

[26] Interview with Nikolaevski in New York (December, 1949); see Steinberg, *Spiridonova*.

stood the Nestor of radical Populism, Mark Natanson, as venerable
a figure as Breshkovskaia and as far to the left in his thinking as
she was to the right. He alone of the first generation of Populists
had come down to 1917 with his outlook unchanged, probably because of the strong racial component in his hatred of tsarism, as
evidenced by his reaction to the news of Pleve's assassination;[27] in
any event the passing years had not softened his bitterness. Natanson
was an old hand at marshaling youthful idealists in the cause of
subversion,[28] and now he was engaged in a contest for power which
in case of success would deliver into his hands an admirable instrument for completing the destruction of the old Russian order. His
dignified appearance and long experience strengthened his hold on
immature zealots and caused him to stand forth in the consciousness
of an icon-minded society as a countersymbol to Breshkovskaia—
that "patented grandmother of the revolution," as a Bolshevik lawyer
once irreverently called her.[29]

With support in the party scattered and of uncertain strength,
and with leadership restricted to the local or provincial level, it was
only natural that Natanson should look upon the Third Congress
as a means of organizing on the national scale those who wanted
immediate peace and intensification of the class struggle. If this
meant fracturing the unity of the PSR by creating a party within a
party, he was not the man to shrink from such a course. To follow
the trail of the left SR's and of Natanson in particular is a difficult
business. They wrote little, and their publications are often inaccessible. Natanson did not like to work in the open; he rarely
spoke and wrote almost nothing. He was a wirepuller par excellence,
"bat-like" in his operations, to borrow Isaac Deutscher's adjective
for Stalin.[30] Less than anyone has Natanson told us how he laid the
foundations of the party of the Left SR Internationalists.

But it was on his initiative that the leftist caucus at the Third

---

[27] See *Pamiati Stepana Nikolaevicha Slëtova*, p. 13.
[28] Numerous references to his activity will be found in Spiridovich, *Histoire du terrorisme russe, passim.*
[29] Antonov-Saratovski, *Pod stiagom proletarskoi bor'by*, I, 92.
[30] *The Prophet Armed: Trotsky 1879-1921* (New York and London, 1954), p. 517.

Congress resolved to set up an "informational bureau" which would keep the scattered elements in touch with each other and coordinate their activities. Seeing in this organ the embryo of a new party in the womb of the old, some of the more moderate leftists raised a cry of protest and Chernov's left center added its voice to theirs. Chernov himself, but recently associated with Natanson in the Zimmerwald movement and now at the height of his popularity, was gravely alarmed at the move, and such was the weight of his disapproval that at the close of the congress he received "formal assurance" that neither then nor in the future would a body of this type be set up. As he ruefully remarked at the Fourth or December Congress, the left had lied to him, for a clandestine bureau did exist from that time onward, coming into the open only on July 9, when a manifesto in its name appeared in No. 85 of the Petersburg *Zemlia i Volia*.[31] Zenzinov corroborated Chernov's account by asserting that the bureau had been formed behind the back of the Central Committee.[32]

There is no doubt as to the existence of the bureau; the only question is whether it consciously aimed at building up a new party at the expense of the old, as Chernov affirms, or merely sought fractional cohesion without any thought of a breakaway, as Kamkov asserted in defending his group against the threat of expulsion.[33] Whatever the original purpose, the result was schism. That the bureau could have led a clandestine existence also arouses some doubt, for a number of moderate leftists or left-centrists who never withdrew from the party belonged to it, so many, in fact, that one of them denied the tie-up between the bureau and the later schismatics.[34] The adhesion of a party wheelhorse like Eugenia Ratner without the knowledge of her friend, V. M. Chernov, is a surprising circumstance, to say the least.

The Third Congress thus witnessed the crystallization of extremist sentiment in definite form. The radicals drew off by them-

---

[31] *Kratkii otchët o rabotakh chetvërtago s"ezda P.S.-R.*, pp. 115-16.
[32] *Ibid.*, p. 71.
[33] *Delo Naroda*, Nos. 97, 101 (July 11, 15, 1917).
[34] *Kratkii otchët o rabotakh chetvërtago s"ezda P.S.-R.*, p. 76.

selves and caucused continually, arousing so much indignation among the champions of unity that one of these, Zenzinov, tore down the placard over the door of the caucus room on the ground that there could be only one type of party member—a plain SR without factional allegiance.[35] But in that room and on the floor of the congress, where the tide of battle went always against them, the radicals were developing the esprit de corps of a group apart. M. L. Kogan-Bernstein has subdivided the left sector of the congress into three groups: the outright maximalists, consciously working for a split; "semi-Bolshevik" intellectuals of the Kamkov type, bold in words but ready to compromise over and over again; and the moderate left, headed by himself.[36] But it will suffice to speak of the extremist left and the moderate left; the former gave battle all along the line, sometimes aided by the moderates and sometimes deserted by them. With the dedicated fanaticism of a minority determined to become the majority and sustained by the knowledge that circumstances were working in their favor, the extremists picked themselves up from each battlefield lost and returned to the charge with unabated energy. Bellicosity and brittleness of temperament, according to Chernov,[37] were their outstanding characteristics. As they were only just finding themselves in the oratorical as well as the organizational sense, they had no one to pit against the spokesmen of the right or the center, so that in tone their speeches suffer in comparison with those of Avksentiev and in content, with those of Chernov. Only Ivanov-Razumnik among the left SR's may be described as thoroughly articulate in the literary and intellectual sense, and he was

[35] *Interview in New York* (December 19, 1949).
[36] "Nashi raskhozhdeniia" (Our Divergences), *Partiinyia Izvestiia*, No. 5 (January 20, 1918), p. 62. Too much weight should not be assigned to the views of Kogan-Bernstein. He obviously disliked Kamkov, perhaps because with the two of them there, left field became crowded. Kogan-Bernstein had a marked proletarian bias, like a Social Democrat; his attribution of the same preference to his group is open to question, for no matter what their differences in other respects, virtually all SR's were as one in regarding themselves as champions of the peasantry. That was the essence of their being. Kogan-Bernstein's attitude was probably no more than a personal deviation from the general pattern.
[37] Manuscript commentary on the minutes of the Central Committee, p. 3.

not even a member of the party.[38] The others had to make up in vehemence what they lacked in polish and background.

The appearance of divisive tendencies on both flanks of the party caused the adherents of unity to organize their own caucus, over the doors of which they posted an invitation to all delegates subscribing, on the one hand, to the "platform of the Zimmerwald Conference" and, on the other, to the "resolution of comrade Abram Gotz on the war."[39] The first limitation excluded the partisans of the extreme right and the second, those of the extreme left. Both concerned the war and afford a very good illustration of how the fortunes of the PSR turned on this problem, in the honeymoon stage of the revolution as well as in the period of dissolution. The center, of course, could count upon all those who were moderate in sentiment, who were disposed to compromise even the most burning of issues, and who saw the party on the threshold of its greatest opportunity, if only it could keep from flying apart; and it enjoyed the support of nearly all of the big names in the party, from Chernov and Gotz to Avksentiev and Rudnev. The prestige of Chernov, his skill at devising formulas which could face both ways at once and satisfy discordant elements, lay unreservedly at the service of the center. His "all-uniting" (*vseob"ediniaiushchie*) resolutions, offered on the floor of the Third Congress and eagerly seized upon by the mass of delegates, were like brilliantly colored paper concealing cracks in the wall—and they lasted about as long. For the cracks ran through the center of the structure as well as between it and the two wings.

The Third Congress had not long been in session before it became apparent that the champions of unity themselves were divided into a right center, which included most of the old-guard leaders, and a left center under V. M. Chernov. Every effort was made, because

[38] This was disclosed only later when he resigned from the editorial board of the *Delo Naroda* (*Kratkii otchët o rabotakh chetvërtago s"ezda P.S.-R.*, p. 72). He desired for moral reasons not to be bound to any particular party. Ivanov-Razumnik's influence upon a section of the St. Petersburg intelligentsia is said to have been considerable, but he offered only inspiration and not leadership. Essentially he was an idealist in revolt against the war, the whole senselessness of which he exposed in elegant and moving prose.

[39] Chernov, manuscript of chapter Partiia S.-R.

of considerations of partisan patriotism, to conceal this rift and present a united front to the extremists, with such success that the full measure of its seriousness was not taken until after the Kornilov affair. In line with this endeavor the vital decisions of the Third Congress were hammered out behind the doors of the centrist caucus and then imposed upon the plenum in lock-step fashion; on two occasions, however, the veil could not be drawn and all could see how deep a fissure ran through the middle of the PSR. The cohesion of the center depended in the last analysis upon the relationship between Abram Gotz and V. M. Chernov: if Gotz had Chernov well in hand, then all was in order, but if Chernov rattled his chains or made as though to assert himself, the vaunted unity dissolved like a wisp of smoke. Neither the left center nor the right center formed a solid bloc, for the moderate left oscillated between Chernov and the Kamkov-Natanson group, preferring in numerous individual cases to caucus with the latter, while Gotz had on his hands in the right center an element that belonged elsewhere but had come to him for tactical reasons.

A word about this latter group. We have seen how the ardor of some of the active participants in the upheaval of 1905 had gradually cooled until little if anything was left of their revolutionary faith; the idealistic void in their natures was filled by the nationalism evoked by the war as well as by the rationalization of their pro-Allied sentiment into a belief that human progress at this stage of development was bound up with the triumph of the Allied cause. Adherents of the new ideology who preferred to take a stand on principle, and were not afraid to show their colors, had constituted themselves as the right wing of the PSR. Others sharing the same ideology refused to go so far; they could see that the *Volia Naroda* group had isolated itself from the heartbeat of the organization and was no longer in a position to influence its decisions, and they desired to remain in contact with the main body of opinion in order to commit it more definitely to a prowar policy, even though the commitment was not as all out as they might have wished. So it was that Gotz acquired on the right side of the centrist caucus an element of support that really belonged to the extreme right but had chosen, for tactical reasons, to march with him in the expectation that he could gradually be inclined in favor of its point of view.

The influence of the rightist camarilla was disproportionate to its numerical backing, for it included some of the most articulate members of the party: Avksentiev, the watchdog of the war party; Bunakov-Fondaminski, a party hierarch linked by marriage to Gotz's family; Rudnev, the newly elected mayor of Moscow; and Vishniak, the party specialist in matters of law and political science. The camarilla had strong support in the intelligentsia—much stronger than in the people—and it had purposeful and determined leadership; it was close to Kerenski, and enjoyed the good will of the Allied embassies. Here was one reason for Gotz's "abrupt deviation" from the Zimmerwald line which proved so upsetting to his colleague Chernov, and here in large measure lay the explanation for the rightward orientation of SR policy at a time when the mass of the Russian people was gravitating steadily leftward. The open right under Argunov had no influence in party councils; the clandestine right in centrist trappings had very great influence.[40]

With factional lines already forming in the manner described, the Third Congress convened on May 25 to elect N. I. Rakitnikov (LC)[41] as its chairman and to choose a praesidium representative of all shades of opinion.[42] Brushing aside less consequential matters with a directness unusual in SR affairs, the congress soon came to the question that was uppermost in everyone's mind: the formulation of policy in respect to the war.

[40] Chernov, manuscript of chapter Partiia S.-R.; Chernov, manuscript commentary on the minutes of the Central Committee, p. 3.

[41] From time to time it will be helpful to designate the factional allegiance or leaning of a party member in cases where it can be established; for this purpose the symbol (R) will denote the right wing (Argunov), (RRC) the clandestine right or right-right-center (Avksentiev, Fondaminski), (RC) the right center proper (Gotz, Zenzinov), (LC) the left center (Chernov), (LLC) the moderate left or left-left-center (Kogan-Bernstein), and (L) the intransigent left (Kamkov, Natanson), which later became a separate party.

[42] *Tretii s"ezd P.S.-R.*, pp. 3 ff., 46.

Three resolutions were offered to establish the principles which the party wished to see incorporated in a final draft: one by Gotz in the name of the center, on behalf of the partisans of unity; one by Kamkov for the antiwar elements; and one, apparently, by the far right. This third resolution, however, was quickly withdrawn before it could figure in the proceedings, presumably because its sponsors did not wish to have their weakness exposed. As between the resolutions of Gotz and Kamkov, the congress decided on May 28, by a vote of 179 to 80 with 5 abstentions, in favor of the former.[43] The entire center, from Avksentiev and Rudnev on the right to Chernov on the left, had lined up in support of Gotz's draft without a ripple of dissent, committing the party, in effect, to a continuation of the war over the protests of a substantial minority. If we may consider the congress as the party in miniature—and there is no good reason for not considering it as such—then between one fourth and one third of the largest socialist party had been unwilling, even in May, to contemplate anything beyond a purely defensive stand in the war. Here was a circumstance which, in conjunction with conditions in the Social Democratic camp, might well have given pause to the champions of all out war, had they been less blind to the temper of the Russian people.

Worse was to follow. Three days after this demonstration of unity by the core of the party, the effect of its action and the stability of its majority alike were called into question when the news leaked out that a fourth resolution, bearing the authority of Chernov's name, had been in the drafting stage at the time when the order of the day had been hurriedly set aside to permit a vote on the two resolutions already before the house. Under the circumstances it was not surprising that a delegate of the left center should move that this buried resolution be exhumed and brought to the floor of the congress. The obvious threat to the unity of the center threw the assembly into an uproar. It is not altogether clear what had gone on behind the scenes. Efforts to get Chernov to talk about his own resolution were like trying to nail down an eel: not only was the subject slippery, he was downright pusillanimous, seeking refuge in the presiding officer's

[43] *Ibid.*, p. 204.

chair from the embarrassing questions that came his way, though not until it had been established that he had intended to introduce, or had introduced, certain parts of his belated draft as amendments to Gotz's resolution, only to withdraw them and present the rest of his resolution, shorn of those parts bearing specifically on the war, as a special resolution on the current moment and tasks of the party. From his confused, in some respects contradictory, and in all respects lame, explanation, the facts that stand out are the delay in drafting his resolution, the suppression of the most controversial passages dealing with the war, and the author's acquiescence in the emascula-tion and transformation of his resolution. From Avksentiev we learn that after the hurried vote of May 28 the center had named a special commission to negotiate with Chernov, and that as a result of these discussions an agreement had been worked out on the basis of certain changes in the text of the adopted resolution.

The congress had now to decide whether to leave things as they were or to reopen the question by debating the relative merits of the Gotz and Chernov resolutions. A motion to permit discussion of the latter tore the center wide open, and with everyone to the right of center arrayed against everyone to the left of center, the motion was lost by the narrow margin between 114 and 108. But a few minutes later, with a score of delegates streaming in from the corridors, the scales were tipped the other way when a motion to permit a reading of the Chernov resolution carried by a vote of 124 to 120. After the reading Kogan-Bernstein moved to set the two resolutions against each other and decide between them. Gotz showed to poor advantage on this occasion; he was essentially a manipulator rather than a tribune, and his talents did not flourish in the broad light of day. The situation might well have gotten out of hand had it been left to him. It was saved (for the right) by Avksentiev, who made a creditable extemporaneous speech in which he emphasized the deference paid to Chernov in revising Gotz's resolution after its adoption and the needless waste of time involved in reopening a matter that had already been settled. This syrup was just what was needed to bring the centrists together again, and after Chernov as presiding officer had helped to rebury his own work by choking off an attempt to examine the propriety of the hurried vote of May 28, the congress resolved by a division of 155 to 99 not to rescind its previous decision.[44]

This incident of the "lost" resolution on the war, so completely ignored in revolutionary literature, even of a party nature, is of the utmost significance in revealing the true state of affairs in the Socialist Revolutionary party. For a brief moment, as though with a surgeon's knife, the body was laid open and the ravages of the war-induced cancer exposed; then the wound was hastily sutured and people chose not to think of what they had seen; but the incision would break open again in September, at the time of Kornilov's coup, and the patient would die in December. Even the dry pages of the minutes reveal clearly enough how desperately the right-centrist leaders strove to keep the ghost of Chernov's resolution[45] in the grave to which their successful maneuvers of May 28 and the pusillanimity of its author had consigned it. The question of unity was no longer so much one of how to bind the extremes to the center as of how to preserve the center from the polarizing influence of the extremes, and the demonstration of the precarious equilibrium of forces in the heart of the organization clearly foreshadowed what would happen when the strain became greater.

The incident also established the pattern of Chernov's conduct in 1917. The resolution had been his feeble attempt to assume the actual as well as the nominal leadership of his party; with its death, he forfeited any claim to leadership and surrendered the reins of power to Abram Gotz. There had been no scandal or contest for power; the stronger personality had simply climbed into the driver's seat, which the weaker personality had not occupied, though everyone had ex-

---

[44] *Tretii s"ezd P.S.-R.*, pp. 313-19.

[45] The text does not even appear in the minutes and remains a mystery, except in its denatured form. It was treated as a dread and dangerous thing. Sukhanov errs in asserting (*Zapiski*, IV, 203) that Gotz opposed his resolutions to Chernov's and emerged victorious. It was precisely the desire to prevent a confrontation of the two resolutions that accounts for the nervous haste of the leaders in whipping through the one before the other was ready and then using the accomplished fact as an argument for shutting off debate; the appointment of a special commission to confer with Chernov likewise betrays their grave concern and the discreet pressure brought to bear upon him not to force the issue.

pected him to, not realizing how weak he was. It had not been necessary to defeat Chernov or even to push him aside—he had settled the
issue by effacing himself. Acquiescing in Gotz's accession to power,
Chernov nonetheless did not relish it. We do not know at just what
point the two men went apart: perhaps earlier in the soviet, when
Chernov's hopes of recruiting an ally in the struggle for peace were
shattered; perhaps only later, in the contentions within the Central
Committee. But in any event the episode at the Third Congress
which revealed to Chernov the unwillingness of the bulk of the
old-guard leadership with Gotz at the head to entrust him with the
formulation of policy on the war undoubtedly contributed to their
estrangement. The refusal to defer to him had been natural, in view
of the very real difference of opinion. And he had no one but himself to blame for the outcome, for if he had chosen to make a stand
for his principles, he quite possibly could have carried the congress
with him, though not by any impressive majority. But a man never
relishes the evidence of his weakness. The sop afforded him of some
changes in Gotz's draft and of acceptance of the shell of his resolution under another label[46] did little to ease the smart, the severity
of which is seen in the fact that even in his most confidential writings
he does not mention the incident. No doubt he rationalized things
and consoled himself with the thought that he had made a sacrifice
to unity—the first of many to a nonexistent god.

Gotz's resolution with Chernov's amendments had been left as the
basis of the final resolution on war and peace; it now had to be
debated, section by section. The delegates followed each point, even
each word, with breathless attention; progress from point to point
resembled a series of pitched battles fought over rough terrain; and
shouts of indignation alternated or were mixed with bursts of frenzied applause. The battles began with the preamble, which branded

[46] The eviscerated resolution repeated the author's thesis of the "third force"
(see chap. IV) and advanced the idea of using war-induced socialism as a
steppingstone to true socialism, thereby shortening the long interval of transition from capitalism hitherto envisaged by the SR's. No one bothered to vote
against the resolution, though twenty-five delegates of the right abstained. Two
delegates protested that its introduction had taken them by surprise. Of course
it had—the resolution had been framed for one purpose and gutted for another.
Text in *Tretii s"ezd P.S.-R.*, pp. 315-17; pertinent discussion, pp. 321, 327.

imperialism as the main, though not the exclusive, cause of the war. The right wished to differentiate in favor of the Allies but could muster in support of its position only a handful of votes. The SR's embraced the soviet formula—peace without annexations or indemnities on the basis of national self-determination—modified by a provision for plebiscites in disputed areas. But how to commit other powers to this formula, first of all, Russia's own allies?

That was the fateful stumbling block which the SR's never succeeded in clearing from their path, either at the Third Congress or on any later occasion. The congress called on the Provisional Government to press this formula upon the Allies and to initiate action looking toward the reexamination and eventual annulment of the secret treaties[47] concluded by the tsarist regime, in the meantime grounding its diplomacy solely on the interests of the toilers of Russia and the world. This seems to have been a concession to Chernov's point of view,[48] but Gotz hastened to rob it of any effective meaning by assuring the party members that nothing in the way of a peremptory demand was intended, only "pressure and persuasion." From the debate it was clear that the leaders would do nothing to embarrass the Allies. The left favored serving them with an ultimatum in the belief that if they could be brought into line the Central Powers would not dare to hold out. But Gotz and Chernov both refused to consider this course as long as public opinion in France and Great Britain had not progressed to the point where such action would strengthen its hand against the regimes in power. Most significant was the stand of Kerenski, who warned against the presumption of lecturing the older, more sophisticated democracies of the West on the evils of imperialism or of expecting them to exorcise it in the same way as the young Russian republic.[49]

The right-wing SR's, in fact, viewed as intolerable any suggestion

[47] The controversy over publication of these treaties had lost much of its edge with the leaking out of information about their provisions, but the left continued to press for publication as a means of confounding such apologists for Allied imperialism as the French socialist Albert Thomas. See *Tretii s"ezd P.S.-R.*, pp. 109, 115.

[48] See *Tretii s"ezd P.S.-R.*, pp. 109, 202.

[49] *Tretii s"ezd P.S.-R.*, pp. 126-28.

of pressure to commit these adulated democracies to the peace program of the Russian Revolution. N. D. Avksentiev was like a knight in armor, bearing the colors of Britain and France and prepared to charge at any moment when an attempt was made to restrict their freedom of action. The special target of his lance was Point VI, in content the heart of the resolution and in execution a monument to casuistry. Its language is classic: while the war continued, revolutionary Russia "moves toward the necessity" (*idët navstrechu neobkhodimosti*) of a united strategic front with the Allies at the same time that it "advances the necessity" of a united political front with them—objectives which constituted the dual aspect of a single cause, the conclusion of peace in accordance with the soviet formula. Chernov undoubtedly had planted this lily in Gotz's garden. Even in the absence in this formula of any adaptation of the Trinitarian dogma of the church, one of Chernov's favorite rhetorical devices (he was frequently as hard pressed as the Fathers to demonstrate unity where there was none), his handiwork could be recognized alike in the elasticity and in the duplicity of the formula. As a delegate exclaimed, it was a baffling business to which one could say neither yes nor no: if a common political front were not worked out, should there be a common strategic front; if Russia and her Allies could not agree on peace terms, should they continue to wage the war together? The best answer Gotz could give was to define the working out of a common political front as a process in which the Russian democracy was then engaged. But in some quarters the language of the draft was construed to mean that military operations were to be suspended until the Allies accepted the soviet formula; the French and British were at this time doing their utmost to stir the Russian army to action, and Avksentiev sprang to his feet to remind the assembly that both Gotz and Chernov had ruled out any attempt at coercion. To prevent misunderstanding he proposed that the language of the resolution be changed from "advances the necessity of" to "attempts to realize" a united political front, thereby upsetting the balance between the two elements in the formula to the advantage of a coordinated military effort with or without an agreement on conditions of peace.

Even in the troubled history of the PSR there had been few scenes to compare to this one. Again the fictitious unity of the center was stretched to the breaking point. Gotz had to defend something that emanated from his rival on the left against the assault of his ally on the right. He said that the resolutions committee had been careful to exclude anything in the way of coercive demands; as for himself, he saw none in the wording under discussion. The congress thereupon rejected Avksentiev's amendment. A few moments later Avksentiev charged again, demanding that the congress formally expunge from the record any possible taint of coercion. . . . [A deafening roar shut him off at this point.] The ties that bound him to the freemasons of France showed through rather plainly on this occasion. Gotz repeated his previous statement, and Chairman Rakitnikov told Avksentiev that he must content himself with the preservation of these words in the official minutes. The sixth point of the resolution on war remained unaltered. Yet it was no more than a windmill against which this Don Quixote had shattered his lance in vain. It left things just as they had been—in a state of paralysis.

Having resolved in effect not to make an attempt to force the Allies into step with the revolution, the party members hastened to block the other way out of the quandary in which they found themselves by refusing to act independently of the Allies. There were no echoes at the congress of the speech which Vladimir E. Trutovski (L) had made at the Northern Regional Conference in favor of a separate peace,[50] but in recent weeks thought of a truce of one sort or another had gained ground in some party circles, and at the Third Petersburg Conference the idea of a general armistice had been advanced by S. P. Postnikov (LC).[51] Acknowledging that it favored a separate armistice, the left went no further at the congress than to offer an amendment calling for the speedy conclusion of a general armistice. Gotz saw nothing terrifying in the proposal but felt that a secondary matter of this sort should not be magnified to the point

---

[50] Delo Naroda, No. 56 (May 24, 1917).
[51] Ibid.; Revoliutsiia 1917 goda (Khronika sobytii), II, 189. Postnikov maintained that the slogan originated with him, and that the Bolsheviks later took it over and made it their own (interview in Prague, August 1, 1935).

of diverting attention from the primary goal of a general peace. With this specious reasoning he kept the left center (though not the moderate left) in line and the amendment was defeated, 122 to 87. The "defensists" greeted the result with wild applause. On the premise that imperialism could be overcome and a peace worthy of the revolution attained only by the concerted action of the toilers of all countries, never by a unilateral withdrawal from the war, the resolution adopted by the congress specifically condemned both a separate peace and a separate armistice. Here no effort was required to hold the center together, for the left center as well as the right always maintained that peacemaking was a collective enterprise.[52]

To stir the concerted action necessary to overcome the resistance of imperialist governments, appeals were to be addressed to the democracies of other countries to follow the Russian example, the International was to be reconstituted, and a socialist peace conference held. In a separate resolution, the congress provided for representation at the international socialist conference which the Petersburg Soviet was trying to organize and at other conferences of an exploratory nature that might be convened beforehand, including the Third Zimmerwaldist. This recognition of Zimmerwaldism infuriated the right and led to a prolonged struggle at the end of the congress, an effort to isolate it from the rest of the resolution failing by a vote of 115 to 32 with 10 abstentions—the high-water mark of rightist strength at the congress.[53]

All factions within the party agreed on the need for a strong army to defend the frontiers of the revolution and to weight its influence in world affairs, and all agreed in condemning any move to end the war by producing a breakdown at the front—neither pacifism nor treason had any foothold in this party—but they could not agree as to how to achieve this objective, the right stressing the preservation of morale by combatting subversive propaganda among the troops, and the left, the elevation of morale by measures to convince the troops that they were now defending their own cause. Foremost

[52] See, for example, the comments of Chernov and others (*Tretii s"ezd P.S.-R.*, pp. 159, 197).
[53] *Ibid.*, pp. 460-71; see also pp. 220-26, 228-37. The clandestine right must have joined forces on this occasion with the *Volia Naroda* group.

among these must be the scrapping of the "false and mutually contradictory" slogans of the hour, born of the hybrid nature—half-imperialist, half-revolutionary—of the February regime, which were confusing the troops and leading them to fear the perpetuation of the old order under a new guise.[54] The left opposed any offensive so long as Russia's allies had not followed her example in renouncing imperialist aims. But they did not push the matter as hard as might have been expected when Kerenski ignored their question on this point and plainly intimated what was brewing in high circles by observing that an offensive would be necessary "sooner rather than later."[55] Avksentiev and Rudnev insisted that the congress must recognize the necessity of putting the army in shape for an offensive effort,[56] and the resolution complied with this demand by sanctioning "active operations . . . in defense of the Russian Revolution and its international policy," and by condemning agitation in the army against any forward movement. At the same time it condemned the agitation of chauvinistic editors—those "heroes of the rear" as Chernov called them—for an offensive at any cost, thus conforming on the whole to the intermediate position of Chernov, who was in no hurry for an offensive but did not wish to tie the hands of the new Russia, on the principle that offense is sometimes the best defense.[57] Nevertheless, the right had gained its point, in substance if not in form, and the Provisional Government could proceed with its plans for an offensive without let or hindrance from the Socialist Revolutionary party. In view of the moral indignation they engendered over the June offensive and its significance in splitting the party, it seems strange that the left SR's should not have made more of an issue of this at the congress.

All aspects of the resolution on war and peace have now been treated.[58] The controversy has been thoroughly analyzed because nothing else aroused so much passion or revealed more clearly the

[54] See especially Kamkov's speech (*ibid.*, pp. 113-14).
[55] *Ibid.*, pp. 129-30.
[56] *Ibid.*, pp. 158-60, 177.
[57] See his comments (*ibid.*, pp. 194-96).
[58] The foregoing discussion is based on *Tretii s"ezd P.S.-R.*, pp. 337-56, 384, 476-78 (text of final resolution), and *passim;* also on the summary in Chernov's manuscript of the chapter Partiia S.-R.

divisions within the party or exposed more glaringly its inability to cope with the great questions of the hour. If final passage were by a vote of 190 to 33 with 35 abstentions, the decisiveness of the margin attested less the unity of the party than the elasticity of the text, in which clarity had been sacrificed to harmony and conviction to expediency, with the result that we have a Janus-like thing, facing in both directions and moving in neither. If any advantage can be said to have been derived from paper formulas obscure to the intellectual and meaningless to the average citizen, then it lay with the right, which in the absence of any discrimination in favor of the Allies had nevertheless managed to have a separate peace or a separate armistice condemned and the door left open for an offensive effort that would help the British and the French. And this was not surprising, in view of the mechanics of the congress. Chernov says that the vital decisions were taken behind the closed doors of the centrist caucus. Available evidence tends to refute his further assertion that in that caucus his left center enjoyed a considerable majority.[59] The maximum voting strength of the left (extreme and moderate) was 87 and of the right 42;[60] while it is not possible because of the fluidity of factional lines and the dwindling attendance to fix a precise ratio of strength, it would seem that the left was at least twice as strong as the right. But on the two occasions at the congress when compromise broke down—the vote on the lost resolution on war and on Kerenski's election to the Central Committee—the result was virtually an even balance between right and left with the center dissolved. No other conclusion is possible than that if the right center could redress the balance in this fashion, it must have been larger than the left center, and that in the united caucus Gotz's more aggressive personality must have been reinforced by a numerically superior following. In any event the equivocal language of this most crucial of resolutions reflected the nearly even division of party opinion. No clear-cut formula would have held the party together, so deep was the cleavage over the war. The SR's chose not to commit

[59] Manuscript commentary on the minutes of the Central Committee, p. 3.
[60] See above, p. 206. The calculation is based on more than these two divisions.

suicide but to mask their affliction and await their fate at the hands of circumstance.

In contrast to the thunder and lightning evoked by the war, the debate on the question of power, second of the four great problems confronting the PSR, proceeded under an all but cloudless sky. One reason for this was that the left SR's, the ginger group of the congress, took the view that, while it was ill-advised for the party to be linked to the Provisional Government and a mistake for socialists to occupy ministerial posts without a free hand, it was an inevitable stage in the revolution that in time would yield to the full-blown socialist stage, making unnecessary an attempt to recall the captive comrades. They insisted merely that the whole Provisional Government, and not just the socialist ministers, should be responsible to the soviet.[61] The opposite point of view was represented by Avksentiev, who devoted his entire career, before, during, and after the revolution, to consummating a "union of all vital forces," in this case for the purpose of keeping Russia in the war on the side of the Allies. Unlike his leftist opponents, who adhered to the traditional SR point of view, Avksentiev had in effect adopted the Menshevik position by assigning a major role in the revolution to the bourgeoisie. His ostensible reason for defending coalition was the fear that if the socialists pretended to all the power large numbers of petty burghers would be driven into the counterrevolutionary camp, thereby bringing the socialists up against the "gray Philistine mass," a much more formidable foe than the old Black Hundreds; but his real purpose was to avert strife that would weaken the war effort. To those who cited the sad experience of Western coalitions, he replied that conditions were not comparable to those in Russia, which had broken out of the old social molds; and to those who viewed socialist ministers as prisoners of the bourgeois majority, he repeated the by now

[61] *Tretii s"ezd P.S.-R.*, pp. 214-18; *Delo Naroda*, No. 57 (May 25, 1917) (report of the Northern Regional Conference).

commonplace assurance—half true and half false—that the real power was lodged in the hands of the socialists.[62]

Thinking to take the congress in tow, Avksentiev had blithely submitted a resolution embodying his point of view when he learned that another current of opinion, also favoring support of the government, had decided to stand on the resolution adopted at the Third Petersburg Conference. This was the group around Chernov. Not caring to fight the issue, the left had agreed to him as its spokesman and the center had done the same. What went on behind the scenes is not a matter of record, but it is a fair conjecture that the core of leadership, and Gotz in particular, being unwilling to entrust Chernov with drafting the resolution on war, had felt obliged to defer to him in a less crucial matter, all the more so since Chernov would do no harm to a body of which he himself was a member. Avksentiev had either not known of what the center was planning or had gone ahead on his own, in any case affording clear evidence that he did not belong to the right center proper but only to the fringe that bordered on the right extreme. He was now in an isolated position, with the ground getting hot under his feet; he faced certain humiliation at the hands of a Chernov backed by both the left and the center. So the clandestine right, having been caught out in the open on this occasion, sought refuge in an agreement for the two men to meet and work out the text of a third or compromise resolution. A comparison of texts[63] discloses the close affinity of the final resolution with that of the Petersburg conference, as could only have been the case in view of Chernov's strong position.

Chernov always claimed to have scored a major triumph on this occasion by forcing the proponents of perpetual coalition to recognize the transitory character of a half-socialist, half-bourgeois government such as now existed in Russia.[64] But what a triumph! Let us listen to the language of the key clause in this remarkable document committing the party eventually to the formation of an all-socialist government: declaring that the coalitional ministry now in office was a necessary step in consolidating the first foothold of the "third

[62] Delo Naroda, No. 57 (May 25, 1917); Tretii s"ezd P.S.-R., pp. 206-13.
[63] Delo Naroda, No. 56 (May 24, 1917); Tretii s"ezd P.S.-R., pp. 478-79.
[64] Manuscript of chapter Partiia S.-R., and elsewhere.

force" in Europe, and that the socialists could take more power only when they had become more of an organized force, the resolution went on to define the present transitional stage as one in which "bourgeois Russia was no longer able to cope with the fateful problems of the day and the party of socialism was not yet obliged to take the power into its hands." The delegates were patient folk, partisans of unity at almost any cost, but this was more than they could stand, and Avksentiev, who had been commissioned, in the interests of harmony, to present the compromise which Chernov had written, was showered with amendments and demands for clarification. One delegate declared the sense of the resolution to be that the power was lying on the street, yet the socialists were not obliged to pick it up, and another protested the whole concept of a period transitory to a purely socialist regime. Once again the exigencies of harmony required Avksentiev to play the hypocrite, and the defense he offered was in keeping with the role. It was not a question of a struggle for power, he explained, but of a "deep organic process." It might even be necessary to take the power, for if the bourgeoisie abandoned it, the socialists would have to assume the burden at a time they considered unfavorable, "since we cannot be without a government."

After this ludicrous spectacle of a man attempting to defend with his mouth what he rejected in his heart, Avksentiev let slip something that would have been worth listening to if he had not already so thoroughly confused his audience. The characterization of the present period as transitory, he said, was not to be taken as implying that the coalition would soon be replaced by a socialist government, even though postponement of the Constituent Assembly might give the Provisional Government a longer lease on life than had been anticipated. In these words Avksentiev clearly intimated that, as far as he and his group were concerned, the coalition would last a long time, and he made known the official attitude toward an early election. It is surprising that he should have been challenged on neither ground.

Chernov would later upbraid the right wing of his party for having violated the decrees of the Third Congress, and specifically for having kept coalition alive much too long, but he never explained why he had done nothing to correct the deviation at the outset, when it had been so clearly foreshadowed in Avksentiev's statement; nor did he explain why he had left things in the hands of his opponent after having been commissioned by both the left and the center to steer the resolution on power through the congress. When it was too late to do anything, Chernov worked out a whole theory of coalition and of its misapplication in 1917,[65] but one searches in vain the resolutions he drafted in May for a timetable or an analysis of conditions which would have enabled his party to judge when coalition had outlived itself and when it was time to proceed to the next stage. He had contented himself with a paper victory and had yielded up the substance to the fetish of unity.

By passing this discreditable resolution—only three votes were cast against it with 32 abstentions—the Third Congress had accepted the principle of coalition and pledged the party's wholehearted support to the Provisional Government so long as democratic control of its actions was assured by the presence of socialist ministers. The specific arrangement whereby Kerenski and Chernov had entered the government with the approval of a special Petersburg conference was ratified, virtually without debate, by a vote of 159 to 27 with 29 abstentions. The congress assumed no responsibility for Minister of Justice Pereverzev, regarded by some as an SR, and the absence of any reference to him in the minutes is evidence that he was not considered a member of the party or at least did not represent it in the government. The two delegated ministers were bound to administer their departments in accordance with the decrees of the congress.[66]

At the Third Congress, as generally at SR conventions in 1917, the questions of war and power aroused so much excitement and set

[65] "Otkliki pressy" (Comments of the Press), *Revoliutsionnaia Rossiia*, No. 32 (December, 1923), pp. 20-21; "Uroki proshlogo" (Lessons of the Past), *ibid.*, No. 42 (April, 1925), p. 15; manuscript of chapter Partiia S.-R.; V. Arkhangelski, "O proshlykh takticheskikh oshibkakh" (Tactical Mistakes of the Past), *Revoliutsionnaia Rossiia*, No. 42 (April, 1925), pp. 10-11; see also below, chap. XII.

[66] Debate and resolutions on the question of power will be found in *Tretii s"ezd P.S.-R.*, pp. 328-35, 374-76, 478-79, and *passim*.

up such acute tension within the party that other matters were pushed into the background, even though these might be scarcely less urgent and of even greater significance from the long-term point of view. It is a remarkable circumstance that the land problem, in conjunction with which this party had grown up and waxed strong, should have suffered from inattention, yet the Third Congress did no more than reaffirm the principle of socialization, leaving the details of implementation to an agrarian commission of the Central Committee and restricting its attention to interim measures pending the convocation of the Constituent Assembly. As if smitten with a bad conscience, the delegates listened to the promise of the agrarian specialist, S. M. Maslov (RRC), that within a month a party council would meet to hear the report of the commission and bring the agrarian program up to date;[67] yet the Seventh Council convened, not in June but in August, and debated not the land question but the war.[68] That is the way things went in this "very biggest of parties," "sovereign of the nation's thoughts"—around and around and around once more, in what the Russians term so aptly a "magic circle." Or a better figure of speech might be that the party was caught in a whirlpool, or a succession of whirlpools, which would carry it to the bottom of the stream.

Among the "details" so conveniently disposed of—ostensibly by reference to a commission but actually by consignment to the grave—was the burning issue of how to reconcile the claims of national or regional autonomy with the determination of the Great Russian peasantry to sweep away all obstructions to a land reform based upon the centralistic, egalitarian principle of the redistribution of all the land among all the toilers.[69] These obstructions might spring from particularist tendencies, as in the Ukraine, or they might be rooted in sectional selfishness, as in Siberia, or in historic privileges,

[67] *Ibid.*, pp. 427, 442.
[68] See below, chap. X.
[69] *Tretii s"ezd P.S.-R.*, pp. 423, 425-26, 429. One notes the relish with which these Narodnik intellectuals (who at bottom were as nationalistic as only they could be) dwelt upon the people's impatience with minority rights, though it is quite likely that in this instance their emotions did not lead them astray in interpreting the popular will.

as in the Cossack lands. The words of Shvetsov,[70] spoken at the First Congress, came back to haunt the delegates at the Third, but they were as little ready as before to grapple with a problem that could cause "rivers of blood" to flow. Another "detail" that the delegates ducked was how to allay the tension between the communal peasants and the individual holders (otrubshchiki), who had taken advantage of the Stolypin legislation to go it alone; according to Rakitnikov, the former would not elect the latter to office even though both groups belonged to the same party.[71] The SR's, of course, preferred the communal peasants, but concerned as always for the unity of the class, they reaffirmed the right of individual as well as collective use of the land and promised not to disturb separate holdings that did not exceed the average allotment.[72] Otherwise they had no plan for healing the rift in the village or preventing the independents from being driven into the counterrevolutionary camp. One "detail" only did the members of the congress decide on the spot, and that was the perennial one of compensation; only three votes were cast in its favor after Rakitnikov had warned that the entire agitation of the party was predicated upon confiscation,[73] but in their hearts the Kadet-loving, all-for-war intellectuals who kept their silence on this occasion were still determined to grant some measure of compensation in order to preserve the "union of all vital forces."

As to the interim measures to be adopted before the Constituent Assembly, the congress had above everything else to decide on a formula that would preserve the land fund against the depredations of the peasants themselves. From encouraging seizures in 1905 the SR's had come to oppose them in 1917: the party was embarrassed by the ghost of its former self, and Rakitnikov, in a nauseous display of hypocrisy, attempted to explain the shift in tactics by the influence of the war, which had drained the village of its working strength and so had slaked the thirst for land (!), instead of honestly admitting that the mass of Narodnik intellectuals had grown older

[70] See chap. II.
[71] Tretii s"ezd P.S.-R., pp. 244-45.
[72] Ibid., pp. 245, 255-56.
[73] Ibid., pp. 430-31.

and more conservative, and that many of them had deserted the shrine of revolution to worship at the shrine of war. Rakitnikov's disbelief in his own explanation is shown by his assertion in one breath that the peasants were now willing to await the Constituent Assembly—a course the party always had favored, even when swept off its feet in 1905—and by his recognition in the next breath that "some action" had to be taken immediately to satisfy their demands. He proposed to stop somewhere between drastic diminution of property rights and the immediate confiscations which the party once had favored.[74]

The congress found the solution in condemning seizures while demanding that the entire land fund be committed to the management (*vedenie*) of the land committees which had been set up by Shingarev, Chernov's predecessor, and which were now to be made thoroughly democratic in order to give them authority in the eyes of the people and to enable them to perform their function of conserving the land fund, livestock, farm equipment, forests, and natural resources until the Constituent Assembly could work out the details of an equitable reform. The unanimity with which this decision was taken is surprising in view of the controversy over seizures at the Northern Regional Conference, where the left had strongly defended them if carried out in an "organized" manner, and had fought Chernov to a standstill over the issue.[75] But at the Third Congress it was silent on seizures. The atmosphere was chilling, it is true, but the left had never hesitated to fight against odds. All factions appear to have been so taken up with the war that they could not generate heat on other issues; the members of the congress plainly did not have their heart in the discussion of agrarian problems, and the commission entrusted with drafting the resolution did not even succeed in preserving a fixed personnel,[76] to say nothing of performing its work in a creditable manner. But if the intellectuals who ran this party were interested only in getting through to the Constituent Assembly, the peasants who constituted its following were deter-

[74] *Ibid.*, pp. 242-44.
[75] *Delo Naroda*, No. 56 (May 24, 1917).
[76] *Tretii s"ezd P.S.-R.*, p. 443.

mined to have action on the matter nearest their heart, and herein lay one of the reasons for the gradual loosening of bonds between the corps of party functionaries and the mass of their rural supporters.[77]

There was still a fourth problem that claimed the attention of the congress, and that was the future of the nationalities which fate had associated with or brought under the yoke of the Russian people; like the agrarian problem, it was shunted aside at the congress, but not before certain basic attitudes had been disclosed. M. V. Vishniak presented a report on the organization of the state, in which the nationalities problem figured prominently. After expressing the view that Russia should become a federal republic on the Swiss model[78] with a collegial executive instead of a president, since a personal symbol of power might serve as a rallying-point for monarchist sentiment,[79] the report went on to declare that this Russian republic should form a single state, a *Bundesstaat* instead of a *Staatenbund*, in which concessions to the various nationalities within the former empire would take the form of mutual agreements between the state as a whole and the parts concerned, never of unilateral decisions by the nationalities themselves.[80] The evolution of national autonomy

[77] For debate on the land question see *Tretii s"ezd P.S.-R.*, pp. 423-43 and *passim.*

[78] The American Constitution, it was asserted, could not possibly find support from a socialist party.

[79] Evidence of a second thought on the part of Populist intellectuals: their elders had extolled the collectivist proclivities of the peasantry; now they were betraying a certain lack of confidence in its elemental democracy.

[80] Vishniak told of an incident that had occurred recently in Penza province. There the Cheremis and other Finnish tribes had held a congress which proclaimed the absolute freedom of these peoples from any measure of outside control. To this the Russian peasants had replied: "If you are absolutely free, so let it be; but if you go to putting up customs barriers we will not recognize your absolute freedom any more than we recognized in the past the freedom of the landowners to do as they pleased" (*Tretii s"ezd P.S.-R.*, p. 309). The reference to customs barriers, a bête noire of the Populist intellectuals, arouses doubt whether the peasants were speaking for themselves or serving as mouthpieces for the intellectuals.

should always be encompassed within the bounds of federation, and should never be permitted to develop into separate statehood. After having thus subordinated the rights of the nationalities, Vishniak with true SR utopianism (he would prefer the term "optimism") proceeded to interpret those rights so broadly that the peoples concerned would inevitably have been tempted to strive for independence, and with some prospects of success: in the case of the Ukraine the report appears to have envisaged a separate coinage and postal system, and even homogeneous Ukrainian regiments, drawing the line only at the erection of tariff barriers.[81] A combination of the prevalent type of European chauvinism, buttressed by national regiments, with a denial of the right of formal independence could not have been better calculated to produce an explosion.

In one case only was independence to be conceded: that of Poland. The Finnish nation was not to be so honored. This glaring discrimination in favor of the hereditary enemy and against a people whose feud with Russia went back only to Alexander III and whose standards of morality, education, and cleanliness were the most elevated in the Russian Empire—higher than those of the Russians themselves and (to speak softly) by no means suffering in comparison with those of the Poles—seems to have troubled the conscience of the author of the report and ought to have troubled that of the assembled delegates a great deal more. Vishniak motivated the discrimination on three grounds: (1) the strategic interests of the Russian people would be impaired by a grant of independence to Finland; (2) territorial interests would be impaired; (3) such a concession to Finland would impart double the force to the separatist pretensions of other peoples than if they had only the Polish precedent to fall back upon. Now this is curious reasoning. To take (2) first, why were the frozen wastes of Lapland or perhaps the empty stretches of Karelia more vital to the territorial interests of Russia than the western borderlands, the status of which would assuredly have been disrupted by a free Poland, as the experience of 1830 and 1863 had shown?

[81] *Tretii s"ezd P.S.-R.*, pp. 291, 308. Kerenski would later agree to the formation of certain Ukrainian units in the army, thereby helping to bring down the first coalition. See below, pp. 275-76.

As to the third argument, if the arithmetic of separatism militated against more than a single grant of independence, why Polish rather than Finnish? Only (1) has any substance in the light of sober analysis: the separation of Vyborg province from the empire and the vulnerability of the approaches to St. Petersburg undoubtedly would pose a threat to the security of Russia.[82]

Legitimate concern for the fate of the capital in the light of war experience may, of course, account for the reversal of the earlier stand in favor of the unconditional right of national self-determination,[83] even in the case of a people who would seem to have had a better claim to independence than any other in the Russian empire. But one cannot be sure. Something else may have been involved, something that could be thought of but never voiced in public. When he was pointedly asked why Polish independence but not Finnish, Vishniak had replied with (3) above. The shallowness of his answer requires no comment, and suggests that we must look deeper into the soul of the right SR's. In a sense Populism and Pan-Slavism were branches of the same plant of Slavophilism. Sharing a common origin, they had a certain affinity. In the years of friendship with France and estrangement from Germany a pro-Polish cult had sprung up in Russia, extending from the Nationalists and right-wing Kadets such as Rodichev, who were chauvinists to the marrow of their bone, through intermediate groups into the right wing of the PSR, which Tsereteli has so aptly described as consisting of "Kadets in disguise."[84] About Breshkovskaia there can be no doubt, and, as we have seen, Vishniak and his colleagues of the hidden right differed in no essential respect from the *Volia Naroda* group of Argunov and Breshkovskaia. Now the Poles were a Slavic people and, moreover, hostile to Germany, the bête noire of the Francophile Populist intellectuals. The Finns, on the other hand, lived in the orbit of Scandinavian and so of Teutonic civilization, and were suspected, not without reason, of being pro-German. Hence in the eyes of these Populist intellectuals they may have become—to bor-

---

[82] For Vishniak report, see *Tretii s"ezd P.S.-R.*, pp. 274-94, 305-10, 490-92.
[83] See chap. II.
[84] Interview in New York (December 23, 1949).

row a puerile phrase from the American public—a "bad people" and unworthy of being elevated to the same level as the brother Poles.

But the Socialist Revolutionary party did not consist exclusively of Francophile Populist intellectuals. Far from it. The whole core of the party, the right center proper under Gotz as well as the left center under Chernov, not to speak of the left itself, held faithfully to the internationalist line and recognized no distinctions among peoples, as demonstrated by the preamble to the resolution on war. Why, then, did the party congress approve Vishniak's theses "in general" and refer them to the Central Committee?[85] Probably for the same reasons that caused it to slight the agrarian problem: haste and preoccupation with other matters. Otherwise it is incredible that a political movement which prided itself on its belief in the brotherhood of nations would have sanctioned even indirectly so flagrant an act of discrimination.

While it would be unfair to attribute the bias of the right to the whole party, it is true that the SR's as a group interpreted the principle of national self-determination in a narrower sense than in 1905. According to Alekseev of Kharkov (L), party members seeking to circumscribe the concept of federalism abounded.[86] Another delegate volunteered the startling information that at the last conference (apparently the Sixth Party Council of April 30) the very principle of self-determination had not passed unchallenged, the proponents of a centralized republic being so numerous as almost to constitute a majority in favor of excluding the nationalities question from the agenda.[87] Inadequate as was the discussion of the problem at the congress, it was easy to detect an undercurrent of feeling indubitably hostile to the dissolution of the imperial entity. Not only was this true of Vishniak and the right but it was also true of Chernov and his group on the left. The acid test came over the procedure to be followed in meeting national claims: should each people be free to formulate its will in a constituent assembly of its own, submitting the result to the federal authority for inclusion in some crazy quilt

[85] *Tretii s"ezd P.S.-R.*, p. 311.
[86] *Ibid.*, p. 413.
[87] *Ibid.*, pp. 303-4.

of union or perhaps none at all, or should the All-Russian Constituent Assembly first trace the bounds within which the regional or national assemblies would do their work? Chernov clearly indicated that the party would champion the second course, and his words were acclaimed by the delegate from Kiev as a blow to Ukrainian separatism.[88] Only the extreme left was prepared to contemplate a dissolution of the bonds of union; the bulk of the party held the view that supreme authority emanated from the will of the people as expressed in the All-Russian Constituent Assembly, through the gates of which every arrangement for national or regional autonomy would have to pass. Whether even Vishniak's Poland would have gotten through those gates is a moot question. The SR's proposed to put their program through the assembly in agreement with kindred national socialist parties,[89] blithely ignoring the fact that the largest of those parties, the Ukrainian SR's, was preparing to assert the sovereignty of the Ukrainian Constituent Assembly. With everything pointing to a clash between mother and daughter, the SR's stubbornly closed their eyes to the facts of life and persisted in thinking that they could count on the Ukrainian SR's to help enact a program that was the primary source of trouble between them. As it turned out, the Bolsheviks destroyed parliamentary government and made it unnecessary for the SR's to see things as they were.

The proceedings of the Third Congress are more important for the attitudes revealed than for the resolutions adopted, because these latter were either so sketchy or so weighted with compromise as to be of little help to the members in steering a course past the reefs of the revolution. It was also the function of the congress to choose a

---

[88] *Ibid.*, pp. 408-9, 412.

[89] *Ibid.*, pp. 481-82. A report dealing with the theoretical aspects of the nationalities problem had been presented by N. V. Briullova-Shaskolskaia, so abstruse and high-flown as to be devoid of significance. The same can be said of the loosely drawn resolution based upon it and adopted virtually without opposition (*ibid.*, p. 426). Much more can be learned from Vishniak's report and the brief remarks of the delegates.

steering committee, and none of its actions proved more fateful for the party's future than the election of the twenty members and five alternates who composed the Central Committee.

The election was accompanied by a major scandal which rocked the party to its foundations. We shall first note the results of the election and the character of the new executive organ, and then proceed to the scandal.

The twenty-five victorious candidates with the votes they received and the symbols[90] of their factional allegiance were:[91]

Central Committee Members	Votes	Allegiance
Gotz, Abram Rafailovich	260	RC
Rakitnikov, Nicholas Ivanovich	258	LC
Arkhangelski, Vasili Gavrilovich	241	RRC
Rusanov, Andrew Iosifovich	241	LC
Chernov, Victor Mikhailovich	240	LC
Vedeniapin, M. A.	237	uncertain
Rosenblum (Firsov), Dmitri Samoilovich	224	RC
Natanson, Mark Andreevich	207	L
Lunkevich, Valerian Viktorovich	202	LC
Gendelman, Michael Iakovlevich	201	RC
Richter, Vladimir Nikolaevich	199	LC
Gerstein, Lev Nikolaevich	193	LC
Zenzinov, Vladimir Mikhailovich	181	RC
Zatonski, Michael Petrovich	177	RC
Avksentiev, Nicholas Dmitrievich	168	RRC
Minor, Osip Solomonovich	157	uncertain
Rubanovich, Ilia Adolfovich	156	uncertain
Fondaminski (Bunakov), Ilia Isidorovich	153	RRC
Rakov, Dmitri Fedorovich	146	LC
Prilezhaev, I. A.	142	uncertain
Alternates	*Votes*	*Allegiance*
Teterkin, I. I.	206	LC
Berg, E. S.	201	RC
Khovrin, A. A.	130	RC
Bykhovski, Naum Iakovlevich	126	RC
Gurevich, Vissarion Iakovlevich	119	RC

[90] See above, p. 198, n. 41.
[91] Izbiratel'naia statistika (an analysis and comparison of the results of the elections of the Central Committee at both the Third and Fourth Congresses, prepared by Chernov in the form of an appendix to the official minutes of the Central Committee; manuscript); *Tretii s"ezd P.S.-R.*, pp. 373-74.

On the supreme organ of a party that prided itself on being the expression of the will of rural Russia there were nineteen intellectuals, one workingman (Zatonski or "Batrak"), and not a single peasant. This was not due, of course, to any prejudice on the part of the intellectuals who composed the congress for their own kind, but to the age-old character of the peasantry, which had caused it always to be dominated and usually victimized by smaller and more articulate groups. Natural as this circumstance was, however, it was also unfortunate, for if it had been feasible to have some authentic sons of the soil on this committee, the direction of party affairs might not have become divorced from the realities of the situation, and the policymakers would have been under less of an illusion as to the temper of the inchoate but seething mass of the people. In view of the prominence of the Jewish question in the revolution, it may be pointed out that eight of the twenty committeemen belonged to that community, a disproportionate number of Jews, though not a majority. Members of the party have told this writer that, in keeping with the spirit of other socialist parties, no attention was paid to ethnic or national origins and that Jews and Gentiles felt as one.

The outstanding feature of the election had been the large amount of voting in the dark. In this respect the SR's had to pay the penalty for an organizational hiatus of ten years, during which they had lost touch with one another and particularly with the rising generation. When they met again in Moscow in 1917, it was largely as strangers, and delegates voted for a man on the strength of his reputation rather than because of his qualifications, or because they were acquainted with his present attitude and found it congenial to theirs. The result was that in many cases they got what they did not want. Chief sufferers from the confusion were the more impulsive radicals of the left, on whose list of recommended candidates could be found no less than seven names to the right of center and no more than four of truly leftist persuasion. On the other hand, the more sophisticated partisans of the right managed to keep their list free of names to the left of center except in three instances. The centrist list was a hodgepodge of one leftist, half a dozen left-centrists, and thirteen individuals who in one degree or another stood to the right of center—

further confirmation of our view that Chernov had only a minority in his own caucus. The centrist list naturally commanded maximum support since it was a morass of compromise and overlapped with the extremist slates on both sides; only two men on it failed of election. Candidates put up by the right alone could not make the grade (Argunov, Rudnev), nor could those who figured only on the leftist slate (Kamkov, Spiridonova—the lady's name, significantly enough, had been advanced by sailor delegates[92]). As to the candidates of the center, the only clear-cut voting came in connection with names prominently identified with one or the other side of the war controversy: thus the right quite obviously refused to vote for Chernov and the left cut Avksentiev, Rubanovich, and Fondaminski, the spread between the vote in question and that for the high man (Gotz) providing a quite accurate indication of the strength of the faction involved.[93] The ticklish problem presented by the "grandmother of the revolution" was deftly disposed of by making Breshkovskaia an honorary member of the Central Committee by acclamation.

The Central Committee chosen by the Third Congress to preside over the destinies of the party during the six most fateful months of its existence consisted of eight members standing to the right of center, eight to the left of center, and four of uncertain tendency. But owing to the fact that these waverers came down more often on the right side than on the left, the committee was characterized during the whole period of its existence by a list to the right. When the alternates were later brought into the committee, the list was accentuated, and Gotz's dominant personality clinched the ascendancy of the more conservative wing of the party. The only member

[92] *Tretii s"ezd P.S.-R.*, p. 368.

[93] Chernov ran 20 votes behind Gotz and the cumulative evidence of events at the congress is that the hard core of rightist strength was about 25. Avksentiev received 92 votes fewer than Gotz; the extreme and moderate left had mustered 87 votes in support of an armistice and could be expected to coalesce again in opposition to so prominent an advocate of war. Balloting for the Central Committee were 270 delegates—the maximum number of votes cast at the congress. These calculations are directly confirmed by Kogan-Bernstein, who placed the strength of the left at one third of the congress. See his article, "O partiinom s"ezde" (On the Party Congress), *Zemlia i Volia* (Petrograd), No. 68 (June 15, 1917).

Gotz could not dominate was Natanson, and he was isolated within the committee. As for Chernov, he had freed himself from the clutches of Natanson only to fall into those of Gotz. Despite the difference in viewpoint he could not bring himself to pose clear-cut alternatives to the policies preferred by Gotz; as one observer has so aptly expressed it, Chernov did not struggle against his party's dominant faction so much as he intrigued against it.[94] Yet at the same time Gotz and his associates found it impossible to steer a resolutely conservative course with a man of Chernov's reputation brooding on the sidelines and two fifths of the committee ready to follow his lead—if ever he should decide to lead. The vagaries of the waverers, and the fluctuating composition of the committee as a result of the call of duty elsewhere, led to unsettled conditions and sometimes produced majorities so slender as to rob decisions of a morally binding effect; the majorities themselves were not stable, and one session might undo the work of another of different complexion on the pretext of "revising" a previously adopted decision. The Central Committee was hard pushed to maintain discipline in its own midst, to say nothing of maintaining it in the party at large.[95]

Twenty men of greater or lesser prominence had been chosen as party directors, but the most prominent man of all had been denied that honor. The story of Kerenski's defeat at the Third Congress, in a wide-open split by a two-vote margin, has never been fully understood, and was soon forgotten in the onrushing tide of revolutionary developments—except in party circles; there it was remembered clearly and vividly. Kerenski's position inside the party did not correspond to his position in public life, even in the heyday of his fame. His aloofness from partisan ties in the past caused him to be re-

[94] Stankevich, *Vospominaniia*, p. 279.

[95] Chernov, Izbiratel'naia statistika (Election Statistics); Chernov, manuscript commentary on the minutes of the Central Committee, pp. 3-4, 65; Chernov, manuscript of chapter Partiia S.-R.; *Kratkii otchët o rabotakh chetvërtago s"ezda P.S.-R.*, pp. 44-45, 90-91; details of the inner organization of the committee in *Delo Naroda*, No. 73 (June 13, 1917).

garded as a fair-weather adherent, as one who claimed equal recognition with the old-guard leaders without having compiled any comparable record of service—in short, as a recruit who would be a general. This attitude found expression in Kogan-Bernstein's denial of immunity from criticism to "leaders who had comparatively recently entered the party."[96] Kerenski could have perhaps lessened the hostility to his person by showing some deference to partisan sentiment, but he pursued just the opposite course, stressing at every opportunity the nonpartisan aspects of his office and even going so far as to declare, before the Petersburg Soviet on May 22, that "parties do not exist for me at present because I am a Russian minister; for me only the people exist and one sacred law—to obey the majority will."[97] On party members imbued with a sectarian spirit such words made a bad impression; to revolutionists they smacked of nationalism, class conciliation, an all-for-war approach, perhaps even of Bonapartism. It was not Kerenski's nonpartisanship so much as his championship of war to a victorious conclusion at the side of the French and British imperialists which earned him the enmity of the left SR's. As Kamkov said, they simply could not stomach such utterances of the war minister as the one about "liberty being brought on the point of bayonets."[98] At the Northern Regional Conference Gotz had found it a thankless task to defend Kerenski before the most radical constituency in Russia,[99] and by the time of the congress the left was boiling mad at Kerenski.[100]

In addressing the congress, Kerenski made no effort to conceal

[96] *Tretii s"ezd P.S.-R.*, p. 79.
[97] *Delo Naroda*, No. 56 (May 24, 1917). See also Shliapnikov, *Semnadtsatyi god*, III, 224, where Kerenski is quoted as telling the All-Russian Soviet Conference that he had consciously put aside partisan considerations in performing the duties of his office.
[98] *Tretii s"ezd P.S.-R.*, p. 200.
[99] *Delo Naroda*, No. 57 (May 25, 1917). The report has Gotz making a frankly apologetic speech. At the congress he charged it had been garbled beyond recognition (*Tretii s"ezd P.S.-R.*, p. 201), but it seems unlikely that the central organ, which followed the line of Chernov rather than that of the extremists, would have willfully distorted his remarks; more likely is it that Gotz, in the chameleon fashion of politicians, had adapted his tone to his audience and gone further in placating the left than he had really desired to do.
[100] Chernov, manuscript of chapter Partiia S.-R.

his nonpartisan approach. It was hard for him to take part in routine political activities, he told the delegates, hard even to give the impression of partisanship, for he had entered the cabinet in the name of the whole democracy and must strive to incorporate in his person the interests of the whole democracy.[101] The left began to snipe at him and asked whether he represented the party in the government, and whether he considered the sanction of the congress essential to his ministerial career. The first time the baited man snapped back that an answer was superfluous, since he was at the congress; prodded again, he observed that the same query should be addressed to other members of the congress—a dig at Chernov.[102] This exchange illustrates Kerenski's uncomfortable position in the party of his nominal affiliation and the outright hostility of a very considerable section of party opinion. But the left did not control the congress, and the general expectation was that Kerenski would be named to the Central Committee.

At the evening session of June 1 the stage was set for the election of the committee. The three factions had caucused separately to discuss candidacies and to draw up rival slates for submission to the plenary session. In all probability the centrist ticket would prevail and the rival slates be successful only in those cases where the candidate had also been picked by the center. Kerenski's name was on the center's list. Things were proceeding in a cut-and-dried fashion when Dekonski, delegate of the extreme left and protégé of Maria Spiridonova, arose to announce that word had just been received of a new decree issued by the war minister which rendered him unfit to sit on the party's executive organ. For Dekonski's zeal there was a special reason: he had been an *agent provocateur* of the tsarist police and now, like a cat, was busily engaged in covering up his traces.[103] Since the rules prohibited discussion of individual candidacies on the floor of the plenum, he moved their suspension to permit consideration of the new development. The congress lost all semblance of order. In the ensuing bedlam Chernov made his way to the platform to protest against the extension of electioneering to

---

[101] *Tretii s"ezd P.S.-R.*, p. 103.
[102] *Ibid.*, pp. 128-29.
[103] He would be unmasked in October.

the hall of the plenum; at the same time he suggested that the best way out of the impasse might be to read without comment the decree in question, since so many of the delegates, including himself, had no knowledge of its contents. While the congress was voting to follow his lead in both respects, Chernov took over the duties of presiding officer, partly because he had a powerful voice, partly because Chairman Rakitnikov had just committed his second parliamentary blunder of the evening.[104] Once in the chair, Chernov took up a newspaper and read the text of the offending decree, which sought to check the epidemic of desertions at the front by pointedly reminding the troops that the law of tsarist times authorizing the infliction of the most drastic punishment in such cases had not been repealed and hence was still in effect. This intimation that the death penalty could be imposed for desertion was certainly a mild action (the death penalty was not actually being imposed) by the standards of any other belligerent power—including the American democracy, now embarking on its holy crusade—but somehow it produced on the left SR's the effect a red flag has on an Andalusian bull. This they never forgot and never forgave.[105]

No discussion of the decree or of Kerenski's responsibility was permitted. The congress proceeded to ballot on the names before it, and that same evening it became known that, whereas Abram Gotz had received 260 votes out of 270 to lead the parade of victorious candidates, the minister of war had failed of election, 134 votes being cast in his favor and 136 against.[106] For the left it was sweet revenge, for Kerenski, an unprecedented humiliation, the first set-

---

[104] It should be noted that the motion to read the decree, submitted in writing by some person other than Chernov, had been entertained by the chair before Chernov occupied it. The latter had merely lent the weight of his authority to this procedure, though whether his suggestion or the written motion came first is not clear.

[105] Chernov, "Istorik ili isterik?", *Volia Rossii* (Prague), III (1925), 96-98; *Tretii s"ezd P.S.-R.*, pp. 365-66.

[106] *Volia Naroda*, No. 30 (June 3, 1917). No attribute of the SR's is more provoking than their ostrich-like attitude toward a scandal; it is characteristic that the minutes of the congress suppress as much of this painful incident as possible, omitting even the vote by which Kerenski failed of election. The *Delo Naroda* is no better. The bleating cry for harmony constrained even the left to adopt a shush-shush attitude: the Petersburg *Zemlia i Volia* printed none of the interesting byplay accompanying the choice of the Central Committee (see No. 60 [June 6, 1917]).

back in his rapid ascent to fame. The whole anomaly of his position within the party was laid bare for the country to see.

The news of his defeat hit the "defensist" element like a thunderbolt, and no amount of reassurance that many had voted against him because the pressure of official duties would leave him no time for party affairs removed the sting of this signal reverse. In the fevered imagination of these people the whole war effort had sustained a setback, not because of the war weariness of the Russian people which had crept into a party congress—that they would never admit —but simply because of intrigue and the machinations of irresponsible elements. Desperately they cast about for some means of retrieving the situation: it was suggested that Chernov should resign from the committee so that neither minister would be on it and the country could be told that the SR's were opposed on principle to having cabinet members as party directors.[107] The sessions were interrupted and the congress broke up into groups holding private conferences. It is not possible to look behind the scenes as the SR's strove to bury their scandal. But on the following day, to give satisfaction to Kerenski's friends, the congress went into executive session, and Chernov made a statement acknowledging that he was equally responsible with Kerenski and the other ministers for the tsarist statute remaining on the books, and that it was a gross injustice to use this as a political weapon against Kerenski. The right had prepared a paper criticizing the composition of the congress, which it desired to have read in open session, but owing to the inadvertence (?) of the presiding officer (Chernov), it was read at the close of the executive session and permission to have it included in the minutes was refused on the ground that it might discredit the work of the congress.[108] Thus we are denied knowledge of a document that may have been one-sided but could not have failed to be interesting. The resolution adopted by the congress specifically approving the min-

[107] Maria Ancharova, "Vseros. s"ezd partii sotsialistov-revoliutsionerov" (All-Russian Congress of the Socialist Revolutionary Party), *Rech'*, No. 130 (June 6, 1917). Even the Constitutional Democratic organ gives less scandal than could have been hoped for, probably in order not to offend a partner in coalition.

[108] *Tretii s"ezd P.S.-R.*, pp. 444-47.

isterial assignments of Kerenski and Chernov[109] seems to have been a further attempt to allay the rancor of Kerenski's friends.[110] And there the matter rested. Ostensibly because of alleged irregularities, the right wanted to annul the election and do the whole thing over again,[111] but this it was unable to bring about. The minister of agriculture stayed on the Central Committee while the minister of war and future premier was denied that honor.[112]

It was in the nature of things that the disgruntlement of Kerenski's friends should focus upon V. M. Chernov. He had succeeded where their idol had failed; his views on the war had always been poison to the "defensists"—had he not told the congress that never, never would he say with some that everything must be laid on the altar of war?[113]—and in the circumstances of Kerenski's defeat there was much that suggested his fine Italian hand. The extreme and moderate left together did not have the strength to keep Kerenski off the committee; the marginal votes could come only from the decomposition of the center, which was backing Kerenski. And the center did go to pieces, for the second time at this congress. As 136 delegates had voted against him, and as the leftist strength did not exceed 90, it is obvious that about fifty votes had come out of the center to insure his defeat, or just about the number which constituted the hard core of Chernov's following. Had these left-centrists moved virtually as one man as the result of fifty individual decisions or had they gotten a cue from their leader? It looked suspicious, to say the least. The enmity that developed between Chernov and Kerenski was poison for the PSR and water on the Bolshevik mill; the question is, how far back did it go, and was it active on June 1, 1917?

As so often happens when personalities are involved, the sources

[109] See above, p. 212.

[110] Volia Naroda, No. 31 (June 4, 1917); Ancharova, "Vseros. s"ezd P.S.-R.," Rech', No. 130 (June 6, 1917). According to these sources the general resolution on coalition was also motivated by such considerations, but because of the time element involved, this would not appear to be correct.

[111] Tretii s"ezd P.S.-R., pp. 377, 468.

[112] Ibid., pp. 371 ff., 382-83, 416; Chernov, "Istorik ili isterik?", Volia Rossii, III (1925), 99.

[113] Tretii s"ezd P.S.-R., pp. 192-93.

contradict one another, and there can be no certainty as to the feelings of the two men on the eve of that fateful day. A. A. Argunov told this author with impressive sincerity that Chernov had conceived a dislike for Kerenski from the very start, referring to him as a "talented novice."[114] Against this must be placed the testimony of Chernov himself, who says that at first both he and the younger Gotz were well disposed toward Kerenski, seeing in him a fresh and vital personality whose mass appeal could be turned to account by the party. They thought to put his popularity beyond the reach of fortune's perversities by signing with his hands the decree safeguarding the land fund against dissipation, thereby linking his name inseparably with the aspirations of the peasantry. Another source states that Chernov also hoped to use Kerenski's influence to advance the cause of peace by having the soviet under his presidency demand that the Provisional Government address a note to the Allies calling on them to institute peace negotiations.[115] Only when it became apparent that Kerenski would do nothing to alienate the good will which he likewise enjoyed among the propertied elements of Russian society did Chernov abandon hope of using him to promote revolutionary policies, but there was nothing in the way of a rupture and Chernov's attitude could be described as one of disillusionment rather than hostility. Chernov continued to cooperate with Kerenski on lesser matters, even going so far as to write for him the letter designed to put in order his relations with the party.[116] Chernov argues with much plausibility that people wished to read the feud that later developed back into this period, creating the legend that relations had always been bad and that Chernov had engineered Kerenski's defeat at the congress.[117]

Yet it is undeniable that the barometer of their relations was already falling. In part this was due to honest differences of opinion. The two men agreed on nothing, neither on the war, nor on the army, nor on coalition, nor on interim measures to tide the country over till the Constituent Assembly. Each had a different concept as

[114] Interview in Prague (June, 1935).
[115] Sukhanov, Zapiski, III, 150.
[116] See preceding chapter.
[117] Manuscript of chapter Partiia S.-R.

to how the other should run his ministry: Kerenski felt that the land office should leave the agrarian problem to the assembly, and Chernov wanted the war ministry to make the army safely republican and revolutionary. Whereas Kerenski came to stress more and more his nonpartisanship, Chernov remained as always the perfect party patriot. In part the trouble was due to a personal element. A British minister once said that socialism has not abolished geography; neither has it abolished human nature. Argunov thought that Kerenski loomed as a serious rival to Chernov in the party,[118] and both had, in fact, become symbols around which rival factions could gather. Chernov may well have envied Kerenski his popularity in the country as well as his devoted following among the SR's, just as Kerenski could envy him his hold on other, and larger, elements of party opinion as well as his intellectual domination of the neo-Populist movement. Whether two such luminaries could be contained in one party had become a question the acuteness of which might have been lessened by the reflection that neither wielded as much influence in this organization as Abram Gotz. Finally, a part of the mischief must be attributed to the bourgeois press, which played up the differences of the two men in order to drive a wedge between them.

But on the surface of things Chernov leaned over backwards at the congress to avoid any appearance of hostility toward his colleague. He took cognizance of the maneuvers of the bourgeois press and denounced them for what they were; he reproved the tendency in leftist circles, where he still was highly respected, to carp at each chance phrase which Kerenski let fall in the performance of his onerous duties[119]—as the spokesman of the left later exclaimed, it had been "the rare good fortune of A. F. Kerenski to find such a champion."[120] The initiative in bringing up the subject of the decree which proved Kerenski's undoing had been that of the extreme left, and the only possible blame attaching to Chernov would come from his suggestion that the decree should be read without comment. Yet his explanation that he honestly believed this to be the best way out

[118] Interview in Prague (June, 1935).
[119] "Istorik ili isterik?", *Volia Rossii*, III (1925), 100; *Tretii s"ezd P.S.-R.*, pp. 192-93; see also Kerenski's remarks on the press campaign (*Tretii s"ezd P.S.-R.*, pp. 121-22).
[120] *Tretii s"ezd P.S.-R.*, p. 200.

of a situation not of his making is at least a plausible one.[121] In taking the chair and reading the decree he had done nothing more than carry out the will of the congress. And at the executive session he had undertaken the defense of his colleague by showing the responsibility of the whole cabinet and shouldering a share of the blame himself.

Of course, as his detractors have claimed, Chernov could have preserved an innocent front while readying the knife in the darkness, using the left SR's as his agents and supplementing his backstage campaign by a seemingly innocuous suggestion on the floor of the congress calculated to impose a fateful handicap upon Kerenski's candidacy. Then, when his purpose had been achieved, he could rise in the post-mortem executive session and play the magnanimous colleague. These were the lines along which the enraged "defensists" were thinking. But the most sensational as well as specific and damning charges were preferred by Kerenski himself, several months later, when events had blown the lid off the SR pot. According to Kerenski, Chernov had deliberately concealed from the congress his own presence and Kerenski's absence at the cabinet meeting at which the decree on desertions had been approved.[122] Chernov said nothing. He allowed the wound to fester and only years later, in a second exile, did he break his long silence to state that, whether because the decree had been considered in the "inner cabinet" (*malyi sovet*) alone, or because the full cabinet had taken it up in his absence, he had learned of it for the first time that evening as a result of Dekonski's action; in his speech in defense of Kerenski before the executive session he had purposely refrained from saying anything about this because the discipline of the Provisional Government forbade the airing in public of differences among its members. Later on, he adds, he learned that Kerenski likewise had had no prior knowledge of the decree.[123] It is clear, therefore, that Kerenski is guiltless in this matter, if, indeed, there had ever been any question of guilt on the part of a war minister who advised deserters that they *could* be shot. It is less clear that Chernov is guiltless. Things may have been as he

---

[121] "Istorik ili isterik?", *Volia Rossii*, III (1925), 98.
[122] *Volia Naroda*, No. 110 (September 5, 1917).
[123] "Istorik ili isterik?", *Volia Rossii*, III (1925), 99n. Bitter polemics with S. Melgunov impelled Chernov to make this statement.

represented them, but his weakness was such that he could have been present at a cabinet session where decisions personally displeasing to him were adopted without any dissent on his part, simply because of his isolation and because a firmer man like Tsereteli, whose lead he would follow, had not chosen to make a stand.

To the criticism that his statement on behalf of Kerenski the day after the election was only an empty gesture, and that it would have had to be made before the balloting if he had really desired to save the situation, Chernov replied by citing his earlier speech at the congress in refutation of Kerenski's critics and by disclosing that he had frequently gone to the left-wing caucus to assume the burden of his colleague's defense against the violent attacks there being made upon him.[124] There are no records of this caucus, and an effort to verify Chernov's assertions by consulting I. Z. Steinberg, the only left SR leader available, had no conclusive result.[125]

Where truth lies in this matter, and where error or falsehood, is not to be decided many years later, after the course of history has set a heavy gravestone over the issues and personalities involved. Suffice it to say that Kerenski was convinced that his party comrade and colleague in the cabinet had intrigued against him to produce this humiliation, and that wounded pride as well as personal inclination confirmed him in his nonpartisanship, loosened the never more than tenuous bonds that connected him with this organization, and made him less than ever willing to heed its injunctions in shaping the policies of the Provisional Government. Within the organization itself, the affair deepened the ideological and tactical cleavage already existing by injecting an element of personal bitterness into the relations of the two most prominent members of the party and their devoted followings.

As though to round out a record of leaving undone the things that would have brought order into party affairs and of doing the things that threw them into disarray, the Third Congress adjourned with-

[124] *Ibid.*, pp. 100-1.
[125] Interview in New York (December, 1949).

out action on the organizational problem. In fact, it did not even come to the matter until the last session, after many of the delegates had already departed and the rest were preparing to leave; in view of the obvious indisposition to grapple with so serious a problem, the congress decided to leave the drafting of a provisional statute on membership to the forthcoming party council, in the meantime recommending observance, when feasible, of the old provisional code of 1907. Ten years of enforced idleness had not sufficed to work out the rules of membership, and six months later, when the Fourth Congress convened, the party was still without any statute, either permanent or provisional, since the intervening party council, to which the agrarian problem had also been referred, had dealt with neither land nor organization but solely with war. Some members of the Third Congress could already discern where this buck-passing was leading, and begged for some standard to go by in determining membership: their prayer went unheeded, and chaos continued.[126]

How bad it was can be seen in the way members were recruited in a village near Moscow. There an SR organizer would ask:

"Are you a peasant?"

"Yes, a peasant."

"Do you want land?"

"Yes, I do."

"Then join our party."

"But I believe I prefer the Bolsheviks," the prospect would sometimes answer.[127]

"Then go with them, but in that case you won't get any land."[128] Not once did a reference to the party program or an attempt to explain its meaning relieve the monotony of this primitive ritual. At a peasants' meeting in Klimenkova village, Voronezh province, on May 19 all thirty-nine of those present became members of the party, simply by paying the initial fee of fifty kopecks.[129] Perhaps this procedure sheds some light on the swollen membership in the fertile

[126] *Tretii s"ezd P.S.-R.*, pp. 449-54.
[127] Bolshevism was prevalent in the partially industrialized countryside around Moscow.
[128] *Ot fevralia k oktiabriu v Moskve*, pp. 258-59.
[129] *1917i god v Voronezhskoi gubernii*, p. 44.

black-earth province, reputed to have been in excess of 100,000.[130] Elsewhere the practice appears to have been even cruder, and the population—presumably adult—of entire villages was enrolled in the organization; a southwestern regional conference in Kiev complained that under such conditions not only nonrevolutionary but even non-democratic elements had managed to worm their way into the party.[131]

In the cities, where, surprisingly enough, a large proportion of the membership was concentrated, recruiting was on a higher plane, though even there it could not be termed satisfactory. The old rule had been that a person must be recommended by someone already a member and then be confirmed by vote of the group or cell; in very few places was this practice still observed.[132] The St. Petersburg organization at first considered anyone a member who declared himself an SR and paid the initial fee. Such a person could be challenged as unsuitable by someone already in, but otherwise there was no way of sifting candidacies. Later on, in an effort to prevent the accumulation of more dead wood, the necessity of a recommendation was restored in the case of candidates whose occupation did not enable them to pass through a qualifying stage of affiliation with some ancillary organization of an industrial or professional character; but even in these instances it was deemed impractical to test the candidates' understanding of the SR program and principles.[133] Whether any improvement resulted may be doubted. Everywhere there seems to have been a gross disparity between enrolled and active membership. In Petersburg a few score, or at best a few hundred, of the thousands of members inscribed on the rolls attended district meetings, and it is estimated that at least half the membership had lapsed into inactivity.[134] In the black-earth farming center of Morshansk less than a dozen of the sixty-odd members fulfilled their

---

[130] Alekseev, *Oktiabr' i grazhdanskaia voina v TsChO*, p. 38.
[131] *Volia Naroda*, No. 16 (May 17, 1917); see also O. L. Chizhikov, "V derevne" (In the Village), *Delo Naroda*, No. 105 (July 20, 1917).
[132] The Iakutsk organization still observed it. See *Volia Naroda*, No. 80 (August 1, 1917).
[133] L. Zeiman, "Po voprosam organizatsionnago stroitel'stva" (Problems in Building an Organization), *Partiinyia Izvestiia*, No. 2 (October 5, 1917), pp. 5-7.
[134] *Ibid.*

obligations,[135] while in the Crimean resort town of Yalta only 154 of the 800 enrollees paid the July levy of one inflated ruble.[136] No wonder the party authorities had decided not to take the variously computed and largely meaningless figures of membership as the basis for distributing seats at the congress.[137]

In Russia in 1917 there was talk of the PSR having a million members. The SR's themselves claimed one hundred thousand in the central black-earth province of Voronezh,[138] with perhaps as many more in the Volga black-earth province of Samara.[139] If the party fathers knew the total membership, they never disclosed it in print or orally to this author, and if they buried it in the archives, then it perished with the archives. The only total ever announced was 22,696 as of July 1, 1917, but this was a ridiculous figure, based upon reports from less than 30 percent of the organizations[140] and not even including the one in St. Petersburg, which alone in that month accounted for 35,000.[141] The fact that only 123 of the 436 locals had complied with the Central Committee's instructions to send in reports, and that among the delinquents was St. Petersburg, the premier organization of the country and the place where the reports were being received and the Central Committee was sitting, is in itself a sufficient commentary on the state of affairs in this party. Straggling reports made at other times furnish a considerable body of statistics on membership, though far from complete and of questionable accuracy. Exact figures are available for only two provinces: there were 268 SR's in Olonets and 2,673 in Vitebsk. For a number of others round figures are given: thus Archangel had 600 party members, Vologda 3,000, Astrakhan 3,000, Tomsk 15,000, Tula 18,000. Certain parts of provinces reported very large totals, as 35,000 for the

[135] Partiinyia Izvestiia, No. 5 (January 20, 1918), pp. 59-60.
[136] Ibid., No. 3 (October 19, 1917), p. 44.
[137] See above, p. 187.
[138] Alekseev, Oktiabr' i grazhdanskaia voina v TsChO, p. 38. A provincial party congress reported this figure.
[139] Leikina, "Oktiabr' po Rossii" (October in Russia), Proletarskaia Revoliutsiia, XLIX (II, 1926), 213-14. No source is given for this estimate.
[140] "Partiinaia zhizn'" (Party Life), Partiinyia Izvestiia, No. 3 (October 19, 1917), pp. 21-24.
[141] Delo Naroda, No. 99 (July 13, 1917).

Taganrog district of the Taurida and 16,264 for portions of the Bakhmut district of Ekaterinoslav province. If it were possible to add up figures for the whole country a total of a million members might well be the result.[142]

But enough has been said to discredit such paper strength. The methods of computing membership differed widely from locality to locality and the figures cited almost certainly do not represent any sorting of active and nominal members, even where relatively high standards of admission were observed. A comparison of the figures discloses their dubious validity: for example, the Taganrog local, which never made any particular mark in SR affairs, claimed a membership of 7,000[143] as against 3,000 returned by the robust organization in Kharkov, a much larger city.[144] Here is where the Third Congress should have stepped in to establish a common denominator as a means of ascertaining the true strength of the party, but this it notably failed to do. Certainly a huge number of individuals affiliated with the PSR in 1917—many to fall away almost immediately—but the conversion of this raw intake into finished fuel for the SR power machine demanded a refining process that was beyond the capacity of the leaders either to work out or to apply.

Viewed from any angle, the Third Congress had been a dismal failure. It had blazed no trail through the maze of difficulties and the need for decisions besetting the party as it grappled with the questions of the hour, or through the tactical situations that arise in the course of a revolution; the questions of war and peace and the construction of power it had muffled in compromise, and those of land and nationalities it had simply shunted aside. Where solutions

---

[142] These figures are taken from reports in the periodical devoted to party life, a very rare publication entitled *Partiinyia Izvestiia*, and more particularly from No. 1 (September 28, 1917), pp. 18 ff.; No. 2 (October 5, 1917), pp. 49-50; No. 3 (October 19, 1917), pp. 35 ff.; No. 5 (January 20, 1918), pp. 56, 59-60. See also *Delo Naroda, passim.*

[143] *Partiinyia Izvestiia,* No. 1 (September 28, 1917), p. 22.

[144] *Protokoly pervago s"ezda P.L.S.-R.,* p. 6.

were needed, it pronounced incantations; where courage was required, it had taken refuge behind a smoke screen of indecision. It
had perpetuated its own divisions and ineffectiveness in the executive organ of its choice, to the curse of the party and the paralysis
of its later efforts. "The Third Congress did not solve any basic
problems and when life demanded an answer . . . the party had
nothing to offer but resolutions and empty pockets"[145]—such was the
verdict of one of the men whom it had placed on that organ. By
refusing to come to grips with organizational problems, the congress
had failed to set the party's own house in order. As to revising in
the light of recent developments the program adopted at Imatra in
1906, the Third Congress was appalled at the magnitude of the task
and did not even make a beginning, preferring to postpone the whole
matter of appointing commissions and engaging in the necessary
spadework to some more auspicious time which never came.[146]

The complacency of the leaders in the face of this record is little
short of amazing. Chernov and Rakitnikov beheld the gage of unity
in the top-heavy majorities accorded the various resolutions[147] without stopping to ask themselves how much substance there was in
these resolutions or what they meant to the average party member—
not to speak of the average Russian. They congratulated themselves
on the number of votes received by resolutions which had been
framed for the purpose of attracting votes through the sacrifice of
convictions and content. Zenzinov congratulated the party on the
instinct of life which had enabled it to overcome the schismatic tendencies so fatal to other sections of the International.[148] The Social
Democrats had chosen to face divisive issues—and to divide—the
Socialist Revolutionaries had preferred to obscure them and to retain
unity. Yet only a little longer, and life would pose the issues for
them. At the Fourth Congress, after the SR's had experienced the
fate of their rivals, nothing more was heard of this holier-than-thou
attitude, and they perceived that the price of unity had been the
loss of the revolution.

[145] *Kratkii otchët o rabotakh chetvërtago s"ezda P.S.-R.*, p. 78.
[146] *Tretii s"ezd P.S.-R.*, pp. 19-20.
[147] *Ibid.*, pp. 426-27, 471-72.
[148] *Delo Naroda*, No. 70 (June 9, 1917).

The work of the Third Congress had proceeded in the spirit of the symbolic kiss exchanged between the internationalist wing under Chernov and the reformist wing under Avksentiev,[149] with Gotz standing over both and holding them together. Or, to look at it in another and even better way, the center of the PSR, aside from two momentary breakdowns, had succeeded in preserving its unity and binding down the extremities, but only at the cost of standing still while events were plunging ahead at a furious pace. The SR's had expended their entire art on uniting, uniting elements that were basically incompatible;[150] the right center and the left center had begun their fateful dance around the totem pole of unity, which would continue as long as there was breath in the party. The Third Congress had provided no solid foundation on which the party could stand in conducting its experiment in coalition; worse still, it had injected so much personal bitterness into the relations of the two SR representatives in the government that any real teamwork, as in the matter of agrarian legislation, was out of the question. If the SR's could not handle their own affairs in better fashion, it was not to be expected that they could set in order the affairs of the nation.[151]

[149] *Kratkii otchët o rabotakh chetvërtago s"ezda P.S.-R.*, p. 89.
[150] *Ibid.*, pp. 91, 99 (speeches of Podvitski [R] and Omelkov [LLC]).
[151] The organ of the extreme right had prophesied on the eve of the congress that compromise would prove the most calamitous solution of all; see *Volia Naroda*, No. 22 (May 25, 1917).

VII

THE FIRST COALITION

DURING the first months of its tenure of power the PSR loomed as the most potent political force in the country and should have wielded a dominant influence in councils of state. Almost every manifestation of the popular will resulted in a triumph for this party. Even in the cities, where rivals championing the bourgeoisie and the proletariat might have been expected to hold the advantage, the SR's swept the field, scoring their most sensational success in the June election of the Moscow city council, in which they received 58 percent of the popular vote and a clear majority of the seats in the council. The eclipse of the parties conventionally regarded as urban may be judged from the returns:[1]

Party	Vote	Percent
SR	374,885	58.00
Constitutional Democrat	108,781	16.85
SD Menshevik	76,407	11.82
SD Bolshevik	75,409	11.66
Popular Socialist	8,132	
Unity (Plekhanov)	1,506	1.67
Liberal Democrat	1,448	
Total	646,568	100.00

These results were startling enough for editors to take up their pencils and engage in post-mortem analyses. From Miliukov's *Rech'* came accusations of demagogy; from Lenin's *Pravda*, predictions of quick disillusionment; from Gorki's *Novaia Zhizn'*, expressions of regret that so many Russians should be swayed by fashion rather than conviction. Closer to the heart of the matter, however, was the comment of the staid and professorial *Russkiia Vedomosti* to the

[1] *Russkoe Slovo*, No. 149 (July 2, 1917).

effect that the election had demonstrated the freshness of ties between this thoroughly Russian city and the Russian countryside.[2] The victors acknowledged the influence of a large element in the population, proletarian in status but still half-peasant in outlook, for whom the Narodnik doctrine of a community of interest between urban and rural toilers had been made to order. According to O. S. Minor, no other point had gone over so well with these urban voters as the promise to still the land hunger of the peasants.[3] The garrison, made up largely of peasants in uniform, had voted 70 percent in favor of the SR's,[4] and the potency of the agrarian factor is established from the negative side by the absence of any names with marked drawing power on the SR ticket and the similarity of their municipal program to those of the other socialist parties.[5] The SR's had known how to play up to the electorate. With a cunningness only too rarely displayed by them, they had contrived to get for their list the number 3, symbolizing not only the tripartite union of the peasants, the manual workers, and the brainworkers, but also the magic word, "land."[6]

The village antecedents of a large part of the city's population, however, do not explain in full measure the SR victory, since it extended to every quarter and encompassed every social element. Probably a Bolshevik observer is right in thinking that for the average voter the Kadets were too academic and conservative and the Bolsheviks too unpatriotic in their stand on the war, while the sacrifice of the terrorist campaign still shed glory on the SR name and

[2] Quoted in *Delo Naroda*, No. 88 (June 30, 1917).

[3] *Ibid.*, Nos. 86, 87 (June 28, 29, 1917). The importance of the agrarian factor is also stressed by the liberal economist, Tugan-Baranovski, in an article in the *Russkoe Slovo*, No. 158 (July 13, 1917).

[4] *Volia Naroda*, No. 134 (September 3, 1917).

[5] "Moskovskaia pobeda" (The Moscow Triumph), *Delo Naroda*, No. 86 (June 28, 1917).

[6] In Russian the word for land is *zemlia*, the first letter of which in the Cyrillic alphabet is made like the number 3. The SR's tried on other occasions to repeat the ruse that had served them well in Moscow, in, for example, the August election in St. Petersburg. See *Delo Naroda*, No. 124 (August 11, 1917). The matter is mentioned by Vishniak in his article, "Partiia i vybory v uchreditel'noe sobranie" (The Party and the Elections to the Constituent Assembly), *ibid.*, No. 121 (August 8, 1917). See also Bernard Pares, *My Russian Memoirs* (London, 1931), p. 452.

the slogan of "Land and Liberty" had not yet lost its romantic appeal.[7] The SR's do not seem to have been under any illusion as to the permanence of their success; in the hour of triumph they were reminded of the adage, "easy come, easy go," and recognized that they had been the beneficiaries of the fashion of the hour, which had brought them adherents both "from conscience and from fear" (*i za strakh, i za sovest'*).[8] Their restraint was well advised: within three months nothing would remain of this victory but a heap of ashes.[9]

In the other great city of Russia, the political situation had been obscured at the outset by the conclusion of a bloc between the SR's and the Mensheviks to contest the election of city district councils (May 27-29).[10] The bloc won upwards of half the vote, leaving most of the remainder to be shared about equally by the Kadets and the Bolsheviks.[11] Though there is every reason to assume that the bulk of the vote cast for the fusion ticket belonged to the SR's rather than to the Mensheviks,[12] the proportions of the triumph were smaller than in Moscow. In a bitter campaign the Kadets accused the SR's of gross demagogy in dangling before the eyes of their proletarian following the prospect of a division of all the land along the Nevski Prospekt on a basis of private ownership![13] Whether the SR's departed from socialist principles to promise their supporters what these in their hearts would most have desired may be doubted;

[7] Voznesenski, *Moskva v 1917 godu*, p. 98.

[8] "Moskovskaia pobeda," *Delo Naroda*, No. 86 (June 28, 1917).

[9] See chap. XI.

[10] Here the procedure was the reverse of that in Moscow. In St. Petersburg the parts of the city elected their councils in May and the whole city its council in August (see chap. X below); in Moscow the central body was chosen in June and the district or ward councils in September. All four of these municipal elections were landmarks in 1917 and attracted much attention.

[11] The complete returns could not be assembled. There were 792,865 votes in all, of which 376,813 fell to the bloc in ten of the twelve districts. The Kadets secured approximately 171,400, and the Bolsheviks 159,500, in all twelve districts. See *Delo Naroda*, Nos. 63, 64, 69, 70, 76 (June 1, 2, 8, 9, 16, 1917); V. E. Trutovski, "Usililis' li bol'sheviki v Petrograde?" (Have the Bolsheviks Grown Stronger in Petrograd?), *ibid.*, No. 165 (September 27, 1917).

[12] In the two districts where they ran separately, the SR's polled 16,729 and 43,465 against 19,045 and 7,144 for the Mensheviks. In all later elections they swamped the Mensheviks.

[13] See *Delo Naroda*, No. 59 (May 27, 1917).

certainly the intellectuals at the top would never have been guilty of such a concession to crude reality.

The trend revealed in the Moscow and Petersburg elections manifested itself in urban centers throughout the country. True, the SR's often had to content themselves with a plurality instead of the absolute majority achieved in Moscow, but in a number of cities they duplicated that feat: in Odessa, Sevastopol,[14] Simferopol, Tambov, Orenburg, Cheliabinsk, Omsk, Irkutsk, and in a number of smaller towns such as Chernov's home of Kamyshin on the Volga and Buguruslan in Samara province; Kharkov, metropolis of the eastern Ukraine, where nationalist friction had not yet sundered the Populist movement, only just missed being in this category. A survey of the results of elections in 240 cities and towns, of which only 84 were clear tests, free of the confusion created by the formation of a (moderate) socialist bloc, showed that in no less than 33 of these 84, the SR's secured 50 percent or more of the vote, and that for all 84 of the urban centers in which they campaigned independently, they obtained 44 percent of the total number of municipal council seats against 28 percent for both branches of the by now hopelessly divided Social Democracy.[15]

The most sweeping success had been achieved in the south, along the Volga, and in Siberia, but there were few localities in which the SR's had not bested their rivals. Only in purely industrial centers like Orekhovo-Zuevo, Ivanovo-Voznesensk, Lugansk, and Tsaritsyn or in military outposts like Revel and Narva did the Bolsheviks come out ahead; only in sleepy provincial towns like Riazan and Ranenburg, where personalities bulked large and liberalism was still in

[14] Here they got 17,000 out of 24,000 votes (see *Delo Naroda*, No. 106 [July 21, 1917]). Nowhere in Russia were the SR's stronger than in the Taurida. The sailors of the Black Sea fleet and the soldiers of the Crimean garrisons were far removed from the centers of Bolshevik contagion, the Russian population was well in hand, and Professor Miliukov's Turkophobe policies delivered over to the SR's the conservative Moslem population as well. See the memoirs of a Kadet physician: Pasmanik, *Revoliutsionnye gody v Krimu*, p. 46.

[15] N. Sviatitski, "P.S.-R. na vyborakh v gorodskiia dumy" (The SR Party in the Elections for the City Dumas), *Partiinyia Izvestiia*, No. 3 (October 19, 1917), pp. 4-10.

vogue, did the Constitutional Democrats prevail.[16] The only Menshevik victory of consequence was in Tiflis,[17] more because of
Georgian nationalism than because of Menshevism, though this party
gained a disproportionate share of seats in the cities where it had
worked out, usually on the basis of parity, a joint ticket with the
SR's. As a result of the many victories in urban territory, most
Russian municipalities in 1917 came to have mayors who were Socialist Revolutionaries instead of the Social Democrats or liberals
whom one would have expected to find: thus G. I. Shreider became
mayor of St. Petersburg, V. V. Rudnev, of Moscow, E. P. Riabtsev,
of Kiev, I. N. Lordkipanidze, of Odessa, A. A. Nikolaev, of Rostov-
on-the-Don, Mukoseev, of Saratov, S. A. Nikonov, of Sevastopol,
and so forth; while O. S. Minor became president of the council in
Moscow and V. A. Karelin, the same in Kharkov.[18]

All this was in the cities. As for the villages of Russia, everyone
had written them off as an SR preserve since the bid of the Kadets
for a conservative solution of the land problem had been decisively
defeated by the SR's through the peasants' soviets, a form of organization they had championed against an attempt with Kadet support
to revive the Peasants' Union of 1905.[19] After the SR's had made the
soviet system the accepted form of organization for peasants as well
as for workers, and had consolidated their partisan control of the
soviets in the First All-Russian Peasants' Congress (May, 1917), they
were confronted with no serious opposition in the villages until division in their own ranks in the fall raised up against them a formidable
threat from the left. For the present, however, every manifestation

[16] V. E. Trutovski, "Zavoevaniia" (Conquests), *Delo Naroda*, No. 100 (July
14, 1917).
[17] Results of the July municipal election in Sef, *Revoliutsiia 1917 goda v
Zakavkaz'i*, p. 203.
[18] Sviatitski, "P.S.-R. na vyborakh v gorodskiia dumy," *Partiinyia Izvestiia*,
No. 3 (October 19, 1917), p. 9.
[19] The story of this struggle is told in the author's unpublished dissertation
(Harvard University, 1939), chap. VII, based upon the account in Bykhovski,
Vserossiiskii Sovet Krest'ianskikh Deputatov, and upon information in the *Delo
Naroda*. Some information on it may also be found in Dubrowski, *Die Bauernbewegung in der Russichen Revolution 1917*, and in A. V. Shestakov, "Krest'-
ianskie organizatsii v 1917 g." (Peasant Organizations in 1917), in *Krest'ianskoe
dvizhenie v 1917 godu*.

of the popular will, whether in the towns or in the country, attested
the primacy of this party and strengthened its claim to a dominant
voice in affairs of state. Yet within the coalition the will of the SR's
was not to prevail.

Their will was not to prevail even in respect to agrarian matters,
the one subject on which all sections of party opinion still agreed.
Chernov had proudly announced that as far as the land problem was
concerned the SR's had assumed power with the intent of becoming
not merely a governing party but *the* governing party.[20] Circumstances beyond his control as well as some that he might have
bettered would thwart his purpose and convert these proud words
into an idle boast. As minister of agriculture from May 6 to the end
of August he bears the primary responsibility for what happened or
did not happen in the realm of agrarian affairs during the heyday of
the coalitional era. At his side he had as deputy ministers N. I. Rakitnikov, one of the founders of the party from his home province of
Saratov, and Panteleimon Alekseevich Vikhliaev, the best brain on
agrarian matters in the ranks of the Socialist Revolutionary party,
though one not free of certain illusions common to all Populist statesmen. Further down the situation was less satisfactory, for Chernov
inherited the unpurged personnel of the old ministry, for whom his
schemes of reform were distasteful if not odious.[21]

The minister of agriculture, of course, did not have the field to
himself. Certain of his duties and powers overlapped those of the
Ministries of the Interior and Food, headed respectively by Prince
G. E. Lvov, who was also prime minister, and A. V. Peshekhonov,
a typical right-wing Populist intellectual who shrank from the revolution he had helped to foment. The minister of agriculture and the
minister of the interior habitually worked at cross-purposes. Then
there was the hierarchy of land committees set up under the law of

[20] Speech to the Northern Regional Conference as reported in the *Delo
Naroda*, No. 57 (May 25, 1917).
[21] See plaint of Bykhovski in *Tretii s"ezd P.S.-R.*, p. 257.

April 21, with volost or cantonal committees at the bottom of the structure and the Head Land Committee in Petersburg at the top. The land committees ran the gamut of political coloration from a rosewater tint of intellectualism to the deep red hue of direct action, the rule being that the closer to the base of the structure the weaker the role of the intellectuals and the greater the degree of radicalism. At all levels the SR's predominated, but they were not all the same kind of SR's, the dirt-soil peasants on the popularly elected volost committees having quite a different outlook from the theoretical revolutionists or technicians on the higher organs, where many of the members sat by appointment. The primary consideration with the former was to get the land before it eluded their grasp again, as in 1905, and with the latter, to bridge over class differences while the war continued. The land committees generally looked up to Chernov and expected from him much more than he gave, but the Head Land Committee was less deferential, staffed as it was with right-wing Populist and Constitutional Democratic agrarian experts, who might squabble incessantly among themselves, yet were as one in their aversion for the "Zimmerwaldist" minister.[22]

Finally as one of the mainsprings of agrarian reform we have the Executive Committee of the All-Russian Peasants' Soviet, elected by the first national congress in May and filled out by representatives of the provincial soviets. Although Chernov received more votes than any other of the thirty core members named by the congress, most of his colleagues in the committee were right-centrist SR's,[23]

---

[22] On the structure and role of the land committees, see especially Pershin, "Krest'ianskie zemel'nye komitety," *Voprosy Istorii*, VII (July, 1948), 70-83; see also Trenogova, *Bor'ba petrogradskikh bol'shevikov za krest'ianstvo v 1917 godu*, pp. 32-36; Alaverdova, "Ocherk agrarnoi politiki," *Sotsialicheskoe Khoziaistvo*, II (1925), 148, 152; Bykhovski, *Vserossiiskii Sovet Krest'ianskikh Deputatov*, p. 160 and *passim*; Chernov, *Great Russian Revolution*, pp. 233-34.

[23] Though Bykhovski's account stands supreme and unchallenged among those that deal with peasant organizations in 1917, he sometimes conveys the wrong impression, as in this instance when he describes the dominant element of the committee as "centrist" (*Vserossiiskii Sovet Krest'ianskikh Deputatov*, p. 124 and *passim*). The practiced eye need only glance at the list to see that it was weighted with right-centrists if not with rightists, and in any event the committee's actions prove the point; there is no need, however, to resort to analysis and indirect proof, for Bykhovski's colleague, V. Ia. Gurevich, confirms its right-centrist cast; see his "Vserossiiskii Krest'ianskii S"ezd," in *Letopis' Revoliutsii*, I, 188, 195.

and it was not until later, when the provincial soviets became restive over the delay in agrarian legislation and began to send up radical-minded delegates, that the left SR's gained any strength in the Executive Committee. At first they were restricted to the delegations from Kazan and a few other extremist strongholds. This state of affairs arose from the mentality of the intellectuals who had long been identified with the peasant movement, as well as from the circumstance that much of the money to put across the soviet system in the villages had come from the cooperative associations,[24] than which there was no more conservative element—in a democratic sense—in Russian society. Determined to have no truck with radicalism and particularly with antiwar sentiment, these ruble-and-kopeck functionaries through their control of the purse strings had seen to it that the peasant soviets were in safe hands. Thus the All-Russian Peasants' Executive Committee remained to the end of its days a nest of war-minded people, one of the sheet anchors of the Kerenski regime, since it spoke not only for the organized minority of peasants affiliated with the SR party but also for the vast nonpartisan majority which shuffled along behind the SR vanguard.[25] In it the tone was set by men of the stripe of N. D. Avksentiev, Ilia I. Fondaminski, N. Ia. Bykhovski, and Gregory A. Martiushin, certainly not by the adherents of V. M. Chernov. The legislative section of the committee was headed by S. L. Maslov (RRC), Chernov's successor in the last coalitional ministry, his factional enemy and personal rival.

The multiplicity of authorities in respect to agrarian legislation would have complicated the task of the minister even in the absence of the factionalism which cursed his party. As it was, he never had the really solid support of the party in his struggle to write its will into law. The left wanted everything at once and the right would never agree to press hard enough on the partners in coalition for him to achieve his major objectives. With the exception of the extreme left, which favored the "organized" taking over of land at

[24] Bykhovski, *Vserossiiskii Sovet Krest'ianskikh Deputatov*, pp. 32-34, 43-44.
[25] At the congress itself (the First or May Congress) nearly half the delegates had attended the SR caucus while the other half, because of an imperfect understanding of rival programs, contracted no partisan ties, though it followed the SR lead (*ibid.*, pp. 65-66, 127n). The vast bulk of the peasantry, of course, resembled this second half of the congress.

once, the SR's generally agreed that basic decisions must await the Constituent Assembly, and that only interim measures to conserve the land fund against panicky or spurious transactions on the part of private owners or against peasant depredations should concern the Provisional Government. Zenzinov defined the agrarian policy of the PSR as purely protective until the Constituent Assembly.[26] That body would decide who was to have the land; the Provisional Government, how in the meantime it was to be used.

This disjunction of objectives in the agrarian sphere had been effected at the Third Congress and—with great difficulty—at the First All-Russian Peasants' Congress, where the intellectuals had managed to restrain the appetite of their peasant followers by providing that the land should be entrusted to the care of the land committees. To the intellectuals this formula meant that the committees would work out a *modus vivendi* between peasants and landowners, preserving the juridical rights of the latter;[27] to the peasants it meant that they would have the land through a subterfuge without waiting for the assembly: "Let there be peace in the capital," they said, "but we shall be masters at home."[28] Thinking to avert a breakdown of the coalition in this manner, the right-centrist bosses with the yeoman assistance of V. M. Chernov[29] had in effect followed their habitual course of purchasing present harmony at the cost of future grief. Besides the latitude it afforded them in negotiations with the representatives of the bourgeoisie, the compromise formula could, of course, be justified from the standpoint of democratic procedure and the economic requirements of an evenhanded agrarian reform. But more was involved in the strategy of leaving basic problems to the Constituent Assembly: the SR's were not ready with their program for socialization of the land. They had a slogan of wondrous appeal

[26] "Podzhigateli" (Firebrands), *Delo Naroda*, No. 125 (August 12, 1917).
[27] Gurevich described the action of the congress, after the leaders had talked the delegates out of the idea of immediate seizure, as susceptible of "interpretation in the proper sense in the course of ensuing discussions" (. . . *moglo byt' istolkovano nadlezhashchim obrazom pri sootvetstvennykh raz"iasneniiakh*). See his "Vserossiiskii Krest'ianskii S"ezd," in *Letopis' Revoliutsii*, I, 194. An outstanding example of how the intellectuals beguiled the simple people.
[28] Bykhovski, *Vserossiiskii Sovet Krest'ianskikh Deputatov*, p. 73.
[29] *Ibid.*, pp. 107-16; Gurevich, "Vserossiiskii Krest'ianskii S"ezd," in *Letopis' Revoliutsii*, I, 193-94.

but no concrete program of action. They had been living on a myth and now suddenly were confronted with the necessity of transforming the myth into actuality. A vague uneasiness gripped them; as one of their leaders said:[30]

It is necessary to bear in mind that while we have an agrarian program in theory, we unhappily do not have a practical plan for its realization, and this, if you please, is the misfortune and, even more, the fault of the party; to neglect the matter further is impossible, for we are being dragged at the tail of events. . . . The fact is that the socialization of land—I do not know, but perhaps other members of the party experience the same sensation—causes a good deal of alarm when you begin to think of proceeding to its practical realization.

No one contradicted this statement, either at the Third Congress or elsewhere, and the man who made it—the agronomist I. A. Prilezhaev —was elected to the Central Committee. The deferment of fundamental issues to the Constituent Assembly was thus not only a matter of choice but also of necessity.

While this decision guaranteed that the Chernov ministry would be concerned mainly with interim measures, the ministry could not ignore the long-range aspects of agrarian reform, since the Constituent Assembly did not lie "on the other side of the mountains." There was need for feverish activity to prepare for it and to compensate for all the time that had been lost. Twenty-four commissions and subcommissions under the general direction of the Ministry of Agriculture were kept at the task[31] and gradually the outlines of socialization began to emerge from the realm of fantasy and faith. One gains the impression that the task exceeded the powers of Chernov and most of his colleagues and that only Vikhliaev possessed the capacity to cloak the ethereal precepts of the Populists in earthly garb. Alone of the men who set their hands to the task, he seems to have worked out a program[32] that was both faithful to principle and flexible enough to fit the diversities of Russian land tenure without offending any broad segment of the rural population or stopping the

[30] *Tretii s"ezd P.S.-R.*, pp. 50-51.

[31] Tsereteli, "Rossiiskoe krest'ianstvo i V. M. Chernov v 1917 godu," *Novyi Zhurnal*, XXIX (1952), 219-20; Chernov, *Great Russian Revolution*, p. 236.

[32] *Kak uravniat' pol'zovanie zemlëi*. Amid an ocean of generalities and a desert of concrete proposals, this slender pamphlet is the one solid contribution to the problem of putting the Narodnik agrarian principles into effect.

wheels of the national economy. That his scheme never officially
became the program of the party, though very likely it would have
been followed had history taken a different course, relieves us of
the necessity of analyzing it, but it is only fair to say that, despite
certain grave economic flaws and even utopian features, it could
have served as a point of departure for the evolution of a new
agrarian system in Russia. For the PSR, however, as for so many of
us, disaster came before decision.

The complexity of the task, and the fact that the SR's were
charmed by the war like birds by a snake, do not fully account for
the state of unreadiness on the eve of the great reform. The sad truth
was that even in matters regarding which the collective mind of the
party had long since been made up, disunity still prevailed, and there
was no assurance that highly placed individuals would defer to the
collective will. The right-wing SR's, so modest in numbers yet so
strong in influence because of their record of service and their knowledge of how to operate, acted as a drag on the solution of the agrarian
problem, just as they impeded action on other matters in relation
to which they had dropped any pretense of being revolutionary.
S. L. Maslov openly proclaimed his rejection of the principle of free
and equal access to the land, to the dismay of old-line leaders like
Rakitnikov and even Bykhovski,[33] and he unquestionably favored in
some degree the principle of compensation for private owners,[34]
though mass sentiment forced him to tread warily in this respect.
Yet his apostasy on the one point and his isolation on the other did
not prevent him from being named to succeed Chernov or from
taking pot shots at his predecessor from the platform of the Fourth
Congress. Far from making any effort to discipline him, the party
actually commissioned him to carry out a program some of the basic
features of which he had pointedly rejected!

As early as the First Congress[35] the SR's had been warned of the
ugly possibilities inherent in an attempt to bring the lands of spe-

[33] *Delo Naroda,* Nos. 149, 153 (September 8, 13, 1917); Lozinski, *Ekonomicheskaia politika,* pp. 174-75.
    [34] *Kratkii otchët o rabotakh chetvërtago s"ezda P.S.-R.,* p. 75 (speech of
Eugenia Ratner); Morokhovets, *Agrarnye programmy rossiiskikh politicheskikh
partii,* p. 105; Lozinski, *Ekonomicheskaia politika,* pp. 176-77.
    [35] See p. 29.

cially privileged population groups within the scope of socialization. Twelve years had gone by without any progress toward a solution of this problem: national minorities with a relatively generous per capita endowment gave the proponents of socialization less concern than the arms-bearing Cossacks, whose claims for preferential treatment were reinforced by the specter of a Russian Vendée on the banks of the Don. The SR's would have desperately liked to sidestep this question, had not the political situation in the Territory of the Don Cossacks been as bad as the economic. There a peasant element comprising 30 percent of the population with one and a half million desiatinas (2.70 acres) of land confronted a Cossack element only half again as numerous (45 percent of the total) but with holdings eight times as great (twelve million desiatinas), a large amount of which was rented out to the peasants on onerous terms.[36] Now if the SR's really believed in leveling, here was a whole mountain of inequity to engage their attention. They approached the problem gingerly, like a cat circling a saucer of hot milk, but the troublesome facts would not yield to platitudes and pious wishes and the peasants virtually to the last man became SR's while the Cossacks remained impervious to their appeal, bringing the problem squarely into the political arena. Only war-weary units at the front leaned to the SR's; the home mass of Cossacks listened to the Constitutional Democrats and the monarchists,[37] sending a chill up the SR leaders' spine. The rank-and-file SR's, however, would not hear of Cossack im-

[36] N. Oganovski, Statistiko-ekonomicheskii obzor (Statistical and Economic Survey), in "Statistiko-geograficheskii obzor Oblasti Voiska Donskogo" (Statistical and Geographical Survey of the Don Cossack Region), in Entsiklopedicheskii Slovar' (Encyclopedic Dictionary) (Granat), Vol. XXX, pp. 386-88 of insert between pp. 384 and 385.

[37] "Kadetizm i kazachii s"ezd" (Kadetism and the Cossack Congress), Delo Naroda, No. 72 (June 11, 1917); see also No. 63 (June 1, 1917) for polemics with the Rech' and the Novoe Vremia. While the sequel would show that the Cossacks were less reactionary than feared, and that they offered only halfhearted resistance even to Bolshevism, they did constitute the only farming community of any consequence which held out against socialism. The social cleavage in the Don Cossack Region is illuminated by the November election returns, which show the Cossacks with 640,000 votes (45 percent of the total—exactly the same proportion as in the population) against 478,901 for the SR's and 205,497 for the Bolsheviks (mainly workers in the towns and the eastern reaches of the Donets Basin); see my study, The Election to the Russian Constituent Assembly of 1917, pp. 13 (n. 8), 79.

munity; as one peasant delegate put it, nothing distinguished the Cossacks from ordinary Russians save their peculiar headgear and their predilection for sour milk.[38] Everything indicated that Cossack privileges would be flattened out by the muzhik steam roller in the Constituent Assembly, whatever the pusillanimity of the SR leaders. With the Cossack Congress bluffly reaffirming the inalienability of Cossack lands,[39] the specter of civil war stalked the southeastern plains.

Under the Vikhliaev plan Cossack holdings would have gone into the pot with all the others, though certain features would have eased the shock. But the PSR as such never said how it would have solved the problem. The issue was soft-pedaled at the Third Congress,[40] and leaders in their public addresses spoke with a forked tongue.[41] The minister himself was disposed to move with caution in the matter, hoping to drive a wedge between the wealthier and the poorer elements of the Cossack population by a gradual leveling process which would avert the solidifying effect of a decree of confiscation. As to national groups with extensive holdings but practicing backward methods of cultivation (Bashkirs, Buriats, etc.), Chernov advocated a policy of forbearance which would seek to raise the level of production before throwing open the surplus lands to settlement.[42] Beyond the enunciation of these guiding principles, however, the minister did not go, and the question was left to the Constituent Assembly, along with other basic aspects of agrarian reform.

Measures to be put into effect in advance of the Constituent Assembly engrossed the attention of the Chernov ministry, especially

[38] F. Klimenko, "Donskaia Federatsiia" (Federation of the Don Region), *Delo Naroda*, No. 125 (August 12, 1917).

[39] *Delo Naroda*, No. 76 (June 16, 1917).

[40] *Tretii s"ezd P.S.-R.*, pp. 423, 425-26, 428-29.

[41] As Avksentiev before the Cossack Congress (see *Delo Naroda*, No. 76 [June 16, 1917]).

[42] See his speech to the Northern Regional Conference (*ibid.*, No. 56 [May 24, 1917]); see also No. 63 (June 1, 1917); Petrograd *Zemlia i Volia*, No. 49 (May 24, 1917). The fuller account in this left SR organ shows that in general Chernov was falling in with Vikhliaev's scheme.

since it was soon locked in mortal combat over even its minimum program. As Chernov surveyed the scene, he concluded that it was both desirable and necessary to fashion a new legal mold in which the spontaneous movement against the existing agrarian order could be contained and turned to constructive purposes.[43] His enemies charged that in so doing he would predetermine the decision of the Constituent Assembly and graft a partisan program on the sovereign will of the nation. History will probably hold that both points of view were justified, that here already were the elements of tragedy, the essence of which is not the conflict of right with wrong but of right with right. If the peasants were going to wait for the orderly processes of the Constituent Assembly instead of taking matters into their own hands, they demanded at least some measures in the interim that would better their lot and ease the burden of war, the full weight of which had fallen upon their shoulders. They also wanted to be very sure that the land fund would not be drawn down in the meantime by legitimate or fictitious deals between estate owners and small or foreign buyers who would be in a better position to claim exemption from confiscatory legislation. The land hunger of the Russian peasants was quite extraordinary, and neither the incantations of the priesthood nor the lullabies of the Populist intellectuals made any more impression than water dripping on granite; while they might wait a little longer for a better reform, the peasants were constantly on the outlook for some form of trickery that would thwart the will of the people.

Chernov understood their psychology and desired to give them satisfaction, not only because he was sympathetic but also because he realized that only through concessions could the land fund be protected from the peasants themselves and the door kept open for a reform that would be fair to all of them, the weak as well as the strong, the soldiers as well as the villagers. The key to SR agrarian policy in 1917, according to Zenzinov,[44] was preservation of the land fund against private encroachment, whether peasant or bourgeois. To this Chernov would add some immediate improvement of the

[43] Great Russian Revolution, p. 240; Tsereteli, "Rossiiskoe krest'ianstvo i V. M. Chernov v 1917 godu," Novyi Zhurnal, XXIX (1952), 225.
[44] "Podzhigateli," Delo Naroda, No. 125 (August 12, 1917).

status of the peasantry as against the landowners. To guard against an increase in the number of private owners which would restrict the freedom of action of the Constituent Assembly, two specific measures were envisaged by the ministry: suspension of the Stolypin legislation providing for the creation of privately owned plots out of communal property, and prohibition of all further transactions involving the purchase and sale of land. To restrain the peasants from anarchic seizures, as well as to provide machinery through which their demands could be met, the ministry undertook to write into law the formula of the peasants' congress and the Third Congress for placing all land under the administration of the land committees, which would decide the conditions of its use while leaving the question of its ultimate disposal open until the Constituent Assembly. These three proposals constituted the heart of Chernov's interim program.

The abrogation of the Stolypin agrarian reform occasioned little difficulty. The effort to individualize Russian agriculture from above had come too late and now was smothered by the collectivist-minded leaders of the peasant movement, only to be revived later from below, by the peasants themselves, and realized on the broadest scale, until this trend, in turn, was reversed by the coercive machinery of the Stalinist state in a campaign without parallel. Chernov's move to halt the conversion of communal holdings into private property could have been expected to encounter the resistance of Kadet ministers, but as a matter of fact the agrarian program of that party was tinctured with Populist solicitude for the commune[45] and its representatives did not choose to make an issue of the matter. For the first and last time a measure proposed by Chernov received the unanimous approval of the cabinet,[46] and by the laws of June 28 and July 19 the land settlement commissions set up under the acts of 1910 and 1911 were abolished, and the issuance of titles confirming individuals in the possession of plots carved from allotment (communal) lands

[45] See my book, *Election to the Russian Constituent Assembly*, p. 10, n. 21.
[46] Tsereteli, "Rossiiskoe krest'ianstvo i V. M. Chernov v 1917 godu," *Novyi Zhurnal*, XXIX (1952), 228.

was discontinued.[47] Thus did the Populists settle accounts with the ghost of the murdered premier who had given them a bad start with his assault upon the commune, which Chernov had proclaimed to be unnecessary to the agrarian program of neo-Populism[48] and then had hastened to rescue at the first opportunity.

The effort to preserve the status quo in respect to land ownership by withdrawing that commodity from the market occasioned far greater difficulty. Here the minister had arrayed against him the entire business community, which held that a ban on land deals would depreciate land values, which in turn would impair the credit structure of banks and endanger the savings of small investors. Needless to say, the Constitutional Democrats offered strenuous resistance to the proposed measure. What had not been foreseen was that the minister-president would make common cause with them. Prince Lvov had hitherto figured as a nonpartisan progressive standing to the left of the Kadets and displaying much more flexibility in his attitude toward the soviet democracy. His socialist colleagues valued his presence in the government, and more particularly at the head of it, because they saw in him a near-ally or at least an impartial mediator in their strife with the Kadets.[49] But when it came to a specific measure restricting property rights, Lvov, who had attained national prominence through the zemstvo organization and was himself a landowner of Tula province, suddenly hardened and took up a position indistinguishable from the Kadets. In the face of this augmented opposition Chernov could not get his projected law through the cabinet and his other measures began to encounter the same resistance. The nonsocialist majority had coalesced against him. Yet there was no more fruitful source of peasant disorders than the rumors of fictitious land deals which would narrow the scope of the future reform, and local organs, which sometimes went ahead on their own

[47] *Izvestiia Glavnago Zemel'nago Komiteta*, No. 1, pp. 23-24, and Nos. 2-3, pp. 3-4; Lozinski, *Ekonomicheskaia politika*, pp. 157-58; Alaverdova, "Ocherk agrarnoi politiki," *Sotsialisticheskoe Khoziaistvo*, II (1925), 169.
[48] Petrograd *Zemlia i Volia*, No. 49 (May 24, 1917) (speech before the Northern Regional Conference); see also discussion above, pp. 82-85.
[49] Tsereteli, "Rossiiskoe krest'ianstvo i V. M. Chernov v 1917 godu," *Novyi Zhurnal*, XXIX (1952), 226.

when laws from the center were not forthcoming, could do nothing in this matter.[50]

To circumvent the obstruction, Minister of Justice Pereverzev volunteered, or was prevailed upon by Chernov, to instruct notaries over the country to withhold acknowledgment of land deals until further notice. The instruction was sent out by telegraph on May 17. In this left-handed manner the socialist ministers thought to accomplish their purpose without provoking a cabinet crisis. But Lvov denounced the step as going behind the back of the rest of the cabinet in a matter that required the action of all, and proposed that the question be referred to an interdepartmental commission. The only effect was that the deadlock was extended from the ministry to the commission. After the impossibility of obtaining an agreement had been demonstrated, Pereverzev, who had already weakened his instruction in the face of reproaches for having usurped a function belonging to the whole government, rescinded it entirely on June 23. For the better part of two months the coalition had contended with the problem and things were now back at the starting point.[51]

Chernov's course in this affair throws light on his character as well as on the conduct of his ministry. He had displayed persistence in pressing for a ban on land deals, but also a deviousness for which he was often reproached. He had not kept faith with the organizations supporting him. As usual, he had preferred to work behind the scenes, and while engaged in a rude struggle with the enemies of socialization in the government, he had lulled his supporters into a false sense of security with assurances which did not correspond to reality, and which contravened his solemn promise to carry his case to the peasants' soviets if his measures were blocked in the cabinet.[52] On May 24 Chernov had told the peasants' congress that the draft law was awaiting the approval of the government.[53] On May 26, in

[50] *Ibid.*, p. 227.
[51] *Ibid.*, pp. 227-28, 241; Chernov, *Great Russian Revolution*, pp. 236-37; Alaverdova, "Ocherk agrarnoi politiki," *Sotsialisticheskoe Khoziaistvo*, II (1925), 164-65; Bykhovski, *Vserossiiskii Sovet Krest'ianskikh Deputatov*, p. 115; Sukhanov, *Zapiski*, IV, 101-3 (somewhat garbled).
[52] Bykhovski, *Vserossiiskii Sovet Krest'ianskikh Deputatov*, p. 68.
[53] *Ibid.*, pp. 115, 119.

reply to a question as to the cause for delay, he told the party congress that more time would be required for its formulation.[54] One would have expected the minister to be, if not more straightforward in his dealings, at least more circumspect in his utterances. And on June 15, after weeks of conflict, Chernov appeared before the Peasants' Executive Committee to excuse the delay on the ground that the government had been weighed down with other urgent matters.[55] The reserve with which he was heard on this occasion shows that the mask of deception he chose to put on when facing his own backers was beginning to wear thin. To preserve a semblance of harmony, at first in the government and then in the party, Chernov sacrificed the vast authority he had enjoyed among the people at the outset of his ministerial career.

If there had been so much trouble over a measure which Chernov termed the most rudimentary of all needed legislation,[56] it will occasion no surprise that the more far-reaching plan to place all land under the administration of the land committees was not even considered by the first coalitional ministry. Chernov is vague about this matter, for reasons that will presently appear. Friction developed between the ministry and the Head Land Committee over the text of the law, delaying its submission.[57] But according to Deputy Minister Rakitnikov, the law was introduced on June 29, to lie without action until August, when it was turned back to the Ministry of Agriculture.[58] In any event it is certain that Chernov made no attempt during the life of the first coalition to carry out the heart of the program adopted by both the First All-Russian Peasants' Congress and the Third Congress of his own party.

Yet this did not prevent a furious controversy from arising in the bosom of the government over the land committees. By June the

[54] *Tretii s"ezd P.S.-R.*, pp. 84, 100.
[55] Bykhovski, *Vserossiiskii Sovet Krest'ianskikh Deputatov*, p. 150.
[56] "Vospreshchenie zemel'nykh sdelok" (Prohibition of Land Deals), *Delo Naroda*, No. 101 (July 15, 1917). Editorials were not signed, but this one was written by Chernov (see under *Delo Naroda* in the bibliography).
[57] *Kratkii otchët o rabotakh chetvërtago s"ezda P.S.-R.*, p. 109; Chernov, *Great Russian Revolution*, p. 239.
[58] "Nasha taktika v zemel'nom voprose" (Our Tactics in the Land Question), *Delo Naroda*, No. 215 (November 21, 1917).

leadership of the movement to improve the status of the peasantry had passed into the hands of these organs, which on the local and district (*uezd*) levels had been constituted on a broadly democratic basis. In the absence of laws from the center, the committees went in for self-action, making use of the vague right to issue regulations which the law of April 21 had conferred upon them: they lowered the payments on rented land, redistributed the labor of prisoners of war, forbade landowners to step up the exploitation of forests while they still had them, took over untilled fields for assignment to peasants, and in general did things which the peasants demanded and the landowners resented. Protests poured into the Ministry of the Interior from all over the country against their irregular and high-handed actions. Prince Lvov responded by inaugurating a campaign to bridle the land committees; he invited the minister of agriculture to set his name to a joint declaration annulling all regulations which overstepped the bounds of existing laws. Chernov replied that since the Provisional Government had failed to provide the necessary legal basis for the activity of the land committees, the effect of the proposal would be to constrain them within the strait jacket of the imperial agrarian code, something that was neither desirable nor possible. The result would be more anarchy instead of less and a broad wave of seizures instead of the isolated excesses hitherto recorded. Chernov refused to subscribe to the declaration, confirming Lvov in his growing conviction that the path of guilt led from the local committees straight to the door of his ministerial colleague.[59]

The following day he called in Tsereteli, most influential of the socialist ministers, as much because of his personality as because of his position in the soviet, and disclosed to him the full measure of his antipathy for Chernov. Not only had Chernov failed to restrain the land committees, according to Lvov, he had abetted their illegal actions, possibly with the purpose in mind of carrying out a *de facto* expropriation and presenting the Constituent Assembly with a *fait accompli*. He had led the committees to believe that they could

---

[59] Tsereteli, "Rossiiskoe krest'ianstvo i V. M. Chernov v 1917 godu," *Novyi Zhurnal*, XXIX (1952), pp. 228-32; Chernov, *Great Russian Revolution*, pp. 237-38; Bykhovski, *Vserossiiskii Sovet Krest'ianskikh Deputatov*, pp. 146-47.

ignore the rights of landowners and decide every conflict in favor of peasants; perpetrators of violence claimed to act under his authority. "Enough of listening to you," the peasants would tell the commissars of the government, "the land is now ours, ours also the minister; in the committee are instructions from him." The minister-president even went so far as to say that he was not at all sure but that the left SR's who were inciting the peasants to seize the estates had the tacit approval of their party chieftain. Tsereteli in rebuttal cited Chernov's record of denunciations of violence in agrarian relations and tried to show how anarchic seizures would defeat the purpose of the SR's, all to no avail; Lvov held to his point of view and ended by saying that the government would have to choose between him and Chernov, which would be all the easier, since neither of them valued too highly the position he held.[60]

The position of Lvov and other opponents of the SR Ministry of Agriculture had some justification, not so much with reference to Chernov personally as to the party he represented. The SR's unquestionably were shaping their interim agrarian program to partisan ends. We have it from no less an authority than N. I. Rakitnikov, one of the founders of the party, a member of the Central Committee, and deputy minister of agriculture, that while the Constituent Assembly would decide the question of ownership, the party upheld the right of the peasants in the meantime to deprive the landowners of all the material advantages of that ownership.[61] The same source tells us that the SR's had taken an active part in forming the land committees so that control of the land would be in trusted hands, leaving no doubt that in respect to their personnel these organs were stacked against estate owners. And no one doubted that, as Lvov's

[60] Tsereteli, "Rossiiskoe krest'ianstvo i V. M. Chernov v 1917 godu," *Novyi Zhurnal*, XXIX (1952), 232-36; see also text of Lvov's letter of resignation in Polner, *Zhiznennyi put' Kniazia . . . L'vova*, pp. 256-57. Kerenski confirmed to the author (1955) that Lvov suspected Chernov of secretly encouraging the left SR's, particularly Kamkov.

[61] "Nasha politika v zemel'nom voprose" (Our Policy on the Land Question), *Delo Naroda*, No. 215 (November 21, 1917). It is true that these words were written after the October Revolution had overwhelmed the SR's, impelling them to take on as radical a coloration as possible, but since they were generally honest, in adversity as in prosperity, and since this statement accords with the facts, there is no reason to question its veracity.

assistant expressed it, "land which in one way or another comes to be used by the peasants will never be relinquished by them, and this will bind the future land reform."[62] All charges of one-sidedness or unfairness, however, the SR's would have countered by denying any conflict between their policies and the sovereign will of the people as it would be manifested in the Constituent Assembly, and the sequel proved them correct—at least for the time being.

The feud between Lvov and Chernov, which was about to upset the first coalition when the Ukrainian question usurped its wrecking function, went deeper, of course, than conceptions of legality or a free hand for the Assembly. All the sources stress the minister-president's friendliness for the peasants and his belief in the justice of their claims, ascribing his campaign against the land committees to the pressure exerted by the *pomeshchiks* (noble landowners).[63] All ignore the most plausible explanation of his conduct: that a belief in abstract principles can go hand in hand with a marked distaste for their application in specific instances. The motivation of armchair liberals is often to be sought for in a conflict between their views and their personal interests. They build a fire, and blow upon it, only to draw back when it begins to spread and threatens to burn them too. Prince Lvov at one and the same time could be willing to concede landed property in general to the peasants and unwilling to have his Tula estates partitioned, at least until after the Constituent Assembly had legislated upon the question. And then he certainly expected to receive some compensation for the land which he would give up and to which he probably felt the same attachment that most people feel who have come into possession of a tract, of whatever size, with its beauties and cares, its trees and its brooks. More than any one else in Russia, V. M. Chernov was the living symbol of expropriation without compensation. How could two such men sit together in a government racked by the strains and passions of revolution?

[62] Alaverdova, "Ocherk agrarnoi politiki," *Sotsialisticheskoe Khoziaistvo,* II (1925), 165.

[63] See, for example, Chernov, *Pered burei,* pp. 327-28, 335; Tsereteli, "Rossiiskoe krest'ianstvo i V. M. Chernov v 1917 godu," *Novyi Zhurnal,* XXIX (1952), 225-26, 229-30, 233.

Why revolutionary leaders in their memoirs have to be so fastidious as not to mention the factor of compensation, when in all probability it lay at the bottom of the feud, is not apparent—the Russian Revolution was not a fastidious affair. But there was also something else involved in this feud. When he first entered the cabinet, Chernov says that he was welcomed cordially and, he thinks, sincerely by Lvov and the other nonsocialist ministers, and invited to make a tour of the front to lift the spirit of the troops. The on-with-the-war politicians wished to use the popularity of the "village minister" to kindle an enthusiasm in the peasant army that notably was not there, and that they themselves had no hope of arousing. But even when Gotz added his importunities to theirs, Chernov maintained that he could not go to the soldiers with empty hands and urge them to sacrifice their lives in the service of a regime that had not yet given them the land or even moved in that direction. He made no tour, and the initial cordiality in the ministerial council gave way to coolness and displeasure.[64] Deep in his heart, however, Chernov held another consideration. The line of the coalition in foreign policy was still in doubt, the attitude of the Allies far from his liking, and while he favored a strong defense and was in no way a defeatist, he felt no urge to go out and prepare Russian peasants to die *ad majorem Britanniae gloriam.*

The conflict over agrarian policy was the fundamental cause for the breakdown of the first coalition but before it could become the immediate cause as well, the Ukrainian question boiled up and precipitated the crisis. The sequence of events was this: on June 23 the minister of justice withdrew his circular instruction suspending the execution of land deeds, bringing the question squarely back into the cabinet, where Lvov secured a postponement until the twenty-seventh; on the twenty-eighth Chernov put through a partial repeal of the Stolypin legislation and on the twenty-ninth introduced the

[64] *Pered burei,* pp. 328-29.

draft code on land committees, evidently in denatured form; a bill on meadowlands and another on fisheries failed of adoption immediately afterwards. But just at this time an acute conflict broke out between the Ukrainian Rada (national council) and the Provisional Government, overshadowing for the moment the less sensational but more serious agrarian problem.

At the root of the trouble in Kiev lay the same development that was destroying the Socialist Revolutionary party—an excess of nationalism in revolutionary trappings. A clash between the Constitutional Democrats with their slogan of "Russia One and Indivisible" and the *samostiiniki* (separatists) with their demand for an independent Ukraine was in any case inevitable, but it might have been hoped that the broad peasants' movement in the Ukraine, in conjunction with that in the rest of the country, would have doused the extremists' fire. Unfortunately, neither in the Ukraine nor in the rest of the country were the peasants masters of their own destinies but everywhere were dominated by intellectuals who were much more likely to be swayed by nationalist prejudice than the peasants themselves. Populism, as we have seen, always contained the seeds of nationalism and these had sprouted luxuriantly in 1917, in Moscow and Kiev, on the Volga and on the Dnieper. The same frame of mind which impelled the right SR's to smooth over points of conflict with the Kadets in the interest of the struggle against Germany, caused the Ukrainian SR's to sink their differences with other national elements in the interest of the struggle against Moscow. The less progress either made in solving basic problems the more nationalist fire they both emitted. Hence there were two SR parties in Little Russia in 1917, each striving to exclude the other from a share of influence in the peasant movement by imposing its own distinctive form of organization. A neutral observer says that the common Narodnik ideology rarely acted as a bridge between them, both being too nationalistic for any sustained collaboration to be feasible.[65] In fact, it is possible to go further and say that their common ideology inflamed the spirit that divided them.

[65] Rafes, *Dva goda revoliutsii na Ukraine*, p. 10. Rafes was a leader of the Jewish Bund.

Political lines in the Ukraine coincided rather faithfully with the Dnieper. The dark amber waters of this swamp-draining river divided the region into two "banks," virtually equal in size and each with four provinces, but differing markedly in respect to history, population, and economy. The right-bank or western Ukraine comprised the provinces of Kiev, Volynia, Podolia, and Kherson; the left-bank or eastern Ukraine, those of Poltava, Chernigov, Kharkov, and Ekaterinoslav. Generally speaking, the right bank was more Ukrainian and agrarian, the left bank more heterogeneous and industrial. The right bank had come to Russia, or come back to her, only at the end of the eighteenth century with the partitioning of Poland, whereas the left bank had passed under the scepter of Moscow in the middle of the seventeenth century and had undergone a more thorough assimilation. The industrial revolution, centering in the Donets Basin of the eastern Ukraine, had strengthened the Great Russian element already present in the rural population by causing an influx of workers from the outside. No comparable development or earlier movement of settlers had occurred on the other side of the river, where Russians and Jews were to be found only in the city of Kiev and in small trading or beet-sugar centers, tiny islands in the sea of the Ukrainian peasantry. As a result of these underlying factors, the revolution assumed a predominantly national character to the west of the river and a predominantly social character to the east. On the right bank diverse social elements of the same nationality coalesced to further the national cause; on the left bank diverse national elements worked in harmony to end the war and expropriate the land and factories. In the conventional political sense, then, the right bank was more conservative and the left bank more radical, helping to fix the troublesome terminology correctly in mind. It should be pointed out, however, that two nonconforming provinces marred this pretty pattern. Kherson belonged politically to the left bank, having a relatively low percentage of Ukrainian stock, while Poltava on the left bank was the most homogeneous and one of the most agrarian provinces, thus fitting the social pattern of the right bank. But otherwise the general pattern held, and the antithesis between the two sections was best exemplified in the populous and opulent provinces of Kiev and Kharkov, Kiev being the symbol of national contention with a truce of classes, and Kharkov that of class strife with a truce of nationalities.[66]

Although scattered groups working with the Russian prototype and also independently dated back to the era of the first revolution, the Ukrainian Socialist Revolutionary party (PUSR) as such owed its existence to the February Revolution. The earlier groups had restricted their propaganda to students and peasants, virtually nothing having been accomplished with respect to the working class—a natural consequence of the fact that most of the workers were not Ukrainian. In the free atmosphere of the February era Ukrainian SR organizations "grew like grass on the steppe," without shedding, however, their embryonic characteristics, for the peasantry continued to form the base, and the intelligentsia the apex, of the party structure.[67] The adherence of virtually the entire intelligentsia of Chernigov province with the schoolteachers' corps in the van had combined with the first stirrings of political consciousness in the villages to make the Chernigov branch of the PUSR a thing of massive proportions.[68] There were special reasons why the peasants would follow Little rather than Great Russian leadership besides language and the numerical preponderance of the Ukrainian intellectuals: the character of the gentry, Polish or Russian in culture if not by antecedents, imparted a nationalist tinge to the struggle for possession of the land,[69] and peasants in the Ukraine feared the imposition of Great Russian forms of communal tenure, as Chernov pointed out.[70]

---

[66] See comment of Rafes, *Dva goda revoliutsii na Ukraine,* pp. 10, 13.

[67] Khristiuk, *Zamitki i materiiali,* I, 35, 37.

[68] Shcherbakov, *Zhovtneva revoliutsiia i roki gromadians'koï borot'bi na Chernigivshchini,* p. 34.

[69] Rafes, *Dva goda revoliutsii na Ukraine,* p. 8.

[70] In his speech before the Northern Regional Conference; see Petrograd *Zemlia i Volia,* No. 49 (May 24, 1917). This was a groundless fear. It lay in the genius of the Vikhliaev plan that socialization could be adapted to household as well as communal tenure or even to private property. In essence, the scheme was broadly democratic and egalitarian rather than socialistic, for, though the land would be "no one's," the peasant who worked a plot not large enough to require hired labor would keep it and receive more if it were below the standard set. See Vikhliaev, *Kak uravniat' pol'zovanie zemlëi,* pp. 16 ff., esp. pp. 20-24.

The towns in the Ukraine were too non-Ukrainian in population for the new party to dominate them, even with the help of the Ukrainian Social Democrats, but it was determined to sweep the villages clean of opposition. Since the SR's had made the soviets the chosen form of peasant organization and since its adoption might help to spread the influence of the urban soviets, controlled by the All-Russian parties, the Ukrainian SR's banned the soviet form of organization and entered the field with their own system, a hierarchy of nationalist peasants' unions known as the Selians'ka Spilka. In this contest between the USR's with their Spilka and the SR's with their soviets the fortunes of war were divided, though the advantage lay with the Ukrainians. The right-bank or western Ukraine was the only part of Russia, aside from the Transcaucasus, where the SR's were thoroughly worsted in a contest for the allegiance of the rural masses. In both instances their own intransigence was wholly or partially to blame, for both the Kievan and Transcaucasian SR's were so nationalistic themselves as to bring on a violent collision with the nationalism of the indigenous population.[71] From their own records we have a concrete example of what happened in the western Ukraine. Having been swept from the field, the SR's tried in the fall to make a comeback in the Uman district of Kiev province by organizing a peasants' congress with representation from 118 of 180

[71] The Transcaucasian SR's were distinguished by their anti-Moslem bias and their partiality for the Armenians. This proved their undoing. To begin with, they got nowhere with the Georgian peasantry because of the power of the Mensheviks, who comprised, in effect, the national party of Georgia. The SR's continually oscillated between an alliance with the Armenian Dashnaktsutiun and a policy of drawing off its truly revolutionary members into their own fold. And they beat the drums for a fight to the finish with Turkey, writing off the Azerbaidzhan Tatars, with minor exceptions, as hopeless in the revolutionary sense. The result was that the Mensheviks took the politically formless Moslems in tow and with their support soundly trounced the SR's and their Armenian allies in the regional peasants' congress (June 20-28) by a vote of 573 to 296—the most signal reverse sustained by the Narodnik land program in the whole course of the revolution. The SR attitude is reflected in the report of preparations for a party conference in Delo Naroda, No. 15 (April 1, 1917); see also Rathauser, Revoliutsiia i grazhdanskaia voina, I, 49, 66-67, 108-9. On the political struggle in the Transcaucasus see S. Bagerian's letter in Delo Naroda, No. 103 (July 18, 1917); also N. Mitsishvili's report in Volia Naroda, No. 75 (July 26, 1917); and especially G. Chubinov, "K krest'ianskomu voprosu v Zakavkaz'e" (The Peasant Problem in the Transcaucasus), Delo Naroda, No. 127 (August 15, 1917).

villages. The congress duly adopted their program and voted to set up a soviet. Immediately the Spilka went into action and in the space of two weeks by dint of tub-thumping nationalism contrived to wreck the whole project and strangle the newborn soviet.[72] Besides showing the superiority of the younger party this incident discloses only too clearly how easily the yokels could be swayed by articulate groups, being inclined now in one direction, now in the other. There was something in the Kadet assertion that the peasants agreed with whoever got to them last, the one exception being the Kadets themselves. But the PSR lacked the strength for a systematic effort, and on the right bank it was pressed back until it became almost purely an urban party, resting on the suffrage of Russian and Jewish workers, soldiers, and petty burghers.[73]

On the left bank, in the part of the Ukraine that was closer to the Muscovite core of Russia and more intimately connected with it, a different situation prevailed. Various factors conspired to reduce national antagonisms and create a common ground that was lacking on the other side of the Dnieper. The Ukranian SR's in the east were drawn from a population less removed from the Great Russian in location, language, and historical tradition. With them the social aspects of revolution outweighed the national. As nearly as can be made out, they sincerely believed in the federalism to which many of the right-bank politicians paid only lip service, and some not even that.[74] On the other hand, the PSR in the eastern Ukraine was predominantly of a radical cast, generously disposed toward the demands of national minorities and seeking collaboration with them in the task of ending the war and furthering the revolution. The Ukrainian SR's and the main-line SR's entertained the same political and social aims and both were less agitated by the

---

[72] *Partiinyia Izvestiia*, No. 5 (January 20, 1918), pp. 58-59.

[73] Khristiuk, *Zamitki i materiiali*, I, 25, 43, 45; I. Prilezhaev, "Verolomnye moskali iz Smol'nago" (Faithbreaking Muscovites from the Smolny Institute), *Delo Naroda*, No. 229 (December 10, 1917); Rafes, *Dva goda revoliutsii na Ukraine*, p. 10.

[74] On the sectional cleavage in the PUSR see *1917 god na Kievshchine*, pp. 111-12, 174-75; Rafes, *Dva goda revoliutsii na Ukraine*, p. 11; *Tretii s"ezd P.S.-R.*, p. 413 (statement of Alekseev).

national problem than their comrades across the river. So peaceful cohabitation was the rule east of the Dnieper. In Kharkov and Poltava provinces, as also in the nonconforming right-bank province of Kherson, the SR organization was in the hands of the left wing, which got along so well with the Ukrainian SR's that the two parties were virtually one, preserving the unity of the peasant movement and presenting a joint ticket in election campaigns. In Kharkov and Kherson there appears to have been no Selians'ka Spilka but only peasants' soviets; in Poltava, no soviets but only the Spilka.[75] Culturally and politically, Kharkov set the tone on the left bank, and so homogeneous were the two big parties in their radicalism, and so tolerant in their national views, that people came to speak of the "Kharkov idyl."

But in the other two provinces of Chernigov and Ekaterinoslav, where the left SR's were not in control, there was the same bickering and the same division in the peasant movement as in the western Ukraine. The initial advantage in Chernigov of the older party is seen in the decision of the first peasants' congress to affiliate with the All-Russian Soviet, just as the later success of the Ukrainian SR's in wresting control from the "Muscovites" is attested by the decision of the second congress in June to switch allegiance to the Spilka. Thereafter the SR's gradually were pressed from the field until by the end of the year they were left clinging only to shreds of their former power and influence, and Bolshevism, brought in on the bayonets of troops streaming back from the front, had become the only real challenge to the dominion of the Ukrainian SR's.[76] In Ekaterinoslav province the SR's stood on firmer ground, maintaining a war on two fronts—against their particularist offshoot

---

[75] Judging from the make-up of the tickets in the election to the Constituent Assembly. See names of candidates and the organizations behind them in *Vserossiiskoe Uchreditel'noe Sobranie*, pp. 116 ff. A Bolshevik source concedes that the influence of the Ukrainian SR's in Poltava province filtered down to the poorest substratum of agricultural laborers—a significant admission, for the Bolsheviks liked to depict nationalism as the affair of the rich peasants, and the hired hands as fit subjects of their own dominion. See Erde, *Gody buri i natiska*, Book I: *Na levoberezh'i 1917*, p. 42, n. 2.

[76] Shcherbakov, *Zhovtneva revoliutsiia i roki gromadians'koï borot'bi na Chernigivshchini*, pp. 33-34; Khristiuk, *Zamitki i materiiali*, I, 43.

in the country, against the Bolsheviks in the towns—and managing to avert a rout even after victory had inclined to their rivals. First in the field, as in Chernigov, they had established peasants' soviets on a solid footing before the Ukrainian SR's began to promote the Spilka, and, aided by the considerable Great Russian element in the population as well as by the Little Russian origin of many of their leaders, the SR's fought tenaciously through the summer and into the fall to hold their advantage. The climax came at the October peasants' congress, where abusive tactics on the part of the Ukrainian SR's, extending even to accusations that a pogrom had been instigated by the Penza SR's against the Ukrainian minority, rallied the mass of delegates to their side and gave them the victory by a vote of 170 to 80. The inevitable bolt followed. By about the same ratio the Ukrainian SR's carried the province in the November election, receiving 556,012 votes against 231,717 for the PSR and 213,163 for the Bolsheviks. Though the Russian SR's eventually lost their commanding position in Ekaterinoslav, they retained a substantial following.[77]

The general rule, therefore, is that everywhere except in the provinces under leftist domination the two kindred parties were more divided by the national issue than they were united by the agrarian; in fact, the unity of the peasant movement had been lost in the heat of national strife. This was worst in Kiev, the center of political turmoil and the hearth of national antagonisms. The sessions of the Rada rang with denunciations of "Muscovite centralism" by Kovalevski, Maevski, Shapoval, and other Ukrainian Socialist Revolutionaries, who found the Russian democracy at fault equally with the bourgeoisie in upholding the unitary concept of the state and in planning to hold the "breadbasket of Russia" in economic servitude to the poorer but more populous sections of the empire; they promised to combat such tendencies by every means in their power, even by terrorism, and predicted the dissolution of existing

[77] See V. Pavlov's report in *Volia Naroda*, No. 146 (October 17, 1917); report to the Head Land Committee in *Delo Naroda*, No. 140 (August 8, 1917); *Partiinyia Izvestiia*, No. 1 (September 28, 1917), p. 18, and No. 3 (October 19, 1917), p. 35; figures for Ekaterinoslav province in my book, *Election to the Russian Constituent Assembly*, p. 79.

ties, dubious in any event, if the Russian attitude remained un-changed.[78] The nationalism of representative SR's in Kiev was just as strong if less strident, since they were not struggling to estab-lish a new order but merely defending one that already existed. Fearing that the Ukrainian national congress in May might take the bit in its teeth and assume power, Nezlobin, chairman of the Kiev soviet, threatened to have it dispersed at the point of bayonets.[79] Nezlobin himself, the mayor of Kiev, Riabtsev, the head of the Kiev military district, Colonel Oberuchev, and the minority representa-tives in the Rada, Sklovski, Sukhovykh, and Zarubin, were all SR's of the right center or beyond, for whom the authority of the Pro-visional Government was as axiomatic as the indissolubility of the empire. They saw themselves as guardians of the new order against wreckers, whereas the Ukrainians saw them as satraps of Muscovite imperialism.

Fundamentally the SR's and Ukrainian SR's were split over the question of whether sovereignty lay with the whole or the part, with the All-Russian Constituent Assembly or with its Ukrainian counter-part. All other points at issue could be reduced to this underlying one. The SR's always held that the All-Russian body must pass the articles of federation, without denying categorically the right of secession—the latter they just brushed aside as of no validity, for who would want to leave an empire converted into a free association of peoples?[80] But the undertone was indubitable hostility to the breakup of the old empire. With reference to the Ukraine specifi-cally, a member of the SR Central Committee would proclaim after Brest-Litovsk that the overthrow of any arrangement impeding the flow of grain, coal, and metal to the industrial north or the move-

[78] *1917 god na Kievshchine*, pp. 111, 287, 288; see also proclamation of, the Petersburg Committee of the PUSR in *Delo Naroda*, No. 129 (August 17, 1917).

[79] Vinnichenko, *Vidrodzhennia natsii*, I, 89-90.

[80] A good example of how the SR's would climb up on a moral perch and sit there, without it being possible to knock them off. A member of the Central Committee later asserted that the Poles would have chosen to remain in the Russian federation if the Bolsheviks had not prostrated their country at the feet of Germany—as though Germany were any more the hereditary enemy than Russia! See O. S. Minor, "Natsional'nyi vopros v 1917-18 gg." (The National Question in 1917-18), in *God russkoi revoliutsii*, p. 96.

ment of manufactured goods southward in exchange was a matter
of life and death for the Russian state.[81] Upon the question of
sovereignty would also depend the distribution of powers, for the
Ukrainian SR's claimed the plenitude of power for the regional
authority, while many SR's would go beyond a reservation of defense and minority guarantees to include the tariff, finance, communications, and the more important aspects of social policy within
the federal competence.[82] Even the territorial delimitation of the
Ukraine was bound up in the question of sovereignty: for the
Ukrainian SR's the inclusion of all eight of the provinces in which
their speech predominated was a matter beyond dispute, and wilder
spirits among them looked beyond to the Taurida and Bessarabia,
at the same time that some members of the PSR begrudged the concession of even five provinces to the Rada,[83] and the left SR's themselves debated for months whether their Kharkov stronghold should
go with the new state or remain outside.[84] With relations already
strained to the breaking point, the SR's averted open hostilities only
by refusing to be pinned down as to where they officially stood on
the territorial limits of the Ukraine, the distribution of powers under
their scheme of federation, and the competence of regional constituent assemblies.[85] Their vagueness purchased a respite at some

[81] A. Eliashevich, "Razrushenie promyshlennosti i rabochii klass" (The
Working Class and the Destruction of Industry), *Narodovlastie*, No. 2, p. 40.

[82] See report on the nationalities section of the Fourth Congress in *Delo
Naroda*, No. 229 (December 10, 1917); compare with the Vishniak report at the
Third Congress (see preceding chapter), which provided for widest decentral-
ization. The party as a whole never took an official stand.

[83] See report of the regional congress of the PSR in *1917 god na Kievshchine*,
p. 201. Some SR's advocated the plebiscite method to determine the status of
territories in which the Ukrainian segment of the population numbered less
than 80 to 90 percent. See N. Briullova-Shaskolskaia, "K ukrainskomu voprosu"
(The Ukrainian Question), *Delo Naroda*, No. 110 (July 26, 1917); I. Sklovski,
"K ukrainskomu uchreditel'nomu sobraniiu" (Toward the Ukrainian Constituent Assembly), *ibid.*, No. 224 (December 5, 1917).

[84] *1917 god v Khar'kove*, p. 57.

[85] Already in May some party members were growing restive over the disinclination to go beyond nebulous phrases: see speech of Alekseev of Kharkov
(L) in *Tretii s"ezd P.S.-R.*, p. 413; see also Briullova-Shaskolskaia, "P.S.-R. i
natsional'nyi vopros" (The SR Party and the National Question), *Delo Naroda*,
No. 55 (May 21, 1917). But the stalling continued, even as late as December,
when the Ukrainian SR's were imperatively demanding an ironclad understanding as to the competence of the All-Russian Constituent Assembly. See
Delo Naroda, No. 234 (December 16, 1917).

cost, however, for even in quarters where the principle of federalism commanded more than lip service, as among the Ukrainian SR's in the east, the suspicion gained ground that the SR's refused to commit themselves because they really did not mean to give satisfaction even to moderate demands for self-determination.

In the late spring of 1917, however, the Ukrainian patriots came up with a practical application of sovereignty that would have defied evasion by the most slippery politician. They proposed to draw together the soldiers of Little Russian origin, scattered throughout the army under the tsarist mobilization plan, into homogeneous national units, to be concentrated eventually on Little Russian soil. That posed the question of sovereignty as nothing else could have, and put everyone on the spot: the moderates in the Rada, the military authorities, Minister of War Kerenski, the Provisional Government as a whole, and even the SR's. No dodging on this issue! We know that the left-wing or Kharkov faction of the Ukrainian SR party had originally opposed the formulation of such a demand, but apparently had been overruled by the right-bank faction or else had receded from its position, for by summer the party delegation in the Rada seemed firmly committed to nationalization.[86] The SR's took just the opposite stand, their representatives in the Kiev soviet being in the forefront of the resistance to the formation of an all-Ukrainian regiment.[87] Even in the mother soviet in Petersburg, where the tone of the party organization was more radical, the SR delegation after an exceptionally heated debate refused to countenance the creation of national units above the platoon and company levels.[88] Only the impact of the October Revolution produced a change in the SR attitude, ostensibly because the armistice (which they other-

---

[86] *1917 god na Kievshchine*, pp. 111, 180-81; Khristiuk, *Zamitki i materiiali*, I, 36. Nationalist agitation created no problem at Kharkov, where troops of all nationalities had been engulfed in a wave of Bolshevism, the spread of which had been facilitated by the inclusion of the area in the Moscow military district (1916). See Oberuchev, *Vospominaniia*, pp. 198-99. Doubtlessly the antiwar stand of the left SR's was also a weighty factor, but sources frequently, and unjustly, make no distinction between Bolshevism and left-wing Social Revolutionism. Troops in the Kiev district proved to be more resistant to disintegrating influences of a social nature, only to succumb to those of a nationalist character.

[87] *1917 god na Kievshchine*, p. 45.

[88] *Delo Naroda*, No. 50 (May 16, 1917).

wise loudly condemned) had dispelled the objections to army reorganization, but actually because they grasped at any straw that held out hope of armed support for the Constituent Assembly.[89]

The two officials most immediately concerned with the question, the commander of the Kiev military district, Colonel K. M. Oberuchev, and War Minister Kerenski, were both nominally members of the PSR and even of the same right-wing faction, yet so poorly were their actions coordinated that the one undermined the authority of the other. Oberuchev was a typical SR from the officers' corps: the revolutionary tradition in which he was rooted had paled as his patriotism became more intense, and in any event it had paid little heed to nationalist distinctions. With him the overriding consideration was to get on with the war, and he resented the intrusion of extraneous matters such as the regrouping of soldiers along national lines, which might serve as an excuse for not going to the front or even for organized desertion (June was the month in which the Provisional Government responded to Allied pressure with an offensive). Feeling that it would be made up largely of deserters from regular units, he had opposed the formation of an all-Ukrainian regiment bearing the name of Hetman Bogdan Khmelnitski,[90] but had been overruled by Kerenski, who recognized it as an accomplished fact with the admonition to undertake nothing further along this line. Yet another regiment, the Paul Polubotok, still wilder in spirit, was already in process of formation. With political freedom in the army, nationally conscious elements in regular units of the front and rear established contacts, and Ukrainian soldiers' congresses were held, the second one being convened in mid-June. Kerenski

[89] "Nasiliia nad natsional'nostiami" (Coercion of the Nationalities), *ibid.*, No. 237 (December 20, 1917); Rathauser, *Revoliutsiia i grazhdanskaia voina v Baku*, I, 124.

[90] Without any desire to disparage Ukrainian nationalism, it may be pointed out that it undoubtedly contained an element of artificiality. The Ukrainian patriots must have been hard pressed for national heroes to accord this honor to a Zaporozhian freebooter who had repeatedly sold out the Ukrainian peasants to the Polish crown. Either the youthful intellectuals who headed the PUSR had no deep feeling for the class they represented or they did not know their history, or knew it only through romantic distortion. For Khmelnitski stripped bare of adornment see W. E. D. Allen's excellent history, *The Ukraine* (Cambridge, England, 1941).

pronounced it "inopportune" and refused to authorize leaves of absence for attendance. As for Oberuchev, he not only found it impossible to obstruct the congress but even helped the sponsors obtain the municipal theater, yet felt obliged by his superior's attitude to turn his back on the proceedings, thereby adding a personal affront to the difference of principle between himself and the Ukrainian military leaders.[91]

Meanwhile the Ukrainian national council or Rada had set up an executive organ called the Secretariat, had issued a proclamation called a Universal, which was something less than a decree and something more than a manifesto, and was making stabs at taking over public functions from the officials of the Provisional Government, including even the power to tax. The current of events flowed more swiftly, Kiev and Petrograd were waiting to see whose nerves cracked first, and a showdown was in the air.[92] Nothing was more certain than the inability of the largest party in Great Russia and the largest party in Little Russia to mediate the conflict, despite their common ideology. A quarrel between relatives can be exceptionally bitter, and these two parties could not work together to allay the strife which in large measure they had engendered. Ninety percent or more of the following of both consisted of peace-loving peasants who, had they been less helpless and inarticulate, might easily have found their way together, but the excess of nationalism among the intellectuals at the top cursed both parties, and cursed especially their followings. The chickens hatched in the Populist incubator were now coming home to roost. People who could not contemplate peace with Germany or Austria also could not contemplate it with their blood brothers, except on their terms. The bluff but well-meaning colonel at Kiev became the symbol of mutual antagonism: the Ukrainian SR's clamored for his dismissal[93] while the SR's in the

[91] *Vospominaniia*, pp. 220-30; A. Shulgin, *L'Ukraine contre Moscou 1917*, pp. 117-18; Chernov, *Great Russian Revolution*, pp. 274-77.
[92] A good summary of developments in English will be found in Reshetar, *The Ukrainian Revolution 1917-1920*, pp. 47 ff.; Chernov's account, though less well organized because of the multiplicity of threads, is full of information (*Great Russian Revolution*, pp. 264 ff.).
[93] *1917 god na Kievshchine*, pp. 180-81.

southwest rallied to his side and renounced any thought of a bloc
with the other party in the November election.[94]

Certain members of the Provisional Government, apparently without benefit of party guidance (which most likely they would have
disregarded in any event), determined to go to Kiev and produce a
détente in the situation through an agreement with the Rada. Partisan
ties rested with equal lightness on Kerenski, Nekrasov, and Tereshchenko, the Masonic trio whose creed emancipated them from sectarian influence and permitted them to balance off the socialists
against the Constitutional Democrats, preserving for themselves the
power of decision. They were joined by Irakli Tsereteli, most influential member of the "star chamber," as the camarilla was called
which ran the workers' and soldiers' soviets, both locally, in St.
Petersburg, and on the all-Russian level. The minister of foreign
affairs, Tereshchenko, Ukrainian in origin but Russian in orientation,
was a wealthy playboy, a connoisseur of the ballet, but Kerenski,
Nekrasov, and Tsereteli were powerful figures who controlled the
dual source of power stemming from the February Revolution and
therewith the destinies of Russia. Had it been a party and not a
personal affair, it would not have been possible to ignore Chernov,
the leading exponent of federalism in the cabinet, who not only was
left out of this but does not seem even to have been consulted. To
read Chernov's account,[95] one would think that he sympathized with
the Ukrainian point of view, yet he took quite a different line at the
time, when he was in the cabinet and could have influenced the
course of events. Perhaps more as a demonstration of solidarity with
the cabinet than as an expression of personal conviction, Chernov
had published in the central organ of his party an attack upon the
"irresponsible actions" of the Rada in presuming to invade, or expecting the Provisional Government to invade, the competence of the
Constituent Assembly in such matters as boundary delimitation and
taxation; the course of the Rada he qualified as "Leninism in the

---

[94] *Partiinyia Izvestiia*, No. 2 (October 5, 1917), p. 46; *Delo Naroda*, No. 165
(September 27, 1917) (report of the Southwestern Front Conference of the
PSR).
[95] In the *Great Russian Revolution*, chap. XIV.

nationalities question."[96] Chernov exerted himself to prove to his detractors that he, too, had the interests of the state at heart and would give no aid or comfort to extremists in this or other questions.

The self-appointed negotiators who went to Kiev, therefore, did not have to worry about any interference from the PSR. They arrived in the mother of Russian cities at the end of June and returned to Petersburg on July 2 with an agreement which they submitted to the rest of the cabinet as the delicate fruit of difficult negotiations which must be eaten without further paring or delay. The Constitutional Democrats were furious, if Chernov was not, at being confronted with a *fait accompli*, and liking the substance still less than the form, their four ministers resigned from the government and put an end to the first coalition. Nekrasov was also nominally a Kadet but he and Miliukov were so far apart that there was nothing illogical in his staying on as minister without portfolio. The two Populist parties reacted in typical fashion: the SR's threw the weight of their influence behind the accord but the Ukrainian SR's would have no part of it, and cut the margin of acceptance in the Rada to the ill-boding ratio of 100 to 70. Chernov does not portray events in their full light; no doubt he would have found it embarrassing to admit that the dominant right-bank faction of the PUSR formed the spearhead of opposition to a compromise settlement.[97]

The agreement itself left many things up in the air, including even the territorial extent of the Ukraine, and could have succeeded only with more good will than was visible on either the northern or southern horizons. It authorized steps towards autonomy while reserving the rights of the All-Russian Constituent Assembly; the General Secretariat would act as the chief governmental agency, but under the control of the Petersburg cabinet as well as the Rada; without accepting the principle of Ukrainian troops on Ukrainian soil, Kerenski acceded to the formation of detachments of one na-

---

[96] "Lozhnyi vyvod iz pravil'noi predposylki" (A False Conclusion from a Correct Premise), *Delo Naroda*, No. 75 (June 15, 1917). This was a signed article.

[97] A. Shulgin, *L'Ukraine contre Moscou 1917*, p. 122; Miliukov, *Istoriia vtoroi russkoi revoliutsii*, I, Part I, 233; see Chernov, *Great Russian Revolution*, pp. 280-81.

tionality if compatible with military requirements. There was nothing in the agreement that could be considered disruptive if the federal principle were taken seriously, but Miliukov's party was not federalist in outlook; rather was it deeply centralistic, with a pronounced anti-Ukrainian bias.

For all of its opposition to the Imperial Government between 1914 and 1917, and disregarding superficial phenomena, the war had caused this party to shift to the right; then the revolution had driven under its skirts all elements more conservative than itself, still further transforming its character, until by the summer of 1917 it may be said to have become the counterpart of National Liberalism in Germany, with which it entered into a competition of follies that might better have caused both to be styled parties of National Decimation and Disaster. The heart of the Constitutional Democrat bled for the Czech and South Slav brothers in Austrian duress, and there was nothing that he would not give the Poles except what Catherine had taken, but he bridled at the mention of the Slavic ethnic group that was second only to his own in numbers and first in point of historical misfortune. Chernov sees in the privileges granted the Poles the source of similar demands on the part of the Ukrainians,[98] who could not understand why people whose forbears had joined Russia of their own accord should be denied the rights enjoyed by a thrice-conquered enemy. The answer lies in the Pan-Slavist aberration of many Russian intellectuals, modified by a touch, or more than a touch, of imperialism. The anti-Finnish, anti-Ukrainian, anti-Turk and Tatar, not to speak of anti-German, bias extended from right-wing Populism to Constitutional Democracy and beyond, gaining in intensity the farther right it went,[99] until in Miliukov and Rodichev we encounter champions of any form of Slavic nationalism that would weaken the Teutonic empires; but when, as with Ukrainian nationalism, the fire turned back on Russia, their Pan-Slavism ceased abruptly, exposing its imperialist essence. To them Ukrainians were Russians masquerading as a separate ethnic group with a dangerous

[98] *Great Russian Revolution*, pp. 269, 272.
[99] A large segment of the right, of course, was not and never had been anti-German (Witte, Durnovo, Gurko, Rasputin).

pro-Austrian orientation, whereas Poles were by no stretch of the imagination Russian and shared their own Germanophobia. Hence the discrimination. Miliukov tells how the Kadet ministers carried into the fateful cabinet session of July 2 the new decision of their party in favor of regional autonomy,[100] but the emphasis was upon regional rather than national autonomy, though in the case of the Ukraine it is difficult to see how even the Kadets could have prevented the one from becoming the other. But this was merely bending before the storm; the leopard cannot change his spots, nor could the Kadet his centralism.

Because the crisis over agrarian policy matured at the same time, it has been argued that the Kadets threw up a smoke screen of patriotism over the Ukrainian question in order to conceal their real motive for leaving the government—dissatisfaction with the economic policies of Chernov and the other socialist ministers. The SR's themselves so construed the action of a party which had identified itself with property interests.[101] But the leaders of Constitutional Democracy were not captains of industry and owners of broad estates; they were primarily professional people—physicians, journalists, civil servants, army officers, and, above all, professors and jurists—for whom the fetish of the state as something above the lives and fortunes of its citizens meant more than other considerations, and caused them to view a threat to territorial integrity as the supreme evil arising from the Pandora's box of revolution, even as it drove them onward in a war which was wrecking the economy of Russia and enraging the social classes upon which, in the last analysis, any state must rest. The Kadet party in 1917 had become, it is true, a very conservative organization, mindful of vested interests in both industry and agriculture, yet the inner shrine at which its devotees worshiped was the State, not Property, and of all the forces threatening to cast down their idol the deadliest was Ukrainian nationalism. For what would it profit them to conquer Galicia and the Straits, Posen and East Prussia, if the south of the Russian matrix were lost—in the

---

[100] *Istoriia vtoroi russkoi revoliutsii*, I, Part I, 236.
[101] *Kratkii otchët o rabotakh chetvërtago s"ezda P.S.-R.*, p. 68 (in the report of the Central Committee to the Fourth Congress).

hearts of its people, if not by actual separation? A keen observer like Sukhanov, despite his Marxian intellectualism, is intelligent enough to recognize the independent force of the Ukrainian question in killing the first coalition.[102] On the other hand, Miliukov, in distracting the reader's attention with minor issues from the influence of the agrarian factor, concedes that the crisis did not break exclusively over the Ukrainian question.[103]

Few mourners wept for the first coalition as it went to the grave. Deadlock rather than achievement had been inscribed on its record. On the agrarian front there was increasing chaos as the laws establishing a new order were held up while peasant sentiment blocked a return to the old. A real effort had been made to find a solution for the most serious of the nationality problems, but only at the cost of destroying the coalition and reopening the question of power. And on the peace front, nothing whatever had been accomplished beyond a disastrous step in the opposite direction in the form of the offensive of June 18, which failed in a few days and left everything worse than before at the front, besides greatly increasing the tension in public life.[104] Other problems of lesser import still awaited a solution, and the preparation for the election to the Constituent Assembly had crawled along at a snail's pace. On the face of things the advantage seemed to lie with the socialists, as two months before when Miliukov retired, for they remained on the battlefield while their enemies withdrew; but whatever advantage they had, they owed to the intermediate elements who held the balance of power. The Kadet reverse was not yet definitive, and it remained to be seen what the socialists would do with their "victory."

[102] *Zapiski*, IV, 369-70.
[103] *Istoriia vtoroi russkoi revoliutsii*, I, Part I, 236.
[104] See following chapters.

VIII

THE JULY CRISIS AND THE BIRTH
OF THE SECOND COALITION

BEFORE the socialists could do anything with their "victory," they faced a formidable revolt within their own ranks against further delay in realizing the program of land and peace or—in simplest terms—against the class truce which lay at the basis of coalition. Petersburg workers and soldiers, stirred by Bolshevik propaganda but without Bolshevik leadership, joined hands with sailors from Kronstadt to force the moderate socialists in control of the soviets to institute an all-socialist government. The July Days are interesting sociologically as marking an attempt of the lower classes to impose their inchoate will on the intellectuals who spoke in their name and for the most part led them around by the nose. The attempt ended as all such attempts end, and even more quickly than most, in popular frustration.

A word about the attitude of the three main socialist parties at this turning point of the revolution. The Bolshevik attitude was dictated by calculation—it favored a seizure of power but not at this juncture, for the party had not yet ousted its Menshevik and SR rivals from enough positions to enable it to swing toilers elsewhere behind the Petersburg vanguard. The Menshevik attitude was dictated by dogma, which told them that nothing was worse than for a socialist party to come to power in a country unready for socialism, for then either it must disappoint its followers or it must embark on an experiment foredoomed to failure. Their dogma was both correct and impossible: correct, as the sequel has shown; and impossible, because the Mensheviks had no way of communicating their own patience and restraint to their working-class following, which sooner or later was bound to desert them.

The SR attitude was dictated neither by calculation nor by dogma; they made no calculations, and had forgotten their dogma. Once again we are reminded that with them the state of mind was everything, the dogma distinctly secondary. When the state of mind changed, the dogma was not revised but allowed to remain as a sort of cocoon, a dry and dusty thing which in no way constrained the form of life that had left it behind. Perpetual coalition was a corollary of the Menshevik belief in the bourgeois character of the revolution but was by no means enjoined by the SR concept of an intermediate order ushered in by socialization of the land, which would break the bourgeois mold of society without as yet establishing socialism. Whether this *narodno-trudovoe* [popular-toil] concept of the revolution was too purely a product of Chernov's mind to have much meaning for other party members, or whether it had consciously been laid aside to smooth the path of coalition, it did not influence the trend of policy in 1917. The SR attitude would seem to have been determined by three other factors. The war had forged a powerful link between the Constitutional Democrats and the right-wing Socialist Revolutionaries; the latter were always ready to submerge differences in order to preserve the union of "all live forces" and to avoid the displeasure of the Western Allies. Party members less willing to sacrifice the social program of the revolution could always console themselves with the thought that the Constituent Assembly was not far away, that it would have to pass on matters in any event and would settle all problems. Faith in the assembly provided wings for a flight from reality. And last but not least, the disparity in leadership between the Menshevik and SR parties meant that in any close association the lesser party would take the larger in tow and make it serve the Menshevik concept of the revolution, whether its members consciously wanted to or not. Precisely the same relationship developed in Kiev,[1] where the Vinnichenkos and Petliuras virtually took over the huge but headless PUSR, though

---

[1] Brief comment on this in Reshetar, *The Ukrainian Revolution*, pp. 62, 135.

these Ukrainian Social Democrats could muster in their own right scarcely a corporal's guard. With the prevalent state of disunity it must be remembered, of course, that there was no one attitude or position in the case of the PSR: the left SR's agreed with the Bolsheviks on throwing coalition out of the window, but wanted the succeeding regime to be one of the proletariat *and* the peasantry. When we speak of SR policy, we mean the majority line, and this had hardened against an assumption of power and in favor of renewing the coalition.

When the breakup of the ministry sparked all the accumulated discontent in the capital and the discontented took to the streets, they could do no better than reecho the Bolshevik slogan of "All Power to the Soviets," only to find that the Mensheviks and SR's in control of the soviets were united in their determination to resist mob tactics and reassert their authority, if necessary by force of arms. While the force was being gathered by Kerenski as minister of war, the soviet leaders decided to send out the "village minister" to talk to the people in the hope that he could quiet these uprooted peasants. Chernov's appeal to the populace must not be underestimated—he was still being used in this fashion on the Volga in 1918, and still with some effect—but his charm did not work on this occasion. His sharp attack on the Kadets failed to engage the sympathy of the crowd; he was hauled down and thrust into a waiting automobile, perhaps to be borne away to his death or else lynched on the spot, had he not been rescued by Trotski's intervention. As often happens on such occasions, no two eyewitnesses formed the same impression of the circumstances of this attempted abduction. The only agreement is that the minister had lost possession of himself and was in a state of "funk" (on this point Chernov is the lone dissenter). But as to the identity of his assailants, there were as many opinions as witnesses. With his powers of perception understandably dimmed, Chernov speaks only of shady characters who had nothing in common with the mass of soldiers and sailors; Trotski is more explicit, ascribing the mischief to agents of the Okhrana (the tsarist secret police), whom he claimed to be able to spot in a crowd of ten thousand; while Midshipman Raskolnikov, a leader of Bolshevik cells in the Baltic Fleet, thought that criminal elements were involved. Sukhanov, on the other hand, sees no provocation but only the fury of the Kronstadt sailors, a factor that Raskolnikov cannot deny.[2]

All these explanations are plausible. In the case of Chernov and even of Trotski, however, we are dealing with men of an idealistic turn of mind who would deny the evidence of their senses if derogatory to the masses, and Trotski's Jewish imagination might lead him to see agents of the Okhrana under the bed. Sukhanov was also a revolutionist, but a more cynical one. Apparently the keenest observer, or the one with the most self-possession, was Second Lieutenant Adam Iablonski, who offered yet a fifth version of the incident: according to him, a band of civilian anarchists, numbering thirty or more and bearing aloft a great black banner symbolic of their movement, had egged the mob on; they comprised the only group to be unmoved by Trotski's appeal.[3] There was no doubt about it, the anarchists were having a big time in 1917, seizing buildings, unfurling their black flags, and engaging in everything from requisitions to executions, which other people termed plunder and murder. On the pages of their organ, the *Burevestnik* (Harbinger of Storm), they preached their message of total subversion and proclaimed their stirring slogan: "On our black banners we shall write with the blood of our enemies." The "village minister" was just as much fair game for them as any other minister, and his blood just as red. They may well have been the culprits.

The rough treatment accorded Chernov was a severe shock to many high-minded but naive people, inside and outside the PSR, who had imagined no evil could come from the masses and who were now being introduced to the facts of life. There would be other chapters in their education. Raskolnikov himself was taken aback at how savagely the sailors had turned upon the lately idolized leader.

---

[2] "Arest V. Chernova v iiul'skie dni 1917 g." (The Arrest of V. Chernov in the July Days of 1917), *Krasnaia Letopis'*, XXI (VI, 1926), 69-72; "V iiul'skie dni" (The July Days), *Proletarskaia Revoliutsiia*, XVII (V, 1923), 70; Trotski, *History of the Russian Revolution*, II, 40-41; Sukhanov, *Zapiski*, IV, 425. Embarrassing questions were put to Chernov, as: why had not the people been given the land? See M. Pokrovski, "Grazhdanin Chernov v iiul'skie dni" (Citizen Chernov in the July Days), *Pravda* (Truth), No. 157 (July 16, 1922).

[3] "Arest V. Chernova v iiul'skie dni," *Krasnaia Letopis'*, XXI (VI, 1926), 73.

To Chernov's comrades, particularly those of the right center, the incident should have served as a warning that the fickleness of the capital might in time be communicated to the provinces if the existing deadlock continued. But men like Gotz and those to the right of him never could free themselves of the illusion that the city mob had no roots in the country, and that the foam of Petersburg would spend itself on the rock of Russia; they never could realize that these "uprooted" or "declassed" peasants from the barracks and battleships were the most important peasants in Russia, who in time would drift homeward and play hell with the party's defenses. It was a process of mutual education: the socialist intellectuals had to learn more about the people, and the people more about the socialist intellectuals. When they marched on the Taurida Palace on July 4, 1917, the rank and file were not conscious of the inconsistency involved in shouting for "All Power to the Soviets" and having voted to send Mensheviks and majority SR's to represent them in those soviets; indeed, in the latter case, there was a special reason for confusion, for the worker or soldier might be swayed by a left SR and cast his vote for a right SR, since he had no means of distinguishing the factional allegiance of a candidate. Two more months in the cities, and longer than that in the provinces, were needed before the foot soldiers of the revolution learned to tell red from pink in their command. Until then, having run into something they did not understand, they lapsed into inactivity, leaving the street to the counter-revolution. All of their bewilderment and exasperation found classic formulation in the action of the workingman who shook his fist in Chernov's face and yelled at him in helpless rage: "Take the power, you son-of-a-bitch, when it's given to you!"[4]

The initial reaction in SR circles had been distinctly favorable to repression. Gotz put the party squarely behind Kerenski in respect to coercive measures, probably even to the extent of sanctioning the dispatch of troops from the front.[5] Vladimir Lebedev, Kerenski's deputy in the Marine Ministry and a prominent right SR, confirmed an order instructing the loyalist submarine fleet to sink any vessel

[4] Miliukov, *Istoriia vtoroi russkoi revoliutsii*, I, Part I, 244.
[5] Sukhanov, *Zapiski*, IV, 450-51, 462-63.

steaming from Helsingfors toward Petersburg with reinforcements.[6] SR's of the right did not doubt that the Bolsheviks had guided this uprising and believed, or affected to believe, that they worked on German gold.[7] The "defensists" entrenched in the All-Russian Peasants' Executive Committee breathed fire against Bolshevism and threw the weight of the committee's authority behind repressive measures, though its historian concedes that the average provincial delegate was not opposed on principle to the Bolshevik slogans, but had merely deferred to his leaders' judgment without sharing their profound indignation—a divergence in point of view that assumed fateful significance in the post-October era.[8] Outside the capital the SR's and the Mensheviks worked together to ban demonstrations and so prevent the extension of the disorders to other parts of the country.[9]

Scarcely had the SR's entered the path of repression, however, than they began to be assailed by qualms and misgivings. A typical reaction was that of their leader Chernov, whose emotions on July 4 ran the gamut from terror to humiliation and from humiliation to anger. At first stunned by the danger to which he had been exposed, he recovered toward evening and unleashed a hurricane of activity. Arriving at the editorial offices of the *Delo Naroda* at 11 P.M., Chernov sat down and composed eight scorching editorials against Bolshevism, of which the editors on duty, Ivanov-Razumnik and S. P. Postnikov, felt that four would be enough for one issue. Chernov even wanted to print the documents in the possession of the Ministry of Justice representing the Bolshevik leaders as German agents.[10] In other words, on the night of July 4-5 he acted like a right SR. But the next day he had calmed down and was back at his left of center position, writing two more editorials in defense of the "inalienable right" of the people to demonstrate and warning his comrades to take care lest in escaping the rain of Bolshevism they

[6] Raskolnikov, "V iiul'skie dni," *Proletarskaia Revoliutsiia*, XVII, 63.
[7] P. A. Sorokin, "Ch'i ruki?" (Whose Hands?), *Volia Naroda*, No. 58 (July 6, 1917); resolution of the Omsk SR's in *Delo Naroda*, No. 99 (July 13, 1917).
[8] Bykhovski, *Vserossiiskii Sovet Krest'ianskikh Deputatov*, pp. 153-55.
[9] For their action in Moscow see *Delo Naroda*, No. 93 (July 6, 1917).
[10] Oral testimony of Postnikov.

fall under the hail of reaction.[11] The powerful SR organizations on the Volga, neither leftist nor rightist but straight centrist in tone, recapitulated in slower tempo the attitude of their fellow provincial, at first sanctioning stern measures against Bolshevism and then, under the impact of the wave of counterrevolution, swinging back toward a united front of socialist parties.[12] The SR's did not come through the upheaval unscathed, for some of their left-wing agitators were arrested along with the Bolsheviks, notably Proshian and Ustinov, who had done as much as any member of the rival party to heat up passions in the Baltic naval centers. While SR opinion as a whole might view these men as harmful fanatics, it betrayed a certain sensitivity to their arrest, particularly in great military and industrial centers, where the tone of the organization had always been to the left of center.[13]

While the demonstrations continued, the SR high command would not hear of political changes. "There can be no thought of a change in the cabinet at the present moment under the threat of machine guns; the ministry remains as before, save for deserters; the socialist ministers stay at their posts"—such was the joint decision of the Central Committee and the party representatives in the two Executive Committees of the All-Russian Soviet.[14] To this was appended the statement that the final decision on the reconstruction of the government would be taken by a national soviet congress, to be convened within two weeks in Moscow, a promise that was soon disregarded. A resolution, sponsored by Gotz and adopted by the Executive Committees around 4 A.M. on July 5, declared that in the meantime the power was vested in the residuary cabinet, which

[11] "Moment obiazyvaet" (The Moment Imposes a Duty), and "Nado razmezhevat'sia" (We Must Draw a Line), *Delo Naroda*, No. 93 (July 6, 1917).
[12] Antonov-Saratovski, *Pod stiagom proletarskoi bor'by*, I, 135-39.
[13] The SR's in the Petersburg Soviet and the city organization as a whole—at its fifth conference—condemned arbitrary arrests and excesses on the part of the military, and in general sought to apply the brakes to the campaign of repression. See *Delo Naroda*, Nos. 99, 104, 106 (July 13, 19, 21, 1917).
[14] *Ibid.*, No. 92 (July 5, 1917).

should exercise it in accordance with the decisions of the soviet congresses.[15] In other words, the SR's and their Menshevik allies seemed to be moving away from the uneasy balance of power existing since February toward an assertion of soviet supremacy, since it was the soviets which would decide the make-up of the new ministry, and since they proposed to subordinate the entire staff of the present ministry, and not just its socialist component as hitherto, to the decrees of soviet congresses. A specific demand for the dissolution of the State Duma and the State Council, the two chambers of the old Imperial parliament, strengthened the impression of a break with the February order. But this demand was accompanied by other and more far-reaching ones which indicated a resolve to break the log jam of the defunct ministry: the legislation proposed by the Agricultural Ministry must be passed, an active peace policy based on the soviet formula must be pursued, and the republic proclaimed. For the Socialist Revolutionaries, these demands were put forward by the Central Committee[16] and the supreme organ of the peasants' soviets;[17] the SR's joined hands with the Mensheviks to cause the workers' and soldiers' organ to take the same steps. The desire to check the drift to Bolshevism growing out of dissatisfaction with the record of the Provisional Government[18] and the calculation that now was a good time, with the Kadets out of the government, motivated this program of action. When its announcement forced the minister-president's resignation, the conjuncture seemed even more favorable.

From the withdrawal of the Kadet ministers on July 2 to the re-constitution of the cabinet on July 25, the government of Russia hung in the balance. Personal politics as well as a conflict of principle account for the protracted crisis. The first phase centered around the effects of the July Days and the minister-presidency, the second concerned most directly Chernov and the Ministry of Agriculture.

[15] *Revoliutsiia 1917 goda*, III, 146, and Appendix No. 44, p. 319; *Delo Naroda*, No. 93 (July 6, 1917).

[16] *Delo Naroda*, No. 95 (July 8, 1917).

[17] Bykhovski, *Vserossiiskii Sovet Krest'ianskikh Deputatov*, pp. 154-55.

[18] This dissatisfaction was freely admitted in a leading editorial, which was written by Chernov, though it did not bear his signature at the time of publication; see "Moment obiazyvaet," *Delo Naroda*, No. 93 (July 6, 1917).

On July 7, five days after the Kadets left the government, Prince Lvov followed them into retirement. The interval afforded proof of the independence of the two events, though none was needed, for the head of the first and second Provisional Governments had always comported himself as a nonpartisan and had usually stood to the left of Miliukov's party. The clash with Chernov and the maturation of the crisis over agrarian policy underlay his decision, but more was involved in his resignation than agrarian policy, much more, indeed.

Lvov had posed the choice between himself and Chernov in categorical terms, yet his letter of resignation mentioned other points of divergence as well, chief among them the attempted subordination of the entire government to the dictates of the soviet, the proclamation of a republic, and the dissolution of the Duma.[19] These last two points had figured in the list of demands submitted by the socialist ministers at the cabinet session of July 7, convincing Prince Lvov that his position as head of the government and minister of the interior was no longer tenable. His resignation had followed immediately. Yet when the program of the government was announced on the following day, no mention was made of a republic and no end put to the Duma, while the statement of agrarian policy had been so toned down that even Miliukov could speak of its moderation.[20] What had supervened to cause a cardinal principle like the form of state suddenly to drop out of sight and the strong line taken by the socialist ministers on one day to be emasculated on the next?

According to both Miliukov and Sukhanov, two primary accounts written from diametrically opposing points of view (though both hostile to Kerenski), the game had been to get Lvov out of the cabinet, after which the issues that had provoked his resignation were treated as subjects of negotiation with the remaining nonsocialist ministers. "It seemed as though the retirement of Prince Lvov was necessary to his colleagues, who proceeded at once to divide his

---

[19] Polner, *Zhiznennyi put' Kniazia . . . L'vova*, pp. 255-57; Sukhanov, *Zapiski*, IV, 510; reports in the *Delo Naroda*, No. 95 (July 8, 1917), and in the *Volia Naroda*, No. 62 (July 11, 1917); Chernov, "K ukhodu kn. L'vova" (The Resignation of Prince Lvov), *Delo Naroda*, No. 96 (July 9, 1917); *Kratkii otchët o rabotakh chetvërtago s"ezda P.S.-R.*, pp. 15, 110. Hesitance on the part of the socialist ministers to sanction the arrest of Bolshevik leaders had been an added source of friction.

[20] *Istoriia vtoroi russkoi revoliutsii*, I, Part II, 20.

inheritance,"[21] Kerenski becoming minister-president and Tsereteli taking over the Ministry of the Interior. Miliukov assigns the leading role to Tsereteli, saying that no sooner was Lvov gone than he receded on two of the points—proclamation of a republic and dissolution of the Duma—in order to mollify Nekrasov and other independents remaining in the cabinet.[22] Sukhanov places the decision to break Lvov at the meeting of the "star chamber" in Skobelev's apartment on the night of July 6-7; according to him, Kerenski arrived around two in the morning to transact big business with Tsereteli, Dan, Chkheidze, Gotz, and Skobelev, the regular members of this powerful but clandestine organ which was the fountainhead of soviet policy in the heyday of the SR-Menshevik era.[23] Chernov agrees with Sukhanov as far as Kerenski's motives were concerned: "Lvov's withdrawal from the ministry merely made a place at the head of the government for Kerenski, and in this conflict he was for the first and last time on Chernov's side."[24] It is not necessary to rely on the testimony of Kerenski's enemies, however, to show that he sought Lvov's replacement; he says as much himself, though in carefully guarded language:

The times had become too difficult for his gentle manner of governing. More firmness was needed in dealing with people, more external compulsion in the method of governing. But it is very hard for me to speak objectively of the causes of Prince Lvov's retirement; first, because it fell to me to take his place, and secondly, because my personal relation to this remarkable man, now deceased, does not permit me to see mirrored in his activity those weak sides of character which, of course, were present, just as they are present in all of us.[25]

[21] *Ibid.*, p. 18.

[22] Miliukov doubtlessly errs in asserting that the Georgian Menshevik at first inclined toward Lvov in the conflict with Chernov. Tsereteli says just the opposite, though without reference, it is true, to this precise juncture. See his "Rossiiskoe krest'ianstvo i V. M. Chernov v 1917 godu," *Novyi Zhurnal*, XXIX (1952), 236-37, 242. Had Tsereteli sided with Lvov, even initially, his relations with Chernov could scarcely have continued to be so cordial.

[23] *Zapiski*, IV, 484-92.

[24] *Great Russian Revolution*, p. 242.

[25] "Iz vospominanii," *Sovremennyia Zapiski*, XXXVIII, 251-52. Though purportedly consisting of excerpts from his book for the foreign reading public, this article is fuller at some points than the book: compare *The Catastrophe*, p. 249; *La Révolution russe 1917* (Paris, 1928), p. 248.

Though Kerenski himself bears the chief responsibility for his displacement of Lvov at the head of the Provisional Government, it is not necessary to convict him, as do his detractors, of being actuated solely or even largely by personal ambition. The break-through of the Russian front at Tarnopol, liquidating in disaster the offensive of June 18 and creating a dangerous situation, had followed hard on the heels of the internal crisis provoked by the disorders in Petersburg, leading Kerenski to feel that a public figure with maximum authority in the eyes of the masses should stand at the head of the state if it were not to go under. No one could deny that his popularity was still greater than anyone else's, even though it had begun to tarnish, as had also the less universal popularity of his rival Chernov. Kerenski desired to become minister-president, profoundly convinced that his elevation would benefit both the country and the revolution at a particularly difficult point in their history. And the man whom he replaced agreed with him: "As a matter of fact," Lvov remarked to a friend the morning after his resignation, "I left because there was nothing further for me to do. In order to save the situation it would be necessary to break up the soviets and fire on the people. I could not do that. But Kerenski can."[26]

The SR and Menshevik politicians had engineered a change at the apex of the political structure. That much is clear. But how could men of their convictions debase a great principle such as the republican form of government into an instrument of personal politics, advancing it one day as a cardinal point in their program and the next day forgetting all about it? It must be remembered that while the Mensheviks accepted republicanism as a matter of course without any particular exaltation, for the SR's, always less economic- and more political-minded than the Social Democrats, the republican principle had never ceased to have an independent value. If the Menshevik Tsereteli had thrown the demand overboard, as Miliukov says, why had his SR allies acquiesced? The proclamation of a republic in a country like Russia was not a matter to be brushed aside even by the Mensheviks, however much they might desire to placate bour-

[26] Polner, *Zhiznennyi put' Kniazia . . . L'vova*, p. 258.

geois politicians in what to them was a bourgeois revolution. Nekrasov had objected to the proclamation of a republic, according to
Miliukov, who represents Tsereteli's action as a concession to him
and the other nonsocialist, non-Kadet ministers.[27] But why should
Nekrasov, that arch-Masonic intriguer and typical radical of the
French type, oppose so strenuously the declaration of a republic
months after the country had become a *de facto* republic? Whose
was the ultimate responsibility for the failure to follow through on
this matter—Nekrasov's, Tsereteli's, or someone else's? These questions deserve an answer, for they indicate that something unaccount-
able, or reprehensible, and in any event interesting, must have taken
place at the source of power.

The mystery began to unravel in September, after the Kornilov
affair had blown the lid off the SR pot. After two months' silence
Chernov, now freed from his ministerial burdens, raised the question
in acute form and dumped all the blame for the failure to proclaim
a republic upon Kerenski, whom he accused of having blocked the
initiative of Tsereteli and the other socialist ministers in the interests
of a renewed coalition with the Constitutional Democrats.[28] Two
days after the publication of Chernov's unsigned editorial, "Honey
and Tar," Kerenski momentarily descended from the eminence of
the minister-presidency to reply through the medium of the right-
wing *Volia Naroda*. The truth, he said, was just the opposite of the
statement printed in the central organ: in the short interval between
assuming the premiership (around noon on July 7) and leaving for
the front (the early afternoon of the same day), he had proposed
that the republic be proclaimed. Tsereteli and "the other leftist
ministers" (a pointed reference to Chernov) had agreed. Then
Kerenski left for the front, entrusting the matter to his colleagues'
care. When he read the declaration of July 8 in his railroad car, he
was surprised to find in it no mention of a republic.[29] The broad
inference is that Chernov himself was responsible. Coming to the

[27] *Istoriia vtoroi russkoi revoliutsii*, I, Part II, 18.
[28] "Mëd i dëgot'" (Honey and Tar), *Delo Naroda*, No. 145 (September 3,
1917).
[29] "Otvet A. F. Kerenskago 'Delu Naroda'" (A. F. Kerenski's Reply to "Delo
Naroda"), No. 110 (September 5, 1917).

defense of Kerenski against a man who—she implied with a touch of feminine venom—was capable of "twisting his soul," Breshkovskaia asserted that the moment had been favorable for such action but "for some reason they (i.e., the other socialist ministers) failed to carry out the agreement; the situation soon changed, and the proclamation of a republic was postponed." Kerenski should not be singled out as the stumbling block; fairness demanded, at the very least, that all the ministers share the blame.[30]

After the bitter recriminations—so many knife-thrusts in the quivering body of the PSR—the question was lost sight of in the course of further and greater catastrophes, until some interesting disclosures were made in the *Red Archives*.[31] It appears that the declaration of July 8 had two authors. One was Nekrasov, generally assumed to have written it by virtue of his position as acting head of the government in Kerenski's absence. The other was Chernov. The "village minister" had written the appeal to the public, extensively edited by Nekrasov, as well as the agrarian section, left unchanged. Nekrasov had formulated the rest of the program. The proclamation of a republic would, under this division of labor, have fallen to his pen. Had he refused to include such a point, confirming Miliukov's reference to his negative attitude? The answer is given by the discovery of a draft in Nekrasov's handwriting of three points for inclusion in the declaration, the first of which read as follows: "The internal policy of the Provisional Government is grounded on the firm conviction that complete and definitive recognition will be accorded by the whole country to the democratic republic."[32] Obviously, he would have assented, if not to the proclamation of a republic, then at any rate to a confession of faith in that principle of government, leaving the formality to the Constituent Assembly. He only needed to be pushed in that direction.

The push was never given. In the letter he addressed to Nekrasov, enclosing his draft of the declaration, Chernov said not a word about

---

[30] "Letopisets" (Chronicler), *ibid*.
[31] "V. Chernov i iiul'skie dni" (V. Chernov and the July Days), ed. M. G. Fleer, *Krasnyi Arkhiv*, V (1924), 268-70.
[32] *Ibid*., p. 270.

a republic. He must have been acting as a spokesman for the soviet contingent in the government, else he would not have written the appeal to the people as well as the agrarian part of the program. And if he had stepped outside the bounds of his office to do that, there is no reason why he should not have at least proposed the declaration of a republic. After all, he was a minister and not a mouse. If, however, the most radical member of the cabinet was content to ignore the subject, there was no reason for Nekrasov to burn his fingers by including it in the program and thus impede the reentry into the government of the Kadet party, the organization to which he until recently had belonged and the only real counterweight to socialism on the horizon. Chernov's post-mortem blast at Kerenski represents an artful attempt to shift the blame onto his opponent's shoulders. The charge and countercharges mentioned above would lead to the conclusion that one party or the other had lied outright. But whatever may be said about their characters or, more particularly, about their political ineptitude, neither Chernov nor Kerenski nor the aging Breshkovskaia were capable of so gross a distortion of the truth, though any one or all three might shift the truth a bit. It is possible to reconcile their statements. Kerenski no doubt opposed the resurrection of the republican issue some days later when he was negotiating with the Kadets for the formation of a new coalition, but had not been responsible for the failure to proclaim a republic on July 7-8, when the interim cabinet was drafting its declaration of intent. This conclusion does not conflict with the testimony of either Chernov or Kerenski and is, in fact, implied in Breshkovskaia's statement.

We are left, then, with two possible explanations of this puzzling episode, so revealing as to the way in which the Russian democrats handled matters of state in their brief period of grace from February to October. To make a bourgeois revolution without the only organized bourgeois force in the country was an absurdity. Tsereteli may well have decided, in keeping with this tenet of Menshevik ideology, to smooth the way for readmitting the Kadets to the cabinet by dropping two of the demands that even Lvov had found intolerable. And having so decided, he needed but to lift his finger, and Chernov would desist from the application of republican principles or any other principles, for the invariable rule is that Chernov moved in Tsereteli's wake. Or the SR minister, having been entrusted with executing the will of the soviet, may have let its demands go by default. This would be in keeping with his character as well as with the conduct of his ministry.[33] The tone of his letter to Nekrasov was obsequious to the point of self-effacement:

Dear Nicholas Vissarionovich:
    I am sending you a draft formula of our agrarian policy; in the general part of it I have formulated nothing independently but am prepared to confine myself to the formula of the Head Land Committee (in working out its resolution Chernenkov, Kornilov, and Kaufman represented the right).
    For purposes of comparison I append the resolution of the All-Russian Soviet Congress of Workers' and Soldiers' Deputies.

Sincerely yours,
VICTOR CHERNOV

P.S. Reedit also my draft of the manifesto which, it is generally felt, should be published at the same time as the business part.[34]

In either case, whether because of his own remissness or out of excessive deference to Tsereteli, the trail of guilt leads after many windings to the door of V. M. Chernov. He was not in a mood to press for further concessions. The Kadets had gone out of the government, and then Lvov had departed, vanquished in their personal tilt, leaving Chernov on the field to celebrate for himself and his party a double victory.[35] Like a contented child, he rested with his candy.

He would not rest for long. Around his head the clouds were gathering, for the Constitutional Democrats with Miliukov in the lead were preparing a signal vengeance, and the poison of Kerenski's defeat at the Third Congress was beginning to work. Naive and filled

---

[33] See below, pp. 330 ff.
[34] "V. Chernov i iiul'skie dni," ed. M. G. Fleer, *Krasnyi Arkhiv*, V (1924), 268.
[35] *Kratkii otchët o rabotakh chetvërtago s"ezda P.S.-R.*, p. 15.

with good will for everyone except landowners and imperialists, Chernov had no inkling of what was brewing in circles of the dethroned reaction, at general headquarters, or even inside the Provisional Government, to the inner ring of which he had never belonged; and little did he suspect that, in the campaign of villification preceding the attempt at a coup d'état, he would be the central figure.

The skeleton cabinet left by the resignations of Lvov, Pereverzev, and the four Kadets, posed of itself the problem of how it was to be filled out, and when. In soviet circles, aside from the Bolsheviks and left SR's, there was no disposition to go it alone: the Mensheviks were opposed on principle to a socialist government; and the SR's, because of the war, because of a fear of power, because of Kerenski, and because of their general helplessness, held in effect the same point of view. A joint party resolution had pledged the support of both Executive Committees to the "government of revolutionary salvation," as Kerenski's rump cabinet was called, and the SR Central Committee had bespoken public confidence for it, provided its foreign policy were framed exclusively in the interests of the Russian Revolution and its domestic policy offered convincing proof to the peasantry of its determination to lay the foundations for the act of the Constituent Assembly giving the land to the people.[36] A few days later the committee backed away from this statesmanlike stand with a shrill cry for "granite-like" support of the government against the dark designs of the German emperor (who was nothing but Ludendorff's puppet) and the machinations of the domestic reaction.[37] The minutes of the Central Committee are not available for this period, having been either lost or buried in the Soviet archives; so there is no way of knowing whether there was a division of opinion on the issue, but the presumption is there was not. In two of his editorials composed on the productive evening of July 4, Chernov had spoken out clearly against a soviet assumption of power "under such circumstances, at such a moment," on the ground that it would discredit the present majority (Menshevik and SR) and pave the

[36] *Delo Naroda*, No. 95 (July 8, 1917); *Volia Naroda*, No. 61 (July 9, 1917).
[37] *Delo Naroda*, No. 98 (July 12, 1917).

way for a dictatorship of the minority (Bolshevik and left SR).[38]
The words in quotation marks indicate that he was hedging, as
always, for he never took a stand without qualifying it, and so never
could impress the people as did Lenin with his ax-like phrases. But
his opposition to a renewal of coalition evidently dates from later in
the month, even though in his heart he had never really accepted the
principle of class collaboration,[39] just as he had never broken spiritually with the opposition to the war, however much he might strive
in public to put distance between himself and his past. Natanson also
was on the Central Committee and no doubt went his own way, on
this issue as on every other, but he was completely isolated in the
committee and had no influence now that Chernov had escaped from
his clutches to fall into those of Gotz.

The left SR's were not taken too seriously at the moment, though
already they were becoming a serious force, and Kerenski need
reckon with no other opposition in the party as he prepared to renew
the experiment in coalition by inviting the Kadets to return to the
cabinet. Like the right SR's in general, Kerenski could not conceive
of a government worthy of the name without representation from
the organization that expressed the will of the upper levels of Russian
society; free-lance radicals such as Nekrasov and Tereshchenko were
not enough. He had flatly refused to form a socialist ministry,[40] and
had the Central Committee insisted, he would have preferred a break
to compliance with its injunction, so independent was his course of
action and so loose the ties that bound him to the party. His attitude
was one reason why the Gotz-Zenzinov core of the Central Committee would not contemplate the abandonment of coalition. Like his
right-centrist friends, Kerenski believed that the exigencies of war
required the collaboration of classes, but unlike them he would have
been pleased to emancipate the Provisional Government from the

[38] "Demagogiia—sestra provokatsii" (Demagoguery—the Sister of Provocation), *ibid.*, No. 92 (July 5, 1917); see also "Osobyi vid doveriia" (A Special
Kind of Confidence), in the same issue.

[39] See "Rossiiskoe krest'ianstvo i V. M. Chernov," *Novyi Zhurnal,* XXIX
(1952), 237, for Tsereteli's comment.

[40] Chernov, *Great Russian Revolution,* p. 283.

tutelage of the soviet.[41] Since he could not gain their assent and could not afford to lose their support, he thought to achieve his purpose by bringing back the Kadets, knowing that they would be eternally at loggerheads with the soviet element in the cabinet, and that he could stand as an arbiter over both, dictating the policy of state. In other words, the Kadets' reentry into the ministry would give him the leverage that he would not have if he were left alone with the socialists, besides which, of course, he did not agree with the policies of the soviet. Conviction propelled Kerenski in the same direction as calculation: he considered that the Kadets were entitled to representation in the government, both because of their social weight and because after the revolution the party had become converted to republicanism, although he was not unmindful of what was hiding behind its skirts.[42]

At the outset he enjoyed a free hand in negotiating with them for the reconstruction of the cabinet on a coalitional basis. The other ministers on July 13 placed their collective resignation in his hands to facilitate the task, and on the next day Kerenski began formal negotiations with the Kadets. At once it became apparent that the crisis would grow worse before it got better. The Kadets set a high price on their collaboration. Not only did they insist on the non-binding character of the declaration of July 8 and on no longer being placed at a disadvantage by majority votes in the cabinet, but they demanded the head of V. M. Chernov on a silver platter. At about the same time a furious press campaign began against this symbol of

[41] Here was the watershed between the right and the right center in the PSR. The former held the government to be accountable solely to the Constituent Assembly for its interim actions, chief among them measures of national defense. For expressions of this point of view, see the editorial in *Volia Naroda*, No. 72 (July 22, 1917), and the resolution of the SR delegation in the Moscow city council, printed in *ibid.*, No. 64 (July 13, 1917), and in the *Delo Naroda*, No. 99 (July 13, 1917). From this community of viewpoint sprang instances of collaboration between the right SR's and the Kadets in forming local unions of national defense, as in the ancient town of Uglich (*Volia Naroda*, No. 72). The right center agreed to having the propertied element in the government but felt that it had to be watched; hence the insistence on soviet supervision and, in effect, on the *dvoevlastie* (dual power) inherited from the February Revolution. This attitude was reflected in the proclamation of the Central Committee referred to above.

[42] "Iz vospominanii," *Sovremennyia Zapiski*, XXXVIII, 252-53.

Zimmerwaldism in a government of national defense. The synchroni-
zation of the Kadet demand with the press campaign, much of which
was carried on in non-Kadet papers, betrays a master plan to end
Chernov's career.

For the bad blood existing between the SR minister and the Constitutional Democrats there was abundant reason. In formally asking
for his removal on July 15 their central committee had charged him
with pursuing, apart from the rest of the government, a "personal"
policy in a matter of "vast importance."[43] At least it can be said for
the Kadets that with habitual Russian honesty they had gone to the
heart of the trouble—Chernov's agrarian policy—and were taking up
where the former minister-president had left off. But more was involved than Chernov's encouragement of the land committees or his
attempt to modify the land tenure system before the Constituent
Assembly. He had become the symbol of agrarian revolution and to
remove that symbol would mean to inflict a moral defeat of the first
magnitude upon the forces working to change the form of Russian
society. At the very least the spearhead of the agrarian movement
would be blunted and the chances for compensation increased. The
Ukrainian issue had aroused the Kadets on its own merits, but the
drift of events in the agrarian sphere had hardened their resolution,
and after the withdrawal of their four ministers, they had centered
their fire on Chernov's administration, holding out in the negotiations
with Kerenski for the *status quo ante* in agrarian relations, in line
with their policy of deferring all basic social reforms to the Constituent Assembly.[44]

Chernov was also the symbol of Zimmerwaldism, of the yearning,
suppressed but powerful, to halt the war short of victory, of opposition to territorial seizures, and of deviation from Russia's allies.
Certainly he owed his reputation as a bête noire of patriotic circles
to the build-up of his enemies rather than to anything he had done
since becoming a minister; indeed, one wonders whether the SR intel-

---

[43] Miliukov, *Istoriia vtoroi russkoi revoliutsii*, I, Part II, 26.
[44] *Ibid.*, pp. 24-25; Bykhovski, *Vserossiiskii Sovet Krest'ianskikh Deputatov*,
pp. 156, 163, 167-68; *Kratkii otchët o rabotakh chetvërtago s"ezda P.S.-R.*, pp.
68, 109-10.

lectuals had not made him minister of agriculture in order to muzzle
him on the war. Although the Kadets were now attacking him in
straightforward fashion for his agrarian policy, they had created the
impression that they could not work with him because of his
"defeatism," thus giving enemies in his own party the opportunity
to press for his retirement on the ground that another SR, free of the
taint of Zimmerwaldism, could either compel the Kadets to cease
their obstruction or expose their insincerity.[45] Eventually this line
of thought would dominate the Central Committee, and Chernov
would be succeeded by S. L. Maslov (RRC). But not for the present.
The hue and cry over Zimmerwaldism undoubtedly served in some
cases as a smoke screen for the protection of vested interests, but the
Kadet intellectuals were not thinking of estates in Tambov or Voronezh, they were thinking of the Straits and Galicia when they so
fiercely berated the SR minister. The link between capitalists and
imperialists has been well advertised, but not enough has been said
about intellectual responsibility for the type of nationalism that
claims everything for itself and concedes nothing to others.

While the Kadets were consorting with right-wing SR's, a running
feud had developed with the Chernov wing of the PSR, at first over
foreign policy and more recently over education. With the Ukrainian
question in the foreground and the land question in the background,
another aspect of the July crisis has been generally overlooked. A
series of articles in the *Delo Naroda* had sharply attacked the Kadet
minister of education, Professor A. A. Manuilov, for blocking reforms in a sphere where the dead hand of tsarist bureaucracy had
rested with baneful effect. No branch of the administration needed
more to be brought into harmony with the times and none had been
less touched by the revolution; in some respects the Manuilov ministry was less responsive to the demands of life than Count Ignatiev's.[46]
On the morning of the day that witnessed the death of the first
coalition, the central organ carried an editorial demanding Manui-

---

[45] "Nedostoinaia igra" (An Unworthy Game), *Volia Naroda*, No. 110 (September 5, 1917). This is the article in which the right-wing organ opened its
guns on Chernov by name. Probably Argunov was its author.
[46] "Ministerstvo inertsii" (The Ministry of Inertia), No. 89 (July 1, 1917).

lov's resignation.[47] The Kadets could scarcely have been under misapprehension as to who had inspired these attacks, whether or not they suspected that Chernov had actually written them.[48] In the light of this situation Tsereteli's suggestion that in the reduced cabinet Chernov should take over education while retaining agriculture[49] acquires more meaning. Kerenski did not act on this suggestion.

There was also in the hostility of the Kadets to Chernov a personal factor. More than any other man he had been responsible for overthrowing the first Provisional Government and driving Miliukov from the cabinet. It was natural for the Kadets to take advantage of a conjuncture which rendered him vulnerable to a charge of Zimmerwaldism to repay Chernov in his own coin. Tsereteli says that Miliukov was the moving spirit behind the campaign of defamation. The Kadet leader acted from conviction as well as rancor: in striking at Chernov, a blow would be delivered at antiwar sentiment and an obstruction removed from the road back to imperialism, for if Chernov had been reduced to silence on Allied war aims, he was still a factor in imposing a self-denying ordinance on Russian diplomacy. In his memoirs Miliukov treats the former defeatism of Chernov as an incontestable fact—an assertion that just as incontestably convicts the Kadet professor of having ceased at this point to be a historian—and leaves open only the question of his relations with the Austro-German authorities, who had made possible the dissemination of his defeatist brochures among Russian prisoners of war.[50] Privately Miliukov alluded to the presence in Allied intelligence files of much that was damning to his opponent, but the only specific charge he adduced was a German agent's attendance at a meeting addressed by Chernov. To this Tsereteli had made the obvious rejoinder: What of it, was Chernov responsible if an agent were in his audience? Miliukov worked through insinuations rather than direct

[47] "Glas naroda o narodnom obrazovanii" (The Voice of the People on Popular Education), No. 90 (July 2, 1917).
[48] Miliukov mentions the campaign against Manuilov but does not attribute it specifically to the SR's (*Istoriia vtoroi russkoi revoliutsii*, I, Part I, 236).
[49] *Delo Naroda*, No. 95 (July 8, 1917).
[50] *Istoriia vtoroi russkoi revoliutsii*, I, Part II, 43. Miliukov concedes the possibility that in this respect the data in the possession of the Russian intelligence service and the suspicions of other ministers may have gone too far.

imputations of guilt, associating Chernov with the Germans without establishing the specific ties that bound him to them.[51] And that, we might add, was the only way in which he could have worked.

In the effort to engineer Chernov's downfall the Kadets would have allies. One could be found on the right wing of Chernov's own party. While the wraps had not yet been taken off in the intraparty polemics and references to personalities were still veiled, it was a secret to no one that Argunov's shafts against the "fog of Zimmerwaldist poison" pervading the socialist camp were aimed at Chernov.[52] But however intense its dislike for Chernov, the *Volia Naroda* did not descend to gutter tactics, being restrained by the desire to remain within the bounds of party propriety as well as by the innate decency of its editor. The same cannot be said of the fringe group of former SR's who cared nothing for the preservation of their party status. These war-heated Populist intellectuals yielded to no one in their rabid nationalism. No term of abuse was too strong, no charge too wild, for them to use against the founder of neo-Populism. At bottom they held against him his reconciliation of Populism with European socialism, which had as a natural corollary the effort to end the war in conjunction with the socialists of other European countries, including, of course, those of Germany and Austria. Dear to their hearts was the old, pre-Chernovian Populism with its socialist froth and nationalist essence. An attack upon the unhappy minister by two of these embryonic national socialists in Plekhanov's *Edinstvo* attracted general attention with its demand that he resign and so permit the government to win the public confidence that it would never enjoy as long as he remained in its ranks.[53] Their campaign was hardly distinguishable from that of the far right, and earned them the plaudits of Miliukov's *Rech'*.[54]

The other ally of the Kadets operated in silence from within the

---

[51] Interview with Tsereteli in New York (December, 1949).

[52] As an example, see the editorial, "Urok koshmarnykh dnei" (The Lesson of Nightmare Days), *Volia Naroda*, No. 59 (July 7, 1917). Though the authorship is not indicated, it presumably was written by Argunov.

[53] See the editorial comment ("Dva dokumenta" [Two Documents]) in *Delo Naroda*, No. 108 (July 23, 1917).

[54] *Ibid.*, No. 115 (August 1, 1917).

cabinet. The clique of middle-class radicals between the Kadets and the socialists had their differences with Miliukov, who had pointedly reminded them that they carried no social weight, had no organization behind them, and spoke for themselves alone; he had plainly intimated that they must make way for authentic representatives of the business world and of conservative political organizations.[55] But they were at one with him in desiring to be rid of Chernov. Nekrasov and Tereshchenko must have had some deeper motivation than Miliukov's pressure, which would more likely have produced on them a contrary effect. When this author asked Tsereteli what or who was behind their offensive, he replied, "Kerenski," thus adding the third and main link to the radical ring which held the balance of power in the Provisional Government. Tsereteli mentioned Kerenski's rancor over his defeat at the Third Congress, which he blamed on Chernov, as the cause of his antipathy. Chernov himself takes a somewhat different line, asserting that Kerenski could not brook independent-minded people around him, and that his enmity settled first on Miliukov, then on Tsereteli, and finally on Chernov, in all three of whom he saw narrow party sectarians incapable of rising to the level of a comprehension of state interests.[56] Both factors no doubt weighed with the new minister-president. When asked whether there were anything behind Kerenski, impelling him onward, Tsereteli gave the hesitant answer: "Well, Miliukov." Kerenski indeed desired to bring the Kadets back into the cabinet—without Miliukov—but otherwise he would not have been influenced by their leader—quite the contrary. That these two enemies should now have been working toward the same end suggests the possibility of a force in the background commanding their common allegiance and coordinating their efforts.

Could perchance His Majesty's Government have been seeking Chernov's removal? Tsereteli denies English instigation of the campaign against his colleague and says Ambassador George Buchanan, correct and cautious in his dealings and not too capable—the latter

---

[55] *Istoriia vtoroi russkoi revoliutsii*, I, Part II, 25-26.
[56] Manuscript of chapter Partiia S.-R.; manuscript commentary on the minutes of the Central Committee, p. 7.

a debatable statement—was not guilty of intervening to procure his downfall. But he admits that Buchanan sympathized with the campaign against Chernov when it was launched and prosecuted, and concedes that Tereshchenko and Nekrasov may have wished to accumulate virtue in English eyes by showing that their influence could rid the cabinet of such a man as Chernov, knowing that his fall would please the British and add to their personal prestige.[57] Now we turn to Buchanan's memoirs and find that when a diplomat writes for posterity he lies less readily than is his custom. Chernov impressed the ambassador at their first meeting as having nothing of the idealist about him, whereas actually he was idealistic to the point of childishness. Buchanan describes him, wrongly, as a "man of strong character" and, correctly, as having "considerable ability." Then he comes to the point: "He was generally regarded as dangerous and untrustworthy, and I found him the reverse of sympathetic."[58] Later on, at the time of which we are speaking (mid-July), Buchanan made known to the foreign minister that he "heartily sympathized" with the Kadet demand for Chernov's resignation.[59] And on September 3 (N.S.) or August 21 in this book, Buchanan wrote to his government that "certain changes ought certainly to be made" in the existing Russian government and "Tchernoff ought more especially to be dismissed."[60] It was not necessary for the British ambassador to issue a command to the Russian foreign minister; a mere wish would send that puppet into action. Whether or not the British instigated the campaign against Chernov, they certainly sustained it.

It is not possible to say whether there was also a French angle. The stinginess of information in the memoirs of the French is in keeping with the national character. Their ambassador tells how Tereshchenko met every morning with the British, French, and American representatives in order to keep in line with them (*pour se concerter avec eux*). He gave them news of the interior as well

[57] Interview with Tsereteli in New York (December, 1949).
[58] *My Mission to Russia*, II, 136.
[59] *Ibid.*, p. 159.
[60] *Ibid.*, p. 173.

as of the front and discussed with them political as well as diplomatic questions.[61] The Italian ambassador had some difficulty in gaining admittance to this charmed circle, no doubt because he represented a weak power which could not command the deference of this French-speaking connoisseur of the dance, who presumed to direct the foreign policy of a great and foundering country at the close of the third year of its agony. But Noulens, the French representative, had nothing to say about Chernov, except that he was the most advanced of the socialist ministers.[62] The members of the managerial core of the cabinet, Kerenski, Nekrasov, and Tereshchenko, were all three Russian Masons, and Avksentiev, whom they were grooming for high office, was a French Mason in his own right;[63] there could have been a connection with the Grand Orient in France, but this author is not of a mind to leave the solid ground of history in order to venture into the swamp of occult relationships, which is without bottom or banks.

More was at stake, of course, than the individual fate of a minister who had offended his country's allies by seeking some better way out of this stupendous and sterile slaughter than by elevating one set of imperialists above the other. There was a scheme afoot, nurtured in the atmosphere of reaction that followed the recent disorders, to give Russia a strong government, free of soviet tutelage and capable of whipping the people back into war. Like the French Directory in 1799, though without its corruption, the existing government was honeycombed with elements which sought its replacement by something more to their liking, whether it be a collegial dictatorship, as Tereshchenko desired, or a cabinet of "yes men" with an all-powerful premier, as Kerenski is said to have envisaged it. Chernov was the Carnot of this combination, an honest, naive man, intensely loyal to the revolution, whose presence restricted the conspirators' freedom of movement and who had to be eliminated lest he discover something and give the game away.

---

[61] Joseph Noulens, *Mon Ambassade en Russie soviétique 1917-1919*, I, 48-49.
[62] *Ibid.*, p. 38.
[63] See chap. IV.

The campaign against the minister of agriculture was carried on inside the government as well as outside, in the more respectable newspapers as in the yellow press, on the boulevards and in the councils of state. The first intimation of an unhealthy situation in the cabinet itself came when Nekrasov gave out a statement to the press on July 13, denying rumors of Chernov's impending resignation.[64] Quite possibly this was a provocative move, for it preceded by two days the action of the Kadet Central Committee in conditioning its reentrance into the government upon Chernov's removal. When its demands were laid before the minister-president, he seemed willing to give satisfaction on questions of program but resolutely refused to pose the question of Chernov's dismissal.[65] Yet just at this moment rumors spread that Kerenski was negotiating with Avksentiev for his appointment as minister of agriculture,[66] and sometime between July 16 and July 19, according to one of his associates, Kerenski had drawn up a list of ministers omitting the name of Chernov but including those of the right-wing socialists Argunov and Plekhanov.[67] The contradiction is easily explained: Kerenski indeed wanted Chernov out of the cabinet but had to tread warily so as not to run afoul of the SR party, hoping, no doubt, that his powerful friends in the Central Committee, Gotz and Zenzinov, would ease Chernov out of the picture in return for the appointment of some right-wing SR. Indirect confirmation of this surmise is seen in Nekrasov's statement deprecating demands for the ouster of this or that minister, since "in that case not the individuals themselves but the powerful organizations behind them would have to be taken into account."[68] Meeting with this outward refusal to dismiss Chernov, the Constitutional Democrats reconciled themselves to his continuance in office provided their other demands were met.[69] But a sudden stiffening in the soviet attitude—Sukhanov says Dan tri-

[64] Volia Naroda, No. 65 (July 14, 1917).
[65] Miliukov, Istoriia vtoroi russkoi revoliutsii, I, Part II, 26.
[66] Sukhanov, Zapiski, V, 42.
[67] Savinkov, K delu Kornilova, p. 9.
[68] Miliukov, Istoriia vtoroi russkoi revoliutsii, I, Part II, 27.
[69] Ibid., p. 26; Burzhuaziia i pomeshchiki v 1917 godu, pp. 243-44.

umphed over Tsereteli in the Menshevik caucus and forced him into line—blocked Kerenski's compliance and resulted in the breakdown of negotiations.[70]

The momentary failure of the Kadet offensive against Chernov did not mean that he was yet in the clear. No sooner had Kadet pressure eased and that party shifted its ground, Rakitnikov told the Petersburg SR committee, than the nonsocialist element in the cabinet had seen fit to revive on its own account the personal issue.[71] Now it was Tereshchenko and Nekrasov who decided to try their hand at removing the obnoxious minister. Not desiring to collide head-on with the soviet, they went to Tsereteli and besought his aid, citing the rumors of Chernov's disloyalty. The Menshevik leader asked them to lay their charges on the table, but warned them beforehand that these were slanderous and that he would brand them as such. The brother Masons pled inability to prefer charges as long as Chernov remained in the cabinet, lest the Provisional Government itself be discredited; let him resign, they said, and then the accusations could be made without shaking the government. Tsereteli replied that he would never play this game, for the effect would be to attaint the largest party in the soviet camp. He would agree, however, that Chernov should leave the government for three days, freeing the hands of his calumniators, who would then either have to put up or shut up; unless substantiation of the charges were forthcoming, Chernov would return at the end of the hunting season. The proposal displeased the two plotters and spoiled their personal relations with Tsereteli.[72]

Meanwhile the boulevard campaign against the Zimmerwaldist ogre in the bosom of the government reached its filthy climax, and Chernov was daily besmirched in the pages of the chauvinistic press, especially in a sheet put out by two exsocialists turned superpatriots, entitled *Bez Lishnikh Slov* (Without Extra Words). Many of the shafts stuck in the soft body of this revolutionary Saint Sebastian,

[70] Sukhanov, *Zapiski*, V, 45-46, 63, 66-68, 80, 82; Miliukov, *Istoriia vtoroi russkoi revoliutsii*, I, Part II, 26-30. Gotz seems to have gone along with the Mensheviks in rejecting any departure from the declaration of July 8, most likely with an eye to the peasants' soviet.

[71] *Delo Naroda*, No. 108 (July 23, 1917).

[72] Interview with Tsereteli in New York (December, 1949).

and it appeared as though he might meet his martyrdom at any moment. Less shrill but scarcely less vicious were the attacks made upon him by the right Kadets, Miliukov and Maklakov, and the reactionary Purishkevich from the podium of the dying Duma: Miliukov lost no opportunity to brand the man who had pulled him out of the Straits as "definitely a defeatist";[73] Maklakov imputed to him the authorship of the slogan for a separate armistice;[74] and Purishkevich arraigned him for raising the peasants against the gentry and the hired hands against the peasants[75]—the last being sheer demagogy, since it attributed to Chernov the Bolshevik aim of dividing the rural toilers, of all that party's plans the most nefarious in SR eyes. Economic fear and chauvinistic passion were so closely entwined that it would be impossible to say which was the stronger motivation behind the attacks on the "village minister." The *Na Chuzhbine* episode in the wartime emigration now rose to plague him, being used by his enemies to establish a link with the German authorities, even to the extent of charging that these had subsidized the journal's publication.[76] Now he was linked with the German espionage system and now with its tsarist counterpart; complicity in the expropriations of 1905 was ascribed to him,[77] the distinction between SR's and SR Maximalists being purposely ignored, so that he would be cast in the role of a bandit as well as a traitor. Chernov also figured in the "campaign against pseudonyms," as the circulation of broadsides with the real and assumed names of revolutionists was called; but the compilers of these lists could not quite bring

[73] *Burzhuaziia i pomeshchiki v 1917 godu*, p. 213.

[74] *Ibid.*, p. 114. At the time of the peasants' congress—certainly a false accusation. As already mentioned, S. P. Postnikov claims to have been the first to enunciate this slogan, and at a Petersburg city conference, where antiwar sentiment was very strong, not at the peasants' congress, where it would have occasioned a scandal.

[75] *Ibid.*, pp. 201, 275.

[76] Chernov had written but one article for the *Na Chuzhbine*, on "Bulgaria and Russia," and this was reprinted in the *Delo Naroda*, No. 109 (July 25, 1917). The same number carried an article by A. Shreider (L) defending the internationalism of the *Na Chuzhbine* against assertions that it had shown partiality to the Central Powers. The younger Shreider, nephew of the SR mayor of Petersburg, had been one of its associate editors; the chief editor had been G. K. Ulianov (L). On the *Na Chuzhbine* episode, see chap. IV.

[77] See his speech to the soviet in *Delo Naroda*, No. 106 (July 21, 1917).

themselves to give this man, who was as Russian in appearance as though he had come dripping from the Volga, a Jewish name—instead they made him a German, not forgetting the noble particle: "von Guttmann."[78] With this the agitation against Chernov had scraped bottom.[79]

Martov and Trotski might accuse him of quitting his post under fire, but to have held on in the face of such abuse, while expecting at any moment to be knifed from behind by his ministerial colleagues, would have required a man with a tougher hide and a stouter heart than V. M. Chernov. He resigned on July 20 and appeared that night before the joint session of the Executive Committees, in a "dejected-triumphant" mood, to announce his decision. The news created a sensation, all the more so since no one in the audience knew about the three-day limit set for his conviction or rehabilitation by Irakli Tsereteli and the SR Central Committee. While powerful forces were being set in motion by the retirement of the "village minister," he himself undertook to force the calumniators into the open by destroying the screen of anonimity and insinuation behind which they had hitherto operated. To the government he addressed a demand for an official investigation of the sources of slander; to reputed holders of incriminating documents, a challenge to lay them on the table; to his enemy Miliukov, a summons to submit the ethics of the *Rech'* to a court of arbitration; and to the minister of foreign affairs, an open letter inviting him to confirm or deny reports of his unwillingness to continue in the cabinet with Chernov, when publicly the latter had been assured of the good will of his colleagues. Tereshchenko lied smoothly, in standard diplomatic fashion: he, of course, was never motivated by personal considerations but only by dictates of principle; he, of course, had no grounds for believing the good name of the minister of agriculture to be attainted by street

[78] One of these lists was reproduced before the United States Senate by the Reverend George A. Simons, a Methodist missionary to Russia, who seems to have been as gullible as most clergymen, whether of advanced or retarded views. See *Bolshevik Propaganda: Hearings*, p. 142.

[79] Bykhovski, *Vserossiiskii Sovet Krest'ianskikh Deputatov*, pp. 145-46, 165, 167; *Delo Naroda*, Nos. 106-109 (July 21-25, 1917); Miliukov, *Istoriia vtoroi russkoi revoliutsii*, I, Part II, 30-31; Chernov, *Great Russian Revolution*, p. 246.

gossip, but at the same time he "fully understood and appreciated his desire to be relieved of the burdens of public office in order the better to defend himself against slanderers."[80] It soon became evident that Chernov's enemies could not prove collusion with the German authorities, and the antiwar tone of his articles prior to 1917 could be explained away on the ground that they had been written before the transformation of the character of the war as a result of the revolution and the renunciation of imperialist aims. No one but the left SR's chose to speak of the failure of Russia's allies to make a similar renunciation, which alone could have bridged the difference in viewpoint between the SR leader and the other ministers and solidified his party behind the Provisional Government. The old make-believe continued. As for the feud with Miliukov, steps had been taken to constitute a court of honor when further developments deprived them of any meaning. For Chernov's rehabilitation was not to remain a private affair.[81]

Rural Russia heard the news of its spokesman's retirement with incredulity and consternation. Once more, it seemed, the crafty landowners had foiled the simple folk; once more the toilers would be denied the land. Expressions of indignation from every part of the country poured into St. Petersburg over the wire. They came most of all from the Volga and black-earth districts, from the peasant heart of Russia, where land hunger was most acute and greed was greatest. One concrete example may be given:

To the Provisional Government. Copy to Exec. Com. All-Russ. Sov. of Peas. Dep. Copy to Minister Chernov. Copy to Central Committee PSR. From Voronezh province. . . . Straight wire. Received July 17, 1917.

Chernov must remain Minister of Agriculture, the peasants' minister. He has our support; in him the peasants believe, and count on realizing, under his leadership, the socialization of the land.

Voronezh Soviet Peas. Dep., Chairman Burevoi[82]

The second peasants' congress of this province (July 20-24) gave

[80] *Delo Naroda*, No. 109 (July 25, 1917); Miliukov, *Istoriia vtoroi russkoi revoliutsii*, I, Part II, p. 43.

[81] Sukhanov, *Zapiski*, V, 87 ff.; *Delo Naroda*, Nos. 106-7, 109 (July 21-22, 25, 1917); Miliukov, *Istoriia vtoroi russkoi revoliutsii*, I, Part II, 31, 42; *Revoliutsiia 1917 goda*, III, 199-200.

[82] *Sovety krest'ianskikh deputatov*, I, Part II, p. 59.

unanimous support to Chernov in his struggle with a recalcitrant government, and organized, in conjunction with the local soviet and garrison, an imposing street demonstration to show that it meant business.[83] From the neighboring province of Tambov the supreme peasant organ telegraphed that "we shall never allow the removal of our peasant minister in furtherance of the nefarious designs of the awakening reaction"[84]—words that struck much closer to the essence of the situation than these provincials probably realized. From Chernov's home province the Saratov committee of the PSR announced that his return was an imperative necessity; his replacement by anyone else, it said, would cause an upheaval in this party stronghold.[85] The peasants' executive committee in Kharkov likewise predicted trouble if Chernov did not resume his post.[86] The Smolensk peasants' soviet reported that Chernov's departure was viewed on every hand as a great *pomeshchik* victory,[87] and Chairman Kutuzov of the Nizhni Novgorod Soviet of Peasant Deputies telegraphed Kerenski that great confusion had arisen in the wake of Chernov's retirement and that he was deemed irreplaceable by the peasants of the province.[88] The army did not lag behind the village in beseeching the minister to stay at his post, and promised him in the struggle with his enemies something more than moral support.[89]

In the cities Chernov's stand on the war as well as his agrarian program told in his favor. Mass meetings were held in the plants and factories to protest his departure; the one in the arsenal at St. Petersburg was attended by 4,000 employees.[90] The SR committee in the capital met with the committees of the districts into which the city was divided to formulate a demand for his reappointment as the best

---

[83] *1917i god v Voronezhskoi gubernii*, pp. 77-79.

[84] *Delo Naroda*, No. 114 (July 30, 1917); Chernov, *Great Russian Revolution*, p. 247.

[85] *Delo Naroda*, No. 107 (July 22, 1917).

[86] *Ibid.*, No. 114 (July 30, 1917).

[87] *Ibid.*, No. 108 (July 23, 1917).

[88] *Volia Naroda*, No. 73 (July 23, 1917). This organ, it will be remembered, was against Chernov.

[89] See expressions of sentiment from the armed forces in *Delo Naroda*, Nos. 111, 113, 128 (July 27, 29, and August 16, 1917).

[90] *Ibid.*, Nos. 107, 111, 114 (July 22, 27, 30, 1917).

means of blunting the counterrevolutionary offensive, although a united front in support of Chernov was not realized until after the left wing, here quite numerous, had censured him for leaving his post under fire.[91]

The *Rech'* refused to be impressed by the flood of testimonials on behalf of Chernov, observing that the Union of Russian People (the Black Hundreds) had also known how to deluge the wires with spurious messages from the provinces—it was notoriously easy to get the peasants to agree to anything. Whereupon the *Delo Naroda* challenged the Kadet organ to get them to approve what Miliukov was saying about Chernov.[92] There was only too much truth in the *Rech'*'s cynical observation: a thousand years of oppression had taught the Russian peasants to dissimulate their feelings, to be one thing and seem another, but on this occasion they were doubtlessly speaking their mind, having been swayed by the intellectuals only to the extent of seeing in V. M. Chernov the gage of expropriation without compensation. Nettled by such disparagement, the Makariev SR group in Kostroma province appended to its demand for Chernov's return a statement that of its 500 members, no less than 400 were grubbers of the soil.[93] There is interesting information in this connection about the peasants' congress in Voronezh province referred to above: whereas the first congress had included some priests and a number of rural intellectuals, at this second congress, which had given unanimous support to Chernov, not a priest could be found and there were only a few representatives of the village intelligentsia among the more than 600 delegates who attended.[94] The "village minister" had the support of the village, whatever the *Rech'* might say. But, then, had not Miliukov's organ always maintained, with true professorial blindness, that this was not a revolution in the real sense of the word until people like Chernov had corrupted what

[91] *Ibid.*, No. 108 (July 23, 1917).
[92] No. 115 (August 1, 1917).
[93] *Delo Naroda*, No. 114 (July 30, 1917).
[94] *Sovety krest'ianskikh deputatov*, I, Part II, 59-60. About one hundred representatives of party organizations were also present without the right to vote. These no doubt guided the deliberations of the congress, but only because the peasants willingly deferred to them.

started out as an outburst of patriotic indignation over the old regime's failure to get on with the war? If the *Rech'* were capable of such self-deception, how could it be expected to see the village as it was?

What did not impress Professor Miliukov was convincing enough to the SR Central Committee. Even had it been of a mind to abandon its comrade, as Sukhanov mistakenly assumes it was,[95] it would have been dissuaded by these manifestations of the will of the party depths. If Nekrasov and Tereshchenko actually intended to give the Kadets Chernov's head as a bribe to reenter the government after the soviet had blocked giving that party satisfaction in other respects, they acted on their own instead of in collusion with high SR circles. About this there is no doubt whatever. On July 21 the central organ of the PSR carried a leading editorial entitled "Against Whom?", in which the whole campaign against Chernov was portrayed as an attempt to overthrow the land program of the PSR and to secure the class position of the bourgeoisie. Firmly identifying the cause of the party with that of Chernov, who was merely the executor of its collective will, the anonymous writer equated the demand for Chernov's scalp with a demand for the exclusion of his party from the coalition, and closed with the admonition that, just as the SR's were as one in respect to their land program, so were they as one in standing behind their comrade.[96] Not a word was said about Chernov's Zimmerwaldism, outwardly, at any rate, the main article in the indictment against him, and for the very simple reason that the SR's were anything but as one in their attitude toward the war. In the file of the *Delo Naroda* preserved in the Russian Archives Abroad in Prague (now no longer abroad), there is written in at the bottom of the editorial, in the hand of V. M. Chernov, the name of A. R. Gotz. With this action the party's real leader had placed the organization solidly behind its nominal leader. For the last time the whole central mass of the PSR coalesced when Gotz and Zenzinov wheeled the right center into line with Chernov's left center to bring insufferable pressure to bear upon Minister-President Kerenski. The Central

[95] *Zapiski,* V, 89-92.
[96] "Protiv kogo?" (Against Whom?), *Delo Naroda,* No. 106.

Committee published its decision[97] giving the Provisional Government three days to probe Chernov's record and conditioning further collaboration upon the restoration of his portfolio. Gotz and Zenzinov bore the demand in person to Kerenski, and neither the quiet manner of their coming nor the friendly tone they employed concealed the fact that the premier had been confronted with an ultimatum from a powerful organization whose support he had hitherto taken for granted. The Peasants' Executive Committee, in the name of rural soviets throughout the country, and for the announced purpose of preserving village peace and quiet, adopted by unanimous vote a similar decision and added the weight of its representations to those of the party.[98] In taking this action the Central Committee, according to its spokesman, had been motivated neither by personal nor by partisan considerations but by the certain knowledge that the country would regard the dropping of Chernov as abandonment of the government's commitment to land reform, and as tacit confirmation of the slanderous attacks upon his character.[99]

The denial of personal considerations was in answer to the protest raised by Argunov in his paper against the confusion of a great Narodnik principle with a personality.[100] The *Volia Naroda*, as we have seen, had taken the line that Chernov should give way to some party member free of his disabilities in respect to the war, thus depriving the Kadets of their patriotic pretext for combating the SR program. That party, in truth, would have been embarrassed by such a maneuver, but not having to worry about it for the moment, in view of the stand of the SR Central Committee, it gleefully seized upon Argunov's articles as evidence of dissension in the opposing camp and did its best to blow the smoke into flame. But the right wing of the PSR was never formidable when standing in isolation

[97] *Ibid.*, No. 108 (July 23, 1917); see further *Kratkii otchët o rabotakh chetvërtago s"ezda P.S.-R.*, p. 68.
[98] Bykhovski, *Vserossiiskii Sovet Krest'ianskikh Deputatov*, p. 165; *Delo Naroda*, No. 109 (July 25, 1917).
[99] V. M. Zenzinov, "Razdeliai i vlastvui" (Divide and Rule), *Delo Naroda*, No. 115 (August 1, 1917).
[100] "K predstoiashchemu sovetu partii" (On the Coming Party Council), *Volia Naroda*, No. 78 (July 29, 1917); "Ob edinstve i fraktsionnosti" (On Unity and Factionalism), *ibid.*, No. 83 (August 4, 1917).

and Argunov did not carry with him even the whole of his own small group in badgering Chernov.[101]

With the party virtually solid behind him, Chernov's vindication was assured—"predetermined" as Nekrasov said in announcing that the official investigation had given him a clean bill of health.[102] In the second coalitional government, constituted on July 25, Chernov was again minister of agriculture. Nekrasov even went out of his way to shake his hand as a testimonial of his regard for the man he had just tried to knife, and, more particularly, of the power of the party behind him. After all the storm over his continuance in office, Chernov's readmission into the cabinet at the conclusion of an investigation of record brevity occasioned scarcely a ripple of dissent. It could not have been otherwise in view of the Central Committee's stand: no Chernov, no coalition.

His resignation had been followed by other developments no less dramatic in character. The resignation of Kerenski himself the next day (July 21) had been followed by a confrontation of all the political groups at a memorable session in the Malachite Hall of the Winter Palace, at which the declaration of July 8 proved to be the chief stumbling block. The Kadets refused to be bound by an action of the rump cabinet taken in their absence, and the SR-Menshevik bloc refused to abandon this "Chernovian document," as Miliukov called it.[103] Finally a way out was found, at Kadet suggestion, by allowing Kerenski to pick a cabinet of his own choosing. The SR Central Committee agreed to give Kerenski a free hand (except in

[101] See the letter of N. Kharitonov, a former volunteer in the French army and associate of the *Prizyv* group of "defensists," in the *Delo Naroda*, No. 109 (July 25, 1917). The memory of past controversies, he wrote, should not lead one to question the sincerity of Chernov's conversion to national defense, now that Russia had been liberated, nor to deny his authority with the mass of the Russian people, who had done much more than "reconcile themselves" to his presence in a position of power.
[102] Miliukov, *Istoriia vtoroi russkoi revoliutsii*, I, Part II, 42-43; *Delo Naroda*, No. 109 (July 25, 1917).
[103] *Burzhuaziia i pomeshchiki v 1917 godu*, p. 213.

relation to the Ministry of Agriculture) but stipulated that the new cabinet must be composed of elements willing to adapt their policies to the principles set forth in the declaration.[104] To create the impression of rank-and-file backing, the SR delegations in both Soviet Executive Committees were assembled in a conference presided over by Gotz, and were persuaded by Avksentiev to ratify the Central Committee's decision.[105]

Had Kerenski been in all respects a free agent, he would not, of course, have included Chernov in the new government. Disliking him as he did,[106] he could not afford to break with the PSR by yielding to the entreaties of the apostate SR, V. S. Miroliubov, and the former anarchist, Prince Peter Kropotkin, who urged him to exclude Chernov despite the ultimatum of the Central Committee.[107] But having bowed to its will in this respect, he proceeded to disregard its injunctions in two other matters, correctly surmising that in relation to them it had taken a less rigid position. Kerenski overcame the deadlock as to a program by simply not having one: he neither repudiated the declaration of July 8 nor bound the new coalition, with its four Kadet members, to its observance, getting around the difficulty either by avoiding pronouncements altogether or by adopting phraseology that was susceptible of varying interpretation.[108] And the SR Central Committee accommodated itself to this tacit emancipation from commitments which were pale enough in any event; a policy of drift was so much according to its nature that it saw nothing wrong with, or even was not conscious of, the same tendency in others.

The second instance of Kerenski's refusal to comply with the wishes of the party to which he at least nominally belonged concerned an appointment of major importance. In the new cabinet of

[104] Delo Naroda, No. 109 (July 25, 1917); Miliukov, Istoriia vtoroi russkoi revoliutsii, I, Part II, 36.

[105] Delo Naroda, No. 109 (July 25, 1917).

[106] Stankevich, Vospominaniia, p. 225.

[107] Zenzinov, "Otvet D. V. Filosofovu" (Reply to D. V. Filosofov), Delo Naroda, No. 164 (September 26, 1917); Chernov, "Kak eto proiskhodilo" (How It Happened), ibid., No. 178 (October 12, 1917).

[108] "Iz vospominanii," Sovremennyia Zapiski, XXXVIII, 256-57; Miliukov, Istoriia vtoroi russkoi revoliutsii, I, Part II, 38, 45-46; Sukhanov, Zapiski, V, 111.

the second coalition Kerenski, in addition to serving as minister-president, retained the portfolios of war and marine, necessitating the appointment of understudies in the two subordinate offices. Kerenski filled the one post in the teeth of party opposition and the other in such a way as to give it very little satisfaction.

As acting minister of war he chose Boris V. Savinkov. The name Savinkov, already known to us from the days of terrorism, is of some significance, not only for the revolution but for the history of Europe in our troubled age. It will not do to fall in with the Communist stereotype and dismiss him as a conspiring reactionary. For this "poisonous flower of our underground past," as Stankevich so admirably describes him,[109] was no Romanov restorationist; he was the prototype of men who, like Benito Mussolini, achieved far greater fame because they lived and operated in countries with a large and desperate middle class. In him could be found the same exalted contemplation of the State, the same confusion of self with the state, the same inner contempt for the masses but outward identification with their passions, the same mouth-patriotism, the same plebeian callousness to means, the same penchant for violence, that constitute the essence of Fascism. Savinkov was a lone wolf, a beast of prey, and was intuitively recognized as such by the PSR, which could never forgive him his apostasy in the years following the Stolypin reaction. In the literature of the time he figures as an SR, but the only reason for regarding him as such was the failure of the Central Committee so far to decree his expulsion. The SR's had steadily opposed his advancement,[110] and Kerenski had as steadily promoted him—a remarkable example either of the minister-president's shortsightedness or of the dearth of competent personnel outside of Lenin's party. Under his pen name of Ropshin—for Savinkov was also a literary figure, and his prose is a pleasure to read—he had published articles in Argunov's paper contrasting the patriotism of the front with the sedition and cowardice of the capital, and representing the former as ready to descend on and clean up the

[109] *Vospominaniia*, p. 226.
[110] Chernov, *Great Russian Revolution*, p. 352.

latter.[111] Savinkov, of course, was merely ascribing to the army his own point of view; in reality the front was not less riddled with subversion than the rear. But the articles breathed fire against Zimmerwaldism and the soviet system.

At the time of the July crisis this bold adventurer functioned as commissar of the Southwestern Front, and it was at his instigation that Kerenski had named General Lavr Kornilov commander in chief.[112] Discerning in the slant-eyed officer a kindred spirit, Savinkov pushed him up the ladder as he went up himself, the ultimate objective of both being a military dictatorship in which one would probably have eliminated the other. Savinkov's unexpected appearance at the session in the Malachite Hall on the night of July 21-22 and his plain intimation of a dictatorship in the offing made the worst possible impression on Chernov and led him to warn the Central Committee that big things were afoot and that Savinkov was probably slated for a ministerial appointment. The right-centrist majority had chosen to disregard the major implication in Chernov's warning but had seized on the Savinkov angle to authorize its representative—presumably Zenzinov—to oppose in its name his admission to the cabinet. This charge had been carried out.[113] Chernov himself tried to work up sentiment for entrusting the direction of the War Ministry to Zenzinov,[114] but with his customary flaccidity did not push hard enough to lift the effort above the level of an intrigue. The alarm in the SR high command was justified, for Savinkov was the mortal enemy, personal and political, of the "village minister," whom he was determined to drive from the government,[115] and he abominated committees of all types and description. But neither the ad-

---

[111] See especially "V deistvuiushchei armii: VIII, Armiia i Petrograd" (In the Active Army: VIII, The Army and Petrograd), *Volia Naroda*, No. 69 (July 19, 1917). Savinkov characterized St. Petersburg (or rather Petrograd, since he would never use a Teutonic-sounding name) as a city of fog—both Neva and verbal. He ventured to say aloud what the Siberian Riflemen were alleged to be muttering: "The citizens of Petrograd are cowards." The tone of his article may be described as strong, even provocative.

[112] Savinkov, *K delu Kornilova*, pp. 8-9; see also pp. 5-6 for Kornilov's earlier appointment to command the Southwestern Front.

[113] *Kratkii otchët o rabotakh chetvërtago s"ezda P.S.-R.*, pp. 90, 118; Zenzinov, "Otvet D. V. Filosofovu," *Delo Naroda*, No. 164 (September 26, 1917).

[114] See V. I. Lebedev's statement at the Fourth Congress as reported in the *Volia Naroda*, No. 185 (December 5, 1917).

[115] Savinkov, *K delu Kornilova*, pp. 13, 18.

monition of the Central Committee nor the cunning intrigue of Chernov—since Zenzinov was a close friend of Kerenski's, yet entirely trustworthy in matters of revolutionary defense—had any effect on Kerenski: "First among revolutionary statesmen he understood the necessity of turning from words to actions and to the organization of a strong authority, and for that reason, overriding the opposition of his party friends and committee, he selected Savinkov as his assistant."[116] It was a fateful appointment, less for the revolution than for the Provisional Government and for its head in particular.

As acting head of the navy Kerenski named V. I. Lebedev, an appointment that evoked no open opposition in SR circles but also no enthusiasm. Lebedev stood so far to the right of the party's center of gravity that he was constantly at odds with the organization, yet was careful to retain his membership. He was an indefatigable "defensist" and quite obviously a man of great honesty and sincerity of purpose, whatever one may think of his position. In accepting an offer made on the personal initiative of Kerenski, Lebedev had not secured the sanction of the Central Committee, nor had he asked for it; when reproved at the Fourth Congress for his independent action, he replied that it was a nonpolitical post, that the offer had come suddenly, catching him unprepared, and that in any event he had not cared to approach the body which harbored at its bosom a defeatist of Natanson's stripe (loud noise in the congress at this point). Nevertheless, had the committee called for his resignation, he would instantly have complied. Lebedev disclaimed any knowledge of an unfavorable attitude in the committee and declared that in conversations with Chernov he had not been informed of any disposition in party circles to question his eligibility; later on, to be sure, he had learned that Chernov and his friends were saying behind his back what they had not been honorable enough to say to his face. The best surmise is that the Central Committee took no stand in the Lebedev matter, leaving the opposition to assume the form of an intrigue on the part of the left center.[117]

The only appointment to a ministerial post in the second coalition

[116] Stankevich, *Vospominaniia*, p. 224.
[117] See report of the congress in the *Volia Naroda*, No. 185 (December 5, 1917); *Kratkii otchët o rabotakh chetvërtago s"ezda P.S.-R.*, pp. 98-99.

on which Kerenski and the party leadership saw eye to eye was that of Avksentiev to the office of internal affairs. His tireless efforts for a union of all live forces, and his predictions of disaster to follow from a socialist assumption of power, had made him *persona gratissima* in circles favorable to coalition,[118] while his chairmanship of the All-Russian Peasants' Executive Committee led to great expectations from his taking over an office whence he could control the police power to the benefit of the land committees, which were everywhere experiencing difficulty with the agents of the Provisional Government.[119] Here it was Kerenski who knew what he was doing and the reformers in the peasants' soviets who were going to be fooled, for Avksentiev was far more interested in sustaining the war effort than in satisfying the demands of the peasants. In view of the commonly accepted notion that the members of the second coalition were the personal choice of A. F. Kerenski and did not represent their parties or organizations as such,[120] it may be noted that on July 23 the SR Central Committee had formally sanctioned the entrance of Chernov and Avksentiev into the government on the understanding that they would answer to it for their actions.[121] Lebedev had assumed office without its approval, and Savinkov, over its strenuous objection. So much for the status of four of the five SR's who held ministerial rank.

But what of Kerenski himself? The Third Congress had delegated both him and Chernov to the Provisional Government, and had done so ostentatiously, as a sop for his stinging defeat in the election to the Central Committee. Long after the events in question, in December at the Fourth Congress, when the affairs of the SR's had ceased to be of much interest to any one except the SR's, the Central

[118] Chernov, manuscript commentary on the minutes of the Central Committee, pp. 37-38.

[119] Bykhovski, *Vserossiiskii Sovet Krest'ianskikh Deputatov*, pp. 168, 171. Avksentiev relinquished the chair in the Executive Committee but clung to the title. At the last moment Nekrasov had desired to become minister of the interior but found the post reserved for Avksentiev. Nekrasov had to content himself with finance. See Miliukov, *Istoriia vtoroi russkoi revoliutsii*, I, Part II, 44.

[120] Miliukov, *Istoriia vtoroi russkoi revoliutsii*, I, Part II, pp. 24, 39, 41, 49; Kerenski, "Iz vospominanii," *Sovremennyia Zapiski*, XXXVIII, 256-57.

[121] *Kratkii otchët o rabotakh chetvërtago s"ezda P.S.-R.*, pp. 68, 111.

Committee announced to the startled delegates that since the session in the Malachite Hall on the night of July 21-22, Kerenski had no longer represented the party in the government, and that, accordingly, from that date onward the committee assumed no responsibility for his actions. The reason assigned for the changed relationship was that since all parties had on that occasion commissioned Kerenski to form a government, he could no longer be regarded as the representative of any one of them. Whether this bland explanation should be accepted at its face value or whether it concealed a recognition on the part even of his friends in the committee that Kerenski's growing impatience with any sort of supervision, party or soviet, required an alteration in his status, is an open question. A certain strain is indicated in the committee's admission that, unlike other SR ministers, Kerenski had not reported to it on his activities. If it had been moved to terminate a relationship which was not producing results and which offended both its dignity and its concept of discipline, the secrecy of the shift would have served the purpose of sparing feelings on both sides.[122]

But such *in camera* proceedings irritated the ordinary members of the party, who had not been initiated into the privy decisions of the Central Committee, and brought down upon that body a hail of criticism. To the right, the procedure followed smacked of dishonorable desertion of a comrade after the tide had turned against him; in good fortune, the party leadership had not challenged Kerenski's actions; in adversity, it was striving to disown him.[123] The left—or rather the moderate left and the left center, since the left now formed a separate party—censured the committee for clandestine operations which had caused the party needlessly to incur the odium of Kerenski's actions. Demanding to know whether he had been excluded from the party, and receiving the answer No, that for such

---

[122] *Kratkii otchët o rabotakh chetvërtago s"ezda P.S.-R.*, pp. 110-11; *Delo Naroda*, No. 224 (December 5, 1917). Incidents of scandal at SR meetings are not fully reported in the official accounts, which must be supplemented, if possible, from other sources.

[123] *Kratkii otchët o rabotakh chetvërtago s"ezda P.S.-R.*, p. 98; *Volia Naroda*, No. 185 (December 5, 1917). Lebedev was Kerenski's chief advocate at the Fourth Congress.

action both a party judgment and the judgment of history were necessary,[124] critics reminded the committee that a member of the party, whoever he was and whatever his rank might be, was always accountable to it for his actions.[125] Vysotski of Petersburg (LC) summed up the criticism from the left when he said that the committee could have rectified the original mistake of delegating Kerenski to the government either by divesting him of his mandate or by securing a change in his policies which would have brought them into harmony with its own; instead, he implied, it had preferred stealthily to revoke his credentials, withholding from its action the publicity which alone could have insured the party against being held responsible for policies over which it had no control.[126] Already in July the leadership, feeling the strain of a relationship which Zenzinov himself would term "deeply abnormal and painful in character,"[127] and reacting in a manner humanly understandable though politically suicidal, had taken advantage of a technicality to end a situation offensive to its conscience without bruising the feelings of its friend or impairing his public position.

Technically speaking, there were five "SR's" in the second coalition.[128] But enough has been said to show what an ill-assorted lot they were. Only two of them (Chernov and Avksentiev) held specific party mandates, one (Kerenski) held the same general mandate he had received from other parties, another (Lebedev) had no mandate, and the fifth (Savinkov) not only lacked authorization but had been included in the slate over the party's strenuous protest. What had happened, of course, was that Kerenski had picked three other SR's like himself and had had Chernov imposed upon him. The minister of agriculture was the only real party man in the lot. Avksentiev was much in the public eye, it is true, but stood too far to the right to exert a determining influence upon the affairs of the organization, toward which he maintained an attitude best described

[124] *Kratkii otchët a rabotakh chetvërtago s"ezda P.S.-R.*, p. 111.
[125] *Ibid.*, p. 95.
[126] *Ibid.*, p. 94.
[127] *Ibid.*, p. 90.
[128] See, for example, the list of ministers in Miliukov's *Istoriia vtoroi russkoi revoliutsii*, I, Part II, 44.

by one of his colleagues when he observed that he did not know of an occasion on which Avksentiev would have deferred to the will of the Central Committee.[129] Since the same state of affairs obtained within the Social Democratic sector, Miliukov is correct in pointing out that the second coalition marked a displacement of strength to the right.[130] If the first coalition witnessed an attempt to write a socialist program with capitalist hands, as he complains, the second would see a conservative course followed by nominal radicals. The socialist ministers in the new government were a pretty bloodless lot, but the parties they imperfectly represented had still to be reckoned with, and in that respect Kerenski was merely repeating the experiment of a mechanical union of incompatible elements. But the second coalition was not vested with any finality in the minds of its architects; it was merely to fill in until superseded by the "strong" government even then being readied behind the scenes by elements bent upon flogging the Russian people back into war.

[129] *Kratkii otchët o rabotakh chetvërtago s"ezda P.S.-R.*, p. 91. Minor's comment is particularly valuable because he was one of the independents in the Central Committee with leanings to the right, and hence cannot be accused of prejudice against Avksentiev.

[130] *Istoriia vtoroi russkoi revoliutsii*, I, Part II, 44-45.

IX

THE STERILE RECORD
OF THE SECOND COALITION

IN the story of the birth of the second coalition will be found the
seeds of its death, as also the key to its lamentable performance.
The congenital sterility of the new ministry makes it easy to deal
with its record, particularly from the standpoint of the SR contribution. Had the ministers of that party been a unit, they would have
had difficulty enough in writing its program into law. There was,
however, not the least cohesion or *esprit de corps* in this group. Four
of its members were committed body and soul to continuing the war
on the side of the Allies, asking nothing in return save material support; the fifth loathed the war and felt that the war aims of the Allies
must be brought into harmony with the soviet peace formula. Four
believed measures of land reform should be left to the Constituent
Assembly, lest the infringement of property rights weaken the arch
of coalition, and had their distaste for interim measures increased
when these were advanced by their party enemy. Responsibility for
this state of affairs must be laid at the door of the Central Committee.
It had taken no commitment from the minister-president in respect
to its demands in the agrarian sphere, perhaps on the supposition
that as a member of the party he was bound by the action of the
Third Congress; and if it could not control the appointments to the
ministries in charge of the armed forces, it ought at least to have
insisted on an enthusiastic proponent of land reform being placed in
the Ministry of the Interior, whence he could have lent support to
Chernov in the cabinet and arranged with him a *modus vivendi* in
the localities that would have secured the status of the land commit-

tees and convinced the rural population that the land would not escape them if they awaited the action of the Constituent Assembly. As it was, in entrusting the execution of the agrarian program to a pair of ministers like Chernov and Avksentiev, the committee was behaving as irresponsibly as the Imperial Government when it confided the invasion of East Prussia to Rennenkampf and Samsonov, two feuding generals at court; and it is an open question whether the SR's or the tsarist authorities achieved the greater disaster.

In this second coalition the minister of agriculture was completely isolated. Not only did he lack political support but he confronted a solid wall of personal ill will. The elimination of his friend Tsereteli, on his own volition or as a result of Kerenski's machinations, or both,[1] deprived Chernov of his only moral support, though scarcely of any assistance in attempting to deepen the revolution. Chernov's most malicious enemy was the dilettante foreign minister, who suspected him of treason; his deadliest enemy was Savinkov, who harbored grudges from the underground but stopped short of believing him personally capable of treason. How bad things were is seen from an incident that occurred in a cabinet meeting addressed by General Kornilov on August 3, when Savinkov passed a note to the premier, asking him whether the military secrets being divulged might not leak to the enemy, the inference being that Chernov would inform the soviet, where suspects were nesting.[2] The incident made upon General Kornilov the worst possible impression and strengthened his determination to stage a coup d'état. On another occasion Kerenski

---

[1] On this matter see especially Chernov, "Kak eto proiskhodilo," *Delo Naroda*, No. 178 (October 12, 1917); Chernov, *Great Russian Revolution*, pp. 247, 283, 399; *Kratkii otchët o rabotakh chetvërtago s"ezda P.S.-R.*, p. 117; Sukhanov, *Zapiski*, V, 112. For a different opinion see Miliukov, *Istoriia vtoroi russkoi revoliutsii*, I, Part II, 27, 41-42.

[2] Kerenski, *Delo Kornilova*, pp. 39-41; Savinkov, *K delu Kornilova*, pp. 12-13; Denikin, *Ocherki russkoi smuty*, II, 17-18; Martynov, *Kornilov*, pp. 47-48. Savinkov says Kerenski passed the note on to Kornilov, who cut short his discourse; Kerenski says he tore up the note and cut in on Kornilov because the general was wasting the cabinet's time with needless details; Kornilov says Kerenski himself first cautioned him in a low whisper, and that a little later he received Savinkov's note to the same effect—three different versions of the same incident.

deemed it necessary to reprove the members of the council for bristling whenever measures proposed by the minister of agriculture came up for consideration.[3] Not only the minister but the ministry as well fell into disfavor.[4] Even during the first coalition there had been indications that personal animosity as well as objections to content figured in the obstruction of its proposals. "More than once we have brought in measures for discussion," Assistant Minister Vikhliaev told the Head Land Committee, "only to have the cabinet crack open and fly apart."[5] It was a most unsatisfactory situation and in the long run an unendurable one.

His isolation within the cabinet and the searing experience of the campaign of slander through which he had passed had its effect upon Chernov's soft and sensitive nature. In the words of a left-wing critic, he became "more quiet than water and lower than grass."[6] At the Moscow State Conference, where his fortunes scraped bottom, he was not even granted the privilege of replying to the impassioned attacks made upon him by right-wing orators, and was too weak to demand that privilege, preferring to sit with bowed head and take the abuse without fighting back.[7] He could at least have resigned, and did, in fact, several times express such a wish to the Central Committee, but each time that body urged him to reconsider lest a major crisis ensue.[8] And so he stayed on at a post he had never really valued,[9] in the interest of perpetuating a coalition in which he had ceased to believe.

In the stifling atmosphere of the second coalition, blanketed by

[3] Demianov, "Moia sluzhba pri Vremennom Pravitel'stve," in *Arkhiv Russkoi Revoliutsii*, IV, 110.

[4] Rakitnikov, "Nasha politika v zemel'nom voprose" (Our Policy on the Land Question), *Delo Naroda*, No. 215 (November 21, 1917).

[5] Alaverdova, "Ocherk agrarnoi politiki Vremennogo Pravitel'stva," *Sotsialisticheskoe Khoziaistvo*, II, 166.

[6] Kamkov, *Kto takie levye sotsialisty-revoliutsionery*, p. 10.

[7] *Ibid.*, pp. 10-11; Bykhovski, *Vserossiiskii Sovet Krest'ianskikh Deputatov*, p. 219; *Kratkii otchët o rabotakh chetvërtago s"ezda P.S.-R.*, pp. 109, 111.

[8] Bykhovski, *Vserossiiskii Sovet Krest'ianskikh Deputatov*, p. 167; Chernov, *Great Russian Revolution*, pp. 249, 356.

[9] See comments of Lvov and Tsereteli in the latter's "Rossiiskoe krest'ianstvo i V. M. Chernov v 1917 godu," *Novyi Zhurnal*, XXIX, 236-37.

his enemies, party or otherwise, he accomplished virtually nothing toward the realization of the SR agrarian program. Such achievements as were recorded came in the period of the first coalition or, more particularly, in the interval of the rump cabinet, after the departure of Lvov and before the return of the Kadets. Thus the laws abrogating the Stolypin reform were enacted on June 28 and July 19, and on July 12 the law suspending land transactions, which had been left hanging in air by the collapse of the first coalition, at length received the assent of the government, not, however, in the prohibitive form proposed by Chernov but in the permissive form favored by Kerenski, so that land deals might still be consummated, but only with the approval of the Ministry of Agriculture, which of course was not forthcoming save in two minor instances.[10] But in the crucial matter of investing the land committees with legal powers which would make them the arbiters of agrarian relations until the Constituent Assembly, Chernov got nowhere at all. A draft of this law was introduced on June 29 but came up for consideration only early in August, prior to the Moscow State Conference, when it was turned back to the ministry for revision. A revised draft was submitted on the very next day but was not honored then or later by the cabinet's attention;[11] in fact, the Provisional Government was considering the draft of Chernov's successor, S. L. Maslov, at the time of its fall.

Seeing that the law was blocked, Chernov had recourse once more to circuitous tactics. On July 16 he, or rather his assistant, Rakitnikov, had issued a circular instruction to the land committees, the purpose of which was to cloak them with the authority of the ministry, encourage them to take action on behalf of the peasants,

[10] Chernov, "Vospreshchenie zemel'nykh sdelok" (Prohibition of Land Deals), *Delo Naroda*, No. 101 (July 15, 1917); Chernov, *Great Russian Revolution*, pp. 242-43; *Kratkii otchët o rabotakh chetvërtago s"ezda P.S.-R.*, p. 109; Sukhanov, *Zapiski*, V, 69-70. Kerenski claims credit not only for the added push necessary to put the law across but also for the initiative in its enactment. See "Otvet A. F. Kerenskago 'Delu Naroda'" (Reply of A. F. Kerenski to "Delo Naroda"), *Volia Naroda*, No. 110 (September 5, 1917).

[11] Rakitnikov, "Nasha taktika v zemel'nom voprose" (Our Tactics in the Land Question), *Delo Naroda*, No. 215 (November 21, 1917).

and raise their morale in the face of the campaign initiated by other agencies of the Provisional Government or by the military authorities to force them back into the strait jacket of the Imperial agrarian code.[12] This effort to fill the void and give some sort of legal status to the land committees by action of one of the departments of state brought the Ministry of Agriculture into conflict with other departments: the Food and Interior Ministries issued decrees, contradictory in spirit if not in letter, and the Ministry of Justice considered indicting the Ministry of Agriculture for attempting to usurp the authority of the government as a whole.[13] Indeed, the acting minister of justice, the Popular Socialist A. A. Demianov, set out to hamstring the rival ministry both centrally and locally by constituting himself a sort of watchdog for the status quo, and official circles were treated to the spectacle of how far Populists could diverge from each other in this clash between the nationalist tendency represented by Demianov[14] and the radical agrarian tendency personified in Chernov. The circular instruction of July 16 played its part in the defamation of Chernov, which was at this moment reaching a crescendo, but when the campaign to exclude him from the government failed, the Kadets raised the question of annulment in the new coalition, only to meet with Chernov's stubborn refusal to rescind the

[12] General Kornilov manifested particular zeal in curtailing the activities of the land committees in the zone near the front. The most sensational case of military intervention was the arrest of Golman, a prominent SR organizer in western Russia and chairman of the peasants' soviet in Mogilev province. See Bykhovski, *Vserossiiskii Sovet Krest'ianskikh Deputatov*, pp. 170, 173-74; Chernov, "Edinstvennyi vykhod" (The Only Way Out), *Delo Naroda*, No. 168 (September 30, 1917); O. Chaadaeva, *Kornilovshchina* (The Kornilov Period) (Moscow and Leningrad, 1930), pp. 29-32.

[13] See Demianov, "Moia sluzhba pri Vremennom Pravitel'stve," in *Arkhiv Russkoi Revoliutsii*, IV, 103-4; Rakitnikov, "Nasha taktika v zemel'nom voprose," *Delo Naroda*, No. 215 (November 21, 1917).

[14] Demianov was so conservative that he even objected to the name "Council of the Republic" for the organ that was set up after the Kornilov affair—something that the right-wing Kadet, Nabokov, accepted with equanimity. See *Arkhiv Russkoi Revoliutsii*, IV, 107; V. D. Nabokov, "Vremennoe Pravitel'stvo," in *ibid.*, I, 70. Further evidence of Popular Socialist hostility to Chernov's policy is given in Morokhovets, *Agrarnye programmy rossiiskikh politicheskikh partii*, p. 122.

circular until the law on land committees should have been enacted.[15] In this situation the land committees knew not what to do. If they went far enough by way of turning over unused lands and fixing rents to pacify the peasants, as the Ministry of Agriculture invited them to do, they risked arrest and criminal prosecution; if they did nothing, they risked surrendering the villages to anarchy. The quandary of the Poltava Provincial Land Committee will serve as an illustration. This committee had carefully adhered to the ministry's instructions and had succeeded in maintaining order, but when it undertook to revise leases weighing heavily upon peasant tenants, it received one telegram from the Ministry of the Interior annulling its decisions and another from Rakitnikov confirming its right to impose a *modus vivendi* when the parties to a contract could not agree among themselves. To crown its misfortunes, the committee ran afoul of the military authorities and was indicted for violating General Kornilov's decrees.[16] Now the instructions inciting the land committees to action emanated from the SR Ministry of Agriculture and the police power restraining them from action was wielded by the SR Ministry of the Interior. How was it, increasing numbers of Russians were asking themselves, that two ministries headed by members of the same party should be pursuing diametrically opposed courses of action? The Russian public was only beginning to be initiated into the mysteries of the Socialist Revolutionary party. It had yet to realize that political figures with the same label, particularly the SR label, might have nothing else in common; that these two men, the ministers of agriculture and the interior, did not speak the same language, did not have the same views, and ought not by any

[15] *Kratkii otchët o rabotakh chetvërtago s"ezda P.S.-R.*, p. 110; Bykhovski, *Vserossiiskii Sovet Krest'ianskikh Deputatov*, pp. 163-64; Alaverdova, "Ocherk agrarnoi politiki Vremennogo Pravitel'stva," *Sotsialisticheskoe Khoziaistvo*, II, 170-71; Morokhovets, *Agrarnye programmy rossiiskikh politicheskikh partii*, pp. 111-13; Lutokhin, "Zemel'nyi vopros," in *Zapiski Instituta*, II, 358; Lozinski, *Ekonomicheskaia politika*, p. 159; Chernov, *Great Russian Revolution*, pp. 243-45; statement of Chernov in *Delo Naroda*, No. 114 (July 30, 1917); *Russkoe Slovo*, No. 238 (October 18, 1917).

[16] A. Altovski, "V derevne—o rabote zemel'nykh komitetov" (In the Village —the Work of the Land Committees), *Delo Naroda*, No. 162 (September 23, 1917).

logical test to have belonged to the same party. It had yet to realize that Minister of Agriculture Chernov was pursuing an agrarian revolution and Minister of the Interior Avksentiev, a truce of classes in order to preserve Russian pressure on the eastern flank of Germany to the benefit of the French Republic. It had yet to realize how completely the war had shattered the unity of this sprawling organization.

But the left SR's and Lenin realized all this already, and determined to make political capital out of it. The situation that gave the left SR's the opportunity to depict Avksentiev as an enemy of the peasant movement gave Lenin a club with which to beat all SR's. A hue and cry arose in radical circles over the country that the SR's were casting land committee personnel into prison. As the SR's were extremely sensitive to this charge, it is not easy to ascertain how much truth there was in it. At the Fourth Congress, Zenzinov officially denied the complicity of party members in these arrests, and asserted that as soon as the Central Committee learned of them, it demanded the release of the detained persons in language equivalent to an ultimatum.[17] He fails to say upon whom the ultimatum was served. Bykhovski, comember with Avksentiev of the Peasants' Executive Committee and therefore in a position to know, but solicitous of his colleague's reputation because of their affinity of viewpoint, contends that the campaign of repression produced more smoke than fire, since in most cases the court summons languished for want of execution; he adds that in the whole period leading up to October, only seventeen to eighteen committeemen were actually deprived of their liberty. He attempts to shift the blame to subordinates or to other agencies. But he cannot deny that Avksentiev, who had been pointedly reminded by the Peasants' Soviet upon assuming office that its chairman would be expected to put an end to intimidation,[18] had in fact brought about no improvement in the situation,

---

[17] *Kratkii otchët o rabotakh chetvërtago s"ezda P.S.-R.*, pp. 68-69.

[18] Avksentiev had been careful to avoid any specific commitments beyond a pledge to the declaration of July 8. In outlining a program for his department, he said nothing about the status of the land committees except for obliquely declaring that all local institutions, new as well as old, must be held to observance of the law. See his statements as reported in *Delo Naroda*, Nos. 110, 119 (July 26, August 5, 1917).

but only a further deterioration, and he admits that the usefulness of the land committees was impaired and the peasants encouraged to take matters into their own hands.[19] In relation to the land committees Avksentiev as minister of the interior walked a tightrope, taking care neither to compromise his position in the Peasants' Soviet by any overt act of hostility nor to disrupt the "union of all live forces" —his favorite phrase—by extending to the committees his protection. In his heart he no doubt regarded their activities with as much disfavor as Chernov viewed them with favor, not, of course, because he sought to preserve the *pomeshchik* system, as Lenin charges,[20] but because there was nothing he would not lay on the altar of war.[21]

The men at the head of the national organization of peasants' soviets also sought relief from the minister-president. After all, he, too, was their party comrade. Kerenski received a peasant delegation on August 4 and listened to its complaint about the tortoise pace of legislation favoring the village. He would do what was possible. The government was not inattentive to the peasants' demands, and he personally was inclined to favor them, but various interests were involved, and in the cause of national defense the government must make every effort to allay class antagonisms. The delegation left feeling depressed: Kerenski was not the man to break out of this "enchanted circle" of no social change because of the quest for victory, and no victory because of mass disgruntlement over the absence of social change.[22] The First All-Russian Peasants' Congress had entrusted the leadership of the peasant movement to the right-centrist or right SR's, simply because the rural delegates had deferred to the intellectuals, most of whom were of that persuasion, and the last thing these people would do was to rock the boat of coalition by bringing really effective pressure to bear for a new agrarian order. Theirs was a complex psychology, compounded of fatuous optimism, a gross miscalculation of social forces, and cynical complacency. They expected in the end to be rescued by the good sense of the propertied classes, which would lead to the acceptance of certain

[19] *Vserossiiskii Sovet Krest'ianskikh Deputatov*, pp. 168-71.
[20] *Sochineniia*, XXII, 314.
[21] On the subject of repression of the land committees see also Steinberg, *Ot fevralia po oktiabr'*, p. 79; Voznesenski, *Moskva v 1917 godu*, pp. 68-70.
[22] Bykhovski, *Vserossiiskii Sovet Krest'ianskikh Deputatov*, pp. 176-78.

unpalatable but inevitable changes in the economic system.[23] They gauged the relative strength of conservative and radical forces in Russian society by their own feeling of inferiority to the Kadet intelligentsia. And they salved their revolutionary conscience with the thought that locally the peasants were taking over the land on their own terms, whether the government in St. Petersburg enacted laws or not.[24] In short, these Populist intellectuals derived secret comfort from the self-action of the peasants which in public they deplored. They sat in their Petersburg offices and imagined the fire would get no larger. They prided themselves on their broad point of view in exalting the interests of the state above those of any component part, even of the class they represented, and they imagined they were serving the Russian state by keeping a prowar coalition in the saddle in St. Petersburg while the bases of Russian society were dissolving in village anarchy. Truly, these Populist intellectuals sowed to the wind and reaped the whirlwind.

On August 23, after the Moscow State Conference, they addressed the government in as yet unheard-of language, censuring it for leaving this legal void in which the forces of order in the village were foundering, and summoning it to choose, once and for all, between the landowners and peasants. But the adherents of the status quo did not take fright—they knew no lightning was mixed with the thunder of the Executive Committee and proceeded to disregard its injunctions. The men at the head of that organ instinctively shrank from the sanctions that would have upset the precarious equilibrium of the second coalition, and the "enchanted circle," or downward spiral, went on and on.[25]

But it would be unfair to lay all the blame for the debacle that overtook the SR land program on the shoulders of the prowar intellectuals. A large measure of blame attaches to Chernov himself. Incredible as it may seem, he emasculated the program by deleting

[23] *Ibid.*, pp. 145-46.
[24] *Ibid.*, pp. 162, 221. The reader is reminded that this information is not drawn from some hostile critic's indictment but from the testimony of one of the most representative of these intellectuals, whose account was sufficiently unrepentant to be torn off the press and destroyed by the Soviet government.
[25] *Ibid.*, pp. 179, 224-27.

from the law on land committees introduced on June 29 the provision for entrusting to them the administration of the land fund.
And he did not restore this provision in the August revision. Its
absence is established by the text of the original law.[26] His personal
responsibility for the deletion rests on the direct charge of an eminent agronomist who was a member of the Head Land Committee,[27]
and is confirmed, without mentioning his name, by his successor in
office, S. L. Maslov, who told the December Party Congress that
upon becoming minister of agriculture he had to withdraw the law
and incorporate this provision.[28] Nowhere, to the knowledge of this
author, does Chernov deny the charge or even discuss it—no doubt
because he found it too embarrassing. It receives added confirmation—if any were needed—from his failure to insert in the declaration
of July 8 any reference to turning over the land to the committees;[29]
he sang in such a minor key on that occasion, in fact, that Miliukov
the historian could speak of the restraint and humility of a document[30] which Miliukov the politician damned as that "Chernovian
program."[31] The minister's default on his obligation before the party
and peasantry is of a piece with his general conduct in 1917. When
the Head Land Committee, reversing the normal roles of conservative committee and radical ministry, proposed to strengthen the law
submitted by the ministry, Rakitnikov sought to dissuade it with the
argument that prospects of passage were poor enough as it was.[32]
But the provincial delegates could see no purpose in land committees
without land, and under pressure from them the Head Committee

[26] *Izvestiia Glavnago Zemel'nago Komiteta*, Nos. 2-3 (August 1-15, 1917),
pp. 23-24. The proposed law restricted the jurisdiction of the committees to
rented or idle lands (Articles 2 and 3).

[27] I. (N. P.?) Oganovski, "Edinstvo fronta" (The Unity of the Front), *Volia
Naroda*, No. 128 (September 26, 1917).

[28] *Kratkii otchët o rabotakh chetvërtago s"ezda P.S.-R.*, p. 104.

[29] See text in *Revoliutsiia 1917 goda (Khronika sobytii)*, III, 327-28. Nekrasov
had accepted Chernov's draft of the agrarian section virtually without change.
See "V. Chernov i iiul'skie dni" (V. Chernov and the July Days), *Krasnyi
Arkhiv*, V, 268.

[30] *Istoriia vtoroi russkoi revoliutsii*, I, Part II, 20.

[31] *Burzhuaziia i pomeshchiki v 1917 godu*, p. 213.

[32] Alaverdova, "Ocherk agrarnoi politiki Vremennogo Pravitel'stva," *Sotsialisticheskoe Khoziaistvo*, II, 170; Lozinski, *Ekonomicheskaia politika*, p. 154.

went ahead with its own draft, in which the SR formula was reinstated.[33]

Such tacit repudiation of his leadership, however, had no effect on Chernov, and it seems that he went out of office without having made an attempt to write into law the core of his party's interim program. He simply could not find the courage to propose a drastic measure to a cabinet that denied him satisfaction in smaller things. His attitude seems to have been that there was no use in trying to thread the eye of the needle with a rope. But the hopelessness of cabinet action was no authorization to cut the heart out of the legislation favored by the PSR. He should have established its hopelessness, and then gone before the party and invited it to change either its coalitional or its agrarian policy. Or if he did not have the backbone to stand alone in the cabinet as the sponsor of a measure formally adopted by the Third Party Congress and the First Peasants' Congress, and therefore doubly binding on himself and the Central Committee, he should have resigned. Several courses were open to him but the one he took has no shadow of justification. A man who prided himself on observing party discipline to the point of self-abnegation had set aside a decision of the highest party instance on a matter of grave importance. A man who did not underestimate the Bolshevik danger, and who knew what it held in store for the peasantry, had made it possible for the Bolsheviks to portray SR promises as empty phrases. After his retirement from office Chernov raised a great noise on behalf of a measure which, during his four months' tenure of the Ministry of Agriculture, he had not lifted a finger to realize.[34] In this matter of putting the land under a public agency, which was the least the peasants could have been persuaded to accept, Chernov had played fast and loose with his party, with the class it represented, and with his own honor.

From all accounts he was a poor minister. He could conceive the theory of a new agrarian order but the application and execution

[33] *Izvestiia Glavnago Zemel'nago Komiteta,* Nos. 2-3 (August 1-15, 1917), pp. 12, 17; Lozinski, *Ekonomicheskaia politika,* pp. 158, 166-67.
[34] See Oganovski, "Edinstvo fronta," *Volia Naroda,* No. 128 (September 26, 1917); Chernov, "Edinstvennyi vykhod," *Delo Naroda,* No. 168 (September 30, 1917).

quite escaped him. The work of the ministry was performed by Vikhliaev while Chernov wrote editorials for the *Delo Naroda*. Very little in the way of systematic work came from his hands during his tenure of office.[35] Political enemies within and without his party have charged that the bills from his ministry were poorly drawn, accounting in part for the obstruction encountered,[36] and Chernov concedes some imperfection when he pleads the impossibility of satisfying jurists trained in the Roman law with measures framed in the spirit of folk concepts, though couched in terms of compromise because of the Provisional Government's refusal to sanction the foundations of a new legal order.[37] His successor spent a week in redrafting the law on land committees,[38] so unsatisfactory was the form in which he found it, and on at least one occasion the council of the Head Land Committee had to revise the form, as distinct from the substance, of a bill introduced by the ministry.[39] The minister-president several times expressed relief over the retirement of Chernov, saying that Maslov was a much easier man to work with,[40] but the subjectiveness of this judgment precludes an evaluation. Kerenski reinforces the impression of weakness received from Chernov's handling of the law on land committees by affirming that during the four months his opponent held office, never once did he cast a dissenting vote, despite his denunciation of the government's record after his retirement from office.[41]

Not only did Chernov write articles when he should have been writing laws, but he indulged his craze for scribbling right in the cabinet meetings. Sometimes Tsereteli would nudge him and say,

[35] Interview with Zenzinov in Paris (September, 1935).

[36] *Kratkii otchët o rabotakh chetvërtago s"ezda P.S.-R.*, pp. 93, 108; "Nedostoinaia igra" (An Unworthy Game), *Volia Naroda*, No. 110 (September 5, 1917); Demianov, "Moia sluzhba pri Vremennom Pravitel'stve," in *Arkhiv Russkoi Revoliutsii*, IV, 110.

[37] Speech at the Congress of Representatives of the Ministry of Agriculture to the Provincial Land Committees, *Delo Naroda*, No. 118 (August 4, 1917).

[38] *Kratkii otchët o rabotakh chetvërtago s"ezda P.S.-R.*, p. 104.

[39] *Izvestiia Glavnago Zemel'nago Komiteta*, No. 1 (July 15, 1917), pp. 24-25.

[40] Interview with Zenzinov in New York (December 25, 1949).

[41] Oral statement (Hoover Library, 1955). The author's recollection is that Kerenski has somewhere made this statement in print, but the source cannot be found.

"Please listen, Victor Mikhailovich; this is important," to which Chernov would answer, "The editorial must be written, and, anyhow, I shall vote the way you do."[42] Here we are dealing, not with a statesman or even a politician, but with a large child.[43] The relationship of the two men is symbolic of the relationship between the sprawling and flabby SR organism and the small but compact Menshevik party, which took it in hand and led it down a path not of its choosing, simply because it could not move down any other under its own power.

The PSR was badly served by its choice as minister of agriculture. But whether it would have given enough backing to another choice to have enabled him to realize its agrarian program is more than doubtful. There was logic, of course, in the nomination of Chernov to this position, since he had conceived (with Vikhliaev) the plan of land socialization. But the possibility is not to be excluded that in giving him this assignment the SR high command—and that means primarily Gotz, to a lesser extent Zenzinov—may have hoped to bridle him with responsibility and cause him to hold his tongue on the war. One is reminded of the desperate maneuver at the Third Congress to keep the drafting of the resolution on war out of the hands of Chernov and in those of Gotz.

If such were the purpose, it was brilliantly successful, for Chernov, the crusader against war, was as effectively buried in the Ministry of Agriculture as in an Egyptian tomb. With the big gun in the antiwar camp spiked, the leadership could sustain a prowar regime despite the sputtering fire of the left SR's. Only in the fall, after the Kornilov upheaval, did that fire become concentrated and deadly.

If the PSR had accomplished so little in the agrarian sphere, in relation to which all members were supposed to be as one, what could it hope to achieve in the field of war and peace, in relation to

[42] Interview with Tsereteli in New York (December, 1949).
[43] This judgment is the author's, not Tsereteli's.

which the members had long since lost their common tongue? It achieved nothing at all, and, in fact, did not even try, since a decisive step in any direction would have disrupted the organization.

The Central Committee, according to its spokesman, had adopted as the basis of policy all three of the principles contained in the soviet formula: the struggle against imperialism (no annexations or indemnities), defense of the revolution, and restoration of the Workers' International.[44] Theoretically, these were objectives on which all sections of SR opinion could agree, yet on no one of them did the party present a united front. The struggle against imperialism bogged down in the question of which set of imperialist powers was obligated to make the next move: the prowar SR's contended that it was up to Germany to follow the Russian example, while the antiwar SR's stressed the impossibility of mobilizing German opinion against its own imperialism until all the Allies, and not just Russia alone, had renounced theirs. The defense of the revolution raised the questions of restoring discipline in the army and resuming offensive operations. Radical SR's would not hear of effective measures to restore discipline until the officers' corps had been purged, and contended that an offensive under existing conditions would be waged in the service of Anglo-French imperialism.[45] Moderate SR's either lacked the zeal for cleaning out the army command or found it impossible to do so without shaking their shibboleth of coalition, in view of the attitude of Kerenski and the Kadets; they supported an offensive both because the enemy occupied Russian territory and because only in this way could the prestige of the revolution be raised in the eyes of friend and foe.[46] The June offensive greatly heightened the tension between the left wing and the rest of the party, foreshadowing the lines along which it would split four months later and embittering the left for the first time against Chernov, who had found it possible, in his ministerial capacity, to

[44] *Kratkii otchët o rabotakh chetvërtago s"ezda P.S.-R.*, pp. 65-66.
[45] As an example of their attitude, the stand of the Kazan Provincial Conference may be cited; see *Kazanskii Oktiabr'*, I, 69.
[46] See statement of Dennis Rosenblum before the Moscow Soviet as quoted in *Ot fevralia k oktiabriu v Moskve*, p. 20; see also articles of Lebedev in *Volia Naroda*, Nos. 47, 50 (June 23, 27, 1917).

reconcile himself to the measure on the ground that offense is sometimes the best defense.[47]

Restoration of the International should have commended itself to all SR's as a means of bringing pressure to bear impartially on both the imperialist camps, but the effort to assemble a socialist congress in the Swedish capital only threw another apple of discord into their midst, due to the circumstances of its failure. During 1917 two members of the Central Committee spent much time abroad, in contact with foreign socialists, A. I. Rusanov as representative of the workers' and soldiers' soviets, and I. A. Rubanovich as representative of the peasants' soviets. The former was left and the latter, right of center; their views on the war were irreconcilable, and they worked at cross-purposes, in standard SR fashion. Rusanov was one of the tireless proponents of the Stockholm Conference, and by August matters had reached the stage where the fate of the congress hinged on whether or not the Allied governments would issue passports to their socialists. The British government opposed the conference, but with its customary finesse, preferred that someone else do the actual knifing. It thought it had lined up a Labor minister, Arthur Henderson, for the purpose of inducing British labor to reject the bid, thus relieving the government of the odium of direct action, but Henderson, having contracted a touch of revolutionary fever on a recent visit to St. Petersburg, crossed up the cabinet by using his influence to win the adherence of the Labor party.

At this juncture His Majesty's Government might have been divested of its raiment of hypocrisy and forced to stand forth in naked repression of a movement for peace had not help come from an unexpected quarter. One reason for caution in killing the Stockholm Conference had been the attitude of the Russian government, which was presumed to be under soviet pressure and hence favorable to the conference. But the July reaction had produced a change.

[47] See his article, "Tezisy s illiustratsiiami" (Theses with Illustrations), *Delo Naroda*, No. 86 (June 28, 1917); *Tretii s"ezd P.S.-R.*, p. 195; *Great Russian Revolution*, pp. 299 ff.; "Ot Zimmerwal'da do revoliutsionnago oboronchestva" (From Zimmerwald to Revolutionary "Defensism"), *Volia Naroda*, No. 45 (June 21, 1917); Lebedev, "Nastuplenie" (The Offensive), *ibid.*, No. 7 (May 6, 1917).

The revolution had left undisturbed the diplomatic corps, and the Russian chargé d'affaires at London, K. D. Nabokov, a Constitutional Democrat, as limited in vision and as inebriated with war as the rest of them, busied himself with reporting the British distaste for the conference to St. Petersburg, in the hope of stiffening the attitude there through an appeal to Allied solidarity and eliciting some expression of opinion which in turn would strengthen the hands of the London cabinet. In his enterprise for mutual strangulation of the conference, the Kadet diplomat was able to enlist help in the highest quarters. Tereshchenko sent a note authorizing him to inform the British that "although the Russian Government does not deem it possible to prevent Russian delegates from taking part in the Stockholm Conference, they regard this Conference as a Party concern, and its decisions in no wise binding upon the liberty of action of the Government." This note, published by the British government with Nabokov's consent, had the desired effect. The rug was pulled out from under Henderson's feet, the back of the pacifist movement broken, and the knell of the Stockholm Conference sounded with the refusal of passports to the British delegates. Tereshchenko had done one other thing: he had informed the French of Kerenski's hostility to the conference, and M. Albert Thomas had lost no time in communicating the news to London.[48]

For this debacle the PSR must shoulder a major share of responsibility, since it was the largest party sponsoring the conference, had a controlling voice in the soviets, and carried Kerenski on its rolls. Yet there was no corporate reaction to the news of the disaster which had overtaken not only the conference but also the party's peace policy, reduced as it had been to this single fragile hope by the inability to agree on anything else. Chernov says that the real authors of the disaster were unsuspected at the time.[49] This is a remarkable

[48] K. D. Nabokov, *Ispytaniia diplomata*, pp. 113-36; Lloyd George, *War Memoirs*, Vol. IV, chap. LVIII, especially pp. 1909-24; Buchanan, *My Mission to Russia*, II, 160-61, 163-64; *The Times* (London), August 13, 1917 (N.S.); Noulens, *Mon Ambassade en Russie soviétique*, I, 56-60; Chernov, *Great Russian Revolution*, pp. 295-98; Sukhanov's account is worthless (*Zapiski*, V, 131-36).
[49] *Great Russian Revolution*, p. 299.

statement even for him to make. One is tempted to say the SR's did not know because they did not want to know. All they had to do was to pick up any English newspaper and read the chilling words: "The Russian Government does not deem it possible to prevent Russian delegates from taking part . . . ," and the further phrases divesting Stockholm of any official sanction whatever. The knife protruding from the back of the corpse bore the trademark of the Russian Ministry of Foreign Affairs and an examination of the finger-prints must have pointed in the direction of the minister-president.[50] It is true that Kerenski tried to redeem the situation by publicly disclaiming any intent to sabotage the conference, promising to regard it as an "important expression of public opinion," and privately asking Buchanan to press for British passports.[51] His party comrades seized upon such protestations of innocence and looked no further. Only the Petersburg organization at its Sixth Conference censured the socialist ministers for not better serving the cause of peace and expressed sharp displeasure with the way the government had acted. The Tereshchenko-Nabokov correspondence, it noted, betokened a turning away from the road to peace. Yet even this radical organization demanded nothing more drastic than a shake-up in the diplomatic corps.[52] The decision lay in the soviets and there the SR's joined hands with the Mensheviks to bury the Stockholm Conference, first choking off Martov's bid for a coroner's inquest and then voicing a pious hope for the conference's future resurrection. In the Petersburg Soviet, Livshits, Burstein, and other SR

[50] Nabokov, in fact, says that due to an error on the part of Lloyd George's chancellery, British journalists came into possession of the French telegram disclosing Kerenski's attitude as well as the note from St. Petersburg (*Ispytaniia diplomata*, pp. 129-30).

[51] *Delo Naroda*, No. 121 (August 8, 1917); Buchanan, *My Mission to Russia*, II, 164. The ambassador says Kerenski never intended to have the government's opposition publicized. Even after the British had let the cat out of the bag, however, he reaffirmed his opposition to the conference in a conversation with the French ambassador. See deciphered telegram, Carlotti to Sonnino, August 17/30, 1917, quoted in N. L. Rubinstein, "Vneshniaia politika kerenshchiny" (Foreign Policy in the Kerenski Period), in *Ocherki po istorii oktiabr'skoi revoliutsii*, II, 433-34. The French ambassador in his memoirs discloses virtually nothing.

[52] *Delo Naroda*, No. 119 (August 5, 1917).

leaders accepted the official version of developments in London and showed a disinclination to pursue the matter further.[53]

Much depended on Stockholm. The SR's with their Menshevik allies had put themselves in a position where it was the last string to their bow. The only consistency about their policy in 1917 was the refusal to contemplate a separate peace.[54] Having closed that door, they could only await a revolution in Germany or a progressive weakening of the will to fight in all the warring countries. On the occasion of presenting the red banner of Land and Liberty to the Baltic Fleet at Revel, Chernov had cried out in desperation for the German and Austrian workers to do what the Russian workers had already done and so end the war[55] (it is doubtful that it would have, and not least because of Chernov's own comrades). But the different social structure and the far stronger spirit of nationalism as yet ruled out in Germany a repetition of the February events in Russia. There remained only the slow and plodding way of mobilizing peace sentiment until it was strong enough to compel the various governments, Allied and enemy, to renounce their predatory designs; and in this endeavor the key role was assigned to Stockholm, which would, it was hoped, restore the unity of the working-class movement and crystallize everywhere the longing for peace. The hope was not as farfetched as it might seem, for war-weariness was increasing everywhere except in the United States, and people as far apart as Marshal Pétain and Ramsay Macdonald were agreed that the conference might make it impossible to go on stoking the fire.[56] Being dead set against a rupture with the Allies and yet sincerely in favor of peace, the controlling SR-Menshevik bloc had to devise some means of bringing Allied war aims into harmony with Russia's; the strategy had been to postpone the inter-Allied conference until after the Stockholm Conference had softened the attitude of the French and

[53] *Ibid.,* No. 124 (August 11, 1917); Sukhanov, *Zapiski,* V, 139-40; *Revoliutsiia 1917 goda (Khronika sobytii),* IV, 21; Bykhovski, *Vserossiiskii Sovet Krest'ianskikh Deputatov,* pp. 227-28.

[54] See official statement of Zenzinov as spokesman of the Central Committee (*Kratkii otchët o rabotakh chetvërtago s"ezda P.S.-R.,* p. 67).

[55] *Delo Naroda,* No. 121 (August 8, 1917).

[56] Noulens, *Mon Ambassade en Russie soviétique,* I, 57.

British peoples, which otherwise would doom the Russian initiative in wiping the Allied slate clean of imperialist aims. In the SR camp only the extreme left had demanded an early Allied conference which would put the British and French on the spot and either force them into line or disclose the incompatibility of their war aims with those of revolutionary Russia. All other sections of the party stood in mortal terror of a rupture. For them Stockholm was the only way out.[57]

Hence in abandoning it so easily, they were taking leave of the only peace policy they had, though they lacked the fortitude to confess what they were doing. From this time onward the official SR line is one of drift, waiting for something to break in other countries. It broke first in Russia, as might have been foreseen, and engulfed all SR's in a common ruin, both those who in effect had abandoned the quest for peace and those who had refused to sit twiddling their thumbs. At the Fourth or December Congress, after it was too late to do any good, the Central Committee came under heavy fire for the bankruptcy of its peace policy. It was justly accused of having failed to focus the party's attention upon the Stockholm Conference and of having neglected to take any serious measures in its defense. In general, during the whole period of coalitional government the leadership had kept the peace problem in the background.[58] The party members who preferred these charges had at last torn the blindfold from their eyes, but even at that late hour they did not seem to understand why the problem had been slighted.

Apparent to everyone, of course, was the sabotage practiced by the diplomatic corps, by all those tsarist functionaries whom the Provisional Government, in accordance with the myth of unbroken succession, had left in their positions. The professional conservatism of these votaries of darkness equaled, if it did not exceed, their political conservatism, and they set themselves with tireless obstinacy to oppose any intrusion of the revolution upon their musty domain.

[57] Snosheniia sovetskoi demokratii s sotsialisticheskimi men'shinstvami voiuiushchikh stran i delo R. Grimma (manuscript), pp. 88-91; Steinberg, *Ot fevralia po oktiabr'*, pp. 39-41, 75-76.
[58] *Kratkii otchët o rabotakh chetvërtago s"ezda P.S.-R.*, pp. 75, 88, 96.

The debacle of the Stockholm Conference gave Nabokov "tremendous moral satisfaction." He was "profoundly convinced" that it "would have led to a peace of compromise, and consequently to what Germany was already desirous of obtaining." And he goes on to say, "If some part of the responsibility for averting this international catastrophe may properly be assigned to me, I shall not cease to be proud of that part."[59] The soviet formula of peace without annexations or indemnities he certainly classified as a "peace of compromise," if not as something worse, and, consequently, as an "international catastrophe." Now the SR's had been clamoring since the early days of the revolution for a purge of the diplomatic service. No voice had been louder than Chernov's in favor of "amputating the tentacles" of the old diplomacy by replacing Imperial appointees with commissars of the Provisional Government.[60] Yet for four months he had sat in the cabinet without initiating any action in that direction, even when the sabotage of his own agrarian policies had revived the cry in the SR press.[61] Now the peace policy had been wrecked by the same unremedied state of affairs, yet the offending diplomat suffered nothing worse than a mild rebuke. Nabokov could not conceal his surprise at the ease with which the Foreign Ministry shielded him from the soviet.[62]

There is a saying in Russian that "a fish begins to spoil at the head," and before getting at obstructionists like Constantine Nabokov it would have been necessary for the revolution to penetrate the Ministry of Foreign Affairs. The SR's had been primarily responsible for Miliukov's fall, but once having achieved this victory—with Kerenski's cooperation and British approval—they rested on their oars and permitted the succession to go to a man who proposed to follow the same course in a less provocative manner. Miliukov went, but his policies remained. Instead of the brusqueness which had offended the socialists, sand was now to be thrown into their eyes, and they were to be lulled to sleep with "gracious verbal conces-

[59] *Ispytaniia diplomata*, pp. 135-36.
[60] "Na dve stezi" (On Two Roads), *Delo Naroda*, No. 30 (April 22, 1917).
[61] See especially the editorial, "Obnovlenie vedomstv i demokratiia" (An Overhaul of the Departments and Democracy), *ibid.*, No. 113 (July 29, 1917).
[62] *Ispytaniia diplomata*, p. 136.

sions," costing little and meaning less. The angular pedantry of the professor gave way to the deceptive grace of the dilettante, but Russian foreign policy continued as subservient to London and Paris as hitherto, even more so, since Tereshchenko did not have Miliukov's obsession with the Straits. Miliukov was an imperialist, but he honestly stated his objectives and was, by his lights, a Russian patriot. Tereshchenko offered everything to the French and British and asked little or nothing in return. For them he was the ideal foreign minister; he knew no higher law than the will of the Western Allies. The minister-president over him also moved in the wake of the British Empire, but Kerenski's ecstatic moods and flights of oratory belied a humane nature that longed for the slaughter to cease.[63] There is no evidence that the foreign minister was capable of deep feeling on any subject, and certainly not for the village youth at the front, whose lot was so remote from his own in the safety and comfort of his Petersburg chancellery. This well-mannered and faultlessly attired sugar magnate with a smattering of French and English culture, exuding opulence and speaking with a smooth and forked tongue, had all the qualifications of a diplomat and none at all of a statesman. In a subordinate position, dealing with matters of protocol and acting as liaison agent, his small talents could have been turned to account, but it was fatal to allow him to climb onto the ministerial level. "During the whole existence of the Provisional Government our international policy was restricted to conversations"—such was the verdict, not of some irresponsible radical, but of the eminently conservative V. D. Nabokov, at one time general secretary of the government and brother of the above-mentioned saboteur. His words reflect, of course, not only upon the revolution's second minister of foreign affairs but also upon the first, who was his friend and party colleague.[64]

This was the man whom the Socialist Revolutionaries tolerated as director of Russian foreign policy from the fall of Miliukov to

[63] Several times he told Buchanan that the war must be shortened (*My Mission to Russia*, II, 173-74).

[64] "Vremennoe Pravitel'stvo," in *Arkhiv Russkoi Revoliutsii*, I, 46-48; Miliukov, *Istoriia vtoroi russkoi revoliutsii*, I, Part I, 167, 170; Chernov, *Great Russian Revolution*, pp. 352-53.

the end of the Provisional Government. He speedily reduced the laurels of their triumph over Miliukov to a small heap of ashes. France and Great Britain would not hear of peace; neither would their puppet in St. Petersburg. "The question of general peace," he remarked to the Japanese ambassador immediately after taking office, "must await the end of the war. In no case will military operations be discontinued."[65] Even when the Provisional Government was falling to pieces and more intelligent conservatives such as Konovalov and Nolde could at least entertain the thought of peace, Tereshchenko remained adamant and clung to the fantasy that by spring Alekseev could have the army back in shape.[66] One can imagine what chance the Stockholm Conference had with the foreign policy of the revolution being molded by such hands. Why did the SR's put up with this state of affairs? It was not simply a question of having the wool pulled over their eyes—if they could not judge policy by the fruits thereof, they had received a plain intimation from Tereshchenko himself as to what his attitude would be when he declared in the Malachite Hall (July 21-22) that "at present no one thinks any more about peace, for all understand that it now is impossible."[67] All the SR chiefs were there, including the "Zimmerwaldist" Chernov, but none reacted to this provocative statement at a time when the government was still in a state of flux. They had demanded the Ministry of Agriculture, and Chernov had been appointed; they had asked for the Ministry of the Interior, and Avksentiev had been named. But never once had they claimed the foreign office, either for themselves or for their Menshevik allies, letting it go more or

[65] Decoded telegram, Utsida to Motono, May 7/20, 1917, "Inostrannye diplomaty o revoliutsii 1917 g." (Foreign Diplomats on the Revolution of 1917), *Krasnyi Arkhiv*, XXIV (V, 1927), 144. After some observation of Tereshchenko, the Japanese diplomat wired his chief that "the present minister of foreign affairs has not escaped the common failing of all Russians, and is extremely loquacious." See decoded telegram, Utsida to Motono, July 16/29, 1917, *ibid.*, p. 153.

[66] The restoration, then, would be performed in the depth of winter, the fourth of the war, and by a general whose outlook led him regularly to refer to the soviets of soldiers' (*soldatskikh*) deputies as the soviets of dogs' (*sobach'ikh*) deputies.

[67] Sukhanov, *Zapiski*, V, 101-2.

less by default to the nonsocialist side of the coalition, which would not move in the direction the party wanted to go.[68]

At the end of the year the retiring Central Committee could find virtually no excuse for its failure to pursue a more active policy on behalf of peace. The best Zenzinov could do was to cite its criticism of Tereshchenko in the editorial columns of the *Delo Naroda*, and he had to admit that the soviet peace delegation abroad, on which Rusanov had served, had been a profitless venture.[69] The defense was so weak, in fact, as to lead to the conclusion that there were some things he could not or did not want to say. We will say them for him. The SR leaders in general could have furthered the cause of peace, and specifically have saved the Stockholm Conference, only at the cost of breaking up the coalition and parting company with Kerenski. Worse still, they would probably have entered into conflict with the Allied governments, for the French government had decided to refuse the passports,[70] and the London cabinet, while more subtle in opposition, would probably have reached the same decision even without the assistance of the Provisional Government; indeed, the role of Kerenski and Tereshchenko may have been but a reflection of the attitude in London and Paris. The SR leaders had no stomach for such a course. The Gotz-Zenzinov clique believed, mildly, in the Stockholm Conference, and would have championed it in other circumstances, but never at the cost of endangering the sacred ties with the Western Allies. Better to let the conference die, and with it their program of peace, even though it was the only one they had. That is why no crisis arose in connection with the Stockholm debacle.

The right-centrist state of mind is illuminated by what happened on August 26 in their stronghold, the All-Russian Peasants' Executive Committee. At this session delegates from the front raised hell over the failure to make any progress toward ending the war, and the customary resolution acknowledging the necessity of continuing

[68] See the cogent criticism of the army delegate Krylov at the December Congress (*Kratkii otchët o rabotakh chetvërtago s"ezda P.S.-R.*, p. 96).
[69] *Ibid.*, p. 66.
[70] Poincaré, *Au Service de la France*, Vol. IX: *L'Année trouble* (1917), p. 224.

it passed only with the help of those who voted for it because of inertia and those who were afraid to vote against it lest they be charged with thinking of their own skins. Actually, the majority of the committee, without saying so, already looked on the war as lost and did not want to fight any longer. Even the Narodnik intellectuals who dominated this organ considered the situation to be all but irremediable, yet refused to draw the only possible conclusion.[71] The fiasco of the conference, which they had done nothing to save, left them without a program on the most crucial of all matters; they could not make war and would not make peace, so they just waited for a crash to come, and it soon obliged them.

The SR record on the other issues besides land and peace which faced the coalition is equally depressing. Thus on the army question there was unity in theory and discord in practice. All factions agreed on the necessity of a strong army, but the type and purpose of that army were questions that divided them bitterly. The right wanted an army of conventional type to join with the Allies in concentric pressure on the hearth of militarism; the left, an army made over on revolutionary lines, standing on the defensive against Germany and ready at any moment to smite the counterrevolution. Everyone agreed that the army coming out of the February Revolution was unsatisfactory. The bulk of opinion held that a purge of the officers' corps was essential, as well as the restoration of discipline in the ranks, but a small yet influential minority dissented and caused SR policy to go on the rocks, where it remained until the Bolsheviks took over. In the first months after the overthrow of the monarchy, while the momentum of change was unarrested and the archconservative Guchkov was actually shaking up the high command, the SR's had been in no hurry to create their new model army. Even at the end of May, Chernov had deliberately applied the brakes to a process that was by no means threatening to run away when he admonished a left-wing audience at the Northern Regional Confer-

[71] Bykhovski, *Vserossiiskii Sovet Krest'ianskikh Deputatov*, pp. 228-30.

ence against imagining that a cleanup at General Headquarters was a simple thing.[72] But two months later he had changed completely, and from advocating patience and piecemeal reform he had come to clamor—anonymously—for speedy action and a purge of the commanding personnel.[73] Chernov's editorials inaugurated a press campaign which went on, without results, all during August and September, and which had for its theme song the impossibility of restoring health to the army as long as the soldiers were not given officers whom they could trust—only then could the source of poison be dried up and the paralyzing dualism of tsarist commanders watched by government commissars be dispensed with.[74] According to Vladimir Utgof, a party specialist on military matters, the Russians would go on being beaten until the regime could be brought to realize the need for drastic changes; there had been much talk, but nothing had been done.[75]

Party organizations lent support to the press campaign. The first SR military conference of the active army (September 4-8) demonstrated its approval by electing Chernov honorary president and called for the elimination of the caste system which blocked the promotion of elements sympathetic to the revolution.[76] The Petersburg branch of the party added its voice to the swelling chorus,[77] and soldier delegates disturbed the complacency of the Peasants' Executive Committee with their flagellations of General Headquarters.[78] Reform of the military establishment along democratic lines was one of the objectives of the military commission of the Central Committee, which claimed to have been aware of the danger nesting

[72] *Delo Naroda*, No. 57 (May 25, 1917).

[73] "Vopros zhizni ili smerti" (A Matter of Life or Death), *ibid.*, No. 105 (July 20, 1917); "Ne po tomu adresu" (Not to That Address), *ibid.*, No. 111 (July 27, 1917).

[74] See especially the article by "an officer of the line," "Reforma armii—vopros zhizni ili smerti" (Reform of the Army—a Matter of Life or Death), *ibid.*, No. 115 (August 1, 1917). Until such a transformation could be effected, the Allies should be bluntly told that offensive action was impossible.

[75] "Prichiny nashikh neudach" (The Reasons for Our Failures), *ibid.*, No. 160 (September 21, 1917).

[76] See the reports in *Delo Naroda*, Nos. 148, 153 (September 7, 13, 1917).

[77] At its fifth conference; see *Delo Naroda*, No. 104 (July 19, 1917).

[78] Bykhovski, *Vserossiiskii Sovet Krest'ianskikh Deputatov*, pp. 180-81, 228-29.

in the officers' corps long before it came to fruition in the Kornilov coup.[79]

But the Central Committee itself took no action, and, once again, the reason was the inability to enlist Kerenski's cooperation and the unwillingness to cross him in a matter that came within the purview of his ministry. The essential conservatism of Kerenski is nowhere better exemplified than in his conduct of the War Ministry, where he made fewer changes than the Octobrist Guchkov. His party comrades had expected much from his assumption of office: the Petersburg military conference in June had petitioned the "comrades at the head of the War Ministry" to include the officer-training schools in the scope of the projected reform,[80] and the military commission of the Central Committee had looked for assistance to "Comrade" Kerenski in the task of building a new army. Never were hopes more misplaced. Though he once boasted that he could clean out the whole general staff in twenty-four hours, Kerenski had announced to Denikin shortly after taking office that in both the civilian and military spheres the revolutionary process had run its course.[81] With a strange perversity he prided himself on "exceptional conservatism" in matters of personnel, naming as commissar at General Headquarters a Polish officer who let it be known that in his eyes each new man was worse than the old, merely because he was new, and who during his whole tenure of office removed only one general.[82]

Other high-ranking SR's shared Kerenski's distaste for change. Of Savinkov, who bears with Kerenski himself the responsibility for advancing Kornilov, there is no need to speak. Colonel Oberuchev, commander of the Kiev Military District and thorn in the flesh of Ukrainian nationalism, condemned Guchkov for summarily dismissing a large number of officers.[83] But the standpat attitude of the SR

[79] M. Broun, "Ocherk deiatel'nosti voennoi komissii pri Tsentral'nom Komitete P.S.-R." (Outline of the Work of the Military Commission of the Central Committee of the SR Party), *Partiinyia Izvestiia*, No. 3 (October 19, 1917), p. 13; *Kratkii otchët o rabotakh chetvërtago s"ezda P.S.-R.*, p. 91.

[80] *Delo Naroda*, No. 80 (June 21, 1917).

[81] Denikin, *Ocherki russkoi smuty*, I, Part II, 181, 183.

[82] Stankevich, *Vospominaniia*, pp. 178, 182.

[83] *Vospominaniia*, p. 169.

element in the army is best illustrated by the conflict that arose in the Caucasus between them and their Menshevik allies. Here the regional army soviet, dominated by D. D. Donskoi and Vladimir Gobechiia, had stifled Bolshevism by denying it either representation or freedom of propaganda, while displaying no inclination to combat the opposite extreme and placing obstacles in the way of the Mensheviks when they wanted to purge the armed forces of unreliable elements. In his home territory the influence of Irakli Tsereteli, which would have guaranteed these right-wing SR's against embarrassment, did not compare with Noah Zhordaniia's, and the patriarch of Georgian Menshevism castigated the SR's for obstructing army reform and sheltering men whose actions could only be qualified as counterrevolutionary.[84] Here in the Transcaucasus conditions of military service in a cockpit of ethnic contention had intensified the nationalism latent in Populism, but in other theaters, also, the concentration of right-wing SR's among army officers seems to have been particularly high and must be considered as a major block in the way of military reform.

With most SR's demanding a new army and a small but highly placed minority resisting any change, the party was suddenly confronted with the decision of the Provisional Government to restore the death penalty at the front. By this means Savinkov and the other advisors of Kerenski hoped to put the officers back in the saddle, the army back in the war, and Russia back in the power game, with the revolution arrested before it could overflow its political banks into the social field. Had the measure been preceded by a drastic shake-up in the army the party might have taken it, but superimposed upon a situation which so many members regarded as unsatisfactory, it seemed a reactionary move and evoked strenuous opposition. Soon broad sections of party opinion, some hitherto quiescent, were in open revolt, and disgruntlement pervaded the organization. The left SR's fought the death penalty as nothing else that came from the hands of the hated coalition, and Spiridonova's flaming feminine oratory with Kamkov's masculine accompaniment won many converts, especially among the soldiers. Within a week

[84] Sef, *Revoliutsiia 1917 goda v Zakavkaz'i*, pp. 84-86, 221-22, 227.

of its enactment, the Petersburg organization condemned the measure,[85] and one of the first actions of the city council elected in August was to petition the government, on the motion of Mayor Shreider (LC), to revoke the penalty.[86] The attitude of the Petersburg organization is not surprising, as it always had been pitched to the left of center. The astonishing thing was the reaction in Moscow, the bailiwick of the right SR's. On July 24 the Moscow city council passed a resolution condemning the imposition of the death penalty, on soldiers, in time of war.[87] In this body the SR's had an absolute majority, and most, if not all, of their deputies stood to the right of center. Moderate by temperament and nationalist in spirit, with a pronounced bias in favor of continuing the war, they nevertheless could not reconcile themselves to a measure which they had imagined to be banished forever along with "Nicholas the Bloody." Whatever one may think of the wisdom of their decision, one cannot deny that it attests the purity of their beliefs.

The most serious aspect of the controversy, however, was the effect upon the "praetorian guard," as the soldier representatives in the soviet were called. Now began the precipitous slide of the SR's in uniform, first to the left-wing opposition, and then on beyond into Bolshevism, the emotions stirred by the death penalty decree having done more than anything else to pry them loose from their moorings and start them on their slide.[88] Months of partisan debate had not shaken them as had this single measure, disclosing to them in graphic fashion the incompatibility of viewpoint beneath the same political label. The most unfortunate aspect of their reaction against Kerenski was that he really did not intend to give them a bloodbath, as Savinkov and the generals were prepared to do. For Kerenski personally the decree was to serve the purpose of a stick in the closet, to be used rarely, if ever. But he could not escape the ostensible import of his action, and in the violence of their reaction against the moderates, the soldier members of the party passed even the Chernov

---

[85] *Delo Naroda*, No. 104 (July 19, 1917). The decision of the fifth city conference was reaffirmed by the seventh; see *ibid.*, No. 152 (September 12, 1917).
[86] *Ibid.*, No. 147 (September 6, 1917). Only the Kadets opposed the motion.
[87] *Ibid.*, No. 109 (July 25, 1917).
[88] See next chapter, pp. 371-73 and chap. XI.

faction by, since everything not plainly labeled left SR had become odious in their eyes; and many did not stop even there, but rushed beyond the confines into Lenin's waiting arms. After Kornilov's abortive coup, when the flowaway became a flood, Kerenski tried to take the heat off himself by disclosing to the Democratic Conference the unanimity of the cabinet decision,[89] greatly to the embarrassment of Chernov, who had to explain why he sanctioned a measure repugnant to some of the right SR's, not to speak of his own following. He did it by citing the recommendation of the political commissars and his own anticipation of army reforms,[90] but he did not explain why he sat in the cabinet for a month and a half, in the absence of any reforms, and observed in silence the efforts of certain authorities to use the measure as a steppingstone to a military dictatorship. In this unhappy affair, Kerenski was not the only sufferer, and the PSR as such emerged gravely weakened.[91]

Having made no impression on the army high command as a result of the willfulness of their leaders, the SR's did not even talk of assaulting another citadel of reaction, the hierarchy of the established church. In part this was due to preoccupation with more pressing matters, in part to fear of the church's influence,[92] though the attitude of soldiers who stabled their horses in its edifices and used its sacred vessels as urinals should have suggested, as it did to General Denikin, that this venerable institution may have slipped in the affections of the people.[93] Members of the party who were much in the

[89] *Volia Naroda*, No. 119 (September 15, 1917); *Delo Naroda*, No. 155 (September 15, 1917).

[90] "Kak eto proiskhodilo," *ibid.*, No. 178 (October 12, 1917).

[91] Long after the events in question the Central Committee let it be known that it had been opposed to so drastic a punishment (see Rosenblum's statement in *Kratkii otchët o rabotakh chetvërtago s"ezda P.S.-R.*, p. 111). That it remonstrated with the government, however, is unlikely, and in any event its attitude is of no political significance.

[92] See S. P. Postnikov, "Litsemerie ili revoliutsionnost'?" (Hypocrisy or Revolutionism?), *Delo Naroda*, No. 5 (March 19, 1917).

[93] *Ocherki russkoi smuty*, I, Part I, 8-10.

public eye, particularly Avksentiev and Mayor Rudnev of Moscow, went out of their way to demonstrate their respect for the church; when the All-Russian Sobor (church assembly) opened in Moscow (August 16), both dignitaries attended, and Rudnev declared that "as long as the Russian nation lives, the Orthodox[94] faith will burn in its soul." The unusual language aroused no comment in his party— the *Delo Naroda* preserved a tomblike silence—and only the Bolsheviks in the city council protested the utterance as unfair to the non-Orthodox part of the Russian people.[95] The minister-president also showed attention to the church, in part, at least, for a special reason: the reactionaries were whispering that the head of state was a Jew, and Kerenski wished to show that he was not. In the rosy dawn of the revolution the SR central organ had carried an editorial lauding the Russian Revolution for the absence of anticlerical excesses such as had marred the French Revolution, and promising that Russian socialists would honor the principle of religious freedom, freethinkers, atheists, and skeptics though they were.[96] The editors should have waited awhile.

Already the rumblings of irrepressible conflict between the old religious and the new political faith could be heard, in Narodnik as in Marxist circles. The bolt of six prelates from the Holy Synod in March as a protest against the "bureaucratic spirit" of the new regime had stirred sarcastic comment in the *Delo Naroda*. Why this sudden interest in a free church, the editor inquired, after two hundred years of abject submission? Quoting the religious precept, "Nest' bo vlast', ashche ne ot boga" (There is no power except from God), he asked whether Lvov's power was not from God as well as Sabler's and Pobedonostsev's. What was lacking? Rasputin?[97] In the proceedings of the congress of clergy and laity, particularly in Bulgakov's speech contrasting the class trinity of the revolution with the Holy Trinity of the church, the SR's saw evidence that the holy fathers

[94] And not the "Christian faith," according to the version in *Revoliutsiia 1917 goda (Khronika sobytii)*, IV, 64.

[95] Interview with Rudnev in Paris (September, 1935).

[96] "Revoliutsiia i svoboda sovesti" (The Revolution and Freedom of Conscience), *Delo Naroda*, No. 17 (April 16, 1917).

[97] Postnikov, "Litsemerie ili revoliutsionnost'?", No. 5 (March 19, 1917).

were returning to form as the handmaidens of reaction.[98] Though the question of church property was not as acute as in Western countries, owing to the secularizations of the eighteenth century, the SR program called for the confiscation of ecclesiastical lands, and in the absence of reaffirmations from more authoritative spokesmen the point was raised by Kamkov with reference to monasteries.[99] Even more than property holdings, the question of secular education would have produced a collision, the negative stand of the All-Russian Sobor drawing the fire of Argunov's *Volia Naroda*,[100] which in the vigor of its anticlerical utterances as in the warmth of its espousal of a school system free of clerical influence, quite surpassed anything in the much more radical *Delo Naroda*. Here the editor's ties with French freemasonry may have had some effect, making him conservative in relation to the war but radical in matters of church and state. In general, however, the SR's did not rush to attack the church, in respect to either the establishment or its property holdings or the spirit of its hierarchy, being content to forego for the time being a purge of prelates in order to concentrate on generals and bureaucrats, although Postnikov, in a vein reminiscent of the Civil Constitution of the clergy, sought the security of the revolution in the popular election of priests and prelates.

During the second coalition the SR's were forced onto the defensive in respect to the nationalities problem. They do not seem to have given it as much attention as previously, probably because of the clamor for strong government, and they offered little resistance to the restrictive measures worked out in the government's legal commission, which was wholly dominated by jurists of a conserva-

[98] "Bludnye syny" (Prodigal Sons), in the section, "Pechat' i zhizn'" (Press and Life), *ibid.*, No. 67 (June 6, 1917).
[99] Speech at the Northern Regional Conference, *ibid.*, No. 57 (May 25, 1917).
[100] "Restavratory tenei proshlago" (Restorers of the Shades of the Past), No. 132 (September 30, 1917). Religious instruction could be given to those who wanted it, but should in no way be made compulsory. State control of vital statistics and civil jurisdiction over marriage and divorce for those who wished it were strongly advocated.

tive cast. For a time all that could be heard was the sound of the Kadet legal worms cutting away the substance of the Ukrainian agreement of July 2. Then, early in August, instead of the instrument of government to which the Ukrainians aspired, an "instruction" was handed down which treated the whole matter as one of "local administration" instead of national autonomy. It restricted the territorial competence of the Ukrainian organs to four and four-fifths provinces out of the nine that were claimed, reduced the executive departments in the General Secretariat and allotted a share of the remainder to non-Ukrainian minorities, and subordinated the whole to the will of the central government. The Kadet jurists had fulfilled their mission of "lessening the harm" done to Russia by the July agreement.[101] Ukrainian nationalism was outraged and the Ukrainian Socialist Revolutionaries branded the instruction a "shameful document," leaving its acceptance to the Social Democrats as all that could be procured under the circumstances. The Russian SR's broke ranks with the other Russian groups in the Rada to oppose the instruction as motivated by a fundamental mistrust of the Ukrainian movement,[102] but their gesture could not efface the impression of unfriendliness produced by a government under the direction of one of their members. It was no doubt with Kerenski in mind that Nicholas Kovalevski, one of the eminent Ukrainian SR's, characterized the instruction as the bastard offspring of the "cohabitation of the Russian SR's with the Kadets."[103]

The Finnish question also boiled up during the second coalition, and the Provisional Government manifested the same insensitiveness to the feelings of subject nationalities, with much less justification. Once more the Kadets set the tone with their stubborn insistence that the powers of the deposed monarch as Grand Duke of Finland had fallen to the Provisional Government instead of to the Finnish Seim, their purpose being to contravene by an excursion into pseudolegality the clear-cut case for Finnish independence that

[101] Miliukov, *Istoriia vtoroi russkoi revoliutsii*, I, Part II, 86.
[102] *1917 god na Kievshchine*, pp. 199-200.
[103] Reshetar, *The Ukrainian Revolution 1917-1920*, pp. 69-76; Miliukov, *Istoriia vtoroi russkoi revoliutsii*, I, Part II, 85-91; Chernov, *Great Russian Revolution*, pp. 283-84.

would arise from recognition of the principle that the authority of the Finnish sovereign had devolved upon the Finnish parliament. Years later a leading Kadet conceded the validity of the Finnish argument, both from the legal standpoint and in the light of the position once occupied by the Kadets themselves, when they were still a liberal party; he acknowledged the baselessness of their contentions in 1917.[104] The last chance to lay the feud so stupidly begun by Alexander III was lost in the imperialist craze of the Kadets and the pusillanimity, if not worse, of the Socialist Revolutionaries, for what can be said for a party that went back on its original purpose and permitted itself to be dragged at the tail of events? At the height of the crisis an editorial appeared in the *Delo Naroda*, sidestepping as of little consequence the legal argument (it would have been interesting to see what the SR's would have done with it) and laying the initial blame for the estrangement on the Finnish Social Democrats. "The Finnish comrades will be gravely mistaken," it declared, "if even for a moment they imagine that they can solve their basic problem outside the boundaries of the Russian Revolution and in defiance of its fate." The soviet had given its promise, and the nationalities, by their excessive demands, would only help to drive it into bankruptcy and prevent the redemption of its bill of credit.[105] But had the Provisional Government made any promise, and why would the independence of Finland have promoted the bankruptcy of the soviet? Rather did its refusal attest the moral bankruptcy of the Socialist Revolutionaries, who by their unwillingness to concede the need for a dissolution of this unhappy marriage, confirmed the worst suspicions of the Finnish democrats and strengthened the Germanophile orientation of the Finnish right.

For the most part the SR's preserved silence in the face of the Finnish conflict, perhaps because they had not yet entirely lost their sense of shame. The Kerenski government dissolved the Finnish parliament and called a new election (what it expected from this election is difficult to see, except a temporary adjournment of the

[104] V. Maklakov, "Iz proshlago" (Out of the Past), *Sovremennyia Zapiski*, XLIV (1930), 442-44.

[105] "Finliandskaia tragediia" (The Finnish Tragedy), No. 127 (August 15, 1917). It would be more significant if we knew who wrote this editorial. The author's guess is that it was written by Vishniak.

controversy, the cost of which would be to make it still hotter later on); it placed a padlock on the doors of their parliament which the Finns promptly broke to hold a forbidden session; and Chernov lamely says that the socialist ministers, prisoners of the coalition, had to be content with the failure to enact reprisals, which the Russian military units in Finland, hotbeds of Bolshevism and left-wing Social Revolutionism, would not in any event have permitted. He makes it clear that the Finns were ready for an accommodation that would have safeguarded Russian interests, but once more he fails to explain why he and his party permitted themselves to be dragged into a position which the Kadet Maklakov himself has compared to that of Stolypin.[106] And once more the explanation is to be sought in the metamorphosis of many SR's from socialists and revolutionists to unadmitted nationalists, for whom the independence of Finland was all the more repugnant because of the need for dissembling their true emotions.

In denying the Finnish claim to independence, the Provisional Government had held that it could not prejudice the rights of the future Constituent Assembly by waiving any of the powers which it claimed to have taken over from the deposed emperor, including those of the Grand Duke of Finland; and many if not most of the SR's agreed in making the freedom of Finland subject to the will of the Russian Constituent Assembly. For all pressing problems that arose in 1917, they had one invariable panacea: wait until the Constituent Assembly, the supreme expression of the will of the Russian people. But having deferred everything to this body, the SR's turned around and deferred the assembly, or rather permitted it to be postponed by a coalition of which they were members. Chernov later pronounced this to be perhaps the most fateful of all their mistakes,[107] yet the decision was made by a cabinet in which he was minister of agriculture, and if his voice was raised in protest, we have no record

[106] *Great Russian Revolution*, pp. 284-86; see also Miliukov, *Istoriia vtoroi russkoi revoliutsii*, I, Part II, 73-77.

[107] "Iz itogov proshlogo opyta" (Some Conclusions on the Basis of Past Experience), *Revoliutsionnaia Rossiia*, No. 23 (December, 1922), p. 4.

of it. By August 9, when this action was taken, everyone agreed that the election could not be held on September 17, the date fixed by the first coalition in June. But why had March, April, May, June, and July—five solid months—gone by and still it was not possible to elect the assembly after a further delay of a month and a half? Technical difficulties, the size of the country, the autocratic past, and the lack of training in democratic processes are not the explanation. France in 1848 knew how to mount an election within two and a half months of the outbreak of revolution, and the disparity in size of the countries is offset by the advance in communications between 1848 and 1917. France before 1848 was no paragon of democracy, nor was Russia before 1917 a desert of despotism—it had elected four national assemblies, the first two on a franchise sufficiently broad to produce a two-thirds majority against the regime. The explanation must be sought elsewhere, and is to be found in the infirmity of purpose of the SR's, as well as in the circumstance that while they might propose in the Provisional Government, it was the Kadets who disposed.

When all is said and done, the Constitutional Democrats did not want an early election because they stood to lose by it, and in one way or another, by indirect if not by direct means, they wrote their will into the decisions of the Provisional Government. They had no more stalwart allies or fruitful collaborators than the right-wing Socialist Revolutionaries, one of whom, M. V. Vishniak, has gone so far as to say that the accusation leveled against them of having dragged out the election is of Bolshevik origin.[108] His case seems to rest on the absence of purposeful obstruction from the Kadet representatives in the Special Commission set up to draft the law for the Constituent Assembly—a commission on which he served as official SR representative—since he cannot deny that the Kadets outside the commission, with Miliukov at their head, favored putting off the election as long as possible,[109] even to the end of the war.[110] But

[108] *Dan' proshlomu*, p. 288.
[109] *Vserossiiskoe Uchreditel'noe Sobranie*, pp. 72-73, 76-78; "Reshitel'nost'" (Decisiveness), *Delo Naroda*, No. 116 (August 2, 1917).
[110] Such was the wish of V. D. Nabokov, though he did not openly avow it at the time. See his memoirs, "Vremennoe Pravitel'stvo," in *Arkhiv Russkoi Revoliutsii*, I, 72; see also Vishniak's article cited in the foregoing footnote.

neither this apologist for the Constitutional Democrats nor any other has ever explained satisfactorily why three months were wasted before this commission held its first meeting (May 25), and why, when at last it did meet, it should have favored November 1 as the date of the election until overruled by the cabinet's selection of September 17. The delay of the soviet in presenting its members for the commission, its reluctance to accept a nonsocialist majority, and the April crisis culminating in the reconstruction of the ministry along coalitional lines, are cited as reasons for this inordinate delay,[111] but the real reason is given by Miliukov when he says that the first Provisional Government came to the conclusion that in the interest of the war the election could not be held before the late autumn, when a lull in operations would set in.[112] If the event were so far removed, one could proceed at a leisurely tempo and active preparations in March and April would be unnecessary. When the Kadet jurists, who easily dominated the Special Commission, tentatively settled on November 1, they were essentially in step with their comrades outside the commission and even with the party leader himself. And if Sukhanov is correct in citing press reports to the effect that Kerenski had declared at General Headquarters that the Constituent Assembly could be convened only after victory,[113] the collusion between the "hostage of the democracy" and the chief nonsocialist party in slowing down the electoral process is apparent.

There was another reason for the reluctance in conservative circles to have an early election, and once more we are indebted to Miliukov for giving it formulation. Protesting against the September date as making the election a farce, the Kadet leader raised the question of a free vote in the village, where the political immaturity of the population laid it open to political manipulation, particularly by the soviets, which had sometimes used their influence to deny the Kadets a hearing. He was unwilling to concede the peasantry to the PSR; political divisions, he felt, had not yet sunk into its consciousness,

---

[111] Vishniak, *Dan' proshlomu*, pp. 286-87; Vishniak, *Vserossiiskoe Uchreditel'-noe Sobranie*, p. 74; Miliukov, *Istoriia vtoroi russkoi revoliutsii*, I, Part I, 69, where still another factor is mentioned.

[112] Miliukov, *Istoriia vtoroi russkoi revoliutsii*, I, Part I, 68-69.

[113] *Zapiski*, II, 286.

and if it seemed to favor the SR's, it was only because these talked the loudest, were first on the spot, and promised so much. With so much at stake in the rural vote, the Kadets insisted that the peasants should have the opportunity to look around and familiarize themselves with other political programs, and that they should be free from pressure in exercising the right to vote. Hence the demand for a model election, surrounded by all possible safeguards against fraud and intimidation.[114] Miliukov makes it clear that in holding out for a slow and cautious approach, the Kadets were not guilty of legal haggling nor of striving for perfection, but were guided by very practical considerations. The village vote was the heart of the matter.[115] It would determine the outcome, and it was only natural for the Kadets to desire to have a better break in respect to it than they could expect at the time. Nor is it possible to deny that the level of political consciousness in the village was low. But if the political education of the peasantry were posed, when could the election be held? In that case it would be necessary for the Provisional Government to become something more than provisional and to come to grips with some of the basic problems posed by the revolution which could not wait interminably for a solution. Solving the land problem more or less according to the will of the peasantry might have enabled the Kadets to cut in on the village vote, for it was not so much the machinations of the SR's as the stand of the Kadets for compensation which barred them from the village. But to distribute the land while the most virile element in the village was at the front would have brought the soldier-peasants home like locusts to a grainfield. And the war was the most sacred of all the shibboleths of Constitutional Democracy. War to victory interdicted a solution of the land problem. And so the Kadets were caught in their own trap, demanding that all basic problems be deferred until the Constituent Assembly but not being willing to risk the election

---

[114] *Burzhuaziia i pomeshchiki v 1917 godu,* pp. 215-17.

[115] It is amazing that Vishniak, who used this source (*Vserossiiskoe Uchreditel'noe Sobranie,* p. 77), should have missed—or chosen not to mention—the essence of Miliukov's discourse.

of that assembly while it still might have coped with the problems.[116] But the SR's were not obligated to accept this formula for disaster. At the very least they could have fought against it. In the rosy dawn of the revolution they thought of the assembly as two or three months away.[117] But thereafter they went to sleep in broad daylight, lulled into a false sense of security by the failure of the right openly to oppose the calling of an election as soon as technical matters could be settled and the local organs of self-government charged with supervision of the voting could be set up. This is admitted by Chernov,[118] and even by Vishniak.[119] Late in May, Chernov complacently told an audience that the election should not be held later than the first part of October.[120] Individual voices were raised in warning even at that time,[121] however, and by summer uneasiness pervaded the party ranks. The setting of the election for September met with general approbation,[122] after which this party went back to bed. Only the July earthquake and the gathering clouds of a military conspiracy, as well as a growing skepticism in the general public, finally aroused the SR's from their long slumber, and on August 3 the editorial columns of the *Delo Naroda* rang with an appeal for

[116] Chernov makes the point that the Kadets, despairing of success under existing conditions, hoped that if the election could be postponed to the end of the war, the upwelling of nationalism in the wake of victory would pry the people loose from the socialists and cause them to turn to conservative leadership (manuscript commentary on the minutes of the Central Committee, pp. 21-24; "Otkliki pressy" [Comments of the Press], *Revoliutsionnaia Rossiia*, No. 32 [December, 1923], p. 21). See also N. Rubinstein, *K istorii uchreditel'nogo sobraniia* (The History of the Constituent Assembly) (Moscow and Leningrad, 1931), pp. 7-11.

[117] See the section on party life in *Delo Naroda*, No. 5 (March 19, 1917).

[118] Manuscript commentary on the minutes of the Central Committee, pp. 18-19.

[119] *Vserossiiskoe Uchreditel'noe Sobranie*, p. 74.

[120] *Delo Naroda*, No. 56 (May 24, 1917).

[121] See V. S. Pankratov's postscript to the letter of protest addressed to the central organ by a number of right-wing SR's (*ibid.*, No. 30 [April 22, 1917]).

[122] Vishniak, "Srok vyborov v Uchreditel'noe Sobranie" (The Date of Elections to the Constituent Assembly), *ibid.*, No. 77 (June 17, 1917); "K sroku sozyva Uchreditel'nago Sobraniia" (The Time of Convocation of the Constituent Assembly), *Volia Naroda*, No. 41 (June 16, 1917).

not a single needless day of delay.[123] By then the realization had dawned that the September date could not be met, and when on August 9 the government postponed the election to November 12-14, and the opening of the assembly to November 28, the SR's acquiesced with a sort of heroic despair. They felt that the election must be so irreproachably conducted that its results would be unimpeachable in the eyes of every section of the population, even though there was already talk that they might be exchanging a live dog for a dead lion.[124] The conservative ministers of the first Provisional Government had concluded that the election could not be held until the late autumn, and late autumn it turned out to be. In this matter, as in so many others, the SR's had simply tailed along behind the Kadets, and the only thing they had accomplished was to dig their own grave.

The record of the second coalition is one of lost opportunities. The suppression of the July disorders had strengthened the government's authority, while warning it that progress must be made toward the realization of revolutionary objectives. Had the second coalition been able to enact constructive measures, it need not have feared the partisans of a military dictatorship, as did one section of the cabinet, or have secretly welcomed them, as did the other. But the Kadets persisted in acting as though there had been no revolution, Kerenski deferred to them, and the SR's to their nominal comrade, while the

[123] "Ni odnogo lishniago dnia otsrochki!" (Not a Single Needless Day of Delay), No. 117.

[124] N. V. Sviatitski, "Tiazhëlaia kolliziia" (A Serious Collision), *Delo Naroda*, No. 114 (July 30, 1917); Vishniak, "Reshitel'nost'," *ibid.*, No. 116 (August 2, 1917). Avksentiev had helped to prepare his party for this bitter decision. As minister of the interior he had general supervision of the voting machinery and could testify to the difficulties that beset the administration. In his opinion the populace should be put through at least one local election before being trusted to vote for the assembly, and it was proving a hard task to get the cantonal (volost) councils elected; in Volynia, for example, a southwestern province and one of the most backward, the peasants had refused to vote. See his remarks to the Seventh Council of the PSR in *Delo Naroda*, No. 121 (August 8, 1917); *Volia Naroda*, No. 88 (August 10, 1917); see also Sukhanov, *Zapiski*, V, 130.

Mensheviks believed on principle that the bourgeoisie should make the revolution, and if it refused to fulfill its function, well, Menshevik theory had no answer to that problem. And so the second coalition perpetuated the supreme folly of the first in refusing either to minister to the needs of a revolutionary society or to hasten the election of the body that could. There would be no further opportunity, for, though a third coalition would be formed, it would exercise from the day of its birth only a shadowy authority. Time had run out for the moderates, and the hour of the extremists was approaching.

X

THE SR DESCENT TO DISASTER

WITH a new crisis in the offing, there was still the question, which set of extremists represented the graver danger to the sway of the moderates? Nearly all of the SR's in July and August would have answered: the right-wing extremists. It was as though they still could not believe that the old regime had been as weak as it seemed in February, and they were constantly on the lookout for some thrust from the right against the new order. Developments after the July Days confirmed their worst fears: the right obviously was pulling itself together in order to make a bid for power. Just because it was very articulate, they thought it must also be very strong. The power of analysis of these Populist intellectuals was inferior to that of the British ambassador, who realized as he strove to preserve the Russian alliance that the best strategy would be for the right to hold its fire until Bolshevism had boiled over a second time, in the hope that antiwar sentiment in organized form could then be so decisively quelled as to enable a strong hand to restore the Eastern Front. But he expected no good to result from the right's taking the initiative— "the Cadets have not got the army with them."[1] The atmosphere of reaction had thickened in St. Petersburg to the extent that the SR's had to postpone the day set aside for soliciting funds in the streets of the capital.[2] Slipping into a Western pattern of thought, they asked themselves: If the tide of counterrevolution was running so strongly in the "red" capital, what must it be like in the provinces? They forgot that in Russia only the middle and upper classes were conservative, not the peasantry, the revolutionary proclivities of which they themselves had been extolling since the spring of 1902.

[1] Buchanan, *My Mission to Russia*, II, 160, 173, 175-76, 185.
[2] *Delo Naroda*, Nos. 101, 113 (July 15, 29, 1917).

So fainthearted had these Populist intellectuals become, and so full of fear, that they no longer had any faith in their own teachings. Just as a wind blowing against the current of a great river can produce by the ripples it raises the illusion of flow in the opposite direction, so in Russia, in the summer of 1917, surface indications of a trend to the right concealed from the SR's the broad undercurrent of sentiment still flowing steadily leftward. And yet, even before the Kornilov fiasco opened their eyes to the true situation, they were to receive two object-lessons in the inaccuracy of their observations, the first within their own organization and the second in a municipal election. Early in August the SR's held their Seventh Council, the chief party gathering between the Third and Fourth Congresses in May and December. And on August 20 the voters of St. Petersburg elected a city council. The first event measured trends in the party; the second gauged the mood of the most sensitive electorate in the country. Proceeding from the simple to the complex, we shall take the second event first.

The August balloting in the Russian capital yielded the following results,[3] in comparison with the preceding election in May:[4]

Parties	Seats	August Votes	May Votes
SR	75	205,666 ⎫	376,813 (incomplete)
SD Menshevik	8	23,552 ⎭	
SD Bolshevik	67	183,694	159,500
Constitutional Democrats	42	114,485	171,400
Unity (Plekhanov)		6,508	...
Toil-Popular Socialists		6,236	...
Republican Democrats		2,855	...
Radical Democrats		1,508	...
Residue		4,875	...
Total		549,379	792,864

The two elections are not strictly commensurate, for the city limits had been extended to take in suburbs like Peterhof, making the potential vote in August considerably larger than in May. That the actual vote was smaller by nearly a quarter of a million is a striking

[3] *Ibid.*, No. 136 (August 25, 1917).
[4] See chap. VII.

testimonial to the absenteeism which this election featured. All parties lost strength, including the Bolsheviks, whose vote within the same limits as in May had declined to 146,400.[5] From this as a point of departure the SR's proceeded to construct a false picture of the election, more because of willful distortion, it would seem, than because of faulty judgment. They could never bring themselves to acknowledge the strength of Bolshevism or the weakness of the propertied classes, and so, shutting their eyes to the plain facts of the situation, they dwelt upon the apathy of the electorate on the assumption that the intelligentsia had somehow failed to turn out while the manual laborers and soldiers had evinced greater interest, thus creating the illusion of extremist strength.[6] At first glance there would seem to be something to this contention, in view of the fact that the Constitutional Democratic vote more than doubled in the November election—until it is remembered that the Bolshevik vote increased in the same proportion. The SR's strained to emphasize the small falling off in the Bolshevik vote within the original city limits while glossing over the catastrophic decline in the moderate socialist vote, which they blandly charged to the Mensheviks' account, refusing to acknowledge that by any rational test the loss could only have been a joint one, and refusing likewise to admit that they owed their position at the head of the poll to the large extremist element in their own ranks, soon to become dominant in the Petersburg organization.[7] But the relative success of the Bolsheviks in holding their lines while the vote of every other party was falling off precipitously left no doubt in the public mind as to the

[5] V. E. Trutovski, "Usililis' li bol'sheviki v Petrograde?" (Have the Bolsheviks Grown Stronger in Petrograd?), *Delo Naroda*, No. 165 (September 27, 1917).

[6] See the report in *Delo Naroda*, No. 133 (August 22, 1917).

[7] See the editorial, "Vybory v tsentral'nuiu dumu" (Elections to the Central Council), in *ibid.*, No. 135 (August 24, 1917). The SR ticket had been a composite of the various factional groupings, with only the extreme right excluded (except for Kerenski) because of the leftist bias of the city organization. Chernov headed the list with Kerenski in second place, followed by Mayor Shreider, Gotz, and Avksentiev. See the list in *ibid.*, No. 129 (August 17, 1917). The Liteiny district, an upper-class area in the heart of the city, had advanced Argunov's candidacy but the Petersburg Committee had stricken his name from the list. See *Volia Naroda*, No. 85 (August 8, 1917).

real victors in this election, and the SR's, as though unconvinced by their own reasoning, hastened to assure their followers that Petersburg was not Russia.[8]

In opposing the "conservative" provinces to the radical capital, as in identifying abstention at the polls with a trend to the right,[9] the party leaders were disregarding evidence of the true state of affairs that wiser men would certainly have taken into account. A report from the south, published in the central organ at precisely the moment when its editors were disparaging the Bolshevik success, made the point that in the provinces the July Days had caused much less of a shift in public sentiment than in the capital, and that while the burghers' attitude had hardened against the soviets, these organs remained secure in the affections of the masses. The indifference everywhere manifest in local elections was not to be interpreted as a revulsion of feeling against the revolution but rather as a growing disillusionment in democratic processes, combined with an inclination to resort to direct action. Reaction was lifting its head all over Russia, it is true, but nowhere did it command the armed strength to make it a serious threat—precisely the point made by the British ambassador in his secret calculations. Evidence was not wanting that by late summer the provinces had caught up with St. Petersburg in the tempo of revolutionary development and had even moved some distance ahead.[10]

The reaction of the SR leadership to the August election in St. Petersburg was what might have been expected, but in relation

[8] See Avksentiev's statement to the press in *Delo Naroda*, No. 136 (August 25, 1917), and the editorial cited in the preceding footnote in No. 135. The local SR organ acknowledged the Bolshevik victory, attributing it to resentment at the wave of repressions after the July Days. See editorial in *Znamia Truda*, No. 4 (August 26, 1917).

[9] Bykhovski, *Vserossiiskii Sovet Krest'ianskikh Deputatov*, pp. 241-42.

[10] Mark Slonim, "Na iuge" (In the South), *Delo Naroda*, No. 134 (August 23, 1917). Compare the telegram of the Balashov district board to Kerenski, Tsereteli, and Chernov on July 24, warning them of the trend in the villages and closing with the admonition: "Comrades! You are far removed from the temper of the villages!" Text of telegram in *ibid.*, No. 115 (August 1, 1917).

to their other object lesson in the growing strength of extremism—the one presented by their own party—no effort at dissimulation was possible, and they could only maintain an embarrassed silence. For them the Seventh Council of the PSR came not so much as a rude awakening as a confirmation of the gnawing fear that the left was making headway. One of the purposes in convening the council, in fact, was to combat the centrifugal tendencies within the party; the other was to prepare for the Constituent Assembly.[11]

The events of the summer and the sterility of coalition had greatly increased the tension among the Socialist Revolutionaries. The left wing of the party had found its bearings at the Third Congress and had set up a clandestine bureau, after assuring Chernov that Natanson's idea of a special informational bureau would be given up in the interests of unity. This initial step on the road to schism had been a deliberate one, according to Chernov, the result of a preconceived plan to utilize the mistakes, misfortunes, and weaknesses of the sheltering organization to form a new party on the "Bolshevik model." The bureau lay low for a while but the events of the summer, principally the June offensive and the July disorders in the capital, brought it into the open. On July 9 a manifesto appeared in the organ of the Northern Regional Committee,[12] chief nest of party radicalism, bespeaking freedom of action for the left in view of the unsatisfactory state of affairs at the party helm, where policy was being shaped by a group which had veered away from the traditional objectives of revolutionary socialism to such an extent as to threaten to shift the social base of the party by alienating the class-conscious toilers. SR's who cherished the principles of their movement no longer could submit passively to a course which had made work among the masses extremely difficult, but must set themselves off from it, without, however, breaking away from the organization. No individual signatures were affixed to the manifesto, which was issued in the name of three groups: the organizational bureau of the left wing of the PSR, formed (clandestinely) at the Third Congress, the left SR fraction of the All-Russian Executive Committee of

[11] See editorial in *ibid.*, No. 120 (August 6, 1917).
[12] *Zemlia i Volia* (Petersburg), No. 85.

Workers' and Soldiers' Soviets, and the left SR fraction of the All-Russian Executive Committee of Peasants' Soviets.[13]

The reaction of the Central Committee was prompt and severe. It decreed the expulsion of the signatory groups, ordered an investigation of the host newspaper to fix the responsibility for opening its pages to such a communication, and summoned the regional committee to change the conduct of the newspaper within a given time—all on the ground that the party had been stabbed in the back at a most critical moment of the revolution.[14] The motion to exclude had been offered by Chernov, perhaps to show the right center what a responsible minister he had become, and the whole Central Committee had supported it, with the exception of Natanson. Party circles buzzed with excitement over the clash between the supreme organ and the extremists. Some passed resolutions upholding the Central Committee, and others asked that its action be reconsidered. The most weighty appeal for moderation came from the fifth conference of the Petersburg organization, which condemned the divisive move of the left but felt that expulsion was too drastic a penalty.[15] Before matters proceeded any further, however, Kamkov wrote to the Central Committee disclaiming on behalf of the bureau any intention of grouping its supporters outside the party and announcing the suspension of its activities, as a result of which, he said, it considered itself as no longer existing.[16] Kalegaev[17] and Algasov made similar recantations and were also received back into the party. The Central Committee had cracked the whip and the left had submitted—for the time being—but actually nothing had changed, for

[13] Zenzinov, and also Chernov, would later say that the manifesto bore the signatures of Kamkov, Algasov, and Kalegaev, by which they probably meant that these were the individuals who acted in the name of the three subscribing groups. See *Delo Naroda*, No. 156 (September 16, 1917); *Kratkii otchët o rabotakh chetvërtago s"ezda P.S.-R.*, p. 115.

[14] *Delo Naroda*, No. 97 (July 11, 1917).

[15] *Ibid.*, No. 100 (July 14, 1917). A Kolomenski district meeting found the guilt of the left extenuated by the sharp turn to the right at the party helm (*ibid.*, No. 106 [July 21, 1917]). A similar meeting in the Vyborg district had split over the issue (*ibid.*, No. 100).

[16] *Delo Naroda*, No. 101 (July 15, 1917).

[17] *Ibid.*, No. 110 (July 26, 1917).

the respective viewpoints were as incompatible as ever and in time would produce another explosion.[18]

The only casualty of this internecine warfare in July was the press organ of the left, the Petersburg *Zemlia i Volia*. Under the lash of the Central Committee's displeasure, the Northern Regional Committee had resigned on July 13, leaving the management of the newspaper to a two-man committee, which the Central Committee hastened to bring under control by imposing two caretakers of its own, Arkhangelski (RRC) and Kapitsa (LC). When Arkhangelski came in, all originality went out of the *Zemlia i Volia*, and henceforth it was as dull and colorless, as stuffy and bloodless as the average SR paper.[19] Worse still, it lost its body along with its soul, since it was ejected from the Senate printing office and had to appear in reduced format from another press.[20] In fact, for a time it even looked as though the 38,000 subscribers might be left without an organ altogether, so unfavorable had the climate become for an extremist newspaper.[21] While the Central Committee failed to subdue the Northern Regional Committee, in view of the nature of its constituency—Spiridonova and others entered the reconstituted committee and made it more intractable than ever—its lost organ was not recovered and the *Zemlia i Volia* remained denatured in content and subservient to the Central Committee. But circumstances soon presented the left SR's with another outlet for their views. In August the Petersburg Committee undertook the publication of a workingman's newspaper,[22] and in September the *Znamia Truda* or *Banner of Labor*, as it was called, passed into the hands of the left SR's when

---

[18] See statements by Zenzinov and Chernov in December before the Fourth Congress in *Kratkii otchët o rabotakh chetvërtago s"ezda P.S.-R.*, pp. 71, 115-16.

[19] Notice of the changeover first appeared in No. 94 (July 20, 1917). Up to then the *Zemlia i Volia* has interest for the historian, though perhaps it had less for its readers. A group of hospital attendants complained that it was only with difficulty intelligible even to students, that sentences of fifteen to twenty lines were no rarity, and that it was heavily salted with foreign terms. See *Delo Naroda*, No. 112 (July 28, 1917). These hospital workers were most likely typical Populist intellectuals who would be prejudiced against anything that was antiwar.

[20] *Zemlia i Volia* (Petersburg), No. 104 (August 1, 1917).

[21] S. Krylov, "Pokhod na 'Zemliu i Voliu'" (The Campaign against *Zemlia i Volia*), *ibid.*, No. 92 (July 18, 1917); see also laconic references to the shake-up in *Delo Naroda*, Nos. 101 and 113 (July 15, 29, 1917).

[22] See notice in *Delo Naroda*, No. 134 (August 23, 1917).

they took over the metropolitan organization. Thereafter it served as the chief mouthpiece of extremism, becoming the central organ of the new party after the schism in October.

Chernov would later brand the backdown of Kamkov and his associates as an "act of political cowardice." Perhaps there was an element of pusillanimity involved, but the chief motivating force was calculation, not fear. The dragon of extremism had come into the open, emitting a burst of flame, and then had retired hastily into its cave, seeing that the time had not come for the consummation of its desires. But the dragon had been more discreet than cowardly, for by lying low a while longer it might hope to do more than tear a limb off the PSR—it might be able to swallow the whole party. Either the center could be freed of its thralldom to the right and pulled back to a revolutionary position[23] or the left could so undercut the support of the rival factions as to gain the upper hand, capture the label, and confront them with the choice of submission or expulsion from the party. As things were going, this was not mere wishful thinking, and the left was justified in deferring a showdown.

Despite superficial indications to the contrary, it was growing in strength. Left-wing Social Revolutionism was above everything else a protest against war; even the promotion of social revolution evoked less ardor than the task of combatting this "senseless and criminal war."[24] The left SR's were beside themselves at the thought that prosecution of the war when the Allies had not followed Russia's example in renouncing predatory aims made their country a handmaiden of alien imperialism and prostituted the revolution at the feet of the English plutocracy. The offensive of June 18, shedding the soldiers' blood in a hateful cause and setting back the peace efforts of the German and Austrian workers, stirred them as had no other action of the Provisional Government, and they joined hands with the Bolsheviks in fighting this "crime against the people."[25] A further

[23] Kamkov, "Dva puti" (Two Paths), *Nash Put'*, No. 1 (August, 1917), pp. 39-40.
[24] Ivanov-Razumnik, "Tretii Rim" (The Third Rome), *ibid.*, No. 2 (1917), p. 5.
[25] Kamkov, *Kto takie levye sotsialisty-revoliutsionery*, pp. 11-12; Ivanov-Razumnik, "Za chto idët voina; za chto voiuet Rossiia" (For What Is the War Being Waged; for What Is Russia Fighting?), *Zemlia i Volia* (Petersburg), No. 43 (May 16, 1917).

stimulus to self-determination, and a further bond of sympathy with Bolshevism, came with the repression of the July disorders, when the authorities struck out at leftist agitators irrespective of party. Kerenski wished to remove Proshian and Ustinov from circulation in the Finnish military centers, and his decision to arrest them met with no obstruction from Chernov.[26] Everywhere the unity of the PSR was strained as the left sided with the Bolsheviks and the rest of the party condemned their bid for power. Here and there the façade of unity gave way, foreshadowing the schism in October, as in the Siberian mining center of Krasnoiarsk, where a demonstration in support of the July uprising, participated in by some of the SR's and boycotted by others, led to a split in the organization and the formation of a separate left-wing group, in which the moving spirit was a girl revolutionary named Ada Lebedeva.[27]

But the development which aroused more indignation among dissident Socialist Revolutionaries, and brought them more political capital—from the short-range point of view—than any other, was the reinstatement on July 12 of the death penalty for military offenses. That soldiers should be shot for refusing to fight in a war foisted by predatory allies upon a renegade socialist government was too much for these SR's, and Maria Spiridonova constituted herself a sort of female angel of vengeance, blasting the Provisional Government in countless meetings over the country for having brought this "greatest shame" upon the revolution. Nothing bore more eloquent testimony to the moral degradation of the revolution, she felt, than this "organized judicial murder," the fruit of the agitation of "the journalist Savinkov" and the negation of everything in the SR program, to say nothing of its spirit. The depth of her feeling against the measure is revealed in the words of a friend, a former terrorist with eleven years of penal servitude behind her, who wrote that she hoped the "socialist" ministers would execute both of them and so help the

---

[26] See the spirited exchange between Chernov and Lebedev at the Fourth Congress (*Kratkii otchët o rabotakh chetvërtago s"ezda P.S.-R.*, pp. 110, 121).
[27] *Khronika grazhdanskoi voiny v Sibiri*, p. 38; *Istoriia grazhdanskoi voiny v SSSR*, II, 107-8. The latter source advances the date of the original split to May.

nation recover its sense of moral values, without which the revolution was doomed.[28]

While some may accuse Spiridonova of impractical idealism and others of feminine hysteria, the fact remains that her agitation produced an effect, and that from this time dates the slide of the "pretorian guard," as the SR military support in the soviets was called, in the direction of left-wing Social Revolutionism, and then on beyond into Bolshevism. As the soldier mass moved to the left, pulling after it a large section of the peasantry, it destroyed in barracks and village alike the sinews of agrarian socialism and prepared the way for the dictatorship of the proletariat. The Black Sea Fleet had from the outset been a stronghold of Social Revolutionism, remoteness or some other factor having preserved it from the extremism rampant in Baltic naval centers; but now, under the impact of capital punishment and multiplying signs of reaction, the sailors became alarmed and would listen only to Bolshevik agitators. There was a swift change in sentiment, and the moderate socialists, fighting to hold their lines, themselves began to waver in their steadfast support of the Provisional Government.[29]

It is in the Petersburg Soviet, however, that the shattering effect of the resurrection of the death penalty upon SR fortunes can best be seen. The SR-Menshevik bloc headed by Tsereteli, hitherto firmly in control, had become more and more dependent on SR soldier delegates as the working class of the capital in one by-election after another manifested its preference for Bolshevism. But on August 8 an unheard-of event occurred. The soldiers' section of the soviet had met to consider routine matters when the Bolsheviks moved that the order of the day be set aside in favor of a discussion of the death

[28] Spiridonova, "O zadachakh revoliutsii" (On the Tasks of the Revolution), *Nash Put'*, No. 1 (August, 1917), p. 9; Spiridonova, "Kazn'" (Capital Punishment), *ibid.*, pp. 32-33.

[29] Telegram of the acting general commissar of the Black Sea Fleet, dated August 21, 1917, and sent to the general staff of the Fleet; see A. Zakova, "Armiia i flot nakanune Velikoi sotsialisticheskoi revoliutsii" (The Army and Navy on the Eve of the Great Socialist Revolution), *Istoricheskii Zhurnal* (Historical Journal), IX (September, 1937), 30.

penalty. The motion carried, 106 to 104.[30] These figures tell us a great deal. The SR's had opposed the motion and had been beaten in their own bailiwick. Henceforth they had no choice but to go along with the mass of their supporters, or see them desert the party fold. A large number of delegates no doubt thought of themselves still as SR's, without any factional distinction; actually they were already left SR's, by instinct if not consciously, and if the left wing had not been there to articulate their opinions, they would soon have gone over to Bolshevism. Some made the shift anyway.

The revolt of August 8 decided the issue for the SR leaders: they resolved to capitulate. On the evening of August 18 the SR delegation switched over and voted with the Bolsheviks to override the presidium and to bring the matter of the death penalty before the soviet. Two resolutions were submitted to this plenary session: one by the SR's and the other by Martov, leader of the Menshevik Internationalists, the only real difference being that the latter censured the All-Russian Soviet Executive Committee for failing to pose the question in negotiations with the Provisional Government. After this feature had been rejected 428 to 377 with 48 abstentions, the Bolsheviks and their allies swung over to support the SR resolution,[31] and it was adopted by the vote of all against four. Among these four was Irakli Tsereteli, the kingpin of moderate socialism, who had seen his SR following desert him on this occasion. As the Georgian's grip loosened on the soviet, the whole structure of coalition was placed in jeopardy. For the SR leaders, the situation had been painful enough—in their hearts they would have preferred once more to

[30] *Delo Naroda*, No. 122 (August 9, 1917).

[31] For once the SR's abandoned the language of compromise and came out in clear and unequivocal terms. Capital punishment in the army was viewed as a means of subjugating the soldier masses to the will of a politically unreliable command and as a prelude to its reintroduction into civilian life—by no means an idle fear, for Savinkov was pressing Kerenski on just this point. Shooting soldiers was no substitute for creating a new army which alone could guarantee both the defense and the internal security of the revolution. The resolution demanded that the government revoke the offensive decree. The SR's were caught as fast as ever in the vicious circle of their unwillingness either to conclude peace or wage war: the requirements of coalition blocked plans for a new army, and the fear of counterrevolution made them unwilling to sanction drastic means of restoring discipline in the existing army.

follow Tsereteli, but the temper of their soldier delegates forced them, as their spokesman frankly admitted, to oppose a measure which "our own comrades," Kerenski and Savinkov, had decreed (his naive confession drew horselaughs from the Bolshevik benches).[32] The final act in the sequence of events set off by the revolt of August 8 came, of course, on the memorable night of September 9, when the split in SR ranks and their own waxing strength enabled the Bolsheviks to unhorse the Menshevik-SR presidium and to take over the direction of the Petersburg Soviet.

Less spectacularly than among the soldiers but none the less steadily, the left SR's had been winning converts in the villages of Russia. In part this was due to the influence of the soldiers on the people back home, but in part, also, it was achieved independently of success in the barracks. The Kronstadt SR organization paid much attention to the peasantry: disposing of considerable means and solidly leftist in outlook, it had already in May dispatched some two hundred agitators to the village.[33] In some provinces remote from the front, however, the left SR's had possessed enough local strength to take over the party apparatus from the start, and it was here, particularly in Kazan province, that they gave the peasants of Russia an object-lesson in how the land question could be solved regardless of the stand of the Provisional Government and the restraints imposed by a policy of coalition at the center of power.

It is doubtful whether in any other province the rural soviets were so solidly entrenched as in the old Tatar stronghold on the Volga, and it is certain that nowhere did they display a more virulent hostility to the landowners. At the head of the Kazan Peasants' Soviet stood A. L. Kalegaev, perhaps the most able of the left SR leaders. Already in May the provincial soviet had decided that privately owned lands should be taken over by the volost land committees, for use by the peasants, but without being parceled out, lest the soldiers' interests should suffer. The Interior Ministry under Prince Lvov had promptly annulled this "decree," only to be answered with defiance

[32] *Delo Naroda*, No. 131 (August 19, 1917); Sukhanov, *Zapiski*, V, 176-82; *Revoliutsiia 1917 goda (Khronika sobytii)*, IV, 69-70.
[33] *Zemlia i Volia* (Petersburg), No. 47 (May 20, 1917).

by Kalegaev, who declared that such measures were necessary to head off anarchy and that the will of the people would be carried out despite threats from the Provisional Government. The ministry had then resorted to armed coercion, causing some of its district commissars to resign, but nothing much seems to have come of its action, for by June 10 peasants' committees were reported to be in full control of estates in Spassk *uezd,* setting an example for other districts to follow, and the landowners of Kazan telegraphed Kerenski in July to protest the ineffectiveness of government measures against seizures, which in Sviiazh *uezd* had led to the full liquidation of private economies and even to the expropriation of household effects. There is no reason to question Kalegaev's assertion, made before an All-Russian conference of peasants' soviets, that by July the land of Kazan province was already in the hands of the peasantry and the soviets were supreme in the villages.[34] The ministerial council at its session of September 28 took up the question of agrarian disorders, especially in Kazan province, and tried to devise a system of mixed councils for public officials to fall back upon in their effort to uphold the law, but by that time peasant communities all over Russia were following the example of the left SR's in Kazan, whether the local party organizations sought to restrain them, or wrung their hands in despair, or acquiesced in the seizures.[35]

Mounting evidence of the inroads of extremism, most palpable in the case of soldiers but not wanting in respect to the peasantry, alarmed the SR leaders and caused them to seek a reaffirmation of

---

[34] Bykhovski, *Vserossiiskii Sovet Krest'ianskikh Deputatov,* p. 159.
[35] "Bor'ba za zemliu v 1917 g. (po Kazanskoi gub.)" (The Fight for Land in 1917 [in Kazan Province]), *Krasnyi Arkhiv,* LXXVIII (V, 1936), 87-89, 96-97; Shliapnikov, *Semnadtsatyi god,* III, 149-53, 353-54; *Kazanskii Oktiabr',* I, 57-59, 69, 87. The Kazan landowners banded together in an effort to group the independent peasants about themselves and play upon the fears of the better-to-do elements in the village (Bykhovski, *Vserossiiskii Sovet Krest'ian-skikh Deputatov,* p. 136). Little came of these efforts, and little could come of them—these islets of individualism were only specks in the gray communal sea of the peasantry.

party unity amid signs of approaching disruption. For this purpose a party council, or congress on a reduced scale, seemed the best means. It would be the seventh in the history of the organization and the second in 1917, and its significance derives from the fact that it was to be the only formal consultation of the membership between the Third Congress in May and the Fourth in December. In summoning the Seventh Council, the Central Committee apparently hoped to center attention on preparations for the Constituent Assembly and commit all factions to a common policy on the agrarian, labor, and nationalities problems (especially the Finnish and Ukrainian), while by-passing the question of war, on which no agreement was possible; but if this was the basic strategy,[36] it was foredoomed to failure, for the Seventh Council no more than any other representative assembly could hope to escape the factional strife engendered by war.

Hardly had the announcement been made (July 27) when the sniping began. The right challenged the authority of a council convened in such haste, since the delegates would be named by existing committees instead of by special meetings of the membership, as provided in the statutes;[37] with only ten days' notice, serious preparation was impossible, and the result would be at best an enlarged conference rather than a council in the true sense of the term. Having thus prepared the ground for contesting an unfavorable decision at the council, the right called on its partisans to take an active hand in the proceedings in the hope of steering the party onto the tracks of revolutionary "defensism" over the obstacles imposed by the "late unfortunate" congress and the "*in camera*" proceedings of the Central Committee. A major objective would be to

[36] An indication may be found in the comment of the *Delo Naroda*, No. 111 (July 27, 1917); see also *Volia Naroda*, No. 86 (August 8, 1917).

[37] Each provincial organization was to have one delegate in its own right and another through the regional organization to which it belonged; each army and fleet would also send one representative; three places were alloted jointly to the SR fractions of the All-Russian Soviet Executive Committees, three apiece to the two metropolitan organizations, and five to the Central Committee. See *Delo Naroda*, No. 111 (July 27, 1917); *Volia Naroda*, No. 78 (July 29, 1917). The principle of proportional representation according to membership was not observed (*ibid.*, No. 86 [August 8, 1917]).

exorcise from the pages of the *Delo Naroda* the Zimmerwaldian spirit still manifest in its "campaign" against the Allies, a spirit that had lingered on in the party's central organ after being banished, in the post-July era, from every other non-Bolshevik source. Here was fair warning that even if the opposite extreme preserved silence, the war controversy would nevertheless be dragged out onto the floor of the council.[38]

The rightist broadside against the Central Committee, the demand for the revocation of many if not most of its decrees as repugnant to democracy in party affairs and politically wrong in any event, and the specific demand for a review of its ultimatum to Kerenski regarding Chernov's retention in the cabinet inspired the Constitutional Democrats to herald the approaching council as a court that would sit in judgment on Chernov. Detecting in this a maneuver of political enemies to deepen the cleavage in the PSR, Zenzinov as spokesman for the Central Committee publicly refuted both the interpretation of the *Rech'* and the initiative of the *Volia Naroda*, declaring that no one in the committee had raised the question of Chernov's political course and that the so-called ultimatum to the Provisional Government did not figure on the council's agenda. In a veiled rebuke to the right, Zenzinov noted that people who were so concerned about the unity of the nation would do well to show some regard for the unity of its largest political organization.[39]

From August 6 to 10 the Seventh Council of the PSR was in session. This is one of the most significant, yet one of the least-known incidents in party history, for the meetings of the council were held in secret and only such information as the leadership chose to divulge found its way into print.[40] The policy had always been to hush up scandal in the party, or to pretend that it did not exist, so that the suppression of compromising details was to be expected, but on this occasion so much was withheld that even the skeleton of the proceedings cannot be reconstructed. From the meager disclosures at

[38] A. A. Argunov, "K predstoiashchemu sovetu partii" (On the Coming Party Council), *Volia Naroda*, No. 78 (July 29, 1917).

[39] "Razdeliai i vlastvui" (Divide and Rule), *Delo Naroda*, No. 115 (August 1, 1917).

[40] See statement in the *Volia Naroda*, No. 88 (August 10, 1917).

the time and snatches of information revealed since, it is possible neither to determine the line-up of the local organizations nor to follow the debate in the council. But certain things we know. The rifts disclosed at the May Congress had deepened, and the sessions, by admission of one of the Central Committeemen, were stormy.[41] The chief target of abuse was Chernov, who got it from both sides, the right and left alternating in shooting barbs into his soft body. Those of Breshkovskaia are said to have been especially venomous. But those from the left must have hurt as badly, for they exposed the unnaturalness of Chernov's position. He was doubtlessly the speaker whom the left had in mind when its spokesman said that "even in the bosom of his party he came with sealed lips," delivering an address in which witticisms and verbal lace replaced substance, and in which no definite stand was taken on any question, least of all in respect to the war.[42] But how could it be otherwise, when Chernov's mouth had to say what his heart denied? Nowhere in his voluminous writings do we find any discussion of the Seventh Council, so it must be concluded that it was another painful episode in his bondage, ostensibly to the Central Committee majority, but actually to his own weakness.

Only fragments of the spirited debate have been preserved. Though the war appears to have been excluded from the subjects to be discussed at the council,[43] it of course dominated the proceedings—for example, it was impossible to discuss economic problems without acknowledging the crushing impact of the war. This consideration led Dennis Rosenblum, one of the members of the dominant right-centrist clique, into a startling admission: conceding that the war was eating up the wealth of Russia at a rate which even the most drastic capital levy could not offset, he was forced to the conclusion that the war must quickly be ended. For the first time a prominent SR "defensist" had looked reality full in the face and had not averted his gaze. But his fellows were taken aback and hastened to disavow

[41] Statement of Rakov before the Tenth Petersburg Conference; see *Delo Naroda*, No. 213 (November 18, 1917).
[42] I. Z. Steinberg, "O edinstve partii" (On Party Unity), *Nash Put'*, No. 2, pp. 36-37.
[43] These are listed in the *Delo Naroda*, No. 121 (August 8, 1917).

his heresy: Bykhovski arose to say that Russia could not end the war on her own, and to deny that the economic situation was so bad—it was not the material side, he said, but the lack of a civil consciousness in the population that constituted the real problem. As though that were any less a reason for trying to do something about the war! The party had reached a pass, however, where some, at least, of its members were beginning to question the old shibboleths: one such delegate in this socialist assembly even went so far as to advocate the development of private industry in order to increase the nation's productive forces.[44]

One of the main duties of the Seventh Council was to hear the report of the Central Committee and to decide whether that body merited a vote of confidence—in other words, to pass on the right-centrist course which had been steered since the Third Congress. Surprisingly enough, the most scathing attack on the committee came not from the left but from the extreme right in the person of Breshkovskaia, who denounced the party leadership in such unbridled terms that even her own organ did not publish the speech as she had delivered it. The basic premise of her arraignment was the equation of antiwar sentiment with Germanophilism—the standard smear used in all Allied countries to stifle dissent. The only difference was that in this case the person who made the charge sincerely believed in it. Breshkovskaia's intense aversion to the *Delo Naroda* derived from its "Germanophile" tendencies and the presence of a questionable character like Mstislavski on the editorial staff. As for the Central Committee under whose auspices it was published, she attributed that body's composition to the ascendancy of the Petersburg element; contrasting the rottenness of the capital with the patriotism of the provinces, Breshkovskaia asserted that the views propagated by the *Volia Naroda* were shared by the great majority of the democracy and by the entire peasantry. Here she was reading a Western pattern into Russian society, where it did not exist and could not prevail. She censured the Central Committee for its arbitrary and secret decisions, its persecution of the *Volia Naroda*, its mismanagement of party finances, and its neglect of the provinces,

[44] *Ibid.*, No. 123 (August 10, 1917).

and concluded by saying that she could not work with a body whose principles and practices were so at variance with her own. So much for the published version of her remarks.[45]

The unpublished was sheer vitriol. She began by noting the presence of "traitors" in the council, and then centered her fire on Chernov as the intellectual fountainhead of everything that was rotten and treasonable and corrosive in the party. It was he who had nurtured the vipers before they attained full poison. Neither the Bolsheviks nor the Black Hundreds ever gave him such a tongue-lashing as he received on this occasion. But he was too flabby to reply, and others struck by this blunderbuss discharge likewise shrank from the challenge. When she had finished, Breshkovskaia stalked out of the hall, leaving a stunned audience behind her. The left prodded Chernov: how would he react to this torrent of abuse, and was it not time for him to decide where he stood?[46]

In one sense Breshkovskaia had overplayed her hand. The violence of her attack and the sweeping nature of her accusations lessened the effectiveness of the indictment, and the Central Committee received a vote of confidence over the protests of the extremists on both sides—by what sort of a margin, we are not told. But from the language of the resolution, which declared that the Committee had faced a complex task without adequate support from the local organizations, and that "in general" it had observed the instructions of the congress, one may infer that the endorsement was not enthusiastic.[47]

While Breshkovskaia's speech was symptomatic of the conditions prevailing in the PSR, and ranks as one of the most painful episodes in its history, the right did not have the votes to sustain her position, and the main struggle at the council was between the left and the center over the resolution on current affairs. There was, of course, no hope of meeting on common ground, so the leadership offered one resolution, written by Dennis Rosenblum, and the left another by Isaac Steinberg, delegate from the Urals. A number of burning

[45] *Volia Naroda*, No. 98 (August 22, 1917).
[46] Interview with Steinberg in New York (December, 1949).
[47] *Delo Naroda*, No. 125 (August 12, 1917).

issues were at stake, including the party's relation to the Provisional Government, but at the heart of the controversy lay the question of the reinstatement of the death penalty for military offenses. For veteran idealists like Spiridonova, this was a moral issue, but for others it was the intensely practical one of whether a coalition of moderates under Kerenski and conservatives under General Kornilov would succeed in bringing the ranks back under control of the officers and so put an end to the revolution. Seen in this perspective, the controversy over capital punishment deservedly occupied the central position in the council's deliberations.

The lines were so tightly drawn over the issue that a schism appeared inevitable. Seeking to lessen the tension, the center asked for an intermission in which to modify the text of the Rosenblum resolution. Apparently the decision was to demand revocation, but at the last moment an amendment was tacked on favoring abolition "at the first opportunity." The left thereupon moved to put the party on record as favoring unconditional repeal of the penalty, and this was voted upon separately. Thirty-eight votes were cast in its favor, 42 against, with 9 delegates abstaining. The moderates owed their slender success to the five votes of the Central Committee, cast in lock-step fashion under the discipline imposed by the right-centrist majority.[48] As he had already let the measure go through the cabinet without dissent, Chernov no doubt found it easier to swallow his convictions on this occasion. The matter was left, then, with the Rosenblum resolution calling for revocation as soon as it should be feasible. Feasibility was not defined, and the bitterness pervading extremist ranks was intensified by the narrow margin of their defeat. It is significant that the official press preserved a gravelike silence on the whole business.[49]

If one wishes to look into the tortured soul of the SR party, he need only read the Rosenblum resolution. Its language will convince him that this party was mired in a swamp, and that it would prob-

[48] Six members of the committee as individuals had declared themselves against capital punishment.

[49] Spiridonova, "O Sovete Partii" (On the Party Council), Nash Put', No. 2, p. 33. This rare publication is the only source of information.

ably drown in the muck of that swamp. Not even Chernov with his long experience had devised a more mealymouthed formula than the one on the Provisional Government, which declared that the party was "obliged" to support it as a "revolutionary government" which "in general" had not defaulted "up to now" on the commitments assumed under the program of July 8. In all this it is impossible to find any real conviction but only the rabbit-like fear of breaking with the coalition, which the spokesman for the committee had fanned with his account of weekly ministerial crises.[50]

The Steinberg resolution, as might be expected, beheld in the Provisional Government the source of most evil: internally, it was killing the revolutionary spirit of the masses with all repression and no reform, while opening the door to reaction through its campaign against the army soviets; externally, it was throwing sand in the eyes of the people with fair words while following the dictates of domestic and foreign imperialism. An honest experiment in coalition was impossible when class differences were so acute; the tasks of the revolution could only be solved by a homogeneous government responsible to the soviets *and* the democratic organs of local self-government (here one will note the difference between the left SR and Bolshevik formulas, the Bolsheviks desiring a government responsible solely to the soviets and the left SR's insisting on mixed control, with both class and democratic organs participating). As an immediate measure, and in order to protect the party's popularity, the left wished the council to disclaim any responsibility for the government or for the presence of Chernov and Avksentiev within it—a proposal calculated to lead to its downfall.[51] Some members of the left were prepared to go much further than the text of their resolution: behind the scenes Spiridonova insisted on a dictatorship of the PSR in the belief that if the party struck out boldly on its own, it would find the strength to scrap the policy of the Provisional Government without admitting the Bolsheviks to power.[52]

[50] The public was not favored with the text or even a résumé of Richter's report.

[51] Steinberg, *Ot fevralia po oktiabr'*, p. 90.

[52] Zenzinov, "Diktatura ili narodovlastie?" (Dictatorship or Democracy?), *Narodovlastie*, No. 2, p. 21.

On the war, the Rosenblum resolution called merely for an active foreign policy to secure peace on democratic principles, whereas the Steinberg resolution advanced the slogan favoring an armistice on all fronts. Here the left, also, was evading the issue, for it did not say what it would do if the slogan were rejected, as it was certain to be. On the land question, the left reiterated the demand for turning all properties over to the land committees. Hitherto this slogan had been chanted in unison by all segments of party opinion, but now the Rosenblum resolution came forth with a proposal for laws that would regulate relations in the village in the spirit of the party program. One wonders what this could have meant to the peasants or, for that matter, to the men who drafted it. The two resolutions were more or less in agreement on the need for democracy in the army, since Rosenblum's favored a change in the high command and advocated strengthening the soldiers' committees (soviets). One of the remarkable features of his resolution was the assertion that, at a time when the war and land problems were digging the grave of the Russian democracy, the center of gravity of the party's work should lie (1) in consolidating the network of soviets, (2) in gaining control of local and provincial councils, and (3) in promoting industrial democracy.[53]

The struggle over the stand on current affairs left wounds that could never heal. The contending factions were divided less by their analysis of the situation or even by their concept of the revolution than by tactical considerations, especially of war and power, the center being determined to demonstrate its political maturity and the left, to have done with military executions, class collaboration, and the government's two-handed game in relation to peace. When it was announced that the Rosenblum resolution had gone through by 54 votes against 35, "a strange silence settled over the hot, stuffy room," and those on the losing side no longer felt anything in common with the majority but "wished to go back to the people whence they had come, leaving the government's party."[54] So intense was the bitterness and so complete the estrangement that the left refused

---

[53] Text of the two resolutions in *Delo Naroda*, No. 124 (August 11, 1917).
[54] Spiridonova, "O Sovete Partii," *Nash Put'*, No. 2, pp. 32-33.

to cooperate in amending the victorious resolution, preferring to let it stand as it was. Although the vote was published,[55] the failure to indicate the organizations represented and the obscurity of most of the delegates robbed the roll call of any significance, except that there were enough familiar names to indicate that the moderate and extreme left had coalesced in support of the Steinberg resolution, while the center had solidly opposed it. Chernov was playing his usual devious game, preserving the unity of the center by going along with the Rosenblum resolution, yet planning to amend it with the help of its enemies, only to have his strategy spoiled by the intransigence of the left, which refused to try to better a bad resolution. The distance between Chernov and his pre-1917 protégés was steadily widening.[56]

The sensation of the council was the strength of the left deviation. That the resolution backed by the Central Committee should pass, occasioned no surprise, but that 40 percent of the council would vote against it, no one had foreseen, not even the left, which was astonished at the number of hands raised in support of its resolution.[57] Here was a reasonably clear indication of the true state of affairs in Russia. Only at the top level of society had there been a lurch to the right in the post-July era; in a mass organization like the PSR the trend was still leftward, and very decidedly leftward, despite superficial signs to the contrary. But the lesson was lost on the men of February, in the high command of the party as in the Provisional Government. They had divested the right of power, but not of authority in their own eyes, and they were fearful lest the power be regained. In the lengthening shadow of the future they looked for the shades of the past. The angry talk on the right filled

[55] *Delo Naroda*, No. 124. The names of the delegates are given, but not the organizations they represented. The author tried with the help of every likely printed source and the oral assistance of Zenzinov, Steinberg, and others to identify the names on the list, but the task proved impossible. Only in relatively few instances could delegate and organization be linked. A list, apparently incomplete, of organizations that sent delegates is printed in *ibid.*, No. 121 (August 8, 1917).
[56] *Kratkii otchët o rabotakh chetvërtago s"ezda P.S.-R.*, p. 115; Spiridonova, "O Sovete Partii," *Nash Put'*, No. 2, pp. 31-33.
[57] Interview with Steinberg in New York (December, 1951).

them with dismay, since it came from gentlemen; the dull roar on the left they dismissed as of little consequence, since it came from the rabble. There is no evidence of the reaction of the Central Committee—if it had any reaction—to the fact that two fifths of the party was dead set against its policies. It continued unperturbed on its course. Perhaps it agreed with Argunov that the council was somehow unrepresentative of the membership, but whatever may be thought of the haste with which the council was convened, and of the manner of selecting delegates, it cannot be denied that the strength of the left wing was much greater than would have been warranted by the half-dozen provincial organizations under its control—Kazan, Ufa, Kharkov, Kherson, perhaps Pskov and Kaluga.[58] No other conclusion is possible than that disaffection was rife in the party ranks *before* the Kornilov upheaval, and that the lack of support from the provinces of which the leadership complained may have been due less to the weakness of organizational ties than to disgruntlement over the policies being pursued.

The very strength of the left delayed the inevitable schism. It had come a long way since the time when a small band of outcasts, mainly Jewish, had been contained with ease in a newspaper office in Geneva. It had become a mass movement, truly Russian in character, and the limits of its growth had not yet been attained. If it stayed on, it might take over the party intact with its machinery and manifold contacts, its name and its good will. The moral unity of the PSR was already lost, and if mechanical union continued, it was because of hesitation on the one side before an operation of such magnitude as excision of the left would entail, and calculation on the other that yet a little patience, and all would be theirs. The agrarian problem likewise exercised a restraining influence. Often berated as the handmaidens of Bolshevism, the left SR's did not have to wait until 1918 to learn what that movement held in store for the peasantry. They realized from the first that its program was to split and subjugate, and they did not underestimate its power; consequently,

---

[58] Doubtlessly as a consequence of the reorganization enforced by the Central Committee, the delegation of the Northern Region was evenly divided; see *Delo Naroda*, No. 120 (August 6, 1917), and compare with the line-up of votes.

they hesitated to break up the party that stood to the peasants as shepherd to sheep. So the left SR's decided to bide their time, demanding only relief from the "prison regime" which had muzzled their adherents in public bodies and debarred them from positions of trust in the party. There was no god-given orthodoxy, they urged, and opinion must be free within the party, even that of the *Volia Naroda*, the rights of which they upheld in order to strengthen their own claim for toleration. It was not easy, in view of its size, to deny recognition to the left as an independent current within the PSR, and the first fruit of its showing at the council was the publication of the minority along with the majority resolution on current affairs. Thus the Seventh Council, though devoid of practical results, marks an important stage in the evolution of the PSR through the crystallization of the left wing into a powerful faction or even embryo party, secure in the knowledge of its strength and possessing in the minority resolution a program about which to rally further support.[59]

From the foregoing examination of party affairs it is apparent that a tremor would suffice to bring the SR structure crashing to ground. It was destined, however, to experience not a tremor but two earthquakes which would leave it a mass of ruins.

The first came at the end of the summer when General Kornilov, commander in chief of the Russian armies by grace of Kerenski at the behest of Savinkov, threw off the mask of obedience to the Provisional Government and declared war on the revolution. It is not proposed to wander here into the bottomless swamp of the Kornilov affair, or even to consider the vexing question of Kerenski's relation to it, but merely to examine the role of the PSR in the crisis and note the far-reaching effects it had on the party's fortunes.

[59] Report of Karelin to the fourth Kharkov provincial congress, *Partiinyia Izvestiia*, No. 2 (October 5, 1917), p. 43; Spiridonova, "O Sovete Partii," *Nash Put'*, No. 2, pp. 33-34, 36; Steinberg, "O edinstve partii," *ibid.*, pp. 37-41; Steinberg, *Ot fevralia po oktiabr'*, pp. 90-92; Steinberg, *Spiridonova*, pp. 177-78. The fact that all five of these citations are left SR shows how little the other SR's liked to dwell on this episode.

For some time the SR's had been disturbed by the accumulating signs of a plot against the revolution centering at General Headquarters. As early as July 12 the Central Committee had warned against the adherents of military dictatorship.[60] The press kept a watchful eye on developments and from time to time lifted up its voice in criticism of the indulgence shown in official quarters to manifestations of counterrevolution. That the *Delo Naroda* should have chided the regime[61] is not surprising, for it had always preserved an air of detachment, even after Chernov had entered the ministry, but an event of greater significance was the appearance in its columns of a signed article by Zenzinov, bosom friend of Kerenski and one of the two main architects of procoalitional policy, who recalled the government to first principles with the pointed reminder that the country expected a revolutionary regime to pursue a revolutionary policy, in default of which disaster was certain.[62] The SR members of the Petersburg Soviet had long been characterized by their moderation but now they demanded that something be done to stem the tide of reaction.[63] These and other public exhortations or even reprimands from the largest political organization supporting the government had no noticeable effect upon its policy.

No better fate attended representations made in private, behind the scenes in the Provisional Government. The military commission of the Central Committee prepared a report on the society that posed the chief threat, the Union of Army and Naval Officers, which enjoyed the favor of headquarters, but the minister-president, to whom the recommendations were submitted on August 3, saw fit to adopt only one of them: the Union was no longer to be permitted the use of staff funds to defray the expenses of publication.[64] If

[60] *Delo Naroda*, No. 98 (July 12, 1917).

[61] See editorials in Nos. 128, 133, 135, 136 (August 16, 22, 24, 25, 1917).

[62] "Strannyia protivorechiia" (Strange Contradictions), No. 114, (July 30, 1917).

[63] See resolution adopted on August 23 and printed in the *Delo Naroda*, No. 135 (August 24, 1917).

[64] M. Broun, "Ocherk deiatel'nosti voennoi komissii pri Tsentral'nom Komitete P.S.-R." (Outline of the Work of the Military Commission of the Central Committee of the SR Party), *Partiinyia Izvestiia*, No. 3 (October 19, 1917), p. 13.

Kerenski brushed aside the advice of a subordinate agency because of the pressure of business, the same cannot be said of his failure to respond to Chernov's intervention, which certainly must have impressed itself upon his mind, not only because of his colleague's standing but also because the two men did not often confer. The circumstances of the Moscow State Conference had convinced Chernov that a military plot was afoot against which precautions should be taken without loss of time. So, sinking his personal differences with Kerenski, he went to him and unburdened himself of his fears, pointing out that certain of the conspirators, or at any rate two-faced people, were occupying cabinet positions. The obstruction of the Kadet party he explained on the ground that it was seeking by blocking reforms to deprive the government of its popularity and to uncover its breast to the militarists' *coup de grâce*. "To force, under the pressure of high army circles, and with the support of the Kadet party, the maximum number of repressions in the absence of positive achievements—that is the plan which is calculated to ruin the Provisional Government."[65] This interview occurred shortly before the upheaval and Chernov's retirement from the cabinet. The intimation of treason in high places was directed in the first instance at Savinkov, the acting minister of war, against whom Chernov had on three occasions warned Kerenski.[66] There is nothing to indicate that the other party representative in the government, Minister of the Interior Avksentiev, associated himself with his colleague's *démarche*; in all probability Avksentiev and Kerenski had the same fundamental approach to the problem, since they desired to strengthen the authority of the Provisional Government and lessen that of the soviets, to continue the war and bridle the revolution, though not, of course, to betray it. For this purpose they wanted to use the officers' corps, but they never intended that it should get out of hand and entertain notions of becoming a political force in its own right. The only clue to Avksentiev's stand at the time was a statement he made to the press in which he predicted an effort on the

[65] *Kratkii otchët o rabotakh chetvërtago s"ezda P.S.-R.*, p. 17.
[66] "Zanaveska pripodnimaetsia" (The Curtain Rises a Little), *Delo Naroda*, No. 151 (September 10, 1917).

part of the reactionaries to make capital out of the fall of Riga and its failure through want of intrinsic strength.[67]

Once more the isolation of Chernov in the government cannot excuse his conduct. If he believed the revolution to be in danger, and could stir none of his colleagues to action, he should have resigned *con brio* and sought to arouse his party and country. But he was never a man for decisive action and for him it was unthinkable to go against the dictates of the Central Committee. Party discipline came first and everything else afterwards. The plans of the conspirators were allowed to mature.

On the evening of August 26 it became known that General Kornilov had cast off the mask of obedience to the Provisional Government and was making a bid for power. The next morning the SR Central Committee assembled and repaired to the Smolny Institute, where the two All-Russian Soviet Executive Committees and the staffs of the other socialist parties were meeting. The SR's had surrendered their foothold in the government when Chernov and Avksentiev resigned along with the other ministers, leaving the power of state in the hands of Kerenski. Now Richter (LC) proposed in the name of his party the reconstitution of the ministry in its original form except for replacement of the Kadet members by men of Kerenski's choice; if, however, it were necessary to institute a directory or other form of government, the PSR would support it, provided it fought the counterrevolution and stood on the Declaration of July 8.[68] Efforts on the part of Savinkov, Miliukov, Alekseev, and others to effect a compromise between Kerenski and Kornilov got no support from the PSR, and the *Delo Naroda* came out against any armistice with Kornilov as merely prolonging an intolerable state of affairs.[69]

For the moment the SR's were less taken up with questions of state than with the military threat to the capital posed by the movement of General Krymov's corps. Being no longer represented in the

---

[67] *Delo Naroda*, No. 136 (August 25, 1917).

[68] *Ibid.*, No. 140 (August 29, 1917).

[69] "Demokraticheskaia respublika ili burzhuaznaia monarkhiia" (Democratic Republic or Bourgeois Monarchy), No. 140 (August 29, 1917).

government, they conducted their struggle from the vantage ground of the soviets and made a substantial contribution to the victory over Kornilov. They joined with the other socialist parties in forming a "committee for struggle against the counterrevolution," at the head of which stood the SR officer, V. N. Filippovski, who once more came into prominence as in the early days of the revolution, and in much the same capacity.[70] It was the last time that an orthodox Socialist Revolutionary would direct the armed forces of the Petersburg Soviet, for this *ad hoc* body was the prototype of the Military Revolutionary Committee, which would come to full flower under Trotski; but six months of experience had caused Filippovski, despite his continued allegiance to Chernov's left-centrist faction, to draw nearer the Bolshevik position in his advocacy of strong measures and in his distaste for the Provisional Government, particularly for the man at its head.[71] How well Filippovski and his associates did their work is not easy to judge—Chernov went out to inspect garrison units entrusted with the defense of the capital and found them deployed in a thoroughly unsatisfactory manner.[72] But one must take into account, first, the state of demoralization in the garrison and, second, the strange action of Kerenski in appointing Savinkov military governor general of St. Petersburg (August 28) in spite of his sympathy for Kornilov's program—though not with its execution— a step that confounded the Socialist Revolutionaries and confused the military situation, since Savinkov and the soviet were certain to issue conflicting orders. Savinkov himself tells how Gotz and Tsereteli insisted on the presence of soviet observers at staff headquarters, "probably to supervise my orders."[73] Nothing reveals the condition into which the Russian democracy had fallen quite like the Kornilov affair.

But victories were won in 1917 by decomposition, not by fighting. The troops dispatched against the capital, including the supposedly impervious Wild Division of Moslem Caucasians, dissolved in a com-

---

[70] See chap. V.
[71] Sukhanov, *Zapiski*, V, 290 ff., 329, 355-56.
[72] *Great Russian Revolution*, p. 368.
[73] *K delu Kornilova*, p. 28.

mon sea of demoralization with those of the Petersburg garrison, the SR's having done much to induce this demoralization. Chernov made the most of his identification in the public eye with land reform: he sped appeals to the advancing troops not to serve as blind tools of the enemies of land reform, and he personally established contact with several Cossack and Caucasian units.[74] The Moslem delegation that was sent out from the garrison to fraternize with the Wild Division has received general recognition, but the agents sent by the Peasants' Executive Committee to work on the hostile forces must also have had their effect. While the city soviet was using the Moslem approach,[75] the Peasants' Committee was appealing to class interest.

It may well be, however, that the SR's made their chief contribution to Kornilov's defeat through the rural soviets. Here they did not share authority with the Social Democrats but had everything their own way. However little stomach they may have had for the class struggle in the midst of war, and however intense their aversion for Bolshevism, the Populist intellectuals dominating these soviets were committed body and soul to the rule of the people, against which sacred principle General Kornilov had raised his blasphemous hand. The members of the All-Russian Executive Committee resolved to fight on the barricades if the enemy burst into the city. For a brief moment the old fire flamed up in the soul of these spent revolutionists, and they telegraphed all subordinate organs to prepare armed resistance to the generals' coup, an action that helps to explain why the enemies of the revolution in the provinces remained on the defensive.[76] Then they turned to Chernov, whose views on the war appalled them but whose prestige they could not do without, and commissioned him to draft an appeal to the peasants, wherever they might be and in whatever guise—in uniform or behind the plow, in the city garrisons, at the front, or on the farms—since the word of the "village minister" still carried the most weight with the rural toilers.

[74] *Great Russian Revolution*, p. 373.

[75] Even the grandson of Shamil was pressed into service—see Dan's comment in Sukhanov, *Zapiski*, V, 322.

[76] Bykhovski, *Vserossiiskii Sovet Krest'ianskikh Deputatov*, pp. 233-34.

In this manifesto,[77] denounced by General Denikin as "infamous,"[78] Chernov made the most of his official position, which he had just given up, to identify the army command with the enemies of land reform in an effort to stir the masses to action. The imputation of reactionary motives to General Kornilov may have been unjust, since he had the lower-class origin, the chauvinism, and the preference for dictatorship over monarchy which characterize more the prototype Fascist than the adherent of the old regime, but Chernov was probably not far wrong in his forecast of the practical effects of a victory for Headquarters. The manifesto was less fulsome in commending the Provisional Government than Sukhanov would have us believe,[79] for its author worked in a backhanded slap at Kerenski's regime for having failed to cast out the handful of generals who were responsible for all the trouble. It is, of course, impossible to gauge the effect of the manifesto, but it seems reasonable to assume that it hit the target of class instinct and was a factor in cutting the ground out from under the conspirators' feet and isolating them from the rest of the country.

There was only one part of Russia where the generals could have gained strong backing, and that was the Don Cossack Territory. Just how this potential Vendée fitted into the scheme of the military is uncertain, but the apprehension in soviet circles was that the Cossacks under Ataman Kaledin would make common cause with Kornilov. The left SR commander of the Tsaritsyn (Stalingrad) garrison, Fedotov, who was himself a Cossack, but a Red one, had caught wind of a grandiose plan whereby Kaledin would seize the line of the Volga, secure his rear, and then strike out to aid Kornilov in subjugating the soviets of northern Russia. First in the line of attack was the Red stronghold of Tsaritsyn with its high-grade steel mills, a lucrative prize for the conqueror. Whether or not this was part of the grand strategy of the conspiracy, the Tsaritsyn official took it and his own danger seriously enough to go to Saratov and

[77] "Ko vsem krest'ianam" (To All Peasants), *Delo Naroda*, No. 140 (August 29, 1917).
[78] *Ocherki russkoi smuty*, II, 15.
[79] *Zapiski*, V, 317.

implore the sister soviet for aid, as a result of which reinforcements were rushed to Tsaritsyn.[80] Another fear current at the time, resting on a threat that he is said to have made at the start of the crisis, but denied by him later on, was that Kaledin would cut the communications between northern and southern Russia. Both this fear and the one regarding Tsaritsyn were fed by the ataman's tour of the northern parts of his territory at the time of the crisis and by certain troop movements, the significance of which has never been clarified.[81]

The soviets of south and south central Russia were just as alert as those on the Volga. In Kharkov, where there was intense resentment against Kornilov for his part in restoring the death penalty, the left SR's joined with the Bolsheviks and left-wing Mensheviks—everything was left in Kharkov—to set up a "revolutionary staff" which simply took over the military functions of the Provisional Government. Indeed, had it not been for the unwillingness of the left SR's to institute a full-fledged soviet regime, the October Revolution would have occurred at the end of August in the eastern Ukraine.[82] The Voronezh Soviet likewise took matters into its own hands and distinguished itself by the energy it threw into its preparations to smother the Cossack fire before it began to spread. M. L. Kogan-Bernstein (LLC) seems to have been the moving spirit in this soviet, which telegraphed an order for Kaledin's arrest to every station "from Liski to Rostov, from Griazi to Tsaritsyn," and instructed the local soviets to impede Cossack troop movements by every means at their disposal, including the destruction of roadbeds along the line of advance.[83] The Cossacks would not permit the arrest of their ataman, but they held aloof from Kornilov's coup.

[80] Antonov-Saratovski, *Pod stiagom proletarskoi bor'by*, I, 131-33. Although the text relates these developments to the end of June, it is obvious that the author's memory is at fault or a misprint has occurred, for concerted action with Kornilov formed the heart of the plan and the latter did not become commander-in-chief till mid-July. The circumstances referred to could only have been those of the second half of August.

[81] See "Delo o generale Kaledine" (The Affair of General Kaledin), in the collection *Kornilovskie dni*, pp. 163 ff.; Miliukov, *Istoriia vtoroi russkoi revoliutsii*, I, Part II, 272-77; *Revoliutsiia 1917 goda (Khronika sobytii)*, IV, 136, 153, 161, 165-66, 174, 176.

[82] Erde, *Gody buri i natiska*, I, 85-87; *1917 god v Khar'kove*, pp. 53-55.

[83] *1917i god v Voronezhskoi gubernii*, pp. 99 ff.

Miliukov writes that misgivings as to the projected action and perhaps reservations in respect to Kornilov himself may have impelled
Kaledin to preserve to the end a free hand,[84] but the fiery girdle of
soviets around the Don Cossack lands must have increased his hesitation to throw in his lot with Kornilov, that man "with the heart of
a lion and the head of a ram."[85]

In all of the instances mentioned, and in many others besides, the
soviets had been able to function smoothly and with maximum effectiveness because the three socialist parties controlling them had seen
fit to sink their differences in the face of a common danger. The
reduction of General Headquarters itself was largely the result of
close cooperation between the SR's in the Supreme Committee of
the Western Front and the Bolsheviks in the Minsk Soviet.[86] But
in the midst of this enforced collaboration the parties did not cease
to think of the morrow, when they again would be fighting each
other. In working with Filippovski's committee and coordinating the
movements of the party's own organization in the army, the military
commission of the Central Committee did not forget to take measures
to keep the extremists in check.[87] The future would disclose how
effective these measures were.

As long as there seemed to be any chance that Kornilov would
succeed, the SR's were too alarmed and too busy to have second
thoughts. But once the danger was over, and the shoot cut down,
they began to probe for the roots of this poisonous plant. And more
than a few of them came to the conclusion that the ultimate responsibility lay with their own party comrade at the head of the government, for had not Kerenski refused to purge the high command,
and had he not appointed Kornilov commander in chief, and had he

[84] *Istoriia vtoroi russkoi revoliutsii*, I, Part II, 273n.

[85] These were the words General Brusilov used in characterizing his colleague
to A. F. Kerenski.

[86] Knorin, *Revoliutsiia i kontr-revoliutsiia v Belorussii*, I, 17.

[87] Broun, "Ocherk deiatel'nosti voennoi komissii," *Partiinyia Izvestiia*, No. 3
(October 19, 1917), p. 14.

not insisted, even in the midst of the crisis, on naming Savinkov to a crucial position in spite of every evidence of his sympathy, if not with the conspiracy, then at any rate with its program? Suspicions that have never been entirely dispelled crept into the minds of some of Kerenski's own friends.[88]

The PSR was shaken to its depths on September 3 when four editorials and one signed article appeared in the *Delo Naroda*, raking the Kerenski administration from stem to stern. The editorials were, of course, anonymous,[89] yet it was enough that they had appeared in the official mouthpiece of the party to which the head of state at least nominally belonged. The article, however, bore the signature of V. M. Chernov[90] and gave the signal, not only for the definitive break between the two party rivals, but also for a declaration of war by the departing minister of agriculture upon the whole policy of coalition as hitherto conceived and executed. The tone of the editorials, the way in which they complemented the article, as well as the polemical skill they revealed, left little doubt in people's minds that they had come from the same pen, and, in fact, at least three, and probably all four, had been written by Chernov. Each of these editorials—"Council of Five," "Course of Zigzags," "Organ of Democratic Control," and "Honey and Tar"—fired a specific shot, while the article loosed the general broadside. The bark of the Provisional Government did not sink at once, but from this time onward it slowly settled.

The burden of the blast was that if the revolution had been saved from its mortal foes, it was due solely to the exertions of the soviet democracy without any help, and indeed in the face of hindrance, on the part of the Provisional Government. What evil spirit possessed Kerenski? Why did he insist on affronting the conscience of the revolution by such acts as the appointment of General Alekseev as chief of staff, when everyone could see the consequences of

---

[88] Interview with Zenzinov in New York (December, 1951). Zenzinov added that he, personally, did not harbor such suspicions.

[89] "Sovet piati" (Council of Five), "Kurs zigzagov" (Course of Zigzags), "Organ demokraticheskago kontrolia" (An Organ of Democratic Control), "Mëd i dëgot'" (Honey and Tar), No. 145.

[90] "Kornilov i Kornilovshchina" (Kornilov and the Kornilov Era).

truckling to such reactionary generals? And why had Krymov not been placed under arrest, so that he could not commit suicide and remove from the scene the one source of information best calculated to shed light on this sordid affair? With the artful insinuation of which he was master, Chernov managed to convey the impression, without making the charge, that Krymov's demise had relieved Kerenski of embarrassing disclosures. Similarly, by accusing Kerenski of unwillingness to rid the army of the Kornilov system along with Kornilov, Chernov implied that conflicting ambitions had had more to do with their disagreement than conflicting principles. The dickering with discredited elements to form a new coalition pointed in the same direction. If the proclamation of a republic were to have any meaning—two months previously the step that Kerenski had just taken would have been widely acclaimed, but now it was scarcely noticed—state policy must be made to conform to the will of the sovereign people. The time had come to put an end to irresponsibility in high places, to government by caprice, and Kerenski must not be left alone in the field but saddled immediately, before the convocation of the Constituent Assembly, with an organ of democratic control.

It was not possible for Kerenski to ignore this challenge. The Krymov angle infuriated him, as also the blame for things done or not done when Chernov had all along been sitting in the government and had not made an issue of these matters. Furthermore, Kerenski was now fighting for his political life against an adversary who might turn the balance in the party against him, since the left SR's were already making serious inroads and Chernov had more prestige than other leaders, although Gotz carried more weight with the organization. And if the SR pillar were removed, the political superstructure would come crashing down. So Kerenski took the obvious line of attack suggested by Chernov's participation in a government the record of which he now so suddenly and loudly denounced. Chernov, of course, had been the prisoner of party policy, but Kerenski repaid him for his insinuations by making his weakness appear as dishonesty. The minister-president also took advantage of the occasion to bring into the open the circumstances of his defeat at the

Third Congress, which he ascribed to dirty politics on the part of Chernov.[91]

The right wing of the PSR leaped to Kerenski's defense. No longer was it necessary to tread softly; Chernov's blast had exploded the fiction of unity. Argunov now proceeded to attack the character as well as the views of Chernov. The title of "village minister" had not been enough to feed his vanity, and by giving free rein to his cabinet-wrecking proclivities he thought to acquire fame as the Russian Clemenceau. Activity along these lines also relieved the frustration of no longer being able to follow the Zimmerwald line so dear to his heart. He had accused Kerenski of a "course of zigzags," but his own course was one continuous zigzag between a negation of "defensism" and participation in a ministry of national defense. He had been a major cause of political instability, and a major obstacle in the way of land reform, by clutching at his portfolio when he should have resigned and made way for another SR against whom the Kadets could not bring the charge of disloyalty.[92] Chernov had been a bad minister, and had capped a record of disservice by stabbing his party colleague in the back.[93] Breshkovskaia did not need the provocation of an attack upon her political idol to incite her against the man she loathed. She resumed where she had left off at the Seventh Council, expressing mild wonderment that Chernov had not been restrained by his collaborators on the *Delo Naroda*, "not all of whom are capable of twisting their souls."[94]

The SR's had always tried to lock up their quarrels in the inner councils of the party, safe from the view of outsiders and their own rank and file. Hitherto only the controversy with the left wing had been publicized, and many branches in their ignorance of the true state of affairs had preserved something of the honeymoon spirit of March. So much greater the shock when the Kornilov affair like a surgeon's knife revealed the ravages of the cancer which had first manifested itself at the Third Congress but which had formed long

[91] "Otvet A. F. Kerenskago 'Delu Naroda'" (A. F. Kerenski's Reply to "Delo Naroda"), *Volia Naroda*, No. 110 (September 5, 1917).

[92] See chap. VIII.

[93] "Nedostoinaia igra" (An Unworthy Game), *Volia Naroda*, No. 110.

[94] "Letopisets" (Chronicler), *ibid.*

before. Party members rubbed their eyes in amazement at Number 145 of the *Delo Naroda,* where the article published over Chernov's signature was a monument of political castigation. Then came Number 110 of the *Volia Naroda,* and their distress was complete. The Alexander Nevski district organization in St. Petersburg spoke for others besides itself when it confessed to having read the latest dispatches with "fear and torment in our souls," and then went on to lament the harm done to morale by these exchanges between "Babushka,"[95] Chernov, and Kerenski, all of whom were held in equal esteem.[96]

The left wing of the PSR had long been all against Kerenski, and the right wing all for him, while the center had regarded him with a greater or lesser degree of indulgence, depending on whether it was the right or left center. Now one section of the center had proclaimed through Chernov that its indulgence was at an end, and it remained to be seen whether the rest of the center had also been alienated by the Kornilov affair or whether its trust in the architect of coalition would survive even this shock and cause it to pull in the other direction, fracturing the unity of the core upon which, in the last analysis, the life of this party depended. In the absence of a congress or council, the issue was fought out in the Central Committee. Fortunately, it is possible to look behind the scenes into the deliberations of this secretive body, for beginning with September the record of its proceedings is available, though only in skeleton form, the minutes for the earlier months having been lost or sequestered in Soviet Russia.[97] The committee at its meeting of September 2 had put aside for the moment the matter of the leftward tide in the party,[98] now running more swiftly than ever, but the bombshell of September 3 claimed its immediate attention. The next day the Committee asked Chernov for an explanation,[99] and at the session of September 6 both he and his adversary Avksentiev—that ill-assorted

---

[95] Party term of endearment for Breshkovskaia meaning "grandmother."
[96] *Delo Naroda,* No. 151 (September 10, 1917).
[97] Chernov, manuscript commentary on the minutes of the Central Committee, p. 4.
[98] *Protokol Zasedaniia Tsentral'nago Komiteta P.S.-R.*
[99] *Ibid.,* September 4, 1917.

pair of representatives in an ill-fated ministry—appeared to fight out the issue.

In a strong defense of his position—that is the way he himself speaks of it—Chernov argued the incompatibility of any other appraisal of recent developments with the SR theory of revolution. But Avksentiev declared that the party must not countenance action reflecting discredit on Kerenski, for he was the only public figure who could provide a broad and stable base for government through his ability to unite the socialist with the nonsocialist democracy. It was just this union of elements that neutralized each other which Chernov felt must now be discarded unless the February regime wished to forfeit the last shred of its popularity and condition the masses for the acceptance of Bolshevism. The immediate result was a victory for Chernov: nine Committee members adjudged his motives in writing the articles to have been correct, two found them reprehensible, and two others did not vote, including himself. One third of the members were not even present.

The very next day another session of the Central Committee, with a slightly different composition and in Chernov's absence, largely undid the work of its predecessor. The decision authorizing the editors of the *Delo Naroda* to publish a statement about the issue of September 3 was set aside in favor of "passing over the incident in silence." The vote was seven to six. Individual members of the staff, however, were to have the privilege of publicly "expressing their disagreement with the articles of Comrade Chernov." A resolution was then passed to the effect that "the Central Committee considers it necessary for the staff of the *Delo Naroda*, while subjecting the government to the most stringent criticism, not to permit the discrediting of individual members of the government who are socialists or to admit personal attacks upon them." This was a backhanded slap at Chernov and a backdoor revision of the previous decision in his favor, and three members of the Committee felt obliged to abstain from the vote on these grounds; two voted against it, and eight in favor. Finally, the Committee refused permission to one of its members, V. V. Lunkevich (LC), to answer the shotgun blasts of Breshkovskaia, which were hitting the whole party; her advanced age was taken into account, and also her past services to the party. The right center was disclosing its hand; it would cleave to Kerenski, and continue the experiment in coalition.[100]

The PSR was a remarkable party. Two members of the editorial staff of the *Delo Naroda*, Zenzinov and Rakitnikov—the latter curiously enough a member of Chernov's faction and his close associate in the agricultural ministry—promptly availed themselves of the opportunity to disclaim responsibility for the provocative articles of September 3, which had not been submitted to the staff before publication, and which were decidedly at variance with their own point of view.[101] The Central Committee, as we have said, had ruled against any corporate expression of opinion. Yet three days later the editorial board published a formal statement disavowing any personal bias against Kerenski but affirming its right to point out and condemn his mistakes—all the more so since he was a party member. The sharpness of recent criticism had been due to the burning issues at stake rather than to any ill will on the editors' part. They regretfully acknowledged, however, that certain passages in recent articles, as well as the intemperate nature of their tone and style, had created a false impression of the newspaper's stand.[102] Then, when Kerenski's defenders at the Fourth Congress asserted that the editors of the *Delo Naroda* had disavowed the attacks, Prilezhaev replied in the name of the latter that only Zenzinov and Rakitnikov had done so. The majority, denying any personal animus toward Kerenski and deploring the tone of Chernov's articles, had nevertheless agreed with them in substance.[103]

The Central Committee had also decreed the suppression of Lunkevich's reply to Breshkovskaia's campaign of disparagement. Yet two days later it appeared,[104] perhaps in watered-down form but in any

---

[100] Chernov, manuscript commentary on the minutes of the Central Committee, pp. 13-14; Protokol Zasedaniia Tsentral'nago Komiteta P.S.-R., September 6, 7, 1917.

[101] *Delo Naroda*, No. 149 (September 8, 1917).

[102] *Ibid.*, No. 151 (September 10, 1917).

[103] *Kratkii otchët o rabotakh chetvërtago s"ezda P.S.-R.*, p. 121.

[104] "Vynuzhdennyi otvet" (A Necessary Answer), *Delo Naroda*, No. 150 (September 9, 1917). The article took Breshkovskaia and the whole right wing severely to task for misrepresentation of the majority's course.

event breaching the wall of embarrassed silence which the Committee had chosen to maintain. These infractions against formal decisions might be set down to the looseness pervading the organization were it not that Lunkevich and other editors of the *Delo Naroda* were themselves members of the Central Committee. Apparently they felt no compunction over violating decisions adopted by a slender margin in the absence of a third of the membership, and apparently the majority agreed with them, for there is no record that it reacted to the infractions or even took note of them.

One would have expected, however, that Chernov would have shrunk from the consequences of his action, particularly in the face of the manifest displeasure of Gotz and his friends, hitherto so effective a factor of restraint; but such was not the case. Throughout September and into October he kept up a drumfire of criticism against Kerenski, unraveling the threads of the Kornilov conspiracy with mounting indignation as the evidence accumulated of complicity within the bosom of the government. He must have been mightily moved to cast off thus the submissiveness of earlier months and stoke the fires of party strife. Whether correctly or not, Chernov became convinced that Kerenski had been privy to the plot and had formed with Tereshchenko and Nekrasov an inner ring within the cabinet, the nucleus of a collegial dictatorship, which had not only kept the other ministers in the dark regarding developments but had gone behind their backs in dealing with General Headquarters. At first disposed to reject evidence of actual collusion between Kerenski and Kornilov,[105] Chernov learned that under the guise of military necessity and without consulting the cabinet, Kerenski had arranged to replace revolutionary units of the garrison with "dependable" units from the front, clearly with political considerations in mind.[106] He learned that when he had acquiesced in the extension of martial law to the capital in the belief that the city was being excluded from General Kornilov's jurisdiction, he actually had been playing into the hands of the conspirators.[107] He learned that official reports of

[105] "Razorvannoe kruzhevo" (Torn Lace), *Delo Naroda*, No. 154 (September 14, 1917).
[106] "Bol'she sveta" (More Light), *ibid.*, No. 156 (September 16, 1917).
[107] See his polemics with Savinkov in *Volia Naroda*, No. 116 (September 12, 1917), and *Delo Naroda*, No. 155 (September 15, 1917).

counterrevolutionary activity in the high command, made as early as August 11, had been disregarded.[108] Kerenski's conduct since the crisis—the continued collaboration with Savinkov and the refusal to arrest him after the final break, the astonishing leniency toward the plotters and the consorting with discredited elements—aroused his gravest misgivings.[109] Ceaselessly goading the minister-president, Chernov declared that the party awaited a clear-cut statement on the Kornilov affair, and an official investigation searching enough to disclose the guilt, not only of the active plotters, but of the accomplices who had deserted before the ship went down.[110]

Gradually he began to discern the outlines of a nefarious design on the part of Kerenski and associates to transform the inner ring of the cabinet into the actual government of Russia with the help of the generals and at the price of admitting Kornilov into the charmed circle, though not in a superior position, as Kornilov himself intended. But whereas Kerenski wished to proceed cautiously, biding his time until the Bolsheviks had taken over some of the more important soviets and rashly provoked another outbreak, the general "with the head of a ram," wishing to butt his way into power immediately, had summoned the premier to go through with his end of the deal before conditions were auspicious. The uwillingness of either to yield to the other the top position had completed their disagreement, and the explosion had followed.[111] To the jealousy existing between Chernov and Kerenski, and their political disagreement, was now added the fire of moral indignation.

An interesting by-product of the baiting of one SR minister by another was the final severance of ties between the party and Boris V. Savinkov. The ex-terrorist had long been estranged from the

---

[108] "Illiustratsiia tvërdoi vlasti" (An Illustration of Strong Rule), *Delo Naroda*, No. 157 (September 17, 1917).

[109] "Zanaveska pripodnimaetsia," *ibid.*, No. 151 (September 10, 1917); "Razgovor dvukh druzei" (Conversation between Two Friends), *ibid.*; "Kurs zigzagov," *ibid.*, No. 145 (September 3, 1917); Savinkov, *K delu Kornilova*, p. 29.

[110] "Eshchë odin dokument" (One Document More), *Delo Naroda*, No. 172 (October 5, 1917); "My zhdëm" (We Are Waiting), *ibid.*, No. 174 (October 7, 1917).

[111] Chernov, manuscript commentary on the minutes of the Central Committee, pp. 9-11.

movement and the impression prevailed that he had long since dropped out of the ranks and gone wild politically. But when the attention of the Central Committee was drawn to his enrollment in an SR organization at the front, it was moved to put an end to an intolerable state of affairs, for Savinkov's role at the time of the crisis and, indeed, for some time previously was too transparent to admit of further inaction. After the first commission set up to investigate the matter[112] had for some reason defaulted on its obligations, a new one was appointed,[113] and now neither Savinkov nor the Central Committee found it possible to evade the issue any longer. Savinkov ignored the summons to appear before the commission on the ground that he did not recognize the competence of a body, some of whose members had returned to Russia across enemy territory while others engaged in political activity detrimental to the country's defense.[114] These shafts were aimed at Natanson and Chernov, respectively. Savinkov conceded that because of his determination to yield in no way to the Zimmerwald spirit, he had not always found it possible to observe the decisions of the Central Committee; furthermore, he had never accepted at face value the conversion to patriotism of people who before the revolution had stood for their country's defeat.[115] Although he left the inference that he might be willing to give testimony to one section of the Central Committee,[116] that body could not but recognize that so gratuitous an insult to two of its members reflected discredit upon the whole group, and so forthwith expelled Savinkov from the PSR.[117]

The revolutionary wing of the PSR had settled accounts with Savinkov but its feud with Kerenski yielded less decisive results.

[112] Protokol Zasedaniia Tsentral'nago Komiteta P.S.-R., September 15, 1917.
[113] Ibid., October 4, 1917.
[114] Letter of October 8 to the Narodnoe Slovo (The People's Word), No. 106, as quoted in Revoliutsiia 1917 goda (Khronika sobytii), V, 51.
[115] Russkoe Slovo, No. 233 (October 12, 1917).
[116] K delu Kornilova, p. 29.
[117] Delo Naroda, No. 176 (October 10, 1917); Kratkii otchët o rabotakh chetvërtago s"ezda P.S.-R., p. 90; Chernov, manuscript commentary on the minutes of the Central Committee, pp. 29-30.

Only the Kamkov-Spiridonova faction would have cast Kerenski out of the party, but the Chernov faction now wanted to clip his wings. After the shattering experience of recent days, it was determined not to allow him a free hand in reconstituting the ministry, and one of Chernov's purposes in raking over the coals of the Kornilov affair must have been to hold before the eyes of the SR's the results of personal government. The political crisis that began with the generals' *putsch* lasted all through September and into October, its protracted character being an indication of how the situation had deteriorated since the similar crisis in July. The basic question concerned the experiment in coalition—whether it would be continued, and if so, in what form. As usual, the SR's did not react as a single party, but as three or four, and every day it became more apparent that their organization had entered the final stage of disintegration.

The position of the extremists was straightforward and clear. The right would leave Kerenski a free hand in putting together a government of all elements supporting the war. The left stood on its formula at the Seventh Council: an end to coalition, the construction of a homogeneous socialist government (just how a union of Marxists and Populists—or, for that matter, of one set of SR's with another— would be homogeneous they never explained), and the subordination of this new government to a mixed authority of soviets and democratically elected bodies, in line with the left SR notion of a dictatorship of the democracy (i.e., of the proletariat *and* the peasantry) as opposed to the Bolshevik idea of a dictatorship of the proletariat alone.[118]

The position of the center was much more involved and in reality consisted of two points of view which superficially approached one another but emotionally were far apart. Chernov's left center did not turn its back upon coalition per se but only upon that form which had twice been tried and twice found wanting. Approaching the problem from the strictly theoretical standpoint, this section of party opinion reasoned that while "predatory-Asiatic" methods of

---

[118] See resolution of the Fourth Kharkov Provincial Congress of the PSR, *Partiinyia Izvestiia*, No. 2 (October 5, 1917), p. 44; reports of the SR caucus at the Democratic Conference in *Delo Naroda*, Nos. 154, 160, 161 (September 14, 21, 22, 1917); Bykhovskii, *Vserossiiskii Sovet Krest'ianskikh Deputatov*, pp. 246-47; *Protokoly pervago s"ezda P.L.S.-R.*, p. 73.

exploitation were now being sloughed off, the role of capitalism in Russia was still far from exhausted, and that while landowners could only be counterrevolutionary, industrial entrepreneurs were still a socially progressive force.[119] With them, it was possible to work; with landowners, it was not. A deal could be worked out whereby the business class would accept socialization of the land and the SR's would agree that there could be no question at present of overturning the whole economic order. All of which, of course, was in accord with the fundamental SR theory of land reform in a capitalist setting. The strategy of Chernov was to clear the tracks for that reform, utilizing the victory over Kornilov to give the peasants satisfaction[120] and letting the workers wait until some future day when success in the agrarian sphere had guaranteed the fulfillment of other class demands. The chief obstacle to this scheme was the Constitutional Democratic party. The revolution had made it the guardian of every form of propertied interest, including the estates of the nobility, and it blocked the progress of the revolution in every sphere, including the agrarian. With it nothing could be done. But if the business interest represented in this party could be separated from the landed interest, the situation would be vastly improved: land reform would become feasible, the Kadet party would be fatefully weakened, and a social matrix provided for the growth of a progressive party which would enlist the services of Nekrasov and Tereshchenko and also, Chernov fervently hoped, of Kerenski himself.[121] But by what means could the sweet dream of laying the basis for a durable coalition, disrupting the Kadet party, and unburdening the PSR of its right wing be realized? By excluding the Kadets from power and offering cabinet positions to representatives of commerce

---

[119] "O postroenii vlasti" (On the Formation of a Government), *Delo Naroda*, No. 143 (September 1, 1917). The stand of the left center at the time is as accurately set forth in this lengthy editorial as it is inaccurately described in Chernov's embroidered analysis in his manuscript commentary on the minutes of the Central Committee (pp. 4-7, 16-17, 43), which was written years after the events in question.

[120] See extract from speech at the joint session of the Executive Committees on September 1 in *Revoliutsiia 1917 goda (Khronika sobytii)*, IV, 149.

[121] Manuscript commentary on the minutes of the Central Committee, p. 46; *Great Russian Revolution*, p. 282.

and industry with a broader point of view. Thus the left center arrived at its formula of coalition without the Kadets.

If no such political realignment could be brought about, however, and if no substantial bourgeois element came forward to participate in an honest coalition, then the left center would accept the alternative of a strictly socialist government. One would have expected that it would assume the initiative in testing its formula, or rather have insisted that the soviets or a representative assembly undertake the construction of such a government, but instead the Chernov faction contented itself with suspending the threat of a veto over any combination that might be worked out which did not accord with its specifications. The effect of this purely negative position was to leave the initiative in the hands of Kerenski, whose past efforts in the field had earned him the unreserved condemnation of the left center. The crisis was severe enough, however, to force Chernov and his friends to take up a clear position on two points: first, Russia could not afford the luxury of another coalition of mutual paralysis, and second, the Kadets were not to be included in the government.[122]

The right center naturally favored a coalition with the more liberal section of the bourgeoisie. It diverged from the left center in respect to the Kadets, not all of whom it was willing to place beyond the pale, since not all of them had been implicated in the Kornilov affair. It would distinguish between the sheep and the wolves, and while not insisting on an agreement with the party as such, it wished to renew the working agreement with such elements as the Moscow Kadets, who had sided with the local SR's in opposing the coup.[123] On the other hand Avksentiev himself proposed the exclusion of the

[122] The position of the left center has been abstracted from the speeches of Chernov and editorials in the *Delo Naroda* (end of August and generally for September), *passim;* manuscript commentary on the minutes of the Central Committee, pp. 4-7, 16-17; manuscript of chapter Partiia S.-R.; Bykhovski, *Vserossiiskii Sovet Krest'ianskikh Deputatov,* pp. 245, 248; Steinberg, *Ot fevralia po oktiabr',* pp. 104-5; Voznesenski, *Moskva v 1917 godu,* p. 117; Chernov, *Great Russian Revolution,* pp. 399-400; see also speech of Chernov reported in the *Delo Naroda,* No. 215 (November 21, 1917). The later writings of Chernov, extremely valuable though they are, do not always faithfully reproduce his position in 1917 and must be compared with what he said at the time.

[123] See Rudnev's speech at the Democratic Conference as reported in the *Delo Naroda,* No. 158 (September 19, 1917).

party center around Miliukov's *Rech'* because of its notorious antipathy to the government at the time of the crisis.[124] SR's of the right center thus favored a "broad coalition" from which only those groups guilty of having betrayed in one way or another their sympathy for Kornilov would be debarred.[125] Attempted subversion rather than obstruction of revolutionary demands would be made the grounds of exclusion.

While striving to salvage as much as possible from the wreck of the second coalition, the right center was prepared to concede to radical opinion in the interval before the Constituent Assembly an organ of public control over the actions of the Provisional Government. Gotz believed this concession necessary to avert the threat of civil war,[126] and even Avksentiev agreed that with so much authority concentrated in a few hands, a measure of control was justified.[127] Just who originated the idea that bore fruit in the Democratic Conference, and then in the preparliament or Council of the Republic, is uncertain: according to the right SR's, it was Chernov who thought up this "absurd project";[128] Chernov himself implies that the impulse came from the friends of coalition;[129] but apparently the first to broach the plan in public[130] was the centrist Menshevik Dan, perhaps the most influential figure among moderate socialists after the Kornilov episode. Be that as it may, the right centrists saw in this measure something more than a sop to extremism or a means to bridle Kerenski's impulses; in the organs that hitherto had exercised a measure of control, the soviets, their influence was slipping, and they were on the outlook for some new arrangement which, by

[124] Speech to the SR caucus at this conference in *ibid.*, No. 154 (September 14, 1917).

[125] See Avksentiev's statement to the Soviet Executive Committees in *ibid.*, No. 142 (August 31, 1917).

[126] *Delo Naroda*, No. 162 (September 23, 1917).

[127] See report of speech at the Democratic Conference in *ibid.*, No. 157 (September 17, 1917).

[128] "Nedostoinaia igra," *Volia Naroda*, No. 110 (September 5, 1917).

[129] Manuscript of chapter Partiia S.-R.

[130] See *Revoliutsiia 1917 goda (Khronika sobytii)*, IV, 104. It was Dan who in the Soviet Executive Committees on August 27 offered the motion in the name of the Mensheviks.

diluting the soviet democracy with more conservative elements, [would provide them with a new basis of power.[131]

It was therefore easy for them to accept the principle of ministerial responsibility, but that was as far as they were willing to go. They would not hear of an all-socialist government, and desired to leave the initiative to Kerenski in forming a new ministry.[132] They were purposefully vague in respect to its program[133] so as not to lessen the chances of a "broad coalition." Even had the right centrists not been so wedded to the idea of class collaboration, and even if they had not feared with Avksentiev that an all-socialist government would arouse hopes of the millennium among the semiliterate masses,[134] they really had no choice in the matter—the Allied governments had decreed the continuance of coalition and Kerenski was under heavy pressure to bring the Kadets back into the picture. Their devotion to the war left these SR's with no freedom of political maneuver; they would have to take what was handed down from above, and if that meant accepting the whole Kadet party, they in the end would agree, the right centrists proper with resignation and the hidden rightists in their midst (Avksentiev, Rudnev, and so on) with alacrity. Avksentiev indicated what was uppermost in their minds when, in an address to the Peasants' Executive Committee, he predicted that the new coalition would have to take over the war policy of the old;[135] and the coalition-at-any-cost mentality is best exemplified in Arkhangelski (RRC), who wished to capitulate right in the beginning by exempting bourgeois ministers from the jurisdiction of the new organ of control because their class would have minority representation.[136] In their approach to the alliance system

[131] Chernov, manuscript commentary on the minutes of the Central Committee, pp. 24-25, 44.

[132] From reports of conversations between Kerenski and representatives of the Democratic Conference in *Delo Naroda*, Nos. 161, 162 (September 22, 23, 1917).

[133] See pertinent comments of Avksentiev in *ibid.*, Nos. 148, 161, 162 (September 7, 22, 23, 1917).

[134] *Ibid.*, No. 160 (September 21, 1917).

[135] *Ibid.*, No. 152 (September 12, 1917).

[136] Bykhovski, *Vserossiiskii Sovet Krest'ianskikh Deputatov*, p. 247.

was to be found the essential difference between right and left center. The war had already all but sheared off the left limb of the PSR; now its iron wedge was being driven into the heart of the organization.[137]

With these premises and predilections the several factions plunged into the post-Kornilov crisis. The left went its own way, consorting with the Bolsheviks. The official leadership at first lost its presence of mind and was prepared to accept any kind of government, directory or otherwise, which would struggle against Kornilov.[138] Never did the SR's show to worse advantage in comparison with the Mensheviks than in high soviet circles on August 27: on the one side there was panic and planlessness; on the other, a businesslike disposition to come to grips with the problem. Having made this zig toward giving Kerenski a blank check to fill in as he saw fit, the Central Committee, as soon as its fright had subsided, then made the zag of forbidding him to include the Kadets in any new ministerial combination. For several weeks thereafter it wavered uncertainly between the two positions. The ban on the Kadets had been moved by Chernov, and the majority had accepted his motion under the impact of a wave of radicalism stirred up by the victory over Kornilov. Years after the event in question Zenzinov disclosed that he and Gotz, as well as Avksentiev, had opposed the motion of exclusion,[139] so that it must have carried through the defection of some of the less prominent right-of-center committeemen.[140]

[137] *Ibid.*, pp. 235-36; report of Avksentiev's speech at the Democratic Conference in *Delo Naroda*, No. 157 (September 17, 1917).

[138] See above, p. 388.

[139] Interview in Paris (September, 1935); interview in New York (December 25, 1949).

[140] Although Chernov nowhere treats of this matter—to the author's knowledge—but only alludes to it (*Great Russian Revolution*, p. 400), he tends to corroborate Zenzinov's statement and this surmise when he writes that September was the honeymoon month of the alliance of Gotz and Zenzinov with Avksentiev, but that they did not carry with them at first all of their supporters (manuscript commentary on the minutes of the Central Committee, p. 39). Sukhanov knew of the decision but possessed no inside information (*Zapiski*, VI, 37).

The effect was soon apparent. On August 31 Nekrasov announced a ministerial slate including certain Kadets who personally had not been compromised by the Kornilov affair and two prominent right-wing Socialist Revolutionaries—Avksentiev as minister of agriculture and Arkhangelski, the coalition-at-any-cost man, as minister of education.[141] Whether this action contravened the decision just adopted or whether it provoked it, is uncertain, since the time sequence cannot be determined,[142] but the news that Avksentiev would fill the post he had abandoned must have been highly unpalatable to Chernov and increased his bitterness against Kerenski. Whatever the details may be, the minister-president and the party were moving in opposite directions and a *démarche* had become necessary.

So on the night of August 31 two emissaries went to Kerenski in the Winter Palace and delivered the charge of the Central Committee, which has been dignified by the name "ultimatum," the second in six weeks' time. Kerenski was told that the Kadets had been so gravely compromised by the military conspiracy that the PSR must refuse to delegate a single representative to a cabinet in which they sat, and that in such a ministry Kerenski himself would lose the right to be considered as in any sense representative of the party.[143] Exclusion of the Kadets was only one point in the ultimatum. The others were that a socialist must head the Ministry of the Interior and an SR, the Ministry of Agriculture. Zenzinov advised the Fourth Party Congress that all three of these demands were accepted by Kerenski but that subsequently the skeleton cabinet was not filled out and thus the crisis was protracted.[144]

What he did not disclose to the congress was the manner in which

[141] *Delo Naroda*, No. 143 (September 1, 1917); Sukhanov, *Zapiski*, V, 336, 346.

[142] As the fragment of the minutes of the Central Committee salvaged from Russia by Chernov begins with the session of September 2, it contains nothing about the matter.

[143] Miliukov first has Gotz leaving the door open to individual Kadets—strictly in accord with the right-centrist position—and then depicts the SR's impersonally as hardening under the impression of the Bolshevik triumph in the Petersburg Soviet (*Istoriia vtoroi russkoi revoliutsii*, I, Part III, 16, 19).

[144] *Kratkii otchët o rabotakh chetvërtago s"ezda P.S.-R.*, p. 69. Other sources mention only the first demand; see Sukhanov, *Zapiski*, V, 350-51; Miliukov, *Istoriia vtoroi russkoi revoliutsii*, I, Part III, 15-16, 18-19.

the party demands had been presented to Kerenski. For the two emissaries were none other than Gotz and Zenzinov himself, and in discharging their mission they had not concealed from the minister-president their personal dissent from the majority decision.[145] Not for the first time in SR history had the execution of a decision been placed in the hands of its opponents, in this instance because they were friends of Kerenski and could break unpleasant news without a scandal, but in general perhaps also because of some tortured concept of unity. Half the force of the ultimatum was lost by the manner of its delivery, and while it had the effect of destroying the combination which had been worked out by Kerenski and announced by Nekrasov,[146] the minister-president knew his SR's and correctly sized up the situation when he decided not to pick a new slate but to leave the question open. He had but to bide his time in the knowledge that eventually the majority of the committee would accept whatever he wanted to do.

All eyes were now turned toward the approaching Democratic Conference as a means of solving the crisis. Whether the original inspiration had been SR or SD, the Central Committee approved both the calling of the conference and the plan of converting it into a preparliament.[147] The next step was to determine what kind of government the SR's wanted, and a week later the committee finally came to grips with the problem. It decided in favor of a coalition with "propertied elements" which would pursue a "firm" foreign policy and acknowledge the principle of accountability. The organ of control was to be a preparliament in which the propertied class would have only minority representation. The first proposition passed by a vote of ten against two; the second, by eight to one with

[145] Interview with Zenzinov in Paris (September, 1935). Fourteen years later and four years before his death, Zenzinov said he could not remember whether they had informed Kerenski of their personal stand (interview in New York, December 25, 1949). It may be noted that as time passed he became confused in his own mind as to whether the incident preceded or followed the Kornilov affair, finally settling on the later date in the Paris interview. His declaration at the Fourth Congress in December, 1917, ends any doubt about the matter.

[146] See comment in "Nedostoinaia igra," *Volia Naroda*, No. 110 (September 5, 1917).

[147] Protokol Zasedaniia Tsentral'nago Komiteta P.S.-R., September 4, 1917.

two abstentions. As a final safeguard, the Central Committee unanimously ruled against any further delay in convoking the Constitutent Assembly and unanimously agreed to impart the force of an ultimatum to this decision.[148] By evading the crucial issue of Kadet participation the committee had tried to hold the center together, and by confronting the Kerenski regime with yet a third ultimatum, and this time a real one, it had afforded the left center some compensation for a long series of decisions in the right-centrist vein.[149] Moreover, the prior ban against the Kadets was neither reaffirmed nor rescinded, and so remained technically in effect,[150] though the committee had begun to back away from it without having touched the hornets' nest.

A further indispensable step in preparing for the Democratic Conference was to tighten up discipline so that the party could speak with a single voice instead of several discordant ones. The committee brandished a stick at the left SR's in threatening "hooligan delegates" with "decisive measures up to and including expulsion from the party." It took more specific action in respect to its own affairs, deciding that its members must act as one, that they must vote as one save for the right of motivated abstention, and that even in closed party gatherings, where committee members were ordinarily free to voice their individual opinions, silence might be enjoined in certain cases. Only one vote was cast against these rules, presumably by Natanson, so that the center as a whole must have favored them. The immediate occasion for their adoption had been a protest from the Moscow branch against Chernov's attacks on Kerenski, reinforced by a similar protest from the Moscow provincial peasants' organization (in Moscow the party's management stood well to the right of center).[151] Yet shortly thereafter the same committee which had encased itself in a strait jacket threw it off completely by granting to members the right to act in the name of other organizations

[148] *Ibid.*, September 12, 1917.

[149] Chernov, manuscript commentary on the minutes of the Central Committee, pp. 18, 24.

[150] Chernov, manuscript of chapter Partiia S.-R.; statement of Richter at the SR caucus of the conference in *Delo Naroda*, No. 154 (September 14, 1917).

[151] Protokol Zasedaniia Tsentral'nago Komiteta P.S.-R., September 12, 1917.

regardless of party instructions.[152] Such an about-face in six days' time seems excessive even in the case of the SR Central Committee, but there was method in its madness, as we soon shall see.

The supreme party organ, of course, could no more still the clangor of factional strife than King Canute could turn back the tide, besides which it lacked the Norse king's sense of limitation. On the eve of the Democratic Conference, which would be the Russian democracy's last chance to straighten out its affairs, party life had degenerated into a state of civil war. Every gathering became a battlefield. Perhaps the best example of how badly the party was torn up is afforded by the caucus of peasant delegates at the conference, part of whom represented the All-Russian Executive Committee in St. Petersburg and part, the local soviets of peasants' deputies. The adherents of coalition were in the majority among the delegates from the Executive Committee, as one would expect, but this majority itself fell apart into a smaller group favoring broad coalition and a larger group which preferred Chernov's formula of coalition without the Kadets. Momentarily, at any rate, Chernov had cracked the citadel of the Provisional Government's support and Chairman Avksentiev was left fighting with his back to the wall. The delegates from the depths of Russia, on the other hand, arrived in bad humor because of the agrarian disorders that had broken out in Tambov and other provinces; they leaned toward the left SR's and opposed any kind of coalition.

A caucus of these discordant elements produced excitement if nothing else. Avksentiev was on hand to warn of an open break with the propertied classes such as had led to disaster in western revolutions. Chernov appeared before the vote was taken to rally his adherents, and the left SR's clamored for an end to coalition as such. First came the vote on the principle of coalition, which yielded an inconclusive result and much noise: 66 affirmative votes were recorded against 57 negative ones and 6 abstentions. Then came the vote on Chernov's formula excluding the Kadets. S. L. Maslov, soon to succeed him as minister of agriculture in the third and last coalition, openly defended this party on the ground that evidence against

[152] *Ibid.*, September 18, 1917.

it in the Kornilov affair was "inadequate," and the die-hards fought to the last to preserve the principle of a "broad" coalition, only to go down in bitter defeat by a vote of 28 to 95 with 6 abstentions. The left wished to take the construction of a new government out of Kerenski's hands and entrust it to the conference, but allowed Chernov to emasculate their forthright stand with his negative formula of no support to a government formed apart from the conference, its program, or organ of control. On the face of it, Chernov had inflicted a signal defeat on the collaborationist wing of his party in what had been the citadel of its strength, but only because of the grudging support of the left SR's, who on this occasion had allowed themselves to be taken in tow. He would not always be so fortunate.[153]

The Democratic Conference, like most revolutionary assemblies in 1917, was a huge and unwieldly affair in which the radicalism of the soviets had been balanced off against the cooperatives, municipalities, rural elective councils, and other bodies composed for the most part of war-minded and collaborationist intellectuals. Many of the delegates had no partisan affiliation, but of those who did, about 365 were SR's and 340 SD's of both kinds.[154] The two Kadets listed in the survey are no indication of the extent of conservative influence in this assembly, for there were many near-Kadets among the nonpartisan delegates and even in the socialist sectors. A lump figure for SR's, of course, had even less meaning in September than before, and the real question is what kind of SR's they were. Here statistics are still less satisfactory, but of a total of 293 for whom information is available, 191 were of the center or undeclared, 58 were "internationalists" or left SR's, 28 "defensists" or right SR's, and 16 Ukrainian SR's.[155]

The SR's formed the largest group at the conference and, if united,

---

[153] *Delo Naroda*, Nos. 156, 158 (September 16, 18, 1917); Bykhovski, *Vserossiiskii Sovet Krest'ianskikh Deputatov*, pp. 242-48.

[154] *Delo Naroda*, No. 156 (September 16, 1917).

[155] *Volia Naroda*, No. 118 (September 14, 1917).

could have wielded a decisive influence. Even if the center had been a solid mass, the effect would have been considerable. But neither of these premises prevailed. The caucus revealed three definite currents: for a broad coalition (with Kadets), for a narrow coalition (without Kadets), and for no coalition at all; or expressed in factional terms, right center and right, left center, and left. The first point of view was championed, without restrictions, by Mayor Rudnev of Moscow and Arkhangelski, and virtually without restrictions, by Gotz and Avksentiev; Chernov defended the second point of view; while Maria Spiridonova, Kamkov, and Mayor Karelin of Kharkov carried the banner for the left SR's. Two significant facts were at once established. The rift in the center, first noted in connection with Kerenski's candidacy at the Third Congress, and then within the confines of the Central Committee in the controversy over Chernov's articles of September 3, had now passed from the level of personalities into the substratum of political issues. The second fact to emerge was that no one of the currents commanded a majority. Thus when Gotz and Avksentiev put through a motion endorsing coalition in principle, it was immediately amended to exclude the Kadets, dissolve the Duma, and abolish capital punishment[156]—a result that satisfied neither extreme but only Chernov and his group in between. Since the decisions of the caucus were made binding on all SR delegates, the vote being 180 to 106 with 15 abstentions,[157] Chernov seemed to be in an enviable position, able to incline the balance at will.

But the left SR's spoiled his game—with the assistance of the Central Committee. With the binding of the SR delegates, the stage was set for divorce proceedings between the left SR's and V. M. Chernov. They had not been living together, in fact, since the return from exile, when Chernov had escaped from the influence of Natanson to fall under that of Gotz, and had thought to demonstrate how responsible a political figure, and later minister, he had become by turning his back on the extremists. The left SR's had remained for some time in the pose of the jilted lover, helpless in their isolation, but since they no longer were either helpless or isolated, their

[156] *Delo Naroda*, No. 156 (September 16, 1917).
[157] *Ibid.*, No. 154 (September 14, 1917).

despondency had yielded to resentment against their faithless mate. Gaining ground everywhere, and since September 10 in control of the big Petersburg local,[158] they were not minded to extend aid to Chernov in his belated break with the right, or on behalf of his weak and shifting positions. His record as minister had exhausted his capital on the left without gaining him any on the right. Spiridonova directly attacked him before the Petersburg SR's for having sat in the government and emasculated the party program; Karelin and Kamkov ridiculed his pet scheme for a progressive middle-class party.[159] The left SR's were determined to force the issues of land and peace at the Democratic Conference; consequently, they refused to be bound by caucus rules and went their own way, depriving Chernov at crucial moments of the strength he needed to commit the SR delegation to a narrow coalition. It had already been intimated to them that such defiant conduct would place them outside the party, when suddenly the Central Committee came to their rescue by granting freedom of action for all three currents at the conference, or, as Chernov bitterly remarked, giving carte blanche to everyone to do as he pleased and in effect dissolving the delegation.[160]

What possessed the Central Committee with its right-centrist cast to perform this service for the "near-Bolsheviks" on the left? Why did Zenzinov, keeper of the party's conscience, give to the left what he would censure it for taking two days later?[161] The answer is not to be found in SR literature—the fact is attested, censure is voiced, but no explanation is given. The only possible conclusion is that more was served by this action than the ostensible beneficiaries. And the clue lies in a parallel and still more extreme decision taken at this same eventful session—the aforementioned permission to members of

---

[158] See next chapter.

[159] *Znamia Truda*, No. 17 (September 12, 1917); *Delo Naroda*, No. 154 (September 14, 1917).

[160] *Kratkii otchët o rabotakh chetvërtago s"ezda P.S.-R.*, pp. 18-19, 91; Protokol Zasedaniia Tsentral'nago Komiteta P.S.-R., September 18, 1917. A right-wing member of the party, Podvitski, had the same thing to say about the committee's action.

[161] "Edinstvo partii" (Party Unity), *Delo Naroda*, No. 159 (September 20, 1917).

the Central Committee to act in the name of other organizations without taking into account party instructions. To understand this strange action, smacking of corporate suicide, it is necessary to know what had just transpired behind the scenes. The minutes of the previous session carry the entry that the committee accepted

the protest of Comrade Vedeniapin against the conduct of A. R. Gotz, who had called a special session of the Central Committee and then had not appeared at it, going off to another meeting where matters were decided which required the previous consideration of the Central Committee; also his protest against the way A. R. Gotz and N. D. Avksentiev had voted in disregard of a ruling of the Central Committee.[162]

Gotz had passed up a committee meeting summoned at his behest to consider a resolution for the SR caucus in order to go directly to the caucus and join Avksentiev in voting for a new coalition based on agreement with the Kadets, despite the previous ban on that party, and despite the unit rule of voting for members of the Central Committee adopted on September 12 at the insistence of Zenzinov and Gotz himself.[163] The dominant clique in the PSR was getting ready to breathe new life into the carcass of coalition. It made rules and set them aside according to what served this purpose to best advantage. The lordly behavior of Gotz shows that he considered himself boss, as indeed he was—of a shrinking fold. He did not have the votes to overcome both Chernov and the left SR's, and if they went together, as in the peasants' section, they could impose the party veto on coalition with the Kadets, which was now his most ardent desire. Hence the strategy of giving the left free rein to follow its own line so that it would not feel obliged to accept Chernov's as the lesser of two evils. The permission to committee members to disregard party instructions when acting in the name of other organizations becomes intelligible in the light of Gotz's selection a few days later as one of the representatives of the Democratic Conference to negotiate with Kerenski for the formation of a new government—with Kadet participation.

[162] Protokol Zasedaniia Tsentral'nago Komiteta P.S.-R., September 17, 1917.
[163] Chernov, manuscript commentary on the minutes of the Central Committee, p. 30.

This combination of centrifugal forces with smart politics caused the SR's to make a sad spectacle of themselves at the Democratic Conference, where they appeared, not as a party, but as three fragments battling for the succession. The first vote showed up all three currents. By an unimpressive margin (766 to 688 with 38 abstentions) the principle of coalition in the abstract received the sanction of the assembly. This vote earned Chernov the derision of Russia. Since an affirmative vote might have been construed as an endorsement of past coalitions, and a negative vote would have contravened the decision of the Central Committee favoring coalition on a restricted basis, he had felt obliged to abstain, and two score of his partisans had chosen to keep him company, making themselves ridiculous in the eyes of the country for the sake of a discipline which Gotz had not scrupled to flout. The bad impression was worsened by the failure to motivate the abstentions—as Chernov says in his private memoirs, because the committee had denied this right to its members.[164] But a glance at the minutes shows that this right was at first specifically recognized,[165] and that it was not withdrawn until the adoption of more stringent rules on September 27,[166] the vote in question having taken place on the nineteenth. It was not any slavish sense of discipline but his flabbiness which had caused him to act in this manner. For some time thereafter he was kept busy explaining away his abstention[167] until bigger events caused people to lose interest in why he had abstained.

After the decision in favor of coalition came the inevitable amendment to exclude the Kadets, and this also carried by a larger majority in a thinner vote, 595 to 493 with 72 abstentions. For a moment it seemed that the dead-center position of Chernov, and also of Martov, his Marxist counterpart, might become the position of the Russian democracy as a result of the nearly equal pull of the extremities, but

---

[164] *Ibid.*, p. 46.
[165] Protokol Zasedaniia Tsentral'nago Komiteta P.S.-R., September 12, 1917.
[166] *Ibid.*
[167] "Uroki soveshchaniia" (Lessons of the Conference), *Delo Naroda*, No. 161 (September 22, 1917); "Moi protest" (My Protest), *ibid.*, No. 215 (November 21, 1917). He gives a different explanation each time, betraying an uneasy conscience.

these quickly coalesced to crush the center. Gotz now threw off the mask. He announced that since no coalition worthy of the name could be formed without the Kadets, his group of SR's would vote against the proposition as amended and wash its hands of the consequences.[168] Spiridonova for the left SR's mounted the tribune to declare their intent of casting a negative vote out of repugnance for the very idea of coalition. The other proponents of coalition and the Bolsheviks reached the same conclusion from opposite premises, and after Chernov had vainly tried to prevent a vote on parliamentary grounds, only to be overruled by the Chkheidze-Tsereteli-Avksentiev presidium, the work of the conference went down the drain, 183 to 813 with 80 abstentions. The result, as Chernov observes, marked the "complete bankruptcy of the revolutionary democracy."[169]

The ensuing confusion enabled the presidium to take over step by step the task of working out with Kerenski a solution to the vexed problem of a new ministry, reducing the role of the conference to that of a recipient of *faits accomplis*. The line of the presidium was foreordained by its composition; already in the rulings accompanying the votes just mentioned, Chernov says, it tried in every way to advance the cause of coalition. Tsereteli dominated the presidium with Gotz and Avksentiev as his assistants. These three, together with Chkheidze, the two big-city mayors, Shreider and Rudnev, and two other men still further to the right, made up the delegation which deliberated with Kerenski over the formation of a new cabinet. Gotz and Avksentiev had in their pocket a ministerial slate prepared by Chernov against the eventuality that the negotiations would fail and Kerenski would decide to resign; on this slate the name of Tsereteli figured as premier and minister of foreign affairs, while Chernov remained on the outside, prepared, however, in case of need to return to his old post of agriculture or assume the duties

---

[168] *Revoliutsiia 1917 goda (Khronika sobytii)*, IV, 240; Miliukov, *Istoriia vtoroi russkoi revoliutsii*, I, Part III, 50; *Delo Naroda*, No. 159 (September 20, 1917). The central organ, characteristically enough, does not have Gotz come right out in favor of the Kadets, though from Berkenheim's reference to his announcement it can be inferred even from this source that he did. Miliukov (pp. 47-48) misrepresents Chernov's whole position in asserting that he and Tsereteli were personally prepared to defend inclusion of the Kadets.

[169] Manuscript commentary on the minutes of the Central Committee, p. 48.

of a new "ministry of nationalities."[170] But there was never any chance that this slate would be produced, even for the purpose of rendering Kerenski more pliant, for of the four SR emissaries, Shreider was the only one who could not safely be characterized as a last-ditch coalitionist, and of the other four, Menshevik or non-partisan, there is no need to speak.

With a delegation of this cast, it is not surprising that Tsereteli should have come back to the Democratic Council, as the shrunken remnant of the conference and the embryo preparliament was called, with an agreement which did not provide for turning land over to the land committees, did not offer any new departure in respect to war and peace, did not establish ministerial responsibility, and did not even dissolve the Imperial Duma. His SR confreres helped in this sell-out of the conference and of the demands of their party. Rudnev had readily agreed with the conservative elements that the conference could not claim to be the source of power[171]—this had been his position all along. Avksentiev had encouraged the other side and weakened the cause he was supposed to represent by conceding that the program advanced by the conference was too broad and would have to be pared down.[172] Gotz must likewise have made a contribution. That an agreement had been reached as a basis for the third coalition was largely due to the "readiness of the representatives of the Democratic Conference to abandon all their positions of principle." These are not the words of some sold-out socialist. They are the words of Professor Miliukov.[173]

The report of Tsereteli, couched in such fuzzy terms that Karelin could reproach him with having told the delegates less than they could learn from the newspapers, evoked impassioned debate and the worst scandal in the SR party since the days of Azef. Behind locked doors the caucus battled ferociously through the night over what stand to take. At first there was no majority for the agreement that had been made and, consequently, for the third coalition. But now

---

[170] Manuscript commentary on the minutes of the Central Committee, p. 48; *Great Russian Revolution*, p. 406.

[171] Miliukov, *Istoriia vtoroi russkoi revoliutsii*, I, Part III, 64.

[172] *Delo Naroda*, No. 162 (September 23, 1917).

[173] *Istoriia vtoroi russkoi revoliutsii*, I, Part III, 65; Chernov, manuscript commentary on the minutes of the Central Committee, pp. 48-49.

the fateful cleavage between the left center under Chernov and the extreme left of Kamkov and Spiridonova appeared in all its force. The state of feeling between the two factions may be judged from an incident that occurred at this time, probably in connection with these proceedings but not necessarily on this specific occasion. The left SR's were having a meeting by themselves when it was noticed that among those present was V. N. Richter, member of the Central Committee and of Chernov's left-centrist faction. He was asked to leave as an "outsider."[174] With such feeling between neighboring factions, to say nothing of those further apart, it was not surprising that on the night of September 23 the left SR's should have decided to pull out of the caucus and go their own way, especially since the Central Committee had built a golden bridge over which they could move into isolation. The sudden withdrawal of twenty-five to thirty votes in this manner left a small majority in favor of coalition and struck from the hands of Chernov the trump he had hoped to use. Not having enough strength of his own to best the Breshkovskaia-Avksentiev-Gotz combination, and desiring to set an example of party discipline—for whose edification, it would be hard to say, since everyone else was flouting it—he resolved not to vote in the plenum, but this time he motivated his abstention in language of quite exceptional vigor, pronouncing a malediction upon the "stillborn" creation and warning the democracy that in repeating an experiment twice found wanting it was committing a blunder that could scarcely be righted. Dan's resolution endorsing the agreement negotiated by Tsereteli then was passed, 109 to 84, the right and right center Mensheviks and SR's voting in favor, the Bolsheviks and left SR's against, while 21 other delegates joined Chernov in not voting at all. The Georgian generalissimo had prevailed once more, and for the last time—by a three-vote margin.[175]

But the worst was yet to come. After Kamenev for the Bolsheviks had brought passions to a white heat with his unsuccessful amend-

[174] I. Prilezhaev, " 'Levaia fraktsiia' sotsialistov-revoliutsionerov" (The "Left Fraction" of the Socialist Revolutionaries), *Delo Naroda*, No. 164 (September 26, 1917).

[175] *Kratkii otchët o rabotakh chetvërtago s"ezda P.S.-R.*, p. 21; *Delo Naroda*, No. 164 (September 26, 1917); Chernov, "Moi protest," *ibid.*, No. 215 (November 21, 1917); Sukhanov, *Zapiski*, VI, 177-79, 181.

ment to knock out the death penalty, the left SR's came forward with a still more crafty motion. Throughout the Democratic Conference and now in its successor, they had pursued the twin objectives of enlarging soviet representation—particularly from the provincial peasant soviets where they were strong—and promoting the agrarian program of the PSR. They now offered as an amendment to Dan's resolution the demand that all land be turned over to the land committees. This was a cruel motion, though one fully justified in the light of party decisions, for it placed Avksentiev squarely on the griddle. To make matters worse, the left SR's announced that they intended to observe how the chairman of the All-Russian Peasant Soviet cast his ballot. The conservative SR's were enraged. Amid Breshkovskaia's denunciation of obstructionists who kept bringing up "remote questions" and cries of "dirty demagoguery" from O. S. Minor, Avksentiev at first tried to slink out of the hall (according to Miliukov) but, reconsidering, he mounted the tribune to announce that the "SR fraction" would accept the amendment provided it did not endanger the coalition, in which case they would be prepared to discard it. Apparently his backers refused to follow through on this maneuver, for the amendment was voted down, but not before Chernov had descended from the dais and walked back and forth past the SR benches, observing how the members voted. This minatory gesture on the part of the dethroned leader provoked an uproar; he was greeted with abuse from the right and derision from the left. It was a never-to-be-forgotten occasion and might have stood as the low-water mark in SR history had not the October hurricane so soon thereafter swept over this unhappy party.[176]

[176] *Rech'*, No. 226 (September 26, 1917); Oganovski, "Edinstvo fronta" (Unity of the Front), *Volia Naroda*, No. 128 (September 26, 1917); Miliukov, *Istoriia vtoroi russkoi revoliutsii*, I, Part III, 72-73; Sukhanov, *Zapiski*, VI, 179-81; *Delo Naroda*, No. 164 (September 26, 1917). The SR press is as close-mouthed as the *Rech'* is loquacious on this juicy scandal; the *Znamia Truda*, organ of the left SR's, which could have been very helpful, has absolutely nothing to say, and Argunov's *Volia Naroda* gives very little, aside from the guarded statements in Oganovski's article. The *Rech'* correspondent lumps Chernov and the left SR's together. Miliukov draws upon this account but without the care one would have expected of so eminent a historian, and is definitely wrong in speaking of the motion as Chernov's; it originated with Alexander Shreider, nephew of the Petersburg mayor and one of the leaders of the left SR's.

The radicals had hit the conservative SR's in a vulnerable spot and maneuvered them into a bad position before the peasants' soviets, as is seen from Gotz's promise at the close of this beastly session to insist in the final negotiations upon acceptance of the SR agrarian formula. But the best he and the others could do was to secure a stylistic concession in the declaration of the new government which stated that farming lands *might be* turned over to the land committees in accordance with subsequent legislation "in so far as their proper exploitation could not be guaranteed under existing conditions" (the words in quotation marks represent Rudnev's interpretation of the official commitment,[177] which neither in scope nor in purpose came anywhere near embodying the SR agrarian formula adopted at the Third Congress). In the ensuing weeks the SR leaders again and again tried to reclaim what they had surrendered in the beginning when they permitted the new coalition to be formed without a hard and fast engagement to go forward on the agrarian front. The reason for their default, of course, was that the Kadets and also the business world which Chernov wanted to include in a new, denatured coalition had turned thumbs down on the proposal that was the heart of their interim agrarian program.[178]

Having labored to bring forth the new coalition and preserve it from the wolves in the improvised parliament of the democracy, the SR trio, who, with Tsereteli, had been the midwives of this abortion, still had to render an accounting to their party. Fortunately for them, in the interval between the Seventh Council in August and the Fourth Congress in December, the tribunal before which they had to appear was the Central Committee, where Gotz reigned supreme. It was no doubt with confidence that he came before it with Avksentiev and Rudnev to report on the negotiations with the Provisional Government. The committee, as might be expected, ruled in their favor, finding "that Comrades Gotz, Avksentiev, and Rudnev have fulfilled the task entrusted to their care in conducting

[177] Letter to *Delo Naroda*, No. 168 (September 30, 1917); see also Miliukov, *Istoriia vtoroi russkoi revoliutsii*, I, Part III, 74.

[178] *Novaia Zhizn'*, No. 136 (September 24, 1917); *Delo Naroda*, No. 163 (September 24, 1917); statement of Rosenblum in *Kratkii otchët o rabotakh chetvërtago s"ezda P.S.-R.*, p. 107.

at the instance of the Democratic Conference negotiations with the Provisional Government for the formation of a cabinet of ministers." But no one, not even a person initiated in the affairs of the SR's and inured to their manner of doing things, would have anticipated the way in which the committee arrived at this decision. Seven members favored its adoption; seven others did not vote at all, feeling that they could not pass on the matter since the previous action of the committee in freeing its members from compliance with party instructions when acting in the name of other organizations had itself been irregular.[179] One other touch to this fantastic scene: V. M. Chernov, who had opposed Gotz at every turn, was not even present to withhold his vote. Had he been there, the abstainers would have been in the majority.[180] And what that would have meant, there is just no telling.

All obstructions had now been cleared away and Kerenski could announce on September 25 the new cabinet, in which no big names from the revolutionary camp figured but only "third-rate forces," guaranteeing, as Chernov said, the colorlessness of the third coalition.[181] But less color did not mean greater sterility—Chernov himself with Avksentiev and others had seen to it that a cabinet of functionaries would in any event not achieve less than the "stars" who had preceded them. Numerous portfolios changed hands, but not that of foreign affairs; minister Tereshchenko remained undisturbed in that outpost of Entente diplomacy. There was one significant omission from the ministerial slate—no minister of agriculture had yet been named. To fill the position vacated by Chernov was a delicate matter, both for Kerenski and for Chernov's own party.

A backward glance at the Kornilov crisis and at the Democratic Conference reveals grievous mistakes and irreparable damage to the

[179] Chernov, manuscript commentary on the minutes of the Central Committee, p. 40.

[180] Protokol Zasedaniia Tsentral'nago Komiteta P.S.-R., September 24, 1917.

[181] Speech to the Democratic Council, *Delo Naroda*, No. 164 (September 26, 1917).

PSR. No wonder Chernov termed the conference a lesson never to be repeated,[182] or Zenzinov confessed to the breakdown of corporate entity and to the action of certain groups with the SR label but not of an SR party.[183] In addition to feeding the fires of extremism, the September crisis had renewed and disastrously deepened the rift in the center which first appeared at the Third Congress in connection with Kerenski's candidacy for the Central Committee and—less clearly—with the resolution on peace and war. The rift had been bridged over with the help of Chernov's elastic formulas; now the bridge was down and the architect of conciliation had himself become a partisan. The opposing stands of Gotz and Chernov in the September conferences signalized the division between the right and left center and created a sensation, for Gotz, unlike Avksentiev, was a true centrist whose veering to the right marked a major displacement of strength within the party. With Gotz and Zenzinov went not only the Central Committee but also control of the organization, for these two leaders supervised the functioning of the apparatus, maintained contact with party workers over the country, dealt with personnel, and in general gathered the threads of power into their hands while Chernov was writing articles. When Gotz joined hands with Avksentiev after the Kornilov upheaval to preserve the principle of a broad coalition in state affairs, a coalition within the party of all elements to the right of center had been formed which took over the helm and put V. M. Chernov in the hole.[184]

The "new course" manifested itself in various actions of the Central Committee, since apparently there was never any prospect of its commanding majority support among the rank and file outside of intellectual circles. The committee favored Avksentiev by advancing his candidacy for a place in the Russian delegation to the projected Allied conference in Paris as a "representative of the Russian revolutionary democracy,"[185] and by backing him for the presidency of

[182] *Kratkii otchët o rabotakh chetvërtago s"ezda P.S.-R.*, pp. 18-19.

[183] "O partiinoi distsipline" (On Party Discipline), *Partiinyia Izvestiia*, No. 2 (October 5, 1917), pp. 1-4; "Edinstvo partii," *Delo Naroda*, No. 159 (September 20, 1917).

[184] Manuscript commentary on the minutes of the Central Committee, p. 30.

[185] Protokol Zasedaniia Tsentral'nago Komiteta P.S.-R., September 27, 1917.

the preparliament, or Council of the Republic as it was now called
(after the Democratic Council had been filled out with bourgeois
elements). A choice more unrepresentative of the state of feeling in
the depths of Russian society or more acceptable to France could
scarcely be imagined. The committee sanctioned the replacement of
Chernov as minister of agriculture by another member of the party,
Simon L. Maslov, who stood much further to the right than his
predecessor had stood to the left, and who in his war-mindedness, in
his devotion to the cult of the state, and his lofty disdain for the will
of the dark and inarticulate masses, typifies the Populist intelligentsia
of 1917. But in picking out a man more in harmony with its own
point of view and much more amenable to Kerenski's leadership, the
committee attached the same conditions that Chernov was loudly
advocating, now that he was no longer minister: handing over the
land to the land committees, and releasing from prison members of
these committees who had been arrested for exceeding their authority
(literally, for "activity in these committees").[186]

Parallel with these actions of public import, the Central Committee adopted a series of measures indirectly or directly aimed at the
muzzling of Chernov. Having set aside discipline when it served their
purpose, the right-right-centrist majority now reinstated it with unprecedented severity as a means of coping with Chernov's campaign
against their policy of coalition. Somehow they seemed to fear this
docile but disgruntled man more than the left extremists, though he
did not conspire against the organization and his blows were like
feather pillows, whereas the left was steering a course toward schism
and Spiridonova would smite opponents with a heavy hand when
she came to power. Seeking in formal discipline the unity that it
lacked in reality, the Central Committee on motion of Zenzinov
adopted the following regulation by a vote of six to two with two
abstentions:

In all of its political activity the Central Committee must appear as a
single whole, and all of its members are bound by an inner discipline;
adopted decisions are carried out by the Central Committee as such, and

[186] *Ibid.*, October 4, 1917; manuscript commentary on the minutes of the
Central Committee, p. 50.

all members of the Central Committee are obliged to adhere to its decrees in each and every action of theirs outside the party, without the privilege of defending the minority's opinion, and without the privilege of voting contrary to the will of the Central Committee.[187]

In other words, no more denunciations of the third coalition, no more personal attacks on Kerenski, and especially no more motivated abstentions as in the Democratic Council on the memorable night of September 23.

Unfolding a quite exceptional activity, the Central Committee in a second session on the same day stormed the citadel of left-centrist opinion by introducing into the editorial staff of the *Delo Naroda* Vishniak of the right, Rosenblum of the right center, and Prilezhaev of the unpredictables.[188] This infusion of a more conservative element guaranteed that the central organ would become even more a swamp of contradictions than previously. Hitherto prevailingly left-centrist in tone—as much because Chernov wrote so much as because of the complexion of the staff—the *Delo Naroda* henceforth would have a balanced board, with four editors to the right of center (Zenzinov, Rosenblum, Vishniak, and usually Prilezhaev), four to the left of center (Rusanov, Lunkevich, Rakitnikov, and Chernov), and a secretary, Postnikov, who also was left of center.[189] Rusanov, Lunkevich, and Rakitnikov like Chernov were members of the Central Committee and bound by the same gag rule, but rules had never rested too heavily on members of the PSR and it cannot be said that there was any drastic change in the tone of the *Delo Naroda* after the addition of three new editors—it always had sung in several voices and continued to do so.

The new staff, however, did promptly disagree over whether to print an article of Chernov's entitled "Lessons of the Conference," which was to be the first of a series devoted to a systematic criticism of the mistakes of the revolution. The Central Committee stepped in to impose its veto[190] over the protest of Chernov, who wanted the

---

[187] Protokol Zasedaniia Tsentral'nago Komiteta P.S.-R., September 27, 1917.
[188] *Ibid.*
[189] See masthead of No. 166 (September 28, 1917).
[190] Protokol Zasedaniia Tsentral'nago Komiteta P.S.-R., September 28, 1917. An article under this title had been published September 22 as the first of a series, but apparently the author either then planned a new series or lost track of the earlier article.

article to be printed with the comment that the committee and the board did not approve of the contents; every party member, he objected, had the right of friendly criticism. But Gotz replied for the committee that Chernov was not "every member" but long the party's recognized leader, whose opinion would be accepted as the party's and would entail embarrassing explanations. "It is the tragedy of the PSR," Gotz went on to say, "that at the most critical moment of the party's life as well as of the revolution, the generally recognized leader of the party and the party itself should cease to understand one another and should go apart." To which Chernov replied that the party and he were one, as before, but that the party's high command had swerved from the SR line, with the result that it was becoming a staff without an army and was providing grist for Lenin's mill.[191] At least that is the reply he attributes to himself. And yet the relationship between these two had been such that one cannot help but wonder whether Chernov had not stood abashed in the presence of the man to whom he had so often deferred, and only later thought of this rejoinder.

In any event the two rivals parted unreconciled. Chernov adopted the strategy of allowing the "new course" free rein in the belief that it would discredit itself in the eyes of the membership. He says that he deliberately abstained from work in the Council of the Republic, considering it to be devoid of any significance, and also took a back seat in the Central Committee.[192] He was preparing to travel around the country and feel out local opinion as a means of testing his conviction that the Central Committee had adopted a course at variance with the will of its constituency, and probably also as a means of lining up support for the Fourth Congress, which would determine which fragment of the center commanded majority support and whether he or Gotz would have the upper hand. The Central Committee had canceled the Eighth Party Council, scheduled for October 1, and had canceled also the economic conference at the end of

[191] Manuscript commentary on the minutes of the Central Committee, pp. 49-50.

[192] From time to time he attended sessions of both, however, and even delivered a major address on peace before the Council on October 20; whether his aloofness was as sustained as he would have us believe is open to question.

September by a vote along factional lines,[193] probably because the adherents of the "new course" did not wish to face in the near future a higher party instance that might reverse their policy.[194] They had a good talking point, however, in claiming that only the highest authority could cope with the existing anarchy in the party—no one would dispute that—and the committee accordingly summoned the Fourth Congress for the interval between the November election and the convocation of the Constituent Assembly.[195] The left center planned to submit the controversy to the congress, in the meantime setting an example of discipline—which it forlornly hoped the left might follow—by holding itself personally at the disposition of the Central Committee and refraining from anything in the way of an "organization within the organization," though it did hold conferences with its supporters in the Petersburg local, where it was also in the minority, not, however, in relation to the right center but in relation to the extreme left.[196] Chernov and his partisans could await the decision of the Fourth Congress; unfortunately, history would not.

[193] Nine to four with three abstentions (Protokol Zasedaniia Tsentral'nago Komiteta P.S.-R., September 24, 1917).

[194] Chernov, manuscript commentary on the minutes of the Central Committee, p. 41.

[195] Partiinyia Izvestiia, No. 2 (October 5, 1917), p. 55; Protokol Zasedaniia Tsentral'nago Komiteta P.S.-R., September 28, 1917. That this claim was a rationalization rather than a reason is indicated by the original announcement in the Delo Naroda, No. 164 (September 26, 1917), where the prolongation of the Democratic Conference and the railroad strike are cited as reasons for canceling the council and the economic conference. This was the conference that was going to put specifications in the party's agrarian program and bring it out of the clouds.

[196] Chernov, manuscript commentary on the minutes of the Central Committee, pp. 50-54; statement of Gerstein in Kratkii otchët o rabotakh chetvërtago s"ezda P.S.-R., p. 90.

XI

THE RISING TIDE OF EXTREMISM

WHILE the SR's were engaged in high politics, their popular support was melting like snow in the sun. The turning away from their flag could be observed in all quarters, but the maximum loss was sustained among those who had been most endangered—among the soldiers, against whom General Kornilov's bid for power was in the first instance directed. Once the mainstay of moderate socialism in the urban soviets, where they wore the SR colors but were marshalled by Menshevik generals, the soldiers reacted violently to the attempt to plunge them back into the nightmare of carnage, repression, and caste degradation from which February had freed them. The cleavage between officers and men, bad in armed forces everywhere, was perhaps worst in the tsarist army, whence the Miliutin reforms had expunged the forms but scarcely the spirit of the lord-serf relationship. The reimposition of the death penalty had started the slide from Social Revolutionism to Bolshevism; the Kornilov affair now greatly accelerated it. The PSR fell into the ill graces of the soldiers because it had supported the Provisional Government, because Kerenski was a member, and because Kerenski had appointed Kornilov. It did no good to point out that Kerenski had denounced and dismissed Kornilov—the Bolsheviks and also the left SR's[1] were on hand to say that the plotters had merely fallen out over the division of the spoils. The story of the slide in the mother soviet of St. Petersburg, resulting in the enthronement of the Bolsheviks at the session of September 9, is well known and need not be recounted

---

[1] In a bristling attack at their first congress, Spiridonova summed up the left SR view on Kerenski's guilt, appealing to Natanson to corroborate her statements (*Protokoly pervago s"ezda P.L.S.-R.*, p. 36).

here.[2] A graphic example of the same process is afforded by the soldiers' section of the Saratov Soviet, which was reconstituted early in September. Before the Kornilov affair the soldiers had been represented by 260 SR delegates, 90 Mensheviks, and 50 Bolsheviks; after the Kornilov affair they were represented by 60 SR, 4 Menshevik, and 156 Bolshevik delegates.[3] Perhaps the most drastic turnover in the country took place among the soldiers of the Moscow garrison in the interval between the two municipal elections of June and September. On the first occasion, the garrison had given 70 percent of its vote to the SR's;[4] on the second, 90 percent went to the Bolsheviks.[5] Everywhere the same slide in the direction of extremism could be observed; only the proportions varied. At the front the SR's seemed to be in a better position, since the army committees were still largely in their hands and could be induced to take a stand against all power to the soviets as late as the second half of October,[6] but invariably in such cases either the front was remote from the furnaces of the revolution or else the committee had not recently been renewed. This discrepancy between the complexion of the army committees and the mood of the men down below was pointed out to the All-Russian Soviet Executive Committees,[7] but the SR and Menshevik leaders did not have the capacity either to see, hear, or listen, and continued to put their faith in the paper resolutions of rootless committees.

The shift within the proletariat was less sensational, because that class had been gravitating to Bolshevism since long before the Kornilov explosion; in fact, in some parts of the country—the textile towns of central Russia, the industrial areas of the Urals—the workers had

---

[2] The reelection of the presidium in the soldiers' section still gave the PSR a slight plurality, with 155 votes being cast for its slate, 138 for the Bolshevik, and 39 for the Menshevik out of a total of 336, but the catch is that the SR candidates were themselves extremists. See *Znamia Truda*, No. 19 (September 14, 1917).

[3] *1917 god v Saratove*, p. 11.

[4] *Volia Naroda*, No. 134 (September 3, 1917).

[5] *Ot fevralia k oktiabriu v Moskve*, p. 78; *Russkiia Vedomosti*, No. 219 (September 26, 1917), where the Bolshevik majority is merely described as "enormous."

[6] *Delo Naroda*, No. 186 (October 21, 1917).

[7] *Ibid.*, No. 181 (October 15, 1917).

been with the Bolsheviks from the start. The SR's had already conceded the majority of the metropolitan proletariat to their rivals.[8] But they had retained a considerable following among the workers and now had to witness this dwindle away. If we may believe the assertion of a radical SR from Voronezh, the name of the "right" (that is, official) SR's had become more odious to the factory workers of his district than that of the Kadets.[9] A woman SR complained that the mass arrest of radicals during Avksentiev's tenure of the Ministry of the Interior had made it very difficult to carry on party work in the factories.[10] In the Obukhovski Works at St. Petersburg, once a stronghold of Social Revolutionism, the reelection of delegates to the soviet resulted in the choice of eleven Bolsheviks and two syndicalists, not a single SR or Menshevik being returned.[11] With the soldiers now joining the workers in trooping over to Bolshevism, or at least to the SR insurgents, the ground in the urban soviets was getting hot under the feet of the regular SR's and they were being confronted with the alternatives of staying on in a humiliating position or withdrawing from the soviets and seeking to find a counterweight such as the leaders thought they had achieved on the national scale when they assembled the Democratic Conference and the Democratic Council. In very many instances the SR's bolted the soviets—they did this in Saratov,[12] in Tsaritsyn,[13] and Kiev,[14] to mention only a few—but their abandonment of these institutions to the extremists did not deprive the soviets of their authority in the eyes of the toilers, for whom these were, with all of their imperfections, still the primary organs of the revolution, not readily to be displaced by elective councils which made their appearance only months after the soviets and were handicapped by being called "zemstvos" and "dumas," which made it seem as though they con-

---

[8] D. Rosenblum, "Voina i revoliutsiia" (War and Revolution), *ibid.*, No. 134 (August 23, 1917).

[9] *Protokoly pervago s"ezda P.L.S.-R.*, p. 19.

[10] *Kratkii otchët o rabotakh chetvërtago s"ezda P.S.-R.*, p. 95.

[11] See the editorial, "Predosterezhenie" (A Warning), *Delo Naroda*, No. 165 (September 27, 1917).

[12] Antonov-Saratovski, *Pod stiagom proletarskoi bor'by*, I, 139-40, 146.

[13] *1917 god v stalingradskoi gubernii*, pp. 103-4, 107.

[14] *1917 god na Kievshchine*, pp. 235-37, 266-67.

tinued to be weighted, as under the tsars, in favor of the propertied classes.[15] By coincidence, the setting up of these democratic organs and the loss of ground in the soviets fell in the same general period of late summer and early fall, so that it would be hard to say whether the SR's, in turning away from the soviets, were prompted more by their dedication to the principle of universal suffrage exemplified in the zemstvos and dumas, or by chagrin at losing out in the class organs of the revolution. Gotz acknowledged at the end of the year that the tactics of withdrawal from the soviets had been grievously erroneous, even "suicidal," but when he says that "we always recognized that boycott tactics only played into the hands of our enemies by . . . cutting us off from the people,"[16] he is guilty of a major distortion, the best proof of which was the partial bolt from the Second All-Russian Congress of Workers' and Soldiers' Soviets at the command of Gotz himself, which resulted in the disruption, not of the soviet congress, but of the SR party.[17]

There had always been a tendency in SR circles, growing stronger with the adverse tide, to discount the will of the soviets as being that of but one segment of the population. The soviet process with its magnification of extremist minorities was contrasted unfavorably with the results obtained when all the people were free to vote according to the dictates of their individual consciences. But if the soviets represented only the toilers, they represented the majority of the people, and the contrast between soviet radicalism and the sober realism of democratically elected organs could be overdrawn. Before September was over the SR's were to receive a dreadful lesson on the chosen ground of universal suffrage as to how much support they had lost in the cities as a result of the experiment in coalition and the adventure of General Kornilov. Since the municipal election

[15] On the negative attitude in many localities to the zemstvos, see especially In. Rakitnikova, "V derevne: vybody v volostnyia zemstva" (In the Village: Elections to the Volost Zemstvos), *Delo Naroda*, No. 160 (September 21, 1917). The peasants in a volost of Tula province declared that "they did not want a zemstvo, as they had had enough of it under the old order."

[16] "Uchred. Sobranie i s"ezd Sovetov" (The Constituent Assembly and the Congress of Soviets), *ibid.*, No. 243 (December 29, 1917).

[17] These events will be described in the author's forthcoming book on the SR's and the October Revolution.

in June,[18] when the all-city council was chosen, Moscow had been looked upon as an SR appanage. The absolute majority in the council had placed responsibility squarely on the shoulders of this single party, and the local organization with its pronouncedly right-of-center cast had given the city a mayor in its own image in the person of V. V. Rudnev, who was so far to the right that he could have been a Kadet except for the sincerity of his democratic convictions. Rudnev, as we have seen, was one of the architects of the third and last coalition, along with his party comrades, Gotz and Avksentiev, and the Menshevik Tsereteli, but even as he was bringing the leaking hulk of coalition safely into harbor, his prestige was being sadly impaired by the results of the election for ward councils in his home city. To the astonishment of the country, the electorate now bestowed on the Bolshevik party the absolute majority which only three months previously it had accorded the SR's, and so badly slashed that party's vote as to cause it to come limping in a poor third, behind the Kadets, who were the secondary victors in this election. The table below will reveal better than words the magnitude of the party's disaster:[19]

Party	Actual Vote		Percentage of Total	
	June 25	September 24	June 25	September 24
SR	374,885	54,374	58	14
Bolshevik	75,409	198,320	12	51
Kadet	108,781	101,106	17	26
Menshevik	76,407	15,887	12	4
Other	11,086	16,160	1	5
Total	646,568	385,847	100	100

Had the SR's been better advised, they would have taken the lesson to heart and objectively analyzed the figures before them. But they were so eager to explain away the disaster that they could see only such superficial phenomena as the apathy and fickleness of the electorate, forgetting that stay-at-homes would have divided more or less in the same manner as participants, and dismissing as evidence

[18] See p. 240.
[19] *Russkoe Slovo*, Nos. 149, 222 (July 2, September 9, 1917); table taken from Radkey, *Election to the Russian Constituent Assembly*, p. 53.

of immaturity what actually was a testimonial to the growing class consciousness of the electorate. For the figures reveal clearly a building up of the extremes at the expense of the center, those who feared to lose from the further course of the revolution deserting the SR's for the Kadets, and those who hoped to gain, forsaking them for the Bolsheviks. The latter had attuned their agitation to the grievances of the poor and are said to have reaped a golden harvest among domestic servants as well as members of the garrison.[20] But whatever the leveling zeal of housemaids and cooks—Russians are an egalitarian people—and the disgruntlement of the soldiers, most of the Bolshevik support no doubt came from the simon-pure proletarians of this great industrial center. The SR's were attacked for having achieved nothing during their tenure in power except an increase in streetcar fares: "Of course, that means nothing to them; they have studied in universities and their income is measured in thousands of rubles, so they can afford to pay more, but they have no thought for the working people."[21] The SR's would concede nothing solid or enduring to their victorious rivals. They consoled themselves with the thought that only miracles could have satisfied so volatile an electorate, and that the lost voters would be no better Bolsheviks now than SR's in the past or anarchists in the future.[22] At first, one of the leading nonsocialist organs agreed with the SR's in predicting the same fate for the victors of the hour,[23] but two months later, after the November election, it revised its dictum and was constrained to admit that the Bolsheviks, like the Kadets, had "solid backing."[24] The dissident SR's on either flank were more inclined than the regulars to look for the causes of the debacle in the party itself: the right stressed the absence of enthusiasm and the lack of unity in the organization,[25] while the left shifted the center of gravity from the organizational to the political plane, contending that for a successful cam-

[20] *Russkiia Vedomosti*, No. 219 (September 26, 1917).
[21] O. S. Minor, "Moskovskiia pis'ma" (Moscow Letters), *Delo Naroda*, No. 168 (September 30, 1917).
[22] *Ibid.;* Mark Vishniak, "Moskovskie pobediteli" (The Moscow Victors), *ibid.,* No. 167 (September 29, 1917).
[23] "Uroki moskovskikh vyborov" (Lessons of the Moscow Elections), *Russkiia Vedomosti*, No. 220 (September 27, 1917).
[24] *Ibid.,* No. 257 (November 24, 1917).
[25] *Volia Naroda*, No. 134 (October 3, 1917).

paign an appealing platform was needed, as well as personnel, and this the party had failed to provide, preferring to live on its inheritance, for it would have starved to death had it tried to live on the miserable capital accumulated since the revolution.[26]

The towns had never been the center of application of SR effort, at least not since 1902, and as the early successes in them had exceeded the party's expectations, the adverse tide now running so strongly could be accepted, if not with equanimity, then at any rate without panic so long as the rural defenses were secure. And the SR's told themselves with a conviction nothing could shake that the village would never desert them. Disquieting signs they refused to recognize and rushed to confute them with wishful thoughts. When a Menshevik newspaper came out with figures purporting to show that 75 percent of the peasant representation at the Democratic Conference had favored coalition, whereas 72 percent of the working-class delegates had opposed it, the SR's found added support for their contention that the proletariat had gotten out of step with the rest of the democracy and was becoming dangerously isolated.[27] In general, they made every effort to depict extremism as an urban phenomenon. But what had the Democratic Conference really disclosed? In order to arrive at the figure of 75 percent as the measure of rural support for coalition, the Menshevik editors had made a composite of three groups, whose members had voted as follows:[28]

Rural Groups	For	Against	Abstaining (with Chernov)
Peasant soviets	102	70	12
Cooperatives	140	23	1
Zemstvos, etc.*	98	23	2

* Including provincial boards (literally, committees).

[26] "Zachem nuzhen s"ezd Sovetov" (Why a Congress of Soviets Is Necessary), *Znamia Truda*, No. 32 (September 30, 1917).

[27] *Delo Naroda*, No. 160 (September 21, 1917); "Golos Demokraticheskago Soveshchaniia" (The Voice of the Democratic Conference), *ibid.*, No. 159 (September 20, 1917).

[28] *Ibid.*, No. 159 (September 20, 1917).

It is at once apparent how the margin for coalition had been inflated by the inclusion of delegates from the cooperatives and zemstvos. Now the personnel of the cooperative societies had been chosen by the peasants as economic functionaries, not as political advisers, and reflected the outlook of the Populist intellectuals, but not necessarily that of the peasants themselves. As for the zemstvos, their title to speak for the peasantry was not as good in reality as on paper, for many had been elected in the face of widespread apathy or even latent hostility on the part of the rural masses,[29] and once elected, they stayed as they were, not being subject to frequent renewal in line with the changing mood of the electors. As the process of election was continuing into the fall, some of them had not as yet been converted from an appointive to an elective basis. While it would be possible to argue from the nonpartisan standpoint that the soviets, also, did not reflect the will of the whole peasantry, but only of its more active elements, it was not possible to impeach their representative character from the SR standpoint, since the party had always regarded these organs as the embodiment of the rural toilers' will and controlled them absolutely. At least the question of Bolshevik influence on the peasant soviets does not yet arise. And if we examine the stand of these soviets on coalition, we find that the margin in favor was by no means overwhelming, being only 55 percent instead of the 75 percent trumpeted by the Menshevik analysts through their SR amplifier.

But that is not the whole story. The delegation was made up from two sources, the All-Russian Peasants' Executive Committee established by the First Congress in May, and the provincial executive committees of peasant soviets, many of which had recently been renewed by provincial congresses of peasant deputies. It was the All-Russian Committee with its partially frozen personnel which had furnished the margin in favor of coalition; the majority of local delegates had been opposed. Few provincial executive committees

[29] Gaisinski, *Bor'ba bol'shevikov za krest'ianstvo*, pp. 119-20; see also comment of M. K. Volski on conditions in Tambov province (*Sovety krest'ianskikh deputatov*, I, Part II, 85); see also I. Rakitnikova, "V derevne: vybory v volostnyia zemstva," *Delo Naroda*, No. 160 (September 21, 1917); Chernov, manuscript commentary on the minutes of the Central Committee, pp. 19-21.

defended the thesis of class collaboration which had brought the peasants so little, but among these few were Kostroma, Moscow, Samara, and the Taurida. On the negative side, opposed to coalition, along with the left SR provinces of Kherson, Kharkov, Ufa, Kaluga, and Pskov, could be found the executive committees of Voronezh, Saratov, and other black-earth provinces, rock-ribbed strongholds of the party where there were no deviations, but only a dense gray mass of centrist SR's. While it is true that black-earth Russia did not speak with a single voice—Samara being one of the fattest provinces, and consistently leaning to the right of center—the stand of the Voronezh and Saratov soviets should have been the danger signal to the SR leaders as they drove headlong toward another coalition. Years later the editor of the peasants' *Izvestiia* admitted that the voice of the provincial delegates had been the authentic voice of rural Russia, that it had sounded the death knell of coalition, and that the SR leaders had disregarded it to their destruction, yet at the time neither he nor his colleagues could free themselves from the hypnosis of a "union of all vital forces."[30]

The welter of contradictions involved in any manifestation of the peasant will gave the SR leaders an excuse for disregarding symptoms of discontent. If Voronezh or Saratov had turned against the prevailing policy, Samara was still in favor. The state of confusion existing in the peasant mind is well illustrated by the action of the Penza provincial congress, which in one and the same breath pledged its support to Kerenski and demanded that he form a government exclusively of socialists.[31] But there was one symptom that no SR could overlook. Early in the fall, just about the time that the Democratic Conference was assembling in St. Petersburg, mass disorders broke out in the black-earth region, centering in Kozlov *uezd* of Tambov province, but spilling over into other districts all the way

[30] Bykhovski, *Vserossiiskii Sovet Krest'ianskikh Deputatov*, pp. 242-49; A.B., "Golos krest'ianstva po voprosu o koalitsii" (The Voice of the Peasantry on the Question of Coalition), *Znamia Truda*, No. 25 (September 22, 1917); Gaisinski, *Bor'ba bol'shevikov za krest'ianstvo*, p. 121. As usual, it is impossible to assemble satisfactory statistics. One source puts Bessarabia on the extreme right; another, on the extreme left. Some provinces were not represented at all; others, apparently, had only partial representation.

[31] *Partiinyia Izvestiia*, No. 3 (October 19, 1917), p. 45.

to the Volga and then becoming general over the country. Clearly the social revolution had begun, not in the towns but in the country, and not in the semiindustrialized countryside around Moscow with its pockets of Bolshevism but in the purely agrarian black-earth region, in the heart of the SR country. The SR's were badly shaken. Not only were the peasants getting out of hand but the seizures and premature parcelings on a purely local scale endangered the principle of equalization around which their whole program was built. The peasants' *Izvestiia* cried out for the laws which the coalitional policy of its publishers had blocked and would continue to block. "It is to the pain and shame of our country that only by bloodshed, insurrection, and arson can legislation in the interests of the people be advanced."[32] The nervousness of the SR's is betrayed in the way they were stung to fury by Lenin when he wrote that "the whole SR scum, up to and including the *Delo Naroda*, has taken to howling about land to the peasants, now that it has been thoroughly frightened by the [Tambov] uprising."[33] He was reminded that the SR's had promised the peasants everything at a time when he—that "twin of Stolypin"—had only the "cut-away lands" to offer, and that at their May Congress the SR's had already moved to put all lands under the land committees at a time when he was just being "unsealed."[34]

The party chieftains in St. Petersburg, still determined not to see the handwriting on the wall, might look for the hand of deserters in the Tambov disorders,[35] but for the local SR's there was no longer room for illusions. And so the whole Tambov organization, together with the soviet hierarchy, stepped out of line with the party center and with the All-Russian Executive Committee, and proposed that the provincial authorities put into effect the agrarian program without waiting for legislation on the national scale, which was never

[32] No. 111 (September 15, 1917), as cited in Bykhovski, *Vserossiiskii Sovet Krest'ianskikh Deputatov*, p. 241.

[33] *Sochineniia*, XXI, 335; Gaisinski, *Bor'ba bol'shevikov za krest'ianstvo*, p. 92.

[34] A. Lezhnev (pseud.), "Gospodinu Leninu" (To Mr. Lenin), *Delo Naroda*, No. 186 (October 21, 1917). The word "comrade" by this time had gone by the boards when the Bolsheviks and SR's addressed each other.

[35] Bykhovski, *Vserossiiskii Sovet Krest'ianskikh Deputatov*, pp. 240-41.

enacted.[36] This was a revolutionary step in defiance of constituted authority, and if it opened up a novel solution of the existing deadlock by combining coalition in the capital with revolutionary action in the provinces, it also marked the crumbling of the main part of the party organization, for, it must be repeated, these were not left SR's in Tambov who had entered the path of decisive and separate action.

This evidence of further disintegration in the central mass of the PSR, broadening and deepening the fissure that had first appeared on the surface when Chernov broke with Kerenski against the will of the Gotz-Zenzinov faction, was by no means the only effect of the Kornilov upheaval upon the party organism. The other was a rapid growth of the left opposition, expressed in battles to take over local organizations and oust the leadership in institutions under party control, particularly the peasant soviets. The left had already given a convincing demonstration of strength at the Seventh Council, and now it lifted its head higher than ever. In the city of Kazan the organization split wide open;[37] the province had been from the start under leftist sway. Information concerning Tomsk province is fragmentary, and the left may already have been in control, but in any event it had gained the ascendancy by fall, in both the party and the peasant organizations.[38] The Tomsk SR's, however, perhaps because of their remoteness, and in spite of the common bond of radicalism, preserved their independence and did not become closely connected

[36] *Partiinyia Izvestiia*, No. 2 (October 5, 1917), p. 45; decision of the provincial party conference in *Delo Naroda*, No. 165 (September 27, 1917); declaration of the provincial authorities and institutions in *ibid.*, No. 168 (September 30, 1917); Chernov, "Edinstvennyi vykhod" (The Only Way Out), *ibid.*, No. 168. The provincial authorities agreed, and issued instructions accordingly.

[37] *Protokol Zasedaniia Tsentral'nago Komiteta P.S.-R.*, September 4, 1917; *ibid.*, September 22, 1917; Chernov, manuscript commentary on the minutes of the Central Committee, p. 16.

[38] *Znamia Truda*, No. 35 (October 4, 1917). The issue contains reports of the congress of peasants' soviets and of the provincial party congress.

with the Kamkov-Spiridonova faction on the European side of the Urals.

The main battleground, of course, was the St. Petersburg organization, largest in the country and with an extremist minority which lacked little of being a majority, even when the tide was running in the other direction. Right SR's did not figure in this organization; the left center had been in control and now had its back to the wall in the struggle to retain its grip. The Seventh Conference had been set for Sunday, the tenth of September. Both sides put forth every effort to muster their strength. Present were 157 delegates representing 45,300 members. There was no question of having Gotz address this convention; he would only have sunk the ship for the moderates. The dominant faction threw Chernov into the breach and in one of the great oratorical efforts of his career, as official spokesman of the convention, he counseled restraint and ordered progress down the road of revolution without sudden lurches to left or right. He counseled against haste in calling a new congress of soviets, protesting against the violation of democratic principles involved in setting the soviets above bodies chosen on the basis of universal suffrage. He stressed the limitations of the former by characterizing them as organs suitable for mobilizing the forces of revolution or for providing political guidance for the masses but not for the business of government. He invited his listeners to peer into the depths of the nation, to consider the enormous number of people who stood apart from the political process, having nothing to do either with the soviets or with the election of public officials, and constituting an unknown quantity upon whom no one could count (implicit in this warning was the fear that the unorganized mass might become a reservoir of reaction instead of revolution). True to the formula he had thought up, Chernov denounced coalition with the Kadets but upheld it with intermediate and less rigid elements.

The extremists, however, were no longer willing to defer to the counsels of their former mentor. A whole battery of speakers arose to refute his arguments: Kamkov saw no sense in seeking a coalition with elements apart from the Kadets, who were not a landowners' party but a bourgeois party, and the only bourgeois party; Dekonski, Trutovski, Alexander Shreider, Algasov, and others demanded a clean break with the class enemy and a purely revolutionary government. The highlight of the counterattack came when Spiridonova characterized the policies of the Provisional Government as a stain on the SR record and personally reproached Chernov with having sat in the government and permitted the party's program to be warped and deformed. She had little confidence in the Democratic Conference, regarding its make-up as unsatisfactory, and if the new government that came from its hands did not give over the land to the land committees and establish workers' control of industry, she proposed to rise up and fight it with arms in hand.

After Zatonski and Boldyrev had spoken for the moderates, the guillotine descended on their remaining orators, Flekkel, secretary of the Petersburg organization, and Postnikov, editor of the *Delo Naroda*, and Chernov was given the floor for rebuttal. He frankly admitted that he had stayed on in the Provisional Government with "pain in his soul" and as soon as circumstances permitted, he had resigned. But he refused to go along with the left on its reckless course. It had demanded the amputation of the right wing of the party. "Do you really think," he asked, "that cutting off Breshkovskaia, Kerenski, and Avksentiev will be a painless operation?" A whole storm had been stirred up when he attacked Kerenski in the columns of the *Delo Naroda*. "I am not minded to take a crowbar and tear down the edifice that we, a handful of people, have built from the ground up, stone upon stone." He was ever the party patriot. Chernov noted that "Comrade Spiridonova hopes to cope with everything. I shall not serve in her dictatorship." Solemnly he adjured his audience, as a man who had seen much, not to enter the path of schism. Later he would talk as though a split had been inevitable between the PSR and what he said was not truly its left wing but an extraneous element to the left of the whole party; and he would confidently assert that the necessary amputation had not created an artificial majority in favor of the right.[39] But at the time he obviously tried to prevent a schism just because he did fear that Gotz and everything to the right of him might profit from the excision of the large and growing extremist minority; in fact, he

[39] "Ochishchenie partii" (Purging the Party), *Delo Naroda*, No. 218 (November 24, 1917).

specifically told his audience that if only they could stay together, meaning the left and the left center, they might straighten things out and save the revolution until the West was ready to come to its aid.

The Petersburg organization, however, rested on a broad stratum of workers and soldiers, and this constituency had been too heated up by the Kornilov episode to listen to counsels of moderation. When the vote was taken, the left prevailed by 83 against 7 with 4 abstentions, and the organization passed into its hands. There are 63 more votes to be accounted for, and where they were, no source explains. Presumably they were centrist delegates who simply withdrew from the proceedings rather than be put in the minority. A bare majority of 83 out of 157 delegates would accord with the virtually even split in the organization at the end of October. A new Petersburg committee was elected, predominantly leftist in make-up; Spiridonova and Kamkov were among those chosen, and also Algasov, Dekonski, Alexander Shreider, Trutovski, and Flekkel.[40] Among the spoils of conquest was the *Znamia Truda*, which now blossomed forth with the list of leftist demands: a general armistice on all fronts, a soviet congress, an end to coalition, workers' control of industry, land for the peasants (via the committees), and long life for the Third International.[41] All of this the right SR's characterized as pure Bolshevism.[42] But it was not Bolshevism because it did not call for all power to the soviets, and within the soviets the peasants' deputies were always to have an equal voice with the workers' and soldiers'. The Petersburg organization had gone leftist but it is a travesty on history to say it had slid into Bolshevism.[43]

[40] There were twelve members in all, the others being Zimin, Katz, Kliushin, Fishman, and Rosenberg. Flekkel and perhaps several others represented the centrist minority.

[41] No. 19 (September 14, 1917). Ivanov-Razumnik, no longer with the *Delo Naroda*, became one of the editors along with Kamkov, Spiridonova, Mstislavski, and others; see No. 20 (September 16, 1917); see also *Delo Naroda*, Nos. 157, 161 (September 17, 22, 1917).

[42] "K organizovannoi bor'be s partiinym bol'shevizmom" (For an Organized Struggle with Bolshevism in the Party), *Volia Naroda*, No. 117 (September 13, 1917).

[43] *Znamia Truda*, Nos. 17, 18 (September 12, 13, 1917); *Delo Naroda*, No. 152 (September 12, 1917). Only these two sources cover the conference and they do not tell everything.

With Bolshevism sweeping the cities, with the peasants getting out of hand, and their own extremists gnawing at the party vitals, how did the regular SR's propose to stem the rising tide of radicalism? Only by decisive action on the international and agrarian fronts could the situation have been retrieved at this late date—if, indeed, it could have been retrieved at all.

In their policy on war and peace the SR's could only move within the narrow limits they had set themselves—concerted action with the Allies abroad, and continued cohabitation with the Constitutional Democrats at home. Anything in the way of independent diplomacy they resolutely rejected, and they had just permitted the third coalition to come into being without taking any definite commitments on foreign policy or, indeed, on anything else. Since they would not move without the Allies, how could they move the Allies toward their goal of a general peace without annexation or indemnities, on the basis of national self-determination? One approach would be to persuade the Allied governments to accept these terms and revise their agreements accordingly, but even the SR's knew that this would be no easy matter. The second approach would be to bring the pressure of public opinion to bear on all the governments by establishing contact with the democracies of the warring powers and inducing them to accept the peace formula of the Russian democracy. The approach to the Allied governments would be through the conference in Paris in the fall of 1917, and the approach to the democracies, through the Stockholm socialist conference.

With reference to the Allied conference, the Central Committee decided on the principle of publicity for all political treaties which might be concluded there, and unanimously demanded that these treaties take the place of those concluded in the past. The conditions of peace should conform to the slogans advanced by the Russian democracy, and if such conditions were not accepted, that democracy should refuse to participate in the conference.[44] The chances were small enough that it would get anywhere walking into

[44] Protokol Zasedaniia Tsentral'nago Komiteta P.S.-R., September 30, 1917.

the lion's den with these demands, even had the Central Committee not already ruined the prospects by designating as its candidate for representative at the conference N. D. Avksentiev.[45] His choice meant standing at the door, hat in hand, and deferentially seeking permission to present the views of the Russian democracy in the least offensive manner, for how could Avksentiev be expected to press anything displeasing upon Poincaré and Clemenceau, the rulers of his second homeland? Moreover, if the Allies were disposed to listen to Russia in her unhappy state, it would be to the Russian government rather than to the unofficial voice of her socialist democracy; and in respect to the Russian government and foreign policy, everything was as it had been, with Tereshchenko still in office and Neratov at his elbow,[46] preserving the spirit and very nearly the personnel of the old diplomacy. When the SR's or rather their leaders accepted the third coalition, they accepted also a foreign policy very little of which was compatible with the principles they had proclaimed. Having fettered their own limbs, about all they could do was to criticize Tereshchenko and reiterate the threadbare demand for an active foreign policy pointed in the direction of peace.[47]

As to the Stockholm Conference, the Central Committee insisted on the issuance of passports and the PSR paid lip service to the idea.[48] But not much seems to have been done on its behalf after the debacle described in Chapter IX. Some members of the party like Avksentiev were determined to avoid even the suggestion of embarrassment to the Allies, while others had lost faith in the conference. Contact with socialist delegations from Western countries had impressed members of all parties with the tenacity of war psychosis in quarters that ought, according to their sociology, to have been free of it, and had convinced them of the hopelessness of expecting an early response to their appeals for peace; but the loss of their illusions had

[45] *Ibid.*, September 27, 1917.
[46] See *Novaia Zhizn'*, No. 124 (September 10, 1917). Gorki's paper, of course, had as its *raison d'être* the propagation of the antiwar point of view, but in this case there seems no reason to question its observations.
[47] *Kratkii otchët o rabotakh chetvërtago s"ezda P.S.-R.*, p. 67.
[48] *Ibid.;* Protokol Zasedaniia Tsentral'nago Komiteta P.S.-R., September 30, 1917.

not caused a reorientation of policy, either in the direction of a separate peace or of unqualified acceptance of the war.[49] Another factor deadening the sense of urgency in respect to peace was the widespread feeling that only the Constituent Assembly could come to grips with the problem in its fundamental aspects, and the tendency to leave it along with every other troublesome matter to the magic of that idolized institution proved too much for the weakly held resolution to advance the cause of peace in the meantime. The German government, of course, had done nothing to meet the Russian Revolution on a common ground of self-renunciation of imperialist ambitions, and here was another potent factor inducing paralysis in matters of war and peace. Imprisoned by their policy concepts, which left them no freedom of movement, and denied succour by either the Allies or Germany, the SR's persevered in their inactivity, waiting for the blow to fall.

Though there was no dearth of dire predictions in their press, it may be questioned whether the imminence of that blow had yet sunk into the consciousness of those who made their party's policy. An incident that occurred at the joint session of the Executive Committees on October 14 illuminates their state of mind. When delegates from the front declared that the situation had become intolerable and clamored for immediate peace, Gotz exclaimed: "I cannot believe that in the Russian revolutionary army there are units which would agree to the shame of a separate peace, and I am confident that in a crisis the Russian revolutionary army will fulfill its duty to the country and the revolution."[50] His words show that he had no understanding of the situation and no plan for coping with it.

If the SR's accomplished nothing at all on the peace front during the final stage of the experiment in coalition, they made a belated effort to put into effect at least a part of their interim agrarian program. Simon L. Maslov, as we have seen, was commissioned on

[49] Stankevich, *Vospominaniia*, p. 110.
[50] Bykhovski, *Vserossiiskii Sovet Krest'ianskikh Deputatov*, p. 268; *Delo Naroda*, No. 181 (October 15, 1917).

October 4 to enter the cabinet as minister of agriculture with the double stipulation that arrested members of the land committees should be freed and that a law entrusting the management of the land fund to the network of land committees should be enacted. Maslov got speedy satisfaction from the minister of justice and from Kerenski himself as to the land committeemen under arrest,[51] but the enactment of the desired legislation was another matter. Maslov labored under none of the disabilities of Chernov—he belonged to the opposite wing of the party, was on good terms with Kerenski and not on good terms with Chernov, knew the technical side of agricultural administration, yielded nothing to Kerenski in devotion to the cult of the state and probably excelled him in zeal for the war. Nevertheless he did not have smooth sailing.

The Maslov land law came before the government in mid-October, so laden with compromise, according to Chernov,[52] that Lenin could seize upon it as evidence of SR betrayal of the peasantry. But according to Maslov, he had to spend a whole week redrafting the law inherited from his predecessor in order to render it feasible and incorporate the basic provision for turning the land over to the committees—an implied rebuke to Chernov which seems to have been justified.[53] If Maslov's account at the Fourth Congress is followed, his bill did not meet with undue obstruction, but the impression conveyed at the time by reports in the press is quite different. He himself is quoted as saying that he anticipated the opposition of certain ministers; there were the stock objections on legal grounds, and the government is reported at first to have been inclined to regard the bill simply as raw material for a new law.[54] With respect

[51] *Kratkii otchët o rabotakh chetvërtago s"ezda P.S.-R.*, p. 104; *Delo Naroda*, No. 183 (October 18, 1917). Chernov contends, however, that many were not released until after the Bolsheviks seized power (manuscript commentary on the minutes of the Central Committee, p. 50). The answer to the contradiction may lie in Maslov's assertion that during his tenure of office no members of these committees were held in prison with the knowledge of the *central* government.

[52] Manuscript commentary on the minutes of the Central Committee, pp. 50-51.

[53] See chap. IX.

[54] *Delo Naroda*, No. 183 (October 18, 1917) in two places: interview with Maslov and report on cabinet proceedings.

to a related law on forests, the Kadets offered such stubborn resistance that Maslov said he could not continue work in the government under such conditions.[55] Bykhovski leaves no doubt as to the presence of obstruction[56] or as to Maslov's reluctance later on to admit the facts because of his extreme conservatism. Nevertheless, the general principle and several sections of the land law had been approved, and further progress was assured, in Maslov's opinion, when the ministry postponed further consideration in order to deal with the imminent Bolshevik rising, or else deliberately set the law aside to avoid the appearance of knuckling under to force.[57] Thus the SR's were denied even the partial realization of their interim agrarian program.

For it must be noted that enactment of Maslov's bill would not have fulfilled that program. Lenin fiercely assailed it as typical bourgeois reform legislation of the Irish type, from which every trace of socialization had been eliminated save social help to the landlord in collecting rent; the restricted scope of the law, the undemocratic character of the higher land committees, and the perpetuation of *pomeshchik* rights were the features he seized upon as constituting betrayal of the peasants' interests. "The SR's are not extinguishing but reinforcing the landowners' property," he wrote in his effort to make the most of the limitations imposed by the exigencies of coalition and the minister's own conservatism.[58] The arraignment on grounds of solicitude for the landowners' interests is without substance and convicts Lenin of demagogy, for the SR's never proposed to abolish private property before the Constituent Assembly; but in attacking the scope of Maslov's law he was on firm ground. The Third Congress had stipulated that all lands without exception should be placed under the land committees[59] and this decision of the congress, binding on him as a party member and doubly binding as the

[55] *Delo Naroda*, No. 179 (October 13, 1917).

[56] *Vserossiiskii Sovet Krest'ianskikh Deputatov*, pp. 264, 270-71.

[57] *Kratkii otchët o rabotakh chetvërtago s"ezda P.S.-R.*, pp. 69, 104; see also Maslov's statement in *Delo Naroda*, No. 193 (October 29, 1917).

[58] "Novyi obman krest'ian partiei es-erov" (A New Fraud against the Peasants by the SR Party), *Sochineniia*, XXI, 357-61.

[59] See chap. VI.

party's commissioned representative in the government, Maslov had coolly disregarded in bringing only the land rented to peasants or cultivated with their equipment or that left idle within the scope of the projected legislation. In general, that portion of privately owned lands which was farmed with the owner's equipment was not to fall within the committees' jurisdiction, and a provision that to a limited extent such property might also be taken over in cases of extreme land hunger is said to have been knocked out in subcommission.[60] While state and appanage lands were to go into the fund that was to be subject to the land committees, allotment lands were not, and the exemption list was swelled by properties devoted to special cultures (viniculture, horticulture, and so forth) and also, apparently, by ecclesiastical properties, unless these are considered as falling within the category of state properties (at least they were not specifically mentioned, although in traditional SR literature they had always been earmarked for socialization). Far from calling the minister to account for his deviation from the party program, the Central Committee did not even take notice of it, and only the *Delo Naroda* spoke of certain deficiencies, "which are quite natural in view of the complexity of the subject."[61] The import of Maslov's legislation was to end the exploitation of peasants by the owners of large estates; the purpose of the party program had been to end the estates. Under Maslov's law, kulaks were to be untouched; under the party program, their surplus land was to go into the common fund or be subjected to a differential tax. If the SR's took their program so lightly, it is not surprising that other people should treat it as window dressing.[62]

The SR's mobilized their remaining strength behind Maslov's law as though it were the answer to their dreams. The Central Commit-

---

[60] Lozinski, *Ekonomicheskaia politika Vremennogo Pravitel'stva*, p. 164.

[61] "Zavoevanie zemli" (Conquest of the Land), *Delo Naroda*, No. 185 (October 20, 1917). Later on a party member condemned the law on the ground that it left the door open to compensation (*Kratkii otchët o rabotakh chetvërtago s"ezda P.S.-R.*, p. 75).

[62] Morokhovets, *Agrarnye programmy rossiiskikh politicheskikh partii*, pp. 112-14; Alaverdova, "Ocherk agrarnoi politiki Vremennogo Pravitel'stva," in *Sotsialisticheskoe Khoziaistvo*, II, 174-75; Rosenblum, "Peredacha zemli v vedenie zemel'nykh komitetov" (Transfer of the Land to the Control of the Land Committees), *Delo Naroda*, No. 183 (October 18, 1917).

tee pronounced it a major step toward the realization of the agrarian program and directed all party organizations to popularize it and agitate for its adoption.[63] Chernov put off his departure from the capital to wage a hot campaign in the *Delo Naroda* for action on the agrarian front. Stressing the imminence of an agrarian revolution, and lashing out partly at Kerenski and partly at the Kadets, he reminded his enemies that the person of the minister of agriculture could no longer be used as an excuse for delay in a matter where one sensible law would be worth any number of punitive expeditions.[64] Others joined in the press campaign, nearly all of them from the same sector of party opinion.[65] The SR's also tried to open up a legislative approach to the problem by having the Council of the Republic (successor to the Democratic Conference) adopt their formula on national defense, in which the collapse of morale at the front was now definitely linked, without further attempt at dissimulation, to the recalcitrance of the government in matters of social legislation. In moving the formula, Rosenblum of the right center addressed the bourgeoisie in language of unusual sternness, accusing them of not yet being willing to recognize the revolutionary democracy and work with it in a loyal manner, but rather of seeking to undermine the partner in coalition in order to reestablish a monopoly on political power.[66] Acceptance of the SR formula would not have produced any drastic change in the situation owing to the failure to endow the council with parliamentary powers, but even this satisfaction was denied the hapless party when the autonomous left SR's spoiled the game by abstaining. As a result the majority SR's and their Menshevik

---

[63] See decree in *Delo Naroda*, No. 184 (October 19, 1917).

[64] "Edinstvennyi vykhod," *ibid.*, No. 168 (September 30, 1917); manuscript commentary on the minutes of the Central Committee, p. 51; see also editorials in the *Delo Naroda* during October.

[65] Arkadii Altovski, "V derevne (o rabote zemel'nykh komitetov)" (In the Village [on the Work of the Land Committees]), *Delo Naroda*, No. 170 (October 3, 1917); N. Rakitnikov, "Voina i zemlia" (War and Land), *ibid.*, No. 174 (October 7, 1917); S. Kallistov, "Zdes' ne mozhet byt' ustupok" (There Can Be No Yielding on This), *ibid.*, No. 182 (October 17, 1917); report from the villages by In. Rakitnikova, *ibid.*, No. 184 (October 19, 1917). From the right of center there is the article by Rosenblum, "Peredacha zemli v vedenie zemel'nykh komitetov," *Delo Naroda*, No. 183 (October 18, 1917).

[66] *Delo Naroda*, No. 179 (October 13, 1917).

allies could muster only 95 votes as against 127 for the nonsocialists and 50 blank ballots cast mainly by disgruntled extremists.[67] Still trying to work through the Council of the Republic, the Central Committee ordered its subcommission to prepare with all possible speed a land bill for submission to the council,[68] but the latter's agrarian section had begun to function only on October 18, after a ten days' delay occasioned by the failure of the nonsocialist groups to send representatives, and the Bolsheviks struck on October 25, leaving far too short an interval to overcome the obstruction that had cursed the Provisional Government every step of the way.[69] Try as they might, the SR's could not make up for lost time and bring their ship in before the port passed into enemy hands.

The oppositional trend in party circles betokened by the press campaign and these activities in the preparliament manifested itself

[67] *Rech'*, No. 246 (October 19, 1917); *Russkiia Vedomosti*, No. 239 (October 19, 1917); *Znamia Truda*, No. 48 (October 19, 1917), and editorial, "'Perekhod'" ("Transition"), in No. 49 (October 20, 1917); *Delo Naroda*, No. 184 (October 19, 1917); Sukhanov, *Zapiski*, VI, 281-84; Miliukov, *Istoriia vtoroi russkoi revoliutsii*, I, Part III, 142 ff.; Steinberg, *Ot fevralia po oktiabr'*, pp. 117-18; Vishniak, *Dan' proshlomu*, p. 311; *Novoe Vremia*, No. 14901 (October 19, 1917). The left SR resolution had received 38 votes. Once more the country witnessed the spectacle of a PSR split three ways. When the representative of the extreme right-wing splinter group, S. V. Vřoček (significantly, a Czech name), arose to announce support of another resolution, Gotz called out from his seat, "How many are you?" Naturally, this bit of information was not printed in any SR paper, where the rule was to hear no scandal, see no scandal, and think no scandal; it comes from the *Rech'*. Miliukov makes one Steinberg-Karelin the left SR leader—first the Jewish name and then the Russian pseudonym, in the usual order. But Steinberg and Karelin were two different people, they both went under their own names, and Karelin was not at all Jewish. As for the *Novoe Vremia*, it viewed the whole battle in terms of a set-to among "Talmudists."

[68] Protokol Zasedaniia Tsentral'nago Komiteta P.S.-R., October 21, 1917.

[69] Bykhovski, *Vserossiiskii Sovet Krest'ianskikh Deputatov*, p. 263. The author was chairman of the agrarian section.

in other ways. Everywhere there was growing restiveness and mounting criticism of the Provisional Government, everywhere irritation with the partner in coalition. Samara province with its kulak horde had steadily inclined to the right of center. The city had the biggest Bolshevik nest on the Volga but the province belonged wholly to the SR's. Yet when E. E. Lazarev, old-line revolutionist and present partisan of war, returned to his native heath he found conditions which to him were terrible—all he could hear were outcries against the Kadets and denunciations of the bourgeoisie. He could discover no sense of external danger—Samara was a long way from the front— but only the fear that the masses would be lost if the SR's ceased to do as the Bolsheviks were doing. No sooner had a decree been issued tightening up discipline than the soldiers deserted by whole commands to the party that promised an immediate end to war.[70] The stunning setback in the armed forces, once the preserve of Social Revolutionism, troubled many party members and bred in them a sense of frustration, as in international and agrarian matters. Army reform seemed as elusive as other objectives on which the great mass of party members were united. On October 20, five days before the final catastrophe, Chernov was still clamoring for the purge of headquarters which he had never ceased to advocate and always failed to attain.[71] Even in small matters it was not possible to obtain satisfaction from the coalitional regime which the PSR had helped to create and was still supporting. Central Committeeman M. A. Vedeniapin, in seeking to translate the remains of Kaliaev, Konopliannikova, Balmashev, and other heroes of the terrorist campaign from Schlüsselburg Fortress, where they had been interred after execution, encountered a stone wall of indifference and procrastination; his petition was first approved and then found defective; the prime minister sent him to the minister of justice and the minister of justice, to the minister of the interior, after which the petitioner's head was whirling and he had lost his sense of direction—and also his hope for action.[72] The petition had been drawn up in the name of the Central Committee. But that sorely tried body had too much other food for thought to experience a sense of humiliation in this connection.

[70] See his letter in the *Volia Naroda*, No. 125 (September 22, 1917).

[71] *Delo Naroda*, No. 186 (October 21, 1917)—in his speech before the Council of the Republic.

[72] "Izdevatel'stvo nad sviashchennymi ostankami" (Mockery of Sacred Remains), *ibid.*, No. 182 (October 17, 1917).

One expedient remained to the SR leaders and their Menshevik allies as the avalanche of extremism gathered headway from day to day. They could go to Kerenski and personally put the screws on him, as had been done with effect at the time of Chernov's resignation in July and again when the premier attempted to reinstate the Kadets immediately after Kornilov's coup. No sooner had the SR's allowed the third coalition to come into being without definite commitments than they resumed the old game of trying to foist their program upon a government recruited, in part, from the enemies of that program with their consent. At the beginning of October Gotz made a report to the Central Committee on negotiations with Kerenski, and it was decided to send a new delegation consisting of Gotz, Rakitnikov, and Arkhangelski, which "would try to prevail upon Comrade Kerenski to agree to the demands of the democracy."[73] The record of the representations they made is blank, but they did not succeed, nor could they succeed because the Constitutional Democrats would have vetoed any concessions the minister-president might have been disposed to make. With their ax on his neck, he would not move.

At the last possible moment, with the machinery of insurrection already in motion, the SR and Menshevik leaders decided on drastic action. Armed with a resolution of the preparliament or Council of the Republic calling for the immediate proposal—through the Allied powers—of a general armistice, the immediate turning over of all *pomeshchik* property to the land committees, and the advancement of the date for convening the Constituent Assembly, Gotz for the SR's and Dan for the Mensheviks went to Kerenski on the evening of October 24 and demanded that an official proclamation conceding these points be printed and posted before morning. To strengthen their representations they took along with them Avksentiev, who only with great reluctance had yielded to the requirements of his position—he was president of the Council—and to Gotz's pointed reminders of party discipline. The Avksentiev-Breshkovskaia or right-wing faction of the PSR had, in fact, hampered the formation

[73] Protokol Zasedaniia Tsentral'nago Komiteta P.S.-R., October 1, 1917.

of an opposition bloc and had obstructed the passage of the resolution in question out of a desire to give Kerenski unconditional support in the struggle with Bolshevism. But probably a deeper reason for hanging back had been the aversion to any proposal that would embarrass the "heroic Allies." During the interview Avksentiev remained silent most of the time and intervened only now and then to take the edge off the statements of Dan and Gotz. But it was all a futile gesture. An open breach was avoided, but no agreement could be reached; the Provisional Government smartly rebuffed the delegation, announcing that it would deal with the rising in its own way, and the socialist spokesmen on their part refused a blanket pledge of support to a regime which consistently turned down proposals that might have stilled the raging waters.[74]

This memorable confabulation found Kerenski indignant, Avksentiev out of character, Gotz taciturn, and Dan businesslike and self-possessed. Never was it clearer how decisions of the revolutionary democracy in the pre-October era were forged by Menshevik hammer on SR anvil. The episode marked the end of the honeymoon stage of the Gotz-Avksentiev marriage and the return of Gotz to a strictly centrist position, though whether under his own steam or as a result of Dan's influence we cannot say.[75] Perhaps Gotz and

[74] Dan, "K istorii poslednikh dnei Vremennogo Pravitel'stva," in *Letopis' Revoliutsii*, I, 167-75; A. F. Kerenski, "Gatchina," in *Izdalëka*, pp. 196-98; Stankevich, *Vospominaniia*, pp. 259-60; Sukhanov, *Zapiski*, VII, 135 ff., 145-47; Miliukov, *Istoriia vtoroi russkoi revoliutsii*, I, Part III, 208-12; *Istoriia grazhdanskoi voiny v SSSR*, II, 222-25. Precedence is given the account of Dan over that of Sukhanov because Dan's is a primary source, because it is far more substantial than Sukhanov's sassy journalism, and because Kerenski confirms its essential features with respect to the SR's.

[75] Owing to the kindness of A. F. Kerenski, sole surviving participant in this conference which preceded the birth of Soviet Russia, it is possible for the author to state definitely that Dan acted as spokesman for the delegation, and not Avksentiev, as one would gather from Sukhanov's garbled version. Dan associates Gotz with his every word and action, and insists, perhaps out of modesty, that both did the talking, whereas Kerenski states that Gotz as well as Avksentiev remained in the background (August 25, 1955, Hoover Library, California). Later he said that Gotz did take more part in the discussion than Avksentiev (September 3, 1955, Alum Rock, California). All sources agree that the initiative in bringing pressure to bear on the government through the formation of a leftist bloc in the preparliament came from Dan. The Menshevik leader carried Gotz with him and Gotz coerced Avksentiev.

Chernov would have found their way together again, reconstituting the poorly handled but numerically imposing center block of the PSR, had not the events of the following days divided them once more. Only by overcoming the rift in the center which began with Chernov's break with Kerenski and deepened at the Democratic Conference could the SR's have made themselves again a dominant factor in Russian political life. One veteran worker had immediately sensed that everything else would depend on the restoration of health at the center.[76] The left deviation sapped the party's strength, but the rift in the center left it nerveless and incapable of any action whatever.

Before the PSR began to recover from the Kornilov disaster, however, it was overwhelmed by the still greater disaster of the October Revolution. The rising tide of extremism had washed away its defenses in the cities and the garrisons, at the front and in the rear. The workers were by now mainly Bolshevik, the soldiers Bolshevik or left SR or on the road to becoming one or the other. Only the peasants remained, and the middle peasants as well as the kulaks felt endangered by the Bolshevik plan to sow dissension in the village through inciting the paupers against their less miserable neighbors.[77] But many peasants had become dissatisfied with the Provisional Government and with the never-ending counsels of patience by the SR's,[78] and these peasants had found a non-Bolshevik means of dissent in the left SR's, who were already strong in some parts of Russia and getting stronger. Moreover, it must always be remembered that, although the largest class, the peasantry was also the weakest.

When news of the impending Bolshevik rising reached the Central Committee, it "took the matter under consideration" and decided to "compose a manifesto."[79] There was little else it could do.

---

[76] In. Rakitnikova, "Eshchë ob edinstve partii" (More about Party Unity), *Delo Naroda*, No. 163 (September 24, 1917).

[77] Bykhovski, *Vserossiiskii Sovet Krest'ianskikh Deputatov*, pp. 272-73. The village SR's, of course, did everything they could to fan this fear.

[78] *Ibid.*, pp. 261-62; *Kratkii otchët o rabotakh chetvërtago s"ezda P.S.-R.*, p. 87. The Bolsheviks summed up SR agrarian policy in 1917 with a single word— "wait." See N. Rakitnikov, "Pobeda ili prestuplenie?" (Victory or Crime?), *Delo Naroda*, No. 212 (November 17, 1917).

[79] Protokol Zasedaniia Tsentral'nago Komiteta P.S.-R., October 15, 1917.

XII

MISTAKES AND WEAKNESSES IN 1917

FEW political movements have faced brighter prospects than the PSR in 1917, and few have ended so dismally. In the beginning everything seemed to be in their favor. People flocked to their standard like crows to a cornfield. The record of struggle against tsarism and the moral eminence of the movement endeared it to the educated classes, its record of service and agrarian program, to the toiling masses. It soon became the mouthpiece of most of the population, at the front and in the rear. Votes and bayonets[1] alike were at its disposal. Every election attested its popularity, every public assembly its power. And it was deservedly popular. An association of men and women more completely dedicated to the service of their fellow-beings and less swayed by personal calculation could nowhere be found, least of all in the older and most sophisticated democracies of the West. Men spoke of the party as "sovereign of the country's thoughts" without evoking dissent save from the hardened partisans of rival causes, which apparently had been left at the post in the contest for popular favor. Few would have ventured to predict that the dominant voice in shaping the destinies of the new Russia would not be that of the Socialist Revolutionaries. Why, then, had they fared so badly? Are they to be viewed as the victims of objective circumstances or as the authors of their own misfortune?

Some of the answers will have suggested themselves in the course of the foregoing discussion. The SR's had entered the Revolution of 1917 a party only in name. Actually they were a conglomerate of discordant elements contending for possession of a label that commanded the good will of rural Russia. The Social Democrats had

---

[1] One of the party's most active workers on the military front spoke of the "enormous preponderance" of SR influence in the army; see statement of V. I. Utgof in *Tretii s"ezd P.S.-R.*, p. 21.

long since chosen to face facts and divide, the factions gaining freedom of action by becoming separate parties; the SR's clung to the fiction of unity at the cost of continued paralysis, since common action was out of the question, and imagined themselves to be in a superior position. All they accomplished was to neutralize one another. Herein lies the explanation of the failure of the right SR's to adopt a firmer course, against which Kerenski inveighs so bitterly—they were preventing the left, or at any rate the left center, from itself adopting such a course. The war, as we have seen, was the great source of dissension in the SR camp. But it was not the only source. In a party that called itself socialist and revolutionary there was an influential element that cared little for socialism and less for revolution, save in a purely political sense, having sowed its wild oats in 1905 and now being desirous of settling down and enjoying the fruits of political liberty produced by the February Revolution; for this element the zeal for war had replaced the zeal for social upheaval. But there was another faction, less influential but with a wider popular following, composed of younger people who only now were having their 1905. These factions were estranged in spirit as well as in regard to the tactical problems posed by the war. They did not belong together and they ought to have separated, but the SR's could not even divide in the absence of leadership capable of taking stock of the situation and instituting divorce proceedings. Such leadership as they had was as infirm in purpose as the mass of the members were deluded in believing that unity could be purchased at any price other than mutual paralysis.

Later on, when disaster had overtaken the party, expressions of regret that the vain quest for unity had been permitted to hamstring its program were common enough, but at a time when the situation might still have been redeemed, too many shared Zenzinov's opinion[2] that the retention of unity constituted a major advantage over the Marxian rival. The absurdity of yoking people who were interested primarily in political liberty with apostles of social revolution came to be realized only in post-mortem analyses, when the explanation was sought either in the absence of a radical democratic party which

---

[2] "Posle partiinago s"ezda" (After the Party Congress), *Delo Naroda*, No. 70 (June 9, 1917).

might have drawn off the first element[3] or in the presence of too many intellectuals at the party helm, to the exclusion of workers and peasants, who might have weighted the scales in favor of social change.[4] However that may be, the fact remains that the PSR as an active revolutionary force staggered under the dead weight of members, often of great personal prestige, whose ardor had been quenched by advancing age or by absorption in the routine of social service, where bookkeeping replaced bomb-throwing and the ruble-and-kopeck mentality of the cooperative societies exorcised the spirit of insurrection more effectively than any means at the disposal of the old regime. As the editor of the central organ expressed it, "the PSR entered the revolution with cadres of practical workers who wanted to do everything gradually."[5] The head of the Voronezh Peasants' Soviet in 1917 observed some years later that "even at the present time the PSR is not a single party but rather a jumble of feuding political groups which could make up a whole parliament; in the early years of the revolution this conglomerate was even more heterogeneous and improbable."[6] He concluded, "The root of the party's misfortune lies in not having split on the eve of the revolution and in grossly exaggerating thereafter the importance of party unity, which actually existed neither before nor after the revolution."[7] But at the time everyone sacrificed on the altar of unity—even the extremists of right and left. They marked time without in any way changing their convictions, so that the unity achieved was of the most superficial kind.

Only strong leadership could have rescued the party from the morass in which it was mired, and such leadership was not available, if indeed one can speak of any leadership at all. It is not necessary to

---

[3] Steinberg, *Ot fevralia po oktiabr'*, p. 26; Spiridonova, "O zadachakh revoliutsii" (The Tasks of the Revolution), *Nash Put'*, No. 1 (August, 1917), p. 4; Chernov, *Great Russian Revolution*, p. 282. The analysis of Spiridonova, it should be pointed out, was contemporary rather than post mortem.

[4] *Kratkii otchët o rabotakh chetvërtago s"ezda P.S.-R.*, p. 64.

[5] Interview with S. P. Postnikov in Prague (September 6, 1935).

[6] Burevoi, *Raspad 1918-1922*, p. 121.

[7] *Ibid.*, p. 125.

go to hostile sources for disclosures concerning the state of affairs at the SR helm; V. M. Chernov himself has made them in terms more damaging than any enemy could. If one listens to Chernov, one would conclude that leadership was somehow out of place in a socialist society, which ought to lead itself with but slight distinction between officers and privates. At the root of his thinking lies the assumption that socialists were in some measure a race apart from the rest of men. When Vishniak asserted, in the course of one of those post-mortem flagellations in which the SR's sometimes engaged, that the party in 1917 had had several leaders and hence no leader at all,[8] Chernov censured him for accepting what in effect was a dictatorial principle, appropriate enough to a political movement built around a single individual, as in the case of Bolshevism or Italian Fascism, but wholly out of place in a democratic society. There the "choir" principle should prevail, as among the Mensheviks with their trio of Martov, Dan, and Tsereteli, the German Social Democrats, with Bebel, Liebknecht, and Kautsky, the French So-cialists, with Jaurès, Guesde, and Vaillant, and the Austrian Socialists, with Bauer, Adler, and Renner.[9] The SR trinity Chernov derived from himself and the two other founders of the party, Gregory Gershuni and Michael Gotz.

Unfortunately for the SR's, their trinity was no longer extant in 1917. The premature deaths of Gershuni and Michael Gotz had shattered the core of leadership and caused the party to enter the revolution with a yawning gap on either side of its chief intellectual force. No one came forward to take their place, and the genius of their surviving comrade lay in another plane, as he realized only too well when he pronounced the words, "orphaned party," over their graves. Gershuni had been the inspiration behind the terror, and his ability to captivate the minds of others had been matched only by his strength of character. Chernov says that Lenin owed his repu-tation as the most strong-willed of the revolutionary leaders to Gershuni's death. The revolution had given the Bolshevik boss his

<hr />

[8] "Tsena soiuza," *Dni*, No. 263 (September 13, 1923).

[9] "Otkliki pressy" (Comments of the Press), *Revoliutsionnaia Rossiia*, No. 32 (December, 1923), p. 19; manuscript of chapter Partiia S.-R.

pass from the underground to a place in the sun; fate had denied that favor to Gershuni. In the original core of leadership of the Socialist Revolutionary party, he had been the field commander, while the elder Gotz had combined the functions of chief of staff and quartermaster-general (he also controlled the purse strings, partly because of his wealth and partly because business ability is always at a premium in a society of idealists); thus relieved of the practical duties of leadership, Chernov could float away into the realm of theory, there to construct the ideology of the movement and formulate its program and the principles of its strategy and tactics. The division of labor was so natural and the relationship so intimate that, truly, a trinity resulted—three aspects of a single whole—in which Gershuni was the will, Gotz the heart, and Chernov the brain.[10]

Whether fate was to blame for disrupting this inimitable combination, while leaving the high command of other parties intact, or whether the qualities of Gotz and Gershuni have been magnified in the memory of their friend and collaborator, only those who combine sober judgment with an intimate knowledge of the personalities concerned could answer. But it may be doubted that men who had been so woefully deceived by Azef could have gauged the depth of social forces a decade later, or that a union forged in the wilderness of irresponsibility could have passed through the fires of war and the assumption of power in 1917 without gravely straining that inner harmony which was its proudest boast.

In any event, there can be no doubt that the surviving member was unequal to the burden. On this, not only the record but also the testimony speaks with rare unanimity. And when Chernov adds his own appraisal of his role in 1917, nothing else is needed. He had never held the threads of organization in his hands nor sought to staff party offices with a hand-picked personnel. In the era of the first revolution Gershuni and the elder Gotz had attended to these matters; in 1917 they devolved upon Zenzinov and the younger Gotz. The party position of Chernov is comparable to that of Lenin only in respect to ideology and literary activity. Here he stands supreme

[10] Chernov, manuscript of chapter Partiia S.-R.

and unchallenged, and Sukhanov is correct in saying that if his work were subtracted from SR literature, almost nothing would remain. But otherwise he made no contribution. While Lenin, with Sverdlov's oft-ignored assistance, fashioned his whole party, organizationally as well as ideologically, Chernov supplied only some of the essential elements. If the machine escaped his control in 1917, it was not surprising.

But we should let Chernov speak for himself. He attributes much of the trouble to his "broad Slavonic nature," which induced complaisance and procrastination, and excessive softness in dealings with others. He lacked a singleness of purpose and the ambition and love of power which in the political arena are essential to success. He was "more a theorist, a man of the writing table and platform, than a professional politician." He made a speech or wrote an article and then rested on his laurels, content with the acclaim of the moment, instead of taking in hand the task of translating oratorical injunctions into party policies. "An inclination to go off into the world of ideas, of social diagnosis and prognosis . . . united in him with a tendency to leave the management of political affairs to others." The original team permitted him to indulge himself without disadvantage, but it was otherwise in 1917, when the ascendancy of the younger Gotz led Chernov to observe that "he had been more trusting in people than is fitting in politics." He freely conceded that his efforts to exemplify the observance of discipline through silence or abstention from voting at decisive moments, when others were acting without regard for the fickle decisions of the Central Committee, had been unavailing, and he regretted that in seeking to ease the strain on party ties and avoid the appearance of personal motives in his dispute with Kerenski he had failed to defend his position with sufficient clarity or vigor. It had been his hope that with restraint and the passing of time his position would be sustained and the party line rectified without painful incidents. "His motives may perhaps be adjudged honorable, but since in the end a party schism—and even schisms—could not be avoided, it must be admitted that to the fetish of an already unattainable unity he sacrificed a vigorous defense of that very line of action which, at his behest, the party had adopted.[11]

[11] Manuscript of chapter Partiia S.-R.; Sukhanov, Zapiski, III, 140-44.

Thus Chernov and his critics are in agreement as to his role in 1917. One competent witness says that he did not struggle against the "defensist" majority of the SR leadership so much as he intrigued against it.[12] Sukhanov's charge that he exhibited not the least constancy, belligerency, or firmness in pursuit of his objectives is nowhere better illustrated than in respect to the purge of the army high command, a measure for which he was clamoring in the fall after having deprecated its urgency in May on the ground that offending generals had already been removed and that to change a whole staff in the midst of war was no simple matter. He had warned that then less than ever was the time to be ruled by impatience.[13] Responsibility for tolerating a mentality at headquarters which would eventuate in the Kornilov affair rests, therefore, not alone on Kerenski's shoulders but also on those of his rival, whose belated campaign for a housecleaning came when the chances of a moderate outcome for the revolution were already hopelessly compromised. The same could be said of other issues equally important if less urgent in character.

To say that the PSR lacked competent leadership in 1917 is by no means to say that it was devoid of political talent. The younger Gotz, Zenzinov, and Avksentiev seem to have been men of rather average ability, but Chernov and his adversary Kerenski, for all of their faults, were outstanding personalities. Chernov had a splendid mind and his powers of social analysis lifted him out of the category of sectarian prophets and deposited him on the same level with Witte and Durnovo. In his thinking there was a strain of pessimism and a sense of limitation which lessened his effectiveness as a revolutionary leader but increased his philosophical stature. If new social orders cannot be instituted without the ruthlessness of a Lenin, neither can they be operated successfully or advance toward their goals without the humanity and distant vision of his despised Narodnik foe. If

[12] Stankevich, *Vospominaniia*, p. 279.
[13] Report of a speech at the Northern Regional Conference in *Delo Naroda*, No. 57 (May 25, 1917).

Chernov could only have had some of the steel in Lenin's character, while remaining himself in other respects, he would have been a force to be reckoned with. But, alas, his intellect and vision were combined with weakness of will, to his own undoing and the ruin of his party.

As for Kerenski, he was never at home in the PSR. Chernov, his enemy, says that he fell like a body from another planet into this party, in the ranks of which he was from start to finish an independent and self-willed quantity,[14] and Zenzinov, his friend, says that Kerenski's whole relationship to the organization was to a high degree abnormal.[15] But it was not simply a one-sided story of the old guard's refusal to accept a newcomer, or of Kerenski's "Duma social revolutionism" versus the orthodox brand of the Central Committee, rooted as it was in the underground (for Kerenski also had connections with the underground). The truth of the matter is that Kerenski assumed a party coloration in 1917 much as a hapless American schoolteacher chooses a church affiliation when he had rather belong to none. It seemed the thing to do, and besides he was already a member. But partisan ties were less binding upon a Duma member in 1916 than upon a minister of state in 1917, and all through the year Kerenski chafed under the necessity of taking into account partisan claims, when in his heart he acknowledged only those of the state. He explained to the comrades in Kiev why he could not become too deeply involved in partisan affairs: "It would be a great mistake if I used my power in the name of party interests."[16] These words go far to explain his failure to cooperate in carrying out the SR program in 1917. Still more significant was his remark on May 22 to the Petersburg Soviet: "Parties do not exist for me at present because I am a Russian minister; the people alone exists, and one sacred law—to obey the majority will."[17] Chernov once remarked to this author that Kerenski's tendency to set the state above classes and parties established a certain affinity between him and fascism,

---

[14] Manuscript of chapter Partiia S.-R.
[15] *Kratkii otchët o rabotakh chetvërtago s"ezda P.S.-R.*, p. 90.
[16] *Volia Naroda*, No. 21 (May 24, 1917).
[17] *Delo Naroda*, No. 56 (May 24, 1917).

though in other respects, of course, his devotion to democracy was not to be questioned.[18] It was not, however, merely his aversion to partisanship which separated Kerenski from the party but also his preference for moderation. Essentially he was neither a socialist nor a revolutionary but a nineteenth- or early twentieth-century radical of the French, or perhaps even more, the British type, a St. Petersburg attorney who consorted with the left without accepting its ultimate objectives. In the words of a not-altogether hostile critic who knew him well, he was rooted in liberal society and neither by inclination nor habit showed himself to be a man of the mass socialist movement.[19] He had once expressed a definite preference for Mirabeau over Danton or Robespierre,[20] and he always had a deep regard for human life which affected his views on war as well as on revolution.

In looking back over the past from the vantage ground of an elder statesman, Kerenski considers his gravest error in 1917 to have been his partisan affiliation,[21] which prevented him from assuming the role which his heart dictated and to which his policies largely conformed—that of an impartial guardian of state interests, an arbiter above the fray, in the interval between the collapse of the monarchy and the convocation of the Constituent Assembly. Now it seems clear that Kerenski committed graver errors than adherence to this ill-fated party, but it is true that nothing violated his conscience more. It would have been better for him and for the party had he followed his inner feelings in the matter and preserved his independence, formally as well as actually. The "great complications," according to Chernov,[22] that arose for the party because of having his name on its rolls would have been obviated, and both sides would have been relieved of the strain of an unnatural connection. It seems unlikely that the absence of partisan ties would have impeded Kerenski's career or kept him from progressing from the Ministry of Justice to the Ministry of War and then to the presidency of the

[18] Prague, 1934.
[19] Sukhanov, *Zapiski*, I, 75-76. See his characterization, pp. 61 ff.
[20] Antonov-Saratovski, *Pod stiagom proletarskoi bor'by*, I, 38-39.
[21] Statement to the author, thirty-eight years after the revolution.
[22] Manuscript of chapter Partiia S.-R.

council; and the SR's could have supported his administration as an interim regime without bearing the responsibility for its actions. Such a course would have been all the more natural since they were deferring most problems to the Constituent Assembly, not so much from calculation as from unreadiness in respect to the execution of their program.

In the last analysis, however, it was not so much his partisan affiliation which handicapped Kerenski in 1917 as his lack of experience. Too often it is forgotten that he was only thirty-five when the revolution began, and only thirty-six when he became head of state; he attained his full powers only later in life, when the opportunity for using them had passed. As an orator he was already supreme, but not yet as a statesman, and the immense though evanescent popularity which his speechmaking brought him was a positive disadvantage in that it caused him to become overconfident and place too much reliance on exhortations, as when he is quoted as telling Professor Hrushevski, "With good will one can get anywhere, a socialist can persuade his people to do anything."[23] Kerenski's activities had been limited to Russia at the time of his assumption of power, and he still had some things to learn about Europe, particularly about France and Great Britain, where surface phenomena are most likely to be deceiving, the culture most seductive for less developed peoples, and the governments most adept in imposing their will upon others. Through much of 1917 he seems to have been under the impression that the leaders of these countries were as honorable in their dealings with others as he was. That he learned his lesson, and learned it well, is apparent from his later writings,[24] but unfortunately the year 1917 had to be a part of his education.

It is, then, obvious that the PSR could derive but little in the way of leadership from its two most talented members, the one without will, and the other strongly nonpartisan in spirit. The year 1917 would establish nothing more clearly than that V. M. Chernov was a knight of the pen rather than a leader of men. As for Kerenski, his real ambition was to lead all parties and not any particular one. In

[23] A. Shulgin, *L'Ukraine contre Moscou*, p. 116.
[24] See especially the collection of articles under the title, *Izdalëka, passim*.

so far as there was a leader of the PSR, it was Abram Gotz, but he had neither the brains, nor the stage presence, nor the prestige of the other two. His control over the right wing was imperfect, and over the left wing, virtually nonexistent. Actually, there was a vacant throne in this huge and disjointed empire, and in the absence of a native pretender, the Menshevik came and sat upon it.

After the revolution, a good deal was said in SR circles about the party having fallen under Menshevik influence. Spiridonova said it at the time. In a strong plea for the SR's to be themselves, she pointed out that to march with the Mensheviks meant to contain the revolution within the framework of a bourgeois order, something that the SR program had never contemplated. Menshevik tactics fitted the Menshevik program, but when SR's aped those tactics, voted for Menshevik resolutions, and acted as one with them in the soviets, they were affronting the "organized conscience" of the working class, a powerful new factor in history which had not been taken into account by Marxist (that is, Menshevik) dogma.[25] The left SR's are commonly regarded as wild-eyed people, wholly utopian in their approach to the problems of the day. Actually, they were not a whit more utopian than the Mensheviks, those sober-minded harbingers of a distant socialism. Was it any more impractical for the left SR's to dream of fashioning a socialist order out of this revolution than for the Mensheviks to stir the proletarian movement and then expect to restrain it from attemping to realize its ultimate objectives?[26] Can a lion be fed on red meat and then be expected to turn vegetarian when the wounded prey is under his paws?

In later years, when nothing could be lost through frank admissions because everything had already been lost, Vishniak for the

[25] "O zadachakh revoliutsii," *Nash Put'*, No. 1 (August, 1917), pp. 5-11; see also *Protokoly pervago s"ezda P.L.S.-R.*, p. 21, for Natanson's comments in a similar vein.

[26] For classic statement of Menshevik position, see Tsereteli's remarks on May 10 in *Revoliutsiia 1917 goda (Khronika sobytii)*, II, 77.

right and Chernov for the center acknowledged the weight of Menshevik influence, though they could not agree on whether the right wing or the rest of the party bore the responsibility for letting it be taken captive and led around by the nose. Pointing out that the SR's had occupied an eminent position only because of their numbers, Vishniak conceded that the Mensheviks had led the revolution, or rather led it through the SR's, because the Marxian party was better organized, richer in human resources, and enjoyed more authority in urban centers. Certainly it is true that the fate of the revolution was decided in the cities, but in view of the fact that the SR's commanded a larger numerical following even there, it is not easy to explain why they should have lagged so badly in respect to quality. Vishniak's suggestion that they were the younger party is no help; after all, there was but a few years' difference in the ages of these parties. Chernov attempts to soften his party's subservience by pointing out that the influence had been mutual, the Mensheviks having been constrained at the first soviet congress to accept the principle of land socialization; but he cannot deny that the Menshevik concept of the revolution had prevailed to the exclusion of the SR, and seeks the reason in the coalition-at-any-price tactics of the right wing of his party, which was dissatisfied with Menshevik hegemony only in so far as it fell short of complete identification with the Kadet position.[27]

Yet it was not just the right wing which held the PSR in thralldom to Menshevism. The center was also responsible for this fateful dependency of the larger party upon the smaller, even to the extent of abandoning its own concept of the revolution. Chernov says the SR's were twice late in respect to coalition, first with its formation, and then with its liquidation.[28] But he also tells us, on an earlier occasion when the impression of the overwhelming catastrophe sustained by his party was fresh on his mind, that at the time of the July crisis the question of a socialist government had been posed

[27] See Vishniak's article, "Tsena soiuza," *Dni*, No. 263 (September 13, 1923), and Chernov's rejoinder, "Otkliky pressy," *Revoliutsionnaia Rossiia*, No. 32 (December, 1923), pp. 19-22.

[28] Chernov, "Otkliky pressy," *Revoliutsionnaia Rossiia*, No. 32 (December, 1923), p. 21.

and had been decided in the negative, partly because the Mensheviks refused to join.[29] A break with Menshevism was by no means desired by many adherents of the center, leftist in inclination.[30] Presumably he numbered himself among these members—he was always friendly to Menshevism. It was at the Tenth Petersburg Conference, however, that he spoke more frankly than on other occasions. He admitted that SR tactics had been framed with reference to Menshevik tactics—sometimes excessively so. He admitted that for the Mensheviks, with their concept of a bourgeois revolution, coalition had been a goal, whereas for the SR's it was only a means. When Tsereteli at the Democratic Conference termed 1905 a failure but this revolution a success, because of the achievement of coalition, Chernov had realized that their paths were fatefully diverging.[31] Need he have waited so long? And why, after the truth finally dawned upon him, should he have thought of Tsereteli as minister of foreign affairs in a government headed by himself?

Superior leadership was not the only reason for the ascendancy of the Mensheviks. Their concept of revolution was as though made to order for the right SR's, whose distaste for social revolution after the achievement of political freedom was as obvious as it was usually unavowed, and whose zeal for war led them to desire above all else a class truce, which could only mean the bourgeois hegemony of the revolution postulated in Menshevik theory.[32] Even in the Peasants' Executive Committee the Menshevik point of view triumphed,[33] the SR intellectuals having sacrificed their own party line to the maintenance of the class truce.[34] The decision to refer controversial problems to the Constituent Assembly removed the agrarian question as a source of dissension, and to the right wing's bid for support in bridling the social revolution was joined the center's fear of the

[29] *Kratkii otchët o rabotakh chetvërtago s"ezda P.S.-R.*, pp. 15-16.
[30] Manuscript of chapter Partiia S.-R.
[31] *Delo Naroda*, No. 213 (November 18, 1917).
[32] *Protokoly pervago s"ezda P.L.S.-R.*, p. 72 (statement of Kamkov); *Kratkii otchët o rabotakh chetvërtago s"ezda P.S.-R.*, p. 80 (statement of Gorvits).
[33] See Ustinov's statement (*Protokoly pervago s"ezda P.L.S.-R.*, p. 51).
[34] Bykhovski, *Vserossiiskii Sovet Krest'ianskikh Deputatov*, p. 227. This source and the one cited in the preceding footnote represent opposing points of view, yet, in effect, they say the same thing.

dictatorship of the proletariat, causing it to view Menshevism as a natural ally in the rude struggle of both against Bolshevism. The cooperation of the two parties extended down to the local level and manifested itself in various ways, among others, in a close coordination of press activities, the invariable rule being for the two never to indulge in polemics with each other; and in some instances the community of views as to the character of the revolution and the tactics to be pursued led to the joint publication of newspapers.[35] It was a strong and stable union, this partnership of the leading Populist party with one of the wings of the Russian Social Democracy, and offers a striking example of how sentiment and temperament transcend theory as determining factors in human behavior. The dry bones of the Marxist-Narodnik controversy, so tiresomely stirred by intellectuals who pursue abstractions and miss the essence of history, opposed no barrier at all to the live union of the Populists with the orthodox but moderate Marxists, both of whom found it far easier to consort with their theoretical adversaries than with the extremists in their own fold. The extremists, moreover, coalesced against them. Clearly, temperament and not theory governed the line-up in 1917, with regular SR's and Mensheviks opposing left SR's and Bolsheviks.

There was one respect in which the intellectual character of the SR leadership would play it false, and from this misconception its Menshevik mentors, for reasons of their own, would do nothing to free it. All through 1917, even after the October disaster, the SR's consistently overrated the Constitutional Democrats and consistently underestimated the Bolsheviks, and the farther to the right they stood, the greater their degree of error. Their mistake, which must be reckoned among the major causes of their undoing, sprang less from theory than from intellectual snobbishness and caste prejudice. If we consider only the upper level of this movement, it would not be too far wrong to say that it was the party of ex-university students and village schoolteachers, and as such, it seems to have looked with

[35] See p. 169.

awe and reverence upon the party of the university professors, much as small-town zealots for learning in America look up to college professors, and with as little reason. Somehow the Constitutional Democracy was regarded as the repository of wisdom and statecraft, of experience and maturity, without whose assistance one could not govern a poor and backward country racked with war and enmeshed in the web of world diplomacy. The Constitutional Democrats had studied Western institutions and bore the standard of Western culture in a land where loud talk in certain intellectual circles about an original path of development concealed a gnawing sense of inferiority. The Kadets spoke French, or even English, and could commune with the "glorious Allies" on a footing of equality. Their "liberalism" could scarcely have commended them to the SR's, for by 1917 this party was liberal in the same sense as were the National Liberals in Germany—i.e., 10 percent liberalism and 90 percent nationalism of the most flamboyant kind. But even as they gathered under their skirts everything that stood farther to the right—the Octobrists and other shadows of the past, figments of Stolypin's franchise—the Kadets became not less, but more, attractive allies, since the SR's not only respected them but also feared them as a source of counterrevolution. Even the victory over Kornilov could not convince these fainthearts of the strength of the revolution or the weakness of reaction; they regarded it as a result of fortuitous circumstances—bad leadership, poor organization—which were not likely to occur again, and they quaked in their boots before the specter of Kaledin and a Cossack Vendée.[36] They thought to appease the Kadets and defer to them in every way, so that the latter would not throw in with the monarchists and reinstate the old regime.

Yet even had the SR's been less misled in their appraisal of the Constitutional Democrats, they still would have had no choice but to go with them—the Allies decreed it so, and for every SR to the right of center there was no higher law than the will of the Western Allies. As one of them says,[37] they were caught in a magic circle:

[36] Manuscript commentary on the minutes of the Central Committee, pp. 43-44; Demianov, "Moia sluzhba pri Vremennom Pravitel'stve," in *Arkhiv Russkoi Revoliutsii*, IV, 81-82.

[37] Bykhovski, *Vserossiiskii Sovet Krest'ianskikh Deputatov*, pp. 235-36.

a separate peace would be ruinous to the revolution, yet the war could not be continued without Allied aid, and the Allies insisted on having the Kadets in the government, viewing them as the bulwark of the state. Kerenski had been under heavy pressure to come to terms with the Kadets. He himself freely concedes the pressure, saying that it assumed outrageous forms during the Kornilov episode, but that he was determined not to make an issue of it in order to avoid a break with the Allies. Now it may be doubted whether the Allies were that impressed with the statesmanlike qualities of a party whose leader, Miliukov, could in one breath blow up the German menace and in the next seriously contemplate a descent on Constantinople with Russia in the throes of revolution and the army on the verge of collapse.[38] What they sought was protection for their loans and a continued flow of cannon fodder to the Eastern Front—purposes which could best be attained by keeping the Kadets in the seats of power.

One will remember that in Populist theory the weakness of the Russian middle class, its hothouse character and subservience to the regime whose favors had called it into being, constituted one of the basic premises for the assumption that Russia must tread her own path of historical development, independently of Western countries. Now in 1917 we find the Populists grossly overrating the strength of the Russian middle class and clinging for dear life to the Western countries, without whose good will and continued support they could not conceive of a fortuitous national development. The closer they were to the original Populism, the further removed from Chernov's neo-Populism, and the weaker their degree of emancipation from Slavophile shibboleths, the ranker their heresy in 1917. Once more the question must be asked, what does Populist theory amount to, and once more the answer must be—to the vaporings of intellectuals, that and nothing more. The Chaikovskis and Breshkovskaias of the far right of Populism, however, were not more inconsistent in these respects than the PSR as a whole in throwing overboard its concept of the revolution and adopting the Menshevik

[38] See brief but pertinent comment by Professor Michael T. Florinski in his admirable study, *Russia: A History and an Interpretation* (New York, 1953), II, 1396. Not even Guchkov and Alekseev had any sympathy with this mad venture.

concept. It is not the theory of the Populists, but their sentiment, that is important; not the search for a distinctive path of historical development, but the latent nationalism that led them to make the search, in prideful exaltation of their people and its destiny.

As badly as the SR's overrated the Kadets, as badly did they underrate the Bolsheviks. Chernov has conceded their error with the admission that only in retrospect did they realize how strong was the tide of radicalism, and how weak the forces of conservatism.[39] There were a number of factors involved in this miscalculation or, as one is tempted to say, this willful self-deception, not least among them the factor of intellectual snobbery, but primarily the SR's seemed convinced that Bolshevism was a form of demagogy sustained by peasants who had been uprooted by impressment into the armed forces, and who had developed an abnormal psychology which would vanish as soon as they returned to the village. It was, therefore, an evanescent phenomenon which could be a serious factor only so long as it took its social base to disintegrate. That the village air might have little effect upon the virus contracted in the army, and that there was more to Bolshevism than the thirst of soldiers for peace, does not seem to have occurred to these shallow reasoners, although they needed only to observe the trend in municipal elections, or in by-elections to any major soviet, to have discerned the direction in which the workers of Russia were moving. One of the more flexible-minded members of the Central Committee, Dennis Rosenblum, conceded as early as August the loss of the workers to Bolshevism, at least in the large cities,[40] but even he persisted in seeing Bolshevism as the political expression of a self-demobilizing army which would soon pass out of existence.[41]

[39] *Kratkii otchët o rabotakh chetvërtago s"ezda P.S.-R.*, pp. 113, 117; manuscript commentary on the minutes of the Central Committee, pp. 43-44; manuscript of chapter Partiia S.-R.

[40] "Voina i revoliutsiia" (War and Revolution), *Delo Naroda*, No. 134 (August 23, 1917).

[41] "Sotsial'nyia osnovy bol'shevizma" (Social Bases of Bolshevism), *ibid.*, No. 240 (December 23, 1917).

The state of mind of the Populist intelligentsia in the hour of the enemy's triumph is revealed in the diary of a member of the Constituent Assembly, N. P. Oganovski, who was, it is true, not a member of the Socialist Revolutionary party, yet owed his election on the SR ticket to the search for experts and the personal favor of M. V. Vishniak,[42] who was nearly as far to the right as Oganovski himself. Desperately the author of the diary casts around for an explanation of the ascendancy of Bolshevism, and the low estate of Populism, and desperately he avoids the obvious conclusion that Bolshevism was strong because it had amassed a popular following, either through its own appeal or through the folly of intellectuals like himself in striving to hold an exhausted people in a war to which these intellectuals had contributed nothing save exhortations from the rear. After the usual charge of dependence upon the soldier scum, the author proceeds to analyze Bolshevism and finds that it was made up of three elements, which like three poisonous snakes were crushing the Russian people within their coils: first, the theoretical Bolsheviks, second, German secret agents, and third, Russian Black Hundred monarchists. Everything is wrong in this analysis, even the figure of speech, since poisonous snakes do not constrict. As for the peasants, our authority says that the contagion got to them only superficially and "is blown away from each soldier returning from the front in a few days." After this display of analytical power, it requires courage, indeed, to sneer at Spiridonova, who, whisked away to prison from a high-school bench, had preserved a mental attitude of the high-school level. A university degree may confer academic distinction but it cannot confer distinction of character. Spiridonova may have been utopian in her views and she may have helped the Bolsheviks into power, but in the flood tide of their success she was not guilty of serving them as was Oganovski.[43]

From this exhibition of rot in the Populist intelligentsia it is a relief to turn to the merely erroneous estimate of Zenzinov, in which he admitted that the masses were following the Bolsheviks, giving them

[42] *Dan' proshlomu*, pp. 299-300.
[43] For his analysis, which betrays a proto-Fascist type of mentality, see pertinent passages in the diary: "Dnevnik chlena Uchreditel'nago Sobraniia," *Golos Minuvshago*, Nos. 4-6 (April-June, 1918), pp. 147-49, 158, 161-62, 164-65, 171.

easy triumphs on the domestic front, yet expressed confidence that a sobering-up process would set in as soon as the promises of immediate land distribution and immediate peace proved illusory.[44] There was nothing spiteful or illogical in this prediction; things just did not work out that way, since an imperfect land reform and a cruel peace nevertheless satisfied the Russian people. But whether they sputtered with rage or tried objectively to analyze the situation, the SR's never succeeded in gauging the depth of the revolutionary tide or the strength of their foes. To the end they persisted in thinking of themselves as stronger than the Bolsheviks, and hence as the rightful heirs of the revolution whom a quirk of fortune had defrauded of their heritage; even the civil war taught them nothing in this respect.[45] As a matter of fact, in point of unity and cohesion, discipline and organization, in leadership and fighting spirit, in everything except mere numbers, the SR's were greatly inferior to their rivals. A Turkish proverb says that "if the enemy be only as an ant, think of him as an elephant." The SR's reversed this principle: they faced an elephant but persisted in seeing in him an ant.

Yet even if their catalogue of errors had been less extensive, it may be asked whether the result would have been any different. The SR's could have enjoyed greater unity and better leadership, they could have been more mindful of their own principles and less dependent on the Mensheviks, less worshipful of the Kadets and more realistic in relation to Bolshevism, and still they would have ended in crashing defeat unless they could have solved the problem of war and peace. And for this problem, it must be admitted in justice to them, there was no easy solution, and perhaps no solution at all. It was their duty, however, to come to grips with it and attempt a solution. Blame

[44] "Upoenie pobedami" (Flushed with Victories), *Delo Naroda,* No. 198 (November 3, 1917).

[45] See Burevoi, *Raspad 1918-1920,* p. 128. The reader is reminded that this is the testimony of a prominent party member who had headed the peasants' soviets in Voronezh province, one of the major strongholds of the PSR.

attaches, not to their failure to solve it, but to their failure to take more than one step in the direction of its solution.

The one step was the acceptance by the great majority of party members of the soviet formula: peace without annexations or indemnities, with right of self-determination for all nationalities. There was nothing wrong in principle with this soviet formula, it was just not acceptable to the beasts in the jungle, and if the Russian socialists who offered it have been punished for the temerity of their idealism, so also has been the world which rejected it. There were, however, two practical disadvantages to the soviet formula: Russia's allies would not accept it, and it menaced with dissolution the enemy power which was most desirous of peace. Austria-Hungary could scarcely press Germany to accede to a proposal that might entail the disruption of the Danubian monarchy, and German imperialists could continue to hypnotize public opinion with arguments of self-preservation as long as England and France did not follow the Russian example. The result was that the soviet formula won no ground in either camp, the foreign ministers of the Provisional Government ceaselessly gnawed at its base in Russia, the war continued, and the Russian people became increasingly restive. In this situation the SR's could find no better course than to sit down and wait for opinion in other countries, and particularly in Germany, to attain the Russian level, forgetting that the revolution had indicated that the strain of war was greater in Russia than elsewhere, and that the Russian people, having been the first to move in the direction of peace, were likely to continue to march in the vanguard, despite the dangers the intellectuals might point to in urging a waiting policy.

Some further step was necessary to unsnag the soviet peace formula and convince the Russian people that the initiative in ending the war had not been surrendered to the Bolsheviks. But could the Mensheviks and Socialist Revolutionaries have taken this step without exposing the young republic to mortal danger, possibly at the hands of its enraged allies, and certainly at those of the Ludendorff junta in Germany, imperialist to the marrow of its bones? And what could this step have been?

It availed little to parade one's virtue in renouncing imperialism so long as Russia continued the war at the side of allies who refused to follow her example and whose real aims were only too well known to Russian socialists through the secret treaties deposited in the Ministry of Foreign Affairs. To influence decisively the populace of enemy countries and bring effective pressure to bear upon their governments, it was necessary for the Russian republic either to bring its allies into line or dissociate itself from the type of war they were conducting. Timidly and hesitatingly the SR's entered upon the first course through their espousal of the Stockholm Conference, but their support was not vigorous enough to produce any result. Here their peace policy was stranded and never subsequently set in motion. To have proceeded further, it would have been necessary to commit the Allies to the soviet peace formula or break with them. And for this drastic action no section of party opinion save the extreme left was prepared.

Both the left center and the right center favored forbearance until a situation more promising for peace developed elsewhere. Gotz agreed with Chernov that all the powers engaged in the war were pursuing imperialist aims, France and Britain as well as Germany and Austria, and Chernov agreed with Gotz on the inadmissibility of confronting the Allies with an ultimatum as long as peace sentiment in those countries had not developed to the point where such intervention would supply the impetus needed to bring the peace party into power.[46] As he told the Third Congress, there was no magic formula for ending the war; it would have to go on until the slogans of the Russian Revolution had undermined the will for a victor's peace in other lands.[47] Essentially, then, SR majority opinion conceived of the situation in terms of an endurance test: could the Russian people stagger on under the cross of war until other peoples signified a willingness to throw theirs down? Whose capacity for suffering would prove the greater, Russia's or the West's? Here was an application of the old antithesis which the early Populists had not foreseen. At first the SR's seemed optimistic; the Third Congress is

[46] *Tretii s"ezd P.S.-R.*, pp. 108-9; Chernov, "Uroki proshlogo" (Lessons of the Past), *Revoliutsionnaia Rossiia*, No. 42 (April, 1925), p. 22.
[47] *Tretii s"ezd P.S.-R.*, p. 71.

said to have cherished the belief that Russia could hold out until European democracy came to her rescue in the matter of peace.[48] But there was also doubt, even in the early days: an editorial in the central organ had warned that the masses might be attracted to Bolshevism by its clear-cut and readily comprehensible stand on the war.[49]

Chernov had said right in the beginning that "either the revolution will consume the war or the war will consume the revolution."[50] Why, then, had he not pressed for a solution instead of letting things take their course? As he later admitted, Russian democracy had been too little aware of the incompatibility of the war and the revolution, and even left-wing elements—here he obviously has in mind his own group—had not realized how essential it was to have peace, for how otherwise could they even for one moment have put up with Miliukov's conduct of foreign affairs?[51] Another error had been the belief that socialism could force the renunciation of war to crushing victory; the optimism of 1917 had vanished, along with much else, and Chernov could not deny that "zoological nationalism" had been altogether too strong with its ability to suborn even the proletariat, and humanitarianism or "healthy internationalism" altogether too theoretical to have entered as yet into the flesh and blood of national communities.[52]

But the failure of the SR's to push their campaign for peace beyond espousal of the soviet peace formula and weak-kneed support of the Stockholm Conference cannot, in the last analysis, be explained by miscalculations or misjudgments nor on grounds of excessive optimism. Whatever illusions may have been cherished at first, the craving of the Russian people for peace had become so overwhelm-

[48] V. G. Arkhangelski, "Ob otkolovshikhsia" (About Those Who Split Off), *Delo Naroda*, No. 223 (December 3, 1917).

[49] "Parlament i protivu-parlament" (Parliament and Anti-Parliament), *ibid.*, No. 67 (June 6, 1917).

[50] "Dvoetsentrie" (Having Two Centers), *ibid.*, No. 42 (May 6, 1917); "Uroki proshlogo," *Revoliutsionnaia Rossiia*, No. 42 (April, 1925), p. 18.

[51] "Uroki proshlogo," *Revoliutsionnaia Rossiia*, No. 42 (April, 1925), pp. 20-21.

[52] "È pur si muove," *Revoliutsionnaia Rossiia*, Nos. 35-36 (June-July, 1924), pp. 2-3; see also Arkhangelski, "O proshlykh takticheskikh oshibkakh" (On Past Tactical Mistakes), *ibid.*, No. 42 (April, 1925), p. 12.

ing by fall that not only moderate socialists, but even moderate imperialists, could no longer deny the evidence of their senses. General Alekseev could speak of the "ruinous psychology" of the majority of the population in desiring peace above all else,[53] and Tereshchenko himself acknowledged that if peace negotiations were opened, it would be most difficult to break them off, even if they took an unfavorable turn, because of the mass psychology.[54] Other peoples might continue to pay the blood toll exacted by imperialism, but the Russian people were groping for a way out of the slaughter pen. Chernov recognized in the February Revolution a convulsive movement on the part of an overstrained organism, directed against the war but in the absence of any clear consciousness of the cause of the strain,[55] while a Kadet leader has confessed the self-deception practiced in official circles in rationalizing the true relationship between the war and revolution into a patriotic manifestation of discontent with tsarist conduct of the war.[56] The "bourgeois" or nonsocialist elements were willfully blind to the need for peace; when Baron Roman Rosen, one of the few clearheaded and stouthearted individuals among them, wished to recall the upper classes to their senses with a few pointed observations, he had to have recourse to Gorki's near-Bolshevik organ[57]—every other press outlet was closed to this eminently respectable gentleman, in whom something of the good sense of the nineteenth century lingered on after being extinguished elsewhere by the surge of chauvinism from above and of class hatred from below. Among the SR's, however, a more flexible attitude could have been expected, since they were under no compulsion to conceal social weakness behind a thick front of patriotism. Yet they, too, had worked themselves into a strait jacket on the war

[53] See his speech before the Council of the Republic as reported in the *Delo Naroda*, No. 177 (October 11, 1917).

[54] "Nakanune oktiabr'skago perevorota: Vopros o voine i mire: Otchëty o sekretnykh zasedaniiakh komissii Vremennago Soveta Rossiiskoi Respubliki" (On the Eve of the October Coup: The Problem of War and Peace: Reports of the Secret Sessions of the Commission of the Provisional Council of the Russian Republic), *Byloe*, XII (VI, June, 1918), p. 27.

[55] "Uroki proshlogo," *Revoliutsionnaia Rossiia*, No. 42 (April, 1925), p. 20.

[56] V. D. Nabokov, "Vremennoe Pravitel'stvo," in *Arkhiv Russkoi Revoliutsii*, I, 57.

[57] *Novaia Zhizn'*, No. 137 (September 26, 1917).

question which left them no freedom of maneuver, and one must search deeper for the reasons for their self-imprisonment.

One reason was the presence in the PSR of what John Adams would have called a French or British faction—a group of citizens who had made a foreign cause their own. These members of the party in their hearts did not want peace so long as Germany was still on her feet and Austria and Turkey still in one piece, and so long as the Allied thirst for vengeance had not been slaked. Perhaps the most extravagant spokesman for this school of thought was Bunakov-Fondaminski, who had told the First Peasants' Congress that for Russia to pull out of the war would be to dishonor herself before the Allies. "Since we must not conclude a separate peace, there is only one thing left to do—continue the war."[58] One will note that not only a separate peace but also any middle course was ruled out by this tub-thumping champion of war, and that for him loyalty to the Allies was the supreme consideration. Less strident in his public declarations but no less emotionally wedded to the Allied cause was Avksentiev, the real leader of the prowar faction in the PSR and a tireless opponent of every manifestation of the will to peace. Even on September 9, after Kornilov's bid for power had insured the disintegration of the army, Avksentiev could still announce before the Peasants' Executive Committee that any hope for peace as envisaged by the Russian democracy had vanished, and that now it must be either war or a separate peace[59]—the same barren alternative that Bunakov had presented several months before.

Avksentiev was always careful to keep considerations of national defense in the foreground, but other members of his faction betrayed their concern for foreign interests. Thus An-ski (Rappoport) wanted to delete the ban on annexations from the soviet peace formula so that Alsace-Lorraine could be restored to France,[60] and Vishniak upheld the principle of reparations, without limiting them to Belgium or otherwise imposing a restraint.[61] Rudnev rejected a purely defen-

---

[58] Quoted in Arkhangelski, "O proshlykh takticheskikh oshibkakh," *Revoliutsionnaia Rossiia*, No. 42 (April, 1925), p. 12.

[59] Bykhovski, *Vserossiiskii Sovet Krest'ianskikh Deputatov*, pp. 238-39.

[60] *Tretii s"ezd P.S.-R.*, p. 142; see also Vishniak, *Dan' proshlomu*, p. 258.

[61] *Dan' proshlomu*, p. 257.

sive motivation in building up the army and battled to keep the door open for offensive action,[62] while Argunov's paper played up the slogan that "offense is the best defense."[63] Great Britain seemed to be less on the minds of these people than France; either she occupied a lower position on the scale of their sympathies or it was assumed that she would take care of herself.[64] Besides France, the Balkan Slavs and Armenia were objects of solicitude for these SR's; in their literature one can find strong sympathy for Serbia and a concept of peace which in effect would have wrecked the Danubian monarchy, since that state would constitute the main, and very nearly the only, field for application of the principle of national self-determination.[65] The zeal with which they would apply it in this instance was notably lacking in the case of the Russian, the French, and the British empires. One can also find in their literature and pronouncements a marked unfriendliness to Germany, extending in particular to the German working class, which was denounced as nonrevolutionary in spirit.[66] It was, in truth—as nonrevolutionary as its SR critics.

These SR's could go to amazing lengths in the effort to reconcile their prejudices with socialist and internationalist principles. An-ski assured the Third Congress that France was not waging a war of imperialism; she was merely striving to redeem national territory which had been occupied by the Germans.[67] Bulanov held that the

[62] *Tretii s"ezd P.S.-R.*, pp. 158-60.

[63] See cartoon and accompanying caption in *Volia Naroda*, No. 17 (May 18, 1917).

[64] B. I. Nikolaevski once remarked to the author that the cultural affinity—with political implications—of the SR's for France and the SD's for Germany had aroused comment in socialist circles. On one occasion English and German comrades expressed regret that SR literature in translation was predominantly in French. See L. Rossel, "Vystavka partiinykh izdanii na Marsel. Kongresse" (Exhibition of Party Publications at the Marseilles Congress), *Revoliutsionnaia Rossiia*, No. 45 (October, 1925). A word of caution, however, is in order: pro-French sentiment, coupled with a certain antipathy for Germany, would seem to have been an attribute of right Narodnik circles; no anti-German bias in left Narodnik circles has ever been detected by this investigator. If there were a national antipathy common to the whole movement, it would be in respect to Turkey.

[65] See, for example, the pamphlet of Bulanov, *Kak mozhno konchit' voinu*, pp. 5-6, 17.

[66] *Ibid.*, pp. 7 ff., 15, 18, 21; *Tretii s"ezd P.S.-R.*, pp. 152-53.

[67] *Ibid.*, pp. 141-43.

Allies were right in expecting aid from Russia: they had refused to abandon her to her fate in 1914 and had incurred devastation on her behalf.[68] His simplification of diplomacy is matched by Oganovski's novel interpretation of French interest in the Ukraine. Fawning upon the Rada as long as it promised to serve as a rallying point against Bolshevism, and cursing it the moment it concluded a separate peace with the Central Powers, this typical right-wing Narodnik intellectual protested first of all the sellout of the oppressed Slavs of Austria and only thereafter the disadvantage to the Ukrainians themselves, who would be called upon to exchange their grain and horses for little pocketknives and mirrors, or at best iron products, from Germany—"and that at a time when the French are prepared to enrich the Ukraine."[69] Scholars will argue whether this or that consideration was uppermost in the minds of MM. Poincaré and Clemenceau as they embarked on their Black Sea venture, but very few besides Oganovski will argue that it was "to enrich the Ukraine."

The presence within the party of these devoted partisans of the Allied cause acted as a brake upon initiative in seeking peace but cannot explain the attitude of the central mass of the PSR, which would have welcomed a general peace but was determined not to conclude a separate one. The reason usually given is that separate action contradicted the principle of international action, which was binding upon the internationalist conscience.[70] Here was a deterrent, there is no doubt. But as Chernov, an opponent of a separate peace in 1917, observes, the interests of humanity did not require the immolation of the one sixth of humanity in the Russian Empire, and he would have been prepared to contemplate a separate peace as a last resort, after any possibility of struggling for a general democratic peace had disappeared.[71] Something else, of a more substantial character, restrained the SR's of the center, and that something, in the

---

[68] *Kak mozhno konchit' voinu*, p. 19.

[69] "Dnevnik chlena Uchreditel'nago Sobraniia," *Golos Minuvshago*, No. 4-6 (April-June, 1918), pp. 162, 168-69 (entries in diary for January 7, 10, 11, 1918).

[70] See statement of Gotz (RC) before the Third Congress (*Tretii s"ezd P.S.-R.*, p. 108); see also statement of Eugenia Ratner (LLC) before the Fourth Congress (*Kratkii otchët o rabotakh chetvërtago s"ezda P.S.-R.*, p. 75).

[71] "Uroki proshlogo," *Revoliutsionnaia Rossiia*, No. 42 (April, 1925), pp. 19-20.

opinion of the investigator, was the fear that Russia's separate exit from the war would throw the victory to Germany and leave Russia more or less at the mercy of the power that was at once the strongest in Europe and the most dangerously situated with respect to Russia. Desiring a decisive victory for neither side, these SR's believed that a separate peace would insure such a victory for Germany.[72] Their fear of German imperialism was fully justified, as Brest-Litovsk would demonstrate. But the situation was not as bad as it seemed to them, and it should have been possible to steer a middle course between surrender to German imperialism and continued inactivity on the peace front, which was equivalent to surrender to Bolshevism.

If the Russian Revolution had broken out a year earlier, the retirement of one of the members of the Entente to the sidelines might actually have spelled victory for Germany. If, on the other hand, it had come a year later, the situation would have been far more favorable, since the process of enfeeblement would have advanced at about the same pace in Germany and in Russia. But the revolution came in between, in February and March of 1917, confronting people of good will and humanitarian instincts like the center SR's with a situation that was difficult and dangerous, but not hopeless or impossible. At about the same time that fate overtook the tsarist regime, another event occurred which did not register as it should have upon the consciousness of Europe: the New World intervened in the feuds of the Old. The British Empire, as well served by its own skill as by the ineptitude of the German ruling class, had picked up a powerful new ally even as an old one was faltering and going down. The plunge of the United States meant that war long would rage in the West, regardless of what happened on the eastern front, regardless even of what happened in France. It meant that Germany, under the fateful handicap of her central position, which only Bismarck

[72] Vladimir Utgof (LC) stated the dilemma for the bulk of the membership in very clear terms at the Third Congress. See *Tretii s"ezd P.S.-R.*, pp. 120-21. He pointed out that one extreme was basing its hope for a change in Germany on a minority of the German Social Democrats, while the other extreme expected a minority of the Entente socialists to curb the imperialism of those powers. Unfortunately, he posed the dilemma without being able to offer a solution.

had fully appreciated, never would have a free hand to exploit her victory over Russia. And if it immeasurably increased the difficulties confronting the young Russian republic in one sense, it lightened its burden in another and opened a possible way out of the war.

American intervention removed any hope that the London and Paris cabinets would accede to the soviet peace formula. On the other hand, it rendered feasible some sort of action by St. Petersburg which might have satisfied the longing for peace of the Russian masses without prostrating the country at the feet of the Reich. The Socialist Revolutionaries could have come forward with a program something like this: they could have announced that since neither the enemy nor the Allies would renounce predatory aims, revolutionary Russia would stand on the defensive and sit out this madness until reason returned in other quarters under the lash of the war and the influence of Russia's example. This announcement would have followed a waiting period during which earnest efforts were made to enlist diplomatic support in other countries or demonstrate the hopelessness of achieving it. Whether enough time would have remained for Ludendorff to seek in the West in 1917 the decision he sought in 1918, after being caught off balance at Passchendaele and dreadfully punished, is more than doubtful; but in any event the United States would have stoked the Western fire, and the SR's, by means of a vigorous army reform and diplomacy addressed toward a separate peace with Turkey and Austria,[73] could have prepared against the eventuality of a German thrust into Russia to escape the effects of the blockade, secure in the knowledge that no matter how far Germany extended her lines, she would still be faced with a two-front war. And need we assume such superiority on the part of the Germans that they could have carved out for themselves, and at Russia's expense, an empire in eastern Europe against the efforts of revolutionaries who had tried to take their people out of war and had proved that it could not be done, and in the teeth of the opposition of the British Empire and of a fresh and powerful America?

[73] Kerenski says that the Provisional Government was working along just these lines, but its design must have been crossed up, late in 1917, by Tereshchenko's attempt to return Russian foreign policy to Miliukov's "Straits" jacket.

Of all the phobias of the SR's in 1917, the most foolish was that the Allies would conclude peace at the expense of Russia, a power whose significance in the war had always been secondary to the feud between Great Britain and Germany, as Durnovo could have told them. It is not contended that the alternative facing the PSR in 1917 was free of danger, or that their road would not have been long and thorny. But in times of danger it is necessary to live dangerously, rather than sit with folded hands.

Of all these implications of the international situation, the SR's seemed blissfully unaware. They had run into a stone wall in the effort to win support for the soviet formula, not seeing that it was America which had doomed their feeble enterprise, and not even dreaming of exploiting the remoter implications of America's crusade against Germany. Inertia and infirmity of will would perhaps have immobilized them in any event, and if not, then the thought of breaking with the Kadets and also with Kerenski in order to implement an independent policy would likely have stayed their hand. Yet at the root of their unwillingness to move further in the direction of peace lay the fear of German imperialism, intensified by a false estimate of the international situation. The exaggeration of German strength and the underestimation of American is clearly seen in the discussion that took place on the eve of the October Revolution in the Foreign Affairs Commission of the Provisional Council of the Republic. Pointing to the extreme war weariness in France, which was "literally bleeding to death," and to the bad situation in Italy, where military disaster had been added to internal difficulties, Gotz asked the foreign minister "whether the intervention of the United States under such conditions could be expected to change to any extent the ratio of strength?" Obviously, Gotz did not expect a great deal from America's participation in the war. And Tereshchenko, who had a better appreciation of its effects, wished to use his superior knowledge, not to reorientate Russian foreign policy in the direction of peace, but to continue a war which he admitted the Russian army was incapable of carrying on. When the question of war aims arose at this session, the foreign minister excused himself with the plea that he must go to the cabinet, whereupon Gotz proposed adjournment and the session ended.[74] This incident reveals how the minister conducted his business and how the SR's let him get away with it.

Many SR's were aware that they had not made the most of the possibilities before them, and tardily repented of the failure. They were by no means restricted to the left or even the left center. One of these critics has conceded that in the question of peace the party displayed no initiative whatever.[75] And Gendelman (RC) told the Fourth Congress that the party either should have secured peace or demonstrated to the Russian people its impossibility.[76] But the most significant admission of all comes from the former minister-president: "At the time of its most terrible trials, the Russian people had no true friends among the great powers of Europe. We note without passion this indisputable historical fact." Observing that Europe and Russia were now free of mutual obligations, Kerenski goes on to say that in the future "Russia must count only on herself and under no conditions sacrifice the vital interests of the Russian people even in the name of the most elevated ideals. The last war has taught us that, once and forever."[77]

Social Revolutionism was conceived in the Populist tradition, though in harmony with twentieth century conditions. It had always prided itself on its moral ties with the Narodnaia Volia, the People's Will group of the preceding century, while shedding its aberrations. In 1917 the people willed peace but the intellectuals at the party helm would not accede to this demand, some because they wished to swim with the surface tide, others because of a sense of obligation to foreign lands, others because a foreign cause had been made their own, but most because of a legitimate though exaggerated fear of the dangers their country faced. Between the SR policy of marking

[74] "Nakanune oktiabr'skago perevorota: Vopros o voine i mire," *Byloe,* XII (VI, June, 1918), pp. 27-28.

[75] A. Bach, "Revoliutsiia i sotsializm" (Revolution and Socialism), in *God russkoi revoliutsii,* p. 10.

[76] *Kratkii otchёt o rabotakh chetvёrtago s"ezda P.S.-R.,* p. 106.

[77] "Orientatsiia na Rossiiu" (Orientation on Russia), *Izdalёka,* pp. 141-42.

time and Lenin's policy of peace at any price lay an untried middle course of keeping the army in being but formally suspending operations, which would have had some prospect of success had it been espoused by the SR's and put into effect early enough in 1917. Such a course would have brought the party the active hostility of the Constitutional Democrats and of its own right wing, without bringing it the support of the Bolsheviks; but the main danger would have been that the Russian soldiers would not have been more than momentarily appeased by a policy of standing still, and later would have insisted on going home. Had the front gone to pieces anyway, the party would at least have had the consolation of having acted in conformity with its principles and would have emerged with a clear conscience and with its unity substantially unimpaired, since the amputation of the small though vociferous right wing would not have compared with the loss of the big left wing in October of 1917.[78] Little would have been lost by a fresh departure and much might have been gained. And even assuming the worst, it would have been defeat in a noble cause, the highest for which men can strive: the elevation of humanity above the jungle level. As the minister said at the bier of Chamberlain, with reference to his efforts for peace, better to have tried and failed than never to have tried at all.

[78] The story of the schism and its aftermath is told in the author's forthcoming study of Social Revolutionism in the era of the October Revolution.

LIST OF SOURCES

SOURCES of minor significance with few citations have been omitted. Society publications and edited works or compilations appear under the title rather than under the sponsoring agency or name of the editor. Only longer articles of considerable significance are listed, and these are always from journals, never from newspapers.

The sources of information are divided into three categories: manuscripts, printed sources, and oral testimony.

MANUSCRIPTS

Argunov, A. A. Pravoe i levoe (Right and Left). 41 pp. [Typewritten manuscript. Used in Prague in 1935 by courtesy of its author and returned to him. Deals with the wartime split in the emigration.]

Chernov, V. M. Izbiratel'naia statistika (Election Statistics). 8 pp. [Typewritten manuscript with unnumbered pages in form of appendix to the minutes of the Central Committee. Placed by Chernov at the author's disposal in Prague in 1934. An analysis of the elections to the Central Committee at the Third and Fourth Congresses, invaluable for the light it sheds on factionalism within the party.]

—— Manuscript commentary on the minutes of the Central Committee of the PSR. 100 pp. [Untitled manuscript, typewritten on legal-size sheets with corrections and additions in author's handwriting. Equivalent of a small book. Used in Prague in 1934 by courtesy of its author and returned to him. Deals with the whole field of the author's experiences in 1917, and not just with the period covered by the fragment of the minutes of the Central Committee *(see below)*. Illuminates the scene as nothing else does. Indispensable source, but not always trustworthy as to Chernov's attitude in 1917; must be checked against his position as recorded in the *Delo Naroda* (The People's Cause).]

—— Partiia Sotsialistov-Revoliutsionerov (Socialist Revolutionary Party). [Typewritten manuscript with unnumbered pages, a chapter from the second volume (unpublished) of the author's *Velikaia Rus-*

skaia Revoliutsiia (The Great Russian Revolution). The chapter has appeared in abridged form in the English edition of the two-volumes-in-one, translated by Philip E. Mosely. Referred to in the footnotes as "manuscript of chapter Partiia S.-R." Placed at the author's disposal by Chernov in 1934. An appraisal of the SR role in 1917 which does not spare Chernov himself.]

—— Partiia Sotsialistov-Revoliutsionerov v epokhu Gershuni (The Socialist Revolutionary Party in the Era of Gershuni). [Typewritten manuscript placed at the author's disposal by Chernov in 1935. Had been published as a chapter of a book in Yiddish on the life of Gershuni.]

Protokol'naia zapis' zagranichnogo soveshchaniia tsentral'nykh rabotnikov PSR po voprosu o linii povedeniia v usloviiakh mirovoi voiny (Minutes of the Proceedings of the Conference Abroad of Central Workers of the PSR to Determine the Line to Be Taken in the World War). 38 pp. [Typewritten manuscript of the minutes of the conference held in Beaugy-sur-Clarens, August 22, 1914. Preserved in the Hoover Library on War, Revolution, and Peace, Stanford University, California. Most of the material was incorporated by V. V. Rudnev in his article published in the *Svoboda* (Freedom).]

Protokol Zasedaniia Tsentral'nago Komiteta Partii Sotsialistov-Revoliutsionerov Sentiabria mesiatsa 2 dnia 1917 goda (Minutes of the Session of the Central Committee of the Socialist Revolutionary Party Held on September 2, 1917) . . . and minutes for succeeding sessions through that of January 30, 1918, followed by minutes for three sessions of subsidiary bodies in 1918. 38 pp. of typewritten manuscript with emendations in the hand of V. M. Chernov. [Placed at the author's disposal by Chernov in Prague in 1935. The terse minutes of the Central Committee, arranged in three columns, need to be supplemented by Chernov's commentary and the information contained in the *Delo Naroda* (The People's Cause) and *Partiinyia Izvestiia* (Party News). The minutes published in the latter source (which is just as rare) for the most part, but not entirely, duplicate this master set, which is but a fragment of the whole, the earlier minutes having been lost in the debacle or seized by the Soviet authorities.]

Snosheniia sovetskoi demokratii s sotsialisticheskimi men'shinstvami voiuiushchikh stran i delo R. Grimma (Contacts of the Soviet Democracy with the Socialist Minorities of the Belligerent Countries and the Case of R. Grimm). [Part of chapter XI of the memoirs of Irakli Tsereteli. Duplicated February, 1953, by the Russian Research Center of Harvard University.]

PRINTED SOURCES

Akhun, M. I., and V. A. Petrov. Bol'sheviki i armiia v 1905-1917 gg. (The Bolsheviks and the Army in 1905-1917). Leningrad, 1929.

Alaverdova, A. "Ocherk agrarnoi politiki Vremennogo Pravitel'stva" (Outline of the Agrarian Policy of the Provisional Government), *Sotsialisticheskoe Khoziaistvo* (Socialist Economy), II (1925), 143-75.

Alekseev, V. Oktiabr' i grazhdanskaia voina v TsChO (October and the Civil War in the Central Black-Earth Region). Voronezh, 1932.

Antonov-Saratovski, V. P. Pod stiagom proletarskoi bor'by: Otryvki iz vospominanii o rabote v Saratove za vremia s 1915 g. do 1918 g. (Under the Banner of Proletarian Struggle: Extracts from Recollections of Work in Saratov in the Period from 1915 to 1918). Moscow and Leningrad, 1925. Vol. I [All that was published. Interesting provincial account.]

Argunov, A. A. "Iz proshlago Partii Sotsialistov-Revoliutsionerov" (From the Past of the Socialist Revolutionary Party), *Byloe* (The Past), No. 10/22 (October, 1907), pp. 94-112.

Bericht der Russischen Sozial-Revolutionären Partei an den Internationalen Sozialistenkongress zu Stuttgart (August, 1907). N.p., 1907.

Boevyia predpriiatiia sotsialistov-revoliutsionerov v osveshchenii okhranki (Terrorist Enterprises of the Socialist Revolutionaries As Viewed by the Okhrana). Moscow, 1918.

Bolshevik Propaganda: Hearings before the Subcommittee of the Committee on the Judiciary, United States Senate, Sixty-fifth Congress. Washington, 1919.

Breshkovskaia, K. Hidden Springs of the Russian Revolution: Personal Memoirs. Stanford, 1931. [Very sketchy; disappointing.]

Buchanan, George. My Mission to Russia and Other Diplomatic Memories. 2 vols. London and Boston, 1923.

Bulanov, L. Kak mozhno konchit' voinu i kakovy spravedlivyia usloviia mira (How to End the War and What Are Just Conditions for a Peace). Petrograd, 1917.

Burevoi, K. (K. S. Sopliakov). Raspad 1918-1922 (The Break-up in 1918-1922). Moscow, 1923.

Burzhuaziia i pomeshchiki v 1917 godu: chastnye soveshchaniia chlenov gosudarstvennoi dumy (The Bourgeoisie and the Landed Gentry in 1917: Private Conferences of Members of the State Duma). Edited by A. K. Drezen. Moscow and Leningrad, 1932. [Significant source with useful annotations.]

Bykhovski, N. Ia. Vserossiiskii Sovet Krest'ianskikh Deputatov 1917 g.

(The All-Russian Soviet of Peasant Deputies in 1917). Moscow, 1929. 438 pp. [One of the basic sources, and the rarest of all. Belonging to the inner ring of the dominant right-centrist faction of the All-Russian Executive Committee of Peasants' Soviets, and editor of the peasants' *Izvestiia* (News), Bykhovski was in a splendid position to observe the political aspects of the agrarian movement. His sober account, conceding the errors that were made in 1917, but reaffirming the unquestionable truth that the PSR (in the broad sense) had commanded the support of the middle peasantry instead of serving as an instrument for kulak interests, proved highly unpalatable to the Soviet authorities when they woke up to what was being printed under their noses; his book was torn from the press and only one copy is said to have found its way abroad. The appendix contains a number of important and otherwise inaccessible documents.]

Byloe (The Past). Old series, 1900-1914 (with some irregularities); 22 nos. (1906-1907); No. 8 (1908). New series, 35 nos., Petrograd, 1917-1926 (irregular numeration); 13 nos. (1917-1918). [Journal devoted to the history of the revolutionary movement. Significant articles and records.]

Chernov, V. M. (Iu. Gardenin, pseud.). Chuzhimi putiami: Sbornik statei (By Roads Not Their Own: A Collection of Articles). Geneva, 1916.

—— The Great Russian Revolution. Translated by Philip E. Mosely. New Haven, Conn., 1936.

—— Internatsional i voina: Sbornik statei (The International and the War: A Collection of Articles). 2d ed. Petrograd, 1917.

—— Istinnye i mnimye porazhentsy: Sbornik statei (Real and Imagined Defeatists: A Collection of Articles). 2d ed. Petrograd, 1917.

—— "Istorik ili isterik?" (Historian or Hysteric?), *Volia Rossii* (The Freedom of Russia) (Prague), III (1925), 92-119. [Polemics with S. P. Melgunov.]

—— Pered burei (Before the Storm). New York, 1953.

—— Rozhdenie revoliutsionnoi Rossii (fevral'skaia revoliutsiia) (The Birth of Revolutionary Russia: The February Revolution). Paris, Prague, and New York, 1934. Vol. I of Velikaia Russkaia Revoliutsiia (The Great Russian Revolution). [All that was published, save for abridged English edition; a study of merit.]

——Voina i "tret'ia sila": Sbornik statei (The War and the "Third Force": A Collection of Articles). 2d ed. Petrograd, 1917.

—— Zapiski sotsialista-revoliutsionera (Memoirs of a Socialist Revolutionary). Berlin, St. Petersburg, and Moscow, 1922. Book I. [All that was published; deals with earliest period of Chernov's career.]

Chernov, V. M. (*Continued*)

—— Zemlia i pravo: Sbornik statei (Land and Law: A Collection of Articles). Petrograd, 1919. [Solid and substantial essays.]

Dan, F. "K istorii poslednikh dnei Vremennogo Pravitel'stva" (On the History of the Last Days of the Provisional Government), in Letopis' Revoliutsii (Chronicle of the Revolution) (Berlin, St. Petersburg and Moscow, Grzhebin, 1923), I, 163-75. [A meaty article.]

Delo Naroda (The People's Cause). 245 nos. Petrograd, 1917. [Daily newspaper. Published by the Central Committee of the PSR. Edited by S. P. Postnikov, V. M. Chernov, V. M. Zenzinov, and others. Most basic of all the sources. Gives the facts as does nothing else, but withholds illumination in matters of tension or scandal. In the file in the Russian Archives Abroad in Prague, the editorials written by Chernov have been signed by him in ink.]

Demianov, A. "Moia sluzhba pri Vremennom Pravitel'stve" (My work in the Provisional Government), in Arkhiv Russkoi Revoliutsii (Archives of the Russian Revolution), IV (2d ed.), 55-120.

Denikin, A. I. Ocherki russkoi smuty (Sketches of Russian Turmoil). 5 vols. Paris and Berlin, 1921-1926. Vols. I (Parts I and II) and II.

Dobavlenie k protokolam pervago s"ezda Partii Sotsialistov-Revoliutsion-erov (Appendix to the Minutes of the First Congress of the Socialist Revolutionary Party). N.p., 1906.

Dubrowski, S. Die Bauernbewegung in der Russischen Revolution 1917. Berlin, 1929.

Dvenadtsat' smertnikov: Sud nad sotsialistami-revoliutsionerami v Moskve (Twelve Prisoners Condemned to Death: The Trial of the Socialist Revolutionaries in Moscow). Berlin, 1922.

Egorov, M. "Krest'ianskoe dvizhenie v Tsentral'noi Chernozëmnoi oblasti v 1907-1914 godakh" (The Peasant Movement in the Central Black-Earth Region in 1907-1914), *Voprosy Istorii* (Problems of History), V (May, 1948), 3-19.

Egorov, N. "Marksistskaia kritika narodnicheskikh vzgliadov na russkuiu obshchinu" (Marxist Criticism of Narodnik Views on the Russian Commune), *Istoricheskii Zhurnal* (Historical Journal), XII (1938), 35-47.

Erde, D. Gody buri i natiska (Years of Storm and Stress). Kharkov, 1923. Book I. Na levoberezh'i 1917 (On the Left Bank in 1917).

Gaisinski, M. Bor'ba bol'shevikov za krest'ianstvo v 1917 g.: Vserossiiskie s"ezdy Sovetov krest'ianskikh deputatov (The Fight of the Bolsheviks for the Peasantry in 1917: The All-Russian Congresses of the Soviets of Peasant Deputies). Moscow, 1933. [Contains a good deal of information, but does not fill, even from the factual standpoint, the void left by the destruction of Bykhovski's book, for which purpose it apparently was intended.]

Gankin, Olga H., and H. H. Fisher. The Bolsheviks and the World War: The Origins of the Third International. Stanford, 1940.

Gerasimov, A. V. Der Kampf gegen die erste russische Revolution: Erinnerungen. Frauenfeld and Leipzig, 1934.

God russkoi revoliutsii (1917-1918 g.g.): Sbornik statei (A Year of the Russian Revolution [1917-1918]: A Collection of Articles). Moscow, 1918. [Contains some significant observations and admissions.]

Gurevich, V. Ia. "Vserossiiskii Krest'ianskii S"ezd i pervaia koalitsiia" (The All-Russian Peasant Congress and the First Coalition), in Letopis' Revoliutsii (Chronicle of the Revolution) (Berlin, St. Petersburg, and Moscow, Grzhebin, 1923), I, 176-96. [Solid article, adding something even to Bykhovski's account.]

International Socialist Committee in Berne. Bulletins Nos. 4 and 5 (April 22, 1916; July 10, 1916). [No. 4 in German, No. 5 in English.]

Istoriia grazhdanskoi voiny v SSSR (History of the Civil War in the USSR). Edited by Maxim Gorki [M. Gor'kii] et al. 2 vols. [with different subtitles]. Moscow, 1935-1943.

Izveshchenie o V-m s"ezde soveta P.S.-R. (Information about the Fifth Assembly of the Council of the SR Party). Geneva, n.d.

Izvestiia Glavnago Zemel'nago Komiteta (Proceedings of the Head Land Committee). 8 nos. Petrograd, 1917.

Izvestiia moskovskago soveta rabochikh i soldatskikh deputatov (Proceedings of the Moscow Soviet of Workers' and Soldiers' Deputies). Moscow, 1917. Nos. 194-233 (October 22–December 19).

Kamkov, B. D. Kto takie levye sotsialisty-revoliutsionery (Who Are the Left-Wing Socialist Revolutionaries). Petrograd, 1918.

Katorga i Ssylka (Penal Servitude and Deportation). 116 nos. Moscow, 1921-1935. [Not all numbers examined.]

Kazanskii Oktiabr': Materialy i dokumenty (The October Revolution in Kazan: Materials and Documents). Edited by E. Grachëv. Kazan, 1926. Part I [all that was published].

Kerenski, A. F. The Catastrophe. New York and London, 1927.

—— The Crucifixion of Liberty. New York, 1934.

—— Delo Kornilova (The Kornilov Affair). Moscow, 1918.

—— Izdalëka: Sbornik statei (1920-1921 g.) (From Afar: A Collection of Articles [1920-1921]). Paris, n.d. [1922]. [Most revealing of Kerenski's writings.]

—— "Iz vospominanii" (From My Memoirs), Sovremennyia Zapiski (Contemporary Notes), XXXVIII, 246-75.

—— The Road to Tragedy. New York, 1935.

Khristiuk, Paul. Zamitki i materiiali do istoriï ukraïns'koï revoliutsiï, 1917-1920 rr. (Notes and Materials for a History of the Ukrainian Revolution, 1917-1920). 4 vols. Vienna, 1921-1922. Vol. I. [Not fully utilized because of language difficulty. Author belonged to PUSR.]

Khronika grazhdanskoi voiny v Sibiri (1917-1918) (Chronicle of the Civil War in Siberia [1917-1918]). Edited by V. Maksakov and A. Turunov. Moscow and Leningrad, 1926.

Knorin, V. Revoliutsiia i kontr-revoliutsiia v Belorussii (Fevral' 1917-Fevral' 1918) (Revolution and Counter-Revolution in Belorussia [February, 1917–February, 1918]). Smolensk, 1920. Part I. [All that was published; information on Minsk province and Western Front.]

Kornilovskie dni: Biulleteni Vr. Voenn. Komiteta pri Ts. Isp. Kom. S.R. i S.D. s 28 Avg. po 4 Sent. 1917 g. (The Kornilov Period: Bulletins of the Provisional Military Committee under the Central Executive Committee of the Soviet of Workers' and Soldiers' Deputies from August 28 to September 4, 1917). Edited by V. A. Kolerov. Petrograd, 1917.

Kosinski, V. A. Osnovnyia tendentsii v mobilizatsii zemel'noi sobstvennosti i ikh sotsial'no-ekonomicheskie faktory (Basic Tendencies in Mobilizing Landed Property and Their Social and Economic Factors). Prague, 1925.

Krasnaia Letopis' (Red Chronicle). 62 nos. Leningrad, 1922-1934. [Only some issues.]

Krasnyi Arkhiv (The Red Archives). 106 vols. Moscow, 1922-1941. [Considerable information of value in form of shorter articles and documents. Contains both diplomatic and revolutionary records.]

Kratkii otchët o rabotakh chetvërtago s''ezda Partii Sotsialistov-Revoliutsionerov (26 noiabria–5 dekabria 1917 goda) (Brief Report of the Work of the Fourth Congress of the Socialist Revolutionary Party [November 26–December 5, 1917]). Edited by V. M. Zenzinov. Petrograd, 1918. 160 pp. [One of the most important sources, and one of the rarest. A mine of information, but Zenzinov had an old maid's attitude toward scandal, and his inadequate reporting of heated scenes must be supplemented by the accounts in the Volia Naroda (The Will of the Nation) and the Delo Naroda (The People's Cause).]

Krest'ianskoe dvizhenie v 1917 godu (The Peasant Movement in 1917). Moscow, 1928. Vol. II of Agrarnaia Revoliutsiia (The Agrarian Revolution).

"K voprosu o teoreticheskom obosnovanii sotsializma" (On the Question of the Theoretical Basis of Socialism), Revoliutsionnaia Rossiia (Revolutionary Russia), No. 36 (November 15, 1903), pp. 1-5. [Anonymous, but unmistakably Chernovian. Probably the most interesting of his writings for theorists, and certainly the most injurious to eyesight.]

Lenin, V. I. Sochineniia (Works). 2d ed., 30 vols. Moscow and Leningrad, 1926-1932. [Preference given to second edition when available.]

Lloyd George, David. War Memoirs. 1st ed., 6 vols. London, 1933-1936. Vol. IV.

Lozinski, Z. Ekonomicheskaia politika Vremennogo Pravitel'stva (The Economic Policy of the Provisional Government). Leningrad, 1929.

Lutokhin, D. A. "Zemel'nyi vopros v deiatel'nosti Vremennogo Pravitel'stva" (The Land Question in the Work of the Provisional Government), in Zapiski Instituta Izucheniia Rossii (Notes of the Institute for the Study of Russia), II, 346-69. Prague, 1925.

Makarov, F. P. Oktiabr' i grazhdanskaia voina v Udmurtii (October and the Civil War in Udmurtia). Izhevsk, 1932.

Martynov, E. I. Kornilov (popytka voennogo perevorota) (Kornilov: The Attempt at a Military Coup). N.p., 1927.

Masaryk, T. G. The Spirit of Russia. 2 vols. London and New York, 1919.

Miliukov, P. N. Istoriia vtoroi russkoi revoliutsii (The History of the Second Russian Revolution). Sofia, 1921-1924. Vol. I, Parts I, II, III. [Always of use, though Miliukov was not at home in SR affairs.]

Morokhovets, E. A. Agrarnye programmy rossiiskikh politicheskikh partii v 1917 godu (The Agrarian Programs of Russian Political Parties in 1917). Leningrad, 1929. [Useful study.]

Mstislavski, S. Piat' dnei: Nachalo i konets fevral'skoi revoliutsii (Five Days: The Beginning and End of the February Revolution). Berlin, St. Petersburg, and Moscow, 1922.

Nabokov, K. D. Ispytaniia diplomata (The Ordeal of a Diplomat). Stockholm, 1923.

Nabokov, V. D. "Vremennoe Pravitel'stvo" (The Provisional Government), in Arkhiv Russkoi Revoliutsii (Archives of the Russian Revolution), I (2d ed.), 9-96. [An honest and searching account. Important contribution.]

Na Chuzhbine (On Foreign Soil). 16 nos. Geneva, 1916-1917. Nos. 1, 10, 11, 13, 14, 15.

Narodovlastie: Sbornik statei chlenov uchreditel'nago sobraniia fraktsii sotsial.-revoliutsionerov (Sovereignty of the People: A Collection of Articles by SR Members of the Constituent Assembly). 3 nos. Moscow, 1918. [Short and rather superficial articles.]

Nash Put': Organ revoliutsionnago sotsializma (Our Path: Organ of Revolutionary Socialism). Edited by M. A. Spiridonova. 2 nos. St. Petersburg, 1917. [A left SR publication, as difficult to come by as most, and with information obtainable nowhere else.]

Nikolaevski, Boris. Azew: Die Geschichte eines Verrats. Berlin, 1932.

Nikolaevski, Boris (*Continued*)

—— Istoriia odnogo predatelia: Terroristy i politicheskaia politsiia (The Story of a Traitor: Terrorists and the Political Police). Berlin, 1932. [Slightly preferable to German edition, but at times was unavailable.]

Noulens, Joseph. Mon Ambassade en Russie soviétique 1917-1919. 2 vols. Paris, 1933. [Gives little.]

Novaia Zhizn' (New Life). 210 nos. Petrograd, 1917. [File partially inspected. Maxim Gorki's newspaper, antiwar and independent leftist.]

Oberuchev, K. M. Vospominaniia (Reminiscenses). New York, 1930.

Obshchestvennoe dvizhenie v Rossii v nachale XX-go veka (The Social Movement in Russia at the Beginning of the Twentieth Century). 3 vols. St. Petersburg, 1909-1914. [A collaborative work from the Menshevik point of view. Vast amount of information.]

Ocherki po istorii Oktiabr'skoi revoliutsii (Studies of the History of the October Revolution). Edited by M. N. Pokrovski. 2 vols. Moscow and Leningrad, 1927. [Strictly Marxist, but substantial investigations.]

Oganovski, N. "Dnevnik chlena Uchreditel'nago Sobraniia" (Diary of a Member of the Constituent Assembly), *Golos Minuvshago* (Voice of the Past), Nos. 4-6 (April-June, 1918), pp. 143-72. [Most revealing.]

Oktiabr' na Odeshchine: Sbornik statei i vospominanii k X-letiiu oktiabria (October in the Odessa Region: A Collection of Articles and Memoirs on the Tenth Anniversary of the October Revolution). Odessa, 1927.

Ot fevralia k oktiabriu v Moskve: Sbornik statei, vospominanii i dokumentov (From February to October in Moscow: A Collection of Articles, Memoirs, and Documents). Moscow, 1923.

Pamiati Stepana Nikolaevicha Slëtova (To the Memory of Stepan Nikolaevich Slëtov). Paris, 1916.

Partiinyia Izvestiia (Party News). 6 nos. Petrograd, 1917-1918. [Published by the Central Committee and edited by V. M. Zenzinov and others. A rare and valuable source. Reports and proceedings of party organizations, shedding light on SR activities in all parts of the country. Illuminating articles on otherwise neglected subjects.]

Pasmanik, D. S. Revoliutsionnye gody v Krimu (Revolutionary Years in the Crimea). N.p., 1926. [Author a Kadet physician. Interesting observations.]

Pavlovich, M. (pseud. of Weltman). "Lenin i es-ery" (Lenin and the SR's), *Pod Znamenem Marksizma* (Under the Banner of Marxism), X (October, 1923), 142-63.

Pershin, P. "Krest'ianskie zemel'nye komitety v period podgotovki Velikoi Oktiabr'skoi sotsialisticheskoi revoliutsii" (Peasant Land Committees in the Period of Preparation of the Great October Socialist

Revolution), *Voprosy Istorii* (Problems of History), VII (July, 1948), 70-83.

Petrogradskii Sovet Rabochikh i Soldatskikh Deputatov: Protokoly zasedanii ispolnitel'nogo komiteta i biuro i. k. (The Petrograd Soviet of Workers' and Soldiers' Deputies: Minutes of the Sessions of the Executive Committee and the Bureau of the Executive Committee). Edited by B. Ia. Nalivaiski. Moscow and Leningrad, 1925.

Poincaré, Raymond. Au Service de la France: neuf années de souvenirs. 10 vols. Paris, 1926-1933. Vol. IX: L'Année trouble, 1917.

Polianski, N. N. Narodnicheskii sotsializm (Narodnik Socialism). Moscow, 1918. [Clarifying essay on Populist theory, trailing off at the end.]

Polner, T. I. Zhiznennyi put' Kniazia Georgiia Evgenievicha L'vova (The Life of Prince George Evgenievich Lvov). Paris, 1932.

Prager, E. Geschichte der U.S.P.D.: Entstehung und Entwicklung der Unabhängigen Sozialdemokratischen Partei Deutschlands. 2d ed. Berlin, 1922.

Prizyv (The Call). 45 nos. Paris, 1915-1916.

Proletarskaia Revoliutsiia (Proletarian Revolution). 113 nos. Moscow, 1921-1931.

Protokoly pervago s"ezda Partii Levykh Sotsialistov-Revoliutsionerov (Internatsionalistov) (Minutes of the First Congress of the Left Socialist Revolutionary Party [Internationalists]). N.p., 1918. 115 pp. [An exceedingly rare source of obvious importance.]

Protokoly pervago s"ezda Partii Sotsialistov-Revoliutsionerov (Minutes of the First Congress of the Socialist Revolutionary Party). N.p., 1906. 368 pp. [The congress at which the program was worked out.]

Protokoly vtorogo (ekstrennago) s"ezda partii S.-Rev. (Minutes of the Second [Extraordinary] Congress of the SR Party). St. Petersburg, 1907. 177 pp. [Chernov said the secretaries were lazy and did not take down his speeches as they should. Presumably the same applies to other speeches.]

Radkey, O. H. "Chernov and Agrarian Socialism," in Continuity and Change in Russian and Soviet Thought. Edited by Ernest J. Simmons. Cambridge, Mass., 1955.

—— The Election to the Russian Constituent Assembly of 1917. Cambridge, Mass., 1950.

Rafes, M. Dva goda revoliutsii na Ukraine: Raskol "Bunda" (Two Years of Revolution in the Ukraine: The Split in the "Bund"). Moscow, 1920.

Rathauser, Ia. Revoliutsiia i grazhdanskaia voina v Baku (The Revolution and the Civil War in Baku). Part I: 1917-1918. Baku, 1927.

Rech' (Speech). Petrograd, 1917. [Some numbers consulted. Daily newspaper. Central organ of the Constitutional Democratic party. V. D. Nabokov was an editor and P. N. Miliukov, a close collaborator.]

Reshetar, John S. The Ukrainian Revolution 1917-1920: A Study in Nationalism. Princeton, 1952.

Revoliutsiia 1917 goda (Khronika sobytii) (The Revolution of 1917: Chronicle of Events). Compiled by N. Avdeev and others. 6 vols. Moscow and Petrograd, 1923-1930. [Valuable for source material as well as for reference.]

Revoliutsionnaia Rossiia (Revolutionary Russia). Old series, 76 nos., 1901-1905. New series, 78 nos., Dorpat, Berlin, and Prague, 1920-1931. [On the closely printed pages of the old series, Chernov worked out the tenets of neo-Populism; on those of the new, he performed an autopsy.]

Rudnev, V. V. "Dvadstat' let tomu nazad" (Twenty Years Ago), *Sovremennyia Zapiski* (Contemporary Notes), LVI, 375-92.

—— "Iz istorii partii (zagranichnoe soveshchanie tsentral'nykh rabotnikov P.S.-R. po voprosu o linii povedeniia v usloviiakh mirovoi voiny" (From the History of the Party [Conference Abroad of Central Workers of the PSR to Determine the Line to be Taken in the World War]), *Svoboda* (Freedom), No. 4 (December, 1935), pp. 13-18; No. 5 (July, 1936), pp. 6-10.

Russkiia Vedomosti (The Russian Record). Moscow, 1917. [Some numbers consulted. Daily newspaper with high standards; staid, professorial, and liberal.]

Russkoe Slovo (The Russian Word). 259 nos. Moscow, 1917. Nos. 148-259 (July 1–November 26, 1917). [Popular newspaper; articles tend to be superficial. But many facts.]

Savinkov, B. V. K delu Kornilova (The Kornilov Affair). Paris, 1919. [Prose that is a pleasure to read.]

—— Memoirs of a Terrorist. New York, 1931.

Sef, S. E. Revoliutsiia 1917 goda v Zakavkaz'i (Dokumenty, materialy) (The Revolution of 1917 in the Transcaucasus [Documents, Materials]). Tiflis, 1927. [Important regional source.]

Sel'skoe khoziaistvo Rossii v XX veke: Sbornik statistiko-ekonomicheskikh svedenii za 1901-1922 g.g. (Agriculture in Russia in the Twentieth Century: A Compilation of Economic Statistical Data for 1901-1922). Edited by N. P. Oganovski. Moscow, 1923.

Shcherbakov, V. K. Zhovtneva revoliutsiia i roki gromadians'koï borot'bi na Chernigivshchini (The October Revolution and the Years of Civil War in the Chernigov Region). Chernigov, 1927. [Substantial account, in which Ukrainian nationalism shows through Communist veneer.]

Shliapnikov, A. Kanun semnadtsatogo goda (The Eve of 1917). 2 parts. Moscow, 1920-?.

—— Semnadtsatyi god (The Year 1917). 4 vols. Moscow and Leningrad, 1923-1931. Vols. I, II, and III. [The Shliapnikov books give only incidental information on the SR's.]

Shulgin, A. L'Ukraine contre Moscou 1917. Paris, 1935.

Shul'gin, V. V. Dni (Days). Belgrade, 1925.

Slavík, Jan. "Ruské strany politické za světové války: Socialisté revolucionáři" (Russian Political Parties during the World War: The Socialist Revolutionaries), Slovanský Přehled (Slavonic Review), XVII, 393-95, 476-83.

Slëtov, S. N. K. istorii vozniknoveniia Partii Sotsialistov-Revoliutsionerov (Toward a History of the Origin of the Socialist Revolutionary Party). Petrograd, 1917. [Basic source for the formative period.]

—— Sto let bor'by za narodnoe delo (One Hundred Years of Struggle for the People's Cause). Helsingfors, 1917.

Sovety krest'ianskikh deputatov i drugie krest'ianskie organizatsii (Soviets of Peasants' Deputies and Other Peasant Organizations). Edited by A. V. Shestakov. Moscow, 1929. Vol. I: Mart-oktiabr' 1917 g. Part II.

Sovremennyia Zapiski (Contemporary Notes). 70 vols. Paris, 1920-1940. [Leading émigré journal with prominent right SR collaborators.]

Spiridovich, A. Histoire du terrorisme russe 1886-1917. Paris, 1930. [A mass of facts and events loosely strung together with little or no attempt at analysis. Nevertheless, this tsarist police official assembled much useful information from the dossiers and other materials at his command.]

Stankevich, V. B. Vospominaniia 1914-1919 g. (Recollections of 1914-1919). Berlin, 1920. [These memoirs are a significant contribution to the history of the period. The author, an army man on the right fringe of Populism, is well informed and objective in his judgments.]

Steinberg, I. Z. Ot fevralia po oktiabr' 1917 g. (From February to October, 1917). Berlin and Milan, n.d. [An informative, well-written survey from the left SR point of view, and for that very reason one of the more significant sources.]

—— Spiridonova: Revolutionary Terrorist. London, 1935. [Biography of a tragic figure. This book does not measure up to the foregoing one.]

Steklov, Iu. Partiia sotsialistov-revoliutsionerov (pravykh eserov) (The Socialist Revolutionary Party [Right SR's]). Moscow, 1922. [This book is put on the list as an example of what not to read. The first lie is right in the title.]

Sukhanov, N. (pseud. of N. N. Gimmer). Marksizm i Narodnichestvo (Marxism and Populism). N.p., n.d. [c. 1915]. [Suggestive essay.]

Sukhanov, N. (*Continued*)

—— Zapiski o revoliutsii (Notes on the Revolution). 7 vols. Berlin, St. Petersburg, and Moscow, 1922-1923. [A source that must always be taken into account, especially for backstage illumination of the soviet scene. Remarkably uneven. Sometimes Sukhanov's keenness of observation or powers of divination are breath-taking; at other times his prejudices or journalistic superficiality throw him wide of the mark. Well written and always interesting; gossipy. Caustic criticism of the "very biggest party."]

Sviatitski, N. "Voina i predfevral'e" (The War and the Pre-February Era), *Katorga i Ssylka* (Penal Servitude and Deportation), LXXV (II, 1931), 7-50. [Very substantial account of a period in the party's history which otherwise is virtually a blank. Novel view on Kerenski's role. In the fifteenth year of the Soviet regime, the author makes Kerenski out as something of a revolutionary hero and opponent of the war.]

Trenogova, T. Bor'ba petrogradskikh bol'shevikov za krest'ianstvo v 1917 godu (The Fight of the Petrograd Bolsheviks for the Peasantry in 1917). Leningrad, 1946. [Some welcome and uncommon information, but weak in analysis. Archival material used extensively, mainly for Northwestern-Lake Region.]

Tretii s"ezd Partii SotsialistovRevoliutsionerov (The Third Congress of the Socialist Revolutionary Party). Petrograd, 1917. 502 pp. [One of the most indispensable sources, and also one of the fattest. The secretaries did better this time, but they still did not like scandal. Inexplicably rare.]

Trotski, L. The History of the Russian Revolution. 3 vols. New York, 1932. [Trotski informed the author these books contained everything he had to say about the SR's. He did not say much.]

Tsereteli, I. G. "Rossiiskoe krest'ianstvo i V. M. Chernov v 1917 godu" (The Russian Peasantry and V. M. Chernov in 1917), *Novyi Zhurnal* (New Journal), XXIX (1952), 215-44. [His colleague and friend sketches Chernov's agrarian policy and reveals the feeling it aroused in the bosom of the Provisional Government.]

1917 god na Kievshchine: Khronika sobytii (1917 in the Kiev Region: Chronicle of Events). Edited by V. Manilov. Kiev, 1928. [Mass of information.]

1917 god v Khar'kove: Sbornik statei i vospominanii (1917 in Kharkov: A Collection of Articles and Reminiscences). Edited by V. Morgunov and Z. Machulski. Kharkov, 1927.

1917 god v Saratove (1917 in Saratov). Saratov, 1927.

1917 god v stalingradskoi gubernii (khronika sobytii) (1917 in the Province of Stalingrad [Chronicle of Events]). Stalingrad, 1927.

1917i god v Voronezhskoi gubernii (khronika) (1917 in the Province of Voronezh [Chronicle]). Edited by B. M. Lavygin. Voronezh, 1928. [One of the better provincial chronicles.]

Vestnik Russkoi Revoliutsii (Herald of the Russian Revolution). 4 nos. Geneva, 1902-1905.

Vikhliaev, P. A. Kak uravniat' pol'zovanie zemlëi (How to Equalize the Use of the Land). Petrograd, 1917. [Socialization of the land brought down to earth.]

Vinnichenko, V. Vidrodzhennia natsii: Istoriia ukraïns'koi revoliutsii (marets 1917r.–gruden 1919r.) (Resurrection of a Nation: The History of the Ukrainian Revolution [March, 1917, to December, 1919]). 3 vols. Kiev and Vienna, 1920. [Could be used only to small extent because of language difficulty.]

Vishniak, Mark V. Dan' proshlomu (A Tribute to the Past). New York, 1954. [An interesting and well-written volume of reminiscences.]

—— "Tsena soiuza" (The Price of Union), *Dni* (Days), No. 263 (September 13, 1923). [Contribution to the party's autopsy.]

—— Vserossiiskoe Uchreditel'noe Sobranie (The All-Russian Constituent Assembly). Paris, 1932. [An authoritative account of preparations for the assembly, but the author's brief for the Kadets is not convincing.]

Voennyi, Victor (pseud.) "K voprosu o prichinakh neudach voennykh vozstanii" (On the Reasons for the Failure of Armed Uprisings), *Sotsialist-Revoliutsioner* (The Socialist Revolutionary), No. 2 (1910), pp. 224-26 (Conclusion).

Voitinski, V. Gody pobed i porazhenii (Years of Victories and Defeats). 2 vols. Berlin, St. Petersburg, and Moscow, 1923-1924.

Volia Naroda (The Will of the People). 206 nos. Petrograd, 1917. [Daily newspaper; organ of the right SR's; published by E. Breshko-Breshkovskaia and edited by A. A. Argunov. A major source.]

Volia Rossii (The Freedom of Russia). 13 vols. Prague, 1922-1934. [Some significant articles, especially from Chernov's pen.]

Voznesenski, A. N. Moskva v 1917 godu (Moscow in 1917). Moscow and Leningrad, 1928. [Intensely interesting, well informed, and objective account.]

Vserossiiskoe Soveshchanie Sovetov Rabochikh i Soldatskikh Deputatov: Stenograficheskii otchët (All-Russian Conference of the Soviets of Workers' and Soldiers' Deputies: Stenographic Report). Edited by M. N. Tsapenko. Moscow and Leningrad, 1927.

Vserossiiskoe Uchreditel'noe Sobranie (The All-Russian Constituent Assembly). Edited by I. S. Malchevski. Moscow and Leningrad, 1930.

Zakliuchenie sudebno-sledstvennoi komissii po delu Azefa (The Conclusion Reached by the Judicial Commission Investigating the Azef Case). N.p., 1911.

Zemlia i Volia (Land and Freedom). 130 nos. (March 21–August 31). Petrograd, 1917. [Daily newspaper, organ of Petrograd Regional Committee PSR. From early May to second half of July definitely left SR in tone. Significance ceased with assumption of control by Central Committee (see No. 94 of July 20). Not to be confused with the Moscow SR newspaper of the same name but opposite tendency.]

Zenzinov, V. Iz zhizni revoliutsionera (From the Life of a Revolutionary). Paris, 1919. [Slender but helpful.]

Znamia Truda (Banner of Labor). 108 nos. (August 23–December 31). Petrograd, 1917. [Began as a daily workingman's paper, published by the Petrograd Committee PSR. Fell to the left SR's when they took over the metropolitan organization in September; became their central organ. Extremely rare.]

ORAL TESTIMONY

Argunov, A. A. Interviews in Prague, June, 1935.

Chernov, V. M. Interviews in Prague, 1934-1935, and in New York, January 4, 1950.

Kerenski, A. F. Interview in Prague, 1934; conversations in California and Texas, 1955-1956.

Nikolaevski, B. I. Interviews in Prague, May, 1935, and in New York, 1948, 1949, 1951, 1954. A Menshevik rather than an SR, Nikolaevski is the thinking archive of the Russian Revolution.

Postnikov, S. P. Conversations in Prague, 1934-1935; interviews there in August and September, 1935.

Rudnev, V. V. Interview in Paris, September, 1935.

Steinberg, I. Z. Interviews in New York, December, 1949, December, 1951, and January, 1954.

Tsereteli, I. G. Interview in New York, December 23, 1949.

Vishniak, M. V. Interviews in Paris, September, 1935, and in New York, January, 1952; conversations in California, 1955.

Zenzinov, V. M. Interviews in Paris, September, 1935, and in New York, December 19 and 25, 1949, December 31, 1951.

INDEX

Agrarian Socialist League, 61n
Alekseev, M. V., 343, 388, 394, 395; and the war, 477 (quoted)
Alekseev, N. N., 219
Alexander II, 48, 59
Alexander III, 48-49, 217, 354
Alexandróvich, Peter (Pëtr Aleksándrovich Dmitrievskii), 91, 116-17, 130, 133; leadership in Petersburg Soviet, 133-34, 136, 191; and the "Petersburg Committee of Socialist Revolutionaries" manifesto, 139-40; as SR leader, 141, 141n, 152
Algasov (pseud. of Bordiukov or Burdiukov), V., 367, 440-41, 442
Allied Conference (Paris, 1917), 424-425, 443-44
Allies, 150-51, 174, 177, 189, 203, 261; and the right-wing SR's, 94-95, 97-98, 198, 203, 204, 208, 209, 280, 345, 375-376, 407, 453, 469-70, 478-80; imperialism of, 103-6, 113, 123, 150, 335, 369; police of, 138; and the peace problem, 154, 158, 160, 178, 204, 230, 322, 474-84; and Russian war policy, 179, 272, 299, 337, 339-40, 341, 346n, 443, 444, 452, 474-84
All-Russian Congress of Soviets of Peasants' Deputies (or All-Russian Congress of Peasants' Soviets), 175, 181, 184, 244, 246, 346, 478; SR's in, 173, 246-47, 306n, 329; and land reform, 183, 248, 254, 256-57, 332
All-Russian Congress of Soviets of Workers' and Soldiers' Deputies (or All-Russian Congress of Workers' and Soldiers' Soviets), 293, 432, 466
All-Russian Executive Committee of

Peasants' Soviets (or All-Russian Peasants' Soviet), 267, 305n, 312, 336, 366-67, 467; SR's in, 136-37, 246-47, 281, 284, 388-89; and land reform, 246-47, 257, 328-29, 330; and the war, 247, 344-45, 407, 445, 478; Avksentiev's chairmanship of, 318, 328-329; and the soldiers, 346, 430; and the Kornilov rebellion, 390; and the third coalition, 412, 436-37; see also All-Russian Soviet Executive Committees
All-Russian Executive Committee of Workers' and Soldiers' Soviets (or All-Russian Workers' and Soldiers' Soviet), 336, 366-67, 372; "group of the presidium," 136-37, 157; SR's in, 137, 274, 281, 285, 349, 388-89; see also All-Russian Soviet Executive Committees
All-Russian Soviet Conference (March-April, 1917), 169, 225n; SR split in, 152
All-Russian Soviet Executive Committees (Peasants', Workers' and Soldiers'), 285-86, 307, 314, 430, 445
Alsace-Lorraine, 478
Altovskaia, Ina (maiden name of Ina Rakitnikova), 52
Altovski, SR leader in Saratov province, 34n
Anarchism, 33, 70
Anarchists, 66, 67, 282
Annenski, N. F., 35n
An-ski (pseud. of S. A. Rappoport), 478-79
Antonov-Saratovski, V. P., 147n, 193
April Days, 160-64

Archangel, SR's in, 236
Arefev, S. V., 52, 57, 58
Argunov, A. A., 73, 79n, 88, 138, 189n, 198n, 479; on competition between Marxists and Populists, 50; position on the war, 91, 93, 97, 98, 118n, 170; as editor of *Volia Naroda*, 189-90, 191, 298n, 300, 312-13, 315, 352; as right SR leader, 197, 218, 223, 304, 364n; on relations between Chernov and Kerenski, 230 (*quoted*), 231, 396
Arkhangelski, Vasili Gavrilovich, 169, 368, 407, 414; as Central Committee member, 221, 452
Armenian Dashnaktsutiun, 38n, 75, 265n
Armenians, 479; and the SR's, 265n
Astrakhan, SR's in, 236
Austria, 95, 110, 121, 156, 276, 369; socialists in, 103, 112, 114, 300, 339, 458; and the war, 273, 474-84
Avksentiev, N. D., 82, 92, 100, 133n, 166, 304, 424, 441; as Central Committee member, 79n, 221, 223, 247, 314, 397-98, 408, 416; position on the war, 91, 93, 94, 95, 102, 170, 197, 198, 204, 328-29, 407, 444-45; as right SR leader, 136, 138, 173, 175, 195-96, 198n, 200, 350-51, 364n, 461, 478; and the Third Party Congress, 204-5, 207, 209-12, 211 (*quoted*), 239; as minister of the interior, 303, 317-18, 320, 321n, 322-23, 327, 343, 360n, 381, 387, 388, 431; and the All-Russian Peasants' Soviet, 328-29, 421; and the third coalition, 405-6, 407, 408, 409, 412, 414, 418, 419, 420-23, 433, 452-53
Azef, E. F., 51, 71-74, 77-80, 87, 419, 458-59
Azerbaidzhan Tatars, 265n

Bakhmut district, 236-37
Bakrylov, V., 189n
Baku, SR's in, 129, 151
Balmashev, S. V., 451
Bashkirs, 252
Beaugy-sur-Clarens Conference, 91-92, 93-94, 100, 107, 118
Berg, E. S., as Central Committee member, 221
Berlin, 51
Bessarabia, 270, 437n

Bez Lishnikh Slov (Without Extra Words), newspaper, 305
Bismarck, Otto von, 481-82
Bitsenko, Anastasia, 192
Black Hundreds, 63, 310, 379, 472
"Bobrov," *see* Natanson, Mark
Boldyrev, SR party worker, 136, 441
Bolshakov, SR workingman, 149n
Bolshevik party, *see* Bolsheviks
Bolsheviks, 3, 63, 93, 117, 129, 170, 229, 315, 345, 379, 393, 401, 468, 473; borrowings from SR's, 6, 116; and the workers, 34, 134, 279, 430-31, 454, 471; and the peasants, 57, 234, 306, 332, 436, 446n, 454; organizational superiority, 64; internationalism of, 89, 113, 152, 189n; tactical intransigence, 102, 279; and the war, 113-15, 120, 205n, 241, 269n, 362, 369, 473, 474, 481, 485; and the soldiers, 131, 171, 243n, 348, 349, 355, 371-73, 429-430, 454, 471, 472; and the Petersburg Soviet, 136, 429-30; and the Provisional Government, 155-56, 170-71, 174, 220, 294-95, 356, 381, 392, 409n; attack on Kerenski, 162-63; theory of revolution, 165, 403; in Moscow city elections (June, Sept., *1917*), 240-42, 430, 432-34; in St. Petersburg municipal elections, 242-43, 363-65; urban strength of, 243, 432-34, 438, 452, 471; and the Cossacks, 251n; in the Ukraine, 267-68, 271n; and the Kronstadt sailors, 279, 281, 284-85; and the July crisis, 281, 286, 287n, 293, 294, 370; and the church, 351; and the third coalition, 420-21; and the soviets, 431-32; growth of power (October), 453-54, 471-73; *see also* Lenin, V. I.; Revolution of 1917; St. Petersburg
Bolshevism, 132, 134, 442, 443, 458, 467-468, 476, 480; Populist influence on, 4-6; agrarian doctrine, 22, 43-44; on revolutionary dictatorship, 42, 43-44; *see also* Lenin, V. I.
Bordiukov or Burdiukov (pseud. Algasov), V., 367, 440-41, 442
Bosporus, *see* Straits, The
Breshko-Breshkovskaia, E. K., 52, 56, 60, 77, 138, 150, 292, 441; as financial angel, 62n, 189n; as right-wing

leader, 165, 189, 192-93, 218, 223, 396 (*quoted*), 397, 398-99, 420, 421, 470; and the July crisis, 290-91 (*quoted*); in Seventh Party Council, 377, 378-379

Brest-Litovsk, Treaty of, 117, 269-70, 481

Briullova-Shaskolskaia, N. V., 220*n*

Brusilov, A. A., 393 (*quoted*)

Buchanan, George, 178, 302, 303, 338, 342*n*, 362, 365

Buguruslan, 243

Bulakov, L. P., 52

Bulanov, L. P., 189, 191, 479-80

Bulgakov, S. N., 351-52

Bunakov-Fondaminski, I. I., 76*n*, 138, 166; as right SR leader, 82, 198, 247; and the war, 91, 93, 97, 100, 119, 478 (*quoted*); on German socialists, 98-99 (*quoted*); on the revolution, 101 (*quoted*); as Central Committee member, 221, 223

Burdiukov or Bordiukov (pseud. Algasov), V., 367, 440-41, 442

Burevestnik (Harbinger of Storm), anarchist organ, 282

Burevoi (pseud. of Sopliakov), K. S., quoted, 308, 457

Buriats, 252

Burstein, SR leader in Petersburg Soviet, 338-39

Bykhovski, N. I., 378; as Central Committee member, 221; and the peasants, 246*n*, 250, 437 (*quoted*), 447; and the All-Russian Peasants' Soviet, 247, 328; as editor of peasants' *Izvestiia*, 437, 489

Capitalism, 4, 298, 404; Imperial Russia's promotion of, 15-16, 82

Caucasus, Mensheviks in, 347-48; SR's in, 347-48

Central Committee of the PSR, *see* PSR Central Committee

Central Powers, 96-97, 106, 114, 153, 203, 480

Chaikin, V. A., 91

Chaikovski, N. K., 83*n*, 470

Cheliabinsk, SR's in, 243

Chernenkov, agronomist, 293

Chernigov, 49, 263; peasants' soviets in, 267-68; SR's in, 264, 267-68

Chernov, Victor Mikhailovich, 49*n*, 52, 79*n*, 138, 168*n*, 198*n*, 210, 386; formulation of SR doctrine, 4-6, 21, 24, 36*n*, 45, 57, 82-85, 86, 116, 230, 300, 424, 459-60, 470; agrarian program of, 4, 26 (*quoted*), 27, 58-59, 174, 177, 215, 245-62, 280, 309, 334; and the village commune, 11-12, 44*n*, 83, 84 (*quoted*), 254-55; on the proletariat, 16 (*quoted*); influence on Lenin, 22, 122-23; on individualism, 26*n*, 85*n*; on political decentralization, 30; on socialization of industry, 33 (*quoted*), 41; on the nationalities problem, 40, 107, 108, 219, 220, 274, 276, 355; on revolutionary dictatorship, 41; Marxist influence on, 45 (*quoted*); ideological influences on, 47, 169; editorship of *Revoliutsionnaia Rossiia*, 51; founding of PSR, 51; and party organization, 56, 128 (*quoted*), 187, 238, 366; and Azef, 73; on the militant policy of the PSR, 79; as party leader, 81, 82, 86-87, 116-17, 180-81, 182, 183, 225*n*, 246, 364*n*, 365*n*, 379, 383, 414-15, 420-23, 427, 440-41, 461-62, 464, 465-67; as internationalist, 89-90, 91-92, 93, 107-111, 117, 118*n*, 124-25, 156, 202*n*, 203, 210-11, 219, 239, 339; proposals for united action in war, 92; on the "defensists," 102, 115, 116*n*, 119, 123; on Russian imperialism, 104-5, 111; Lenin's influence on, 110-12, 115; and the Third International, 111; and the war, 111-12 (*quoted*), 113, 115, 150, 207, 261, 297-98, 299-300, 303, 308, 309, 313, 475-77, 476 (*quoted*), 480; on the defeatists, 113-114, 115, 116, 261; charge of pro-Germanism, 114; on Bolshevism, 116*n*, 398; on Zimmerwald Manifesto, 117-18, 156; and the February Revolution, 131 (*quoted*); and the Petersburg Soviet, 136, 172; as minister of agriculture (first coalition), 136, 174-76, 177, 181-82, 212, 231, 232-233, 245-61, 277, 286-87, 324-25; "dual power" doctrine, 144; relations with Kerenski, 146, 159-60 (*quoted*), 182, 226, 229-33, 239, 290, 292, 333, 391, 401, 454, 460, 462-63; attack on

Chernov, Victor Mikhailovich (*Cont.*)
Miliukov, 155-64, 162 (*quoted*), 174-175; and the April Days, 161-62; and first coalition government, 181, 183, 184, 210-12, 248, 295, 299; and the Third Party Congress, 185, 194, 195, 196-97, 208, 210-12, 226, 256-57; and the Fourth Party Congress, 194; and the center SR's, 196, 222-23; relations with Gotz, 197, 198, 201-3, 311-12, 333, 400, 414, 424, 426, 453-54; and resolution on the war at the Third Congress, 199-202; failure of leadership of, 201-2, 256-57, 330-34, 388; as Central Committee member, 221, 223-24, 228, 367, 369; minimum land reform program (*1917*), 252-54, 297, 332; conflict with Lvov, 258-61; and the Ukrainian problem, 274-76; and the Kronstadt sailors, 280-81; and the masses, 281-82, 289, 308-10; and the July crisis, 287, 288 (*quoted*), 291-93, 294-95, 316-17, 370; and the declaration of July 8, 291-93, 331; letter to Nekrasov, 293; Kadet campaign against (July), 293-313, 326; resignation from ministry episode, 307-13, 376; as minister of agriculture (second coalition), 313, 322-34, 334 (*quoted*), 340, 415; retirement from second coalition, 333, 452; and the second coalition war policy, 334, 335-39, 341, 343, 400; and the army, 345-46, 349-50, 391, 451, 461; and the Constituent Assembly, 355-56, 359; and the Seventh Party Council, 376-77, 379, 380-81; and the Kornilov rebellion, 387-88, 389, 390-91; attack on Kerenski's administration, 393-402, 403, 411, 414, 439, 442; Manuscript commentary on the minutes of the Central Committee of the PSR, 404*n*, 486; and controversy over the third coalition's composition, 404-5, 408, 412-13, 416, 417-18, 418 (*quoted*), 420-23, 424, 440; and the third coalition, 423, 425, 446*n*; "Lessons of the Conference," 426-27; and the move toward schism, 441 (*quoted*), 441-42; and the third coalition land reform policy, 446, 449; and SR leadership

problem, 458 (*quoted*), 458-61; self-appraisal, 460 (*quoted*); and the Mensheviks, 466-67
Chernov, Vladimir M., 189
Chernyshevski, N. G., 4, 47
Chita, 144, 192
Chkheidze, N. S., 136, 168*n*, 288, 418
Clemenceau, Georges, 444, 480
Coalition, *see* Provisional Government, first coalition, second coalition, third coalition
Committee of Soldier's Soviets of the Western Front, 171
Committeee on Civic Education in Free Russia, 189*n*
Commune (*obshchina*), village, 8, 22, 82, 84, 214; as bridge to socialism, 10-12, 28, 44, 48; and capitalism, 12-15; stagnation in, 59-60; collectivism in, 82, 84, 254; and Provisional Government land program, 254-55
Congresses and councils of the PSR, *see under* PSR
Constantinople, 178, 470
Constituent Assembly, 139, 143, 144, 169, 230, 269, 271-72, 280, 366, 375, 395, 406, 445, 463, 464; and the nationalities problem, 39, 219-20, 269, 275-76; and the republic issue, 140, 147, 291; and land reform, 181, 213-215, 247-48, 249, 252, 253, 254, 258, 260, 294, 297, 322-23, 325, 447, 467-68; postponement of, 211, 355-60, 411, 452; Provisional Government's accountability to, 296*n*, 355
—— election for, 43, 147-148, 267*n*, 278, 472; in Don region, 251*n*; in the Ukraine, 268, 273-74
Constitutional Democratic party, *see* Kadets
Cooperative associations, 247
Cossack Congress, 252
Cossacks, 213-14; and the land reform problem, 251-52; and Kornilov rebellion, 390, 391-93
Council of the Republic, 406, 424-25, 426, 427, 431, 449, 450, 452, 453*n*; agreement on the third coalition, 419-22; Foreign Affairs Commission of, 483
Crimea, SR's in, 235-36

Dalin (pseud. of M. A. Levenson), 91, 116, 126

Dan, F. I., 136, 167-68, 169, 288, 304-5, 406, 420, 421, 452-53, 458

Dardanelles, *see* Straits, The

"Defensism," 94-95, 375, 396

"Defensists," 67, 89-90, 131, 136, 189*n*; 317; émigré, 91-92, 93-94, 99, 138, 188; relation to the revolution, 92-93, 98, 100-103, 284; nationalism of, 94, 106, 170; attitude toward the Allies, 94, 177-78, 179; hostility toward Germany, 95-96; position on the war, 96-99, 102-3, 113, 124, 149-55, 156, 166, 177, 377; and the Mensheviks, 118-19, 166; criticism of *Na Chuzhbine*, 121; and *Volia Naroda*, 189-90; at the Third Party Congress, 207, 228; support for Kerenski, 228, 229, 232; *see also* "Defensism"; Intelligentsia; Nationalism

Dekonski, Peter P., 226, 232, 440-41, 442

Delo Naroda (The People's Cause), newspaper, 136, 145*n*, 156, 188, 196*n*, 227*n*, 333, 368*n*, 438, 490; on SR party resolutions, 141*n*, 145*n*; on the Provisional Government, 158, 344; Gotz's defense of Kerenski, 225*n*; on the Bolsheviks, 284-85, 365; attacks on Manuilov, 298-99; on Chernov's resignation, 309, 310, 311; and the church, 351, 352; on the Finnish question, 354; on election of the Constituent Assembly, 359-60; Balashov district board telegram, 365*n* (*quoted*); on the war, 375-76, 378; and the Kornilov rebellion, 386, 388; Chernov's attack on Kerenski's administration, 394, 396-97; on Chernov's attack on Kerenski, 398-400; Central Committee reorganization, 426-27; Chernov on schism, 441; on land reform, 448, 449; Alekseev on the war, 477

Demianov, A. A., as minister of justice, 326

Democratic Conference, 350, 406, 428*n*, 431, 437, 441, 467; SR's in, 410-12, 413-15, 416-19, 421, 423-24, 454; Kadets in, 413; composition of, 413-414, 435-37; negotiations on the third coalition at, 416, 418-19, 422-23; decision on the third coalition, 417-18; presidium of, 418-19; *see also* Council of the Republic

Democratic Council, 419-22, 424-25; *see also* Council of the Republic

Den', newspaper, 145*n*

Denikin, A. I., 347, 350, 391

Deriuzhinski, V. L. (pseud. Vladimir Utgof), 346, 481*n*

Dnieper River, 262-63, 266-67

Dobronravov, P. A., 56

Don Cossacks, *see* Cossacks

Donets Basin, 251*n*, 263

Don region, 54*n*, 251, 391-92, 393; November election results in, 251*n*

Donskoi, D. D., 348

Dulebov, Egor, 70*n*

Duma, 161, 286, 287, 288, 414, 419; First, 36, 63, 76, 77; Second, 28, 36, 76-77, 99, 102, 129; Third, 76*n*; Fourth, 76*n*, 139, 166, 306; Fourth, Provisional Committee of, 132-33, 139, 143-44, 146; Fifth, 129

Durnovo, P. N., 64, 69, 76, 116, 461, 483

East Prussia, 277-78, 323

Edinstvo, Plekhanov's, 300

Egorov, A., 42*n*, 50*n*

Ekaterinoslav, 49, 263; SR's in, 236-37, 267-68; peasants' congress (October), 268

England, 95, 109, 138, 148, 208, 464; imperialism of, 105, 160, 225, 369; and Russian war policy, 150, 177-78, 179, 203-4, 340, 341, 343, 474-84; and the campaign against Chernov, 301-2; and the Stockholm Conference, 336-340, 344

Eniseisk province, 167

Fascism, 70, 315, 458, 462-63

February Revolution, *see* Revolution of 1917, February

Fedotov, left SR, 391

Fifth Party Congress of the SD's, *see under* SD's

Fifth Party Council of the PSR, *see under* PSR

Fighting Organization, 68, 69, 71

Filippovski, V. N., 132, 173, 389

Finland, 40, 75, 184; independence issue, 216n, 217-18, 353-55, 375; Grand Duke of, 353-54, 355; Seim, 353-55
Finnish Social Democrats, 354
First coalition, see Provisional Government, first coalition
First Party Congress of the PSR, see under PSR
Fishman, left SR, 442n
Five-Year Plans, 27, 44
Flekkel, B. O., 141, 441, 442
Fondaminski, see Bunakov-Fondaminski, I. I.
Fourth Party Congress of the PSR, see under PSR
France, 95, 101, 109, 117, 119, 138, 208, 218, 356, 464; Radical Socialist party, 44; imperialism of, 105, 160, 225, 475, 480; and Russian war policy, 150, 178-79, 203-4, 328, 340, 343, 424, 474-84; and the campaign against Chernov, 302-3; and the Stockholm Conference, 337, 339-40, 344; socialists in, 458
Freemasonry, 160, 205, 290, 303
French Revolution, 41, 47, 48
Fundamental Laws of the Russian Empire, 77

Galicia, 105, 156, 277-78, 298
Gendelman, M. Ia., 90, 129, 138, 144, 484; as Central Committee member, 221
Geneva (Switzerland), 138, 149n, 384
Georgia, 244; Mensheviks in, 265n; SR's in, 265n
Gerasimov, A. V., 71, 72n, 74
Germany, 67, 104, 110, 113, 115, 122, 218, 262, 284; socialists in, 17, 36n, 98-99, 109, 114, 124-25, 300, 339, 458, 481n; and Russian war policy, 94, 95-96, 106, 121-22, 153, 177-78; imperialism of, 103, 109, 114, 121, 150-151, 178, 474; working class in, 109, 112-13, 339, 369; Independent Socialists in, 109, 124-25; Majority Socialists in, 109, 124-25; and the war, 116, 178, 269n, 273, 335, 346, 445, 474-84; National Assembly (1919), 124-25; Communists in, 125; and passage of Russian émigrés, 138-39; National Liberals in, 276, 469

Gershuni, Gregory, 51, 52, 60, 62, 73, 77, 185, 458-59
Gerstein, L. N., as Central Committee member, 221
Gimmer, N. N., see Sukhanov, N.
Gobechiia, Vladimir, 348
Godnev, I. V., 164n
Golman, SR party worker, 326n
Gorki, Maxim, 240, 477
Gotz, Abram R., 133n, 134, 138, 146, 181, 198n, 289, 440, 441, 450n (quoted); and Zimmerwaldism, 90, 168n; as SR leader, 136, 173, 175, 180, 197, 231, 283, 311-12, 364n, 395, 406, 424, 432 (quoted), 459-60, 461, 465; resolution at Second Petersburg City Conference, 152-53, 154-55, 196; and the war, 152, 165, 167, 219, 261, 344, 445 (quoted), 475, 483 (quoted); and the Mensheviks, 168, 169, 288; and Third Party Congress, 196-206, 210, 239; and the resolution on the war at the Third Congress, 199-204, 204 (quoted), 207 (quoted), 334; as Central Committee member, 221, 223-24, 227, 295, 408, 416, 417, 427 (quoted); and Kerenski, 225, 230; and the July crisis, 285-86, 304, 305n, 312, 314; and the second coalition, 334; and the third coalition, 408, 409n, 410, 414, 418, 419, 420, 422, 423, 433; and the October crisis, 452-54
Gotz, Michael R., 51, 73, 77, 458-59
Great Russia, see Peasants; Ukraine
Group of Toil, 36, 37, 363 (table)
Guchkov, A. I., 172, 345, 346
Guchkov-Shulgin mission, 147
Gukovski, A. I., 14-15, 38, 188, 189; on populism, 14 (quoted)
Gurevich, V. I., 246n, 248n; as Central Committee member, 221

Helsingfors (Finland), 283-84
Henderson, Arthur, 336, 337
Herzen, A. I., 4, 40
Hrushevski, M. S., 464

Iablonski, Adam, 282
Ignatiev, N. P., 298
Imatra (Finland), 24, 185

Imperialism, 103, 105, 158-59, 202-3, 206, 276, 298, 335, 477; see also Allies; Austria; Central Powers; England; France; Germany; Russia, Imperial; United States

Intelligentsia, 16, 47-48, 49, 188, 198, 276, 424, 472; and the peasants, 59, 85n, 246, 248, 262, 283, 310, 329-30, 390; and terrorism, 69-70; prowar sentiments of, 88, 89, 329-30, 413; and the February Revolution, 127-28; and the workers, 279; see also SR's

Internationalists, see SR Internationalists

International Socialist Bureau, 91

Irkutsk, 167, 169; SR's in, 243

Iskra, SD organ, 38

Ivanovo-Voznesensk, SR's in, 243

Ivanov-Razumnik, R. V., 89, 191, 195-196, 284, 442n

Izmailovich, Alexandra, 192

Izvestiia, peasants' (ed. Bykhovski), 437, 438, 489

Izvolski, A. P., 159

Japan, 94; government contributions to Russian extremist groups, 75

Jewish Bund, 262n

Jews, 62, 70, 71, 105, 116, 119n, 142, 263, 266, 351, 450n

July Days, 279-320 passim, 365

Kachinski, V. M., 91

Kadets (Constitutional Democrats), 36-37, 163, 164, 166, 218, 364, 432, 466, 473; concentration in cities, 53; in the first coalition government, 169-70, 175, 176, 178-79, 292; neo-Kadetism, 170; and the war, 170, 281, 298, 299, 335, 358, 362, 485; Central Committee of, 179n, 304; and SR Third Party Congress, 228n; in St. Petersburg municipal elections, 242-243, 363-64; urban strength of, 243-244, 430, 433-34; and the land reform problem, 244, 246, 254, 255, 266, 277, 326-27, 358, 404-5, 422; and the Cossacks, 251; and the Ukrainian problem, 262, 274, 275-78, 297, 353; and the nationalities problem, 276; leadership of, 277; and breakdown of the first coalition, 277-78; in the July crisis, 281, 286-87, 290, 292-93, 296-302, 304-8, 310-13; in the second coalition, 304-5, 311, 313-14, 325, 326, 330, 360-61, 387, 388; and the Finnish problem, 353-55; and the Constituent Assembly, 355-60; and the peasants, 357-58, 446-47, 449, 451; and the Seventh PSR Council, 376; and the Kornilov rebellion, 387-88, 405-406, 412-13; and the third coalition, 404-6, 407, 408, 409, 411, 412-13, 414, 416-18, 440, 443, 452; appraisal of, 468-71; see also Miliukov, P. N.

Kakhovskaia, Irina, 192

Kaledin, A. M., 391-93, 469

Kalegaev (also Kolegaev), L. A., 192, 367; as leader of the Kazan Peasants' Soviet, 373-74

Kaliaev, Ivan P., 451

Kaluga, 437; SR's in, 384

Kamenev, L. B. (pseud. of Rosenfeld), 420-21

Kamkov, B. D. (pseud. of Katz), 91, 138, 195n, 198n; as left SR leader, 116, 141, 183, 194-95, 259n, 367, 369, 414, 415, 419-20, 440, 442; and the war, 152, 153, 192, 199, 348; criticism of Kerenski, 225, 403

Kamkov-Natanson group, see Kamkov, B. D.; Natanson, Mark; SR's, left

Kamyshin, 52n, 243

Kapitsa, M. P., 368

Karelia, 217

Karelin, V. A., 192, 244, 414, 415, 419, 450n

Katz, see Kamkov, B. D.

Katz, E. N., 442n

Kaufman, A. A., 293

Kazan, 70-71, 374; SR's in, 143, 192, 247, 373-74, 384, 439; peasants' soviet of, 373-74

Kerenski, A. F., 81, 90, 99, 133n, 147n, 168, 351, 456, 483; and Petersburg Soviet, 136, 139-40, 146-47, 148, 225 (quoted), 230; as SR leader, 141, 173, 203, 365n, 439, 441, 461-64; SR opposition to, 145, 146-47, 224-26, 317-18, 376, 426; "nonpartisanship" as Provisional Government minister, 145-146 (quoted), 147, 163-64, 172, 212,

Kerenski, A. F. (*Continued*)
225 (*quoted*), 226, 233, 319-20, 462-64
(*quoted*); as minister of justice, 147-
148; and the war, 154-55, 166, 203,
207, 335, 342, 344, 470, 482*n*, 484
(*quoted*); attack on Miliukov's foreign policy, 159-60, 162-63, 178, 341;
and the note of April *18*, 162-63; as
first coalition leader, 174, 178-79,
182; as minister of war and marine,
175-76, 177, 217*n*, 225 (*quoted*), 231,
232, 346-50, 370; and the Third
Party Congress, 198, 207, 212; defeat
at Third Party Congress, 208, 224-33,
293, 301; decree on desertions, 226-
227, 231-32; criticism of Chernov,
232, 259*n*, 333, 395-96; as Prime
Minister, 247, 287, 289, 314-15, 322-
323, 360-61, 372*n*, 373, 380, 385, 394-
402, 424, 429; and the Ukrainian
problem, 271, 272-76, 353; and Kronstadt sailors, 281, 283; and the July
crisis, 285-92, 295-97, 301, 311-21; re-
constitution of ministry (July), 295-
296, 301, 303-5, 311-21; and the
Chernov resignation episode (July),
304, 309; resignation episode, 313;
and second coalition agrarian policy,
325, 329, 374; and the Stockholm
Conference, 337, 338; and the Constituent Assembly, 357; and the Kornilov rebellion, 386-89, 391, 393-95,
400, 461; and controversy over composition of the third coalition, 403,
404-5, 406-7, 408, 409-10, 413, 416,
418-19; and the peasants, 437, 449;
and the growth of extremism (October), 452-54; self appraisal, 463
Kharkov, 58, 91, 263, 270, 271*n*; city,
49; SR's in, 129*n*, 192, 237, 243, 244,
267, 271, 364*n*, 384, 392; peasants'
soviet of, 309, 392, 437
Kherson, 263, 264, 437; SR's in, 192,
267, 384
Khmelnitski, Bogdan Hetman, 272
Khovrin, A. A., as Central Committee
member, 221
Kienthal conference, 118-19
Kiev, 49, 262, 263, 264, 271*n*; SR's in,
18*n*, 143, 220, 244, 265, 280-81, 431,
462; city, 263, 268, 273, 274, 275;
Uman district, 265-66; soviet, 269,
271; military district, 272

Kliushin, left SR, 442*n*
Kogan-Bernstein, M. L., 91, 195, 198*n*,
392; and Third Party Congress, 200,
223*n*; criticism of Kerenski, 225
(*quoted*)
Kolegaev, *see* Kalegaev, L. A.
Kolomenski district, 367*n*
Konopliannikova, Zinaida, 76*n*, 451
Konovalov, A. I., 164*n*, 343
Kornilov, agronomist, 293
Kornilov, Lavr, 391; and second coali-
tion ministry, 316, 323, 326*n*, 327,
343*n*, 347, 380, 385, 388, 392, 393-94,
400, 401
Kornilov rebellion, 157, 346-47, 350,
363, 384, 385-93, 403-6, 409, 412-13,
423-24, 429-30, 432, 442, 461, 469, 478
Kosinski, V. A., 13*n*
Kostroma, 437; SR's in, 310
Kovalevski, Nicholas, 268, 353 (*quoted*)
Kovarski, right SR, 166
Kraft, P. P., 52
Krakovetski, (A. A.), 167
Krasnoiarsk, and the July crisis, 370
Krasnyi Arkhiv (The Red Archives),
291, 492
Kronstadt, SR's in, 373
Kronstadt sailors, 279, 281-85, 289
Kropotkin, Peter, 314
Krymov, A. I., 388, 395
Kursk, 49, 54*n*
Kutuzov, M. N., 309

Land and Liberty (Zemlia i Volia),
organization, 50, 60
Land committee system, 245-46, 248,
254, 297, 318, 322-23, 382, 419, 421,
422, 425, 438; Head Land Committee, 246, 257, 293, 324, 331-32, 333;
and the first coalition, 257-60; accomplishments, 258-59; and the second coalition, 325-34, 373-74; and
the third coalition, 446-48
Land fund, *see* Land committee system
Land reform, *see* Bolshevism; Chernov, Victor Mikhailovich; Kerenski, A. F.; Land committee system;
Marxism; Peasants; Populism; Provisional Government; Social Revolutionism; SR's
Lapland, 217

Lavrov, P. L., 4, 47; on progress, 9 (*quoted*); on the role of the intelligentsia, 9

Lazarev, E. E., 188, 451

Lebedev, V. I., 96, 189, 191, 283-84, 317, 318, 320

Lebedeva, Ada, 370

Left Socialist Revolutionaries, *see* Left SR's

Left SR's, 67, 81, 90-91, 130*n*, 189*n*; *see also* SR's, left

Lenin, V. I. (Vladimir Ilich Ulianov), 19, 82, 116, 168, 240, 458-60, 461-62; use of Populist ideas, 5, 21-22; popular appeal, 34, 295, 349-50; on revolutionary dictatorship, 42; views on terrorism, 67*n*; criticism of the SR's, 85-86, 125-26, 328, 329, 438 (*quoted*); on the SR's land program, 85-86, 446-47, 447 (*quoted*); on the war, 110-11, 115, 122-23, 484-85; and the "sealed train" episode, 139

Levenson, M. A. (pseud. Dalin), 91, 116, 126

Lezhnev, A., 438 (*quoted*)

Liebknecht, Karl, 99, 458

"Liquidators," *see* Pochinists

Little Russia, 51, 85, 192; *see also* Peasants; Ukraine

Livshits, N., 136, 338-39

London Conference of Allied socialists (*1915*), 118

Lopukhin, A. A., 73

Lordkipanidze, I. N., 244

Ludendorff, E. F., 294, 482

Lugansk, SR's in, 243

Lunkevich, V. V., 426; as Central Committee member, 221, 398-400

Lvov, G. E., 160, 164, 173, 179, 351; and land reform, 249, 255-56, 287; and dispute over land committees, 258-61, 373-74; retirement from government, 287-89, 289 (*quoted*), 292, 293, 294

Lvov, V. N., 164*n*

Maevski, Ukrainian SR, 268

Mainov, I. I., 189, 191

Maiorov, Ilia A., 192

Maklakov, V. A., 306, 355

Malachite Hall, Winter Palace, 313, 316, 319, 343

Maltsevo circle, 192

Manuilov, A. A., 298-99

"March Socialist Revolutionaries," *see* SR's

Martiushin, G. A., 247

Martov, L. (pseud. of Iu. O. Tsederbaum), 137, 138-39, 307, 338, 372, 417-18, 458

Marx, Karl, 12, 13, 45, 47

Marxism, 3, 4, 5, 6, 17, 18, 22, 44-45, 49, 72, 118-19, 126, 465, 468; revisionist, 4, 5, 15; interpretation of history, 7, 10, 11, 12-13, 21-22, 49-50; role of the proletariat, 8, 9; role of the peasants, 13, 15; criticism of Populism, 15; theory of politics, 15, 17, 42; tactical doctrine, 16-17, 67; on capitalism, 25, 33; revision by Lenin, 41; *see also* Bolshevism; Menshevism

Marxists, *see* SD's

Maslov, P. P., 64

Maslov, S. L., 189*n*; as minister of agriculture, 247, 250, 298, 325, 331, 333, 425, 446*n*; as right SR leader, 250, 412-13; land law of, 445-50

Maslov, S. M., 213

Maslov, S. S., 189

Maximalists, *see* SR Maximalists

Melgunov, S. P., 232*n*

Melnikov, M. M., 52

Mensheviks, 3, 6, 21, 42, 63, 102, 131, 473; party program, 24; relations with SR's, 102-3, 135-37, 152, 166-70, 172-73, 242-44, 280-81, 284, 286, 288-289, 294-95, 313, 334, 338-40, 343-44, 371, 449-50, 452-53, 465-68; leadership of, 103, 136-37, 166, 167, 280, 408, 458, 466, 467; and problem of coalition government, 164-69, 170-72, 173; in Moscow municipal elections (June, Sept., *1917*), 240-42, 430-32; in St. Petersburg municipal elections, 242-43, 363-64; urban strength of, 244; and the peasants, 265*n*, 436, 466; in July crisis, 281, 283, 286-89, 294, 304-5; role in soviets, 281, 283, 392; and Kronstadt sailors, 281, 284; and the republic issue, 289-90; and the war, 338-40, 347-48, 474; and the soldiers, 372-73, 429-30; and the third coalition, 419, 420, 452-53; and the workers, 431; *see also* Menshevism; St. Petersburg

Menshevism: Populist influence on, 5; interpretation of Russian history, 10; on the peasants, 43, 44; theory of revolution, 102, 165, 166-67, 209, 279-280, 292, 360-61, 465, 466, 467, 469-70

Miakotin, V. A., 35; on Marxism, 45 (quoted)

Michael, Alexandrovich, Grand Duke, 147-48

Mikhailovski, N. K., 4, 47

Miliukov, P. N., 147-48, 174, 240, 275, 276-78, 300, 393, 421, 450n; as foreign minister, 155-64, 160 (quoted), 164, 177, 179 (quoted), 180, 243n, 341-42, 470, 476, 482n; ouster of, 176-180, 299, 341, 342-43; and the July crisis, 287-88 (quoted), 289-90, 291, 293, 299, 301; and the land reform problem, 287, 331; and the second coalition, 306, 307, 310-11, 313, 321; as Kadet leader, 356-58, 388; and the Democratic Conference, 418n, 419 (quoted)

Min, General, 76 n

Minor, O. S., 32, 241, 244, 421; on expropriation without compensation, 32 (quoted); as Central Committee member, 221, 321; and the Moscow SR's, 434 (quoted)

"Minority of initiative" group, 81

Minsk, 393; SR's in, 143, 151

Miroliubov, V. S., 314

Mobile Detachments of Combat, 69

Mogilev Peasants' Soviet, 326n

Molotov, V. M., 140n

Moscow, 49, 51, 53, 90-91, 138, 144, 184, 185, 222, 262, 437, 438; SR's in, 90, 129, 151-52, 244, 349, 411; SR regional congress, 171; city council election (June), 240-42, 244, 430; September municipal election, 242n, 430, 432-34; military district, 271n; State Conference, 324, 325, 330, 387; city council, 349, 351; soldiers in, 430

Moslems, and the SR's, 243n, 265n

Mstislavski, S. D., (pseud. of S. D. Maslovski), 90-91, 128, 132, 148, 155, 378, 442n

Mukoseev, mayor of Saratov (1917), 244

Nabokov, K. D., 337-38, 341-43; on the Stockholm Conference, 341 (quoted)

Nabokov, V. D., 163, 179n, 326n, 342 (quoted), 356n; on Tereshchenko, 179

Na Chuzhbine (On Foreign Soil), periodical, 121-22, 191, 192, 306, 493

Narodnaia Volia (People's Will Group), 22, 42n, 48-49, 50, 55, 56, 59, 60, 67, 68, 484

Narodniki, see Populists

Narodnye Sotsialisty, see Popular Socialists

Narva, 243

Natanson, Mark ("Bobrov"), 73, 79n, 91, 92, 116, 117, 138, 198n, 317, 414; "defeatist" position of, 93; and Zimmerwald Conference, 117-18; at London Conference of Allied socialists, 118n; on return of émigrés, 138-139; as left SR leader, 183, 192-93, 429n; in the Third Party Congress, 193, 366; as Central Committee member, 221, 223-24, 295, 367, 402, 411

Nationalism, 20, 276, 298, 359n, 476; see also "Defensists"; Imperialism; Populism; Provisional Government; Russia, Imperial; Social Revolutionism; SR's; Ukraine; Ukrainian SR's

Nationalists (party), 218

Nekrasov, N. V., 147-48, 160, 164, 168, 400; and the Ukrainian problem, 274-75; and the July crisis, 288, 290, 291-93, 291 (quoted), 295, 331n; campaign against Chernov, 301-5, 311, 313 (quoted); and the third coalition, 404, 409, 410

Neo-Populism, see Social Revolutionism

Neratov, A. L., 159, 494

Nezlobin, SR leader in the Ukraine, 269

Nikolaev, A. A., 244

Nikolaevski, Boris, 71-74, 479n

Nikon, Bishop, 98

Nikonov, S. A., 244

Nizhni Novgorod, 49; SR's in, 129, 143; peasants' soviet of, 309

Nolde, B. E., 343

Northern Regional organizations, see under SR's

"Northern union" (Union of Socialist Revolutionaries), 51

Noulens, Joseph, 303
Novaia Zhizn' (New Life), newspaper, 240, 477, 494
Novoe Vremia (New Times), 450n

Oberuchev, K. M., 269, 271, 272-74, 347
Obshchina, see Commune, village
Obukhovski Works (St. Petersburg), 431
October Manifesto (*1905*), 76
October Revolution, *see* Revolution of 1917, October
Odessa, 49; SR's in, 151, 243, 244
Oganovski, N. P., 421n, 472, 480 (*quoted*)
Okhrana, *see* Police, tsarist
Olonets, SR's in, 236
Omsk, 243
Orekhovo-Zuevo, SR's in, 243
Orenburg, SR's in, 243
Orthodox Church, 57, 350-52; Holy Synod, 351; All-Russian Sobor, 351, 352

Pankratov, V. S., 189, 191
Pan-Slavism, 218, 276; *see also* Slavophilism
Pares, Bernard: *Russia and Reform,* 40n
Party of the Socialist Revolutionaries ("southern union"), 51
Pavlodar, 56
Peasants, 5, 19, 216n, 222; antagonism of, toward gentry, 8; land tenure of, in Great Russia, 10, 11, 28, 85, 213, 264; and land reform, 25, 29, 37, 82, 213-15, 241, 246, 248, 253-55, 278, 373-74, 438; land tenure of, in Little Russia, 28, 85, 264; political alignments of, 36-37, 133, 357-58, 362, 435-439; support for SR's, 37, 42-43, 54, 56-57, 60-62, 64, 135, 183, 188, 192, 215-16, 244-45, 247n, 435-39, 454; egalitarianism of, 44, 84; loyalty to the throne, 57; unrest among, 57-59, 255-56, 330, 412, 437-39; participation in terrorism, 69-70; and the war with Germany, 89, 97-98, 117; initiative in the February Revolution, 127; and the Cossacks, 251-52; and land committees, 257-59, 327, 328-

330, 373; in the Ukraine, 262-66, 268; declassed, 283; support for Chernov, 308-9, 310; and the third coalition, 435-39; *see also* All-Russian Congress of Soviets of Peasants' Deputies; All-Russian Executive Committee of Peasants' Soviets; Chernov, Victor Mikhailovich; Commune, village; Intelligentsia; Land committee system; Peasants' movement; Peasants' soviets; Populism; Provisional Government; Social Revolutionism; SR's; Ukrainian SR's; Zemstvos; and "peasant" entries under names of specific parties
Peasants' movement, 48, 254
Peasants' soviets, 256, 286, 318, 373-74, 412, 421, 422; and the Kornilov rebellion, 390-93; *see also* under names of specific provinces
Peasants' Union of the PSR, 60, 244
Penza, 70-71, 216n, 437; SR's in, 268
People's Will Group, *see* Narodnaia Volia
Pereverzev, P. N., 175-76, 180, 212; as minister of justice, 256, 261, 294
Perm province, 49
Peshekhonov, A. V., 35n, 73, 174-75, 176, 181; as minister of food, 245
Peterhof, 363
Petersburg Committee of Socialist Revolutionaries, manifesto, 139-40
Petersburg Soviet, *see* St. Petersburg
Petliura, Simon, 280-81
Petrograd, *see* St. Petersburg
Pilsudski, Joseph, 75n
Plekhanov, G. V., 102, 300, 304
Pleve, V. K., 68, 69, 70n, 71, 73; assassination of, 193
Pobedonostsev, K. P., 351
Pochin, Pochinists' organ, 81
Pochinists, or "liquidators," 81-82, 86, 102, 130, 166
Podolia, 263
Poincaré, Raymond, 444, 480
Poklevski-Kozel, S. A., 159
Poland, 263; and the separatism issue, 38-39, 40, 217-18, 220, 269n, 276-77
Police, tsarist (Okhrana), 131, 138; and the Azef affair, 71, 73, 74, 78; and the espionage system, 129; infiltration into SR's, 129-30; and the July Days, 281-82

Polish Socialist party (PPS), 75

Polner, T. I., 289

Poltava, province, 57-58, 263; city, 49; SR's in, 267; Provincial Land Committee, 327

Popular Socialists (Narodnye Sotsialisty), 3, 81, 82n, 99, 135, 189n, 363; rejection of terrorism, 17, 65; on land expropriation without compensation, 32, 65; on the dynastic problem, 35; criticism of SR's, 46; political tenets, 65; secession from the PSR, 65, 67; and coalition government, 171-72, 174-75, 176, 181; in Moscow city council election (June, 1917), 240-42

Populism, 6, 18, 47, 72, 83, 118-19, 189, 218, 262, 468, 484; evolution of, 3-6; utopianism in, 4, 84; interpretation of history, 6-7, 10, 20, 21-22, 470; differences from Bolshevism, 6-17; individualism in, 6-7, 19, 48; differences from Marxism, 6-17, 82; and class struggle, 7, 8, 11, 13-15; role of intelligentsia, 8, 9-10, 47-48; concept of "toil," 8, 11-12; role of peasants, 8-10, 11, 13-15; role of proletariat, 9; and the political regime, 10, 15-17, 49; agrarian system as revolutionary force, 10-15, 43, 82, 86; role of village commune, 11-15, 47; on capitalism, 11-17, 22; tactical doctrine, 16-17; and terrorism, 16-17, 19, 42n, 49, 50n, 86; nationalism in, 67, 88, 94, 262, 348, 471; see also Chernov, Victor Mikhailovich; PSR; Social Revolutionism; SR's

Populists (Narodniki), 3, 4, 135, 188, 193; domination by intelligentsia, 18-19, 368n; origins of, 48-51; sources in Narodnaia Volia, 49; rejection of Marxism, 49-50; fusion into one party, 51-52; see also Narodnaia Volia; Party of the Social Revolutionists; SR's; V narod ("into the people") movement

Posen, 277-78

Postnikov, S. P., 89, 205, 284, 306n, 352, 426, 441, 457 (quoted)

PPS (Polish Socialist party), 75

Pravda, Lenin's, 240

Prilezhaev, I. A., 399, 426; as Central Committee member, 221, 249; on land reform, 249 (quoted)

Prizyv (The Call), periodical, 102, 190, 495

Prizyv group, 120

Progressive Bloc, 142-43

Proletariat, 16, 19; in Moscow uprising, 76, 78; antiwar position, 89; internationalism of, 89; in February Revolution, 131; in St. Petersburg, 160; see also subheads on "workers" under names of specific parties

Proshian, P. P., 192, 285, 370

Provisional Council of the Republic, see Council of the Republic

Provisional Government, 103, 114, 233, 406; amnesty of, for émigrés, 138; relation to soviets, 139-40, 143-44, 161-64, 281, 283, 285-87, 295-96, 318, 338-39, 372-74, 421; precoalition ministry of, 144-48, 157, 159-60, 161, 162; and the monarchy, 147-48, 150-151; precoalition foreign policy of, 155, 164; declaration of March 28, 1917, 156, 159, 160, 163; note of April 18, 1917, 160-63; Foreign Ministry, 340-44; and the Kornilov rebellion, 386-92; and the war, 474-485; see also Constituent Assembly; Duma; and under names of specific leaders and parties

—— first coalition: support by the SR's, 142-44, 155-56, 160-61, 207, 209-212; war policy of, 152-53, 160, 178-180, 203, 206-7, 230, 369-70; Menshevik support of, 155-56, 160-61; formation of, 164, 172, 357; ministry, 164-84, 232, 275, 321, 360; dispute over cabinet posts, 173-77; foreign policy, 176-80, 261; and the land reform problem, 245-61, 277-78; and Chernov's minimum land program, 253-60; breakdown of, 260, 261, 275, 277-78, 281; and the Ukrainian problem, 260, 261-62, 271-78; mission to Ukrainian Rada, 274-76; accomplishments, 278

—— second coalition: Menshevik support of, 280-81, 283-84, 286-89; support by the SR's, 280-81, 283-89; formation of, 285-320; ministry, 285-286, 314-20, 321; and the republic

issue, 287, 289-93, 395; declaration of July *8*, 290-92, 296, 305*n*, 313, 314, 328, 331, 381, 388; middle-class radicals in, 301; war policy of, 303, 321, 322, 334-45, 348; and the land reform problem, 312, 322-34, 374; agrarian policy of, 322-34; law on land committees, 326-27, 330-32, 333; and the army, 343, 347-48, 350, 370; and the nationalities problem, 352-55; Special Commission (on Constituent Assembly), 356-57; postponement of Constituent Assembly election, 356-60, 361; evaluation of 360-61
—— *third coalition*, 451; conflict over composition of, 409-13, 418-19, 422-423; and land reform policy, 422, 445-50; formation of, 423; and the war, 444; and the growth of extremism, 452-54
Pskov, 437; SR's in, 384
PSR (Socialist Revolutionary party): origin, 47-60; formal founding (*1901*), 50-51; early organic growth, 53; development, 60-67; effect of Popular Socialists' secession, 65; relations with the Duma, 76*n*, 129; leaders in exile, 79, 90, 91-93, 94, 97-98, 99, 138; decline in membership, 79-80, 128; demoralization, 79-87, 129-30; membership (*1917*), 234-237; in Moscow municipal elections (June, September, *1917*), 240-42, 244, 430, 432-34; in St. Petersburg municipal elections, 242-43, 363-65; *see also* Chernov, Victor Mikhailovich; Populism; Populists; SR's; and city and regional branches by name
—— *party program* (*1906*), 47, 66, 238; adoption, 24; maximum, 24, 32-34, 41, 82; minimum, 24-32, 33-41; problem of implementation, 27, 28-30
—— *party congresses:*
First (Imatra, Finland, *1906*), 20, 24, 29, 30*n*, 31, 35, 36*n*, 37, 38, 39, 40, 41, 45, 65, 75-76, 88, 185, 214, 238, 250-51
Second (*1907*), 46, 63, 185
Third (May, *1917*), 46, 127, 145-47, 165, 166, 175-76, 184, 212, 363, 375, 377, 396-97; selection of delegates, 187, 236; role of the right, 188-91,
197-98, 199, 200, 203-4, 205, 206, 208, 210, 211-12, 228-29; role of the left, 192-96, 203, 205-6, 207, 208, 209, 210, 211-12, 366-67; role of the right center, 197-98, 200, 210; convened, 198; and war policy, 198-209, 219, 237, 334, 424, 475-76, 479, 481; role of the center, 199, 200-201, 205, 206, 208, 210, 211-12; role of the left center, 199, 206, 208; issue of participation in the government, 209-12, 237; and land reform, 213-16, 237, 248, 249, 252, 254, 256-57, 322, 332, 422, 447-48; and the nationalities problem, 216-220, 237; election of Central Committee, 220-24; Kerenski's defeat at, for Central Committee, 224-33, 318, 395, 396, 414, 424; and the organizational problem, 234-37; evaluation of, 237-39
Fourth (December, *1917*), 46, 194, 238, 250, 317, 328, 363, 375, 422; organizational problems, 234, 427-28; criticism of Kerenski, 318-20, 399; and the land reform problem, 331, 446; and the war, 340, 484; and the composition of the third coalition, 409-10
—— *party councils:*
Fifth (May, *1909*), 79
Sixth (April, *1917*), 187, 219
Seventh (August, *1917*), 183, 363, 366, 422; precouncil controversy, 374-76; representation in, 375*n*; role of the right, 375-76, 377; Central Committee's role in, 375-76, 378-79, 380, 383; attack on Chernov, 377; and the war, 377-78, 382; role of Provisional Government, 378-81; role of the center, 379, 380; role of the left, 379, 380, 381, 382-85, 403; Rosenblum resolution, 379-83; Steinberg resolution, 379-83; land reform problem, 382; resolution on current affairs adopted, 382-83, 385
PSR Central Committee, 63, 68, 70, 71, 73, 74, 77, 79, 126, 130, 194, 202, 236, 259, 402, 462; Delegation Abroad, 126, 187, 213, 219; vote on, 221; composition of, 221-24, 226, 384; dominance of the right of center, 223-24; and the war, 269-70, 335,

PSR Central Committee (*Continued*) 344, 350*n*; and the July crisis, 285 (*quoted*), 286, 294, 295, 296*n*, 304, 307, 311; opposition to Chernov, 297, 425-28; ultimatum to Provisional Government, 311-13, 376; and the second coalition, 313-14, 316-21; 322-323, 324, 328, 332, 388; and the Stockholm Conference, 333, 340, 444-45; military commission of, 346-347, 386, 393; and the left SR's, 367, 368, 411 (*quoted*); efforts for party unity, 375-76, 414; and the Kornilov rebellion, 386, 388; and Chernov's attack on Kerenski, 397-400, 398 (*quoted*); party discipline in, 399-400, 414-18, 416 (*quoted*), 422-23, 425-26 (*quoted*), 427-28, 460; and the third coalition, 408, 409-12, 415-417, 422-23 (*quoted*), 424, 451, 452 (*quoted*); and the Allied Conference, 424-25 (*quoted*), 443-44; and third coalition land reform policy, 448-50; and the October crisis, 454 (*quoted*)

Pugachëv, Emilian, 54; rebellion, 9

Pumpianski, N. P., on the coalition ministry, 144 (*quoted*)

Purishkevich, V. M., 306

PUSR (Ukrainian Socialist Revolutionary party), *see* Ukrainian SR's

Rada, Ukrainian, *see* Ukrainian Rada

Radek-Lenin resolution (Zimmerwald), 118

Radical Democrats, 363

Rafes, M., 262*n*

Rakitnikov, N. I., 34*n*, 52, 60, 79*n*, 138, 399, 426; as Central Committee member, 90, 221, 452; and Third Party Congress, 127-28, 198, 205, 227, 238; on Kerenski's joining the ministry, 145 (*quoted*); on land reform, 214-15, 245, 250, 257, 259; and the July crisis, 305; as deputy minister of agriculture in second coalition, 325-26, 327, 331

Rakitnikova, Ina (née Altovskaia), 52

Rakov, D. F., as Central Committee member, 221

Ranenburg, 243-44

Rappoport, S. A. (pseud. An-ski), 478-479

Raskolnikov, F. F., 281-82

Rasputin, Gregory, 351

Rataev, L. A., 72*n*

Ratner, Eugenia, 194

Razin, Stenka, 54

Rech' (Speech), newspaper, 240, 300, 307, 310-11, 376, 405-6, 421*n*, 450*n*, 495-96

Red Archives, see *Krasnyi Arkhiv*

Rennenkampf, P. K., 323

Republican Democrats, 363

Revel, 243

Revoliutsionnaia Rossiia (Revolutionary Russia), 496; Old Series, 51, 56*n*, 58*n*

Revolution of *1905*, 56, 66-67, 456, 465; Moscow uprising, 76

Revolution of *1917*, 66-67, 150, 204, 207, 261, 276, 335, 354, 445, 466, 475; April Days, 160-64; Jewish question, 222; July Days, 279-320 *passim*, 365; *see also* Kornilov rebellion; Kronstadt sailors; Provisional Government

—— *February*, 127-28, 149, 166, 185, 274, 296*n*, 339, 456, 477, 481; role of revolutionary parties, 89, 90, 127-128, 131-32, 264; threat of counter-revolution, 142-43, 150, 164-65, 285, 345, 362, 365, 383-84, 403-4; Ukrainian SR's in, 264

—— *October*, 30*n*, 78, 271-72, 392, 450, 454

Riabtsev, E. P., 244, 269

Riazan, 243-44

Richter, V. N., as Central Committee member, 221, 388, 420

Riga, 387-88

Riurik (ship), 72*n*

Rodichev, F. I., 218, 277

Rodzianko, M. V., 132, 147-48

Roman law, 26

Ropshin, *see* Savinkov, B. V.

Rosen, Roman, 477

Rosenberg, SR party worker, 442*n*

Rosenblum, D. S., 129, 138, 377-78, 426, 471; as Central Committee member, 221, 449

Rosenfeld (pseud. L. B. Kamenev), 420-21

Rostov-on-the-Don, 244
Rubanovich, I. A., 91, 118n, 336; as Central Committee member, 221, 223
Rudnev, V. V., 76n, 94, 99n, 418, 419, 422 (*quoted*), 433; on national self-determination, 39 (*quoted*); on the war, 91, 93, 97 (*quoted*), 123, 198, 478; condemnation of Liebknecht, 99; as right SR leader, 196, 197, 207, 223, 244, 350-51, 351 (*quoted*), 407, 414
Rumania, 106-7
Rusanov, N. S., 90, 133n, 336, 344, 426; on Kerenski, 145; as Central Committee member, 221
Russia, Imperial, 15, 16, 38, 105, 114, 116, 178, 217, 263, 431-32, 480; and the war, 113, 117, 323; war industrial committees, 120; diplomatic service, 159, 337, 341-42; imperialism of, 178-80, 182, 354; policy on SR's, 185; agrarian code, 258, 326; and education, 298; *see also* Russian Army; Stolypin, P. A., and under the individual names of tsars
Russian Archives Abroad (Prague), 311
Russian Army, 131, 261, 271-73, 315, 316, 335, 345, 351, 355, 382, 445, 485; Semenovski Regiment, 132; Paul Polubotok Regiment, 272; Ukrainian soldiers' congresses, 272-73; General Headquarters, 345-46, 347, 357, 386, 391, 393, 400; SR's in, 347-48, 430, 451; Wild Division of Moslem Caucasians, 389-90; Miliutin reforms, 429; prerevolutionary, 429; *see also* Kornilov rebellion; Soldiers
Russian Navy: Black Sea Fleet, 371; *see also* Kronstadt sailors; Sailors
Russkiia Vedomosti (The Russian Record), newspaper, 240-41, 496

Sabler, V. K., 351
Sailors, as participants in terrorism, 69-70; *see also* Kronstadt sailors
St. Petersburg (also called Petrograd), 49, 54, 80, 89, 120, 168, 218, 316n, 336; SR's in, 89, 90-91, 130-31, 133, 139-40, 141, 151, 182-83, 187n, 191-92, 196n, 235, 236, 244, 305, 309-10, 346,

348-49, 362, 363, 378, 415, 440-42; SR's first city conference, 140 (*quoted*), 141 (*quoted*), 145; SR's first regional conference, 140-41, 145; SR's city committee, 141, 190; SR's second city conference, 145, 149n, 152, 154, 182, 188; SR's third city conference, 205, 210; August election in, 241n, 242n, 363-66; May municipal election, 242-43, 363-64; revolutionary force in, 283, 365; SR's fifth city conference, 285n, 367; SR's sixth city conference, 338; and the Kornilov rebellion, 389-90; Alexander Nevski district SR's, 397 (*quoted*); SR's seventh city conference, 440-42; SR's tenth city conference, 467
—— Soviet, 132, 139, 143-44, 147, 157, 162, 206, 429-30, 462; workers in, 132, 133-34; military section, 132-34, 148, 371-72; SR's role in, 132-37, 171-73, 181-82, 271, 274, 285n, 338-39, 371-73, 386; Executive Committee, 133, 135, 136, 148, 157, 161, 163, 171-72, 173, 176; SR's split in, 133-34; Mensheviks in, 134, 135, 136, 338-39, 371-73; representation in, 134n; and the agrarian issue, 135; Bolsheviks in, 173, 371-73, 389; and military death penalty issue, 372-73; Military Revolutionary Committee, 389; "committee for struggle against the counter-revolution," 389, 393; and the Kornilov rebellion, 389-90
Samara, 54n, 78, 236, 243, 437, 450-51; city, 70-71, 150, 451
Samsonov, A. V., 323
Saratov, 49, 57, 58, 64, 75, 78, 245, 391-92; city, 51, 52, 53, 58n, 60, 89, 138, 147n, 244; condition of peasants in, 54; SR's in, 309; Soviet, 430, 431, 437
Savinkov, B. V., 74, 77, 91, 100, 138, 189, 316n; as acting minister of war, 315-17, 318, 320, 323, 347, 348, 349, 372n, 373, 385, 387, 388, 393-94, 401; as military governor general of St. Petersburg, 389 (*quoted*); expelled from PSR, 401-2
Sazonov, S. D., 70n, 72, 159
Schlüsselburg Fortress, 451

SD's (Social Democrats), 3, 6, 18, 24, 41, 44, 50-51, 60, 61, 66, 124, 155, 170-71, 321, 410, 413, 479*n*; domination by intelligentsia, 18-19; debt to Populism, 21-22; on the nationalities problem, 38; concentration in cities, 53, 243, 244, 390; "economism" among, 54*n*, 289; Fifth Party Congress (*1907*), 63; strength in *1905*, 63, 76; attitude toward SR doctrine, 75; in the February uprising, 131; in Petersburg Soviet, 135; split in, 152, 198, 238, 455-56; in Eniseisk group, 167; in the Ukraine, 265, 280-81, 353; *see also* Bolsheviks; Lenin, V. I.; Mensheviks

Second coalition, *see* Provisional Government, second coalition

Second International, 88, 89, 92, 94, 107, 110, 167, 238; SR proposal for reconstitution of, 206; restoration of, 335, 336

Second Party Congress of the PSR, *see under* PSR

Seim (Finnish), 353-54

Selians'ka Spilka, 265-66, 267, 268

Serbia, 479

Sergius Alexandrovich, Grand Duke, 68, 69, 73

Sevastopol, SR's in, 243, 244

Seventh Party Council of the PSR, *see under* PSR

Shapoval, Ukrainian SR leader, 268

Shingarev, A. I., 176, 215

Shliapnikov, A., 131, 133, 134

Shreider, A. A., 306*n*, 421*n*, 440-41, 442

Shreider, G. I., 244, 349, 364*n*, 418, 419

Shvetsov, SR party worker, 29, 214

Siberia, 29, 79, 213, 243

Sibir' (Irkutsk), newspaper, 167

Sibirskii Zhurnal, 167-68

Sibirskoe Obozrenie, 167-68

Sigov, A. S., 189, 191

Sigov, I. S., 189, 191

Simbirsk, 70-71

Simferopol, SR's in, 243

Sipiagin, minister of the interior, 69

Sixth Party Council of the PSR, *see under* PSR

Sklovski, I., 269

Skobelev, M. I., 288

Slavophilism, 15, 22, 23, 160, 189, 470; *see also* Pan-Slavism

Slëtov, S. N., 49*n*, 56, 73, 91, 119-20; and terrorism, 73*n*, 74

Slëtova, A. N., 49*n*, 56

Smolensk Peasants' Soviet, 309

Smolny Institute, 388

Social Democrats, *see* SD's

Social Democrats, Finnish, 354

Socialism, 37, 66, 114, 117, 124, 153; and the intelligentsia, 47-48; Western, 114, 117-18, 144, 444, 458, 479*n*; *see also* Bolshevism; First International; Marxism; Menshevism; Populism; Second International; Social Revolutionism; Third International; Zimmerwaldism; and under names of specific countries

Socialist Revolutionaries, *see* SR's

Socialist Revolutionary party, *see* PSR

Social Revolutionism (also called neo-Populism), 4, 5, 82, 99, 105, 166, 185-86, 352; interpretation of history, 7, 24, 38; and personal rights, 19, 85*n*, 155*n*; Populist background of, 19-23, 49, 83; on economic individualism, 20, 28; and nationalism, 20-21, 22-23, 38, 39, 197; Marxist influence on, 21-22, 45-46; primacy of peasants, 22-23, 34, 42-43; on capitalism, 25, 26*n*, 42, 43, 44; concept of land ownership, 25-27; land socialization plan, 25-32, 28 (*quoted*), 33, 37, 41, 42, 43, 45, 82, 83, 84-85, 134, 135, 165, 181, 213-16, 251-52, 280; roots in tradition, 26*n*, 42*n*, 50-51, 484; on the village commune, 28-29, 31, 37, 214; problem of land-use equalization, 29-31, 44, 84; political decentralization, 30-31, 35-37, 43, 213; land expropriation without compensation, 31-32, 65, 214-15, 250, 260-61; socialization of industry, 32-34, 41, 43; separation of church and state, 34; direct democracy, 34-35, 36; political principles, 34-37, 88, 216-17; republicanism, 35, 37, 65; and the nationalities problem, 37-40, 203, 216-20; messianism of, 39; revolutionary dictatorship, 41, 42; collectivization, 41, 82; utopianism in, 43, 217; on the class struggle, 45, 193,

241; *see also* Chernov, Victor Mikhailovich; "Defensism"; Internationalism; Zimmerwaldism

Soldiers, 131, 485; as participants in terrorism, 69-70; in February Revolution, 127, 132; in the Ukraine, 271-273; support for Chernov, 309; radicalism among, 371, 429-30

Sopliakov (pseud. Burevoi), K. S., quoted, 308, 457

Sorokin, P. A., 188, 189

"Southern union" (Party of the Socialist Revolutionaries), 51

Soviet Union, enforced collectivization of land, 27

Spassk district, 374

Spiridonova, Maria, 138, 192, 223, 226, 348, 442n, 465, 472; as left SR leader, 368, 370-71, 370 (*quoted*), 403, 415, 425, 429n, 439-40, 442; and Seventh Party Council, 380, 381, 382 (*quoted*); and the third coalition, 414, 418, 420, 441

SR Internationalists, 67 (*quoted*), 89-90, 96, 480; émigré group, 91-94, 130, 149n; Bolsheviks' influence on, 102, 110, 115-18, 118-19, 152; evolution of, 103; position on the war, 103-9, 119-20, 124-25, 149-55, 219; Lenin's influence on, 110, 115-18; and revolution in wartime, 110-14, 177; propaganda of, 120-22; criticism of "defensists," 123-24, 149; and return of the émigrés, 138, 139; *see also* Socialism; Zimmerwald Conference; Zimmerwaldism

SR Maximalists, 76n, 81, 306; political platform, 65-66; secession from the PSR, 65-66, 67

SR's (Socialist Revolutionaries), 3, 11, 12, 14, 49n, 131; ideological confusion, 3, 25-26, 30, 40; criticism of Marxists, 6, 18, 19; role of intellectuals, 19, 20, 31n, 52, 55-56, 59, 88, 89, 128, 129, 130, 141, 213n, 214, 215-16, 218-19, 222, 242-43, 253, 273, 423-24, 456-57, 484; organizational problems, 19, 61-64, 68, 73, 78, 128-30, 137, 139-42, 185-87, 222, 234, 384, 411-12; liberal political goals, 19-20, 55, 56, 85, 140; hostility to bourgeoisie, 30-31, 36, 43, 169-70, 184, 440; agrarian

policy, 34, 54-55, 132, 245-61, 280, 286, 311, 324-25, 328, 330-32, 334, 404, 422, 445-50; and the peasants, 36-37, 42n, 44-45, 55-60, 75, 77, 80, 132, 165, 173, 195n, 214, 222, 241, 246, 265n, 390, 435-39, 451, 454; and anarchism, 36n; and the Saratov circle, 52, 53, 78, 89, 90; black-earth and Volga region base, 53, 54, 80, 129-30; use of terrorism, 55, 61, 67-74, 79, 241-42; and the proletariat, 55-56, 58, 61, 133-34, 141, 160-61, 165, 183, 188, 222, 241, 283, 430-31, 454, 471; role of theory, 58-59, 185, 280, 468, 470-71; and the students, 61, 129; bourgeois support, 62, 170, 186, 404; strength in *1905*, 62-63, 75-76, 77; and the Jews, 63, 70, 71, 222; schisms of *1906*, 64-67; and the war issue, 67, 88-91, 94-95, 102-3, 118-26, 143, 148-155, 164-65, 180, 193-94, 199, 203, 206-8, 215, 250, 286, 327-28, 407-8, 443-45, 469-70, 473-85; and the Russo-Japanese war, 67, 94; role in the Revolution of *1905*, 67-68, 76-78; leadership of, 68, 73-74, 77, 78, 81-82, 90, 127, 136-37, 165n, 172, 175n, 185, 192, 408, 427, 456-65; and E. F. Azef, 73, 419, 459; attempted subversion of armed forces, 75; preparations for agrarian insurrection, 75-76, 77; internal crises, *1907-14*, 79-82, 128; factionalism among, 82n, 88-94, 122-26, 180, 187-88, 194-95, 196-97, 201, 207-8, 238-39, 250, 327-28, 335, 345, 369, 382-83, 396-97, 408, 412-13, 424, 455-57; South Russian committee, 91; October (or November) schism (*1917*), 90, 141-42, 154-155, 335-36, 369, 370, 460, 485; alliance with Mensheviks (*1917*), 102-3, 135-37, 152, 166-69, 170, 172-73, 242-243, 244, 280-81, 284, 286, 288, 289, 294-95, 313, 334, 338-40, 343-44, 371, 449-50, 452-53, 465-68; volunteerism of, 119-20; and the soldiers, 134-35, 139, 141, 157, 160-61, 171, 241, 243n, 349-50, 371, 429-30, 451, 454, 471; Northern Regional organizations, 141, 190, 205, 215, 225, 345-46, 366, 368, 384n; and problem of first coalition government, 142, 144-48,

SR's (*Continued*)
164-84, 228-29, 239; and the "dual power" doctrine, 143; in Eniseisk group, 167-68; relation to Kadets, 169-70, 468-71; role in first coalition cabinet, 174-84; urban strength of, 240-44, 432-35, 454, 471; and the soviets, 244, 265-66, 267-69, 281, 283, 431-32, 436-39, 440, 442; and the Cossacks, 251-52; relations with Ukrainian SR's, 262, 265-75, 353; and problem of the second coalition, 280-81, 314, 317-20, 322, 327-28, 332, 360-61, 380-81, 388; and Kronstadt sailors, 281-85; in July crisis, 280-89, 294, 359, 362, 370; and the republic issue, 289-90; and the second coalition war policy, 334-45; and the Stockholm Conference, 337-40, 475, 476; and the army, 345-50; first military conference, 346; and the church, 350-52; and the nationalities problem (second coalition), 352-55, 375; and the Constituent Assembly, 355-60; fear of rightist reaction, 362-65, 383-84, 403-4, 469; move toward schism, 366, 374, 375, 439-40, 454; and the Kornilov rebellion, 385-93, 396-97, 454; and problem of the third coalition, 403-8, 413-14, 417-23; role in the third coalition, 443, 450-54; and the growth of extremism, 452-54; misappraisal of Bolsheviks, 468, 471-73; *see also* Chernov, Victor Mikhailovich; "Defensists"; Intelligentsia; SR Internationalists; SR Maximalists; Peasants' Union of the PSR; PSR; St. Petersburg; Social Revolutionism; SR headings below; Teachers' Union; Ukrainian SR's; Zimmerwald Conference; and city and regional branches by name
—— center, 86-87, 172, 195, 196, 239; and the coalition government, 164-165, 166-67, 169; rift in, 197, 200, 229, 454; and Central Committee election, 222-23, 229; and Kerenski, 226, 229, 397; and the Kronstadt sailors, 285; and the third coalition, 403, 414, 424; and the peasants, 437; and the Mensheviks, 466-67; *see also* "Defensists"

—— left, 65, 66, 86-87, 91, 117, 131, 142, 171, 173, 174, 195, 196, 456, 465; growth in power (*1917*), 116, 191-193, 383, 384, 395; and the Bolsheviks, 116-18, 369-70, 372, 384, 408, 468; and the war, 117-26, 149-55, 203, 205, 219, 271n, 308, 334, 335-36, 339, 345, 369-70, 415, 485; and coalition government, 164, 209, 281, 294-95; and the workers, 191-92; and the peasants, 192, 215, 373-74, 384-85, 412, 437; leadership of, 192-93; "informational bureau," 193, 366-67; manifesto of July 9, 194, 366-67; on the nationalities problem, 219-20, 270, 355; and Central Committee election, 222-23; criticism of Kerenski, 225-26, 229, 231, 232, 397, 402-3; and land reform, 247-48, 259, 415, 449, 450n; and the Kronstadt sailors, 285; and the second coalition, 328, 370, 381, 397, 429; and the military death penalty issue, 348-50, 370-73; and the third coalition, 403, 412-13, 414-15, 416, 418, 419-22; opposition to Chernov, 414-15, 420-21; move toward schism, 425, 439-42, 454; and the Moscow elections, 434-35; at Seventh Petersburg City Conference, 440-42; *see also* SR Internationalists
—— left center, 93, 117, 194, 195, 196, 197, 219, 239, 456; and the second coalition, 317-18, 319-20; and the third coalition, 403-5, 414, 419-20, 424; attack on Kadets, 404-5; and the move toward schism, 428; and the war, 475
—— right, 81, 102-3, 154, 157, 171, 173, 195, 196, 239n, 456; beginnings, 81, 100; and the war, 118-26, 149-55, 170, 197, 203, 262, 280, 345, 376, 407, 478-80, 485; and the coalition government, 164, 182n, 188, 209, 296n; move away from revolutionary beliefs, 165-66, 169, 188, 250, 355, 442; and the *Volia Naroda*, 188-90, 197, 206n; debate on secession, 190-91; and the Polish issue, 218-19; and Central Committee election, 222-23; and land reform, 246, 247, 329-30, 450n; and the Ukrainian problem, 269, 272; and the Kadets, 280, 295,

296n, 298, 300, 356; attacks on Chernov, 300-2, 312-13, 396-97, 406; and the army, 348; and Kerenski, 397; and the third coalition, 403, 404-5, 413, 414, 421-22, 424, 425-26, 452-53; and the workers, 431; and the Moscow elections, 434; and the Mensheviks, 466-67

—— right center, 93, 100, 156, 168n, 196, 219, 239, 246-47, 248, 283; and the coalition government, 296n, 316; and the war, 344, 403, 475; and the third coalition, 405-8, 414, 415, 418, 421-22, 424, 425-28

SR Union of the Left, 81

Stalinski, E. A., 121, 189, 191

"Star chamber" group, 168, 274, 288

State Council, 286

Steinberg, I. Z., 90-91, 149n, 183, 233, 377 (quoted), 383n, 450n

Steklov, Iu. M., 133, 136

Sternberg, L. Ia., 189

Stockholm Conference, 336-41, 343, 344, 443, 444-45

Stolypin, P. A., 64, 69, 73, 76-77, 158, 255, 315, 354, 469; land legislation, 14n, 44n, 82, 85, 86, 87, 214, 254, 262-63, 325

Straits, The (Bosporus and Dardanelles), 104-5, 156, 178, 179, 277-78, 298, 306, 342, 482n

Sukhanov, N. (pseud. of N. N. Gimmer), 4-5, 133, 141n, 146n, 168n, 175n, 176, 181, 201n, 278, 282, 357, 391, 453n, 459-60, 461; on PSR leadership, 137; and the July crisis, 287-288, 304-5, 311; and the third coalition, 408n

Sukhovykh, K. A., 269

Supreme Committee of the Western Front, 393

Sverdlov, Ia. M., 460

Sviatitski, N. V., 90, 141; on lack of party unity, 126 (quoted), 130 (quoted)

Sviiazh district, 374

Switzerland, 138, 216

Taganrog district, 236-37

Tambov, 49, 298, 412; SR's in, 243, 438-439; Peasants' Soviet, 309 (quoted)

Tambov group, 56-57

Tambov uprising, 437-39

Tammerfors, 185

Tarnopol, 289

Taurida, 270, 437; SR's in, 236-37, 243n

Taurida Palace, 283

Teachers' Union, 61

Tereshchenko, M. I., 160, 164, 174, 404; as foreign minister, 178-80, 295, 342-344, 343 (quoted), 400, 423, 444, 482n, 483-84; and the Ukrainian problem, 274-75; campaign against Chernov, 301-3, 305, 307-8, 311; and the Stockholm Conference, 337 (quoted), 338 (quoted)

Terrorism, 17, 42n, 48, 50, 67-74, 192; see also Narodnaia Volia; Populism; SR's

Teterkin, I. I.; as Central Committee member, 221

Thiers, L. A., 41

Third coalition, see Provisional Government, third coalition

Third International, 111, 151, 442

Third Party Congress of the PSR, see under PSR

Thomas, Albert, 178-79, 203n, 337, 338n

Thompson, William B., 189n

Tiflis, SR's in, 151, 244

Timofeev, E. M., 167

Tiutchev, N. S., 189, 191

Tomsk, 29; SR's in, 143, 236, 439

Transcaucasia, 39; SR's in, 151, 265, 348

Treaty of Brest-Litovsk, 117, 269-70, 481

Triple Entente, 96, 105

Troitski, SR party worker, 78

Trotski, Lev D., 132, 281, 282, 389; and Chernov, 307

Trudoviks, 76n, 99, 171-72

Trutovski, V. E., 153, 205, 440-41, 442

Tsaritsyn, 391-92; SR's in, 243, 431

Tsarskoe Selo, 148

Tsederbaum, Iu. O., see Martov, L.

Tsereteli, Irakli G., 155-56, 157, 167-68, 289, 477; as Menshevik leader, 136, 137, 348, 365n, 371-73, 458; and Chernov, 169, 323, 333-34 (quoted), 467; as coalition minister, 174, 180-181, 233, 258-59; and the Ukrainian problem, 274-75; and the July crisis, 288, 289-90, 292-93, 299, 301 (quoted),

Tsereteli, Irakli G. (*Continued*) 304-5, 307; and the third coalition, 418-19, 420, 422, 432-34
Tugan-Baranovski, M. I., 241*n*
Tula, 255; SR's in, 236
Turkey, 265*n*, 478, 479*n*, 482
Tver, SR's in, 151

Ufa, 437; SR's in, 192, 384
Ukraine, 213, 217, 243, 260, 480; nationalism in, 220, 262, 263, 265, 267*n*, 271, 272*n*, 276, 347, 375; Great Russians in, 263, 264, 266, 268; political geography of, 263-69; soviets in, 265-66, 267-69; and the second coalition government, 353
Ukrainian Constituent Assembly, 220
Ukrainian national congress (May), 269
Ukrainian Rada (national council), 262, 268, 269, 270, 271, 274, 353, 480; and the national autonomy issue, 269-75, 276; Secretariat of, 273, 276
Ukrainian Socialist Revolutionary party (PUSR), *see* Ukrainian SR's
Ukrainian SR's, 21, 43*n*, 262, 280-81, 413; and Ukrainian nationalism, 220, 266, 268, 269-71, 273; intellectuals among, 264, 272*n*, 273; support by peasants, 265-66, 267; on the Dnieper right bank, 265-66, 271, 275; factions among, 266-67; on the Dnieper left bank, 266-67, 271; and army reorganization, 271-72; rejection of Provisional Government agreement, 275, 353; *see also* Selians'ka Spilka
Ulianov, G. K., 306*n*
Ulianov, V. I., *see* Lenin, V. I.
Uman district (Kiev), 265-66
Union of Army and Naval Officers, 386
Union of Maximalists, 33, 34*n*
Union of Public Schoolteachers, 61
Union of Socialist Revolutionaries ("northern union"), 51
United States: Republican party, 54-55; support for SR's in, 62, 189*n*; and the war, 178, 481-83
Unity party (Plekhanov): in Moscow city council election (June, *1917*), 240-42; in St. Petersburg city council election (August, *1917*), 363

Ural Mountains, 52, 430-31
Ustinov, A. N., 192, 285, 370
Utgof, Vladimir (pseud. of V. L. Deriuzhinski), 346, 481*n*
Utsida, quoted, 343*n*

Vedeniapin, M. A., 78, 138, 451; as Central Committee member, 221, 416
Vestnik Russkoi Revoliutsii (Herald of the Russian Revolution), 56*n*, 499
Viatka, 49, 52
Vikhliaev, P. A.: and land reform, 30*n*, 245, 249-50, 252, 264*n*, 334; *Kak uravniat' pol'zovanie zemlëi*, 30*n*, 499; and second coalition land reform policy, 324 (*quoted*), 333
Vinnichenko, V. K., 280-81
Vishniak, M. V., 90, 129, 138, 197, 216*n*, 426, 458, 465-66, 472, 478; on the nationalities problem, 216-20, 354; and election to the Constituent Assembly, 356-57, 358*n*, 359
Vitebsk, SR's in, 236
Vladimir, 49
V narod ("into the people") movement, 48, 56; *see also* Populists
Vnorovski, Boris, 70*n*
Voennyi, Victor (pseud.), 78 (*quoted*)
Volga *druzhina* (armed band), 70-71
Volga River, 262, 391, 392, 437-38, 452
Volga valley, 52, 54, 243
Volia Naroda (The Will of the People), newspaper, 188-90, 190 (*quoted*), 191, 218, 376, 378-79, 385, 421*n*, 479, 499; Kerenski on the July crisis, 290; attacks on Chernov, 298*n*, 300, 312, 397; and the church, 352
Vologda, 52; SR's in, 236
Volski, V. K. and M. K., brothers, 56
Volynia, 263
Voronezh, 49, 54*n*, 91, 298; SR's in, 234, 236, 431; second peasants' congress of, 308-9; Peasants' Soviet, 309 (*quoted*), 310, 392 (*quoted*), 437
Vřoček, S. V., 450*n*
Vyborg province, 218, 367*n*
Vysotski, A. D., 320

White Russia, SR's in, 183*n*
Witte, S. Iu., 4, 60, 64, 69, 76, 108, 461

Yalta, 235-36

Zarubin, Alexander, 269
Zatonski, M. P., 441; as Central Committee member, 221
Zemlia i Volia (Land and Liberty), organization, 50, 60
Zemlia i Volia (Land and Freedom), Moscow newspaper, 158, 189n, 500
Zemlia i Volia (Land and Freedom), St. Petersburg newspaper, 194, 366, 368, 500; on the Third Party Congress, 227n; denatured, 367, 368
Zemstvos, 59, 80, 255, 431-32, 436
Zenzinov, V. M., 71-72, 76n, 79n, 80, 90, 129, 133, 138, 168n, 198n, 383n, 472-73; on the revolution, 128 (quoted); leadership of, in Petersburg Soviet, 133-34, 136; as SR leader, 141, 194, 399, 439, 459, 461; support for Kerenski, 146, 462; on the war, 156; and factionalism, 195, 238, 424, 425-26, 456; as Central Committee member, 221, 304, 328, 344, 367n, 376, 408, 415, 416; on land reform, 248, 253; and the second coalition, 311-12, 316-17, 320 (quoted), 333, 386; and the third coalition, 408, 409-10
Zhordaniia, Noah (Noi Nikolaevich), 348
Zimin, SR party worker in St. Petersburg, 442n
Zimmerwald Conference, 110, 111, 118-19, 174-75; SR cleavage at, 117-118; Third, 206
Zimmerwaldism, 90, 117, 121, 149, 156, 159, 194, 197, 296-97, 316, 375-76; "Siberian," 167; rightists' criticism of, 296-98, 299-300, 305, 311, 396, 402
Zimmerwald Manifesto, 117-18, 125-126, 196
Zinoviev, G. E. (or E. A.?), 112
Znamia Truda (Banner of Labor), newspaper, 189, 365n, 368-69, 421n, 442, 500